MACHINE
INTELLIGENCE 15

MACHINE INTELLIGENCE

Machine Intelligence 1 (1967) (eds N. Collins and D. Michie) Oliver & Boyd, Edinburgh

Machine Intelligence 2 (1968) (eds E. Dale and D. Michie) Oliver & Boyd, Edinburgh

(1 and 2 published as one volume in 1971 by Edinburgh University Press) (eds N. Collins, E. Dale and D. Michie)

Machine Intelligence 3 (1968) (ed. D. Michie) Edinburgh University Press, Edinburgh

Machine Intelligence 4 (1969) (eds B. Meltzer and D. Michie) Edinburgh University Press, Edinburgh

Machine Intelligence 5 (1970) (eds B. Meltzer and D. Michie) Edinburgh University Press, Edinburgh

Machine Intelligence 6 (1971) (eds B. Meltzer and D. Michie) Edinburgh University Press, Edinburgh

Machine Intelligence 7 (1972) (eds B. Meltzer and D. Michie) Edinburgh University Press, Edinburgh

Machine Intelligence 8 (1977) (eds E. W. Elcock and D. Michie) Ellis Horwood, Chichester/Halsted, New York

Machine Intelligence 9 (1979) (eds J. E. Hayes, D. Michie and L. Mikulich) Ellis Horwood, Chichester/Halsted, New York

Machine Intelligence 10 (1982) (eds J. E. Hayes, D. Michie and Y.-H. Pao) Ellis Horwood, Chichester/Halsted, New York

Machine Intelligence 11 (1988) (eds J. E. Hayes, D. Michie and J. Richards) Oxford University Press, Oxford

Machine Intelligence 12 (1991) (eds J. E. Hayes, D. Michie and E. Tyugu) Oxford University Press, Oxford

Machine Intelligence 13 (1994) (eds K. Furukawa, D. Michie and S. Muggleton) Oxford University Press, Oxford

Machine Intelligence 14 (1996) (eds K. Furukawa, D. Michie and S. Muggleton) Oxford University Press, Oxford

MACHINE INTELLIGENCE 15

Intelligent Agents

edited by

K. FURUKAWA

Keio University, Tokyo

D. MICHIE

Turing Institute, Glasgow

and

S. MUGGLETON

Oxford University Computing Laboratory

OXFORD
UNIVERSITY PRESS

OXFORD
UNIVERSITY PRESS

Great Clarendon Street, Oxford OX2 6DP

Oxford University Press is a department of the University of Oxford
It furthers the University's objective of excellence in research, scholarship,
and education by publishing worldwide in

Oxford   New York

Athens Auckland Bangkok Bogotá Buenos Aires Calcutta
Cape Town Chennai Dar es Salaam Delhi Florence Hong Kong Istanbul
Karachi Kuala Lumpur Madrid Melbourne Mexico City Mumbai
Nairobi Paris São Paulo Singapore Taipei Tokyo Toronto Warsaw

with associated companies in Berlin Ibadan

Oxford is a registered trade mark of Oxford University Press
in the UK and in certain other countries

Published in the United States
by Oxford University Press Inc., New York

A catalogue record for this book is available from the British Library

Library of Congress Cataloging in Publication Data
(Data available)

ISBN 0 19 853867 7 (Hbk)

Typeset by Newgen Imaging Systems (P) Ltd., Chennai, India
Printed in Great Britain
on acid-free paper by
Bookcraft (Bath) Ltd.
Midsomer Norton, Avon

PREFACE

The Machine Intelligence series (see http://www.cs.york.ac.uk/mlg/ for an overview), founded in 1965 by Donald Michie, is probably the most venerable and prestigious book series in the Artificial Intelligence (AI) literature. Many of the best known papers in AI were published in this series. The series has had fourteen previous volumes to date. Each volume in the series is associated with a particular by-invitation-only workshop. Machine Intelligence 15 was held at St. Catherine's College Oxford in July 1995 and included papers by some of the most eminent figures in AI including John McCarthy, Donald Michie, Alan Robinson, Robert Kowalski and Mike Genesereth. The theme of the workshop was 'Intelligent agents'.

The workshop papers represent a wide range of topics, including representations of consciousness (John McCarthy, Stanford University and Donald Michie, Edinburgh University), SoftBots (Bruce Blumberg, MIT Media Lab), parallel implementations of logic (Alan Robinson, Syracuse University), machine learning (Stephen Muggleton, Oxford University), machine vision (Andrew Blake, Oxford University), and machine-based scientific discovery in molecular biology (Mike Sternberg, Imperial Cancer Research Fund).

November 1998   Stephen Muggleton,
                                                                  Executive Editor

ACKNOWLEDGEMENTS

The Machine Intelligence 15 workshop was generously supported by the Daiwa Anglo-Japanese Foundation under an agreement concluded in 1991 between the Turing Institute, UK and the Japan Society for Artificial Intelligence, Tokyo. The Foundation provided funding, covering Workshops 13, 14, and 15 to defray travel and attendance costs for six Japanese and six British scientists nominated by the respective parties. The workshop was also partly supported by an Anglo-Japanese grant from the Royal Society and the British Council entitled 'Computational Aids to Intellectual Discovery'.

St Catherine's College Oxford kindly provided support and facilities for the Machine Intelligence 15 workshop. Like its predecessor, Machine Intelligence 13, this volume reflects the vigour with which the subject is being advanced in Japan.

CONTENTS

FORMALISMS AND MODELS OF LEARNING

APPLIED SCIENTIFIC DISCOVERY

CONCURRENT DECLARATIVE PROGRAMMING

HISTORY OF COMPUTING

CONSCIOUSNESS AND CAUSATION

1

Making robots conscious of their mental states

John McCarthy

Computer Science Department,
Stanford University,
Stanford, CA 94305,
USA
e-mail: jmc@cs.stanford.edu

Abstract

In AI, consciousness of self consists in a program having certain kinds of facts about its own mental processes and state of mind.

We discuss what consciousness of its own mental structures a robot will need in order to operate in the common-sense world and accomplish the tasks humans will give it. It's quite a lot.

Many features of human consciousness will be wanted, some will not, and some abilities not possessed by humans will be found feasible and useful.

We give preliminary fragments of a logical language a robot can use to represent information about its own state of mind.

A robot will often have to conclude that it cannot decide a question on the basis of the information in memory and therefore must seek information externally. Gödel's idea of relative consistency is used to formalize non-knowledge.

Programs with the level of consciousness discussed in this article do not yet exist.

Thinking about consciousness with a view to designing it provides a new approach to some of the problems of consciousness studied by philosophers. The advantage is that it focusses on the aspects of consciousness important for intelligent behavior.

1   INTRODUCTION

In this article we discuss consciousness with the methodology of logical AI. McCarthy (1989) contains a recent discussion of logical AI. The *Remarks* section has a little about how our ideas about consciousness might apply to other AI methodologies. However, it

3

seems that systems that don't represent information by sentences will be limited in the amount of self-consciousness they can have.

McCarthy (1959) proposed programs with common sense that represent what they know about particular situations and the world in general *primarily* by sentences in some language of mathematical logic. They decide what to do *primarily* by logical reasoning, i.e. when a logical AI program does an important action, it is usually because it inferred as sentence saying it should. There may be other data structures and programs, but the main decisions of what to do are made by logical reasoning from sentences explicitly present in the robot's memory. Some of the sentences may get into memory by processes that run independently of the robot's decisions, e.g. facts obtained by vision. Developments in logical AI include situation calculus in various forms, logical learning, nonmonotonic reasoning in various forms, theories of concepts as objects (McCarthy, 1979b) and theories of contexts as objects (McCarthy, 1993). McCarthy (1959) mentioned self-observation but wasn't specific.

There have been many programs that decide what to do by logical reasoning with logical sentences. However, I don't know of any that are *conscious* of their own mental processes, i.e. bring sentences *about* the sentences generated by these processes into memory. We hope to establish in this article that some consciousness of their own mental processes will·be required for robots to reach a level of intelligence needed to do many of the tasks humans will want to give them. In our view, consciousness of self, i.e. introspection, is essential for human-level intelligence and not a mere epiphenomenon. However, we need to distinguish which aspects of human consciousness should be modelled, which human qualities should not and where AI systems can go beyond human consciousness.

For the purposes of this article a robot is a continuously acting computer program interacting with the outside world and not normally stopping. What physical senses and effectors or communication channels it has are irrelevant to this discussion except as examples.

In logical AI, robot consciousness may be designed as follows. At any time a certain set of sentences is directly available for reasoning. We say these sentences are in the robot's *consciousness*. Some sentences come into consciousness by processes that operate all the time, i.e. by *involuntary subconscious processes*. Others come into *consciousness* as a result of *mental actions*, e.g. observations of its consciousness, that the robot *decides* to take. The latter are the results of *introspection*.

Here's an example of human introspection. Suppose I ask you whether the President of the United States is standing, sitting or lying down at the moment, and suppose you answer that you don't know. Suppose I then ask you to think harder about it, and you answer that no amount of thinking will help. [See (Kraus, Perlis and Horty, 1991) for one formalization.] A certain amount of introspection is required to give this answer, and robots will need a corresponding ability if they are to decide correctly whether to think more about a question or to seek the information they require externally.

We discuss what forms of consciousness and introspection are required and how some of them may be formalized. It seems that the designer of robots has many choices to make about what features of human consciousness to include. Moreover, it is very likely that useful robots will include some introspective abilities not fully possessed by humans.

4

Two important features of consciousness and introspection are the ability to infer nonknowledge and the ability to do nonmonotonic reasoning.

Human-like emotional structures are possible but unnecessary for useful intelligent behavior. We will also argue that it is best not to include any that would cause people to feel sorry for or to dislike robots.

2 WHAT CONSCIOUSNESS DOES A ROBOT NEED?

In some respects it is easy to provide computer programs with more powerful intro-spective abilities than humans have. A computer program can inspect itself, and many programs do this in a rather trivial way. Namely, they compute check sums in order to verify that they have been read into computer memory without modification.

It is easy to make available for inspection by the program the manuals for the pro-gramming language used, the manual for the computer itself and a copy of the compiler. A computer program can use this information to simulate what it would do if provided with given inputs. It can answer a question like: 'Would I print "YES" in less than 1 000 000 steps for a certain input?' A finite version of Turing's argument that the *halting problem* is unsolvable tells us that a computer cannot in general answer questions about what it would do in n steps in less than n steps. If it could, we (or a computer program) could construct a program that would answer a question about what it would do in n steps and then do the opposite.

Unfortunately, these easy forms of introspection are not especially useful for intelli-gent behavior in many common-sense information situations.

We humans have rather weak memories of the events in our lives, especially of intellectual events. The ability to remember its entire intellectual history is possible for a computer program and can be used by the program in modifying its beliefs on the basis of new inferences or observations. This may prove very powerful.

To do the tasks we will give them, a robot will need at least the following forms of self-consciousness, i.e. ability to observe its own mental state. When we say that something is *observable*, we mean that a suitable *action* by the robot causes a sentence and possibly other data structures giving the result of the observation to appear in the robot's consciousness.

We will give tentative formulas for some of the results of observations. In this we take advantage of the ideas of McCarthy (1993) and give a context for each formula. This makes the formulas shorter. What *Here, Now* and *I* mean is determined in an outer context.

- Observing its physical body, recognizing the positions of its effectors, noticing the relation of its body to the environment and noticing the values of important internal variables, e.g. the state of its power supply and of its communication channels:

$$\ldots : c(Here, Now, I) : lowbattery \wedge in(screwdriver, hand3). \qquad (1)$$

[No reason why the robot shouldn't have three hands.]

5

- Observing that it does or doesn't know the value of a certain term, e.g. observing whether it knows the telephone number of a certain person. Observing that it does know the number or that it can get it by some procedure is likely to be straightforward:[1]

$$c(Now, I) : \neg know(Telephone\ Clinton) \qquad (2)$$

$$c(Now, I) : \neg know\text{-}whether(Sitting\ Clinton). \qquad (3)$$

Deciding that it doesn't know and cannot infer the value of a telephone number is what should motivate the robot to look in the phone book or ask someone.

- Keeping a journal of physical and intellectual events so it can refer to its past beliefs, observations and actions.

- Observing its goal structure and forming sentences about it. Notice that merely having a stack of subgoals doesn't achieve this unless the stack is observable and not merely obeyable.

- The robot may *intend* to perform a certain action. It may later infer that certain possibilities are irrelevant in view of its intentions. This requires the ability to observe intentions.

- Observing how it arrived at its current beliefs. Most of the important beliefs of the system will have been obtained by nonmonotonic reasoning, and therefore are usually uncertain. It will need to maintain a critical view of these beliefs, i.e. believe meta-sentences about them that will aid in revising them when new information warrants doing so. It will presumably be useful to maintain a pedigree for each belief of the system so that it can be revised if its logical ancestors are revised. *Reason maintenance systems* maintain the pedigrees but not in the form of sentences that can be used in reasoning. Neither do they have introspective subroutines that can observe the pedigrees and generate sentences about them.

- Not only pedigrees of beliefs but other auxiliary information should either be represented as sentences or be observable in such a way as to give rise to sentences. Thus a system should be able to answer the questions: 'Why do I believe p?' or alternatively 'Why don't I believe p?'.

- Regarding its entire mental state up to the present as an object, i.e. a context. McCarthy (1993) discusses contexts as formal objects. The ability to *transcend* one's present context and think about it as an object is an important form of introspection, especially when we compare human and machine intelligence as Roger Penrose (1994) and other philosophical AI critics do.

- Knowing what goals it can currently achieve and what its choices are for action. We claim that the ability to understand one's own choices constitutes *free will*. The subject is discussed in detail in McCarthy and Hayes (1969).

---

[1] However, observing that it doesn't know the telephone number and cannot infer what it is involves getting around Gödel's theorem. Because, if there is any sentence that is not inferrable, a system powerful enough for arithmetic must be consistent. Therefore, it might seem that Gödel's famous theorem that the consistency of a system cannot be shown within the system would preclude inferring non-knowledge except for systems too weak for arithmetic. Gödel's (1940) idea of *relative consistency* gets us out of the difficulty.

The above are only some of the needed forms of self-consciousness. Research is needed to determine their properties and to find additional useful forms of self-consciousness.

2.1 Understanding and awareness

We do not offer definitions of understanding and awareness. Instead we discuss which abilities related to these phenomena robots will require.

Consider fish swimming. Fish do not understand swimming in the following senses.

- A fish cannot, while not swimming, review its previous swimming performance so as to swim better next time.
- A fish cannot take instruction from a more experienced fish in how to swim better.
- A fish cannot contemplate designing a fish better adapted to certain swimming conditions than it is.

A human swimmer may understand more or less about swimming.[2]

We contend that intelligent robots will need understanding of how they do things in order to improve their behavior in ways that fish cannot. Aaron Sloman (1985) has also discussed understanding, making the point that understanding is not an all-or-nothing quality.

Consider a robot that swims. Besides having a program for swimming with which it can interact, a logic-based robot needs to use sentences about swimming in order to give instructions to the program and to improve it.

The *understanding* a logical robot needs then requires it to use appropriate sentences about the matter being understood. The understanding involves both getting the sentences from observation and inference and using them appropriately to decide what to do.

Awareness is similar. It is a process of appropriate sentences about the world and its own mental situation coming into the robot's consciousness, usually without intentional actions. Both understanding and awareness may be present to varying degrees in natural and artificial systems. The swimming robot may understand some facts about swimming and not others, and it may be aware of some aspects of its current swimming state and not others.

3 FORMALIZED SELF-KNOWLEDGE

We assume a system in which a robot maintains its information about the world and itself primarily as a collection of sentences in a mathematical logical language. There will be other data structures where they are more compact or computationally easier to process, but they will be used by programs whose results become stored as sentences. The robot

---

[2]One can understand aspects of a human activity better than the people who are good at doing it. Nadia Comenici's gymnastics coach was a large, portly man hard to imagine cavorting on a gymnastics bar. Nevertheless, he *understands* women's gymnastics well enough to have coached a world champion.

decides what to do by logical reasoning, not only by deduction using rules of inference but also by nonmonotonic reasoning.

We do not attempt a full formalization of the rules that determine the effects of mental actions and other events in this paper. The main reason is that we are revising our theory of events to handle concurrent events in a more modular way. There is something of this in Costello and McCarthy (1998).

Robot consciousness involves including among its sentences some about the robot itself and about subsets of the collection of sentences itself, e.g. the sentences that were in consciousness just previous to the introspection, or at some previous time, or the sentences about a particular subject.[3]

We say subsets in order to avoid self-reference as much as possible. References to the totality of the robot's beliefs can usually be replaced by references to the totality of its beliefs up to the present moment.

3.1 Mental situation calculus

The *situation calculus*, initiated by McCarthy and Hayes (1969), is often used for describing how actions and other events affect the world. It is convenient to regard a robot's state of mind as a component of the situation and describe how mental events give rise to new situations. (We could use a formalism with a separate mental situation affected only by mental events, but this doesn't seem to be advantageous.) We contemplate a system in which what *holds* is closed under deductive inference, but *knowledge* is not.

The relevant notations are:

- $holds(p, s)$ is the assertion that the proposition p holds in the situation s. We shall mainly be interested in propositions p of a mental nature.

- Among the propositions that can hold are *know p* and *believe p*, where p again denotes a proposition. Thus we can have

$$holds(know\ p, s). \tag{4}$$

- As we will shortly see, sentences like

$$holds(know\ not\ know\ p, s) \tag{5}$$

are often useful. The sentence (5) asserts that the robot knows it doesn't know p.

- Besides knowledge of propositions we need a notation for knowledge of an *individual concept*, e.g. a telephone number. McCarthy (1979b) treats this in some detail. That paper has separate names for objects and concepts of objects and the argument of knowing is the latter. In that paper, the symbol *mike* denotes Mike himself, the function telephone takes a person into his telephone number. Thus *telephone mike* denotes

---

[3]Too much work concerned with self-knowledge has considered self-referential sentences and getting around their apparent paradoxes. This is mostly a distraction for AI, because human self-consciousness and the self-consciousness we need to build into robots almost never involves self-referential sentences or other self-referential linguistic constructions. A simple reference to oneself is not a self-referential linguistic construction, because it isn't done by a sentence that refers to itself.

Mike's telephone number. The symbol *Mike* is the concept of Mike, and the function *Telephone* takes the concept of a person into the concept of his telephone number. Thus we distinguish between Mike's telephone number, denoted by *telephone mike* and the concept of his telephone number denoted by *Telephone Mike*. This enables us to say

$$holds(knows\ Telephone\ Mike, s) \tag{6}$$

to assert knowledge of Mike's telephone number and

$$holds(know\ not\ knows\ Telephone\ Mike, s) \tag{7}$$

to mean that the robot knows it doesn't know Mike's telephone number. The notation is somewhat ponderous, but it avoids the unwanted inference that the robot knows Mary's telephone number from the facts that her telephone number is the same as Mike's and that the robot knows Mike's telephone number.[4] Having the sentence (7) in consciousness might stimulate the robot to look in the phone book.

3.2 Mental events, especially actions

Mental events change the situation just as do physical events.

Here is a list of some mental events, mostly described informally.

- *learn p*. The robot learns the fact *p*. An obvious consequence is

$$holds(know\ p, result(learn\ p, s)) \tag{8}$$

provided the effects are definite enough to justify the *result* formalism. More likely we'll want something like

$$occurs(learn\ p, s) \supset holds(F\ know\ p, s), \tag{9}$$

where *occurs(event, s)* is a *point fluent* asserting that *event* occurs (instantaneously) in situation *s*. *F p* is the proposition that the proposition *p* will be true at some time in the future. The *temporal function F* is used in conjunction with the function *next* and the axiom

$$holds(F\ p, s) \supset holds(p, next(p, s)). \tag{10}$$

Here *next(p, s)* denotes the next situation following *s* in which *p* holds. (10) asserts that if *F p* holds in *s*, then there is a next situation in which *p* holds. (This *next* is not the *next* of some temporal logic formalism.)

- The robot learning *p* has an effect on the rest of its knowledge. We are not yet ready to propose one of the many *belief revision* systems for this. Indeed we don't assume logical closure.

---

[4]Some other formalisms give up the law of substitution in logic in order to avoid this difficulty. We find the price of having separate terms for concepts worth paying in order to retain all the resources of first-order logic and even higher-order logic when needed.

- What about an event *forget p*? Forgetting p is definitely not an event with a definite result. What we can say is

$$occurs(forget\ p, s) \supset holds(F\ not\ know\ p, s). \tag{11}$$

In general, we shall want to treat forgetting as a side-effect of some more complex event. Suppose *foo* is the more complex event. We'll have

$$occurs(foo, s) \supset occurs(forget\ p, s). \tag{12}$$

- The robot may decide to do action a. This has the property:

$$occurs(decide\text{-}to\text{-}do\ a, s) \supset holds(intend\text{-}to\text{-}do\ a, s). \tag{13}$$

The distinction is that *decide* is an event, and we often don't need to reason about how long it takes. *intend-to-do* is a fluent that persists until something changes it. Some call these *point fluents* and *continuous fluents* respectively.

- The robot may decide to assume p, e.g. for the sake of argument. The effect of this action is not exactly to believe p, but maybe it involves *entering a context* (see McCarthy (1993)) in which p holds.

- The robot may infer p from other sentences, either by deduction or by some non-monotonic form of inference.

- The robot may see some object. One result of seeing an object may be knowing that it saw the object. So we might have

$$occurs(see\ o, s) \supset holds(F\ knows\ did\ see\ o, s). \tag{14}$$

Formalizing other effects of seeing an object require a theory of seeing that is beyond the scope of this article.

It should be obvious to the reader that we are far from having a comprehensive list of the effects of mental events. However, I hope it is also apparent that the effects of a great variety of mental events on the mental part of a situation can be formalized. Moreover, it should be clear that useful robots will need to observe mental events and reason with facts about their effects.

Most work in logical AI has involved theories in which it can be shown that a sequence of actions will achieve a goal. There are recent extensions to concurrent action, continuous action and strategies of action. All this work applies to mental actions as well.

Mostly outside this work is reasoning leading to the conclusion that a goal cannot be achieved. Similar reasoning is involved in showing that actions are safe in the sense that a certain catastrophe cannot occur. Deriving both kinds of conclusion involves inductively inferring quantified propositions, e.g. 'whatever I do the goal won't be achieved' or 'whatever happens the catastrophe will be avoided'. This is hard for today's automated reasoning techniques, but Reiter (1993) has made important progress.

3.3 Inferring non-knowledge

Let p be a proposition. The proposition that the robot does not know p will be written *not know p*, and we are interested in those mental situations s in which we have *holds(not know p, s)*. If *not p* is consistent with the robot's knowledge, then we certainly want *holds(not know p, s)*.

How can we assert that the proposition *not p* is consistent with the robot's knowledge? Gödel's theorem tells us that we aren't going to do it by a formal proof using the robot's knowledge as axioms.[5] The most perfunctory approach is for a program to try to prove *holds(not p, s)* from the robot's knowledge and fail. Logic programming with negation as failure does this for Horn theories.

However, we can often do better. If a person or a robot regards a certain collection of facts as all that are relevant, it suffices to find a model of these facts in which p is false.[6]

Consider asserting ignorance of the value of a numerical parameter. The simplest thing is to say that there are at least two values it could have, and therefore the robot doesn't know what it is. However, we often want more, e.g. to assert that the robot knows nothing of its value. Then we must assert that the parameter could have any value, i.e. for each possible value there are models of the relevant facts in which it has that value. Of course, complete ignorance of the values of two parameters requires that there be a model in which each pair of values is taken.

It is likely to be convenient in constructing these models to assume that arithmetic is consistent, i.e. that there are models of arithmetic. Then the set of natural numbers, or equivalently Lisp S-expressions, can be used to construct the desired models. The larger the robot's collection of theories postulated to have models, the easier it will be to show ignorance.

Making a program that reasons about models of its knowledge looks difficult, although it may turn out to be necessary in the long run. The notion of *transcending* a context may be suitable for this.

For now it seems more straightforward to use second-order logic. The idea is to write the axioms of the theory with predicate and function variables and to use existential statements to assert the existence of models. Here's a proposal.

---

[5]We assume that our axioms are strong enough to do symbolic computation which requires the same strength as arithmetic. I think we won't get much joy from weaker systems.

[6]A conviction of what is relevant is responsible for a person's initial reaction to the well-known puzzle of the three activists and the bear. Three Greenpeace activists have just won a battle to protect the bears' prey, the bears being already protected. It was hard work, and they decide to go see the bears whose representatives they consider themselves to have been. They wander about with their cameras, each going his own way.

Meanwhile a bear wakes up from a long sleep very hungry and heads South. After three miles, she comes across one of the activists and eats him. She then goes three miles West, finds another activist and eats her. Three miles North she finds a third activist but is too full to eat. However, annoyed by the incessant blather, she kills the remaining activist and drags him two miles East to her starting point for a nap, certain that she and her cubs can have a snack when she wakes.

What color was the bear?

At first sight it seems that the color of the bear cannot be determined from the information given. While wrong in this case, jumping to such conclusions about what is relevant is more often than not the correct thing to do.

Suppose the robot has some knowledge expressed as an axiomatic theory and it needs to infer that it cannot infer *that* President Clinton is sitting down. We immediately have a problem with Gödel's incompleteness theorem, because if the theory is inconsistent, then every sentence is inferrable, and therefore a proof of non-inferrability of any sentence implies consistency. We get around this by using another idea of Gödel's – *relative consistency*.[7]

Gödel (1940) proved that if Gödel–Bernays set theory is consistent, then it remains consistent when the axiom of choice and the continuum hypothesis are added to the axioms. He did this by supposing that set theory has a model, i.e. there is a domain and an $\in$ predicate satisfying GB. He then showed that a subset of this domain, the constructible sets, provided a model of set theory in which the axiom of choice and the continuum hypothesis are also true. Cohen proved that if set theory has any models it has models in which the axiom of choice and the continuum hypothesis are false. The Gödel and Cohen proofs are long and difficult, and we don't want our robot to go through all that to show that it doesn't know that President Clinton is sitting.

For example, suppose we have a first-order theory with predicate symbols $\{P_1, \ldots, P_n, sits\}$ and let $A(P_1, \ldots, P_n, sits)$ be an axiom for the theory. The second-order sentence

$$(\exists P_1', \ldots, P_n' sits') A(P_1', \ldots, P_n', sits') \tag{15}$$

expresses the consistency of the theory, and the sentence

$$(\exists P_1', \ldots, P_n' sits')(A(P_1', \ldots, P_n', sits') \wedge \neg sits'(Clinton, s)) \tag{16}$$

expresses the consistency of the theory with the added assertion that Clinton is not sitting in the situation s.

Then

$$(15) \supset (16) \tag{17}$$

is then the required assertion of relative consistency.

Sometimes we will want to assert relative consistency under fixed interpretations of some of the predicate symbols. This would be important when we have axioms involving these predicates but do not have formulas for them, e.g. of the form $(\forall x \, y)(P(x, y) \equiv \ldots)$. Suppose, for example, that there are three predicate symbols $(P_1, P_2, sits)$, and P_1 has a fixed interpretation, and the other two are to be chosen so as to satisfy the axiom. Then the assertion of consistency with Clinton sitting takes the form

$$(\exists P_2' P_3') A(P_1, P_2', sits') \wedge sits'(Clinton, s). \tag{18}$$

The straightforward way of proving (18) is to find substitutions for the predicate variables P_2' and $sits'$ that make the matrix of (18) true. The most trivial case of this would be when

---

[7]Our approach is a variant of that used by Kraus, Perlis and Horty (1991).

the axiom $A(P_1, P_2, sits)$ does not actually involve the predicate *sits*, and we already have an interpretation $P_1, \ldots, P_n, sits$ in which it is satisfied. Then we can define

$$sits' = (\lambda x\ ss)(\neg(x = Clinton \wedge ss = s) \vee sits(x, ss)), \qquad (19)$$

and (18) follows immediately. This just means that if the new predicate does not interact with what is already known, then the values for which it is true can be assigned arbitrarily.

3.4 Observing its motivations

Whatever motivational structure we give to robots, they should be able to observe and reason about it. For many purposes a simple goal-subgoal structure is the right thing. However, there are some elaborations to consider.

1. There often will be auxiliary goals, e.g. curiosity. When a robot is not otherwise occupied, we will want it to work at extending its knowledge.
2. The obverse of an auxiliary goal is a constraint. Maybe we shall want something like Asimov's science fiction laws of robotics, e.g. that a robot should not harm humans. In a sufficiently general way of looking at goals, achieving its other goals with the constraint of not harming humans is just an elaboration of the goal itself. However, since the same constraint will apply to the achievement of many goals, it is likely to be convenient to formalize them as a separate structure. A constraint can be used to reduce the space of achievable states before the details of the goals are considered.

3.5 Robots should not be equipped with human-like emotions

Some authors, e.g. Sloman and Croucher (1981), have argued that sufficiently intelligent robots would automatically have emotions somewhat like those of humans. We argue that it is possible to give robots human-like emotions, but it would require a special effort. Moreover, it would be a bad idea if we want to use them as servants. In order to make this argument, it is necessary to assume something, as little as possible, about human emotions. Here are some points.

1. Human reasoning operates primarily on the collection of ideas of which the person is immediately conscious.
2. Other ideas are in the background and come into consciousness by various processes.
3. Because reasoning is so often nonmonotonic, conclusions can be reached on the basis of the ideas in consciousness that would not be reached if certain additional ideas were also in consciousness.[8]
4. Human emotions influence human thought by influencing what ideas come into consciousness. For example, anger brings into consciousness ideas about the target of anger and also about ways of attacking this target.

---

[8]These conclusions are true in the simplest or most standard or otherwise minimal models of the ideas taken in consciousness. The point about nonmonotonicity is absolutely critical to understanding these ideas about emotions. See, for example McCarthy (1980, 1986).

5. Human emotions are strongly related to blood chemistry. Hormones and neurotransmitters belong to the same family of substances. The sight of something frightening puts certain substances in our blood streams, and these substances may reduce the thresholds of synapses where the dendrites have receptors for these substances.[9]

6. A design that uses environmental or internal stimuli to bring whole classes of ideas into consciousness is entirely appropriate for lower animals. We inherit this mechanism from our animal ancestors.

7. According to these notions, paranoia, schizophrenia, depression and other mental illnesses would involve malfunctions of the chemical mechanisms that bring ideas into consciousness. A paranoid who believes the Mafia or the CIA is after him and acts accordingly can lose these ideas when he takes his medicine and regain them when he stops. Certainly his blood chemistry cannot encode complicated paranoid theories, but they can bring ideas about threats from wherever or however they are stored.

These facts suggest the following design considerations.

1. We don't want robots to bring ideas into consciousness in an uncontrolled way. Robots that are to react against people (say) considered harmful, should include such reactions in their goal structures and prioritize them together with other goals. Indeed we humans advise ourselves to react rationally to danger, insult and injury. 'Panic' is our name for reacting directly to perceptions of danger rather than rationally.

2. Putting such a mechanism in a robot is certainly feasible. It could be done by maintaining some numerical variables, e.g. level of fear, in the system and making the mechanism that brings sentences into consciousness (short-term memory) depend on these variables. However, human-like emotional structures are not an automatic byproduct of human-level intelligence.

3. It is also practically important to avoid making robots that are reasonable targets for either human sympathy or dislike. If robots are visibly sad, bored or angry, humans, starting with children, will react to them as persons. Then they would very likely come to occupy some status in human society. Human society is complicated enough already.

4 REMARKS

1. We do not give a definition of *consciousness* or *self-consciousness* in this article. We only give some properties of the consciousness phenomenon that we want robots to have together with some ideas of how to program robots accordingly.

2. The preceding sections are not to be taken as a theory of human consciousness. We do not claim that the human brain uses sentences as its primary way of representing

---

[9] Admittedly referring to 'reducing the thresholds of synapses' is speculative. However, it may be possible to test these ideas experimentally. There should be a fixed set of these substances and therefore definite classes of ideas that they bring in.

information. Allen Newell (1981) introduced the term *logic level* of analysis of a person or machine. The idea is that behavior can be understood as the person, animal or machine doing *what it believes will achieve its goals.* Ascribing beliefs and goals then accounts for much of its behavior. Daniel Dennett (1978) first introduced this idea, and it is also discussed by McCarthy (1979a).

Of course, logical AI involves using actual sentences in the memory of the machine.

3. Daniel Dennett (1991) argues that human consciousness is not a single place in the brain with every conscious idea appearing there. I think he is right about the human brain, but I think a unitary consciousness will work quite well for robots. It would likely also work for humans, but evolution happens to have produced a brain with distributed consciousness.

4. Francis Crick (1994) discusses how to find *neurological correlates* of consciousness in the human and animal brain. I agree with all the philosophy in his paper and wish success to him and others using neuroscience. However, after reading his book, I think the artificial intelligence approach has a good chance of achieving important results sooner. They won't be quite the same results, however.

5. What about *the unconscious?* Do we need it for robots? Very likely we will need some intermediate computational processes whose results are not appropriately included in the set of sentences we take as the *consciousness* of the robot. However, they should be observable when this is useful, i.e. sentences giving facts about these processes and their results should appear in consciousness as a result of mental actions aimed at observing them. There is no need for a full-fledged Freudian unconscious with purposes of its own.

6. Should a robot hope? In what sense might it hope? How close would this be to human hope? It seems that the answer is yes. If it hopes for various things, and enough of the hopes come true, then the robot can conclude that it is doing well, and its higher level strategy is OK. If its hopes are always disappointed, then it needs to change its higher level strategy.

To use hopes in this way requires the self-observation to remember what it hoped for.

Sometimes a robot must also infer that other robots or people hope or did hope for certain things.

7. The syntactic form is simple enough. If p is a proposition, then *hope* p is the proposition that the robot hopes for p to become true. In mental situation calculus we would write

$$holds(hope\ p, s) \qquad (20)$$

to assert that in mental situation s, the robot hopes for p.

Human hopes have certain qualities that I can't decide whether we will want. Hope automatically brings into consciousness thoughts related to what a situation realizing the hope would be like. We could design our programs to do the same, but this is more automatic in the human case than might be optimal. Wishful thinking is a well-known human malfunction.

8. A robot should be able to wish that it had acted differently from the way it has done. A mental example is that the robot may have taken too long to solve a problem and might wish that it had thought of the solution immediately. This will cause it to think about how it might solve such problems in the future with less computation.

9. A human can wish that his motivations and goals were different from what he observes them to be. It would seem that a program with such a wish could just change its goals.

10. Penrose (1994) emphasizes that a human using a logical system is prepared to accept the proposition that the system is consistent even though it can't be inferred within the system. The human is prepared to iterate this self-confidence indefinitely. Our systems should do the same, perhaps using formalized transcendence. Programs with human capability in this respect will have to be able to regard logical systems as values of variables and infer general statements about them. We will elaborate elsewhere (McCarthy, 1995) our disagreement with Penrose about whether the human is necessarily superior to a computer program in these respects. For now we remark only that it would be interesting if he and others of similar opinion would say where they believe the efforts outlined in this article will get stuck.

11. Penrose also argues (p. 37 *et seq.*) that humans have *understanding* and *awareness* and machines cannot have them. He defines them in his own way, but our usage is close enough to his so that I think we are discussing how to make programs do what he thinks they cannot do. I don't agree with those defenders of AI who claim that some computer programs already possess understanding and awareness to the necessary extent.

12. Programs that represent information by sentences but generate new sentences by processes that don't correspond to logical reasoning present similar problems to logical AI for introspection. Approaches to AI that don't use sentences at all need some other way of representing the results of introspection if they are to use it at all.

Acknowledgements

This work was partly supported by ARPA (ONR) grant N00014-94-1-0775 and partly done while the author was Meyerhoff Visiting Professor at the Weizmann Institute of Science, Rehovot, Israel.

Thanks to Yoav Shoham and Aaron Sloman for email comments and to Saša Buvač and Tom Costello for face-to-face comments.

This document is available via the URL: http: http://www-formal.stanford.edu/jmc/.

REFERENCES

Crick, Francis (1994): *The Astonishing Hypothesis: The Scientific Search for Soul*, Scribners.
Dennett, Daniel (1978): *Brainstorms: Philosophic Essays on Mind and Psychology*, Bradford Books.
Dennett, Daniel (1991): *Consciousness Explained*, Little, Brown and Co.

Gödel, Kurt (1940): *The Consistency of The Axiom of Choice and of the Generalized Continuum-Hypothesis with the Axioms of Set Theory*. Princeton University Press.

Kraus, Sarit, Donald Perlis and John Horty (1991): "Reasoning about Ignorance: A Note on the Bush–Gorbachev Problem". *Fundamenta Informatica*, XV, 325–332.

McCarthy, John (1959): "Programs with Common Sense", in *Proceedings of the Teddington Conference on the Mechanization of Thought Processes*, Her Majesty's Stationery Office, London. Reprinted in McCarthy (1990).

McCarthy, John and P.J. Hayes (1969): "Some Philosophical Problems from the Standpoint of Artificial Intelligence", in D. Michie (ed.), *Machine Intelligence 4*, American Elsevier, New York, NY. Reprinted in McCarthy (1990).

McCarthy, John (1979a): "Ascribing Mental Qualities to Machines" in *Philosophical Perspectives in Artificial Intelligence*, M. Ringle (ed.), Harvester Press. Reprinted in McCarthy (1990).

McCarthy, John (1979b): "First Order Theories of Individual Concepts and Propositions", in D. Michie (ed.), *Machine Intelligence 9*, University of Edinburgh Press. Reprinted in McCarthy (1990).

McCarthy, John (1980): "Circumscription – A Form of Non-Monotonic Reasoning", *Artificial Intelligence*, 13, Numbers 1, 2, April. Reprinted in McCarthy (1990).

McCarthy, John (1986): "Applications of Circumscription to Formalizing Common Sense Knowledge", *Artificial Intelligence*, April. Reprinted in McCarthy (1990).

McCarthy, John (1989): "Artificial Intelligence and Logic" in R. Thomason (ed.), *Philosophical Logic and Artificial Intelligence*, Kluwer Academic.

McCarthy, John (1990): *Formalizing Common Sense*, Ablex, Norwood, New Jersey.

McCarthy, John (1993): "Notes on Formalizing Context", IJCAI-93. Morgan-Kauffman. Also accessible from http://www-formal.stanford.edu/jmc/.

McCarthy, John (1995): "Awareness and understanding in computer programs". *Psyche, a refereed electronic journal*, 2. Part of a symposium on Shadows of the Mind by Roger Penrose, also available as http://www-formal.stanford.edu/jmc/reviews/penrose2.html.

McCarthy, John and Tom Costello (1998): "Combining Narratives", in *Proceedings of Sixth Intl. Conference on Principles of Knowledge Representation and Reasoning*. Morgan Kaufman.

Newell, Allen (1981): "The knowledge level". *AI Magazine*, 2(2): 1–20. Originally delivered as the Presidential Address, American Association for Artificial Intelligence, AAAI80, Stanford, CA, August 1980.

Penrose, Roger (1994): *Shadows of the Mind: A Search for the Missing Science of Consciousness*. Oxford University Press.

Reiter, Ray (1993): "Proving properties of states in the situation calculus". *Artificial Intelligence*, 64: 337–351.

Sloman, Aaron (1985): *What Enables a Machine to Understand?*, in Proceedings 9th IJCAI, pp. 995–1001, Los Angeles.

Sloman, Aaron and Monica Croucher (1981): "Why Robots will Have Emotions". Proceedings 7th IJCAI.

2

A framework for verbalizing unconscious knowledge based on inductive logic programming

Koichi Furukawa

Graduate School of Media and Governance,
Keio University,
5322 Endoh,
Fujisawa-shi,
Kanagawa, 252
Japan
e-mail: furukawa@sfc.keio.ac.jp

Abstract

In this paper, we discuss the problem of verbalizing unconscious knowledge. Since there is no way to observe brain activities directly, it is rather difficult to clarify the mechanism of such intelligent behaviour as speaking natural language. A new approach to this problem is proposed. We select the domain of string instrument performance because of the possibility for getting objective data associated with intelligent activities. It is rather easy to measure various muscle movements during the performance. To elicit the secrets of miraculous performance by virtuosos, we need to analyse elaborately the measurements associated with their performance to explain them in terms of primitive muscle movements. We propose inductive logic programming as a very promising candidate for such analysis because of its capability of associating measurements with such basic facts as the structure of the human body and of muscle links.

1 INTRODUCTION

Verbalization of unconscious knowledge is one of the main issues of artificial intelligence. A well-known example of verbalization of unconscious knowledge is knowledge acquisition from experts. The difficulty of the problem is known as the 'Feigenbaum bottleneck' in developing expert systems. Another example (or non-example) is the inability to explain the origin of the behaviour of a neural network. It is also not known

18

how humans can speak natural language. All these problems are related to the problem of verbalization of unconscious knowledge. Since there is no way to observe brain activities, it is rather difficult to clarify the mechanism of such intelligent behaviour as speaking natural language. In this paper, we propose a new approach to this problem from two aspects: the selection of target domains and a scientific method of verbalization. We select the domain of string instrumental performance because of the possibility of getting objective data associated with intelligent activities. It is rather easy to measure various muscle movements during the performance. In such activities as playing string instruments, the precise movements of arms and hands seem directly to reflect intelligent brain activities which control every movement of the muscles. In contrast, in language speaking, for example, it is rather difficult to measure intelligent activities directly.

To elicit the secrets of miraculous performance by virtuosos, we need to analyse elaborately the measurements associated with their performance in order to explain them in terms of primitive muscle movements. There has been much work on behavioural cloning to obtain cognitive skill models by applying machine learning technologies to performance data (Michie *et al.*, 1990), (Sammut *et al.*, 1992), (Michie *et al.*, 1995). We propose inductive logic programming as a very promising candidate for such analysis because of its capability of associating measurements with such basic facts as the structure of the human body and of muscle links.

2 THE ROLE OF PRACTICE

Practice works as a process to acquire the unconscious knowledge needed for playing instruments. Even in the process of acquiring unconscious knowledge, relevant verbal suggestions by teachers help learners to learn skills efficiently. There are several kinds of notes or remarks given by teachers to learners: those concerning position, posture of arms and hands, muscle strength, movement of arms and hands, and so on. In the following, we consider the performance of the cello and give more concrete examples of these pedagogical notes.

2.1 The importance of form

Like natural language, there are two aspects of playing string instruments: form and content. At first, we follow form just as we follow syntax in learning foreign languages. By form, we mean the physical posture of our body in playing string instruments. There are several important parts of the physical posture affecting the performance: body position, arms position, hand position and shape, and so on.

Throughout a lesson, the most important caution given by a teacher is to maintain a good body position. One has to sit forward in a chair keeping the spine straight. The most important point is to keep the two arms completely free for their movements. The arms must not be used to keep the body's balance. I personally suffered from this very simple bad 'disease' for a long time, and it caused a constant bias noise added to a right control signal for positioning the left hand, producing a constant bias of higher pitch every time I tried to change my hand position. Very recently, I realized that I unconsciously had been using my arms to keep my body balance and that it had prevented me from controlling my left hand precisely. In the case of violin lessons, teachers apply pressure to learners' backs to check whether they are standing straight enough so as not to move against the teachers' push. In holding a string instrument, the arms should have their best positions against the instrument. Note that the body position affects substantially the determination of the relative position of the instrument and the body.

The shapes of arms and hands are the next important points taught by teachers. Arms should be raised 'naturally' by the elbows (not shoulders) with no extra force given to any muscles. Wrists should not be heavily bent. The fingers are shaped as if grasping eggs carefully.

When one holds the cello, its height and angle are the next important issue. It depends on one's physical constraints (such as height, thigh length, sitting height) and also one's degree of progress. The height of the cello can be adjusted using the end-pin. When one puts his/her left hand on the instrument, the best shape is obtained by just grasping the neck of the cello, putting the lower arm at a right angle to the neck by raising the elbow.

2.2 Basic practice for playing the cello

2.2.1 The practice of the left hand

For beginners, the most difficult thing for the left hand is to control each finger independently. The strengths of fingers are different, and also for most people it is very difficult to move the third finger freely. Sometimes one even cannot put the fingers at equal intervals on the strings. The training of the fingers to make them independently controllable is the first thing to be done. It is a problem of articulation of fingers which will be described in more detail later.

In order to change the position correctly, we need to control the movement of the left hand very precisely. We locate the left hand by the upper arm muscles which seem to remember the exact position to be moved. For the precise positioning, relative addressing regarding current finger position is very important. I need to concentrate my consciousness to the location of the current finger position for measuring the destination. For rapid positioning, we need to achieve it by a smooth muscle movement of the left upper arm, avoiding unnecessary force to be put on the muscle. It is very important to know what are necessary forces of muscles and what are not. Weak muscle causes problems to make other muscles help for recovering the weakness. Sometimes it is even useful for training muscles by dumbbells, newspaper graspings, and so on.

2.2.2 The practice of the right hand

The manner of holding the bow is much more difficult than the preparation of the left hand. Basically, the bow should be held softly enough to make it possible to transmit the control signal through the muscles directly to the strings with which the bow is in contact. The bow should be located at right angles to the string (as a first-order approximation). The selection of strings is done by the height of the right elbow. The basic movement of the bow is driven by the stretch and shrinking movement of the upper right arm's muscles.

The first elementary practice of the bow is to make a continuous sound by a single bow action from the bottom of the bow to the top and vice versa. One should maintain an equal amount of sound during the movement. Next, one should try to move and stop repeatedly in a single down- or up-movement of the bow. It is important to achieve a smooth change of the bow direction (from down-bow to up-bow and vice versa).

Very recently I found it was very important to 'feel' the place where the bow touches the string just as blind people feel the tip of the stick as a part of their body. This makes it possible to control the bow very precisely. The quality of the sound produced by the string heavily depends on very precise bow control.

3 ARTICULATION OF THE MUSCLE MOVEMENTS

In order to achieve a good cello performance, independent control of different muscle movements is required. This is analogous to the articulation needed for speaking natural language.

One example of such articulation of muscle movements is the correct placement of the left hand in changing positions controlled by the upper arm. The upper arm's muscle remembers the angle needed to achieve the proper position. This knowledge is acquired by supervised learning in which the target correct position is obtained by pitch detection by one's ears.

My conjecture is that muscles speak a kind of (good) language for a good performance. We need to extract the vocabulary in which muscles speak. Examples of such vocabulary may include such high-level notions as *smoothness, conservation of momentum, flexibility, finger sensibility* and so on. These 'words' in the vocabulary act as compound or 'defined' concepts which in turn may be 'explained' by lower level primitive 'words' such as each muscle's amount of stretch or shrinking.

4 IMPORTANCE OF VERBALIZING UNCONSCIOUS KNOWLEDGE

Verbalization sometimes plays the role of 'eureka' in improving one's performing skill drastically.

One example of such verbalization involves the height of the chair one sits on when playing the cello. I found it essential to make it lower, in order to make the instrument have a smaller angle with the floor. (It is possible to change this angle by adjusting the length of the cello's end-pin. However, my cello had only a short end-pin and its length was not enough to make a desirable angle.) The change of the angle of the instrument by using a shorter chair allowed the removal of the extra force from the back muscles used to keep the spine straight while leaning a little backwards (to achieve a lower angle without adjusting the end-pin length). This extra force had been a source of constant bias noise added to the control signal and made the positioning of the left hand always a little higher than expected.

Another example showing the importance of consciously verbalizing unconscious knowledge is paying explicit attention to the finger pressures to keep each of them equal. Finger pressure must be soft enough in order to be able to feel the finger tip consciously. I found that the force of the middle finger had been much stronger than others, and this in turn made it difficult to keep the spine straight, too.

The third example of verbalization concerns the angle of the bow against the string. As explained previously, the first-order approximation is to keep it at right angles to the string. However, more precisely speaking, it must be slightly different from a right angle in order to produce a force vector component in the direction of the bridge for attracting the bow to the bridge. This can be described as a dynamic characteristic of the bowing behaviour and is regarded as a second-order approximation.

The last example is paying explicit attention to the contact point of the bow to the string, as we described before. The conscious verbalization of this is very important. It improved my performance greatly. I could now solve many problems including that of playing a very rapid passage while keeping a good sound, and playing double strings clearly and smoothly.

5 VERBALIZATION OF UNCONSCIOUS KNOWLEDGE BY ILP

For the process of conscious verbalization of unconscious knowledge, a promising candidate is to apply machine learning techniques to a set of measurements taken during playing the cello. There have been several applications of machine learning of a set of qualitative rules for controlling given targets in the field of dynamic systems control (such as the inverse pendulum and autopilots). We propose to apply the most advanced machine learning technique, that of inductive logic programming (ILP), to extract a set of rules for good cello performance, corresponding to the conscious verbalization of the secrets underlying the excellent performance of professional players.

The reasons why ILP is most appropriate for verbalization are: (1) it can relate good performance to lower level muscle activities automatically by inductive inference; (2) the results are expressed by a set of rules which can be interpreted and understood naturally by a human; (3) the expressive power of ILP is rich enough to represent skill and 'know how'.

An essential issue in using ILP is the selection of input data. We need to measure appropriate attributes in order to learn a set of rules for performance successfully. We need to consult experts to get advice for this problem. My personal experience suggests the importance of the muscular electrical signals of the upper arms and the finger pressure on the strings. The grasping power of the right hand is also very important. A professional cellist has suggested the importance of the shoulder blades also, and the position and angle of the bow relative to the strings are important. In order to measure such data, new sensors are required. The development of suitable sensors is one of the most difficult problems in this research. A sensor which measures position and angle of the bow relative to the strings has been developed by Gershenfeld (1991) in a 'hypercello' project carried out by Machover (1992).

22

The right selection of background knowledge is also critical for the success of an ILP application. There are several different sources of possible background knowledge. One is the muscle structure of the human body which defines relationships among muscles. Another is the structure and the physics of the instrument. The third is the definition of 'high-level' notions in terms of primitive ones. It may be quite difficult to define them and it may be a challenge for machine learning to find these definitions.

The selection of positive examples and negative examples depends on what we choose as a target concept in the experiments. One obvious target concept is the method for playing better. Then a professional player's performances become positive examples and those of an amateur negative examples. Another approach might be based on remembering a good performance when one gets into a slump. Then positive examples are obviously performance data taken when one is playing well and negative examples those in a slump. We could even restrict the target to good playing in a particular way, such as a very fast passage or a single bow staccato.

6 CONCLUSION

In this paper, we propose a new research area of applying ILP to verbalization of unconscious knowledge. The area covers many research topics such as analysing the physical performance of the human body, including playing musical instruments and playing sports; finding verbal explanations for a neural network trained to perform a particular task; analysing human language understanding and speaking mechanisms, and so on.

In particular, we pay attention to the problem of analysing muscle movements for playing musical instruments because of the fact that we can directly measure the outcome of very intelligent activities during the play. The muscle movements reflect what our brain plans and directs us do to the muscles. In the case of natural language understanding or speaking, it is rather difficult to observe what is happening in the brain during such activities.

We need real experimental studies to promote further research. There are many difficulties in realising the experimental studies, ranging from developing appropriate sensors for measurement, to designing proper positive examples, negative examples and background knowledge for the input to ILP.

We believe that this research area is a very important and promising area for ILP technologies to be applied because of its scientific nature of revealing underlying secrets by giving a set of rules which can be interpreted by humans.

The most difficult issue related to semantics or appreciation of aesthetic value is not discussed here. It may be the most important for a human being to learn such skills as playing musical instruments. One cannot learn properly if one does not have a good sense of aesthetic value appreciation which acts as oracles in a supervised learning framework. It is related to a deeper brain activity which is not yet measurable. It may be possible to measure alpha or beta waves in the brain but there still remains the problem of relating the measurements to human controllable and understandable activities.

REFERENCES

Gershenfeld, N. Sensors for real-time cello analysis and interpretation, Proceedings of the ICMC. Montreal, 1991.

Machover, T. Hyperinstruments – A Progress Report 1987–1991. MIT Media Laboratory, MIT, 1992.

Michie, D., Bain, M., and Hayes-Michie, J. E. Cognitive models from sub-cognitive skills. In M. Grimble, S. McGhee, and P. Mowforth (Eds.), Knowledge-base Systems in Industrial Control. Peter Peregrimus, 1990.

Michie, D. and Sammut, C. Behavioural Clones and Cognitive Skill Models. In K. Furukawa, D. Michie, and S. Muggleton (Eds.), Machine Intelligence 14. Oxford University Press, 1995.

Sammut, C., Hurst, S., Kedzier, D., and Michie, D. Learning to Fly. In D. Sleeman and P. Edwards (Eds.), Proceedings of the Ninth International Conference on Machine Learning, Aberdeen. Morgan Kaufmann, 1992.

3

Legal responsibility and causation[1,2]

I. J. Good

Department of Statistics,
Virginia Polytechnic Institute and State University,
Blacksburg,
Virginia 24061-0439,
USA

Abstract

Convincing explications are quoted for the degrees to which an event F tends to be necessary, or sufficient, for a later one E, and are called the *necessitivity* or *necessitude* (Q_{nec}) and *sufficientivity* or *sufficitude* (Q_{suf}) *of F for E*. They pertain to ethical responsibility. Formulaic relationships between Q_{nec}, Q_{suf}, W (weight of evidence), and probability, are mentioned thus gluing the concepts together. (Hence causal networks $\approx$ probability networks.) Their legal interpretations are considered. An explication for 'legal responsibility' is mentioned, and is a plausible explication of the degree to which F *actually* (physically) caused E.

This nation is too great to look for mere revenge.
—James Garfield.*

The totality of the causes of events is inaccessible to man's mind. But a desire to discover causes is innate in man's soul.
—Tolstoy (1922/23, Book 13, p. 299).

A desire to avoid probability is innate in a child's soul.
—Bon mot based on research by Piaget.

If controversies were to arise ... it would suffice [for philosophers] ... to say ... Let us calculate.
—Leibniz (according to Russell, 1946, p. 615).

Art is long, life short; judgment difficult, opportunity transient.
—Goethe

---

[1] This chapter is based on Good (1993a; 1994a; 1995a; 1994b).
[2] The notes are an essential part of this chapter.
* Said in his speech on the assassination of Lincoln in 1865. Garfield was himself assassinated in 1881.

1 INTRODUCTION

My topic is the philosophy of probabilistic causality, and, in particular, degrees of ethical and legal responsibility which are distinct concepts. I do not have a law degree but ignorance of the law is no excuse for not talking about it nor for not serving on a jury. The law is too important and difficult to be left entirely to lawyers.[3] (For an extensive discussion of the meaning of 'responsibility', and its relation to punishment, with an emphasis very different from that in the present work, see Hart, 1968.) The concepts of subjective (personal) probability and physical probability are central to the discussion.

2 THE UNIVERSAL INTEREST IN CAUSATION

The law is in part a soft inferential science and is very much concerned with cause and effect and with degrees of causality.[4] In fact the Greek word for *cause*, from which *etiology* is derived, originated in connection with legal responsibility. (See *Great Books of the Western World*, 1952, Vol. 2, p. 155.) Of course the interest in causality is not restricted to legal matters. That the second sentence of the Tolstoy quotation applies to most souls is supported by Table 1 which shows the authors cited by *Great Books of the Western World*. I have indicated by an asterisk the names of the few authors who were *not* cited in the chapter on causality in the *Great Books*. Let's largely explain away those few in order to strengthen the case for Tolstoy's comment. It is understandable that

---

[3]The great mathematician Hilbert once said that physics is too difficult for physicists. Perhaps that generalizes to all professions: religion is too difficult for theologians, judgment is too difficult for jurors, etc. It could be said of the jury system what Churchill said of democracy that it is the worst of all systems except the other systems that have been tried from time to time. Both systems would be improved by giving more votes to the more intelligent voters and by punishing lawyers' flammery more than lying if that were practicable. By 'flammery' I mean the making of a statement that is true but deliberately misleading – such a statement is not a genuine contribution to 'the whole truth' and is more reprehensible than lying because it takes sneaky advantage of a loophole in the law.

Although I agree with much in Dershowitz (1996), I know he was guilty of defense-a-flammery when he said at least twice in broadcast interviews that batterers seldom murder their wives, for he didn't then add the qualification (on his p. 105):

It is of course, also true that a high proportion of wives who have been battered by their husbands . . . , and are then found dead were killed by those batterers, but it is equally [??] true that a high proportion of women who have *not* been battered and are found dead were killed by their husbands . . . .

He used this statement to argue that the knowledge of battery should be 'inadmissible' in a murder trial. If judges were thereby lured into conceding the point, batterers would be encouraged to murder their wives. But Dershowitz's qualification and other statements on this topic in Dershowitz (1996, pp. 108, and 117) are seriously mistaken. Actually, if the wife is murdered the odds of the guilt of a 'representative batterer' (one who battered his wife about once per year) are about 8 (which could conveniently be taken by the jury as the prior odds), whereas they are, according to 1992 statistics, only about 1/7 for a mere husband. (This of course ignores all other information.) Thus, given that a man is the husband, the information that he is a representative batterer provides the very large Bayes factor of roughly 56 in favor of his guilt (Good, 1996a, b). Dershowitz's slightly subtle mistake, explained in the cited references, therefore leads to the conclusion that 1 is approximately equal to 56!

[4]The words *causation* and *causality* are almost synonymous and I am often unsure which of them should be used.

Table 1. Authors and books in *The Great Books of the Western World*.

4. Homer	19. Thomas Aquinas I	38. Montesquieu
5. Aeschylus*	20. Thomas Aquinas II	Rousseau
Sophocles*	21. Dante	39. Adam Smith
Euripides	22. Chaucer	40. Gibbon I
Aristophanes*	23. Machiavelli	41. Gibbon II
6. Herodotus	Hobbes	42. Kant
Thucydides	24. Rabelais*	43. American
7. Plato	25. Montaigne	State Papers*
8. Aristotle I	26. Shakespeare I	The Federalist
9. Aristotle II	27. Shakespeare II	J. S. Mill
10. Hippocrates	28. Gilbert	44. Boswell
Galen	Galileo	45. Lavoisier
11. Euclid*	Harvey	Fourier
Archimedes*	29. Cervantes	Faraday
Apollonius*	30. Francis Bacon	46. Hegel
Nicomachus*	31. Descartes	47. Goethe
12. Lucretius	Spinoza	48. Melville
Epictetus	32. Milton	49. Darwin
Marcus Aurelius	33. Pascal	50. Marx
13. Virgil	34. Newton	Engels
14. Plutarch	Huygens	51. Tolstoy
15. Tacitus	35. Locke	52. Dostoevsky
16. Ptolemy*	Berkeley	53. William James
Copernicus	Hume	54. Freud
Kepler	36. Swift	
17. Plotinus	Sterne	
18. Augustine	37. Fielding	

*Apart from the ten authors or books marked with an asterisk all of the authors were cited in the chapter on causality in *The Great Books*. This demonstrates the almost universal interest in causality among great writers of the past. There were twenty authors not cited in the chapter on chance, namely Aristophanes, Galen, Euclid, Archimedes, Apollonius, Nichomachus, Ptolemy, Copernicus, Kepler, Gilbert, Galileo, Descartes, Swift, American State Papers, Boswell, Lavoisier, Fourier, Faraday, Engels, and Dostoevsky.

the four people represented in Book 11 were not cited, for, in their writings, they were primarily concerned with the geometry of two and three dimensions which do not involve time. Of course causality is intimately connected with the passage of time. Archimedes was interested also in statics but not in dynamics. Ptolemy was interested in kinematics, not dynamics which involves forces which we usually regard as causes. Rabelais, in his bawdy humor, was not much concerned with causation, but he might have been in his capacity as a physician. And finally, even *American State Papers*, though not cited in the chapter on causality in the *Great Books*, says, in the first paragraph of the Declaration of Independence, that 'they [Americans] should declare the causes [reasons] which [that] impel them to the separation [independence of Great Britain].'

3 DEGREES OF RESPONSIBILITY

The law has to take into account *degrees* of responsibility for determining degrees of punishment and magnitudes of awards. English law is also concerned with *apportionment* of responsibility, for example between the captains of two ships that have collided. (See *Apportionment* in the index of Hart and Honoré, 1959.) We would like to have a measure for degrees of causality for its philosophical interest, especially for the philosophy of the law, and for its probable eventual practical interest in statistics, in computerized diagnosis, in the construction of robots, and in the understanding of artificial or living neural networks. Quantitative considerations always shed light on the structure of qualitative matters, a point that is often ignored by the 'qualitativists'. The influence in the opposite direction is never ignored by the 'quantitativists'. It is worth emphasizing that a formula does not require that the quantities represented have precise values, although it might seem to, but one merges from the quantitative to the qualitative depending on the degree of imprecision. To talk of murder of the first and second degrees strikes me as 'quantito-qualitative'. Of course discretionary sentencing by the judge has many more than two degrees.

Consider the case of Peter and Paul where Peter had committed a murder whereas Paul had merely stolen a crust of bread. Peter wasn't necessarily more responsible than Paul, but he was responsible for more. Naturally, rewards and punishments depend on the values (utilities) of what is probably or actually caused or prevented as well as on degrees of responsibility. But degrees of responsibility for specific events depend not on values but on degrees of causality. I am ignoring the fact that people are not always responsible for their actions.

4 CAUSATION, WEIGHT OF EVIDENCE, AND PROBABILITY

It has been shown, I think convincingly, from a Bayesian perspective (Good, 1994a), that weights of evidence, probabilities, and degrees of tendency to cause an event, can be expressed in terms of one another formulaically and I shall quote the appropriate formulae.[5,6] The existence of these formulae shows that these concepts are even more

---

[5]The frequencies of published usage of words associated with two concepts give some idea of their relative importance in our printable thoughts. A list of word frequencies, in a corpus of a million words of edited texts printed in 1961, was published by Kučera and Francis (1967). It was based on 16 genres of texts. In accordance with Good (1953, formula (9)), the probability is about 1/40 that a word chosen at random from running text of English is a word not in their sample, in other words about one word per four lines of print. (This is only an approximation because the formula should strictly be applied to each genre separately.) So the sample is small for some applications (as W. F. Twaddell stated in the Foreword of that book), but it is adequate for the present application.

Two difficulties in using this method for comparing the frequencies of concepts are that words can be more or less related to a concept and they can also have more than one meaning. But here is my attempt to compare the frequencies of usage of the concepts of causality and probability in American publications:

Causality: caus . . . , 306 (the sum of the frequencies of all words beginning 'caus'); effect . . . , 540; because, 883; conseq. . . . , 103; induce, induced, induces, inducing, 29; generat . . . . ('generation' not included), 53; agent . . . , 84; stimul . . . , 62; objective, 91; *total:* 2151.

closely intertwined than has usually been thought. The concepts are all fundamental in AI, in medicine, and in forensic science.

5 DEGREES OF CAUSALITY AND DEGREES OF MURDER

Suppose that an event F (such as the Firing of a gun), or its negation, might occur earlier than an event E (such as the Ending of a life).[7] I assume throughout that the person M, the agent who performs the 'act' F or the 'act' $\bar{F}$ (not F), can have no further influence on whether E occurs. *Provisionally*, let $Q(E : F)$ denote the *tendency* of F to cause E and let $\chi(E : F)$ denote the extent to which F *actually* (physically) caused E. (Physical probabilities are discussed in Note 24.) An example of this distinction is that between attempted murder and actual murder. For avoiding complicating the notations *I will always denote an explanandum and its explanans (explication) by the same notation* and will rely on the contexts to resolve the ambiguities. These provisional notations were used also by Good (1961/62), as *abbreviations*, and they can be abbreviated still more to Q and χ. I don't know whether the important distinction between Q and χ had been made or emphasized before 1961. (In my numerous scribblings on probabilistic causality, some of which are listed in the References, I have tried to use fairly consistent

---

Probability: probab . . . , 341; perhaps, 307, chance, chanced, chances, 158; likel . . . , 161; maybe, 134; odds, 15; expect . . . , 380; anticipat . . . , 62; unlikely, 21; presumably, 40; improbable, improbably, 3; *total*: 1622.

The total for probabilistic words would increase to 2473 if 'seem . . .' were included. These figures show clearly enough that there is not much difference in frequency of printed usage of the concepts *causality* and *probability*.

[6]Bayesianism has at least $2 \times 6^6 = 93,312$ shades of meaning, where I have here doubled the number given by Good (1971) to allow for 'dynamic probability' (axiom A4' in Good, 1950, or see Good 1977b). They all depend on the use of either logical or subjective (personal) probability, and on forms of the addition and product axioms even when probabilities are regarded as partially ordered (interval-valued, or 'upper and lower'). Subjective or personal probability is the main kind used implicitly or explicitly by honest jurors. Whether a personal probability should be regarded as a judgment of a (metaphysical?) logical probability, or as a more fundamental concept, is largely a matter of taste. For some twentieth-century books dealing with espistemic probability (personal or logical) see, for example, Keynes (1921), Jeffreys (1939/61), Carnap (1950), Good (1950, 1983), Savage (1954), Jeffrey (1965/83), Zellner (1971), Box and Tiao (1973), de Finetti (1974/75), Kyburg and Smokler (1980), Hartigan (1983), Berger (1985), Eatwell *et al.* (1990), and the proceedings of the five 'Valencia' conferences entitled *Bayesian Statistics* edited by J. Bernardo *et al.* (1985).

[7]It is convenient to interpret an *event* in a very general sense. Raining, if defined adequately, is an event. Not raining is also an event. *An event is something that can occur or not occur.* (For a Bayesian, aiming at the greatest generality, axioms are best expressed in terms of *propositions* which can refer to events, mathematical statements, and hypotheses or theories. In forensic science, most events are also hypotheses.) Nearly always an event is a union of a large number of more detailed events, or, in propositional terminology, a logical disjunction. For example, an event could occur to various degrees and durations, such as more or less rain. In some cases it is natural to describe the detailed events as microevents. Mathematicians will see the parallel of this definition of an event with that of the technical term 'event' described as a measurable set, for example, by Loève (1963, p. 149). A Bayesian might say that it is a (measurable) set equipped with a probability distribution over the set, whereas a non-Bayesian would usually not assume the existence of this probability distribution. In a Bayesian perspective, the negation $\bar{E}$ of an event E is also an event equipped with a probability distribution over its microevents. Compare Good (1961/62, p. 309) or (1983, p. 200). Note that a Bayesian can use an expression like $P(E|H)/P(E|\bar{H})$, a *Bayesian* likelihood ratio, more freely than a non-Bayesian can. The adjective 'Bayesian' in this definition is often omitted, but it is a bit misleading to do so, partly because 'likelihood ratio' often means the ratio of two maximum likelihoods.

notations.) In most of this chapter I discuss Q rather than χ, but χ will be very briefly discussed at the end.

To exemplify degrees of murder, suppose that M, a potential murderer, throws a stone at a victim V and V dies. The degree of the murder, or degree of M's resolve to kill, then depends partly on the size and shape of the stone and on its momentum when it hits the victim. M's intention could be to cause injury or alarm to V with appreciable probability, but to cause V's death with only a small probability. If M throws a small pebble which happens to enter one of V's eyes and V dies, then, in a civilized country, M would probably not be accused of murder unless M was known to be an extraordinarily accurate thrower of pebbles, or perhaps if the person killed was a VIP.

6 NECESSITY AND SUFFICIENCY AND DEGREES THEREOF

When thinking about causation it is easy to overlook the distinction between sufficient causes (sufficient for a specified effect) and necessary causes (necessary for the effect), obvious though the distinction is. (It is not at all unusual to overlook the obvious.) Hart and Honoré (hereafter referred to as H & H'), in their interesting book *Causation in the Law*,[8] refer to necessary causes or conditions as *conditio sine qua non*.[9]

To exemplify the distinction between 'somewhat necessary' causes and 'somewhat sufficient' causes, let us consider a firing squad. Suppose there are six marksmen, all fairly good shots, and consider one specific marksman. The firing of his gun is hardly necessary for the death of the victim but it is almost sufficient. Perhaps his gun is the one that contains a blank shot, but nobody knows whether this is so. (This example is treated quantitatively in Note 25.) His degree of *ethical* responsibility depends partly on his estimate of the probability that his gun contains a blank whereas his degree of *legal* responsibility depends on more than his ethical responsibility. For example, it depends on whether the victim dies. From the *physical* point of view the presence or absence of the blank is fully determined before the gun is fired. Thus, in this example, neither

---

[8] Hart and Honoré (1959), which will be cited as H & H', is intended somewhat more for lawyers and legal historians than for philosophers, and it cites about 800 legal cases.

[9] A cause F that is strictly sufficient to cause E is one that is necessarily followed by E (or makes E necessary) where both F and $\bar{F}$ are possible sequels of U (and E does not necessarily follow from $\bar{F}$). (U is defined in Section 7). This assumption commits us to indeterminism or to a branching-universe (many-worlds) theory for which see Everett (1957) and, for some prehistory and speculation (Good, 1962/63, pp. 154–155 and 326–329). Again, if F is strictly necessary to cause E, then the occurrence of E is sufficient to imply that F occurred. So there is scope for terminological confusion, and H & H' (page 386) mention a historical usage that exemplifies this confusion. They say

At the beginning of the nineteenth century lawyers generally took the view that a cause in law meant a 'necessary' cause in the sense that, given the alleged cause, the alleged consequence necessarily followed.

In my terminology this is a *sufficient* cause because it is *sufficient to cause the consequences* or sufficient *for* the consequence. It is the *consequence* that is necessary, not the cause! Thus, in 1800 or so, legal causation was usually intended to mean strict sufficiency. The avoidance of probabilistic aspects shows that most of the lawyers at that time must have had, in this respect, the mentality of Piaget's eight-year olds. The law must have been somewhat of 'a ass, a idiot' (Mr. Bumble in *Oliver Twist*). H & H' (page 387) say in effect that the view just expressed 'fell into discredit' and I hope that the early nineteenth century usage of the expression 'necessary cause' has fallen into the same place.

ethical nor legal responsibility can be the same as degree of physical causality, but they should be estimates of it (if it is definable) perhaps by means of a weighted average of the possible physical degrees.[10]

For the present, I am thinking of the causal chain from the marksman to the victim as consisting of only one causal link. Cases where there is more than one link, forming a chain or network, will be considered later. I shall return to the legal aspects also.

7 MORE ON NOTATIONS

As before, let E and F be two events (sometimes F is better described as the *circumstances*) each of which can occur or not occur. (The same symbols denote the corresponding propositions.) Their non-occurrences are denoted by $\bar{E}$ and $\bar{F}$ read 'not E' and 'not F' or 'E bar' and 'F bar'. I assume that the user of the theory *chooses* the meanings of E, F, $\bar{E}$ and $\bar{F}$. *When we say that F is a cause of E we imply that F, as compared with, or as against $\bar{F}$, is a cause of E rather than of $\bar{E}$.* The personal choice of the meanings of the negations already suggests that χ, degree of physical causality, will not be easy to explicate uncontroversially.

Suppose F occurs, or $\bar{F}$ occurs, earlier[11] than the occurrence of E. (In legal problems the event E is usually known by the public before F is known if F is ever known.) Let U denote the state of the universe,[12] including all laws of nature, just before the occurrence of F or $\bar{F}$. (I'll soon say more about this grandiose-sounding concept, U.) Let $Q_{\mathrm{nec}}(E:F|U)$ and $Q_{\mathrm{suf}}(E:F|U)$ denote the degrees to which F has a tendency to be necessary and respectively to be sufficient to cause E given U. The colon is assumed to be more binding than the vertical stroke so we don't need to write $(E:F)$ with parentheses.[13] The mere introduction of U accounts in principle for the distinction between causation and mere association (which can be due to a common cause that belongs to U). It is in the spirit of the first sentence of the Tolstoy quotation because the universe is a big place. Of course, when judging degrees of causality one thinks about only a small part of the universe. For example, a physicist thinks about initial and boundary conditions. I use U to ensure that everything is covered. It is not necessary to drag in the whole universe, but it is sufficient in principle for the purpose of solving the problem of 'association versus causation' with a 'stroke of the pen'. In specific cases

---

[10]In the example the sum would contain two terms with weights 1/6 and 5/6 multiplied by the two corresponding possible physical necessitudes (or sufficitudes) for which proposed definitions are briefly discussed later in the text.

[11]For some applications to twentieth century physics, 'earlier than' can be interpreted as 'in the backward light cone of' but this point is irrelevant for forensic science.

[12]The universe is often called the *world*, but I prefer the less cozy but more specific term. For some discussion of the meaning of 'state' see Good (1961/62) or (1983, p. 217).

[13]The vertical stroke is now the standard notation for 'given' or 'assuming' in books on mathematical probability. This notation was introduced by Harold Jeffreys in 1931. I often use the oblique stroke to mean 'as contrasted with' as in $Q_{\mathrm{suf}}(E:F_1/F_2|U)$. The oblique stroke is more 'binding' than the colon. The notation $Q_{\mathrm{suf}}(E:F|U)$, used in this chapter, is an abbreviation of $Q_{\mathrm{suf}}(E:F/\bar{F}|U)$ and, for rigor, both F and $\bar{F}$ require careful definitions.

many difficulties remain: as every physicist knows, to solve a problem 'in principle' is only part of a practical solution.[14,15]

8 BAROMETERS SELDOM AFFECT THE WEATHER

For an example of the use of the notation U, let F denote the event that you observe the reading on a barometer, and let E denote the event of wet weather somewhat later. Then $Q_{nec}(E : F|U) = Q_{suf}(E : F|U) = 0$ (or virtually zero) apart from far-fetched cases.[16] In this example E and F are statistically correlated but you know they are physically independent conditionally on the meteorological circumstances, without even knowing those circumstances. You can sometimes make reliable probability judgments without being God. Conditional independence (as well as dependence) is an important concept when discussing causality; see, for example, the discussion of causal or inference networks in Good, 1961/62, p. 45, or 1983, p. 211, Pearl (1988); Lauritzen and Spiegelhalter (1988); and Kadane and Schum (1996).[17] It is also important for the simplification of the analysis of multidimensional contingency tables (Good 1976, p. 1172). Dawid (1979) has also emphasized the importance of conditional independence in statistics, with several examples.

---

[14]H & H', page 12, imply that the distinction between causes and conditions is one of the main sources of the difficulties in understanding the causal concepts with which the lawyer works. Our solution is to regard 'conditions' as part of U because the conditions are usually in place before the event (or act) begins. In this way, again with a stroke of a pen, we cope 'in principle' with some of the lawyer's difficulties.

[15]In experimental, as distinct from observational science, the experimenter controls a small part of U. A statistician, when designing a controlled experiment, often uses a randomized design, such as in the assignment of treatments ('causes') to plots on a field, in the hope of most probably 'eliminating' the effect of unknown systematic properties of the unmodified U such as the spatial pattern of the quality of the soil related to past plowing of the field. In any specific application, the number of possible equally probable randomizations should be much larger than the number of plausible unknown appreciably systematic designs. These numbers depend on personal judgment at present (which is one reason for saying that everybody is implicitly a personalistic Bayesian) but Kolmogorov's definition of a 'random finite sequence' (as being impossible to describe more briefly in a specified programming language) should eventually be helpful in principle because it eliminates systematic and partially systematic designs. The inequality just mentioned should be appended to Kolmogoroff's definition, otherwise (0, 1), for example, would be called a random sequence! In statistical mechanics this inequality is usually satisfied, when entropy is maximized, because the number of molecules in most applications is extremely large. If there is any discernible pattern, such as unstirred milk in a cup of tea, we say that entropy has not yet been maximized.

If the inequality just mentioned were not satisfied then there would be too high a probability that the actualized randomization would itself exhibit a systematic pattern. If it happens to do so, and is known to have done so, the design should not be used. This reduces the number of permissible designs, and changes the P-value, but statisticians are busy and usually ignore this point. They attain 'objectivity' by throwing away some evidence (Good, 1950, p. 102; 1974, p. 124 = 1983, p. 88; and 1974). (For more on this see Good, 1974.) The statistician often assumes further a mathematical model of part of U such as an additive model or a normal distribution of a random variable (and in principle should test the model). Compare Stone (1993) and Good (1995b). (Indeed everybody makes models of reality but they are not usually mathematical.) This is not the place to expand further on the discussion of experimentation.

[16]Far-fetched exceptions or quibbles are possible for almost any proposition. Imagine an insane president who reads a barometer and, according to the outcome, decides whether to press a button that Ends all human life on earth (event E). The event F could be defined as the reading of the barometer plus the pressing of the button, and $\bar{F}$ as doing neither.

[17]The latter authors base their work largely on Bayesian thinking and on very early work on inference networks in the law by John H. Wigmore dating back to 1913.

9 NECESSITY IS NOT ENOUGH

H & H', p. 85, state that many modern writers insist that 'the only factual [as distinct from logical] element' [regarding 'extent of liability'] is whether the harm, our event E, would have happened without the act, our F. In other words these modern writers think F is irrelevant unless it is *sine qua non*, i.e. necessary for the occurrence of E. If so, then those modern writers are wrong and misleading. For example, throwing a pebble might be almost necessary but barely sufficient, and hence of low liability regarding the death of the victim. Note, in fairness to H & H', that later, on pages 108–122, they point out that not every cause is *sine qua non* so they disagree with the 'many modern writers'. (See also footnote 2 on their page 85.)

10 THE *MEANING* OF STRICT CAUSATION

Much has been written about strict causation but it is possible to define it in 70 words (plus a definition of U), while at the same time making the distinction, so often overlooked, between necessary and sufficient causes. (Compare Keynes, 1921, p. 276.) This can be done (see Note 9) in the following manner:

Assume that U alone does not imply E or its negation, and assume, as before, that F or its negation occurs earlier than E or its negation. (i) *If $E \cdot U$ logically implies F, or equivalently if $\bar{F} \cdot U$ implies $\bar{E}$, then F is said to be strictly necessary to cause E.* (ii) *If $\bar{E} \cdot U$ implies $\bar{F}$, or equivalently if $F \cdot U$ implies E, then F is said to be strictly sufficient to cause E.* (The difficulties in applying this definition are in describing the relevant parts of U.)

Our definitions of degrees of probabilistic causation ought to be, and are, generalizations of (i) and (ii). These generalizations and their justifications were presented in Good (1994a).

11 TERMINOLOGY

It would be unwieldy to use repeatedly the expression 'the degree to which F has a tendency to be sufficient (or necessary) to cause E conditionally on the state U of the universe just before F or $\bar{F}$ occurred'. So it is convenient to use a pair of neologies. In Good (1993a,b; 1994a; 1995a) I used the almost self-explanatory terms *sufficientivity* and *necessitivity* (based on the suffix *-ivity* which is in the OED and was previously used in the neology *explicativity*, in Good, 1977a). But Suppes and others did not like these somewhat clumsy terms so I am switching to the pair *sufficitude* and *necessitude* which are almost as self-explanatory and more euphonious.[18] We can then refer to the sufficitude of F for (producing) E, and similarly the necessitude of F for (producing) E.

Sufficitude and necessitude can be expressed in terms of probability (Good, 1994a). It helps my intuition to express them first in terms of weight of evidence, which generalizes

---

[18]I have resurrected the word *necessitude* which became obsolete when its meaning was different. *Sufficitude* is not yet in the *OED*.

strict implication (which corresponds to infinite weight of evidence), and separately to express weight of evidence in terms of probability. This procedure leads to simple expressions for Q_{nec} and Q_{suf} in terms of probability, and these expressions again have strong intuitive appeal. (The derivation in Good, 1994a, differs somewhat.)

12 CAUSALITY AND WEIGHT OF EVIDENCE

Let $W(H : A|B)$ denote the weight of evidence in favor of a hypothesis H (where the hypothesis could be that some proposition is true or that some event occurred) provided by evidence A assuming background knowledge B all along. The notation is conveniently read in words from left to right. To understand this notation think of Themis, the goddess of justice, dropping weights of evidence into her two scales. This concept is uniquely captured by a specific explication of weight of evidence, whether or not the concept was familiar to some ancient Greeks. I'll soon spell out this explication of W which I have mentioned or discussed in about fifty publications some of which deal with the history which dates back at least to a few sentences by Peirce (1878). Implicit in his exposition was the special assumption that the prior odds of H were 1 so he did not quite capture the concept $W(H : E|G)$ as defined below in equation (3). But he thought that a formalization of his concept of weight of evidence from an 'argument' provided the main justification for the use of subjective ('conceptual') probability. Otherwise he did not favor the use of subjective probability in science although he must have used it implicitly because all scientists do whether they know it or not. (Leibniz's dream of total objectivity has not yet been attained.) Given a couple of natural desiderata, the correct explication is unique up to a choice of unit (see, for example, Good 1994a) if the product axiom for epistemic (logical or subjective) probabilities is accepted.[19]

The explication of Q_{nec} is

$$Q_{nec}(E : F|U) = W(F : E|U). \tag{1}$$

In words, the necessitude of F for producing E is equal to the weight of evidence in favor of F provided by the occurrence of E, or by the proposition stating that E occurred, given U all along. For example, if F is entirely necessary for E to occur (if that were

---

[19]The product axiom is $P(A\&B|G) = P(A|G) \cdot P(B|A\&G)$ where A, B, and G denote propositions, events, or hypotheses. I am using sharp probabilities for the sake of simplicity although I have 'always' (for over fifty years) believed that subjective (personal) probabilities are only partially ordered, i.e. they are interval-valued at best: see Good (1950, 1962) and the *two* subject indexes of Good (1983). Perhaps better than an interval estimate is an estimate of log-odds and of its standard deviation. Compare the use of a hierarchy of types of probability as in Good (1952) and in many later publications by others and myself ('hierarchical Bayes'). As I said in Good (1952), 'the higher the type the woolier [= fuzzier] the probabilities ... [but] the higher the type the less the woolliness [fuzziness] matters ... '. Later writers on fuzzy logic perhaps ignore this comment.

For a brief review of the properties and history of weight of evidence, see Good (1985b). For scores of further references, see 'weight of evidence' in the subject indexes of Good (1983). Expected weight of evidence is often called 'cross-entropy' or 'Kullback expression'. It was used by Turing and myself in World War II, and it was developed in much detail later by Kullback and myself, especially by Kullback who told me his work was kindled by an unpublished paper of mine.

possible in the real world), then the occurrence of E provides infinite evidence that F occurred. Then again

$$Q_{\text{suf}}(E : F|U) = W(\bar{F} : \bar{E}|U) \tag{2}$$

the weight of evidence against F if E does not occur (possibly counterfactually). For example, if the victim V had not dropped dead, that would have been some evidence that M did not throw a stone at V. In normal circumstances (the local part of U), throwing a mere pebble, as compared with throwing nothing, would have high necessitude but low sufficitude for the dead-dropping. But, as compared with throwing a rock, it would have negative necessitude (as well as negative sufficitude). This shows that the user of the theory has to choose the meaning of $\bar{F}$ even if F has already been defined. 'Negation' is often an ambiguous concept. This is a source of difficulty in a legal trial because there are usually many possible perpetrators of a crime apart from the defendant. A full-dress Bayesian approach is to define $\bar{F}$ as the logical disjunction of all possible alternatives to F together with a probability distribution over those alternatives. This very important point was made in Note 7.

If F is entirely sufficient for E, then the nonoccurrence of E would provide infinite weight of evidence against the occurrence of F. In practice, weight of evidence is always finite though it is often called conclusive in common parlance just as *certainty* and *impossibility* have formal and informal meanings. In a court of law one would not distinguish between probabilities of 10^{-1000}, $10^{-1000\,000}$, and zero, but to identify them in a mathematical theory would quickly lead to contradictions. (It would be like assuming there is a largest number.) Strict causality is a limiting case of probabilistic causality. This is analogous to the fact that Newtonian mechanics is a limiting case of quantum mechanics which in most formulations denies strict causality. (In quantum mechanics, this is usually called the Correspondence Principle.)

Convincing arguments for the explications (1) and (2) were presented in Good (1994a), my chapter in the Festschrift for Patrick Suppes, which chapter was followed by favorable comments and a useful summary by Suppes. These arguments will not be repeated here but it will be essential to mention the explication of $W(H : A|B)$ which is the logarithm of a *Bayes factor* (*the factor by which the odds of a hypothesis are multiplied by some evidence*). The two main theorems about weight of evidence are

$$W(H : A|B) = \log \frac{O(H|A \cdot B)}{O(H|B)} = \log \frac{P(A|H \cdot B)}{P(A|\bar{H} \cdot B)}, \tag{3}$$

in which the first equation is a *definition*, and

$$W(H : A \cdot B|G) = W(H : A|G) + W(H : B|A \cdot G), \tag{3A}$$

where O denotes odds, $P/(1 - P)$, and where the dot denotes *and*, also called logical conjunction.[20] (The logarithm is discussed later. The base of the logarithms determines the unit in terms of which W is measured.) It would take only a few sentences to justify

---

[20]The definition of W is meaningful to most Bayesians, though it is not necessarily easy to estimate. Jurors are implicit Bayesians but not necessarily good ones. When A and B are independent, both given H

the definition in (3) but to put the justifications into this chapter would be too repetitive of what I have said elsewhere several times. (See, for example, Good, 1984; 1987a; 1991; 1994a; 1995a.) It is worth emphasizing that, *to switch from strict causality to probabilistic causality, we simply replace implication by weight of evidence.* Philosophers, even when of a Bayesian persuasion, do not yet all accept the explication or explanans (3) but that's because many of them are not yet familiar with its simple justifications, and perhaps because some philosophers are 'qualitativists', and, for a few, "'whatever it is, they're against it'". I call that 'Grouchomarxism'.[21]

13 PROBABILITY AND DEGREES OF CAUSALITY

We can use (3), substituted into (1) and (2), to express Q_{nec} and Q_{suf} directly in terms of probability. We get the basic formulae

$$Q_{nec}(E : F|U) = \log \frac{P(E|F \cdot U)}{P(E|\bar{F}U)} = \log \frac{p}{q}, \tag{4}$$

and

$$Q_{suf}(E : F|U) = \log \frac{1 - P(E|\bar{F} \cdot U)}{1 - P(E|F \cdot U)} = \log \frac{1 - q}{1 - p}, \tag{5}$$

where $p = P(E|F \cdot U)$ and $q = P(E|\bar{F} \cdot U)$. (I assume that neither p nor q is exactly equal to 0 or 1. This assumption is always true in the real world.) Note that both Q_{nec} and Q_{suf} are functions of the two arguments $P(E|F \cdot U)$ and $P(E|\bar{F} \cdot U)$, as one would naturally require, but of course they are distinct functions. Both Q_{nec} and Q_{suf} vanish when $p = q$, if $p \neq 0$, $p \neq 1$, and otherwise they have the same sign. Apart from that constraint they are mathematically independent. Let us write

$$n = Q_{nec}^{mult}(E : F|U) = P(E|F \cdot U)/P(E|\bar{F} \cdot U)$$

$$= \frac{p}{q} = \frac{1 + \bar{O}}{1 + O} \cdot (O/\bar{O}) \tag{4M}$$

and given $\bar{H}$, equation (3A) simplifies in that A can be omitted from the second term on the right. In the law, approximate independence can be achieved, for example, from testimony from witnesses, fingerprints, DNA, motivation, behavior of the defendant, Dick, in court combined both with his earlier claim to be a good liar and his demonstration of that fact in court, and, if available, previous convictions. (See, for example, Good, 1987a, page 540.) When estimating the weight of evidence from testimony, one should take into account the behavior of the witness Joe, the size of his fee or bribe, and whether *he* has previously been convicted!

Defense lawyers seem to hate adding weights of evidence together. They try to get the jurors and the judge to reject any piece of evidence that is not by itself decisive.

[21] The 'triple quotes' are intended to indicate an inexact quotation. Groucho Marx, as a college president in *Horsefeathers*, after shaving on the platform, sang 'Whatever it is, I'm against it'. I could be accused of Grouchomarxism because of my failure to refer to Eells (1991) and to the works of Nancy Cartwright, D. B. Rubin, B. Skyrms, E. Sober, D. H. Mellor, and others. This is because art is long and life is short especially for octogenarians who are too undisciplined to focus on a single discipline.

The expression *Bayes factor* is standard in the Bayesian literature. Many writers are satisfied with having multiplicativity instead of the additivity of weights of evidence which completely captures the ordinary English meaning of the expression. The basic assumption is that W depends only on $P(A|H \cdot B)$ and $P(A|\bar{H} \cdot B)$ from which it follows quickly that it is a function of their ratio. Then the desire for additivity fixes the explication.

where $O = O(E|F \cdot U)$, $\bar{O} = O(E|\bar{F} \cdot U)$, and

$$s = Q_{\text{suf}}^{\text{mult}}(E : F|U) = P(\bar{E}|\bar{F} \cdot U)/P(\bar{E}|F \cdot U) = \frac{1-q}{1-p} = \frac{1+O}{1+\bar{O}} \qquad (5M)$$

which have multiplicative properties corresponding to various additive properties of Q_{nec} and Q_{suf}. For these additive properties, see for example, Good (1961/62), where causal networks are emphasized, and especially Good (1994a). We may call $Q_{\text{nec}}^{\text{mult}}$ and $Q_{\text{suf}}^{\text{mult}}$ *multiplicative* necessitude and multiplicative sufficitude. By analogy one could regard a Bayes factor as a multiplicative weight of evidence W^{mult}.[22]

These expressions for n and s are very simple, so it is hardly surprising that, when U is dropped, not just as an abbreviation, the corresponding measures of association in 2×2 contingency tables were proposed long ago in addition to a number of other measures. Sheps (1959) cites papers in medical journals by T. Francis, Jr. *et al.* and by E. C. Hammond and D. Horn, in 1955 and 1954 respectively which use p/q and $(1-q)/(l-p)$ (in my notation). Sheps says that the choice between them is often arbitrary. But we now know that they are not arbitrary when they can be interpreted in terms of necessitude and sufficitude.[23]

When p and q are both close to 0 or both close to 1, one should hold in mind what may be called the 'Ratio Principle': it is often more difficult to judge the values of very small probabilities than to judge their ratio. (This point is essential in the philosophy of science: see Good, 1975; but it is usually overlooked in that context. It is also essential in legalistic theory. It might be a general approximate law of perception of physical intensities; see Dember and Warm (1979, 87–89.) Therefore it might sometimes be less difficult to judge n and s directly, once these concepts become familiar, instead of by using formulae (4M) and (5M).

Equations (4) and (5) can be solved, to express $P(E|F \cdot U) = p$, and $P(E|\bar{F} \cdot U) = q$ in terms of n and s. (This aspect of the unification of probability and causality was not possible when there was only one measure for degree of causal tendency.) The solutions (Good, 1994a) are

$$p = \frac{ns - n}{ns - 1}, \qquad q = \frac{s - 1}{ns - 1} \qquad (6)$$

as the reader can readily verify, and the corresponding odds are given by

$$O(E|F \cdot U) = \frac{n(s - 1)}{n - 1}, \qquad O(E|\bar{F} \cdot U) = \frac{s - 1}{s(n - 1)}. \qquad (7)$$

---

[22] Suppes (1994) abbreviated these notations to Q'_{nec} and Q'_{suf}. Of course abbreviations are often convenient. The symbols n and s are even more abbreviated. A conformable notation for a Bayes factor would then be W' instead of BF which I used in Good (1994a). The notation Φ would appeal to those who write Ω for odds.

[23] For various measures of association (in contingency tables), see Goodman and Kruskal (1979) (who emphasize that a measure of association should have an interpretation), Good and Mittal (1987), and Good (1985a). One measure which dates back to Peirce (1884) is $p - q$ in my notation. It is discussed by Good and Mittal (1987, p. 698), with some further references. (One way to see that it cannot measure necessitude or sufficitude is by considering the cases where p and q are both small or both close to 1.) In a medical context it measures the superiority or inferiority of one treatment as compared with another and could be interpreted as proportional to an expected gain in utility. Utilities are relevant to degrees of punishment, but not to degrees of responsibility *for what occurred*, as mentioned above in relation to Peter and Paul.

The distinction and relationship between probability and odds is shown in the following table:

$P = O/(1 + O)$	0	1/10	1/4	1/3	1/2	2/3	3/4	9/10	1
$O = P/(1 - P)$	0	1/9	1/3	1/2	1	2	3	9	∞

(The odds of a negation $\bar{A}$ are equal to the reciprocal of the odds of A.) In Tables 2a and 2b, the values of n and s are shown as functions of $O(E|F \cdot U)$ and $O(E|\bar{F} \cdot U)$.

According to Jean Piaget (Gruber and Vonèche, 1977, p. 247), 'Before the age of 7–8 the child seeks . . . to eliminate chance from nature'. Of course Piaget didn't claim that the child succeeds in this search. His assertion is roughly equivalent to saying that the young child wants to believe in strict causation and only later understands that probabilistic causation is more important.[24] So it might be argued that the concept of strict causation is psychologically more primitive than that of probability at the conscious level. But the concepts of probability and probabilistic causation evolve together as the infant grows up, and also as philosophy develops, just as chicken eggs and chickens evolved together. See also Note 5.

It might be possible, with practice, to use judgments of causality to improve one's body of beliefs by using formulae (6) or (7), or formulae (1)–(5M), or tables based on these formulae. This would be consistent with the 'Black Box' philosophy of subjective (personal) probability (Good, 1950, 1962) in which a variety of kinds of judgments and discernments can respectively be the input and output of the Black Box. (The output can be fed back to the input.) It is difficult to judge whether or when the (quantitative) concepts of necessitude and sufficitude, and their multiplicative forms, will become as familiar as the quantitative and semiquantitative concepts of probability and odds. If they do become familiar, then judges, lawyers and detectives will be able to switch from one set of concepts to the other. This way of 'thinking' might first become standard

---

[24]Most adults, even some philosophers and lawyers, like Piaget's child, have the desire to avoid mentioning probability. For example, grown-up lawyers talk as if someone is either a suspect or is not, without mentioning the threshold probability of guilt that defines the term. Physicists were mostly determinists up to the advent of quantum mechanics (although it can be given a deterministic interpretation as in a branching-universe theory; see Note 41). Poincaré believed in determinism but knew the importance of probability and wrote a book on that topic (Poincaré, 1912). On his page 4 he attributed probability, from a pragmatic point of view, to the phenomenon of extreme sensitivity to initial conditions. He said 'Une cause très petite, qui nous échappe, détermine un effet considérable que nous ne pouvons pas ne pas voir, et alors nous disons que cet effet est dû au hasard.' Freely translated – a cause too small to notice can produce a considerable effect that we cannot overlook and we then say that this effect is due to chance. (Poincaré gave several examples; another one is a supersaturated solution.)

Maxwell (and presumably earlier workers on statistical mechanics) was another determinist who used probability, as in the Maxwell–Boltzmann distribution.

'Sensitivity to initial conditions' is familiar outside physics; for example, there were some small events that led to the birth of Hitler and then to world-wide suffering. As Benjamin Franklin said in 1758 'A little neglect may breed mischief . . . for want of a nail the shoe was lost . . .'. One could call this the horseshoe effect corresponding to the familiar 'butterfly effect' in meteorology. (See, for example, Gleick, 1987.)

The effect could also be called 'indeterminism emerging from determinism': see Good (1974, p. 129; 1983, p. 92) where I said in relation to statistical mechanics, '. . . to predict a time T ahead . . . I think we would need to know [the initial conditions] to a number of decimal places proportional to T.' (Perhaps in 1974 I had been influenced unconsciously and indirectly by Poincaré.) It is mainly in Poincaré's or Franklin's sense, or the butterfly or horseshoe sense, that I talk of physical probability in forensic matters. The indeterminism of quantum mechanics is something extra.

Table 2a. Values of n (multiplicative necessitude) in terms of $O = O(E|F \cdot U)$ and $\bar{O} = O(E|\bar{F} \cdot U)$. The corresponding table for (additive) necessitude (or sufficitude) world be skew symmetric.

$O \backslash \bar{O}$	1/1000	1/100	1/10	1	10	100	1000
1/1000	1	1/10	1/90	1/500	1/900	1/990	1/1000
1/100	10	1	1/9	1/50	1/90	1/100	1/100
1/10	90	9	1	1/5	1/10	1/11	1/11
1	500	50	5	1	1/2	1/2	1/2
10	900	90	10	2	1	1/1.1	1/1.1
100	990	100	11	2	1.1	1	1
1000	1000	100	11	2	11	1	1

Table 2b. Values of s (multiplicative sufficitude).

$O \backslash \bar{O}$	1/1000	1/100	1/10	1	10	100	1000
1/1000	1	1	1.1	1/2	1/11	1/100	1/1000
1/100	1	1	1/1.1	1/2	1/11	1/100	1/990
1/10	1.1	1.1	1	1/2	1/10	1/90	1/900
1	2	2	2	1	1/5	1/50	1/500
10	11	11	10	5	1	1/9	1/90
100	100	100	90	50	9	1	1/10
1000	1000	990	900	500	90	10	1

for intelligent machines (which presumably will not be wishful thinkers). For numerical examples see Note 25. In Good (1986) I suggested, somewhat facetiously, that computers would recommend appropriate punishment by the year 2501. Judging by the advances

---

[25]Consider three numerical examples.

(i) F: a dog goes out-of-doors. E: the dog is injured by a vehicle. Assume $p = P(E|F \cdot U) = 10^{-4}$, $q = P(E|\bar{F} \cdot U) = 10^{-9}$.

Then, if logarithms to base 10 are used,

$$n = Q_{\text{nec}}^{\text{mult}} = \frac{p}{q} = 10^5$$

$$s = Q_{\text{suf}}^{\text{mult}} = \frac{1-q}{1-p} \approx 1.0001$$

$$Q_{\text{nec}} = 5, \qquad Q_{\text{suf}} = 0.0000434.$$

As one would expect, the necessitude of F for E is large and the sufficitude is small. The owners of the dog do not deserve much blame although the sine-qua-non-itude (necessitude) is large.

(ii) *The marksman.* Suppose there are six marksmen in a firing squad and we consider a specific marksman named Jones. $F =$ Jones shoots. $\bar{F} =$ Jones does not shoot (counterfactually). $E =$ the victim dies. U contains the information that the captain has said 'Fire'. Given U, each marksman without a blank has an independent probability 0.9 of killing the victim, and we assume that all marksmen obey orders. Precisely one marksman has the blank, each with probability 1/6. Assume that the marksmen fire simultaneously. We have, again with logs to base 10,

$$p = P(E|F \cdot U) = 1 - 10^{-5} = 0.99999$$

(because five marksmen do not have a blank)

in Bayesian analysis in the law, with computer aid, as described by Kadane and Schum (1996), we might not have to wait that long for the computers to take over.

The reason for using logarithms is of course to give necessitude and sufficitude several additive properties (not repeated in the present paper) and to make them vanish when $p = q$.[26] These properties justify the expression *causal calculus* which Leibniz would have liked. It has been speculated that our brains contain neural circuits for doing additions and subtractions (Uttley, 1959, p. 144;[27] Good, 1961, p. 128); and the

$$q = P(E|\bar{F} \cdot U) = \frac{1}{6}(1 - 10^{-5}) + \frac{5}{6}(1 - 10^{-4})$$

$$= 1 - \frac{51}{6} \times 10^{-5} = 0.999915$$

$$n = Q_{\text{nec}}^{\text{mult}} = \frac{p}{q} = \frac{1 - 10^{-5}}{1 - \frac{51}{6} \times 10^{-5}} = 1.0000750$$

$$Q_{\text{nec}} = 0.00003257$$

$$s = Q_{\text{suf}}^{\text{mult}} = \frac{1 - q}{1 - p} = \left(\frac{51}{6}\right) 10^{-5}/10^{-5} = 8.5$$

$$Q_{\text{suf}} = 0.929.$$

The calculations can be checked by means of equations (6).

Thus the necessitude is small and the E sufficitude is appreciable, as is intuitively reasonable. If the firing squad is illegal, then Jones would be held responsible. But, if his gun were later found to have fired a blank, he might be accused only of attempted murder unless perhaps as part of a conspiracy. But common sense suggests that 'divine law' should be used in this situation, that is, his intentions should count more than whether he had a blank.

A similar but slightly simpler calculation can be applied to the *captain* of the firing squad. He has large sufficitude *and* necessitude.

(iii) *The battered woman (see also Note 3)*. A woman had a choice of marrying a 'representative batterer' (event F) or a nonbatterer (event $\bar{F}$). In say 1994 she is murdered by somebody (event E). Let U denote the state of the universe just before she made her choice of husband. Then, by using official statistics for 1992, it can be shown (Good, 1996a, b) that

$$p = P(E|F \cdot U) \approx 1/2000, \qquad q = P(E|\bar{F} \cdot U) \approx 1/20,000.$$

For the criminal O. J. Simpson case, Dershowitz confused *the probability per battery with that per batterer*, in other words the probability per year, for a 'representative batterer' with the probability in the long run. The latter is an order of magnitude greater than 1/2000.

Thus, approximately $n = p/q = 10$, $s = 1.000450$, $Q_{\text{nec}}(E : F|U) = 1$ ban, $Q_{\text{suf}}(E : F|U) = 120$ microbans. So marrying the batterer had appreciable necessitude but very small sufficitude for getting murdered in 1994. (Compare Example i.) If the day (or only the decade) of the murder were specified, then p and q would both be divided by 365 (or multiplied by about 10) so the necessitude would be roughly unchanged. The sufficitude would become 1/3 microban (or 1.2 millibans). Similarly, to be killed in an air crash it is almost necessary to travel by air but far from sufficient!

The sensitivity of the sufficitude to the precise description of E can only be cured by a weighted integration of the sufficitudes over all events similar to E as explained in relation to Example (a) in the main text.

[26]If U is dropped, one obtains new additive and corresponding multiplicative properties for measures of association in multidimensional contingency tables, but these measures are perhaps meaningful only when they can be interpreted in terms of probabilistic causality.

[27]Uttley suggested that the difference between two estimated log-probabilities might be represented by a time-delay in the nervous system. He did not consider an analogy with heterodyning in which sums as well as differences could be represented. The sums are needed for combining independent log-probabilities or independent weights of evidence. A natural conjecture would be, in other contexts, that summations of logarithms of physical intensities are effected by the *summing of frequencies of firing of neurons*. This conjecture could perhaps be tested experimentally. Of course, like most laws, it must break down under extreme conditions.

Weber–Fechner 'law', though not accurate except for pitch, might be relevant. [28,29,30] Perhaps our unconscious minds, or neural networks, embody the formulae of this paper in a rough manner. This would help to explain the value of common sense, and hence why the jury system is not entirely without merit.[38]

Let us now consider the multiplicative explications (where the logarithms are dropped). We have the basic definitions which can hardly be overemphasized:

Multiplicative necessitude is the factor by which the probability (not the odds) *of E is multiplied by the occurrence of F, as contrasted with $\bar{F}$, and multiplicative sufficitude is the factor by which the probability of the failure of E is divided by the occurrence of F* (again as contrasted with $\bar{F}$). (Note, for example, that if the prior probability of E is close to 1, then the multiplicative necessitude is bound to be small as it clearly should be.) These properties are somewhat easier to grasp in terms of an example. Consider attempted murder by shooting. The multiplicative necessitude is the factor by which the probability of the death of the victim is multiplied by firing the gun. The multiplicative sufficitude is the factor by which the probability of survival of the victim is divided by the firing. The simplicity of these facts again supplies intuitive support for the explications and I believe that at present, and for several decades to come, most jurors, lawyers, judges, detectives, and doctors will prefer not to have to use logarithms. The explications of necessitude and sufficitude, in their additive and multiplicative forms, are compelling, not allowing for the partial ordering of epistemic probabilities, i.e. the use of upper and lower probabilities (for example, Keynes, 1921, and dozens of publications by Good).

The magnitudes of the necessitude and sufficitude depend very much on what is meant by $\bar{F}$. The definitions of n and s do not absolve us from the need to consider the probabilities of various explanations for the occurrence of E. Technically, if utilities are not introduced, the best theory is perhaps the one of highest 'explicativity' which is a 'quasiutility' (Good, 1969, 1977a).

---

[28]Peirce (1878) regards the Weber–Fechner 'law' as 'in harmony' with conceptual log-odds. The 'law' states that a subjectively least discernible difference in a physical quantity is proportional to the physical intensity or energy of the quantity when the intensity is not too small or too large. This leads naturally to the formulation that a physiological reaction, perhaps the frequency of the output of a neuron, is proportional to the logarithm of the physical intensity, apart from ends of the ranges. This justifies the use of logarithmic measures for sound (decibels) and for star magnitudes. For a critique of the Weber–Fechner law see, for example, Stevens (1982) or Dember and Warm (1979, pp. 51–54). A 'deciban', Turing's unit for weight of evidence (see, for example, Good, 1991), or half a deciban, is I believe approximately a least discernible difference in weight of evidence when the weight of evidence, in absolute value, is not extremely small or extremely large.[29,30] Presumably the corresponding facts apply to 'decicasats' (a unit suggested by Good, 1988a, and earlier) because necessitude and sufficitude can be expressed as weights of evidence. In fact the 'decicausat' could reasonably be called a 'deciban'. 'Grades' A, B, C, D, and F, or 0, 1, 2, . . . , 10, or 'starrages' might also be used. Empirical research would be required for approximate calibration purposes, as in other experiments in psychology. Such research is largely concerned with *how people use language*, for example, when they say that one sound is 'twice as loud' as another.

[29]The half-deciban (hdb) was used for an important cryptanalytic technique, called Banburismus, in World War II (Good, 1994c, p. 158), in which many independent weights of evidence were added together. According to Anon (1976, p. 1239, col. ii) about 280 intensity levels of sound can be distinguished in a range of 120 decibels, so half a decibel is about the least distinguishable difference just as half a deciban might be.

[30]It would be interesting to know the thresholds of weights of evidence below which judges consider them unworthy to contribute to 'the whole truth', or to be 'more prejudicial than probative'. Their attitude to 'lie detectors' (polygraphs) gives some information on this point where the expected weight of evidence, under pass-fail usage, is only 1.5 decibans (Toulmin, 1984; Good, 1991). I think the standard deviation is about 4 db. The research (and the law) should be updated to allow for *degrees* of failure.

14 A STRAW MAN

An opponent, a straw man, who has not seen the arguments in Good (1994a) in favor of the explications (4M) and (5M) for $Q_{\text{nec}}^{\text{mult}}$ and $Q_{\text{suf}}^{\text{mult}}$, might say incorrectly that $P(E|F \cdot U)/P(E|\bar{F} \cdot U)$ is intuitively no better than $O(E|F \cdot U)/O(E|\bar{F} \cdot U)$ as an explication of $Q_{\text{nec}}^{\text{mult}}$ and that $P(\bar{E}|\bar{F} \cdot U)/P(\bar{E}|F \cdot U)$ is likewise no better than $O(\bar{E}|\bar{F} \cdot U)/O(\bar{E}|F \cdot U)$ for $Q_{\text{suf}}^{\text{mult}}$. Apart from knowing already that this suggestion is wrong, it is refuted by noting that

$$\frac{O(E|F \cdot U)}{O(E|\bar{F} \cdot U)} = \frac{O(\bar{E}|\bar{F} \cdot U)}{O(\bar{E}|F \cdot U)}. \tag{8}$$

Thus, the opponent's suggestion would equate $Q_{\text{nec}}^{\text{mult}}$ and $Q_{\text{suf}}^{\text{mult}}$ (or Q_{nec} and Q_{suf}) and we already know this must be wrong.

Another way to refute this opponent's suggestion for $Q_{\text{nec}}^{\text{mult}}$ is to consider the case where p and q are both close to 1. Then the event E cannot be made much more probable by the occurrence of F rather than $\bar{F}$, that is, F is hardly necessary for producing E. To produce E it is hardly necessary to raise its odds from say a billion to a trillion, so in this case $Q_{\text{nec}}^{\text{mult}}$ should be small, not large. It would be large if the probabilities in formula (4M) were replaced by odds as the straw man proposed.

Similarly, if p and q were both small, the 'action' F would have been of little help to cause E to occur, so Q_{suf} should be small. But this again would not apply if P were replaced by O in (5) (or (5M)). Thus the straw man is blown away.

15 ETHICAL RESPONSIBILITY

When considering the agent M's ethical responsibility for the act F, it is M's *estimate* of $Q(E : F|U)$ that should be taken into account. That is a reason why a child is usually considered to be less culpable than a sane adult for the performance of essentially the same type of crime. Judea Pearl, in a private communication (June 1998), suggests that U could well have a subjective distribution and then $Q(E : F|U)$ should be replaced by its expectation. Indeed, Good (1961/62, p. 308) said that the exact state has a probability distribution. Compare the proposal in Good (1961/62) of replacing the negation of F by a distribution over all alternatives of F; and a suggestion in Good (1993a, p. 102) for a distribution of possible states U_t'; and yet again, the weighted average of sufficitudes over all events similar to E mentioned in Note 25 and in Section 20. All of these ideas are consistent with my view that a degree of probabilistic causality is a physical concept that often has to be judged subjectively.

To avoid misunderstanding, note that Pearl's writings on causation are based on the assumption of physical determinism, as are the writings of A. P. Dempster, D. B. Rubin, Richard Stone, and others. I regard such a model or theory of causation as an important special or limiting case of a theory of probabilistic causation. Pearl doesn't agree. See the end of Section 10.

16 MULTIPLE EFFECTS

From now on, let us concentrate mainly on legal matters. Then the event F usually describes or includes an act by an agent. The act is an event F. The law is concerned with the legal responsibility of this act in causing an event E, or in causing each of two or more events $E_1, E_2, \ldots$. For example, in the film *From Russia With Love*, the world chess champion Kronsteen might try to kill James Bond (event E_1) under orders from SPECTRE, the Special Executive for Counter Intelligence, Terrorism, Revenge, and Extortion. The event E_2 might be Kronsteen's survival. If Kronsteen succeeds, then he has high legal responsibility for E_1 and also for E_2 (saving his own life). His legal responsibility for E_1 was not decreased by the fact that he was acting under duress, but his legal punishment, as distinct from his Spectral punishment, would reasonably be decreased for that reason. For example, he might be merely hanged instead of being hanged, drawn, and quartered. In other words, the punishment can depend on the responsibility of F for E_2 as well as on the responsibility for E_1.

The topic of multiple causes is at least as interesting as that of multiple effects. A medical example, relating to smoking and living in a smoky district, was used by Good (1961/62, 1994a) as an illustration of an additive formula.

17 THE JURY'S RESPONSIBILITY

Suppose that an accused man (defendant) is on trial for causing E, such as the death of a woman, and that he is alleged to have perpetrated some act F, such as throwing a pebble, which had some sufficitude for E. Apart from E there will be other evidence E' which could be included in a juror's updating of the juror's estimate of the state of the universe. Part of E' would be whether the accused, or a witness Joe, appears truthful in court and, even more, whether he appears truthful when he is known to be almost certainly lying! I take it that, at least implicitly, the jury makes a multisubjective[31] ('dodecasubjective'?) estimate of the posterior probability $P(F|E \cdot E' \cdot U)$, an estimate denoted here by

$$\mathrm{jury}\,P(F|E \cdot E' \cdot U) \qquad (9)$$

[31] If several people give honest estimates of their personal odds of a hypothesis, after interpersonal deliberations, then these estimates could perhaps be usefully combined by first rejecting outliers and then taking the geometric mean, i.e. by averaging the log-odds instead of relying on a straight vote. (Odds judged as zero or infinity, being too dogmatic, should be regarded as outliers unless the verdict is almost unanimous.) A weighted average of the log-odds could be used, with the weights equal to the marks attained in preliminary examinations. This method might *eventually* become realistic. At present, personal odds might not be explicit enough, and jurors, influenced by politicians, might not be honest enough.

Similar considerations apply in a medical or machine-maintenance context, as of a computer or car. The level of *necessitude (plus the initial log-odds) helps to determine a conviction in the legal context*, and a diagnosis in the medical context and in the context of machine maintenance. The sufficitude is related to the magnitude of the legal sentence and to a medical or machine treatment. The jury corresponds to a team of doctors or of maintenance engineers. The need to combine judgments of odds can arise in all three contexts.

(or the jurors might prefer to use odds instead of probability). How else could the jury ever arrive at an honest conviction? In a Bayesian model they arrive at (9) by adding

$$\text{jury}\, W(F : E \cdot E'|U) \tag{10}$$

to the initial log-odds of F, etc. But this procedure is usually only implicit and approximate and is performed at a subconscious or unconscious level. I think, more typically, a juror J makes judgments of intermediate rather than prior odds. For example, part way through a trial, or through an argument, J might think the guilt of the defendant is 'odds on', and thereafter, in a rough and ready way, J multiplies the odds by judged Bayes factors obtained from evidence presented later in the trial. By using Bayes's theorem in reverse J can discover J's own initial probability. J can also use the 'device of imaginary results' (see Good, 1950 and the two subject indexes of Good, 1983). For more on these matters see Good (1986, 1987b).

We can write (10) as

$$\text{jury}\, Q_{\text{nec}}(E \cdot E' : F|U), \tag{11}$$

and a future juror's judgment might be helped by knowing that (10) and (11) should be equal.

In addition, the jury or judge must estimate the *accused's* estimate of the sufficitude of F for E because they are supposed to take the *intent* of the accused into account. So they arrive at

$$\text{jury}[\text{accused}\, Q_{\text{suf}}(E : F|U)]. \tag{12}$$

At first, I thought that perhaps the jurors should consider whether some function of (9) and (12) exceeds some threshold for 'determining' a conviction. But this would not be appropriate. Instead they should decide whether (9) by itself exceeds some threshold, such as 0.99, on which the verdict largely depends, and, if it does, then they or the judge could use (12) as a partial measure of the '*degree*' of the murder. Of course, if this degree were small enough the crime would be 'determined' or guessed as, at worst, manslaughter, or at best a misdemeanor.

Moreover, when an accused man is contemplating a crime, not knowing E', he might use his judgment of the jury's judgment of his judgment of the necessitude, somewhat as in the theory of games. He might try to allow for a probability distribution over the possible sets of evidence E'; for example, he might avoid leaving fingerprints.

In practice, F would often be a disjunction of many possible mutually exclusive acts (by the accused) $F_1 \vee F_2 \vee F_3 \vee \ldots$, with posterior probabilities say $\pi_1, \pi_2, \pi_3, \ldots$ (as implicitly judged by the jury), where

$$\pi_1 + \pi_2 + \cdots = \text{jury}\, P(F|E \cdot E' \cdot U), \tag{13}$$

and I think (12) should be replaced by

$$\text{jury}\left[\sum_i \pi_i\, Q_{\text{suf}}(E : F_i|U)\right]. \tag{14}$$

The sum here has the form of an expected weight of evidence. If allowance is made for a variety of E's, say E_1, E_2, $E_3, \ldots$, then there could be several expressions like (14), one for each E_j, as in the Kronsteen example.

Note that, according to this analysis, the jury should not combine the necessitude and sufficitude into a single number. The *verdict* depends largely on the size of the *necessitude* because this contributes to the weight of evidence in favor of F (the guilt of the accused) provided by $E \cdot E'$. To obtain the posterior (final) log-odds of F, the total weight of evidence provided by $E \cdot E'$ should be added to the prior (initial) log-odds of F which unfortunately can vary greatly from one juror to another and is usually only implicit.[32] After a verdict of guilty (decided by the jury), the *sentence* (decided I hope mainly by the judge[33]) depends largely on the *sufficitude* of F to cause E, partly on the extent of the damage, and partly on additional evidence mentioned in the next paragraph.

When sentencing the convicted person, the judge allows for previous convictions or good or bad behavior of the accused. Officially the jury is not supposed to take previous bad behavior of the defendant into account in its verdict unless that behavior is obviously causally relevant as, for example, battery followed by murder. (Re this example, see Good, 1996a, b for a quantitative analysis in which a claim by Dershowitz is shown to be mistaken, as explained in Note 3.) In any case, a knowledge of previous convictions would affect the prior probability of guilt, prior to the other evidence received in court. At least in England the defending attorney usually tells the jury if the defendant has had no previous convictions. When the attorney does not do so a knowledgeable juror infers that the defendant *has* been previously convicted. The lawyers for the defense hope that jurors are not that knowledgeable. Sometimes, the judge uses this additional evidence to decide the severity of the punishment but justice might already have been denied if the defendant has been acquitted by a jury that was kept in the dark. I believe the law is wrong and that the jury *should* be told about previous convictions, – the advantages might well outweigh the disadvantage of having numerous recidivists at large.

18   REVENGE

Consider again the example of murder. The event F is, for example, that someone fires a gun pointed at the victim. The event E is the ending of another's life. From an ethical

---

[32] The interpretation of 'beyond a reasonable doubt' might also vary a lot from one juror to another. My opinion is (i) final odds of 50 (50 to 1 on), or at least 200 in a capital case, should be enough for a verdict of 'guilty beyond a reasonable doubt', (ii) final odds between 1 ('evens') and 50 should imply a verdict of 'unproven' (in the language of Scottish law), (iii) between 1/50 ('50 to 1 against') and 1 imply 'innocent', and (iv) less than 1/50, 'innocent beyond a reasonable doubt'. I haven't seen this matter of threshold odds of guilt in criminal law worked out quantitatively in terms of maximizing expected utility or errors of the first and second kinds. The legalese 'not guilty', meaning 'not guilty beyond a reasonable doubt', greatly misleads the public and has even misled at least four lawyers on American television (the Geraldo Rivera show on CNBC) who interpreted 'not guilty' to mean 'innocent'. Two of them quickly corrected themselves, while the other two either wanted to mislead or didn't want to admit error or perhaps would fall back on the sanctimonious slogan 'presumed innocent until proven guilty'. (Here 'proven' means 'said by the jury to be'.)

[33] This was roughly true in California in the first part of the twentieth century (Friedman, 1993, p. 409) and I assume it to be true in some of the text for the sake of brevity. For a very interesting historical discussion of sentencing in America see Friedman (1993, pp. 409–417). The book is highly readable yet scholarly.

point of view what matters most is the attempt or the degree of resolution of the attempt, but human law, as distinct from divine law, regards it as especially important that the victim died (the event E). Part of the justification for this might be the need to decrease the complexity of the law. Another justification is that murder is strong evidence for attempted murder! H & H' (pp. 354–355), citing H. Wechsler and J. Michael, say 'a completed crime awakens more social resentment than an attempt'. Also 'the judge ... who takes account of ... public sentiment ... does not thereby embrace the popular theory'. It seems that H & H' are reluctant to concede that revenge against the criminal is one of the main functions of the law, at least implicitly. (No country is as great as Garfield claimed, although some individuals are.) *Revenge* is a dirty seven-letter word and is not in the index of their book. There is one index entry for 'retributive theory'. (Lawyers, like doctors, prefer unemotional language.) They argue that greater leniency for a mere attempt does not diminish the deterrent effect of the law because the criminal does not know in advance that his attempt will fail. Their argument is convincing when the attempt is entirely resolute, but it does not apply, for example, to the case of throwing a small pebble, or punching the victim on the jaw, where the agent is not much deterred by the possibility of the maximum penalty.[34]

19 LEGAL RESPONSIBILITY OR 'CULPABILITY'

But if it is so important whether E occurs (the completed crime), then, for the sake of consistency, *intermediate* events should also be highly relevant. This requirement, which χ should also satisfy, is attained by the expressions $C_{nec}(E : F)$ and $C_{suf}(E : F)$ about to be described (Good, 1993a). They are defined only if F and E both occur. They appear also to be reasonable candidate explications for χ_{nec} and χ_{suf}.

The expressions C_{nec} and C_{suf}, when applied to causal chains, express the notion that the strength depends on the weakest link. In England, if the victim survives more than a year and a day, the law regards the causal chain as cut and the defendant is then acquitted of murder (H & H', p. 63 or 88). My suggestions are less arbitrary (but less simple) and are intended to be a normative expression of the *spirit* of the law rather than its letter. These suggestions are based on the assumption that the agent was attempting

---

[34]Neither 'revenge' nor 'retribution' occur in the index of Friedman (1993). I have noticed the word 'revenge' on pages 73 and 74 of Hart (1968) (though not in the index) but he does not condone this hormonal feature of men and animals. Whether we like it or not, a desire for revenge is innate in man's soul (to parody Tolstoy). The other cheek usually belongs to the other man! The desire for revenge has the function of discouraging one's enemies so it can be explained by Natural Selection. Even a wasp attempts revenge when it chases a person who has disturbed it. Charles Darwin, in Chap. III of *The Descent of Man*, said 'Many, and presumably true, anecdotes have been published on the long-delayed and artful revenge of various animals'. His examples referred to monkeys. Of course revenge is an extremely frequent theme in literature. The Count of Monte Cristo is an outstanding example.

The concept of revenge is also powerfully treated in the film 'Fury' (1936) with Spencer Tracy and Sylvia Sidney. The character acted by Tracy tries to get revenge against the mob who tried to kill him by setting fire to the gaol in which he had been unjustly locked up. They thought they had succeeded. 'Tracy' tries to suppress the fact that he had escaped. The mob was ethically exactly as much at fault as if it had succeeded, yet 'Tracy' too was attempting murder because the mob would have been hanged if he had succeeded in his plan. They did not ethically deserve to be hanged, not because Tracy escaped but because they thought *he* was guilty. They certainly deserved *severe* punishment.

to achieve E, or was not taking reasonable precautions to prevent it. The suggestions, at least for causal *chains*, are *legalistic sufficitude* or *sufficientive culpability*,

$$C_{\mathrm{suf}}(E : F|U) = C_{\mathrm{suf}}(E : F) = \min_t \log \frac{P(\bar{E}|\bar{F} \cdot U_t' \cdot U)}{P(\bar{E}|F \cdot U_t \cdot U)}. \tag{15}$$

(unless the numerator and denominator both vanish) and *legalistic necessitude* or *necessitive culpability*

$$C_{\mathrm{nec}}(E : F|U) = C_{\mathrm{nec}}(E : F) = \min_t \log \frac{P(E|F \cdot U_t' \cdot U)}{P(E|\bar{F} \cdot U_t' \cdot U)}. \tag{16}$$

Here U_t denotes the state of the universe at time t after F occurs (and before E occurs), and U_t' denotes what the state would have been if F had not occurred, that is, in the example, if the gun had not been fired. In Good (1988b), where I offered a definition of χ_{suf} (denoted there by χ), this idea was called 'carrying along the negation (of F)'.[35] I am reminded of a remark by Trevor-Roper (1980), 'History is not merely what happened, it is what happened in the context of what might have happened'. In other words, the historian, say Hugh, is interested in Causation, otherwise he would be only a chronicler. Like the lawyer, the historian is usually, but by no means always, more interested in proximate causes than in remote causes.[36]

The notion of updating U gradually or piecemeal (in the notations U_t and U_t') is somewhat analogous to what Salmon (1984, pp. 196–200) calls, in connection with the concept χ, 'the method of successive reconditionalization', but his concept is qualitative and he does not consider taking the minimum over time.

The expressions (15) and (16) define physical concepts but they would have to be judged subjectively by the judge, the lawyers and each juror, and these judgments would often be complicated. Moreover, it is necessary in both (15) and (16) to average the logarithms over all possible sequences U_t', weighted with their probabilities, thus obtaining cross-entropy expressions. For remote causes especially, the complexities could be overwhelming for humans and for computers of the next several decades.[37] This is a sufficient

---

[35] The quantities minimized, in formulae (17) and (18), are generalizations of weight of evidence. They are actual weights of evidence if $\bar{F} \cdot U_{t'}$, is regarded as the negation of $F \cdot U_t$.

[36] As an example of a remote cause according to a television programme, ancient Egyptians buried Tutankhamun with meat for his afterlife. This meat developed into a deadly mold which much later killed some archaeologists and some less respectable grave robbers. (The 'curse of Tutankhamun'.) Were the ancients guilty of unwitting manslaughter? Ignorance of the laws of nature *is* an excuse.

A disadvantage of looking for temporally remote causes is that it can greatly increase the difficulty of envisaging all possible meanings of U_t'. The roots of the backward tree of causation can branch out exponentially until they cover the earth (compare Good, 1994d). Even for fairly proximate causes it is necessary in practice to categorize the possible histories from F to E into a small number of groups. Of course such categorization is necessary for all our thinking; in statistics it is called 'modeling'.

[37] Verdicts are therefore left to twelve somewhat haphazardly chosen people, six being the expected number of whom are below median intelligence, irrespective of the definition of intelligence. The reliance on the jury system is a little like telling the time by averaging the times on the faces of twelve second-hand clocks. Perhaps potential jurors should take multiple-choice examinations. They should eventually be required to know the distinction between probability and odds, and also the definition of a Bayes factor. A child of 14, and also lawyers, could be taught these things. In a later year at school, the technical definition of weight of evidence could be given and justified – it would incidentally make the notion of logarithms more interesting for the youngster. (Of course logarithms are still important though not for the reason they were first introduced.)

explanation of why historians and lawyers are mainly concerned with proximate rather than with remote causes. (The averaging is theoretically appealing because of the additive property of logarithms just as for cross-entropies.)

If multiplicative forms $C_{\text{nec}}^{\text{mult}}$ and $C_{\text{suf}}^{\text{mult}}$ are preferred we can simply drop the logarithms. (The operations min and log are interchangeable.) Then geometric means (weighted by 'powering') would replace the averages just mentioned.

Roughly speaking, C_{nec} is the minimum weight of evidence in favor of F, provided by the occurrence of E, during the period of time between the occurrences of F and E. Again roughly speaking, C_{suf} is the minimum weight of evidence against F, during the same time period, provided by the (counterfactual) nonoccurrence of E. The more completely the causal chain is cut, the smaller C_{suf} becomes.

The use of counterfactual propositions is essential in the philosophy of causation and also in that of explanation (Good, 1977a, p. 303; or 1983, p. 219). When a counterfactual proposition occurs to the right of the vertical stroke in the probability notation, it is better to read the vertical stroke as *assuming* rather than *given*. It is more general to read it as 'conditioned upon'. It might be objected that one should never condition on a proposition of zero probability, to which one can reply that no *empirical* proposition has physical probability smaller than the reciprocal of

$$10\text{xp}(10\text{xp}(10\text{xp}(10))),$$

where $10\text{xp}(a)$ means 10^a, just as $\exp(a)$ means e^a. Therefore a rational subjective estimate of the probability of an empirical proposition also cannot be exactly zero. To argue that it can be zero 'for all practical purposes' would be a mistake because one practical purpose is to use the calculus of probability to deal with counterfactuals!

Let us consider two examples of culpability. The two examples in Note 25 need no mention of minimization over time.

20 EXAMPLE (A)

An example of a short causal chain of forensic interest occurs in the Babylonian Talmud (Kirzner, 1964, pp. 26b, 27a) and was brought to my attention by M. I. Heiligman in 1994. I give this example with some embellishment:

A man M_1 throws a child named Jacob from the roof of a building (act F_1), intending to commit infanticide. Just before Jacob hits the ground, a man M_2, whose presence was unknown to M_1, kills Jacob with a sword (act F_2). Who was legally responsible for Jacob's death in the way it occurred (event E)? The Talmud says there was a difference of opinion. The 'dream team' for M_1 could argue that the 'sufficientive' causal chain from F_1 to E was cut by M_2, so M_1 was guilty only of *attempted* murder, but the Rabbis argued that M_2 was also not guilty of murder because Jacob would soon have died even if F_2 had not occurred. But R. Judah said M_2 was guilty of murder because F_2 was the immediate cause of the death: we see here the emphasis on proximate causes as in modern times. Indeed H & H' have 33 index entries to that topic but they somewhat down-play the importance of proximate causes in the law. Jacob's mother might put aside the pilpul and would demand maximum revenge against both M_1 and M_2 (assuming she was not one of them) although there was no conspiracy. Common sense[38] agrees with the mother and this agreement can be justified by some further simple pilpul, namely by replacing E by E^* defined simply as Jacob's *death*. The action F_1, led more or less inevitably to E^* though not to E whereas F_2 led to E (the more precise manner of the death). So M_1 and M_2 were both guilty of murder. Note that $C_{\text{suf}}(E : F_1|U)$ is small, because of the 'min' in formula (17), but $C_{\text{suf}}(E^* : F_1|U)$ is large. The action by M_2 did not cut the sufficientive causal chain from F_1 to E^*, only that from F_1 to E. The distinction between E and E^* explains why the Rabbis disagreed with R. Judah.[39]

Similarly, suppose that a man M shoots a woman, while aiming at her heart, and she dies although the bullet missed her heart. (For a discussion of problems with a similar logical structure, see H & H', pp. 355–359, who refer to a tentative draft of the English Model Penal Code.) Even M's nightmare team would 'know' that M committed murder although the manner of death was not precisely as M had intended.[40] It was close enough by common sense standards. If the event E were defined with absurd precision, the sufficitude of F could be made arbitrarily small, but the necessitude would be almost unaffected. Convicted defendants would not be punished! The theoretical solution to this 'paradox' is to express the observed event as a logical disjunction or bundle of microevents $E_1 \vee E_2 \vee E_3 \vee \ldots$ and take a weighted sum of the sufficitudes of each of them, where the weights would depend on how far each microevent was from the event intended by the agent. (Compare the concept of 'substantialism' in Good 1965 in connection with the evaluation of clusters. Formula (B2) therein requires a correction. I used this concept in a Bayesian manner for an important cryptanalytic procedure in WWII, only recently declassified and so not mentioned in Good, 1994c.) This suggestion, combined with a limiting operation, is intended to be analogous to the definition of a Riemann integral. This approach would be needed for defining χ_{suf} as a physical concept; but in a legal trial the judge has to fall back on common sense in which the microevents are lumped into at most three classes.

21 EXAMPLE (B)

(This example is from Good, 1993a, with slight change of wording.) A man is not guilty of murder unless he attempted the murder (event F) and succeeded (event E). But if the chain of causation is nearly or completely cut at any time then the *degree* to which he is responsible can be small or zero. (For example, a surgeon might put the victim V in a reasonable state of health and thereby decrease the probability that V will die within a year from 0.95 to 0.05. If V nevertheless dies within that period the murder could no longer be

---

[38] H & H' have a chapter on causation and common sense.

[39] The analysis would be different if M_2 had first saved Jacob's life and then cut his throat. In that case the chain of causation from M_1 to E^*, as well as to E, would also have been cut, and M_1 would have been guilty only of attempted murder.

[40] To 'know' is usually assumed to mean 'to have justified true belief', but in customary parlance the term is ambiguous for the same reason that 'certainty' is ambiguous, as discussed earlier in the main text. Perhaps strict knowledge is impossible.

regarded as of the 'first degree' *if* the law is self-consistent. Then again, if the surgeon's scalpel slips and the victim dies, the assailant might be told 'you have retrospectively committed murder'. Clearly this is unfair because there had previously been a chance of saving the victim.) The degree can also be negative. In the Holmes–Moriarty–Watson example (Good, 1961/62), Moriarty was trying to kill Holmes by pushing a boulder over the edge of a cliff, at the foot of which Holmes was sitting, and Watson immediately tried (event F) to increase the speed of the boulder to *prevent* the murder. Here C_{suf} is negative (and therefore so is C_{nec}) although Watson's attempt was unsuccessful because a banana skin had been dropped in his path by a chimpanzee. (When I first recounted this tale I forgot to mention the chimpanzee.) Although Watson's action was an important part of the *physical* causal net that led to Holmes's death, I think the reader will agree that Watson could reasonably be described as an *attempted negative* murderer or attempted savior, because, when Watson made his decision, he didn't know about the banana skin, just as the marksman, mentioned earlier and in Note 25, didn't know whether his gun had the blank shot. Both for the marksman and for Dr. Watson, the judge and jury would try to take into account the extenuating circumstances of Watson's incomplete knowledge of U as well as his intentions. Watson was analogous to M_2 in the Talmud story and to the surgeon who botched the operation on the victim. Moriarty was analogous to M_1 and he was guilty of murder because the chain of causation closely resembled what Moriarty had intended. His action had extremely high necessitude and substantial sufficitude for the death of Holmes. The judged value of C could perhaps be regarded as a subjectively weighted average of all possible values of χ.[41]

22 CAUSAL NETWORKS

A causal chain is a special case of a causal network which, I shall assume, consists of a finite number of events or nodes, connected by causal links or branches. Each event either occurs or does not occur at a certain moment. Each link is associated with an arrow pointing in the direction of increasing time. A given moment in time can be regarded as defining a line or plane that might pass through some of the causal links. This assumes that simultaneity has an objective meaning so the model is nonrelativistic. The network is assumed, given F and also given $\bar{F}$, to be a probability network. Then C_{suf} and C_{nec} can be defined by the formulae (15) and (16) just as in the special case of a causal chain. Moreover, I believe we can reasonably define χ_{suf} and χ_{nec} by

$$\chi_{\mathrm{suf}} = C_{\mathrm{suf}}, \qquad \chi_{\mathrm{nec}} = C_{\mathrm{nec}}. \tag{17}$$

---

[41]This is reminiscent of Feynman's sum over all paths in quantum theory. See for example, Feynman (1948) and Schweber (1994, p. 389–396). (Good, 1980, is perhaps suggestive, but half-baked.) Feynman says, in the Conclusion of his Princeton thesis of 1942, 'The interpretation of the formulas from the physical point of view is rather unsatisfactory.' (See Schweber, 1994, p. 393.) I believe his idea can be given an interpretation in terms of the branching-universe theory by adopting the very natural assumption that the universes take a nonzero but very small time (like 10^{-24} sec.) for each separation. This interpretation should appeal to those, like Popper (1982, p. 46), who, believe in *realism* in physics but *pseudorealism* might be a better term in the present context. Combining paths that *coexist*, if only for a short time, is consistent with this kind of physical realism; unlike combining paths that *might* have existed but did not as in Feynman's model.

This definition of χ_{suf} is different from but similar to the one in Good (1988b) where it was called simply χ. The χ of Good (1961/62) was refuted in the Appendix of Good (1988b) and in more detail by Salmon (1988a), and Good (1988b) was my response. A third attempt is given by equations (17).

As in the special case of a causal chain, a user of the theory cannot know χ_{suf} and χ_{nec} with certainty but can make estimates of them.

23 EXAMPLE (C)

The Devil's pin-table (Compare Good, 1988a, p. 44.) The Devil's pin-table has only one exit, and when the ball Exits (event E) it causes an Explosion. Setting the ball in motion is the Foolhardy event F. Clearly $P(E|F \cdot U_t \cdot U) = 1$ (or very close to 1) at all relevant times t, even if the path of the ball happens to be very improbable. Thus $C_{\text{suf}}(E : F) = \infty$, agreeing with the values of Q_{suf} and χ_{suf} if χ_{suf} is properly explicated.

The analysis of boiling a kettle of water, in terms of statistical mechanics, is very similar, and we again find that $C_{\text{suf}} = \infty$ (or 'very close to ∞').

24 EXAMPLE (D)

A pinball machine where skill is involved Consider a pinball machine in which skill is involved. At the end of a game it registers a score. Soon after the player leaves the hall a witness William sees the score but knows only that the player was A or B ('events' F and $\bar{F}$). If it was A then A had an alibi for a murder that occurred elsewhere. From previous experience the probability functions for the scores are known for both players, say p_s, and q_s. The Bayes factor in favor of A having an alibi is p_s/q_s. The witness William is hard to find, and the decision of whether to look for him depends on the expected weight of evidence, or cross-entropy

$$\sum_s p_s \log(p_s/q_s). \tag{18}$$

The ball had many conceivable routes so, from a more complete physical point of view we are dealing with a complicated causal network, but we naturally simplify by relying on the score s alone even if the route taken were recorded on a video tape. (This is analogous to the use of an insufficient statistic in ordinary statistical practice.) This example illustrates once again that it can be extremely difficult to know the values of physical probabilities.

Because complete physical description can be extremely difficult or impossible, it is fortunate that, *when deciding whether to perform an act F*, necessitude and sufficitude are much more important that χ_{suf} and χ_{nec}.

Acknowledgment

Donald Michie told me in 1992 that he thought χ could be defined in terms of Q and he encouraged me to write this paper and Good (1993a) although he was working on the same topic.

51

I. J. GOOD

APPENDIX

My chapter on causation in this volume, and the first draft of Donald Michie's chapter, were written independently, and he has invited me to write an appendix discussing the relationship between the two chapters. There are some differences of notation and terminology but I will not mention them all.

Background

Good (1961/62) emphasized the distinction between the explicanda Q ('tendential causation') and χ (actual causation) *both being intended to apply to a specific occasion*. (I repeat that, at some risk, I use the same symbols for the explications.) That article introduced the symbol U for the state of the universe (or 'world') just before the occurrence of the 'cause' F or $\bar{F}$. This symbol serves to distinguish causation from mere association. There was a separate symbol denoting all true laws of nature known or unknown, but the laws of nature are now included in the symbol U. The arguments in that paper for the explications (explanantia) depended on the consideration of the explicanda of Q and χ in an intertwined manner. A clear requirement is that Q shouldn't depend on what events happen after F or $\bar{F}$ occurs, but it should depend on their probabilities if they belong to the causal network joining F or $\bar{F}$ to E or $\bar{E}$. But χ (meaningful only if F and E occur) should depend on whether these intermediate events occur and on their probabilities before they occur. Further, χ depends also on the *meanings* of $\bar{F}$ and $\bar{E}$ (as well of course on the meanings of F and E), and on what would have happened if F had not occurred.

In the appendix of Good (1988a) I expressed very strong doubts about the explication of χ proposed by Good (1961/62). (That appendix was submitted just before Salmon expounded his refutation of that explication.) Those doubts might then have been extended to Q (because of the abovementioned intertwining), but, as far as I know, the explication of Q has never been questioned. It has turned out that Q is the same as Q_{suf} which, with Q_{nec}, was convincingly explicated by Good (1994a, 1995a).

Good (1988b) proposed a new candidate for χ using a concept called 'carrying along the negation of F.' This candidate has not yet been ruled out, but the problem remained of finding a *convincing* explication for χ. The notion of 'carrying along the negation' has influenced my present work as have the forensic discussions.

In 1992 Michie told me that he thought χ could be explicated in terms of Q (although he did not yet have an explication), but he knew that I wanted to find a convincing explication of χ and he encouraged me to compete with him in that project. Our efforts resulted in the two chapters written for the present book. They are closely related in many ways and different in other ways. His article depends on subjective probabilities alone and he makes no judgement about whether physical probabilities exist. I have always regarded causation as a physical phenomenon and that therefore probabilistic causality should be explicated in terms of (single-case) physical probability (propensity). In fact the definitions of causation and causality in the OED refer unambiguously to physical phenomena. Subjective probability is involved when judging the values of the physical

52

probabilities and when making judgements about the relevant part of U, for example when choosing models in statistics.

David Hume, whose philosophy seems to me to be close to operationalism, questioned the existence of physical causation, so it is appropriate to describe Michie's article as somewhat Humean. On the other hand, I agree with Bertrand Russell's argument against Hume's skeptical attitude to the concept of physical causation (Russell, 1948, p. 473). I leave it to the reader to consult Russell's book on that matter. Then again, de Finetti (1974/75, p. x) said 'Probability does not exist'. He was referring to physical probability. I consider that it is at least convenient to talk as if physical probability exists: it either exists or is a 'useful fiction' in the sense of Jeremy Bentham (Ogden, 1932/1959) or Hans Vaihinger (1911/1924). Ogden (1959, p. xxxii) summarizes Bentham's ideas by means of the quotation 'To language, then – to language alone – it is that fictitious entities owe their existence; their impossible, yet indispensable existence'). Perhaps this can be expressed by saying that metaphysics cannot be completely avoided. A little metaphysics can avoid a lot of wordage. (The wordage is better than the metaphysics when the number of words is small, but how small is bound to be controversial.) See also Note 24 in my chapter, especially Poincaré's expression 'nous disons'. Apparently he was a kind of Benthamite without knowing it.

The concept of (single-case) physical probability might not be entirely indispensable but I think it is at least very convenient for ease of communication with most people. In some cases, when communicating with the cognoscenti, the mention of physical probability can be avoided by making use of de Finetti's representation theorem. Max Born's (and Popper's) propensity interpretation of quantum mechanics is too useful to be discarded on the grounds that it is metaphysical. (It might be false if a branching-universe theory is true, as I think is epistemically probable, but it is useful even if false.) Perhaps my position should be called 'moderate fictionalism'. Even subjective probability can be regarded as metaphysical if we adopt Jimmie Savage's approach. He showed that, given some rather convincing assumptions about rational actions ('decisions'), a completely rational organism behaves *as if* it uses subjective probabilities and utilities and maximizes its expected utility.

Although I adopt the interpretation of causation as a physical phenomenon, I believe that 'in so far as physical probability can be measured it (its measurement) can be done only in terms of subjective probability' (Good, 1961/62, Introduction). My approach then is first to express everything in terms of physical probability and, when that task is complete, to consider how to estimate in practice the physical probabilities and causal tendencies. Likewise, whether in statistical or forensic practice, one has to make personal judgements about the relevant parts of the state of the universe and of the laws of nature. I discussed the subjective aspects, for example, when pointing out that the ethical aspects of behavior depend on the actor's *estimates* of Q_{nec} and Q_{suf}. In 'divine law' that is what matters whereas, in human law, the estimates by judge and jury are also relevant, both of Q and χ. It is part of my philosophy that these judgements usually allow for the cost of thinking: rationality of type II. Michie has avoided the concept of physical probability and goes straight to what I prefer to call the estimation problem. He makes this especially clear from his paragraph 'Return to Good's Q_{suf}' where his 'curly U' is an estimate of U. That paragraph and his ($Q2$) show that at first his R_{suf} is an estimate of Q_{suf}. He extends this definition in his next paragraph where he says 'We conjoin to Ω additional background information . . . subsequent to the moment at which . . . Ω was finalized' as in Good (1988b) and in my chapter. He denotes the updated estimate of Q_{suf} by R_{suf} and offers this as an explication of χ_{suf}. This goes a long way to agreeing with my proposed explication C_{suf} (as well as with Good, 1988b) but it doesn't include 'min$_t$'. The reason I included 'min$_t$' was to allow explicitly for a 'degree of cutting' of a causal chain or net. If a causal net is cut, χ_{nec} and χ_{suf} should vanish, regardless of what happens after the moment of cutting, and, more generally, degrees of cutting should not be ignored.

Nevertheless Michie shows that R_{suf} makes sense for the problem of the desert traveller. His argument would apply I think also to C_{suf} (in my notation). To make his application he had to go outside one's initial understanding of the problem. This he did by allowing for events of very small probability, events chosen by common sense in my opinion, and entered in his 'statistician's logbook'. It can be difficult to estimate the small probabilities of competing hypotheses but less difficult to estimate their ratios or to put them in order of magnitude. The need to allow for the 'Ratio principle', as I called it in my chapter, is clear in theoretical science (Good, 1960, 1975) and is even clearer in most cases in a court of law where the probability of the evidence can very well be as small as 10^{-100} (Good, 1991, p. 92).

Michie's discussion of the desert traveller could be applied, with small modifications, to the Talmud example in my chapter. The two criminals were clearly guilty at least of attempted murder in both examples. In the Talmud example, one could allow for events of very small probability, such as the ground's having a mound of mulch on it that could break the child's fall and save his life. The second criminal M_2 killed the child before that could happen and therefore had higher sufficitude than M_1 for the death of the child, but lower necessitude. In forensic terminology the act by M_2 was the more proximate cause of the death. To convict both criminals of murder, they could both be indicted under more than one interpretation of E.

It would be an onerous and lengthy task to analyze the precise analogy between the desert-traveller problem and the Talmud problem.

Miscellaneous comments

(i) The example of chess in Michie's appendix is reminiscent of my discussion in Good (1968 and 1977). Chess programming is an excellent example for a discussion of dynamic probability in AI. Chess programming would ultimately shed more light on human thought processes if the brute force of the machine was made less brutal (Good, 1993). For example, the machine could be allowed to examine no more than say a thousand positions at each move. This limitation would encourage programmers to make more accurate evaluations of positions. Before 1968 the discussions didn't recognize the relationship of evaluations to dynamic probability and to rationality of type II.

(ii) The odds form of Bayes's theorem, although not formulated by Bayes, has a long history. I think it is implicit in Laplace's work, and was the basis of Jeffreys's work on the philosophy of science and of Turing's work in World War II on a cryptanalytic process called Banburismus. My contribution was that of acting as Turing's 'Boswell' and of developing his ideas in many works. (Turing never published his ideas on this topic.) Some of my ideas, such as those of dynamic probability and type II rationality (used and acknowledged in Michie's chapter), were largely original I believe. Michie's eponymous description 'Turing–Good theory of evidence' is only partly appropriate, but he has obeyed Stigler's law (Stigler, 1980), according to which eponymy is always wrong. Stigler was anticipated by God (c. 200 BC) as senior author. Stigler and God exaggerated somewhat. Good (1962/63, Appendix) modified God's law to 'There is no *single* idea that is absolutely new under the sun.'

(iii) When Michie says 'In an empirical domain, some certainties are more certain than others', I would prefer to say that in ordinary conversation the term *certain* is used loosely and usually means 'with high odds'. I think it is better to avoid this usage in a technical discussion. For the informal meaning 'nearly certain' and 'practically certain' are appropriate, but not 'almost certain' which has a technical meaning. The concepts of 'Practical certainty' and practical impossibility are discussed by Good (1950, pp. 39, 67, 68).

(iv) Good (1993a) said that the concept C would be inappropriate as an explication of χ, but I now think it is appropriate. Legal thinking is an ideal field for understanding the concepts of both tendential and actual causation.

REFERENCES[42]

(The numberings of my publications are included here for general convenience)

Anon (1976). 'Hearing and the ear', in *Van Nostrand's Scientific Encylopedia*, fifth edn., pp. 1237–1243.

Aitken, C. G. G. and Stoney, D. A., eds. (1991). *The Use of Statistics in Forensic Science* (New York: Ellis Horwood).

Berger, J. O. (1985). *Statistical Decision Theory and Bayesian Analysis*, 2nd edn. (New York: Springer-Verlag).

Bernardo, J. J., DeGroot, M. H., Lindley, D. V. and Smith, A. F. M., eds. (1985). *Bayesian Statistics 2: Proceedings of the Second Valencia International Meeting, September 6/10, 1983* (North Holland: Valencia University Press).

Box, G. E. P. and Tiao, G. C. (1973). *Bayesian Inference in Statistical Analysis* (Reading, Mass.: Addison-Wesley).

Carnap, R. (1950). *Logical Foundations of probability* (Chicago: University of Chicago Press).

Cherry, E. C., ed. (1961). *Information Theory: Fourth London Symposium* (1960) (London: Butterworth).

Dawid, A. P 1979). 'Conditional independence in statistical theory', *J Roy. Statist. Soc. ser. B, 41*, 1–31.

Dershowitz, A. M. (1996). *Reasonable Doubts* (New York: Simon and Schuster).

Dember, W. N. and Warm, J. S. (1979). *Psychology of Perception*, 2nd edn. (New York: Holt, Rinehart and Winston).

Eatwell, J., Milgate, M., and Newman, P., eds. (1987). *The New Palgrave: a Dictionary of Economics*, Vol. 4 (London: Macmillan).

---

[42]There are many references to I. J. Good because I have read everything written by that inkslinger, and this has diminished the time available for reading the works of other quill drivers. There are several references on this list that I have read only very incompletely. I apologize for having listed some books that have no indexes.

Eatwell, J., Milgate, M., and Newman, P., eds. (1990). *Utility and Probability* (London: Macmillan). A collection of forty articles from the four 1987 volumes.

Eells, E. (1991). *Probabilistic Causality* (Cambridge: Cambridge University Press).

Elcock, E. W. and Michie, D., eds. (1977). *Machine Intelligence 8* (Chichester: Ellis Horwood).

Everett, H. J. III (1957). ' "Relative state" formulation of quantum mechanics', *Rev. Mod. Physics, 29*, 454–462.

Feynman, R. P. (1948). 'Space-time approach to non-relativistic quantum mechanics', *Rev. of Mod. Physics 20*, 367–387. (Reprinted in Schwinger, 1958.)

de Finetti, B. (1974/75). *Theory of Probability*, two volumes (New York: Wiley). Trans. by Antonio Machí and Adrian Smith from the Italian of 1970.

Friedman, L. M. (1993). *Crime and Punishment in American History* (New York: Basic Books).

Galavotti, M. C. and Gambetta, G., eds. (1988). *Epistemologia ed Economia* (Bologna: CLUEB).

Gleick, J. (1987). *Chaos: Making a New Science* (New York: Penguin Books).

God (c.200 B.C.). Ecclesiastes, 1:9.

13 Good, I. J. (1950). *Probability and the Weighing of Evidence* (London: Charles Griffin; New York: Hafners).

26 Good, I. J. (1952). 'Rational decisions', *J. Roy. Statist. Soc. B. 14*, 107–114. Republished in Kotz and Johnson (1991), 365–377, preceded by an introduction by Lindley.

38 Good, I. J. (1953). 'The population frequencies of species and the estimation of population parameters', *Biometrika 40*, 237–264.

191 Good, I. J. (1960). Review of K. R. Popper 'The Logic of Scientific Discovery', *Math. Rev. 21*, 1171–1173.

221 Good, I. J. (1961). 'Weight of evidence, causality, and false-alarm probabilities', in Cherry (1961), 125–136.

223 Good, I. J. (1961/62). 'A causal calculus', *British J. Philosophy of Science 11*, 305–318; *12*, 43–51; *13*, 88. Republished in Good (1983) with misprints corrected.

230 Good, I. J. (1962). 'Subjective probability as the measure of a non-measurable set', in Nagel *et al.* (1962), 319–329. Republished in Good (1983) and in Kyburg and Smokler (1980).

339 Good, I. J., general ed. (1962/63). *The Scientist Speculates* (London: Heinemann; New York: Basic Books).

411 Good, I. J. (1965). 'Categorization of classification', in *Mathematics and Computer Science in Biology and Medicine* (London: Her Majesty's Stationary Office), 115–128, with discussion.

521 Good, I. J. (1968). 'A five-year plan for automatic chess', in *Machine Intelligence 2* (E. Dale and D. Michie eds.; London: Oliver and Boyd), 89–118.

618 Good, I. J. (1969). 'What is the use of a distribution?', in Krishnaish (1969), 183–203.

765 Good, I. J. (1971). '46656 varieties of Bayesians', letter in *American Statisticians 25*, 62–63. (Republished in Good, 1983.)

815 Good, I. J. (1974). 'Random thoughts about randomness', in Schaffner and Cohen (1974), 117–135. (Republished in Good, 1983.)

846 Good, I. J. (1975). 'Explicativity, corroboration, and the relative odds of hypotheses', *Synthese 30*, 39–73. Republished in Good (1983).

929 Good, I. J. (1976). 'On the application of symmetric Dirichlet distributions and their mixtures to contingency tables', *Annals of Statistics 4*, 1159–1189.

1000 Good, I. J. (1977a). 'Explicativity: a mathematical theory of explanation with statistical applications'. *Proc. Roy. Soc.* (London) *A 354*, 303–330. Republished in Zellner (1980) and in Good (1983).

938 Good, I. J. (1977b). 'Dynamic probability, computer chess, and the measurement of knowledge', in Elcock and Michie (1977), 139–150. (Republished in Good, 1983.)

1333 Good, I. J. (1980). 'Feynman's path integrals and Sewall Wright's path analysis', in *J. of Statist. Comput. and Simul. 12*, 74–77.

1364 Good, I. J. (1983). *Good Thinking: The Foundations of Probability and its Applications* (Univ. of Minnesota Press). (Out of print but I have some copies.)

1575 Good, I. J. (1984). 'The best explicatum of weight of evidence', C197 in *J. Statist. Comput. and Simul. 19*, 294–299.

1636 Good, I. J. (1985a). 'Mathematically natural generalizations of some measures of association and dependence for contingency tables', C236 in *J. Statist. Comput. and Simul. 22*, 93–97.

1515 Good, I. J. (1985b). 'Weight of evidence: a brief survey', in Bernardo *et al.* (1985), 249–269, with discussion.

1710 Good, I. J. (1986). 'The whole truth', *The Institute of Mathematical Statistics Bulletin 15*, 366–373. (An editor's invited column.)

1673 Good, I. J. (1987a). 'Subjective probability', in Eatwell, Milgate, and Newman (1987), 537–543. Republished, with a few additional misprints, two being in formulae, in Eatwell, Milgate, and Newman (1990), 255–269.

1709 Good, I. J. (1987b). 'Some checks on the consistency of probability judgments and a conjectured method for improving those judgments', C277 in *J. Statist. Comput. and Simul. 28*, No. 1, 63–71.

1606B Good, I. J. (1988a). 'Causal tendency: a review', in Harper and Skyrms (1988), 23–50.

1606C Good, I. J. (1988b). Response to Salmon (1988a). In Harper and Skyrms (1988), 73–78. (A few numerical corrections for p. 76 were pointed out by Harper in 1989 and can be supplied.)

1828 Good, I. J. (1991). 'Weight of evidence and the Bayesian likelihood ratio', in Aitken and Stoney (1991), 85–106, with an editors' introduction, 83–84. Also as a Technical Report, 89-16 (July 11, 1989).

2001 Good, I. J. (1993a). 'A tentative measure of probabilistic causation relevant to the philosophy of the law', C400 in *J. Statist. Comput. and Simul. 47*, 99–105. Also Technical Report 93-4 (March 4).

2131 Good, I. J. (1993b). Updated notes for a colloquium on Probabilistic Causality in the Statistics Dept., Va. Tech on 1993 September 23, pp. 16. Technical Report 93-17 (October).

2125 Good, I. J. (1993c). 'Limited competition', *ICCA Journal 16*, No. 2 (June 1993), 118.

2000 Good, I. J. (1994a). 'Causal tendency: necessitivity and sufficientivity: an updated review', in Humphreys (1994), 293–315. Also issued as Technical Report 93-10 (1993 July 8).

2158 Good, I. J. (1994b). 'Legal responsibility and causation'. Technical Report 94-4, Statistics Dept., Va. Tech., Blacksburg, VA 24061, USA (June 7).

2117H Good, I. J. (1994c). 'Enigma and fish', in Hinsley and Stripp (1994), 149–166.

2130 Good, I. J. (1994d). 'The flybutter effect: the obverse of the butterfly effect', *J. Statist. Comput. and Simul. 49*, 237–238.

2101 Good, I. J. (1995a). 'The mathematics of philosophy, a brief review of my work', in Jarvie and Laor (1995), 211–238.

2157 Good, I. J. (1995b). Review of R. Stone (1993), *Math. Rev. 95F*, 3546–47.

2230 Good, I. J. (1996a). 'When batterer becomes murderer', *Nature 381*, 481. Not to be confused with a version in *Nature 375*, 541.

2240A Good, I. J. (1996b). 'Fattori di Bayes, mariti violenti, assassini ed avocati', *KOS* (Milan) *nuova ser.* nos 131/132 (Aug./Sept.), 25–29. An Italian translation of Technical Report 96-4, May 6.

1616 Good, I. J. and Mittal, Y. (1987). 'The amalgamation and geometry of two-by-two contingency tables', *Annals of Statistics 15*, 694–711. There is a longer unpublished version numbered 1616A.

Goodman, L. A. and Kruskal, W. H. (1979). *Measure of Association for Cross Classification* (New York: Springer-Verlag). (A collection of four papers from 1954 to 1972.)

Gruber, H. E. and Vonèche, J. J., eds. (c. 1977). *The Essential Piaget* (New York: Basic Books). (The date of publication is not printed.)

Harper, W. and Skyrms, B., eds. (1988). *Causation, Chance, and Credence* (Dordrecht: Kluwer). Proceedings of a conference held in 1985 at Irvine, California.

Hart, H. L. A. (1968). *Punishment and Responsibility* (Oxford University Press).

Hart, H. L. A. and Honoré, A. M. (1959). (H & H'.) *Causation in the Law* (Oxford: Clarendon Press). (Chapter III is entitled "Causation and responsibility".)

Hartigan, J. A. (1983). *Bayes Theory* (New York: Springer-Verlag).

Hinsley, F. H. and Stripp, A., eds. (1994). *Codebreakers: The Inside Story of Bletchley Park* (Oxford University Press) paperback, a corrected form of the 1993 hardback, a fact not mentioned by the publishers. The very important correction on page 156, lines 4–7, was supplied by Joan Murray (née Clarke).

Humphreys, P., ed. (1994). *Patrick Suppes: Scientific Philosopher*, Vol. 1 (Dordrecht: Kluwer).

Hutchins, R. M., ed. in chief (1952). *Great Books of the Western World* (Encyclopaedia Britannica, Benton, Chicago, Illinois, U.S.A.).

Jarvie, I. C. and Laor, N., eds. (1995). *Critical Rationalism: Metaphysics and Science. Essays for Joseph Agassi*. Vol. 1 (Dordrecht: Kluwer).

Jeffrey, R. C. (1965/83). *The Logic of Decision* (New York: McGraw-Hill).

Jeffreys, H. (1939/61). *Theory of Probability* (Oxford: Clarendon Press).

Kadane, J. B. and Schum, D. A. (1996). *A Probabilistic Analysis of the Saccho and Vanzetti Evidence* (New York: John Wiley).

Keynes, J. M. (1921). *A Treatise on Probability* (London: Macmillan).

Kirzner, E. W. (1964). *Baba Kamma*. English trans. from the Hebrew of the Babylonian Talmud second to sixth century, C. E. (I. Epstein, ed., revised by M. Ginsberg; London: Soncino Press).

Kotz, S. and Johnson, N. L. (1991). *Breakthroughs in Statistics*, Vol. 1 (New York: Springer-Verlag).

Krishnaiah, P. R. (1969). *Multivariate Analysis-II* (New York: Academic Press).

Kučera, H. and Francis, W. N. (1967). *Computational Analysis of Present-Day American English* (Providence R.I.: Brown University Press).

Kyburg, H. E. and Smokler, H. E., eds. (1980). *Studies in Subjective Probability*, 2nd edn. (Huntington, NY: Robert E. Krieger). Contains a republication of Good (1962) on pp. 133–146. (Figure 1 omitted in error.)

Lauritzen, S. and Spiegelhalter, D. (1988). 'Local computations and probabilities on graphical structures and their application to expert systems', *J. Royal Statist. Soc. ser. B 50*, 157–224.

Lloyd-Jones, H., Pearl, V., and Worden, B., eds. (1982). *History and Imagination: Essays in Honor of H.R. Trevor-Roper* (New York: Holmes & Meier).

Loève, M. (1963). *Probability Theory* (Princeton, N.J.: Van Nostrand).

Nagel, E., Suppes, P., and Tarski, A., eds. (1962). *Logic, Methodology and Philosophy of Science, Proc. of the 1960 International Congress* (Stanford University Press).

Ogden, C. K. (1932, 1959). *Bentham's Theory of Fictions* (London: Routledge and Kegan Paul; and Patterson, N.J.: Littlefield, Adams).

Pearl, J. (1988). *Probabilistic Reasoning in Expert Systems* (San Mateo, Calif: Morgan Kaufmann).

Peirce, C. S. (1878). 'The probability of induction', *Popular Science Magazine*, republished in *The World of Mathematics 2* (J. R. Newman, ed.; New York: Simon and Schuster, 1956), 1341–1354.

Peirce, C. S. (1884). 'A numerical measure of success in prediction', *Science 4*, 453–454.

Poincaré, H. (1912, 1923). *Calcul des Probabilités*. 2nd edn. (Paris: Gauthiers-Villars).

Popper, K. R. (1982). *Quantum Theory and the Schism in Physics* (London: Hutchinson).

Russell, Bertrand (1946). *History of Western Philosophy* (London: George Allen and Unwin).

Russell, Bertrand (1948). *Human Knowledge: its Scope and Limits* (London: George Allen and Unwin).

Salmon, W. C. (1980). 'Probabilistic causality', *Pacific Philosophical Quarterly 61*, 50–74.

Salmon, W. C. (1984). *Scientific Explanation and the Causal Structure of the World* (Princeton, NJ: Princeton University Press).

Salmon, W. C. (1988a). 'Intuitions – Good and not-so-Good', in Harper and Skyrms (1988), pp. 51–71. For an Italian translation see Salmon (1988b).

Salmon, W. C. (1988b). 'Intuizioni. Sulla teoria della causalità probabilistica di I. J. Good'. In Galavotti and Gambetta (1988), 189–209.

Savage, L. J. (1954). *Foundations of Statistics* (New York: Wiley).

Schaffner, K. F. and Cohen, R. S. (1974). *PSA 1972: Proceedings of the 1972 Biennial Meeting of the Philosophy of Science Association* (Dordrecht: D. Reidel).

Schweber, S. S. (1994). *QED and the Men Who Made it: Dyson, Feynman, Schwinger, and Tomonaga* (Princeton, N. J.: Princeton University Press).

Schwinger, J., ed. (1958). *Selected Papers on Quantum Electrodynamics* (New York: Dover).

Sheps, M. C. (1959). 'An examination of some methods of comparing several rates or proportions', *Biometrics 15*, 87–97.

Stevens, S. S. (1982). 'Psychophysics', in *Encyclopedia of Psychology* (H. J. Eysenck, W. Arnold, and R. Meili, eds.; New York: Continuum), 867–871.

Stigler, S. M. (1980). 'Stigler's law of eponymy', *Trans. New York Acad. Sc.*, Ser. II, *39*, 147–158.

Stone, Richard (1993). 'The assumptions on which causal inferences rest', *J. Roy. Statist. Soc. B*, *55*, 455–466.

Suppes, P. (1994). Discussion of Good (1994a), in Humphreys (1994), 312–315.

Tolstoy, Leo Nikolaevich (1922/23). *War and Peace* (The World's Classics, Oxford University Press). Translated by Louise and Aylmer Maude from the Russian of 1868/69.

Toulmin, G. H. (1984). 'Lie dector lies', *Nature 309*, 203.

Trevor-Roper, H. R. (1980). 'History and imagination', a Valedictory Lecture delivered before the University of Oxford. In Lloyd-Jones, H., *et al.* (1982), pp. 356–369, esp. p. 364.

Uttley, A. M. (1959). 'Conditional probability computing in the nervous system', in *Mechanization of Thought Processes*, National Physical Laboratory, Symp. No. 10 (London: Her Majesty's Stationary Office), 119–152 (with discussion); with a reference to an unpublished paper by G. Russell.

Vaihinger, H. (1911). *Die Philosophie des Als-Ob*, translated by C. K. Ogden as *The Philosophy of As If*. 2nd edn. reprinted (New York: Barnes and Noble, 1968).

Zellner, A. (1971). *An Introduction to Bayesian Inference in Econometrics* (New York: John Wiley).

Zellner, A., ed. (1980). *Bayesian Analysis in Econometrics and Statistics: Essays in Honor of Harold Jeffreys* (Amsterdam: North Holland Publishing Co.).

4

Adapting Good's Q theory to the causation of individual events

Donald Michie

University of Edinburgh,
UK
email: D.Michie@ed.ac.uk

> One man's mechanism is another man's black box.
> Patrick Suppes, in *A Probabilistic Theory of Causality*.

Abstract

The notion of causality is embedded in scientific language. I. J. Good's 'Q_{suf}' for sufficient causation and 'Q_{nec}' for necessary causation satisfactorily formalize the general idea of causal tendency in an additive framework of Bayesian weights of evidence. But there remain difficulties in characterizing the causes of *individual* events. In this paper Good's theory is combined with an explicit treatment of individual events as sets, and is specialized to the management by resource-bounded agents of causal belief, both about tendencies and about individual events. The approach is strictly statistical and treats cause as a degree of rational inferrability, without commitment to whether or not causality is a physical law, i.e. an objective property of external reality.

R_{suf}, an adaptation of Q_{suf}, is tested with satisfactory results on an open problem of Suppes' concerning individual events. R_{suf} and R_{nec} are also used to show the feasibility of machine-generated causal comments on individual event sequences.

1 APPROACH AND TERMINOLOGY

Published treatments have found difficulty in seeing how a *single* history's condition–outcome pair is to be confidently related to a causal tendency. For other problems involving dependencies among variables including binary variables, logicians and statisticians have used *consistent with* or *sampled from* to relate individual instances to general laws. A medical scientist is ordinarily happy to interpret in causal language a sufficiently large and well-controlled set of case histories in each of which a 'vaccinated'/'not-vaccinated' entry is paired with a 'flu'/'no-flu' outcome. He or she may even express numerically the strength of preventive tendency inferrable from such a dataset. He or she will however be at a loss if asked to specify the numerical degree to which the vaccination on September 2nd of case no. 31, 192 prevented the flu which this subject was later known either to have contracted or not to have contracted. Neither logic nor statistics nor AI have to date supplied vocabularies and agreed procedures for answering such a question; but the distinction was greatly emphasized by Good (1961, 1962). I shall labour the point with a second, more complex, example.

Suppose that a certain casino features a table bearing two roulette wheels where a 'Grand Accumulator' play comprises two phases. In the first phase, wheel 1 is spun and bets are laid in the normal manner, there being 37 possible results of a spin. For the second, each player who has won in the first has his or her original stake, augmented by winnings, transferred to the same number on the second wheel for the croupier's second spin. Payouts on this second spin are accompanied by a bonus chip as a motivator for entering the Grand Accumulator in the first place.

A gambler conjectures that the result of the first spin causally influences the second in such a way as to make repetition of the first result less likely. Only repetitions result in payouts. So if the tables had been crocked so as to yield a shortage of repetitions, this would tend to recoup the casino's bonus chips. Being also a statistician he decides before venturing on the gaming table to construct a logbook, collecting in the course of time a million histories and recording the results of each Grand Accumulator play. His original idea was to use 1/37 as the null-hypothesis probability of a repetition. Analysis of his logbook, however, shows that each wheel has its own statistically significant pattern of very small deviations from the random expectation of $P = 1/37$ or 0.027 for each of the 37 numbered outcome. He therefore calculates the null-hypothesis frequency of repetitions from the empirically estimated frequencies of the individual outcomes, i.e. as the sum from $i = 1$ to $i = 37$ of $p_i \cdot p_j$ where $i = j$, the p_i's and p_j's being estimated from the logbook. Let us suppose that the sum of these products $p_i \cdot p_j$ does not sufficiently vary from 1/37 to reject the use of the pure theory-derived repetition frequency, leading to an expectation of 27 027 cases of repetition in the sample of 1 000 000 double plays. Since for each individual event-pair the expectation of its being a repetition is small, the null hypothesis (no causal influence) indicates an approximately Poisson distribution of the million cases with a mean equal to 27 027. The standard deviation around the mean is estimated as its square root, namely 164.4. The statistician then notes that there are only 25 388 repetitions in his logbook, a shortfall of 1639, i.e. nearly ten standard deviations. The probability of so large a shortfall in the absence of the conjectured linkage is almost inconceivably small.

He concludes (i) that there is indeed a tendency of the first spin's result to inhibit occurrence of the same number on the second spin, and that the tendency amounts to a reduction from random expectation by about 1639 parts in 27 027 or about 6 per cent, and (ii) that if in an individual double play the number 17, say, comes up from the first spin, the conditional probability that a 17 will be delivered by the second wheel is diminished from 1/37 in this same degree, i.e. by about 6 per cent. (In view of the above-stated 'significant pattern of very small deviations' from 1/37 shown by the empirical p_i's and p_j's, he or she may wonder whether the conditional probability estimate can be improved by using just his logbook's entries for the case 'wheel 1 gave 17', represented in future as '$w_1 = 17$'. We return to this point after completing the broad idea.)

When wheel no. 2 is now actually spun, there are two scenarios:

1. The result is a 17. Comment: 'In view of the first spin's result, this occurrence was *to some degree in spite of* the inhibition. In the light of it, the outcome becomes *to some degree more unexpected* (less expected).'

2. The result is not a 17. Comment: 'In view of the first spin's result, this occurrence was *to some degree because of* the inhibition. In the light of it, the outcome becomes *to some degree less unexpected* (more expected).'

The statistican may feel uncomfortable about the lack of an established method of putting numbers to these degrees. He might also ask to examine the table for hidden wires or other interconnections between the two roulette wheels, or between the croupier and wheel 2.

A point illustrated above is that routine statistical parlance uses separate vocabularies, on the one hand for discussing *populations* and *samples* (e.g. the theory-derived population parameter 1/37 and the sample statistic $\sum p_i \cdot p_j$), and on the other hand for discussing *individual occurrences* (e.g. the *conditional probability* of the occurrence of a 17). In the same spirit, I use a hygienic separation between the levels at which causal statements are made. The terms 'causation' and 'causativity' are reserved for general causal tendency, and 'cause' for an individual history's condition–outcome link.

Returning to the query raised above, surely the gambler-statistician can get a better estimate of $P(w_2 = 17|w_1 = 17)$ directly from the logbook frequency of $(w_2 = 17|w_1 = 17)$? What does a statistical theory of causes buy the user in exchange for risks of blurring predictive accuracy?

First, note that the gambler-statistician who foregoes the concept of causality is landed with an unwieldy theory, containing 37 individual statements. If moreover he wants his theory to help him evaluate $P(w_2 = n|w_1 = m)$ for all m and n in the 1–37 interval, then he has a theory of 1369 components comprising the cells of a 37×37 contingency table. The leading diagonal is picked out by the causal statement under consideration. Consider two cases:

Case 1. The 'very small deviations' are sufficiently small that the result of increasing the prediction error by, in effect, pooling the off-diagonal p_{ij}'s, remains within rounding error for the number of decimal places used to express posterior probabilities. A causally expressed theory may then enjoy an outright preference, on grounds of succinctness and ease of application.

Case 2. The preset error bounds on prediction are 'soft'. That is, they may be traded against a theory's simplicity and ease of use. Situations will arise in which gains from simplification exceed losses in predictive accuracy.

2 RELEVANT BACKGROUND

In Bayesian reasoning, probabilities represent degrees of rational belief. An axiomatization for modern use was introduced in I. J. Good's (1950) 'Probability and the Weighing of Evidence', which offered two variant options for the definition of 'rational'. Specifically, optional replacement of Good's axiom A4 with his A4′ (see below) supplies a basis for what he subsequently termed 'type-2 rationality', similar to Simon's (1979) more vaguely expressed concept of 'bounded rationality'. The resulting definition allows consistent probability judgements to be made by rational agents with limited resources of memory and calculation. A theory of type-2 rational belief makes it practical to model human-type problem-solving in intelligent artifacts.

Good (1961, 1962) and Suppes (1970) broke new ground by treating causality as a branch of the mathematical theory of probability. The distinction between causal tendency and specific causation was somewhat clarified by Good (1992) who also characterized a 'point event' as an event of small spatial and temporal 'diameter'. Of such individual events Good further remarks that 'in ordinary usage, an event (meaning "individual event", DM) is regarded as a bundle or disjunction of many more specific events that might be called *microevents*'. Good uses 'specific' here, not in the sense of an individual event, but for an event's unobserved microcomponents. Of these microevents, suppose that a particular one, e, actually occurred. In the usage of this paper, we then assert the occurrence of the 'bundle or disjunction' containing it, i.e. the individual event E where e is a microevent in E. Suppose that no member of the 'bundle or disjunction' occurred. We then say that the event E did not occur. Although we may loosely speak of the probability of an event, in our treatment probabilities attach strictly to propositions E^+ or E^-. These state that of all the possible microevents satisfying E's description and falling within a specified observational time interval either just one occurred (positive instance of E) or none occurred (negative instance of E).

Good expressly limited his Q_{suf} and Q_{nec} theories of probabilistic sufficient and necessary causation to causal tendency, and supplied a clear method for deriving the two measures (Good, 1992). For actual (i.e. as opposed to 'tendential') causation of *individual* events, Good (1961, 1962) went on to develop a separate χ calculus. Later he expressed dissatisfaction with this. The present approach extends and modifies Good's Q theory of probabilistic causation by an overtly set-theoretic interpretation of individual events, while taking Good's Bayesian orientation to the limit. It seems that the scope of interpretation of Q can be extended in such a way as to do the job for which Good had intended χ.

3   EVENTS AND MICROEVENTS

We represent each individual 'bundle or disjunction' as a *set* of elemental microevents which are not individually distinguished in the statistician's logbook, and cannot be since they are either below the level of observability or not included in the recording instructions. To illustrate the latter, consider a causal experiment in chess of the kind described in the appendix. If the statistician's statement of task includes recording occurrences and non-occurrences of the condition 'Black's move is a separating move' and of the outcome 'Black now has a lost position', but does not include recording individual moves, then the latter count as unobserved microevents until such time as a new experiment with new ground rules is declared. As illustration of non-observable, as opposed to non-observed, microevents, members of an intensionally defined set may all satisfy the same description, yet be mutually distinct in ways not feasibly accessible to inspection. In my revised calculus of causes, every individual event is conceived as labelled with a unique time-and-duration stamp enclosing not only the microevent that may actually have occurred but also arbitrarily many non-occurring microevents satisfying the same intensional description. Satisfaction of descriptions is checked by an observer considered to be located in space and time at the effect end of the cause–effect relation. Occurrences at the cause end are stamped at the effect end according to the arrival times of their sensed signals. This sufficiently meets the need to relativize strict temporal antecedence to speeds of signal propagation. For example, because of the relatively slow speed of sound, the firing of a starting gun at a distance of a mile takes about 200 milliseconds to arrive. Hence it cannot causally explain an observation that within a few tens of milliseconds of the firing the runners in the observer's locality begin to run. Assuming that the flash or discharge of smoke was not visible to them, nor the sound conveyed to them by radio, there must have been some other cause, for the reason that the arrival of the starting signal is logged as subsequent to the beginning of the running.

Time-interval stamping does not in general have to be accurate so long as relations of antecedence are conserved. The overall effect is to reduce the task of assigning causal responsibility to that of annotating the statistician's logbook by filling in and quantifying the missing causal linkages. The intent is to transform histories into explanatory narratives. We want, for example, an artificial golf coach to be able to say: 'You sliced your drive *because* you brought your head up during the down-swing, and then you recovered from the bunker *in spite of* taking too much sand.'

4 CAUSATION AND BELIEF

The revised and extended theory, which I shall call R_{suf}, places causation on the same subjective basis as belief. Causation is defined as the amount of *rationally inferrable influence linking known prior events to subsequent ones*, – rationally inferrable, that is, by a defined observer from events known to that same observer. In line with Good's (1977) dynamic probability and Michie's (1977) theory of advice, 'rational' is relativized to a rational agent's computational resources. Computations are non-monotonic in the sense, for example, of Ginsberg (1987). This leads to a notion of dynamic causality, in which rationally inferred allocations of cause are successively revised as further information comes to hand. The practicality of this is later illustrated with a court-room scenario, in which inferred causes of an event undergo sequential revision as the information available to the jury is incremented or qualified.

5 BOUNDED RATIONALITY

The basic axiomatic stance is that earlier referred to in terms of a substitution of A4′ for A4, as follows.

Axiom A4: If E and F are logically equivalent (i.e. they imply one another) then $P(E|H) = P(F|H)$ and $P(H|E) = P(H|F)$ for any H.

Axiom A4′: *If you have seen that E and F are equivalent then $P(E|H) = P(F|H)$ and $P(H|E) = P(H|F)$.*

The 'you' in 'If you have seen...' denotes the 'rational agent' that underpins Bayesian theory. Under A4′, rationality is bounded by the time available for calculating, including the calculation involved in accessing stored information. Hence rational agents differentially constrained by resource bounds, as also rational agents possessed of different amounts of background information, may validly arrive at different degrees of rational belief about the same hypotheses, even in fully deterministic worlds. A pre-existing body of belief, $\mathcal{B}$ (background information), was specified by Good for use with A4 as including not only the explicitly known facts and laws of probability and logic, together with scientific facts and laws, but also all their implications, i.e. everything in principle inferrable from $\mathcal{B}$'s explicit contents. Under the alternative axiom A4′, the implications to be included in $\mathcal{B}$ are restricted to those inferrable in practice. A4′ offers a closer approximation to real-life causal assessment, and is adopted here.

As in subjective probability, so also in subjective theories of causality, different rational agents (with different background knowledge and/or computational resource) can validly infer different causal connections and strengths from the same set of observed events. The point will be illustrated via resolutions of a paradox of which I first learned from a talk at Stanford in 1962 by Patrick Suppes.

6 A PARADOX FROM SUPPES

A traveller, T, sets out from the middle of a waterless desert, unaware that two enemies have secretly and independently interfered with his preparations. Enemy 1 has put cyanide in his water bottle (event C_1). Enemy 2, ignorant of this, takes aim from a distance and shoots a hole in the bottle before the traveller has had a chance to drink from it, rendering it empty (event C_2). In course of time T's dead body is found in the desert. Initially we make the simplifying assumption that its state is such as to preclude forensic tests. The set of possible outcomes is thus summarized by the statement: the traveller died, in some way or another, in the desert (event E_T). As already explained, an individual event is represented as a set *defined by a predicate*.

Both enemies later confess to their respective deeds. There is no hint of collusion between them, so they are individually sent to be tried for murder in separate courts. The courts operate in parallel, and every material fact that emerges in one court-room is immediately made available to the other. Each jury is instructed that, for a finding of murder, it is necessary to establish both that the accused willed his act *and that the act was a sufficient cause* of the victim's death. Intent has already been admitted by both accused, so that only questions of causation remain.

The poisoner's defence argues that his action was deprived of causal responsibility for the traveller's death by the subsequent holing of the bottle. While admitting intent, he denies specific causation. The marksman's defence points out that the only identifiable consequence of *his* action was to prolong the traveller's life, and thereby to increase whatever infinitesimal chances of rescue T might have had.

Each jury is asked to determine if the given defendant's admitted act was a sufficient cause of the desert traveller's death.

7 GOOD'S THEORY OF SUFFICIENT CAUSATION

I. J. Good defines Q_{suf}, the tendency of C^+ to be sufficiently causative of E^+, as the weight of evidence for the *non-occurrence* of C that would be contributed by the *non-occurrence* of E. Q_{nec}, *the tendency of C to be necessarily causative*, is the weight of evidence for the *occurrence* of C that would be contributed by the *occurrence* of E. As they stand, the definitions are intended to apply only to complete causal domains, from which many (C, E) histories could in principle be sampled. I have sought a revised version, R, with its own interpretations tuned to specific causation.

Proposition E^+ asserts that e is in E and E^- denies it, where e is a microevent that has actually occurred. Note that e is not directly observed in the sense of full specification, but only to the extent necessary to determine whether it satisfies E^+ or E^- and to log an E-occurrence or non-occurrence accordingly. Each logged entry itself is thus regarded as a labelled black box with its microstructure disregarded. The same conventions apply to C. W is the 'weight of evidene', i.e. the logarithm of the Bayes factor. In the absence of time-interval stamping, $Q_{suf}(E^+ : C^+|U)$ denotes the general tendency of occurrences which satisfy C's description to cause occurrences which satisfy E's description, given in the background information that the state of the Universe prior to all of C's possible instances $c_1, c_2, c_3, \ldots$, satisfies some description U:

$$Q_{suf}(E^+ : C^+|U) = W(C^- : E^-|U) \tag{Q1}$$

The right-hand side of the equation is to be read 'the weight of evidence for the non-occurrence of C provided by the non-occurrence of E, given U'. The function symbol W for 'weight of evidence' resembles P for 'probability' in being defined over propositions that assert occurrence or non-occurrence of events, which are in this case not time-interval stamped. Hence both sides of the equation refer (as they should) to populations of events, not to individual events. Note, however, that the vertical bar leaves space to its right for introducing further particularization to any degree we please, and thus to set up new problems of causal estimation over subsets of the original data. In the flu vaccination survey the statistician might prepare two separate tabulations, having randomly split the original E's into two samples, E_1 and E_2, perhaps as a consistency check. Taking 'C_1 **part** C' to mean 'C_1 is a random partition of C' the causal strength estimated above can be applied to such subsets, as below:

$$Q_{suf}(E_1^+ : C_1^+|U \ \& \ C_1 \ \textbf{part} \ C) = W(C_1^- : E_1^-|U \ \& \ C_1 \ \textbf{part} \ C)$$
$$Q_{suf}(E_2^+ : C_2^+|U \ \& \ C_1 \ \textbf{part} \ C) = W(C_2^- : E_2^-|U \ \& \ C_1 \ \textbf{part} \ C).$$

It is important to bear in mind that the quantity attributed to such subsets is the underlying causal influence under which they came into being, not the degree of causal association that now, perhaps after repeated selections and subselections of the data, the final and possibly small end-samples may appear to manifest. An analogous distinction is between, say, the mean stature in a regiment and the mean for one of its platoons. Assuming a stature-neutral policy of allocating recruits to platoons and of their subsequent treatment, once the regimental mean is known, the *expected* mean for a platoon can be stated. Further it remains unaffected by subsequent knowledge of the actual platoon mean. This expected value, for example, remains the optimal predictor of the stature of the platoon's next recruit. Similarly, provided that the probability estimates used in the above two causality statements continue to be derived from the original population parameters, then further specializations can be added to the right of the vertical bar, *up to and including the time-interval stamps of C and E.* Both sides of the equation now designate only one single individual event-pair, or history, thus completing the forbidden adaptation of Q from being a measure of tendencies to being descriptive of individual occurrences.

Rather than apply someone else's notation to an unsanctioned purpose, I have introduced the symbol R to replace Q when attributing causal influence to individual events. Meanwhile, to illuminate the structure of Bayesian inference, a brief refresher follows on the axiomatic roots of Bayes' theorem. The refresher also includes a logodds formulation emphasized by Turing and Good that facilitates the weighing of evidence.

8 THE TURING–GOOD THEORY OF EVIDENCE

Probability theory rests on three basic axioms, to do respectively with

A1. Conjunction of propositions–multiplicative law;

A2. Disjunction of propositions–additive law;

A3. Negation of propositions–complementation law.

A1 and A3 suffice for our purposes, which can be expressed as two schoolroom tasks.

Task 1. Derive Bayes' theorem directly from the axioms of probability.

$$P(H^+ \ \& \ E^+) = P(H^+) \times P(E^+|H^+) \quad \text{from A1} \tag{P1}$$

$$P(E^+ \ \& \ H^+) = P(E^+) \times P(H^+|E) \qquad \text{from (1) by substitution.} \tag{P2}$$

Hence

$$P(H^+) \times P(E^+|H^+) = P(E^+) \times P(H^+|E^+)$$

from (1) and (2) and the identity $A \ \& \ B = B \ \& \ A$.
Hence

$$P(H^+|E^+) = P(H^+) \times P(E^+|H^+)/P(E^+) \quad \text{by rearrangement.} \tag{P3}$$

Interpret H^+ as the proposition that a hypothesis, H, is true. H^- is the proposition that H is false. Interpret E^+ as a proposition asserting occurrence of an instance of E, and

E^- as its negation. With these interpretations, (P3) is seen to be the classical form of Bayes' theorem.

Task 2. Show that the odds form of the theorem follows from its classical form.

$$P(H^-|E^+) = P(H^-) \times P(E^+|H^-)/P(E^+) \quad \text{from (P3) by substitution} \quad \text{(P4)}$$

Hence

$$P(H^+|E^+)/P(H^-|E^+) = [P(H^+) \times P(E^+|H^+)/P(E^+)]$$
$$/[P(H^-) \times P(E^+|H^-)/P(E^+)] \quad \text{from (3) and (4).}$$
$$\text{(P5)}$$

Hence

$$P(H^+|E^+)/P(H^-|E^+) = P(H^+) \times P(E^+|H^+)$$
$$/P(H^-) \times P(E^+|H^-) \quad \text{from (5) by cancellation.}$$
$$\text{(P6)}$$

A3 says that $P(H^+) = 1 - P(H^-)$. From A3 and the definition of 'odds' it follows that

$$\text{Odds}(H^+|E^+) = \text{Odds}(H^+) \times P(E^+|H^+)/P(E^+|H^-) \quad \text{(P7)}$$

In words:

> The posterior odds = the prior odds times the Bayes factor, f,

where $f = P(E^+|H^+)/P(E^+|H^-)$.

Incremental updating. One convenience of the odds representation is that there may be many events $E_1, E_2, \ldots, E_i, \ldots, E_n$, perhaps sequential. If the individual effects on the posterior probability are mutually independent ('naive Bayes' assumption) then the combined effect can be got from a single application of the global factor F, calculated as $f_1 \times f_2 \times \cdots \times f_i \times \cdots \times f_n$, i.e. as the product of the individual factors.

Transformation into logarithms yields an additive system in which logodds $P(H^+)$ is called the prior plausibility of H^+, and logodds $P(H^+|E_i^+)$ is the posterior plausibility of H^+ after noting that the ith observation yielded an instance of E_i. The formula for the posterior plausibility after taking into account the first independently sampled k observations is

$$\text{Posterior plausibility}(H^+) = \text{prior plausibility}(H^+) + \log f_1$$
$$+ \log f_2 + \cdots + \log f_k. \quad \text{(P8)}$$

The quantity $\log f_i$ can be written in the expanded form $W(H^+ : E_i^+|\mathcal{B})$ where the symbol $\mathcal{B}$ ('curly B') is Good's symbol for the Bayesian reasoning agent's background body of beliefs. It is interesting to read as early as 1950 of the use of the Bayesian calculus to effect what in artificial intelligence today is called 'non-monotonic reasoning' (see for example Ginsberg, 1987). In such reasoning the inferrable conclusions can change from one inference to the next. Good writes: '... the immediate purpose of a theory of probability is to enlarge $\mathcal{B}$'. This symbol $\mathcal{B}$ corresponds essentially to my use of $\mathcal{U}$ below to adapt $\mathcal{B}$ to the case of 'bounded rationality' (Good's axiom A4').

$W(H^+ : E_i^+|\mathcal{B})$ is 'the weight of evidence in favour of H^+ provided by the ith observation, given $\mathcal{B}$'. Weights can be negative, as also plausibilities. We can speak about a negative weight as 'the weight of evidence against H^+' or equivalently as 'the weight of evidence in favour of H^-', and of a negative plausibility as 'the degree of rational disbelief that H^+' or equivalently as 'the degree of rational belief that H^-', all in logodds measure.

In the light of the above, the posterior plausibility of H^+ can be stated as:

$$\text{Plaus}(H^+|E^+ \& \mathcal{B}) = \text{Plaus}(H^+|\mathcal{B}) + \log[P(E^+|H^+ \& \mathcal{B})/P(E^+|H^- \& \mathcal{B})] \quad \text{(P9)}$$

which in the earlier-introduced notation can be written:

$$\text{Plaus}(H^+|E^+ \& \mathcal{B}) = \text{Plaus}(H^+|\mathcal{B}) + W(H^+ : E^+|\mathcal{B}). \quad \text{(P10)}$$

To prepare for talking about causal influences linking individual events to individual events, we reemphasize the interpretation of Bayesian inference as operating in a world of propositions. Recall that 'events' are now *sets*, intensionally defined by propositions to which (non-monotonically modifiable) probabilities are attached. To reinforce this, I shall depart from the neutral choice of symbols used in expounding elementary Bayesian probability. For the purpose now in hand, all symbols for propositions follow an alphabetical convention in expressing time-ordered events. Thus propositions C^+, E^+ assert the occurrence of a strictly earlier event C and a strictly later event E.

Changing symbols accordingly in (9) and (10) above, and reversing truth values, we write:

$$\text{Plaus}(C^-|E^- \& \mathcal{B}) = \text{Plaus}(C^-|\mathcal{B}) + \log[P(E^-|C^- \& \mathcal{B})/P(E^-|C^+ \& \mathcal{B})] \quad \text{(P11)}$$

$$= \text{Plaus}(C^-|\mathcal{B}) + W(E^- : C^-|\mathcal{B}). \quad \text{(P12)}$$

The final subexpression $W(C^- : E^-|\mathcal{B})$, 'the weight of evidence for C's *non-occurrence* contributed by the *non-occurrence* of any member of E', is Good's $\text{Q}_{\text{suf}}(E^+ : C^+|\mathcal{B})$ with $\mathcal{B}$ in place of U.

9 RETURN TO GOOD'S Q_{suf}

$\text{Q}_{\text{suf}}(E^+ : C^+|U)$ in Good's treatment was defined with respect to background information (i) that the state of the Universe prior to C satisfied some description U and (ii) scientific and mathematical laws not explicitly shown. Causality is treated as an expression of the universe's objective physical laws, implicit in the laws of physics but requiring separate and logically redundant elaboration for convenient application, and also requiring subjective estimates in practice. Good's background information presents a 'God's eye view'. While developed directly from Good's, the present paper leans towards an agent's eye view, substituting the symbol $\mathcal{U}$ ('curly U'), thus:

$$R_{\text{suf}}(E^+ : C^+|\mathcal{U}) = W(C^- : E^-|\mathcal{U})$$
$$= \log[P(E^-|\mathcal{U}\ \&\ C^-)/P(E^-|\mathcal{U}\ \&\ C^+)]. \qquad (Q2)$$

$\mathcal{U}$ denotes what the agent, presumed rational, already knows of the state of the universe and the laws of science, *together with those laws of mathematics and logic that might reasonably be known to the agent for feasibly reasoning with such rules of inference as are also in* $\mathcal{U}$. A rational agent is one that calculates consistently with the laws of logic and probability.

10 AGENT-CENTRED INTERPRETATION

Having established an agent-centred frame, the next move is to have agents assess causal influences by performing 'thought-experiments', e.g. hypothesizing the four possible individual two-event history-descriptions $(C^+, E^+), (C^+, E^-), (C^-, E^+), (C^-, E^+)$ of which only one can be satisfied by any given individual history. We conjoin to $\mathcal{U}$, as defined above, additional background information that becomes available to the causality-assessor subsequent to the moment at which the world-description $\mathcal{U}$ was finalized. This allows different assessors, equipped with the same $\mathcal{U}$, to have access to different qualifying circumstances. Differential access may arise either from variations in external availability of the information, or from variations in internal information-processing resource. The latter is parameterized in R_{suf}'s causal formulae (see later): two rational agents may have in $\mathcal{U}$ the same method for calculating the decimal expansion of π, but in response to a request for the parity of its nth digit, one may be a sufficiently fast mental calculator for the information to be effectively available, while the other is forced to substitute a probability judgement. Explicit and implicit restrictions on availability of information may operate simultaneously, as will be illustrated.

11 APPROACH TO SUPPES' PARADOX

With these modifications we take R_{suf} as expressed in (Q2), and apply it. The relevant propositions are as follows:

C_1^+ is the proposition: Enemy 1 poisoned the water bottle;
C_2^+ is the proposition: Enemy 2 holed the water bottle, rendering it empty;
E_T^+ is the proposition: the traveller was found dead in the desert.

In the statement of the problem C_1^+ and C_2^+ have probabilities equal to unity, conventionally expressed as '$P(C^+) = 1$', equivalent in mathematicians' usage to 'C^+ is almost certain'. E_T also has probability equal to 1. Conspicuously absent, however, from the problem statement so far is the 'statistician's logbook'. In the make-believe world of such mathematical puzzles one might of course choose to postulate the existence of encyclopaedic judicial records. From these could then be induced the assumed causativities needed in the solution of this particular problem. But here these have to be supplied by derivation and lookup from $\mathcal{U}$. All that remains of the logbook is the fill-in-the-blanks structure into which the available details of individual cases could in principle have been entered. This is equivalent to the 'statement of the problem' in more formal work, where all variables and constants (logbook-headings), together with definitions, rules of inference and background facts ($\mathcal{U}$), are set out before the solving process can begin.

Required: an estimate of the respective degrees to which a member of C_1 (the microevent c_1 which actually occurred) and a member of C_2 (the c_2 that actually occurred) specifically caused the occurrence of some member of the set E_T (the microevent e_T that actually occurred). So long as we know nothing further about the microevent that actually occurred in each case, other than its membership of C_1, C_2 or E_T as the case may be, we regard each as a fair sample of its set. Hence probability statements applied to the particular instance distinguished by the phrase 'the one that actually occurred' also characterize the containing set. A direct analogy would be to say, on drawing a playing card from a full deck and laying it face down, that 'the probability that the drawn card is a black picture card is 6/52'. Here the 'event' is the union of unit sets: $X = \{x \mid x$ is a black picture card$\} = \{\{x \mid x$ is the Queen of Spades$\} \cup \{x \mid x$ is the Jack of Clubs$\} \cup \ldots \}$, and the conditional probability (conditioned, that is, by the information conveyed in the initial statement of the problem) remains the same regardless of which particular instance of the event turns out to be the one that actually happened, and regardless of whether the observer ever obtains, or could obtain, this precise information.

Likewise with the desert traveller, the event E_T consists of all rationally conjecturable instances of 'the traveller died in some way or another in the desert'. To apply Bayesian analysis to the problem, we ought strictly to supply a logical axiomatization of the relevant facts in $\mathcal{U}$, such as that a non-empty water bottle is a source of water, that x is non-empty iff x is not empty, that without a source of water people always die, that after drinking cyanide people also always die, that cyanide dissolves in water, etc. I have excused myself this potentially onerous chore, and have left the needed gap-filling to the reader's own world-knowledge.

Substituting in (Q2):

$R_{suf}(E_T^+ : C_1^+ \mid \mathcal{U} \,\&\, C_2^+)$ is the weight of evidence for C_1's non-occurrence that would be provided by the non-occurrence of E_T (i.e. T does not die), given the occurrence of C_2. (Q3)

$R_{suf}(E_T^+ : C_2^+ \mid \mathcal{U} \,\&\, C_1^+)$ is the weight of evidence for C_2's non-occurrence that would be provided by the non-occurrence of E_T, given the occurrence of C_1. (Q4)

Recall that adoption of sets to represent events means that phrases such as 'C_2 occurred' and 'E_T did not occur' are shorthand for 'some microinstance of C_2 occurred' and 'no microinstance of E_T occurred', etc.

Note also the expanded representation of background information. $\mathcal{U}$, which includes the state of the world known to the jurors immediately prior to the earliest of the events in question, is incrementally conjoined with relevant additional information acquired between then and verdict time. In thought experiments, relevant sequels also include

71

occurrence of hypothesized samplings of combinations of C_1, C_2 and E_T, *including sequels in which the traveller does not die*. Such 'might-have-beens' are called by philosophers 'counterfactuals'. The following note shows that they can be assimilated into subjective probability and causation without contradiction.

12 NOTE ON 'COUNTERFACTUALS'

Subjective probability does not bar worlds containing events with zero probabilities, such as C_1^- and C_2^- in the present case. The technical interpretation of the statement $P = 0$ concerning an empirical statement S is that S is *almost impossible*. But we still need protection against having to divide by zero. A mode of protection which turns out to confer additional benefits is explained below.

A probability is represented by a real number in the unit interval. In subjective probability, assertions characterized by $P = 0$ and $P = 1$ have conventional interpretations 'almost false' and 'almost true', respectively. The corresponding events are described as 'almost impossible' and 'almost certain'. These probabilities are not to be equated with the contradictions and tautologies recognized by purely logical systems which employ simply 'false' and 'true'. We now make the empirical-versus-logical distinction explicit in the notation, reserving the integer symbols 1 for 'logical certainty' (e.g. given arithmetic, the probability that 43 is prime is equal to 1, and the probability that it is a square is 0) while otherwise employing the notations $P = 0^+$ and $P = 1^-$. These two extremal values are interpreted as denoting $0 + \varepsilon$ and $1 - \varepsilon$ respectively, where the 'minitesimal' ε stands for the discrepancy between truth in logic and truth in science. Science's 'certain' predictions are given subjective probability $0.99999 \ldots$ where the succession of 9's is long but terminating, which we denote by 1^-. Similarly science's 'impossibilities' are characterized by long but terminating complementary expressions which we denote by 0^+.

Some scientific certainties are more 'certain' than others, and some impossibilities more scientifically 'impossible' than others. The present treatment allows inequality of probabilities between different near-impossibilities and between different near-certainties, drawing as needed on distinguishing symbols $\varepsilon_1, \varepsilon_2, \varepsilon_3, \ldots$. The practical usefulness for the topic in hand will emerge in further consideration of the desert traveller problem.

13 RESUMPTION OF THE CASE

Putting (Q3) and (Q4) together with (P11) and (P12) we get

$$R_{suf}(E_T^+ : C_1^+ | \mathcal{U} \ \& \ C_2^+) = \log[P(E_T^- | \mathcal{U} \ \& \ C_1^- \ \& \ C_2^+)/P(E_T^- | \mathcal{U} \ \& \ C_1^+ \ \& \ C_2^+)] \tag{Q5}$$

$$R_{suf}(E_T^+ : C_2^+ | \mathcal{U} \ \& \ C_1^+) = \log[P(E_T^- | \mathcal{U} \ \& \ C_1^+ \ \& \ C_2^-)/P(E_T^- | \mathcal{U} \ \& \ C_1^+ \ \& \ C_2^+)]. \tag{Q6}$$

The replacement of $\mathcal{B}$ by $\mathcal{U}$ requires further comment. In Good's original axiomatization, $\mathcal{B}$ was the rational agent's body of pre-existing beliefs, in the form of judgments of inequality among various hypotheses applicable in the given domain, together with the basic laws of mathematics and logic. It was accompanied by a separate symbol, not reproduced here, to denote knowledge of scientific laws. The U of Good's recent papers specifies a comprehensive snapshot of the world at a given moment, together with all laws of nature (known or unknown). We bundle all of the above into our definition of $\mathcal{U}$, after relativizing to the computational resources of the given rational agent, or agents (juries in the present case). We thus include in $\mathcal{U}_A$ (where A is some agent) only that knowledge of the relevant world-state, its relevant laws and of its immediate history, which A actually possesses. On the other hand, 'rational' predicated of A according to Good's usage implies that U already incorporates the basic laws of mathematics and logic, and all their in-principle inferrable implications, both analytic and in application to the above-mentioned world-snapshot. Good's U-equipped rational agent would seem to have in-principle knowledge of all mathematics and all science, past, present and future. I postulate a 'boundedly rational' agent, parametrizing the bound with the symbol β as in Michie (1977). β is here a computational time-bound set by the requester of causal judgements from the agent. For example, in the law court, a deadline might be set by the judge to the jury. The pure theory expresses β in computational rather than chronological units, e.g. in binary discriminations per second. β constrains the quality of judgements. Small values (hurried deliberations) correspond to shallower judgements, and large values to deeper judgements. A hurried judgement can be β-rational, i.e. as rational as β's value permits, as in Grandmaster B's judgements in the appendix.

The bounded-rationality reformulation of R_{suf} for the desert traveller problem is:

$$R_{suf}(E_T^+ : C_1^+ | \mathcal{U} \ \& \ C_2^+ \ \& \ \text{bound} = \beta)$$
$$= \log[P(E_T^- | C_1^- \ \& \ C_2^+ \ \& \ \mathcal{U} \ \& \ \text{bound} = \beta)$$
$$/ P(E_T^- | \mathcal{U} \ \& \ C_1^+ \ \& \ C_2^+ \ \& \ \text{bound} = \beta)] \qquad (Q7)$$

$$R_{suf}(E_T^+ : C_2^+ | \mathcal{U} \ \& \ C_1^+ \ \& \ \text{bound} = \beta)$$
$$= \log[P(E_T^- | C_1^+ \ \& \ C_1^- \ \& \ \mathcal{U} \ \& \ \text{bound} = \beta)$$
$$/ P(E_T^- | \mathcal{U} \ \& \ C_1^+ \ \& \ C_2^+ \ \& \ \text{bound} = \beta)]. \qquad (Q8)$$

For problems in which β is uniformly more than sufficient for full evaluation of all the causal expressions, explicit mention of the bound $= \beta$ condition will in future be omitted. Although not required for most of our desert traveller scenarios, in other contexts it can dominate. For example its essential role in causal reasoning in chess is illustrated in the appendix.

First case: enemy1, C_1 as cause of E_T. To what degree was the poisoner's act a cause of T's death, given that the marksman subsequently emptied the water bottle?

Equation (Q7) asks us to consider the probability that T survives if enemy 1 *doesn't* poison the water bottle, given that enemy 2 subsequently empties it, in ratio to the probability that T survives if enemy 1 *does* poison the water bottle, given that enemy

2 empties it. Since both probabilities are the same, namely equal to the probability that with an empty water bottle T survives, the ratio is 1 and the weight of evidence, and hence R_{suf}, is zero. No sufficient cause of T's death can be attributed to the poisoner's act.

Second case: enemy 2, C_2 as cause of E_T. (Q8) addresses the probability that T survives if *enemy 2 doesn't* empty the water bottle, given as background that enemy 1 has poisoned it, in ratio to the probability that T survives if enemy 2 *does* empty the water bottle, given as background that enemy 1 has poisoned it. Here the two probabilities are not necessarily the same. The numerator is equal to the probability that with a poisoned water bottle T survives, while the denominator is equal to the probability that with an empty water bottle T survives. Of course, in each case the jury 'knows' that T does *not* in fact survive: both eventualities are 'almost impossible', that is $P = 0^+$ in both cases. But we distinguish the two minitesimals, ε_1 and ε_2 respectively, and argue that, if only because the longer expected period of survival might be associated with increased, even if still very small, rescue chances, the denominator exceeds the numerator, i.e. $\varepsilon_1 < \varepsilon_2$. So the logarithm of the ratio, i.e. the weight of evidence required by (Q8), is a negative quantity. Conclusion: the marksman's act was a weak sufficient negative cause of T's death: in other words, his action had a weak preventive effect, as indeed this accused had argued in court.

So much for the bare bones. Solutions so far were obtained without overt involvement of the β resource-bound parameter beyond the assumption that its value was sufficiently generous for the required chain of inference. How well does the model correspond to intuition and to the normal usage of these concepts? The results certainly do not seem self-evidently unreasonable.

14 MODIFIED SCENARIOS

1. What if forensic tests had replaced E_T^+ with E_2^+: 'T *died of thirst* in the desert'?
2. What if forensic tests had replaced E_T^+ with E_1^+: 'T *died of cyanide*'?
3. What of a joint event? Can one say that the *conjunction* C_1^+ & C_2^+ was a sufficient cause of E_T^+?
4. What of the *disjunction*, C_1^+ or C_2^+?
5. What if the jury, although otherwise rational, cannot hold both C_1^+ and C_2^+ in simultaneous mental review, either through incapacity or because of *time pressure*?

Each of the above will be analysed.

14.1 Scenario 1: T dies of thirst

The jury is informed on the basis of forensic tests that T died of thirst. They are required, as before, simply to determine whose act, if anyone's, *was a sufficient cause of T's death*. Their thought experiment then takes the form of asking themselves the same question as before and arriving at the same negative weight as before: $\log(\varepsilon_1/\varepsilon_2)$.

But consider the unlikely case that the juries are asked to decide whether the respective defendants' acts were causes of the outcome T *died of thirst*. They may well object that an extra cause has been smuggled into the event-description, the full chain being first that someone *causes T to be waterless* and second that being waterless *causes T to die*. However, the courts rule that the final outcome be treated as a unitary black-box event, 'T dies-of-thirst'. Note that the 'statistician's logbook' device (see the first three sections for this concept) renders the effect of such a ruling precise, corresponding to a specification of what is and is not entered in the logbook. Good (1988a) mentions the perils of overspecification: 'The assassin is not tried in court for shooting the victim in the third rib from the top, four inches from the sternum; he is tried for murder', and recommends common sense as the means of weeding out counterproductive detail. The 'statistician's log' gives us a basis for causal assessment of whatever has been recorded, independent of common-sense judgements on its level of detail. Thus in statistical data analysis the selective collection of data and its analysis are treated as separate tasks. The 'statistician's log' also cuts through tangles that can be engendered by postulating freakish but unrecorded, or separately recorded, happenings intervening between cause and effect.

It is convenient to represent the traveller's death E_T as the union of disjoint events, $E_T = E_1 \cup E_2 \cup E_R$, where E_1 is the event describable as 'T dies of cyanide', E_2 corresponds to 'T dies of thirst', and E_R is the residual subset: 'T dies in the desert in some other way'. We assume $E_1 \cap E_2 \cap E_R = \phi$. In this new scenario the event-hypothesis is E_2^+. We enquire how much evidence its negation would contribute to

(i) the hypothesis C_1^- (enemy 1 did *not* add cyanide), and how much evidence would be contributed to

(ii) the hypothesis C_2^- (enemy 2 did *not* empty the water bottle).

First consider (i). The negative proposition E_2^- is equivalent to E_1^+ or E_R^+ or E_T^-, i.e. 'T dies from cyanide, or from some other alternative to thirst, or not at all'.

The relevant equation is

$$R_{suf}(E_2^+ : C_1^+ | \mathcal{U} \, \& \, C_2^+)$$
$$= \log[P(E_2^- | C_1^- \, \& \, C_2^+ \, \& \, \mathcal{U} / P(E_2^- | C_1^+ \, \& \, C_2^+ \, \& \, \mathcal{B}] \qquad (Q9)$$

$$= \log[P(E_1^+ \, \text{or} E_R^+ \, \text{or} E_T^- | C_1^- \, \& \, C_2^+ \, \& \, \mathcal{U}$$
$$/ P(E_1^+ \, \text{or} E_R^+ \, \text{or} E_T^- | C_1^+ \, \& \, C_2^+ \, \& \, \mathcal{U}]. \qquad (Q10)$$

R_{suf} evaluates, as in the previous case, to zero. This can be seen by separate inspection of the numerator and the denominator of the Bayesian factor enclosed in the square brackets of (Q10). The two are equal, as before, since each expresses the same quantity, namely the probability that with an empty water bottle, T will die from cyanide, or from some other alternative to thirst, or not at all. Their ratio is thus 1, and R_{suf} is therefore equal to the logarithm of 1, i.e. to zero.

Now consider (ii). The relevant equation is

$$R_{suf}(E_2^+ : C_2^+ | \mathcal{U} \& C_1^+)$$
$$= \log[P(E_2^- | C_2^- \& C_1^+ \& \mathcal{U}/P(E_2^- | C_2^+ \& C_1^+ \& \mathcal{U})] \qquad \text{(Q11)}$$

$$= \log[P(E_1^+ \text{ or } E_R^+ \text{ or } E_T^- | C_2^- \& C_1^+ \& \mathcal{U})$$
$$/P(E_1^+ \text{ or } E_R^+ \text{ or } E_T^- | C_2^+ \& C_1^+ \& \mathcal{U})]. \qquad \text{(Q12)}$$

It is now apparent that the two probabilities used to form the Bayesian factor are by no means equal, but on the contrary highly unequal. The numerator is the probability that with a cyanide-poisoned water bottle T dies from cyanide, or from some other alternative to thirst, or not at all. The first of the three disjuncts dominates, and the probability is high. The denominator is the probability that with an empty water bottle T dies from cyanide, or from some other alternative to thirst, or not at all. The probability, as in the case involving E_T rather than E_2, is infinitesimal. The sufficient causal responsibility allotted to the marksman for the observed outcome 'T dies-of-thirst' is therefore overwhelming.

Disregarding parameters assumed constant throughout, the whole calculation can be recapitulated in English as follows. The degree to which enemy 2's shooting act is specifically responsible in the sense of sufficient cause for 'T dies of thirst' (given knowledge of enemy 1's poisoning act) is equal to the weight of evidence that the discovery that T has *not* died of thirst (given knowledge of enemy 1's poisoning act) would contribute to the hypothesis that enemy 2 never emptied the bottle after all. This in turn is equal to the logarithm of a ratio of two probabilities, namely:

- the probability that T dies of cyanide or in some other way (not thirst) or survives, given that enemy 2 does *not* empty the water bottle and enemy 1 has poisoned it, and

- the probability that T dies of cyanide or in some other way (not thirst) or survives, given that enemy 2 *does* empty the water bottle and enemy 1 has poisoned it.

The first probability is clearly very high, since the first of the three disjuncts dominates. The second is very low. C_2 turns out to be have sufficient causal responsibility for E_2 in overwhelming degree. And this is how it should be. The marksman's act is not a cause of the undifferentiated fact of T's death, except to the extent that it acted as a weak preventative, see earlier. *But it is a powerful cause of the form which it takes.* In a normal criminal process, of course, the jury's task would not be narrowed in this way, other than as a subgoal in assessing causal responsibility for the undifferentiated event.

14.2 Scenario 2: T dies of cyanide

The juries are informed on the basis of forensic tests that the event for which they have to determine the cause is E_1, 'T dies-of-cyanide'. They become uneasy and object to the explicit reference to cyanide in the outcome-description, and ask instead to work with E_T. They request that the forensic lab report (that 'the state of the body is consistent with cyanide poisoning') be placed with the other items of evidence along with enemy 1's confession of C_1^+ and enemy 2's confession of C_2^+. They know from C_2^+ that the water bottle lost its poisoned contents *before* T had a chance to drink from it. There is a feeling astir that one at least of the 'almost certainties', including perhaps even reliance on the forensic lab report, F, may have to be revised. Both judges deny the request, pointing out that this would involve placing a post-mortem event, F, among condition-events which by definition precede the outcome, and directing that the court is bound to hold the coroner's forensic lab report above possibility of doubt. F's presence in the logbook is now redundant since its sole consequence was the court's replacement of E_T by E_1.

Each jury must now decide whether the given defendant was responsible for E_1. It is convenient to represent the traveller's death E_T as the union of disjoint events, $E_T = E_1 \cup E_2 \cup E_R$, where E_1 is the event describable as 'T dies-of-cyanide', E_2 corresponds to 'T dies-of-thirst', and E_R is the residual subset: 'T dies in the desert in some other way'. We assume $E_1 \cap E_2 \cap E_R = \phi$. In this new scenario the event-hypothesis is E_1^+. We enquire how much evidence its negation would contribute to (i) the hypothesis C_1^- (enemy 1 did *not* add cyanide), and how much to (ii) the hypothesis C_2^- (enemy 2 did *not* empty the water bottle).

We consider (ii) first:

$$R_{\mathrm{suf}}(E_1^+ : C_2^+ | \mathcal{U} \ \& \ C_1^+)$$
$$= \log[P(E_1^- | C_1^+ \ \& \ C_2^- \ \& \ \mathcal{U})/P(E_1^- | C_1^+ \ \& \ C_2^+ \ \& \ \mathcal{U}]. \tag{Q13}$$

The formalism is in line with the intuition that C_2^+ cannot be a cause of E_1^+. The only possible world in which jury 2 can see enemy 2's act as a cause of T's ingesting cyanide, is one in which it was self-administered to escape the agonies of thirst. Before returning a 'not guilty' verdict they enquire whether any other containers than the empty water bottle were found among T's possessions. They are told 'no'.

Next consider jury 1's approach to (i). The negative proposition E_1^- is equivalent to E_2^+ or E_R^+ or E_T^-, i.e. 'T dies from thirst, or from some other alternative to cyanide, or not at all'.

The relevant equation is:

$$R_{\mathrm{suf}}(E_1^+ : C_1^+ | \mathcal{U} \ \& \ C_2^+)$$
$$= \log[P(E_1^- | C_1^- \ \& \ C_2^+ \ \& \ \mathcal{U})/P(E_1^- | C_1^+ \ \& \ C_2^+ \ \& \ \mathcal{U}]. \tag{Q14}$$

We separately inspect the numerator and the denominator of the Bayesian factor enclosed in the square brackets of (Q14). Both numerator and denominator reduce to the same probability, namely that with an empty water bottle T will die of thirst or in some other way (not cyanide) or survive. Hence enemy 1 has no causal responsibility for T's having met his death by cyanide. But the jury trying this case also has an event E_1, to which they cannot assign a cause and this impels them to notice that their inference is predicated on the constant assumption of C_2^+. Moreover, if E_1^+ is to be accepted as certain, in compliance with the court's directive, then C_2^+ cannot be. Since C_2^+ has (infinitesimally) lesser status than E_1^+, namely '*almost* certain', they entertain the possibility that enemy 2's confession is false. Methods exist for Bayesian inference in the case that one or more of the conditions is a probability statement of the form $P(C_2^+) = p$ (see Good, 1981). Substitution of any probability less than 1 leads to the verdict that enemy 1 is guilty, but with a reservation. Jury 1 enters a rider to the effect that their conclusion was perforce derived from an 'almost inconsistent' set of assumptions.

14.2.1 Reasoning from 'incoherent' condition-sets

The root of the trouble is that, with reasonable $\mathcal{U}$, the body of knowledge and belief to the right of the vertical bar is inconsistent with E_1^+, and vice versa. In particular C_2^+ & F^+ are mutually contradictory. If the forensic lab report is true then T must have drunk from a non-empty bottle and therefore enemy 2 cannot have emptied it. If enemy 2 emptied it, then T must have died of thirst and the forensic lab report is erroneous. C_2^+ had to give way on account of its lower order of certainty.

Instead of speaking of logical consistency we need a probabilistic concept of 'degrees of consistency' that I shall call 'coherence'. Just as in predicate logic inconsistency allows the derivation of the empty clause, so a maximally incoherent set of probabilistic conditions denotes the *almost impossible event*. Given a reasonable $\mathcal{U}$ and the premises $(P(C_2^+) = 1^-$ and $P(F^+) = 1)$, $P(C_2^+$ & $F^+) = 0^+$ is inferrable. The conjunction is rendered 'almost impossible' by $\mathcal{U}$. No rational agent can be satisfied with a verdict based on something that almost certainly did not happen.

The first step in the quest for a more solid base must be to consider the prior probabilities associated with the conditions. The juries might rebel and enquire into the relative frequencies of false confessions and erroneous coroner's lab reports. Suppose that the statistics indicate that F should preferentially be disregarded, and the court reverses its ruling. Then (Q7) and (Q8) are reinstated and the reconvened juries deliver innocent verdicts accordingly. A possible qualification is that although F^+ has been rejected, the level of certainty of C_2^+ (the proposition validated by enemy 2's confession) may be felt to have been somewhat impaired by the appearance of F^+ in the record, even to the extent of C_2^+'s now having a probability strictly less than 1^-. It is technically possible to perform multi-condition Bayesian inference with conditions that are probabilistically expressed. This is required, for example, for weighing evidence gathered from error-prone sensors (see I. J. Good, 1981). The basic method is to evaluate the Bayesian expression for all combinations of extremal confidence-settings for the probabilistic conditions (each combination corresponding to a 'possible world'), and to combine the evaluations at the end by weighting according to the calculated prior probability of each world. If, alternatively, the C_2 event were disregarded in the light of F, then the line of reasoning expressed in (Q14) below applies and enemy 1 is found guilty and enemy 2 acquitted. In all of this there seems nothing out of line with intuition.

14.2.2 Last resort: Rejection of the model

Should erroneous forensic lab reports and false confessions both turn out to be equally and sufficiently infrequent, for example neither having ever been reported, the two juries would be justified in refusing to work from so incoherent a base. T died from cause or causes unknown. Coroners and data analysts alike will find in this a familiar ring. This concludes the most exacting of the tests of R_{suf}'s performance.

14.3 Scenario 3: The conjuction of C_1^+ & C_2^+

To what degree does the *conjunction* C_1^+ & C_2^+ constitute a sufficient cause of E_T^+? In the generic template illustrated by (Q5) and (Q6) we substitute as follows:

$$R_{\text{suf}}(E_T^+ : C_1^+ \ \& \ C_2^+ | \mathcal{U})$$
$$= \log[\, P(E_T^- | \mathcal{U} \ \& \ (C_1^- \ \& \ C_2^+ \ \text{or} \ C_1^+ \ \& \ C_2^- \ \text{or} \ C_1^- \ \& \ C_2^-)$$
$$/ P(E_T^- | \mathcal{U} \ \& \ C_1^+ \ \& \ C_2^+)]. \tag{Q15}$$

For evaluating the numerator of the Bayesian factor within the square brackets, the causality assessor first considers the prior probabilities of the three alternative events of which the set-complement of $C_1 \cap C_2$ is composed. Lacking accurate frequency estimates for such occurrences in desert travel, the assessor merely notes that $P(C_1^- \ \& \ C_2^-)$ dominates, so that the numerator as a whole must be close to unity. But the denominator is the probability that T survives with an empty water bottle, which we have earlier represented by ε_2, only infinitesimally greater than zero. So the conjunction comes out as strongly responsible for T's death in the sense of being a sufficient cause, in line with common sense.

14.4 Scenario 4: The disjunction C_1^+ or C_2^+

This time the appropriate substitutions yield:

$$R_{\text{suf}}(E_T^+ : C_1^+ \ \text{or} \ C_2^+ | \mathcal{U})$$
$$= \log[\, P(E_T^- | \mathcal{U} \ \& \ C_1^- \ \& \ C_2^-) / P(E_T^- | \mathcal{U} \ \& \ C_1^+ \ \text{or} \ C_2^+)]. \tag{Q16}$$

The right-hand side's numerator is slightly closer to unity than in (Q15), since C_1^- & C_2^- is now the only conjunction of non-occurrences that it considers, instead of just the dominating one. Further, the denominator is infinitesimally closer to zero since it involves ε_1 as well as ε_2. Recall that $\varepsilon_1 < \varepsilon_2$ (the probability that T survives the poisoner's act in the case that the water bottle is not emptied is even less than his probability of surviving with an empty water bottle). The strength of the disjunction's causal responsibility for T's death is thus even greater for the disjunction than for the conjunction. The intuitive interpretation of the Bayesian analysis is that the disjunction gives some play to the poisoner, while his act causally nullifies the conjunction.

14.5 Scenario 5: Memory constraints and pressure of time

Oversimplified thinking is not uncommon, and indeed is to a degree necessitated by the brain's relatively slow data-processing and meagre bound on the number of items that can be held in working memory (Miller, 1956). Schoolteachers encourage pupils to make 'scratchpad' records of intermediate results as an aid to offsetting these limitations – a tactic that can be defeated by lowering the time-limit, β, for deliberation. In multi-causal systems such as economics or politics, it is normal to drop a sufficiently large subset of the possible factors to permit mental review of what remains. As the β-bound shrinks, perceived causation tends towards the single-factor assessment widely encountered in the unavoidably simplistic causal reasoning of people in a hurry.

(Q7) and (Q8) are the relevant formulae for the original desert traveller problem. We suppose that both juries are barred by the court from taking written notes, and are set a time limit for deliberation corresponding to a very low β value.

In trying enemy 1, jury 1 drop (Q7)'s references to C_2, giving:

$$R_{\text{suf}}(E_T^+ : C_1^+ | \mathcal{U} \ \& \ \text{bound} = \beta)$$
$$= \log[P(E_T^- | \mathcal{U} \ \& \ C_1^- \ \& \ \text{bound} = \beta)/P(E_T^- | \mathcal{U} \ \& \ C_1^+ \ \& \ \text{bound} = \beta)]. \quad (Q17)$$

The probability of T's surviving with a poisoned water bottle is so low that the verdict is delivered with overwhelming confidence: 'Guilty'.

Jury 2, trying the marksman, drops (Q8)'s references to C_1, obtaining

$$R_{\text{suf}}(E_T^+ : C_2^+ | \mathcal{U} \ \& \ \text{bound} = \beta)$$
$$= \log[P(E_T^- | \mathcal{U} \ \& \ C_2^- \ \& \ \text{bound} = \beta)/P(E_T^- | \mathcal{U} \ \& \ C_2^+ \ \& \ \text{bound} = \beta)]. \quad (Q18)$$

The probability of T's surviving with an empty water bottle is sufficiently low for a verdict with a confidence that is nearly as overwhelming: 'Guilty'.

These time-pressured verdicts do not correspond to the allocation of causes that would result from a deeper analysis. In even a relatively small end-game of chess (see the appendix), almost all judgements are time-pressured relative to the exhaustive analysis of microevents that is technologically feasible. Microevent exhaustion renders causal statements *logically* redundant. However, for boundedly rational agents, such as grandmasters, causal statements retain their full utility. Time-pressured verdicts sometimes cohere with a related notion encountered in human affairs that is distinct from causality. I. J. Good (Chapter 3 above) recently used the term 'culpability'. Here an act's intent dominates over its effects. An application to the desert traveller is the following. Enemy 1 poisoned the water bottle with the intent that T should die. He also knew, correctly, that his action guaranteed with strong probability that T would indeed die. Enemy 1 is therefore strongly culpable. By similar reasoning enemy 2 is deemed to be nearly as strongly culpable. A morally suitable end to the story might be that, faced with two discrepant court findings, a superior court declares mistrials, followed by a new trial that finds both malefactors innocent of murder, but guilty of attempted murder. For reasons already explored concerning the inequality $\varepsilon_1 < \varepsilon_2$, enemy 1 receives the longer prison sentence.

15 GENERATING CAUSAL COMMENTS ON OUTCOMES

The following tabulation displays the anatomy of probabilistic sufficient and necessary cause in terms of after-the-event comments on individual outcomes.

	E_1	E_2	
	a	b	$a+b$
C_1	$R_{suf} = \log[d/(c+d)]$ $- \log[b/(a+b)]$	$R_{suf} = \log[c/(c+d)]$ $- \log[a/(a+b)]$	
	$R_{nec} = \log[a/(a+b)]$ $- \log[c/(c+d)]$	$R_{nec} = \log[b/(a+b)]$ $- \log[d/(c+d)]$	
	c	d	$c+d$
C_2	$R_{suf} = \log[b/(a+b)]$ $- \log[d/(c+d)]$	$R_{suf} = \log[a/(a+b)]$ $- \log[c/(c+d)]$	
	$R_{nec} = \log[c/(c+d)]$ $- \log[a/(a+b)]$	$R_{nec} = \log[d/(c+d)]$ $- \log[b/(a+b)]$	
	$a+c$	$b+d$	N

In the table's four cells, a, b, c, d represent frequencies of occurrence of the four history-types in a logbook sample of N histories. Assume N to be sufficiently large that they are close to the (possibly unknown, possibly deducible) population frequencies. Inspection of any given individual history identifies just one of the four cells (corresponding to a (C, E) pair) as satisfying the conjunction $(C^+ \& E^+)$, i.e. this is the event-type that the new occurrence exemplifies, the one that actually occurred. We therefore associate with it the corresponding cells's R_{suf} and R_{nec} estimates of degrees of sufficient and necessary causal tendency. According as $ad > bc$ or $bc > ad$, one of the two diagonals is identified as the positive diagonal, i.e. its contents exemplify positive causation of outcomes rather than negative causation (prevention). To generate comments on a new individual outcome, proceed as follows:

First obtain the R_{nec} formula from the appropriate cell of the table (the one containing the new history, denoted by (C^+, E^+)).

Case 1. The selected cell is on the positive diagonal.

Assert 'To degree $R_{nec}(E^+ : C^+)$, E^+ occurred *because of* C^+'.

Case 2. The selected cell is on the negative diagonal.

Assert 'To degree $R_{nec}(E^+ : C^+)$, E^+ occurred *in spite of* C^+'.

It would be nice to derive equally useful comments from the R_{suf}'s. To do this, it is necessary to switch from commenting on an outcome's *explainability*, as above, to its *expectedness*. A critical property now is C's role as a predictor of E. Obtain the R_{suf} formula from the appropriate cell. Note that when (C, E) is on the negative diagonal, the R formula comes from the horizontally *adjacent* cell, corresponding to the event that (predictively speaking) should have happened but did not.

Case 1. The selected cell is on the positive diagonal.

Assert 'To degree $R_{suf}(E^+ : C^+)$, E^+'s *expectedness* was increased (unexpectedness was decreased) by C^+.

Case 2. The selected cell is on the negative diagonal.

Assert 'To degree $R_{suf}(E^- : C^+)$, E^+'s *unexpectedness* was increased (expectedness was decreased) by C^+.'

For the most natural linguistic effect, select from synonymous alternatives as follows. If E^+'s conditional probability exceeds 50%, then describe C^+'s impact on E^+'s expectedness, otherwise C^+'s impact on E^+'s unexpectedness.

16 DISCUSSION

Treatment of cause as probabilistic inferrability might suggest that the analysis is suited only to non-deterministic worlds. But in Bayesian inference imperfect information in the model is as potent a source of probabilistic uncertainty as is random noise in the modelled world. I have accordingly added an appendix which considers causal inference in chess. The latter shows that a finite and fully deterministic game with complete information is amenable to precisely the same kinds of causal inference. Beyond a certain complexity level, access to the microevent structure of a given (C^+, E^+) history (inaccessible in most real-world domains) does not take a resource-bounded agent's predictive grasp any further beyond what he, she or it can do with a causal calculus based on subjective probability judgements and a body of relational background knowledge.

Even simplified worlds of games and ultrasimplified subgames fully extend human powers of explanatory narrative. Such powers are as yet negligible in AI's grandmaster-strength programs (see Michie 1995). Yet Internet agents capable of causally phrased self-reporting can expect an eager market. Satisfaction of demand seems unlikely until (1) there is wide availability of satisfactory formalizations of causality and (2) they can be made easy to understand and apply. The requirement is for a calculus for reasoning about causal responsibility for individual events. Pearl (1998) has recently applied a counterfactually-based definition of 'actual cause', after extension to cover notions of 'sufficient' in addition to 'necessary' cause, to the Desert Traveller problem. He concludes, as we do, that neither enemy's act was a sufficient positive cause. Pearl's treatment is not taken through the gamut of variant scenarios explored here, nor applied to deterministic worlds such as that of the appendix of this paper, nor used to generate causal commentaries from logged histories. The criteria for any comparison of the two calculi must be applicability and clarity in practice. Suppes (1994) recently remarked: 'As yet, it is fair to say, the literature on probabilistic causality has not had much impact on the actual practice of statistical inference about causal matters, although it has had an impact on the conceptual discussion of causality by statisticians. There is a chance that Good's new concepts will have a more direct influence.' The present paper's aim is to further this.

Acknowledgements

I learned what I know about Bayesian probability from my wartime colleague I. J. Good. Subsequently, at Virginia Polytechnic Institute and State University in 1992, I enjoyed a spell of renewed collaboration and embarked on the present work. During its recent finalization Professor Good has once more been a source of helpful criticism, pointers to the literature and stimulating suggestions. My second debt is to Patrick Suppes. As a visiting worker at Stanford University, I attended a lecture on probabilistic causality in 1962. In outlining his approach to the desert traveller problem, the lecturer, Professor Suppes, invited the audience to try it as an exercise. My response comes with apologies for lateness. I am also indebted to Professor Ross Quinlan of Sydney University for identifying a flaw in an earlier version, and to James Cussens of the Oxford University Computing Laboratory for pointers to the recent literature.

APPENDIX: CAUSALITY IN CHESS

The tendency has always been strong to believe that whatever received a name must be an entity or being having an independent existence of its own. And if no real entity answering to the name could be found, men did not for that reason suppose that none existed but imagined that it was something peculiarly abstract and abstruse.

John Stuart Mill

The foregoing theory is to be understood in a sense which can be illustrated from a small deterministic and finite universe that has a complete specification, namely the laws of chess. These constitute its 'physics'. The laws define legality of moves and positions, and lay down the move-alternation rule, and the conditions for terminating games and assigning outcomes.

Consider, now, the *riskiness* of a chess move under the assumption of a game-theoretically infallible opponent. Given only that the side considering the move has bounded calculational resource, the riskiness of a move is definable in a sense intelligible to other rational agents subject to similar bounds. Yet nothing resembling the concept of riskiness is to be found in the 'physics', i.e. in the laws. Riskiness is a complex, agent-centred, abstraction.

Example. The state-space of the endgame king and rook against king and knight (black to move) has been exhaustively enumerated by computer, and complete lookup tables of optimal moves for both players have been constructed. The majority of the approximately 200 000 positions in the space of legal positions are found to be won for white – by convention the side with the material advantage. In positions of the drawn subset it is by definition always possible for black to find a move which preserves the game's drawn status. But in most cases he has at least one alternative which is a 'mistake', i.e. a move which changes the game from drawn to lost-for-black (there are effectively no won-for-black positions). Over the years certain rules of thumb have been developed by students of the endgame to help the defender avoid such losing moves. One of them is: 'Do not separate king and knight.' Adherence to this precept does not eliminate *all* losing moves. Indeed Kopec and Niblett's (1980) exhaustive analysis revealed freak positions in which the only *non*-losing move for black is a separating move. In other words, instead of avoiding a forced loss, in these special cases following the rule of thumb guarantees it. Their paper's Figure 8 reproduces an intriguing sample of eight such positions. But in the problem space as a whole, it is neglect of the rule rather than adherence to it that correlate strongly with losing lines of play.

Let us now suppose that a human grandmaster, G, starting from a drawn position, faces a game-theoretically infallible opponent, in the form (let us say) of a computer armed with an optimal move-lookup table. Let us suppose that G practises daily, starting from a position randomly selected from the space of draws, taking the black pieces against the computer. Hence the respective frequencies with which his separating and non-separating moves are losers are already known and documented in his chess club who, shall we say, have retained Kopec and Niblett as consultants. G makes a separating move. Onlooker A without revealing the precise move, comments on the phone to a distant grandmaster B 'He's separated king and knight'. B replies 'That's extremely risky!'

But in the computer's book, all is predestinate. *Every* defending move, including the hypothesized separating move, is precategorized as either a mistake or not a mistake. So it could be argued that a probabilistic notion like *risk* cannot validly characterize black's move. The agent-centred approach resolves the dilemma. From the computer's viewpoint, black's move is either a mistake or it is sound, and the database 'knows' which. But neither the player G nor the onlookers, nor for that matter grandmaster B, possess this knowledge. Their bounded calculational powers disallow extensive lookahead analysis, and their memories preclude storage of more than a small fragment of such a vast lookup table. Under these conditions the theory of subjective probability can assign to B's comment 'That's extremely risky!' a straightforward meaning in Bayesian (subjective) probability. In the terminology of the main paper, 'the statistician's log' does not include the exhaustive database but only what B can infer from $\mathcal{B}$, the laws of chess, together with his relevant experience of practical play and from the club's statistical summaries of G's track record.

H is the hypothesis that black's move loses. $\mathcal{B}$ consists of the laws of chess. E is the set of separating moves that can be made from the position in question. Given that G has just made a separating move, what *now* is H's probability, i.e. H's posterior probability? It is more convenient to consider H's posterior *plausibility*, using (P9) from the main paper:

$$\text{Plaus}(H^+|E^+ \,\&\, \mathcal{B}) = \text{Plaus}(H^+|\mathcal{B}) + \log[P(E^+|H^+ \,\&\, \mathcal{B})/P(E^+|H^- \,\&\, \mathcal{B})]. \quad (P9)$$

$\text{Plaus}(H^+|\mathcal{B})$, is the prior plausibility, when we still don't yet know what black's move is, of the hypothesis that it is a losing one. It was earlier mentioned that a good historical summary is to hand, so we proceed to the remaining term, which requires two quantities, namely:

$P(E^+|H^+ \,\&\, \mathcal{B})$ expresses the probability of E^+ ('G made a separating move') given the knowledge that it was a loser. It can be estimated, supposing such records to exist, from the frequency with which separating moves occur among G's game-losing mistakes, and $P(E^+|H^- \,\&\, \mathcal{B})$ can be estimated from the frequency with which separating moves occur among G's draw-preserving moves. This empirical frequency information is included in $\mathcal{B}$ in the statistician's logbook. From this together with (P9) the inferrable posterior probability that G has made a losing move is very high.

At this juncture the computer discloses that G still has a drawn position (it wasn't after all a losing move). A fresh problem is defined for B, namely to evaluate $R_{\text{suf}}(H^- : E^+|\mathcal{B})$, i.e. the degree to which the cause of G's obtaining a drawn position is to be sought in the fact that G's move was a separating one. Informally, R_{suf} says: 'If instead he had got a lost position, what weight of evidence would that have given *against* his having made a separating move?' The answer is a negative weight, and this makes sense. G got a drawn position not *because* his move was a separating one but *in spite of* it. The cause of his maintaining the draw must be sought in some other feature of the move, perhaps expressible as an 'exception to the rule'.

Now let us consider a further problem. The information recorded in the statistician's logbook now narrows the event E by elaborating its description until E becomes the unit set containing just the move that G actually made. Grandmaster B is not only told that G has separated king and knight but is given the actual move. With the same $\mathcal{B}$, his comment will be as before, since $\mathcal{B}$ contains nothing to give him a handle on the newly added elemental information. This would require that $\mathcal{B}$ be augmented with a list of specific exceptions taken from the database (real-world grandmasters do not know this list, nor do they for the most part even know of its existence), against which he could match the telephoned move. Then, and only then, could he say: *the cause of getting a drawn position was making this particular move, countertypical of the tendency of separating moves to be a sufficient cause of lost positions.*

This is a substantive point for causality theory. If refining a condition so as to specify the particular microevent that actually occured has in general no effect on calculation of its cause (for notation see main paper) then this holds a fortiori for the real-world case where the micro-events are not even observable. In propounding a golfing puzzle, Suppes (1970) remarks: that 'hitting the branch in exactly the way it did was essential to the ball's going into the cup'. This is precisely on a par with 'separating king and knight in exactly the way he did' except that in golf 'in exactly the way it did' is not accurately observable or describable. To speak of causal description being in some sense changed by unobservable variables not even named in the initial problem description is far removed from any known statistics paradigm. If microspecification, even when it is possible, has no consequences for a rational agent's causal description of events, then its introduction into causality analyses seems closer to metaphysics than to science.

REFERENCES

Ginsberg, M. L. (ed., 1987) *Readings in Nonmonotonic Reasoning*, Los Altos, CA: Morgan Kaufmann.

Good, I. J. (1950) *Probability and the Weighing of Evidence* (London: Charles Griffin; New York: Hafners).

Good, I. J. (1961) A causal calculus (1). *Brit. J. Phil. Sci.*, **11**, 305–118.

Good, I. J. (1962) A causal calculus (2). *Brit. J. Phil. Sci.*, **12**, 43–51; **13**, 88.

Good, I. J. (1977) Dynamic probability, computer chess and the measurement of knowledge. In *Machine Intelligence 8* (eds. Elcock, E. W. and Michie, D.), Edinburgh: Edinburgh University Press.

Good, I. J. (1981) The weight of evidence provided by uncertain testimony or from an uncertain event. *J. Statist. comput. Sim.*, **13**, 56–60.

Good, I. J. (1988a) Causal tendency: a review. In *Causation, Chance and Credence* (eds. Skyrms, B. and Harper, W. L.), Vol. **I**, 23–50. Dordrecht: Kluwer.

Good, I. J. (1988b) Response to Salmon. In *Causation, Chance and Credence* (eds. Skyrms, B. and Harper, W. L.), Vol. **I**, 73–78. Dordrecht: Kluwer.

Good, I. J. (1992) The mathematics of philosophy. a brief review of my work. Technical Report No. 92-3, Blacksburg, VA: Dept. of Statistics, Virginia Polytechnic and State University. Published in *Critical Rationalism: Metaphysics and Science, Essays for Joseph Agassi*, Vol. **1** (eds. I. C. Jarvie and Nathaniel Laor), Boston Studies in the Philosophy of Science, 1995, pp. 211–238.

Good, I. J. (1994) Causal tendency, necessitivity and sufficientivity: an updated review. In *Patrick Suppes: Scientific Philosopher*, Vol 1 (ed. P. Humphreys), Dordrecht: Kluwer Academic Publishers, pp. 293–315.

Kopec, D. and Niblett, T. (1980) How hard is the play of the King-Rook-King-Knight ending? In *Advances in Computer Chess 2* (ed. M. R. B. Clarke), Edinburgh: Edinburgh University Press, pp. 57–81.

Michie, D. (1977) A theory of advice. In *Machine Intelligence 8* (eds. Elcock, E. W. and Michie, D.), Edinburgh: Edinburgh University Press, pp. 151–168.

Michie, D. (1990) Personal models of rationality. *J. Statist. Planning and Inference*, Special Issue on Foundations and Philosophy of Probability and Statistics, **21**, 381–399.

Michie, D. (1995) Game mastery and intelligence. In *Machine Intelligence 14* (eds. K. Furukawa, D. Michie and S. Muggleton), Oxford University Press.

Miller, G. A. (1956) The magical number seven, plus or minus two. *Psych. Review*, **63**, 81–97.

Pearl, J. (1998) Probabilities of causation: three counterfactual interpretations and their identification. *Technical Report R-261*, Computer Science Department, University of California, Los Angeles, CA 90024.

Simon, H. A. (1979) *Models of Thought*. New Haven, CT: Yale University Press. [The phrase "bounded rationality" is from Simon's introduction to the first section of this collection of his papers.]

Suppes, P. (1970) A probabilistic theory of causality. *Acta Phil. Fennica*, **24**, Amsterdam: North Holland.

Suppes, P. (1994) Comments by Patrick Suppes. Addendum to Good (1994).

Suppes, P. (1970) A probabilistic theory of causality. *Acta Phil. Fennica*, **24**, 5–130.

86

COMPUTER VISION

5

Making robots see

Andrew Blake

Department of Engineering Science,
University of Oxford,
Parks Road,
Oxford,
UK
Web: http://www.robots.ox.ac.uk/~ab

1 INTRODUCTION

Progress in vision for robots over the past two decades since the seminal work of Ambler *et al.* (1975) exhibits several distinct strands. Firstly, deeper understanding of the applications of differential geometry (DoCarmo, 1976; Giblin and Weiss, 1987; Cipolla and Zisserman, 1992) and perspective geometry (Koenderink and Van Doorn, 1975; Koenderink and Van Doorn, 1978; Ullman, 1979; Longuet-Higgins and Pradzny, 1980; Huang and Tsai, 1981; Waxman and Ullman, 1985; Maybank, 1985; Faugeras *et al.*, 1987; Murray and Buxton, 1990) to visual motion analysis allow the three-dimensional structure of the world to be analysed, on-the-fly, as a robot moves around its environment. Secondly, modelling of specific prior knowledge of objects and motion, often using statistically based models, allows robots to see anticipated objects remarkably robustly (Gelb, 1974; Bar-Shalom and Fortmann, 1988; Fischler and Elschlager, 1973; Kass *et al.*, 1987; Dickmanns and Graefe, 1988; Grenander *et al.*, 1991; Bennett and Craw, 1991; Szeliski and Terzopoulos, 1991; Terzopoulos and Metaxas, 1991; Yuille and Hallinan, 1992; Harris, 1992). This is in marked contrast to the general and overambitious aims of earlier research (Marr, 1982) which sought to compete with the highly developed visual systems of humans and animals. Finally, with the advent of adequate processing power, it has become possible to regard cameras as visual sensors in control systems, allowing robots to react to visual events in real time (Dickmanns, 1992; Brown *et al.*, 1992; Murray *et al.*, 1992; Krotkov, 1989; Ballard and Ozcandarli, 1988).

In this chapter, we report some recent progress, within the broad paradigm described above, towards building a visually guided robot arm that is able to grasp and transport objects across an obstacle-strewn environment. A CCD camera is mounted on the wrist of an ADEPT robot and a computer continually monitors visual signals. Deliberate, exploratory motions are coordinated with visual computation so as to explore the shape of three-dimensional, curved obstacles (Giblin and Weiss, 1987; Blake and

89

Cipolla, 1990; Vaillant, 1990; Arbogast and Mohr, 1990; Cipolla and Blake, 1992). The visual computation itself is based on *dynamic contours* (Kass *et al.*, 1987; Curwen and Blake, 1992) which are strongly focussed on obstacle silhouettes and hence efficient. The combination of focussed attention and parallelism leads to real-time performance. This in turn allows integration of perception with control systems for action (Figure 1). Coordinated, sequenced perception and action drives the robot to reach around obstacles towards a goal (Blake *et al.*, 1991, 1992), as in Figure 2.

Given that a robot may be able to reach around obstacles and retrieve objects, it is then necessary for it to be able to control a gripper. Complex, anthropomorphic hands have been built (Salisbury and Roth, 1983) but, for control purposes, the simplest gripper is a two-fingered one. The fingers may open and close either with parallel motion or with hinged motion. They may either be plates or thin cylinders. Of course the human hand has a wide repertoire of grasps (Elliot and Connelly, 1984). The assumptions of our model are

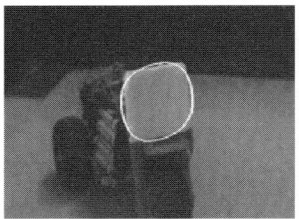  

Figure 1. A dynamic contour visual tracker follows the motion of a model vehicle. The camera is mounted on the wrist of an ADEPT robot which rotates the camera to maintain the contour in the center of the image. The dynamic contour, a computed B-spline, is shown in white, overlaid on the images. (Figure by courtesy of R. Curwen.)

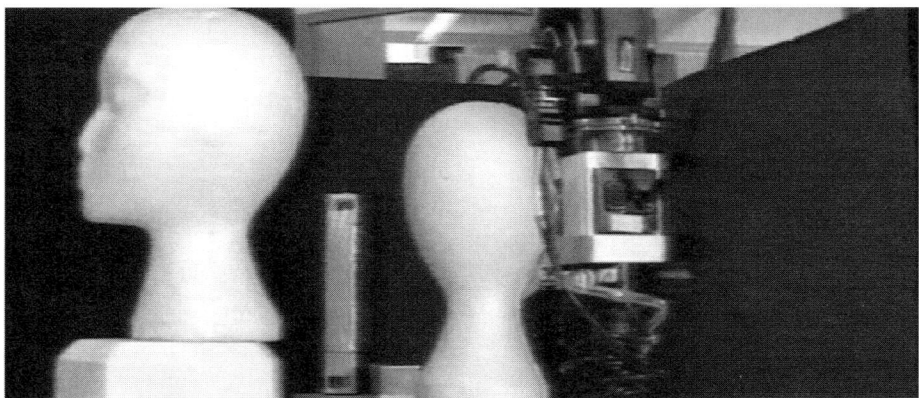

Figure 2. The robot directs the camera's gaze towards one of two obstacles, attempting to plan a path between them. The goal object is marked by the vertical white column in the distance. (Figure by courtesy of A. Zisserman.)

probably closest to the *index roll*, a grip between thumb and index finger. It is desirable to relate the control of a two-fingered gripper to the information available directly from visual dynamic contours. We build on the notable work of Faverjon and Ponce (1991), extending it to obtain *qualitative rules* for stable grasp based on contour shape. The result is a computational procedure for obtaining locally optimal finger positions, based on an elementary use of differential analysis, of the kind used by Bruce and Giblin in their taxonomy of symmetry sets (Bruce and Giblin, 1984). Indeed the classification of grasps turns out to be tightly coupled to symmetry properties.

2 VISUAL ANALYSIS OF CURVED SURFACES

Recent work has shown that, by combining differential geometry (DoCarmo, 1976) and static contour analysis (Koenderink, 1984) with analysis of visual motion (Longuet-Higgins and Pradzny, 1980; Maybank, 1985) local surface curvature can be computed from moving images. The apparent contour is the boundary of the image of a smooth surface. It is the perspective projection of a smooth curve – an 'external boundary' – onto the image plane (Figure 3). Figure 4 demonstrates the ability to discriminate qualitatively between rigid features and extremal boundaries on smooth surfaces. Despite much effort, attempts over the last two decades to make this distinction by photometric analysis have been relatively unsuccessful. However, by allowing small camera motions and observing the resulting contour deformations the distinction can be made reliably. Particularly important for collision-free motion, the 'sidedness' of apparent contours is computed,

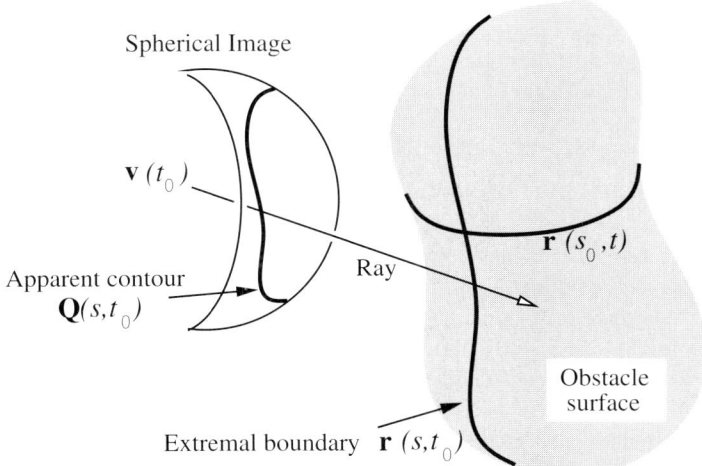

Figure 3. For a given vantage point, $\mathbf{v}(t_0)$, the family of rays emanating from the viewer's optical centre that touch the surface defines an s-parameter curve $\mathbf{r}(s, t_0)$ which is the extremal boundary from vantage point t_0. The spherical perspective projection of this extremal boundary – the apparent contour, $\mathbf{Q}(s, t_0)$ – determines the direction of rays which graze the surface.

91

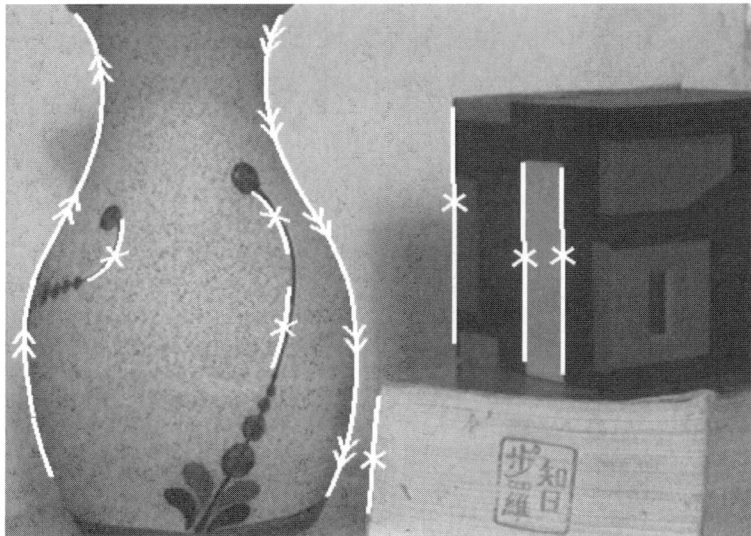

Figure 4. Vase and block, one frame from an image sequence with a moving camera. Labels on contours display results of qualitative curvature analysis. A cross denotes a rigid feature, a surface crease or marking. A double arrow indicates an 'apparent contour' or silhouette. The obscuring surface is to the right of the arrowed direction. (After Cipolla and Blake, 1992.)

that is, which side is solid surface and which is free space. Useful quantitative analysis of apparent contours is also possible, yielding full information about local surface curvature. Details of the algorithm that does this are given elsewhere (Blake and Cipolla, 1990; Cipolla and Blake, 1992).

3 CIRCUMNAVIGATION OF SINGLE OBSTACLES

Practical navigation is somewhat flexible to the positioning of an obstacle, using the convergence of the dynamic contour tracker, run at coarse scale for target-acquisition, to lock onto the apparent contour. Then the camera scans horizontally with the contour tracking at fine-scale. Resulting motion is analysed and used in several ways. First the *sign* of the estimated normal curvature κ_n determines the *sidedness* of the apparent contour – which side is free-space and hence navigable. Second, the magnitude of κ_n is used to extrapolate a smooth path around the object. Third, error in $1/\kappa_n$ from the regression analysis is 'added on' to the path to ensure safe clearances. Uncertainty is simply incorporated into the procedure of the previous section by using a value for the radius of curvature which exceeds $1/\kappa_n$ by the appropriate tolerance. This results in a motion along a *parallel surface* (DoCarmo, 1976) to the true obstacle surface.

Performance is limited, currently, by vibration of the robot (of approximate amplitude 0.1 mm). This means that the movement of the robot necessary for visual computation

Front view   Side view

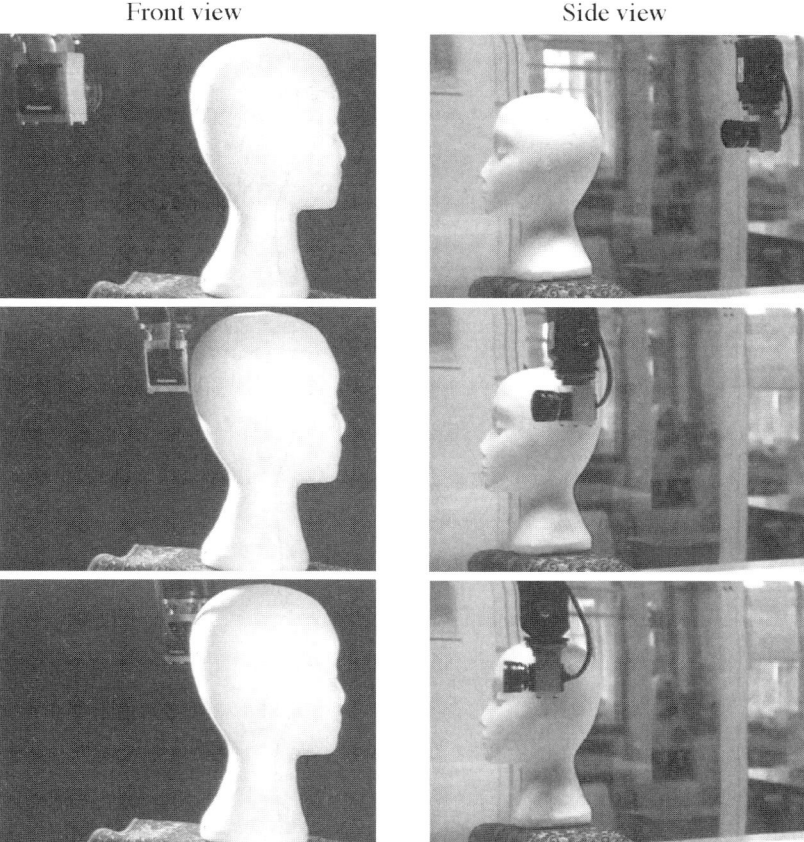

Figure 5. Three frames from a sequence shows the arm-mounted camera following a planar path around a curved obstacle.

of curvature is somewhat extended, lasting for about 5 seconds at a visual sampling rate of 25 Hz. Recursive least squares analysis of the image motion limits the effects of vibration somewhat. The result is that distance λ to the apparent contour can be computed quite accurately from visual motion, typically 200 ± 0.5 mm. Curvature, as expected from theory, is less accurate. Radius of curvature $1/\kappa_n$ is typically measured to within ± 10 mm. The accuracies quoted above are quite sufficient to assist path-planning. Figure 5 shows the arm with camera moving from start to goal, along a horizontal planar path, around a curved obstacle. A second example (Figure 6) shows navigation along a geodesic path using the pitch angle α obtained from normal curvature and geodesic torsion.

3.1 Freespace representation

Freespace is explored visually (Blake *et al.*, 1992). Since the portion of our SCARA robot that penetrates the working volume is approximately a vertical cylinder it is reasonably

Figure 6. An approximated geodesic path. This sequence shows the robot driving the camera over the central helical section of an approximated geodesic path, touching the obstacle surface.

efficient to project 3D freespace onto a horizontal plane. Path-planning is guaranteed safe but not necessarily optimal, in common with well-known heuristic approaches such as Brooks' freeway method (Brooks, 1983). Within the plane, freespace is represented as a union of triangles (Figure 7). The robot then translates on one horizontal plane (Lumelsky's (1986) assumption for a Cartesian arm).

Visual exploration however must involve vertical scanning (using camera tilt) as well as horizontal. Thus the robot is frequently seen eyeing a particular visual feature up and down. Clearance at all heights within the workspace can be determined by projecting the ray at each point of the obstacle's silhouette onto the freespace plane, as a line. Making use of the visually inferred sidedness of the silhouette (see earlier), the line becomes the boundary of a free half-plane. The intersection of such half-planes sweeps out an area that is guaranteed free for robot-motion. (Note that the sweeping process need not actually be performed point by point but can be computed analytically for each span of the dynamic contour.)

3.2 Two-fingered grasps

Contour trackers readily deliver smooth, closed curves bounding the object to be grasped, as in Figure 1. It is therefore reasonable to assume a smooth curve for grasp-planning purposes. However, the theory presented in this chapter can be readily adapted to the case of piecewise smooth curves, should they be available.

We assume that a thin, planar object bounded by a closed curve is to be grasped by a two-fingered gripper. The fingers are thin, frictional cylinders. Parallel jaws are also dealt with as a special case. Grasps are analysed in terms of 'force closure' (Reuleaux, 1876; Latombe, 1991). A grasp has force closure if any force and couple applied externally to

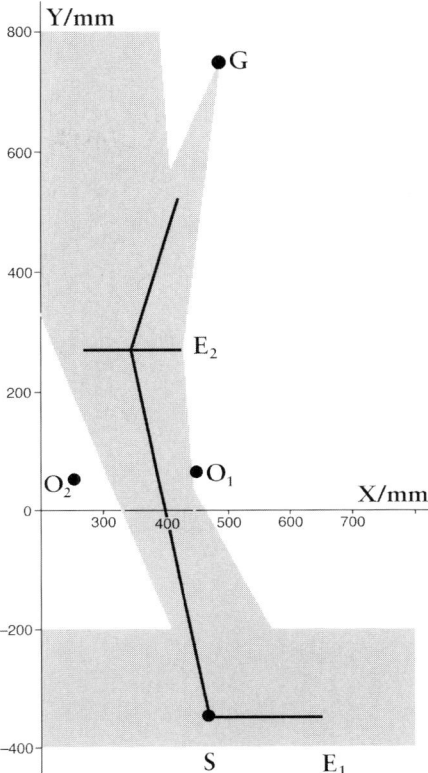

Figure 7. This freespace map is built incrementally by the active robot as it explores its environment, in search of the goal G. Initially the robot is at S, in an area of guaranteed freespace (the rectangle at the bottom). The robot directs its gaze toward the goal and, fails to find it. It then pans until it finds an image feature. It moves along the line E_1 to recover the distance to the obstacle feature O_1, identify it as an extremal boundary and compute surface curvature. It then pans towards obstacle O_2, clearing an area of freespace sufficient to move through. Then it plans a new vantage point (where there should be a clear view of the goal if there are no further obstacles) including a free line E_2 for exploratory motion. From there it looks towards the goal, finds a feature, makes an exploratory motion to compute distance and hence verifies that the goal has been sighted. There is a clear path to pick up the object. (Figure by courtesy of A. Zisserman.)

the object can be cancelled by some set of positive forces at the fingers. Markenscoff and Papadimitriou (1988) show that a minimum of three fingers are required to guarantee force closure in the plane, for a piecewise smooth curve. For a smooth curve, however, two fingers are sufficient (Chen and Burdick, 1992). Force closure of a particular grasp is established via the friction cone construction (Nguyen, 1988), in Figure 8.

Faverjon and Ponce (1991) have shown how sets of force closure grasps can be mapped out in the configuration space for a two-fingered gripper – 'grasp configuration

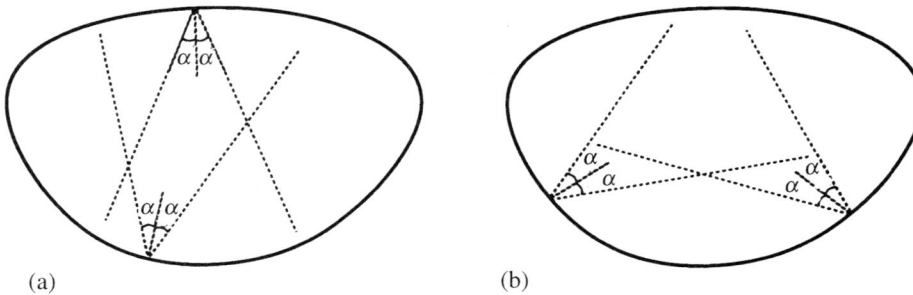

Figure 8. A two-fingered frictional grip is in equilibrium when force closure is satisfied as in (a). The fingers contact the two points shown on the contour. Each point lies within the friction cone of the other (semi-angle $\alpha = \tan^{-1}(\mu)$, where μ is the coefficient of friction). In (b) force closure is not satisfied.

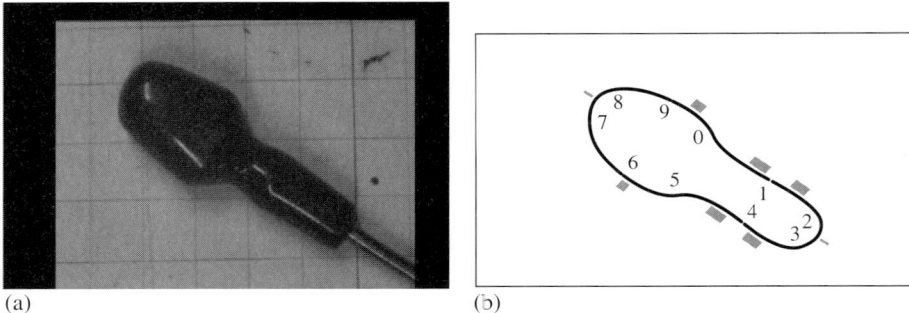

Figure 9. Primary grasps for the screwdriver outline (a) are shown in (b) as opposing pairs of rectangles. The width of each rectangle indicates a measure of the tolerable uncertainty in position, obtained by considering sensitivity, for one finger in a particular grasp, with a given coefficient of friction (0.05 in the case illustrated).

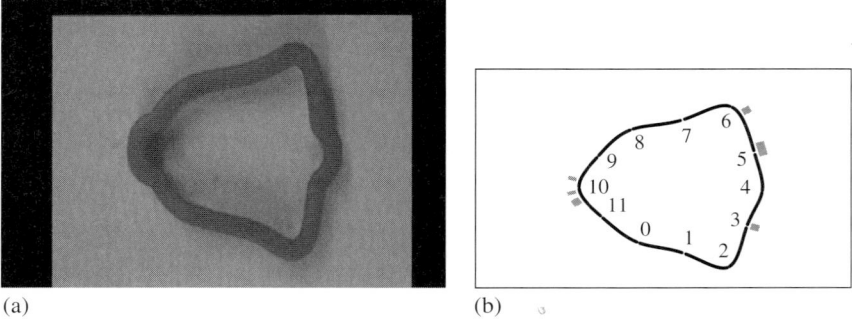

Figure 10. This bell-shaped cookie-cutter (a) has 11 primary grasps of which the 3 most stable are displayed in (b) with sensitivity measures as before.

space' (Hong *et al.*, 1990) – for a given coefficient of friction. A more general method exists (Blake, 1992; Blake *et al.*, 1993) that does not require prior knowledge of the coefficient of friction. Discrete sets of 'extremal grasps' are generated, constituting grasps which are locally optimal or pessimal in the sense of requiring least or greatest friction for force closure. The resulting theory is driven by local object symmetry. All extremal grasps lie either on the 'symmetry set' of Bruce and Giblin (1984) or on the 'anti-symmetry set' (Blake, 1992), relating to reflectional and rotational symmetries, respectively. The theory is extended to include a simple analysis of grasp stability and sensitivity. Results of an implementation of the theory using a robot vision system are shown in Figures 9–11.

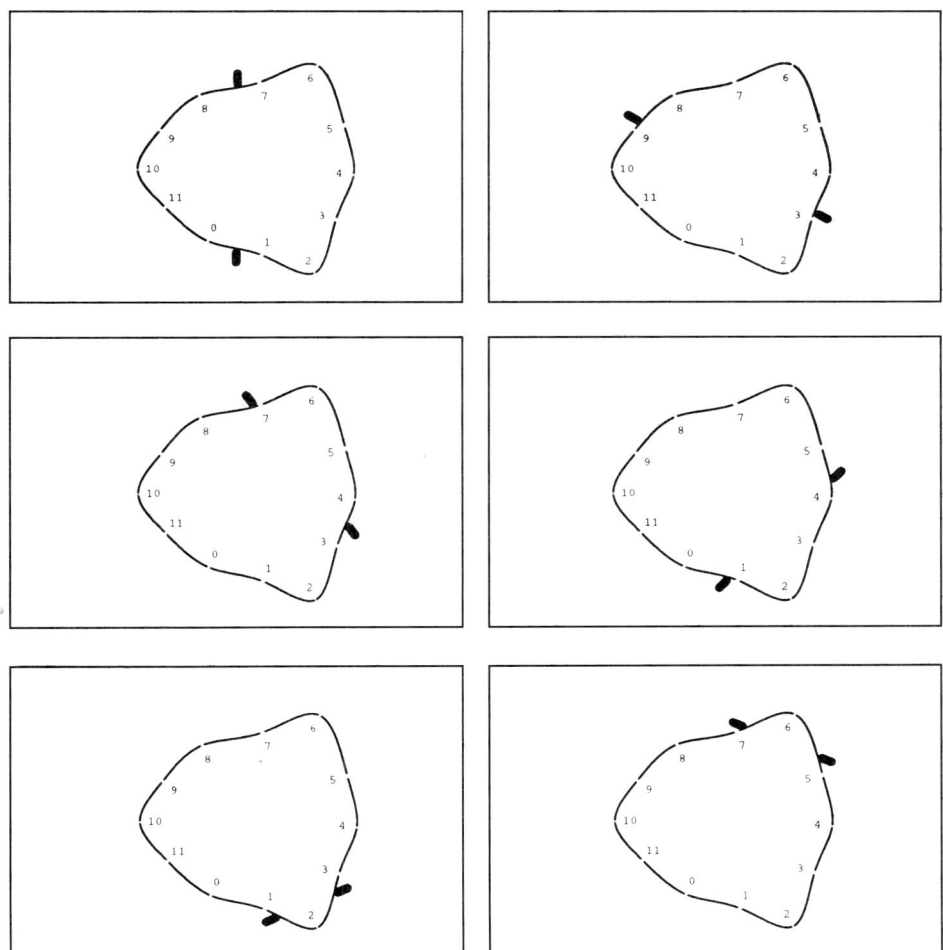

Figure 11. The bell-shaped cookie-cutter in Figure 10 has, in addition to its primary grasps, several secondary grasps, of which the six shown here have minimum coefficients of friction below $\mu = 1$.

REFERENCES

Ambler, A., Barrow, H., Brown, C., Burstall, R., and Popplestone, R. (1975). A versatile system for computer controlled assembly. *Artificial Intelligence*, 6: 129–156.

Arbogast, E. and Mohr, R. (1990). 3D structure inference from images sequences. In Baird, H., ed., *Proceedings of the Syntactical and Structural Pattern Recognition Workshop*, pp. 21–37, Murray-Hill, NJ.

Ballard, D. H. and Ozcandarli, A. (1988). Eye fixation and early vision: kinetic depth. In *Proc. 2nd Int. Conf. on Computer Vision*, pp. 524–531, Tampa, FL. IEEE Press.

Bar-Shalom, Y. and Fortmann, T. (1988). *Tracking and Data Association*. Academic Press.

Bennett, A. and Craw, I. (1991). Finding image features for deformable templates and detailed prior statistical knowledge. In Mowforth, P., ed., *Proc. British Machine Vision Conference*, pp. 233–239, Glasgow. Springer-Verlag, London.

Blake, A. (1992). Computational modelling of hand-eye coordination. *Phil. Trans. R. Soc*, 337: 351–360.

Blake, A., Brady, J., Cipolla, R., Xie, Z., and Zisserman, A. (1991). Visual navigation around curved obstacles. In *Proc. Int. Conf. Robotics and Automation*, volume 3, pp. 2490–2499, IEEE Press.

Blake, A. and Cipolla, R. (1990). Robust estimation of surface curvature from deformation of apparent contours. In Faugeras, O., ed., *Proc. 1st European Conference on Computer Vision*, pp. 465–474. Springer-Verlag.

Blake, A., Curwen, R., and Zisserman, A. (1993). Affine-invariant contour tracking with automatic control of spatiotemporal scale. In *Proc. 4th Int. Conf. on Computer Vision*, pp. 66–75, IEEE Press.

Blake, A., Zisserman, A., and Cipolla, R. (1992). Visual exploration of freespace. In Blake, A. and Yuille, A., eds., *Active Vision*, pp. 175–188. MIT Press, Cambridge, MA.

Brooks, R. (1983). Solving path planning by representation of freespace. *IEEE Trans. Sys. Man. Cyb.*, 13: 190–197.

Brown, C., Coombs, D., and Soong, J. (1992). Real-time smooth pursuit tracking. In Blake, A. and Yuille, A., eds., *Active Vision*, pp. 123–136. MIT Press, Cambridge, MA.

Bruce, J. W. and Giblin, P. (1984). *Curves and Singularities*, Cambridge University Press.

Chen, I.-M. and Burdick, J. (1992). Finding antipodal point grasps on irregularly shaped objects. In *Proc. Int. Conf. Robotics and Automation*, pp. 2278–2283, IEEE Press.

Cipolla, R. and Blake, A. (1992). Surface shape from the deformation of apparent contours. *Int. Journal of Computer Vision*, 9(2): 83–112.

Cipolla, R. and Zisserman, A. (1992). Qualitative surface shape from deformation of image curves. *Int. Journal of Computer Vision*, 8(1): 53–69.

Curwen, R. and Blake, A. (1992). Dynamic contours: real-time active splines. In Blake, A. and Yuille, A., eds., *Active Vision*, pp. 39–58. MIT Press, Cambridge, MA.

Dickmanns, E. (1992). Expectation-based dynamic scene understanding. In Blake, A. and Yuille, A., eds., *Active Vision*, pp. 303–336. MIT Press, Cambridge, MA.

Dickmanns, E. and Graefe, V. (1988). Applications of dynamic monocular machine vision. *Machine Vision and Applications*, 1: 241–261.

DoCarmo, M. (1976). *Differential Geometry of Curves and Surfaces*. Prentice-Hall.

Elliot, J. and Connelly, K. (1984). A classification of manipulative hand movements. *Developmental Medicine and Child Neurology*, 26: 283–296.

Faugeras, O., Lustman, F., and Toscani, G. (1987). Motion and structure from motion from point and line matches. In *Proc. 1st Int. Conf. on Computer Vision*, pp. 25–34, IEEE Press.

Faverjon, B. and Ponce, J. (1991). On computing two-finger force-closure grasps of curved 2d objects. In *Proc. Int. Conf. Robotics and Automation*, volume 3, pp. 424–429, IEEE Press.

Fischler, M. A. and Elschlager, R. A. (1973). The representation and matching of pictorial structures. *IEEE. Trans. Computers*, C-22(1).

Gelb, A., ed. (1974). *Applied Optimal Estimation*. MIT Press, Cambridge, MA.

Giblin, P. and Weiss, R. (1987). Reconstruction of surfaces from profiles. In *Proc. 1st Int. Conf. on Computer Vision*, pp. 136–144, London, IEEE Press.

Grenander, U., Chow, Y., and Keenan, D. M. (1991). *HANDS. A Pattern Theoretical Study of Biological Shapes*. Springer-Verlag. New York.

Harris, C. (1992). Geometry from visual motion. In Blake, A. and Yuille, A., eds., *Active Vision*, pp. 263–284. MIT Press, Cambridge, MA.

Hong, J., Lafferriere, G., Mishra, B., and Tan (1990). Fine manipulation with multifinger hands. In *Proc. Int. Conf. Robotics and Automation*, pp. 1568–1573, IEEE Press.

Huang, T. and Tsai, R. (1981). Image sequence analysis: Motion estimation. In T. S. Huang, ed., *Image sequence analysis*. Springer-Verlag, New York.

Kass, M., Witkin, A., and Terzopoulos, D. (1987). Snakes: Active contour models. In *Proc. 1st Int. Conf. on Computer Vision*, pp. 259–268.

Koenderink, J. (1984). What does the occluding contour tell us about solid shape? *Perception*, 13: 321–330.

Koenderink, J. and Van Doorn, A. (1975). Invariant properties of the motion parallax field due to the movement of rigid bodies relative to an observer. *Optica Acta*, 22(9): 773–791.

Koenderink, J. and Van Doorn, A. (1978). How an ambulant observer can construct a model of the environment from the geometrical structure of the visual inflow. In Hauske, G. and Butenandt, E., eds., *Kybernetik*. Oldenburg, Munich.

Krotkov, E. P. (1989). *Active Computer Vision by Cooperative Focus and Stereo*. Springer-Verlag.

Latombe, J.-C. (1991). *Robot Motion Planning*. Kluwer.

Longuet-Higgins, H. and Pradzny, K. (1980). The interpretation of a moving retinal image. *Proc. R. Soc. Lond.*, B208: 385–397.

Lumelsky, V. (1986). Continuous motion planning unknown environment for a 3D cartesian arm. In *Proc. Int. Conf. Robotics and Automation*, pp. 1050–1055, IEEE Press.

Markenscoff, X., Ni, L., and Papadimitriou, C. (1988). Optimum grip of a polygon. *Int. Journal of Robotics Research*, 8(2): 61–74.

Marr, D. (1982). *Vision*. Freeman, San Francisco.

Maybank, S. (1985). The angular velocity associated with the optical flow field arising from motion through a rigid environment. *Proc. R. Soc. Lond.*, A401: 317–326.

Murray, D. and Buxton, B. (1990). *Experiments in the Machine Interpretation of Visual Motion*. MIT Press, Cambridge, MA.

Murray, D., Du, F., McLauchlin, P., Reid, I., Sharkey, P., and Brady, M. (1992). Design of stereo heads. In Blake, A. and Yuille A., eds., *Active Vision*, pp. 303–336. MIT Press, Cambridge, MA.

Nguyen, V. D. (1988). Constructing force-closure grasps. *Int. J. Robotics Research*, 7(3): 3–16.

Reuleaux, F. (1876). *The Kinematics of Machinery*. Macmillan (republished by Dover, 1963).

Salisbury, J. and Roth, B. (1983). Kinematic and force analysis of articulated mechanical hands. *ASME J. Mechanisms, Transmissions and Automation in Design*, 105: 35–41.

Szeliski, R. and Terzopoulos, D. (1991). Physically-based and probabilistic modeling for computer vision. In Vemuri, B. C., ed., *Proc. SPIE 1570, Geometric Methods in Computer Vision*, pp. 140–152, San Diego, CA. Society of Photo-Optical Instrumentation Engineers.

Terzopoulos, D. and Metaxas, D. (1991). Dynamic 3D models with local and global deformations: deformable superquadrics. *IEEE Trans. Pattern Analysis and Machine Intelligence*, 13(7): 703–714.

Ullman, S. (1979). *The Interpretation of Visual Motion*. MIT Press, Cambridge, MA.

Vaillant, R. (1990). Using occluding coutours for 3D object modelling. In Faugeras, O., ed., *Proc. 1st European Conference on Computer Vision*, pp. 454–464. Springer-Verlag.

Waxman, A. M. and Ullman, S. (1985). Surface structure and three-dimensional motion from image flow kinematics. *Int. Journal of Robotics Research*, 4(3): 72–94.

Yuille, A. and Hallinan, P. (1992). Deformable templates. In Blake, A. and Yuille, A., eds., *Active Vision*, pp. 20–38. MIT Press, Cambridge, MA.

AGENTS THAT LEARN

6

A framework for behavioural cloning

Michael Bain and Claude Sammut

School of Computer Science and Engineering,
University of New South Wales,
Sydney,
NSW 2052,
Australia
e-mail: mike@cse.unsw.edu.au and claude@cse.unsw.edu.au

Abstract

This paper describes recent experiments in automatically constructing reactive agents. The method used is behavioural cloning, where the logged data from skilled, human operators are input to an induction program which outputs a control strategy for a complex control task. Initial studies were able to successfully construct such behavioural clones, but suffered from several drawbacks, namely, that the clones were brittle and difficult to understand. Current research is aimed at solving these problems by learning in a framework where there is a separation between an agent's goals and its knowledge of how to achieve them.

1 INTRODUCTION

Behavioural cloning has been successfully used to construct control systems in a number of domains (Michie *et al.*, 1990; Sammut *et al.*, 1992; Urbancic and Bratko, 1994). Clones are built by recording the performance of a skilled human operator and then running an induction algorithm over the traces of the behaviour. The most basic form of behavioural cloning results in a set of situation–action rules that map the current state of the process being controlled to a set of actions that achieve some desired goal.

This formulation of the problem has several weaknesses.

- The rule sets generated are very often large and difficult to understand.

- The controllers may not be robust with respect to changes in initial conditions and disturbances in the environment.

In this paper, we describe some attempts to solve these problems. The main theme running through the work described here is that greater structure is added to the problem as compared with the original formulation. In particular, we examine the following techniques:

- decomposing learning into two tasks: learning goals and learning the actions that achieve those goals;
- constructing high-level features;
- providing a mixed-mode of automated learning and interactive knowledge acquisition.

These techniques are illustrated using the domain of learning to fly an aircraft in a flight simulator. The following section describes the original 'learning to fly' task and subsequent sections introduce each of the above techniques for structuring the problem.

2 LEARNING TO FLY

Sammut, Hurst, Kedzier and Michie (1992) modified a flight simulation program to log the actions taken by a human subject as he or she flies an aircraft. The log file is used to create the input to an induction program. The quality of the output from the induction program is tested by running the simulator in autopilot mode where the autopilot code is derived from the decision tree formed by induction.

The central control mechanism of the simulator is a loop that interrogates the aircraft controls and updates the state of the simulation according to a set of equations of motion. Before repeating the loop, the instruments in the display are updated.

2.1 Logging flight information

The display update was modified so that when the pilot performs a control action by moving the control stick or changing the thrust or flaps settings, the state of the simulation is written to a log file. Three subjects each 'flew' 30 times.

At the start of a flight, the aircraft points North, down the runway. The subject is required to fly a well-defined flight plan that consists of the following manoeuvres:

1. Take off and fly to an altitude of 2000 feet.

2. Level out and fly to a distance of 32 000 feet from the starting point.

3. Turn right to a compass heading of approximately 330°. The subjects were actually told to head toward a particular point in the scenery that corresponds to that heading.

4. At a North/South distance of 42 000 feet, turn left to head back towards the runway. The scenery contains grid marks on the ground. The starting point for the turn is when the last grid line was reached. This corresponds to about 42 000 feet. The turn is considered complete then the azimuth is between 140° and 180°.

5. Line up on the runway. The aircraft was considered to be lined up when the aircraft's azimuth is less than $5°$ off the heading of the runway and the twist is less that $\pm 10°$ from horizontal.

6. Descend to the runway, keeping in line. The subjects were given the hint that they should have an 'aiming point' near the beginning of the runway.

7. Land on the runway.

During a flight, up to 1000 control actions can be recorded. With three pilots and 30 flights each, the complete data set consists of about 90 000 events. The data recorded in each event are:

on_ground	boolean: is the plane on the ground?
g_limit	boolean: have we exceeded the plane's g limit
wing_stall	boolean: has the plane stalled
twist	integer: 0 to $360°$ (in tenths of a degree, see below)
elevation	integer: 0 to $360°$ (in tenths of a degree, see below)
azimuth	integer: 0 to $360°$ (in tenths of a degree, see below)
roll_speed	integer: 0 to $360°$ (in tenths of a degree per second)
elevation_speed	integer: 0 to $360°$ (in tenths of a degree per second)
azimuth_speed	integer: 0 to $360°$ (in tenths of a degree per second)
airspeed	integer: (in knots)
climbspeed	integer: (feet per second)
E/W distance	real: E/W distance from centre of runway (in feet)
altitude	real: (in feet)
N/S distance	real: N/S distance from Northern end of runway (in feet)
fuel	integer: (in pounds)
rollers	real: ± 4.3
elevator	real: ± 3.0
rudder	real: not used
thrust	integer: 0 to 100%
flaps	integer: $0°$, $10°$ or $20°$

The elevation of the aircraft is the angle of the nose relative to the horizon. The azimuth is the aircraft's compass heading and the twist is the angle of the wings relative to the horizon. The elevator angle is changed by pushing the mouse forward (positive) or back (negative). The rollers are changed by pushing the mouse left (positive) or right (negative). Thrust and flaps are incremented and decremented in fixed steps by keystrokes. The angular effects of the elevator and rollers are cumulative. For example, in straight and level flight, if the stick is pushed left, the aircraft will roll anticlockwise. The aircraft will continue rolling until the stick is centred. The thrust and flaps settings are absolute.

When an event is recorded, the state of the simulation at the instant that an action is performed could be output. However, there is always a delay in response to a stimulus, so ideally we should output the state of the simulation when the stimulus occurred along with the action that was performed some time later in response to the stimulus. But how do we know what the stimulus was? Unfortunately there is no way of knowing. Human responses to sudden piloting stimuli can vary considerably but they take at least one second. For example, while flying, the pilot usually anticipates where the aircraft will be in the near future and prepares the response before the stimulus occurs.

Each time the simulator passes through its main control loop, the current state of the simulation is stored in a circular buffer. An estimate is made of how many loops are executed each second. When a control action is performed, the action is output, along with the state of the simulation as it was some time before. How much earlier is determined by the size of the buffer.

2.2 Data analysis

Quinlan's C4.5 (Quinlan, 1993) program was used to generate flight rules from the data. Even though induction programs can save an enormous amount of human effort in analysing data, in real applications it is usually necessary for the user to spend some time preparing the data.

The learning task was simplified by restricting induction to one set of pilot data at a time. Thus, an autopilot has been constructed for each of the three subjects who generated training data. The reason for separating pilot data is that each pilot can fly the same flight plan in different ways. For example, straight and level flight can be maintained by adjusting the throttle. When an airplane's elevation is zero, it can still climb since higher speeds increase lift. Adjusting the throttle to maintain a steady altitude is the preferred way of achieving straight and level flight. However, another way of maintaining constant altitude is to make regular adjustments to the elevators causing the airplane to pitch up or down.

The data from each flight were segmented into the seven stages described previously. In the flight plan described, the pilot must achieve several, successive goals, corresponding to the end of each stage. Each stage requires a different manoeuvre. Having already defined the subtasks and told the human subjects what they are, the learning program was given the same advantage.

In each stage four separate decision trees are constructed, one for each of the elevator, rollers, thrust and flaps. A program filters the flight logs generating four input files for the induction program. The attributes of a training example are the flight parameters described earlier. The dependent variable or class value is the attribute describing a control action. Thus, when generating a decision tree for flaps, the flaps column is treated as the class value and the other columns in the data file, including the settings of the elevator, rollers and thrust, are treated as ordinary attributes. Attributes that are not control variables are subject to a delay, as described in the previous section.

C4.5 expects class values to be discrete but the values for elevator, rollers, thrust and flaps are numeric. A preprocessor breaks up the action settings into subranges that can be given discrete labels. Subranges are chosen by analysing the frequency of occurrence of action values. This analysis must be done for each pilot to correctly reflect differing flying styles. There are two disadvantages to this method. One is that if the subranges are poorly chosen, the rules generated will use controls that are too fine or too coarse.

Secondly, C4.5 has no concept of ordered class values, so classes cannot be combined during the construction of the decision tree.

An event is recorded when there is a change in one of the control settings. A change is determined by keeping the previous state of the simulation in a buffer. If any of the control settings are different in the current state, a change is recognised. This mechanism has the unwanted side-effect of recording all the intermediate values when a control setting is changed through a wide range of values. For example, the effects of the elevator and rollers are cumulative. If we want to bank the aircraft to the left, the stick will be pushed left for a short time and then centred, since keeping it left will cause the airplane to roll. Thus, the stick will be centred after most elevator or roller actions. This means that many low elevator and roller values will be recorded as the stick is pushed out and returned to the centre position.

To ensure that records of low elevator and roller values do not swamp the other data, another filter program removes all but the steady points and extreme points in stick movement. Control engineers are familiar with this kind of filtering. In their terms, the graph of a control's values is differentiated and only the values at the zero crossings of the derivative are kept.

2.3 Generating the autopilot

After processing the data as described above, they can be submitted to C4.5 to be summarised as rules that can be executed in a controller.

Decision tree algorithms are made noise tolerant by introducing *pruning*. If the data contain noise, then many of the branches in a decision tree will be created to classify bad data. The effects of noise can be reduced by removing branches near the leaves of the tree. This can either be done by not growing those branches when there are insufficient data or by cutting back branches when their removal does not decrease classification accuracy.

The flight data are very noisy, so decision trees are generated using conservative settings for pruning and then tested in the simulator. Pruning levels are gradually increased until the rule 'breaks', i.e. it is no longer able to control the plane correctly. This procedure results in the smallest, and thus most readable, rule that succeeds in accomplishing the flight goal.

2.4 Linking the autopilot with the simulator

To test the induced rules, they are used as the code for an autopilot. A post-processor converts C4.5's decision trees into if-statements in C so that they can be incorporated into the flight simulator easily. Hand-crafted C code determines which stage the flight has reached and decides when to change stages. The appropriate rules for each stage are then selected in a switch statement. Each stage has four, independent if-statements, one for each action.

When the data from the human pilots were recorded, a delay to account for human response time was included. Since the rules were derived from these data, their effects should be delayed by the same amount as was used when the data were recorded. When a rule fires, instead of letting it effect a control setting directly, the rule's output value is stored in a circular buffer. There is one for each of the four controls. The value used for the control setting is one of the previous values in the buffer. A lag constant defines how far to go back into the buffer to get the control setting. The size of the buffer must be set to give a lag that approximates the lag when the data were recorded.

Rules could set control values instantaneously as if, say, the stick were moved with infinite speed from one position to another. Clearly this is unrealistic. When control values are taken from the delay buffer, they enter another circular buffer. The controls are set to the average of the values in the buffer. This ensures that controls change smoothly. The larger the buffer, the more gentle are the control changes.

2.5 Flying on autopilot

An example of the rules created by cloning is the elevator take-off rule generated from one pilot's data:

```
elevation > 4 : level_pitch
elevation <= 4 :
|  airspeed <= 0 : level_pitch
|  airspeed > 0 : pitch_up_5
```

This states that as thrust is applied and the elevation is level, pull back on the stick until the elevation increases to 4. Because of the delay, the final elevation usually reaches 11 which is close to the values usually obtained by the pilot. pitch_up_5 indicates a large elevator action, whereas, pitch_up_1 would indicate a gentle elevator action.

A more complex case is that of turning. Stage 4 of the flight requires a large turn to the left. The rules are quite complex. To make them understandable, they have been greatly simplified by over-pruning. They are presented to illustrate an important point, that is that rules can work in tandem although there is no explicit link between them. The following rules are for the rollers and elevator in the left turn.

```
azimuth > 114 : right_roll_1
azimuth <= 114 :
|  twist <= 8 : left_roll_4
|  twist > 8 : no_roll
twist <= 2 : level_pitch
twist > 2 :
|  twist <= 10 : pitch_up_1
|  twist > 10 : pitch_up 2
```

A sharp turn requires coordination between roller and elevator actions. As the aircraft banks to a steep angle, the elevator is pulled back. The rollers rule states that while the compass heading has not yet reached 114, bank left provided that the twist angle does not exceed 8. The elevator rule states that as long as the aircraft has no twist, leave the elevator at level pitch. If the twist exceeds 2 then pull back on the stick. The stick must be pulled back more sharply for a greater twist. Since the rollers cause twist, the elevator rule is invoked to produce a coordinated turn. The profile of a complete flight is shown in Figure 1.

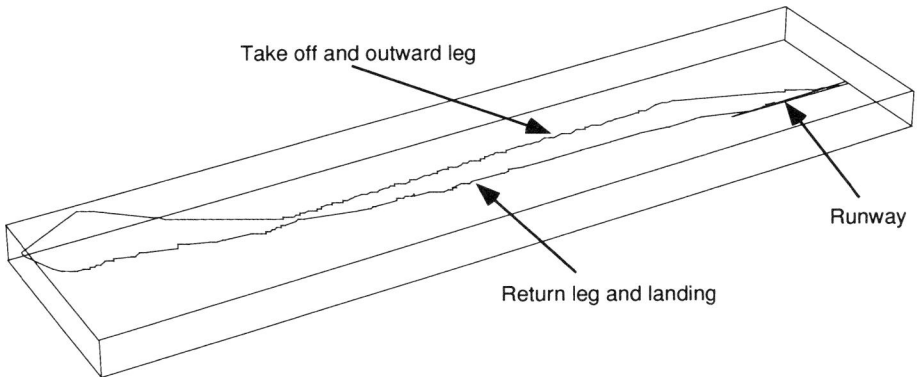

Figure 1. Flight profile.

Like Michie, Bain and Hayes-Michie (1990), this study found a 'clean-up effect'. The flight log of any trainer contains many spurious actions due to human inconsistency and corrections required as a result of inattention. It appears that the effects of these inconsistent examples are pruned away by C4.5, leaving a control rule which flies very smoothly.

3 LEARNING TO ACHIEVE GOALS

One of the interesting features of behavioural cloning is that the method can develop working controllers that have no representation of goals. The rules that are constructed are pure situation–action rules, i.e. they are reactive. However, this feature also appears to result in a lack of robustness. When a situation occurs which is outside of the range of experience represented in the training data, the clone can fail entirely. To some extent, a clone can be made more robust by training in the presence of noise. However, because the clone does not have a representation of how control action can achieve a particular goal, it cannot choose actions in a flexible manner in totally new situations.

3.1 CHURPS

CHURPS (or Compressed Heuristic Universal Reaction Planners) were developed by Stirling (1995) as a method for capturing human control knowledge. Particular emphasis was placed on building robust controllers that can even tolerate actuator failures.

Where behavioural cloning attempts to avoid questioning an expert on their behaviour, Stirling's approach is to obtain from the expert a starting point from which a controller can be generated automatically. The expert is asked to supply 'influence factors'. These are numbers in the range 0 to 1 which indicate how directly a control input affects an output goal. This is illustrated in Figure 2 below. Here, control action, A, has an influence of 0.8 on goal variable, X. This means that A is the main effector

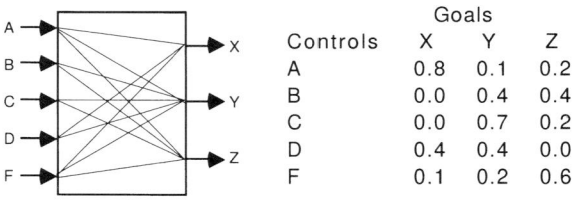

Controls	Goals		
	X	Y	Z
A	0.8	0.1	0.2
B	0.0	0.4	0.4
C	0.0	0.7	0.2
D	0.4	0.4	0.0
F	0.1	0.2	0.6

Effector set allocations

SET	X	Y	Z
UE	—	—	—
ME	A	C	F
SE	D,F	B,D,F,A	B,A,C

Figure 2. A CHURPs model. (a) An example of a process; (b) perceived influences between control inputs and output goals; (c) agent's effector view of system.

that influences that value of the measure variable, X. Action A also has lesser effects on variables Y and Z. A is also classed as the main effector for goal vaxiable X. From the influence matrix, control actions are grouped into three sets for each goal variable:

Unique Effector (UE) is the only effector which has any influence on a goal variable.

Maximal Effector (ME) has the greatest influence over a particular goal variable. However, other effectors may have secondary influence over that goal variable.

Secondary Effectors (SE) are all the effectors for a goal variable, except the main effector.

The UE, ME and SE sets are used by Stirling's Control Plan generator (CPG) algorithm to generate operational control plans. The algorithm assigns appropriate effectors to control various output goals in order of importance. Informally, the CPG algorithm is:

Create an agenda of goals which consist of output variables
    whose values deviate from a set point.
The agenda may be ordered by the importance of the goal variable.
    <u>while</u> the agenda is not empty
      select the next goal
      <u>if</u> deviation is small then
        attempt to assign an effector in the order, UE, SE, ME.
      <u>if</u> deviation is large then
        attempt to assign an effector in the order, UE, ME, SE.
      examine influencees of the effector that was invoked and
        add them to the agenda.
      remove selected goal.

The selection of an effector is qualified by the following conditions:

- A controller which is a UE of one goal should not be used as an ME or SE for another goal.

110

- When choosing an SE, it should be one that has the least side-effects on other goal variables.

This procedure tells us which control actions can be used to effect the desired change in the goal variables. However, the actions may be executed in a variety of ways. Stirling gives the following example. Suppose variables X, Y and Z in Figure 2, are near their desired values. We now wish to double the value of Y while maintaining X and Z at their current levels. Following the CPG algorithm:

1. Y initially appears as the only goal on the agenda.

2. Y had no unique effector and since the required deviation is large, we try to apply an ME, namely, C.

3. Since C also effects Z, Z is appended to the agenda.

4. Since Y is the current goal and an effector has successfully been assigned to it, Y is removed from the agenda.

5. Z becomes the current goal. Let us assume that the deviation in Z is small.

6. We attempt to assign as SE to control Z. B is selected since C is already assigned to control Y. A could have been selected, but it would have a side-effect on variable X, causing a further expansion in the agenda.

7. The agenda is now empty and terminates with the assignments {Y/C, Z/B}, which can be read as 'control goal Y to its desired state via effector C and control goal Z to its desired state via effector B'.

This plan can be executed sequentially, by first using C to bring Y to its desired value and then using C to bring Z to its desired value. A loop would sample the process at regular intervals terminating each phase when the desired value is reached. Alternatively, both actions could be executed in parallel. The first strategy corresponds to one that might be followed by a novice, whereas experts tend to combine well practised behaviours since they do not have to think about them.

As a model of human subcognitive skill, the CPG method does not capture the notion that pre-planning is not normally carried out. That is, a skilled operator would not think through the various influences of controls on outputs, but would act on the basis of experience. This is usually faster than first trying to produce a plan and then executing it. To try to simulate this kind of expert behaviour, Stirling used the CPG algorithm as a plan generator which exhaustively generated all combinations of actions for different possible situations. This large database of plans was then compressed by applying machine learning to produce a set of heuristics for controlling the process. The architecture of this system is shown in Figure 3.

Figure 3. CHURPS architecture.

To create the input to the learning system (Quinlan's C4.5) each goal variable was considered to have either a zero, small or large deviation from its desired value. All combinations of these deviations were used as initial conditions for the CPG algorithm. In addition, Stirling considered the possibility that one or more control action could fail. Thus plans were also produced for all of the combinations of deviations and all combinations of effector failures.

Stirling devised a 'goal centred' control strategy in which learning was used to identify the effectors that are required to control particular goal variables. Thus if there is a deviation in goal variable Y, a decision tree is built to identify the most appropriate control action, including circumstances in which some control actions may not be available due to failure. An example of a tree for goal variable X is shown below:

```
if (control A is active)
   if (deviation of X is non-zero)
      use control A
   else
      if (control D is inactive)
         use control A
      else
         if (control F is active)
            use control D
         else
            use control A
else
   if (control D is active)
      use control D
   else
      use control F
```

Once the control action has been selected, a conventional proportional controller is used to actually attain the desired value.

The CHURPS method has been successfully used to control a simulated Sendzimir cold rolling mill in a steel plant. It has also been used to control the same aircraft simulation used by Sammut *et al*. Like that work, the flight was broken into seven stages. However, one major difference is that CHURPS required the goals of each stage to be much more carefully specified than in behavioural cloning. For example, the original specification of stage 4, the left turn was:

At a North/South distance of 42 000 feet, turn left to head back to the runway. The turn is considered complete when the compass heading is between 140 and 180°.

In CHURPS this is translated to

At a North/South distance of 42 000 feet, establish a roll of 25 ± 2 and maintain pitch at 3 ± 5, airspeed at 100 knots ± 40 knots and climb speed at 1 ft/sec ± 5 ft/sec.

When the plane's compass heading is between 140 and 180°, return the roll to 0±2 and maintain all other variables at the same values.

112

Recalling that the influence matrix was constructed by hand, CHURPS requires much more help from the human expert than behavioural cloning. However, so far, CHURPS have produced smoother and more robust controllers. The question arises, can some combination of behavioural cloning and the CHURPS method be used to produce robust controllers requiring minimal advice from the expert?

4 LEARNING EFFECTS AND GOALS WITH BEHAVIOURAL CLONING

In this section we discuss work on extending the framework of behavioural cloning. A simplified scheme for a control system is assumed, such as that shown in Figure 4. In this scheme the process is a black-box and the controller is an autonomous agent whose memory contains a set of control rules and a buffer of process variables. The original formulation of the behavioural cloning technique requires learning rules of the form:

$$action\text{-}variable \leftarrow process\text{-}variables.$$

The antecedent is a subset of the set of all process variables, and may include state and action variables. Therefore a set of such rules is an example of process control as depicted in Figure 4. Usually standard machine learning algorithms for classification are used to learn a behavioural clone. The induced rule-set or theory partitions the space defined by the set of all process variables, classifying each region of this space in terms of the action typically applied by a skilled operator. Reactive control can then be implemented by installing the rules in a controller as in Figure 4 to output actions given process states and actions.

However, for complex control tasks the use of 'classical' behavioural cloning presents problems (Arentz, 1994; Urbančič and Bratko, 1994). What is perhaps worse, the successful execution by a clone of even a relatively simple control task can result in behaviour which appears 'mindless' (Michie, 1995).

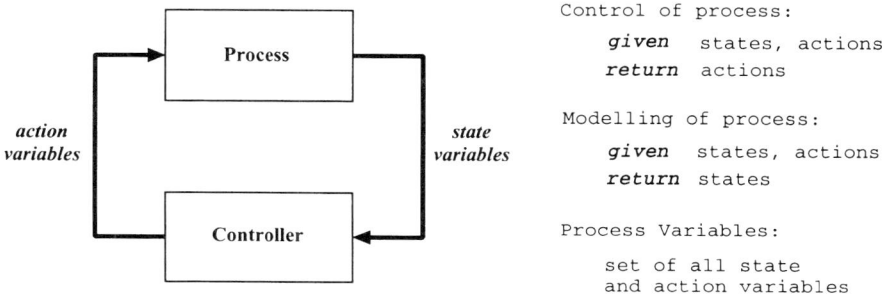

Figure 4. Schematic diagram of a simplified control system.

113

4.1 Grail

To address these shortcomings we have reformulated behavioural cloning in a method called GRAIL, which stands for **G**oal-directed **R**eactive **A**bduction from **I**nductive **L**earning. A GRAIL controller comprises an **effects level** and a **goals level**. Both levels are based on theories built by inductive learning from the traces of skilled operators. In this sense the technique of behavioural cloning is continued in the new method. However the method extends behavioural cloning as follows. Rule-sets can be hierarchical, or structured. Also, we allow for the possibility of adding user-supplied rules to the theories. This is mainly intended for adding high-level rules about the control task at the goals level. Additionally we expect that user-supplied or machine-invented predicates ('controller variables') may be useful in extending the vocabulary for describing process variables and controller states. These extensions could apply at both the effects level and the goals level. So far they have not been used in our experiments, since we have concentrated on the learning of theories for each of the effects and goals levels. The theory for the combined effects and goals levels will be referred to as the 'task theory'. The method is summarised in Figure 5 as an algorithm sketch.

4.1.1 Inductive learning of task theories

The target theories to be learned at each level are slightly different from those of classical behavioural cloning. At the effects level we have rules of the form:

$$state\text{-}variable \leftarrow process\text{-}variables.$$

An effects theory can be thought of as approximating *the operator's model of the effects on the process of applying certain control-actions.* As such it is a form of operator-centred process model as depicted in Figure 4.

The goals level is intended to enable the incorporation of rules referring not only to states of the process but also states of the controller. In particular, reference to the goals of the controller is allowed. To this end we suppose a set of controller variables distinct from the process variables of Figure 4. The combined set of process variables and controller variables will be referred to as 'task variables'. Therefore at the goals level we have rules of the form:

$$task\text{-}variable \leftarrow task\text{-}variables.$$

These rules may include variables from plans or other background knowledge, or they may contain only process variables. A goals theory can be thought of as approximating *the operator's model of the goals directing their control of the process at any given time.*

As for behavioural cloning, the inductive learning step of GRAIL is done offline from recorded traces of the execution of control tasks by skilled operators. The induced rules are in the form of definite clauses, and the task theory can therefore be understood as a logic program. Our work so far has dealt only with rules containing propositional variables, although we discuss below ways in which first-order learning methods may be used to improve our approach.

The GRAIL method:

Offline stage: (Inductive Learning)
    From behavioural traces learn theories for:
        • *goals level;*
        • *effects level.*

Online execution: (Goal-directed Reactive Abduction)
    During each sample period:
        • *update values of state variables in knowledge base;*
        • *update top-level goal, then use it to derive*
            low-level goals by backward-chaining on task theory;
        • *for each of the low-level goals do*
            • *if low-level goal is:*
                an action expression then
                    action = goal value;
                an effects expression then
                    actions = select-rule(effects expression);
                an indirect-effects expression then
                    derive an effects expression;
                    actions = select-rule(effects expression);
        • *controller applies actions to process;*
        • *update knowledge-base to record actions applied.*

select-rule(effects = val)
    Let R be the set of effects rules in knowledge base.
    Find $r_i \in R$ such that head(r_i) is "effects = val_i", each
    condition "state-variable = val_s" in body(r_i) is satisfied
    in knowledge base and $|val - val_i|$ is minimised for all such r_i.
    If there is more than one such r_i, pick the one with highest coverage
    on training data.
    return set of conditions "action-variable = val_a" from body(r_i).

Figure 5. GRAIL: a method for behavioural cloning.

4.1.2 Goal-directed reactive abduction

To implement control we take advantage of the fact that the theories for both effects and goals are logic programs. The task theory is structured so that actions which can be performed by the controller are included in the bodies of effects rules as 'abducible goals', i.e. goals (in the logic programming sense) which can be 'made' true (by executing the associated control action). The rules in the remainder of the task theory reduce higher-level goals to lower-level goals using Prolog-style execution.

The controller is presumed to be an autonomous agent linked to a black-box process which is to be controlled. The controller possesses a knowledge base containing the task theory. This knowledge base also contains facts about: the current state of the process (state variables); the current action settings (action variables); possibly other sensory or perceptual information; and a history of previously known facts. These facts are updated at predefined regular time intervals. The time between successive intervals is referred to as the sample period. The sample period is assumed to be sufficient for execution of the task theory with respect to the updated knowledge base, as follows.

Within each sample period a top-level Horn goal $\leftarrow G$ which represents the controller's current task is invoked on the updated knowledge base. Using Prolog-style execution this top-level goal is reduced to a set of low-level goals. In our experiments to date the goals theory is constructed so as to always reduce to a set of *goal_variable = value* expressions, where each *goal_variable* is one of a predefined set based on a subset of the process variables. These are the low-level goals of Figure 5.

The low-level goals are the 'set points' for the controller. If the low-level goal is an action expression, i.e. *goal_variable* relates to an action variable, then an assignment of *value* to the corresponding action variable is made. For example, the statement goal_throttle = 100 leads to the assignment throttle = 100. Otherwise, the low-level goal is an effects expression or an indirect-effects expression. This is explained as follows.

Before learning any rules, a representation must be chosen. Process variables are usually pre-determined. However, we must select which of these variables to include in the effects theory. Usually, this requires some knowledge of the domain, or is subject to a degree of trial-and-error. A state-variable selected to be the target-attribute for learning will appear in the heads of a set of effects rules and is referred to as an *effects_variable*. An effects expression is of the form *effects_variable = value*. An indirect-effects expression involves a state variable other than an *effects_variable*, from which an effects expression can be derived using a user-supplied pre-defined procedure.

For example, in our experiments in the flight domain it was found convenient to use the low-level goal *goal_elevation*, but to learn effects rules for *elevation_speed*. By taking the difference

$$goal\_elevation\_speed = goal\_elevation - elevation$$

we derive an effects expression from the indirect-effects expression in terms of *goal_elevation*. The effects expression in terms of *goal_elevation_speed* is then used to select an effects rule (see Figure 5).

In the remainder of this section we give examples of learning effects and goals in the flight domain, and discuss the relations between our method and other approaches.

4.2 Learning effects

At this level we require a rule-based model of the effects on certain state variables of control actions. As for the goals level of our controller, the effects rules are inductively learned from trace examples. In the case of flight the system variables can be subdivided into a number of distinct types. For example, the orientation of the aircraft can be described in terms of pitch, roll and yaw. The corresponding controls are elevators, ailerons and rudder. In our simulator the position is slightly simplified by disabling rudder (on advice that its operation is incorrectly simulated). Consequently changes in yaw, or heading, are treated as side-effects of changes in roll and pitch (twist and roll).

In a simplified formulation of an effects model we have a set of rules of the form

```
Effects_variable = Effects_value ←
            Action_variable = Action_value
```

The action variables are abducibles, in the following sense. Given a desired effect and a rule in the model whose head matches the effect, the control variable is assigned a value which will 'cause' the required effect. The rule body could also contain extra literals imposing conditions under which the action will cause the effect.

As an example, take a simple theory for elevation speed defined in terms of elevators. This was induced from instances from the trace in Figure 6. Note that since the elevators are a *rate* controller, the effects variable chosen is elevation speed. This can be linked to the more natural goal of elevation by differencing between target and actual values as described above.

```
Elevation_speed = 3 ← Elevators = −0.28
Elevation_speed = 1 ← Elevators = −0.19
Elevation_speed = 0 ← Elevators = 0.0
Elevation_speed = −1 ← Elevators = 0.9
```

Data was pre-processed using AWK to select variables. Learning was carried out using C4.5. Decision trees were then converted into rules for particular abducibles by AWK scripts, as our rules have a more complex syntax than that generated by C4.5 rules.

A similar effects rule was found for the relation between rollers and roll speed. The picture is more complicated when it comes to other effects in the domain, such as airspeed. Airspeed is mainly influenced by throttle, although this is conditional on elevation and other system variables. Additionally, the time delay in the effect of throttle changes on airspeed seems to be greater than the delay in other effects. This is the subject of our current work on learning effects.

4.3 Learning goals

The problem of learning goals can be seen in terms of conjecturing which variables must be attended to and what values must be assigned to those variables in order to achieve the desired outcomes for system control. Clearly this is a difficult task. However, unless goals can be specified in sufficient detail possession of a robust and accurate effects model will not be enough to implement the complex behaviours required. In the flight domain we have begun to learn goals rules which determine system variables in terms of external environment variables. An example theory of this type is given below.

```
if (Distance > −4007.66) Goal_elevation = 0;
else if (Height > 1998.75) Goal_elevation = 20;
else if (Height > 1918.65) Goal_elevation = 40;
else if (Height > 67.61) Goal_elevation = 100;
else if (Distance <= −4153.4) Goal_elevation = 40;
else Goal_elevation = 20;
```

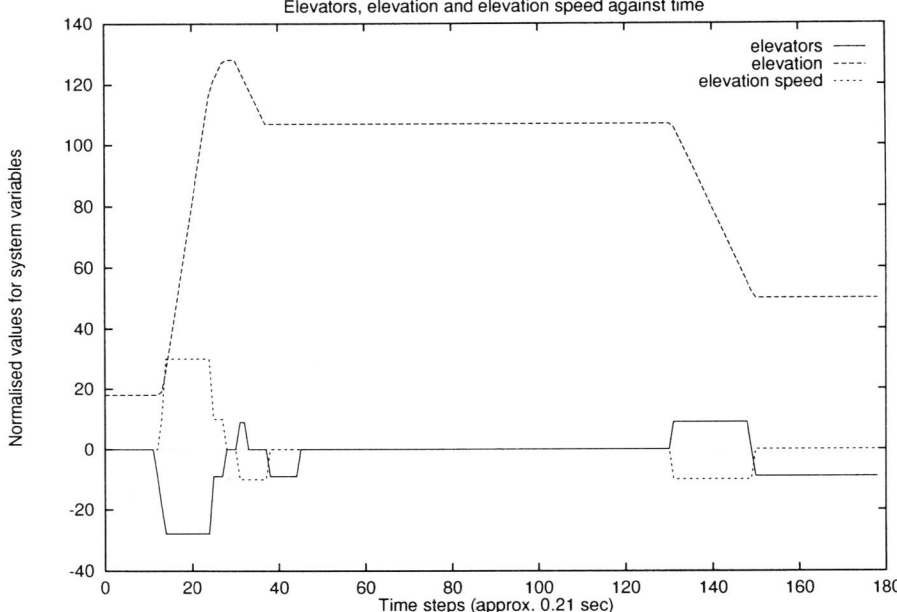

Figure 6. Comparing the effects of elevators on elevation and elevation speed.

This work is in a preliminary stage, but we hope to improve the method of learning goals in a number of ways. For example, in the example above elevation is set relative to distance from and height above the runway. While this may be adequate for certain manoeuvres, in general it is not a sufficiently powerful representation, since it lacks many of the features a human pilot might use to set goals. Below we discuss how this could be extended where necessary to include high-level features based on background knowledge and relational information pertaining to visual perception.

4.4 Control with effects and goals

Currently the GRAIL approach to behavioural cloning is in development. However, we have evidence from initial investigations that it allows for machine-learned rule-based controllers to be 'cloned' from trace examples, and that the induced theories are more compact on a lines-of-code measure than those obtained by a previous behavioural cloning method.

The figures in the comparison of traditional with GRAIL behavioural cloning are for the first stage only of the standard flight plan, i.e. take off and climb to an altitude of 2000 feet then level out. Theory sizes are measured in lines of C program code.[1]

---

[1] This tends to overestimate the complexity of the theories compared with their C4.5 representation but by a factor of less than two.

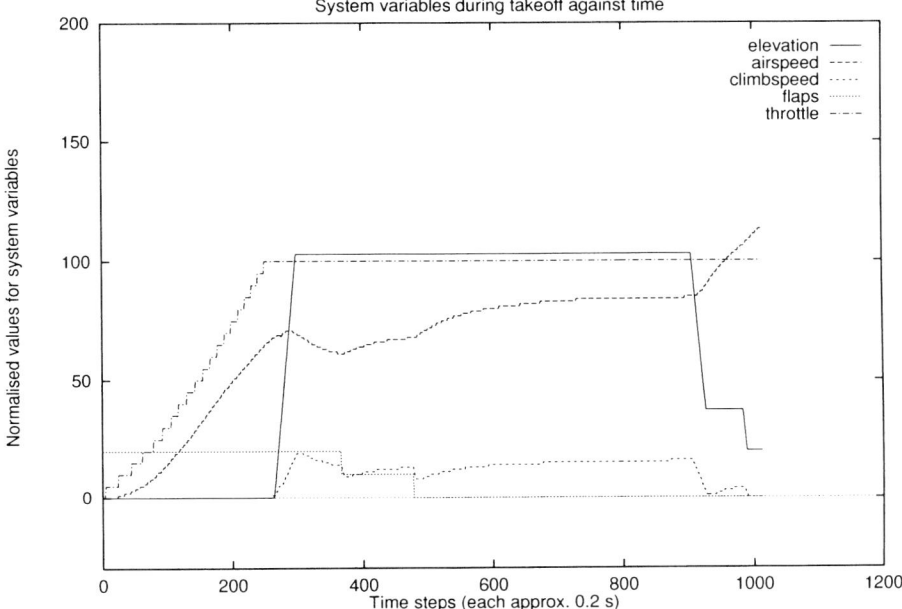

Figure 7. Comparing the system variables during takeoff.

Evaluation (Takeoff)	Cloning method	
	Traditional	GRAIL
Theory size	221	65
Examples	1804	1014
Traces	30	1

Note that only one trace is required for the GRAIL method compared with thirty for the traditional method, although the total number of examples used are of the same order of magnitude. This is due to the different sampling schemes employed. In (Sammut *et al.*, 1992) an example was recorded only when the pilot changed the setting of one of the four control variables. In contrast, due to the requirement of building an effects model for the GRAIL method, a fixed rate sampling scheme is employed. In the current work a sample was recorded approximately once every 0.2 seconds (see Figure 7).

We have also used GRAIL to learn simple but general manoeuvres such as climbs and turns. Currently we are working use GRAIL to complete the most difficult flight plan stage accomplished by the traditional method, namely the approach to landing. GRAIL has not yet matched the performance of the earlier method by landing, but its approach to the runway is reasonable and, as seen from the table below, the theory sizes are smaller.

Evaluation (Landing)	Cloning method	
	Traditional	GRAIL
Theory size	8542	680
Examples	8428	3072
Traces	30	5

4.5 Further work

Whilst the flight of the GRAIL clones has not yet fully matched that of the earlier 'best clone' built by the traditional method, it does already have the advantages described above in terms of reduced sizes of rule-sets. We have some reason to suppose it may also prove more robust to variations in initial conditions during testing when compared to the traditional method, although this needs to be substantiated. However, we believe it is the possibility of extending GRAIL to use structured theories and background knowledge via first-order learning that is most likely to further improve the performance of behavioural cloning.

In other related work Benson (1996) has adapted the framework of teleo-reactive programs for agent control proposed by Nilsson (1994) to the flight domain. This method has some very interesting aspects for agent control, such as the modelling of durative actions and the use of circuit semantics. The machine learning component of Benson's thesis addresses learning action models for use in the control of a teleo-reactive agent. The agent planning system utilises a formalism for operators called TOPs (for teleo-operators). The TOPs framework is closely related to effects rules in GRAIL, but includes the ability to represent the effects of durative actions. TOPs also allow for representation of side-effects in terms of state changes due to the application of actions. However, the application to the flight domain only covered a subset of the stages of the standard flight plan used in our behavioural cloning experiments.

Interestingly, Benson (1996) noted that one difficulty with the application of his learning method to the flight domain was the lack of any temporal reasoning ability in the teleo-reactive formalism. Kowalski (1995) has proposed a framework for combining reactive and rational agency in work which uses abduction to realise agent actions. The method is similar to the goal-directed reactive abduction approach of GRAIL. However, the meta-logical approach of Kowalski provides a very general and powerful framework for planning and reacting which uses an explicit representation for time or resources. Additionally, knowledge assimilation is incorporated via the mechanism of integrity constraints. Aspects of this logic programming framework for agency could provide a basis for methods of first-order learning to be used in behavioural cloning.

5 CONSTRUCTING HIGH-LEVEL FEATURES

Decomposing learning into two stages is one way of structuring the problem domain so that more effective behavioural clones can be built. Another, complementary approach

Table 1. Background predicates.

pos(P, T)	position, P, of aircraft at time, T.
before (T1, T2)	time, T1, is before time, T2.
regression (ListY, ListX, M, C)	least-square linear regression, which tries to find for the list of X and Y values.
linear (X, Y, M, C)	linear (X, Y, M, C):- Y is M*X+C.
circle (P1, P2, P3, X, Y, R)	fits a circle to three points, specifying the centre (X, Y) and radius, R
$\leq, \geq$, abs	Prolog built-in predicates

is to construct high-level features that improve the expressiveness of the language used to describe the control strategies.

In the original 'learning to fly' experiments, only the raw data from the simulator were presented to the learning algorithm. While these data are complete in the sense that they contain all the information necessary to describe the state of the system, they are not necessarily presented in the most convenient form. For example when a pilot is executing a constant-rate turn, it makes sense to talk about trajectories as arcs of a circle. Induction algorithms, such as C4.5, can deal with numeric attributes to the extent that they can introduce inequalities, but they are not able to recognise trajectories as arcs or recognise any other kind of mathematical property of the data.

Srinivasan and Camacho (1998) have shown how such trajectories can be recognised by making use of background knowledge with Progol (Muggleton, 1995). The program was applied to the problem of learning to predict the roll angle of an aircraft during a constant rate turn at a fixed altitude. To do this effectively, the target concept must be able to recognise the trajectory as an arc of a circle. The predicates shown in Table 1 are included in the background knowledge.[2]

The pos predicate is the input to the learner since it explicitly describes the trajectory of the aircraft as a sequence of points in space. These points are derived from flight logs. The before predicate imposes an ordering on the points in the trajectory. The mode declarations in Srinivasan's version of Progol are not typical of the declarative bias found in other ILP systems. Srinivasan's modes permit the user to specify that some arguments should be lists of values collected over the entire data set. Thus, the mode declaration for regression specifies that the first two arguments are lists which described the sequence of pairs of coordinates for the aircraft during the turn. That is, the coordinates from all the examples in the data set are collected. The mode declaration causes Progol to generate these lists and invokes regression which performs a least-square regression to find the coefficients of the linear equation which relates roll angle and radius. Regression must be accompanied by another background predicate, linear, which implements the calculation

---

[2]In practice, it is necessary to include error terms since the regression equation is unlikely to fit new data exactly. However, we omit these here for the sake of clarity.

of the formula. The theory produced is:

```
roll_angle(Radius, Angle):-
    pos(P1, T1), pos(P2, T2), pos(P3, T3),
    before(T1, T2), before (T2, T3),
    circle(P1, P2, P3, _,_, Radius),
    linear(Angle, Radius, 0.043, -19.442).
```

The circle predicate recognises that P1, P2 and P3 fit a circle of radius, *Radius* and *regression* finds a linear approximation for the relationship between Radius and Angle which is:

$$Angle = 0.043 \times Radius - 19.442.$$

The _ arguments for circle are don't cares which indicate that, for this problem, we are not interested in the centre of the circle.

This example illustrates an ILP system's ability to use background knowledge to generate high-level features that permit the learning system to refer to meaningful components of a flight. Just as we can describe turn as above, we could also apply linear regression to fit a line to a pilot's approach to the runway, thus discovering the glide slope used. In the following section, we describe an alternative method of invoking complex background knowledge.

5.1 Refinement rules

Cohen (1996) introduced refinement rules as a method for constructing new literals to be added to clauses during a general-to-specific search. In his FLIPPER program, Cohen used a restricted second-order theorem prover to interpret these rules. The advantage of refinement rules is that they can give FLIPPER users fine control over how background knowledge is applied in order to create new literals to refine a clause. However, the second-order theorem prover is limited to a simple function-free language.

The system described here is a component of *iProlog* (Sammut 1997). This is an ISO compatible Prolog interpreter with a variety of machine learning tools embedded as built-in predicates. Since the full power of Prolog is available, the refinement rules we implement can invoke arbitrary Prolog programs.

Two types of refinement rule may be defined. A *head rule* has the form:

$$\langle A, Pre, Post \rangle$$

where A is a positive literal, *Pre* is a conjunction of literals and *Post* is a set of positive literals. A body rule has the form:

$$\langle \leftarrow B, Pre, Post \rangle$$

where B is a positive literal and *Pre* and *Post* are as above.

There must only be one head rule. This indicates that A should be used to create the head of the clause being learned, provided that the condition *Pre* is satisfied. After A has been constructed, the literals in *Post* are asserted into Prolog's database. There may be any number of body rules. The literals generated by these rules can be added to the body of the clause under construction. Literals in the precondition of these rules can invoke any Prolog program.

Suppose we wish to create a saturated clause (Rouveirol and Puget, 1990; Sammut, 1981; Sammut and Banerji, 1986) based on the same data as Srinivasan and Camacho. The left-hand side of the following rule is the template for the head literal.

```
roll_angle(Radius, Angle)
  where
    true.
```

The *where* part of the rule is the precondition. Refinement rules are invoked in a forward chaining manner. The head rule matches an example fact, say, roll_angle(1000, 2). Since there are no preconditions, the head of the new clause is created.

The refinement rules for body literals are as follows:

```
:- pos(P, T)
  where
    pos(P, T)
  asserting
    time(T).
:- TI < T2
  where
    time(T1),
    time(T2).
:- circle(P1, P2, P3, X, Y, Radius)
  where
    pos(P1, _),
    pos(P2, _),
    pos(P3, _),
    P1 \ = P2, P1 \ = P3, P2 \ = P3.
:- Angle is M * Radius + C
  where
    roll_angle(Radius, Angle),
    coefficients(M, C).
coefficients(M, C) :-
  findall(X, pos(point(X, Y, Z), T), Xlist),
  findall(Y, pos(point(X, Y, Z), T), Ylist),
  regression(Ylist, Xlist, M, C).
```

The first rule introduces the *pos* literal. That is, a literal of the form $pos(P, T)$ is introduced into the clause if there is a corresponding fact in the example database. After creating the literal, the postcondition is $time(T)$. This is useful as a typing mechanism for later refinement rules.

The *time* predicate is used by the next refinement rule. This introduces the *before* literal. In this case, we simply use numeric *less than* to represent *before*. The assertion from introducing the *pos* literal ensures that, in this case, only comparisons between times are permitted.

We assume that predicates for *circle* and *regression* have already been defined. The *circle* literal in introduced if there are three distinct position facts in the example database.

The final refinement rule introduces a linear relation between roll angle and radius. Note that the preconditions invoke a call to the regression program. The *coefficients* predicate collects the *X* and *Y* values of the aircraft's position and passes the lists to the regression program. Again, we have left out error terms to simplify the discussion.

This refinement rule mechanism is implemented in *iProlog* and can be used, as Cohen originally intended, that is to generate literals for a general-to-specific search. They can also be used to produce a saturated clause to be used in a specific-to-general search. This is the manner in which they are currently used. The thing to note is that refinement rules provide a mechanism for invoking quite complex background knowledge.

5.2 Recognising trajectories

Geometric shapes such as circles and lines are suitable for simple trajectories like turns and climbs, but very often trajectories are much more complicated and therefore more difficult to describe and match. Pearce and Caelli (1995) have devised an instance-based learning algorithm for recognising trajectories.

The first step in their algorithm is to fit a polygonal approximation to a curve (Figure 8).

The system then extracts relations between the lines fitted to the curve. For example,

$$angle(p_2, p_3, 92)$$

indicates the angle between two of the lines. Each instance of a trajectory is stored in the system's database. Identification of new trajectories is performed by a constrained graph matching algorithm that is capable of handling relations.

Because of the flexibility offered by the refinement rules described earlier, it is possible to include this kind of case-based matching as background knowledge. Thus, where we previously had a *circle* predicate for identifying a circular trajectory, we can also have a more sophisticated matching algorithm for irregular trajectories.

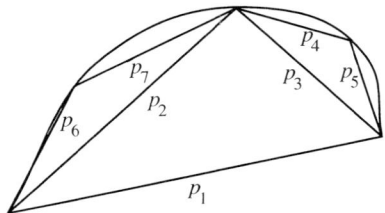

Figure 8. Polygonal approximation of a trajectory.

124

6 COMBINING MACHINE LEARNING AND ADVICE TAKING

Although many skills are performed subconsciously, it may still be possible to verbalise some aspects of the skill. For example, as well as acquiring the basic motor skills for controlling an aircraft at a particular instant, pilots must also learn to plan flights, to navigate according to the plan, they must learn about way points and landmarks, etc. Thus, while the low-level skills that a pilot employs may not be available to introspection, higher-level tasks may be. It is therefore reasonable to acquire behaviours be a mixed strategy of machine learning and advice taking.

Shiraz and Sammut (1997) have developed a knowledge acquisition system for piloting aircraft in a flight simulator that combines the interactive method of Compton's ripple-down rules (Compton and Jansen, 1988) with a machine learning algorithm. Shiraz's system, called *Parvaz*, behaves as follows:

- The autopilot flies the aircraft.
- If the aircraft does not follow the desired trajectory, the human trainer can intervene in either of two ways:

  1. The trainer may enter a rule editing environment, permitting new control rules to be constructed; or
  2. the trainer may take over the flight and provide examples of the correct behaviour.

We will briefly describe ripple-down rules before reviewing Shiraz's work.

6.1 Ripple-down rules

The basic form of a ripple-down rule (RDR) is as follows:

if condition **then** conclusion **because** case **except**
  if condition **then** conclusion **because** case **except**
    if . . .
else **if** . . .

Initially an RDR may consist of the single rule:

if true **then** default conclusion **because** default case

That is, in the absence of any other information, the RDR recommends taking some default action. For example, in a control application it may be to assume everything is normal and to make no changes. If a condition succeeds when it should not, then an exception is added (i.e. a nested if-statement). Thus the initial condition is always satisfied so when the do nothing action is inappropriate, an exception is added. If a condition fails when it should succeed, an alternative clause is added (i.e. an else-statement). The new condition in the exception or alternative clauses is easy to determine.

With each condition/conclusion pair, RDRs store the cornerstone case, i.e. the case that caused the new condition to be created. When a new case is incorrectly classified, it is compared with the cornerstone case of the incorrect condition and the differences are used to construct the new condition. Usually, the difference list is presented to the expert so that he or she may select the most relevant differences or generalise the conditions. That is, the trainer never has to explicitly construct a new rule to insert into the RDR; instead, the knowledge acquisition system presents the trainer with two cases and asks which features distinguish the cases. The system then builds the rule and adds it into the appropriate place in the RDR.

6.2 Parvaz

A ripple-down rule system has been added to the same flight simulator that was used by Sammut *et al.* (1992) in their 'Learning to fly' experiments. Four RDRs are used to control each of the four control actions. Initially each RDR consists of the default rule described above. That is, do nothing unless circumstances warrant an action.

Starting on the runway, the aircraft will do nothing, so the trainer intervenes and creates a rule to increase the throttle to 100%. This rule will cause the plane to travel down the runway, but when it does not lift off because no flaps have been applied and the stick has not been pulled back, the trainer again intervenes. The aircraft will then continue to climb. When it fails to level out, the trainer must provide further advice to the autopilot.

In each intervention, the system displays to the trainer the instrument readings at the time the flight was paused. It also displays the readings for the situation that caused the currently active rule to be created. By indicating the significant differences between the two sets of readings, the trainer assists the RDR system in building a new rule.

Shiraz tested the system by asking several subjects to build autopilots for the same flight plan as defined by Sammut *et al.* (1992). The subjects were able to construct rules 'manually' for most of the flight. However, some subjects found it was easier, in particularly difficult parts of the flight, to simply take over control and provide examples of the appropriate actions. That is, many stages of the flight are sufficiently simple that control rules can be easily verbalised, however, actions performed in other stages, especially landing, are much more difficult to describe and so teaching by example becomes easier.

In the next section we describe Shiraz's learning algorithm.

6.3 Learning ripple-down rules

The learning algorithm also builds ripple-down rules. This permits the automated learner to extend RDRs built manually and vice versa. When the autopilot makes a mistake, the trainer provides a single trace of the correct behaviour. The data are segmented and preprocessed just as in Sammut *et al.* (1992). The system executes the RDRs for each control action on the trace data. Where the RDRs conclusion differs from the action taken by the trainer, a new rule is added to the RDR to correct the error. The method for creating a new rule is now described.

Attributes are assigned a priority for each action in order to implement a heuristic to limit the number of conditions in a rule. Initially, all attributes may be given equal priority. For each attribute in the priority list, the algorithm compares the attribute's previous direction with its next direction. If there is a change in direction (e.g. it was increasing and becomes steady) then:

1. Create a test for the attribute. The test is based on the attribute's current value and its previous direction. The test always has the form:

$$attribute \textbf{ op } value$$

    where op is '$\geq$' if the previous direction was increasing and '$\leq$' if it was decreasing. *Value* is the value in the current record.

2. If the new test succeeds for the new case and fails for the cornerstone case, the test is added to the new rule, otherwise the test is discarded.

3. Increment the attribute's priority.

4. If the number of tests in the condition reaches a user-defined maximum, scan the rest of the attributes and just update their priorities if their direction has changed. The maximum was set to 3 for these experiments.

Intuitively, the priority reflects a causal relationship between a variable and an action and is related to Stirling's influence matrix.

Shiraz found that all of his subjects were able to construct working controllers by a combination of learning from behavioural traces and ripple-down rule's semi-automatic knowledge acquisition method. His subjects ranged from novices who were not previously familiar with flight simulators or RDRs, to those skilled in flying game simulators and who understood RDRs.

7 DISCUSSION

In this paper, we have reviewed recent research in the application of symbolic machine learning techniques to the problem of automatically building controllers for dynamic systems. We have shown that by capturing traces of human behaviour in such tasks, it is possible to build controllers that are efficient and robust. This type of learning has been applied in a variety of domains including the control of chemical processes, manufacturing, scheduling, and autopiloting of diverse apparatus including aircraft and cranes.

Recent extensions to the original formulation of behavioural cloning have the common theme of adding greater structure to the representation of the problem. The style of control achieved can be characterised by Nilsson's term *teleo-reactive*, which means that the controller is goal-directed, taking into account and reacting to the current environment. Further progress in this direction is possible, we believe, by continuing to improve the representations and structures available to the learner, to take greater advantage of the abilities of the trainer.

Acknowledgement

Michael Bain is supported by the Australian Research Council.

REFERENCES

Arentz, D. (1994). *The Effect of Disturbances in Behavioural Cloning*. Computer Engineering Thesis, School of Computer Science and Engineering, University of New South Wales.

Benson, S. (1996). *Learning Action Models For Reactive Autonomous Agents*. Ph.D. Thesis, Dept. of Computer Science, Stanford University.

Benson, S. and Nilsson, N. J. (1995). Reacting, planning and learning in an autonomous agent. In K. Furukawa, D. Michie and S. Muggleton (Eds.), *Machine Intelligence 14*. Oxford University Press.

Cohen, W. W. (1996). Learning to classify English text with ILP methods. In L. De Raedt (Ed.), *Advances in Inductive Logic Programming*. IOS Press, pp. 124–142.

Compton, P. and Jansen, R. (1988). Knowledge in context: a strategy for expert systems maintenance. In *Proceedings of the Australian Artificial Intelligence Conference*.

Kowalski, R. A. (1995). Using meta-logic to reconcile reactive with rational agents. In K. Apt and F. Turini (Eds.), *Meta-Logic and Logic Programming*. Cambridge, MA: MIT Press.

Michie, D. (1986). The superarticulacy phenomenon in the context of software manufacture. *Proceedings of the Royal Society of London*, **A 405**, 185–212. Reproduced in D. Partridge and Y. Wilks (1992). *The Foundations of Artificial Intelligence*, Cambridge University Press, pp. 411–439.

Michie, D., Bain, M. and Hayes-Michie, J. E. (1990). Cognitive models from sub-cognitive skills. In M. Grimble, S. McGhee, and P. Mowforth (Eds.), *Knowledge-base Systems in Industrial Control*. Peter Peregrinus.

Michie, D. and Camacho, R. (1994). Building symbolic representations of intuitive real-time skill from performance data. In K. Furukawa. D. Michie, and S. Muggleton (Eds.), *Machine Intelligence 13*. Oxford: Clarendon Press, pp. 385–418.

Michie, D. (1995). Building symbolic representations of intuitive real-time skill from performance data. In S. Wrobel, N. Lavrac (Eds.), *ECML95*. Berlin: Springer.

Muggleton, S. H. (1995). Inverse entailment and Progol. *New Generation Computing*, **13**, 245–286.

Nilsson, N. J. (1994). Teleo-reactive programs for agent control. *Journal of Artificial Intelligence Research*, **1**, 139–158.

Pearce, A. and Caelli, T. (1995). On the efficiency of spatial matching. In *Proceedings of the Second Asian Conference on Computer Vision*, pp. 79–82. Singapore.

Quinlan, J. R. (1993). *C4.5: Programs for Machine Learning*. San Mateo, CA: Morgan Kaufmann.

Rouveirol, C. and Puget, J.-F. (1990). Beyond inversion of resolution. In *Proceedings of the seventh International Conference on Machine Learning*, pp. 122–130. Morgan Kaufmann.

Sammut, C. (1981). Concept learning by experiment. In *Proceedings of the Seventh International Joint Conference on Artificial Intelligence*, pp.104–105. Vancouver.

Sammut, C. and Banerji, R. (1986). Learning concepts by asking questions. In R. S. Michalski, J. G. Carbonell and T. M. Mitchell (Eds.). *Machine Learning: An Artificial Intelligence Approach, Vol 2*. Los Altos, California: Morgan Kaufmann, pp. 167–192.

Sammut, C., Hurst, S., Kedzier, D., and Michie, D. (1992). Learning to fly. In D. Sleeman and P. Edwards (Eds.), *Proceedings of the Ninth International Conference on Machine Learning*, Aberdeen: Morgan Kaufmann.

Sammut, C. (1997). Using background knowledge to build multistrategy learners. *Machine Learning* **27**, 241–257.

Schoppers, M. J. (1987). Universal plans for reactive robots in unpredictable domains. In *Proceedings of IJCAI-87*. San Francisco: Morgan Kaufmann.

Shiraz, G. M. and Sammut, C. (1997). Combining knowledge acquisition and machine learning to control dynamic systems. In M. E. Pollack (Ed.) *Proceedings of the International Joint Conference in Machine Learning*. Nagoya: Morgan Kaufmann, pp. 908–913.

Srinivasan, A. and Camacho, R. (1998). Inductive logic programming applied to an area of flight control. In S. Muggleton, K. Furakwa and D. Michie (Eds.), *Machine Intelligence 15*. Oxford University Press.

Stirling, D. and Sevinc, S. (1992). Automated operation of complex machinery using plans extracted from numerical models: Towards adaptive control of a stainless steel cold rolling mill. In *Proceedings of the 5th Australian Joint Conference on Artificial Intelligence*,

Stirling, D. (1995). *CHURPs: Compressed Heuristic Universal Reaction Planners*. Ph.D. Thesis, University of Sydney.

Urbančič, T. and Bratko, I. (1994). Reconstructing human skill with machine learning. In A. Cohn (Ed.), *Proceedings of the 11th European Conference on Artificial Intelligence*, John Wiley.

7

Control skill, machine learning and hand-crafting in controller design

Ivan Bratko

Faculty of Computer and Information Science,
Ljubljana University,
and
J. Stefan Institute,
Ljubljana,
Slovenia

Tanja Urbančič

J. Stefan Institute,
Ljubljana,
Slovenia

1 INTRODUCTION

Consider a dynamic system, such as a crane or a plane, and an operator who has acquired the skill of operating that system. Suppose then that the operator is asked to design an algorithm for automatically controlling the system. The operator may try to design such an automatic controller by reconstructing his or her subcognitive skill through introspection, or by other means, e.g. by reasoning about the system and engineering the controller. The main question investigated in this paper is, how would different operators go about this task, and how does the success depend on various factors affecting the task? These factors include:

1. The level of the operator's skill;

2. To what degree is the control skill amenable to introspection?

3. Is there a machine learning tool available to help the subject reconstruct the skill?

4. Does the operator know what the controlled system is? That is, does the operator have some mental model of the system which would allow him to reason about control from 'first principles'?

Here, a 'model' is not necessarily a proper physics model, e.g. in terms of differential equations. Rather we mean the common-sense knowledge of what the controlled system is and correspondingly some naive physics understanding of the system's dynamics. In the case of no model, the controlled system is a complete black box from the operator's point of view, when the operator can only observe the state variables of the system, without knowing the physical meaning of these variables. We will be referring to a black box also as *instrument representation* (the operator can only see 'instruments' showing the current values of the state variables). The opposite to instrument representation is 'pictorial representations' (i.e. non-black-box) when the operator can see a graphical animation of the system on the screen.

We investigated experimentally how these factors affect the operators' development of automatic controllers. We also considered the case when the controller designer does not have the skill to operate the system. However in any case, whether having the control skill or not, the controller designer is assumed to be 'naive' in the sense that he is not familiar with any mathematical model of the system, and does not have any knowledge of the systems control theory.

We carried out a series of experiments designed to systematically explore various aspects of the problem. But first we describe an initial experiment (Section 2) that increased our interest in the problem and invoked some motivating initial hypotheses. One of these hypotheses concerns the role of machine learning in skill reconstruction.

2 INITIAL 'BLACK-BOX' EXPERIMENT

In this experiment, the popular pole-and-cart control task was used. The system consists of a pole hinged on a cart which moves on a track of limited length and can be controlled by a force pushing to the left or to the right. Eight students were asked to learn the task of controlling a simulated pole–cart system, using the instrument representation. That is, they did not know at all what the controlled system was. Instead, they could only see the current values of four state variables A, B, C and D displayed as a bar chart. These variables were actually the pole–cart's state variables x (position of the cart), $\dot{x}$ (velocity of the cart), θ (angle of the pole), and $\dot{\theta}$ (angular velocity). The parameters of the simulated pole and cart were the same as used by most of the researchers in previous studies in this domain [6]: mass of the cart $M = 1\,\mathrm{kg}$, mass of the pole $m = 0.1\,\mathrm{kg}$, length of the pole $l = 1$ m. The start state was: $x = -2m$ or $+2m$, $\dot{x} = \theta = \dot{\theta} = 0$. The control task was to bring the cart into the middle of the track ($x = 0$) and stay inside a small neighbourhood of $x = 0$ for 2 s. The control regime was that of bang-bang with switching the control force between $+10\,\mathrm{N}$ and $-10\,\mathrm{N}$, pushing the cart to the right or left.

The subjects were allowed 150 trials to experiment with the system and acquire the control skill. To make the task easier, the simulator was slowed down by a factor of 8. A trial either ended successfully, or was terminated with failure because of one of the following reasons: the cart went outside the track limits (-2.4 m, $+2.4$ m), or the angle became too large (± 45 deg), or the time limit was reached (15 simulated seconds, that is 120 actual seconds after the slow-down).

131

Having finished all 150 trials, two of the subjects had at least one successful trial and the remaining six none. In the quickest successful trial, the task was accomplished in 4.7 s of simulated time. All the subjects believed that they more or less knew a correct control strategy. They all believed that variables A and C (i.e. x and θ) were the most important control parameters. They had very different physical interpretations of the simulated system, none of them correct.

The two subjects (M.M. and A.Z.) who had at least one successful trial were then asked to translate their skills into a control algorithm. More precisely, they were asked to write a Pascal function E(A, B, C, D) where E is the control force. Their prevailing method was introspection and experimentation with the simulator. They wrote several control programs and numerous versions of their refinements. Their typical program consisted of some 30 lines of Pascal code. None of these programs could complete the control task. After a total of about one week of these trials, they produced a final version that was close to success. It moved the cart to $x = 0$ in 6.5 s of simulated time. However, the problem with that version was that at the moment when x reached 0, the cart's velocity was rather high when it should ideally be 0. Trying to reduce $\dot{x}$, the controller then quickly collapsed in the next half-second because of pole crash.

This inability to handcraft a controller on the basis of skill appears paradoxical in view of the fact that there exists a controller that can be written as one line of Pascal. Namely, a classical control theory solution (obtainable after linear approximation of the corresponding differential equations) is:

$$F = 1.09x + 2.17\dot{x} + 26.53\theta + 6.78\dot{\theta}.$$

There are many successful combinations of the values of the coefficients in the linear control rule above. This control rule can be successfully executed in the bang-bang regime at, say, 50 Hz by simply taking the sign of F above as the direction of the control force.

M.M. and A.Z. stated in their final report the difficulties they felt contributed to their failure to reconstruct a successful controller: 'We found it difficult to translate our control strategy into a program. Some of our control decisions are reflex and we are probably not aware of them. Another difficulty is that the control program can only use the *current* values of the four variables, but cannot, for example, take into account how long a variable has not changed its direction. In manual control we found this information quite significant.'

Later one of the two students (A.Z.) was given a regression tree learning program RETIS [3] as a tool to help him in cloning his own skill. A.Z. took the usual approach to behavioural cloning by means of machine learning [1,5,8]. He took the sequences of state-action pairs from his own traces as sources of examples to induce rules for action as a function of state variables. So the machine learning task was to induce the function $F = F(x, \dot{x}, \theta, \dot{\theta})$ where in the usual ML terminology F is the class and $x, \dot{x}, \theta, \dot{\theta}$ are the attributes. His learning set consisted of the concatenation of two of his control traces, starting from the opposite sides on the track. He chose the first 10 seconds of simulated time of each of the traces (Figure 1). These two traces provided enough variety for reliable induction of good control rules. He thus induced several successful controllers which were typically much simpler than the control programs he hand-crafted

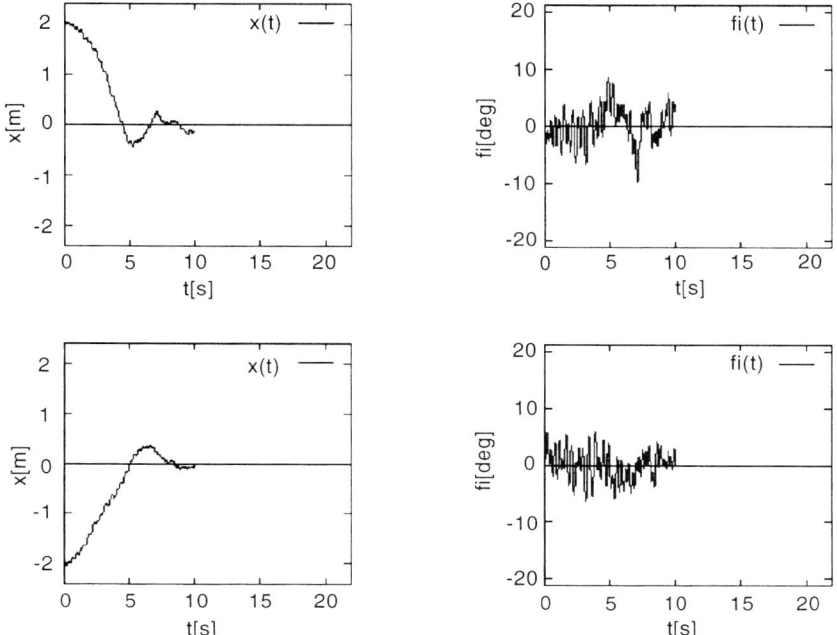

Figure 1. Two human control traces, starting at opposite ends of the track, used as a learning set. The left hand side diagrams show the position of the cart, the right hand side diagrams show the angle of the pole.

previously [12]. However, some care was necessary in setting the parameters of RETIS. The main parameters in RETIS are:

- Use of linear regression in the leaves of the tree: yes or no.

- Parameter m: This is the parameter in the m-probability estimation formula [2]. m may take any non-negative real value, when large m corresponds to high noise in the learning data, and low m to low noise. Correspondingly, in post-pruning RETIS prunes more when m is set high. Thus m is used to set the degree of pruning.

Regarding linear regression in the leaves, good control rules were obtained in both cases: with linear regression and without it. However, the appropriate degree of pruning was surprisingly just the opposite in both cases. In the case of linear regression, a high degree of pruning was desirable (large m). In the case of no linear regression, little or no pruning was desirable. In general, the performance was better with linear regression in the leaves, when a large interval of m very stably produced good control rules. Figure 2 illustrates success of control with various settings of RETIS. Figure 3 shows a typical induced regression tree.

133

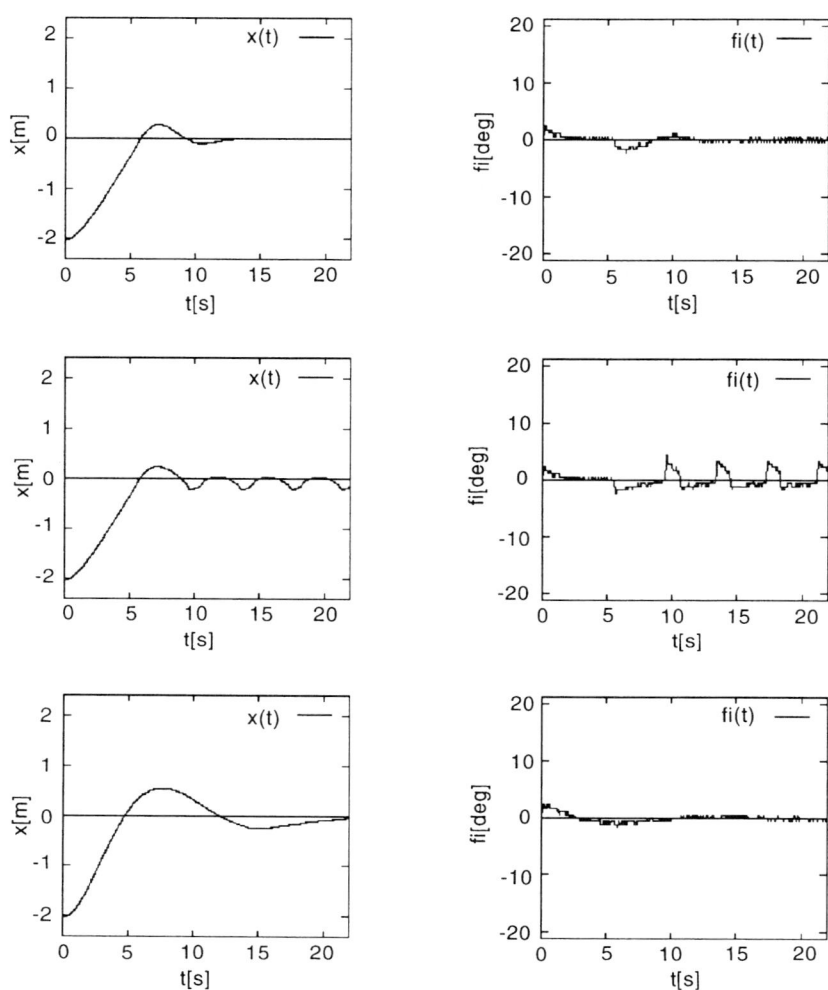

Figure 2. Control of pole and cart with three different regression trees induced by RETIS from the learning set of Fig. 1. The left hand side diagrams show the position of the cart, the right hand side diagrams show the angle of the pole. All the three trees were obtained with linear regression in the leaves and different settings of parameter m. Top diagrams: $m = 0$ (tree size = 93 leaves); middle diagrams: $m = 20$ (19 leaves); bottom diagrams: $m = 200$ (1 leaf).

As for unsuccessful attempts, induction *without* linear regression did not produce a completely correct control tree for $m > 1$. On the other hand, induction *with* linear regression produced correct control trees for all $m \geq 20$, and for no $m \leq 10$. In the cases reported here, the control rules were executed in the bang-bang regime by simply taking force $10\,\mathrm{N}$ in the direction of the sign of the real value predicted by the regression tree.

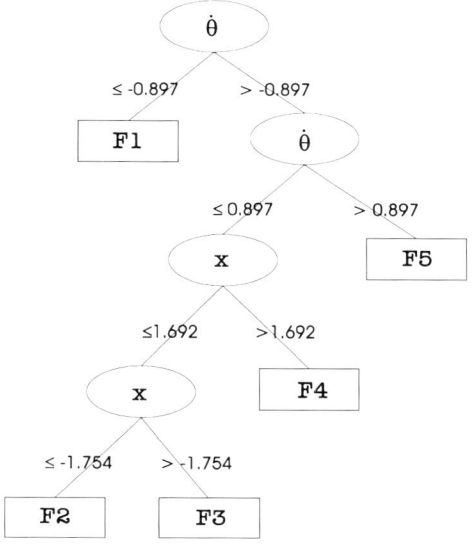

$$F1 = -0.5$$
$$F2 = 5.5 + 3*x - 2*\dot{x} + 19*\theta - 0.62*\dot{\theta}$$
$$F3 = 0.6*x + 0.9*\dot{x} + 8*\theta + 1.2*\dot{\theta}$$
$$F4 = -1.06 - 0.78*x - 0.86*\dot{x} + 17*\theta - 0.14*\dot{\theta}$$
$$F5 = 0.5$$

Figure 3. A regression tree and the corresponding five linear regression formulas in the leaves of the tree, induced by A.Z. from traces of his manual control. RETIS was used with parameter $m = 50$.

This early experiment indicates a hypothesis that skill reconstruction with machine learning (ML) is easier than through hand-crafting and introspection. There are several related questions that we investigated by further experiments in this paper:

- Is skill reconstruction with machine learning easier than by introspection, or by hand-crafting in general?
- Are there characteristic differences between rules obtained with ML and rules obtained by introspection or hand-crafting?
- Can (*formal*) control rules be *reliably* reconstructed by ML? If yes, how? How about *skill* reconstruction?
- For humans, is learning to control using instrument representation easier than with pictorial representation?

This last question was suggested by an observation by Michie and Chambers [6]. They investigated human learning to control pole and cart using both kinds of representation.

Contrary to intuition, they found that pictorial representation did not help in their case.

3 STUDIES WITH A POLE–CART SIMULATOR

In this section we present two studies in control reconstruction with machine learning: reconstruction of automatic controllers, and reconstruction of human control skill. Although we are primarily interested in reconstruction of human skill, we here begin with reconstruction of automatic controllers. Reconstruction of an automatic controller does not bear any particular practical importance. The only objective of this study was to test the approach under very controllable conditions: should this test fail, every application to more demanding problems would be questionable from the very beginning. If we could not reconstruct a simple and consistent, fully specified controller with no delay and no noise, how could we approach human skill, where the following factors present additional difficulties:

- Operator's skill is more or less subcognitive. We cannot fully rely on their verbal descriptions of this process. We do not even know what would be a suitable formalism for defining a strategy underlying a skilled performance.

- Usually we do not know what subgoals subjects have in mind, how they order them, when they change them, etc.

- Even more, we sometimes do not know what the main reason is for their decisions and actions, what kind of information they use, which relations they observe, how they combine visual and numerical information, etc.

- Personal style makes the skills of different subjects difficult to compare.

- Experience and development make the skill of the same subject change in time.

- Several natural and subjective factors, which cannot be fully avoided, make the skill execution inconsistent also in the short term.

3.1 Reconstruction of automatic controllers with machine learning

3.1.1 Experimental materials

Two students (M.B. and M.F.) were asked to reconstruct two simple controllers from traces of their performance. They knew that the controlled system was a pole and cart simulator, but they were not told anything about the controllers. We believe that it was essential in this exercise that it was done by two 'naive' users of an ML program on a problem they were not familiar with. By this, we believe we eliminated a possible bias of an expert user who could, guessing a solution in advance, accordingly tune the learning program. All that the two students were given, was:

- A simulator of the cart and pole system;
- traces of successful control representative of both controllers;
- the RETIS learning program.

There were 2×5 traces of successful control (2 different controllers, each starting from 5 different initial states: $x = -2m, -1m, 0m, 1m, 2m$, all the other state variables having initial value 0). A trace was a sequence of (*State*, *Action*) pairs, where *State* was described by the current values of x (position of the cart), $\dot{x}$ (velocity of the cart), θ (pole inclination) and $\dot{\theta}$, and *Action* was -1 or 1, or meaning push to the left or right, respectively. The control task was to bring the system from the initial state to the middle of the track without a crash, and to keep it within the target region in an upwards position for a specified period of time.

As a curiosity, we report on the fact that the students were originally given 3×5 traces, where the third set of five traces was produced by a human operator instead of an automatic controller. Very soon the students distinguished this set of data as more difficult (odd, as they said), and decided to start with the other two controllers.

The controllers that produced the given execution traces were the following:

1. Makarovič's controller (a decision tree constructed by Andrej Makarovič [4], given as an if-then-else rule in Figure 4);

2. a bang-bang variant of a linear control rule:

$$F = \text{sign}(0.147x + 0.319\dot{x} + 3.911\theta + \dot{\theta}).$$

3.1.2 Results for Makarovič's controller

The students decided to merge traces from two different initial states ($x = -1m$ and $x = 1m$) into a set of 979 learning examples. They applied RETIS to this learning set and varied the parameters of RETIS. The results are given in Table 1. Note that even in the case of linear regression in the leaves, the induced rules were executed under the bang-bang regime (taking the sign of the predicted value).

3.1.3 Results for bang-bang variant of linear controller

In the case of the bang-bang variant of the linear controller, the students merged traces from the five different initial states. They applied RETIS with all the mentioned options to this learning set, and obtained the results, given in the bottom part of Table 1.

```
if DTheta < -5 then F := -10 else
if DTheta >  5 then F :=  10 else
if Theta  < -2 then F := -10 else
if Theta  >  2 then F :=  10 else
if DX   <  -0.1 then F := -10 else
if DX   >   0.1 then F :=  10 else
if  X   <   0    then F := -10 else F := 10
```

Figure 4. Control rule for pole and cart problem, constructed by A. Makarovič [4]. Angle Theta is in degrees. DX is the velocity of the cart, D Theta is the angular velocity of the pole.

Table 1. Reconstruction of Makarovič's controller and linear bang-bang controller. Tree size is shown as the number of leaves. 'yes' means successful control from the corresponding start position, '—' means failure.

Original controller, with/out linear regression	m	Tree size	$-2m$	$-1m$	0	$+1m$	$+2m$
Makarovič,	0	14	yes	yes	yes	yes	yes
without	1	14	yes	yes	yes	yes	yes
	2	14	yes	yes	yes	yes	yes
	3	13	yes	yes	yes	yes	yes
	4	12	yes	yes	yes	yes	yes
	8	11	yes	yes	yes	yes	yes
	12	10	yes	yes	yes	yes	yes
	20	9	yes	—	yes	yes	yes
	30	7	yes	—	—	—	—
	40	4	—	—	—	—	—
Makarovič	0	12	yes	yes	yes	yes	yes
with	10	11	yes	yes	yes	yes	yes
	20	10	yes	yes	yes	yes	yes
	30	9	yes	yes	yes	yes	yes
	40	8	yes	yes	yes	yes	yes
	56	7	yes	yes	yes	yes	yes
	60	3	yes	yes	yes	yes	yes
	300	1	—	yes	yes	yes	—
Linear,	0	88	yes	yes	yes	yes	yes
without	1	86	yes	yes	yes	yes	yes
	2	69	yes	yes	yes	—	yes
	3	57	yes	—	yes	—	yes
	5	37	yes	—	yes	—	yes
Linear,	0	32	—	yes	—	—	—
with	1	26	—	yes	yes	—	—
	5	23	—	yes	yes	—	—
	10	14	yes	yes	yes	yes	—
	20	6	yes	yes	yes	yes	yes
	40	4	yes	yes	yes	yes	yes
	60	3	yes	yes	yes	yes	yes
	125	1	yes	yes	yes	yes	yes

3.1.4 Summary and discussion of the results

Let us first discuss the cases when no linear regression was used in the leaves.

The findings were similar in both cases, in the reconstruction of Makarovič's rule and in the reconstruction of the bang-bang variant of the linear controller. In both cases, no pruning and a small degree of pruning resulted in trees that worked as controllers from all of the five testing initial states. By increasing the parameter m (increased pruning

```
if DTheta >  4.98 then F :=  10 else
if DTheta < -4.98 then F := -10  else
if DX  <  -0.098  then
    if  Theta > 2.01 then F := 10 else F := -10  else
if Theta  < -1.98 then F := -10 else
if X  >  0.015  then F := 10 else
if DTheta >  1.56 then F := 10 else F := -10
```

Figure 5. Makarovič's rule as reconstructed from performance traces with RETIS.

of the regression tree) we can find the smallest tree which still works without failure. Reconstructing Makarovič's control rule, the smallest working tree induced by RETIS had 10 leaves, obtained by setting parameter $m = 1$. This tree, written as an if-then-else statement, is shown in Figure 5. It is trivial to rewrite it in a form that enables direct comparison with the original rule. It slightly differs from the original tree only in numerical parameters. Further increasing of pruning parameter m resulted in trees that did not solve the control problem for all the testing initial states. (They even failed from the initial state $x = -1m$, although this was an initial state in the traces that were used for learning.)

Also in the case of the bang-bang variant of the linear controller, at a certain point, increased pruning deteriorated performance. In fact, in this case it was not possible to preserve correctness and reduce the tree below 86 leaves. This difference between the cases can be explained by the level of similarity between the form of RETIS trees and the language defining the original controllers. While this was very similar in the case of Makarovič's controller, it differs significantly in the case of the linear controller. Therefore, in the latter case, it was possible to achieve practically identical performance, but the hypothesis language limitations did not allow the reconstruction of the original structure. Reconstruction succeeded in the behavioural sense, but did not contribute to the understanding of the original controller.

Now we look at the results obtained *with* linear regression.

In the case of Makarovič's rule, reconstruction with RETIS with linear regression in the leaves, the tree with seven leaves performed in a way very much the same as the original controller. The tree with three leaves differed more. The main difference, which could be desirable in many cases, is smootheness in the performance of the reconstructed controller, contrasted to very jerky traces characteristic of the original. Failures of the extremely pruned tree in this case (1 leaf) from the initial state $x = -2m$ and $x = 2m$ could be due to the fact that learning examples did not cover these cases. (Nevertheless, these cases were also solved successfully when there was no regression.)

With linear regression, it was possible to prune substantially also in the case of the bang-bang variant of the linear controller. Actually, pruning was necessary to get working controllers. While up to the trees with 14 leaves tests reported failure for some initial states, further increase of pruning produced better results. Trees with six leaves or less all worked from the five initial states. Due to the similarity of the description language, in this case it was possible to reconstruct also the structure of the controller. The result

$$F = \text{sign}(0.128x + 0.240\dot{x} + 4\theta + \dot{\theta})$$

again differs from the original in the numerical details, but fully reflects the logic of the controller. It should be noted that RETIS discovered a continuous variant of the rule, without signum. Due to the fact that control was bang-bang, the real number predicted by RETIS was interpreted as a push left or right, according to the sign.

At first sight it is surprising that linear regression helps in the bang-bang regime. After a careful analysis we found an explanation for this phenomenon, which is given in Section 5.

After the positive results of this study we proceeded with the reconstruction of *human* control skill with machine learning, as described in the next subsection.

3.2 Reconstruction of human control with machine learning

To investigate the repeatability of Zalar's results described in Section 2, two other students (D.M. and V.S.) were asked to learn to control the same pole-and-cart simulator as used in the previous exercise. The task was also the same: bring the cart from the initial position to the middle of the track with the pole in the upward position, and maintain the system within a narrow target region for a certain period of time. First they had to learn to control it manually by using a *pictorial* representation of the system's behaviour on the screen. Since it is extremely difficult to control the simulator in real time, the simulation was slowed down by a factor of 8 with respect to simulated time. This slow down factor was chosen experimentally. After acquiring the manual skill, the students had to follow Zalar's findings and reconstruct their own skill from traces of their performance. The main objective of this exercise was to test the robustness of the approach by replication in the same domain, but with other subjects and other traces.

The subjects succeeded in learning to control the system manually. On average, they needed 30 trials before the first success. This took 450 simulated seconds which corresponds to 3600 seconds of real time. Notice that the human learning here was much more effective than in the experiments of Section 2 when the *instrument* representation was used. When they attained reliable skill, they recorded 11 trials, some from the initial state $x = -2m$ and some from $x = +1m$ (Table 2). The recordings consisted of snapshots (*State, Action*), which were taken with the frequency 50 Hz and served as a source of learning examples. As in the previous exercise with reconstruction of automatic controllers, *State* was described by the current values of x (position of the cart), $\dot{x}$ (velocity of the cart), θ (pole inclination) and $\dot{\theta}$, and Action was -1 or 1, meaning push to the left or right, respectively. For learning, the state from the previous snapshot was attached to the current action. This time shift between state and action aimed at simulating the operator's delay in reacting to a new state. The appropriateness and the amount of such a delay is debatable [9]. In any case we believe that the chosen small delay in this experiment produced results that would be very similar to those obtainable

140

Table 2. Manual control of pole-and-cart simulator, performed by subjects V and D. Times to finish are *simulated* execution times; the actual subjects' times were eight times greater because of the simulator's slow-down.

Trace	Initial position	Time to finish
V−21	−2m	5.88
V − 22	−2m	5.32
V − 23	−2m	6.10
D − 21	−2m	6.20
D − 22	−2m	10.74
D − 23	−2m	6.56
V + 11	+1m	12.00
V + 12	+1m	10.34
V + 13	+1m	4.82
D + 11	+1m	6.58
D + 12	+1m	5.78

with no delay. The shortest time needed for manual control from $x = 1m$ was 4.82 seconds, and from $x = -2m$ the best result was 5.32 seconds. As shown in Table 2, times vary significantly also for the same subject.

3.2.1 Learning with RETIS without linear regression

First, 11 learning sets were formed as described above, so that in one learning set there were only examples from one trace. Only in two cases, namely V − 21 and D + 11, were successful trees learned by RETIS without pruning and without linear regression in leaves. The execution times obtained by these two trees were 15.64 s and 15.46 s from the initial state $x = 1m$. In the next step, the corresponding two learning sets were merged into one set with 643 learning examples. Trees with much better execution times were obtained from the composed learning set. For example, the task with initial state $x = 1m$, which was solved by humans in approximately 15 seconds, was now solved in times that varied from 3.84 to 15.22 seconds, depending on the level of pruning. Note that substantial improvement was obtained in this case by merging traces of different subjects. Table 3 gives the details of this experiment. The observed improvement is interesting in the view of the common belief in skill reconstruction that traces from different subjects should not be mixed together. It is commonly believed that mixing examples from different control strategies would only confuse the learning program.

The smallest tree which still controlled the system from the five testing positions had 17 leaves.

3.2.2 Learning with RETIS with linear regression

When linear regression was used, 8 out of 11 traces (when used separately as sets of learning examples, i.e. without merging) resulted in trees that controlled the system from

Table 3. Learning from two traces of manual control (one from $x = -2m$ and one from $x = 1m$), obtained from two different subjects. Traces were merged into a single set of learning examples. RETIS without linear regression in leaves was used for learning. '—' means unsuccessful control from the corresponding start position; for successful control, the given numbers are simulated times to finish.

m	Tree size	$-2m$	$-1m$	0	$+1m$	$+2m$
0	42	9.45	7.42	2.02	4.30	9.98
1	32	9.44	7.42	2.02	4.30	9.98
2	30	6.60	8.70	2.02	6.64	10.62
3	29	—	8.70	2.02	3.84	11.08
4	28	—	9.18	2.02	3.84	10.08
5	26	—	8.96	2.02	4.40	8.52
6	25	—	15.68	6.86	8.76	18.64
7	20	—	15.68	6.98	8.76	18.64
8	18	14.04	8.10	11.56	7.14	12.64
10	17	11.62	8.74	2.02	15.22	11.62
12	10	—	—	—	—	—
20	8	—	—	—	—	—
25	6	—	—	—	—	—
35	4	—	—	—	—	—
100	2	—	—	—	—	—

Table 4. The most successful trees obtained from traces of manual control by RETIS with linear regression in leaves. Whenever there was more than one tree that solved the task from all the five initial states, we present the smallest of them. When there was no tree that would solve the task from the five initial states, we show the smallest one, successful for 4 (or 3, if this was a maximum) initial states.

Trace	m	Tree size	$-2m$	$-1m$	0	$+1m$	$+2m$
V − 21	20	1	8.24	7.42	2.02	7.42	8.42
V − 22	16	1	5.78	5.64	2.02	5.64	5.78
V − 23	30	1	12.42	5.86	2.02	5.86	14.66
D − 21	15	1	6.12	6.02	2.02	6.02	6.12
D − 22	16	4	5.88	4.26	2.02	—	—
D − 23	15	1	5.92	5.78	2.02	5.78	5.92
V + 11	15	6	13.62	9.94	2.02	6.62	9.94
V + 12	30	1	5.88	5.66	2.02	5.66	5.88
V + 13	22	1	4.42	4.18	2.02	4.18	4.42
D + 11	4	11	—	2.68	9.18	5.42	13.84
D + 12	10	2	—	—	2.02	4.38	5.46

all the five testing start positions. Typically, some pruning was needed to obtain such trees. Details are given in Table 4.

The three remaining traces which did not give fully successful trees all belonged to the same subject (D). We did not investigate this fact in more detail, but it could support the hypothesis that some subjects' traces are more suitable for reconstruction than others. Still, these trees proved to be successful for at least three out of five initial states.

3.3 Hand-crafting a control rule

In this exercise, another student (A.B.) was asked to learn to control the pole–cart simulator with pictorial representation (white box). So while learning, he could use his common-sense understanding of the dynamics of the controlled system. Then he was asked to hand-craft a controller, that is, write a control program in Pascal. The handcrafting method consisted of playing with the simulator and using his own control experience in whatever way he found most useful. He was not given any ML tool.

It should be noted that this student was naive in the sense that he did not have any knowledge of differential equations or concepts from control theory. So his search for a controller was limited to common-sense intuitive ideas and was not biased by knowing any principles from control theory.

We believe that the hand-crafting of the controller mainly consisted of qualitative reasoning about a common-sense model of the pole and cart, and tuning the intuitive control rules on the simulator. Perhaps surprisingly, it only required about one day of work to systematically design a successful control program in this way. This program works reliably although it performs far from optimally regarding the time needed to carry out the control task. The program, written in Pascal, is shown in Figure 6. It can clearly be interpreted in terms of the causalities in the system. The control program implements the following qualitative control rules:

- If $|\dot{\theta}|$ is too high then take immediate corrective action to reduce it.

- If cart is 'far left' from the middle then attain $\dot{x} = 0.5$ m/s; analogously for cart 'far right'

- If cart is left and 'close' to the middle then attain $\dot{x} = 0.1$ m/s; analogously for cart right and 'close' to middle.

- To attain $\dot{x} = \dot{x}_{desired}$ do:
  if $\dot{x}$ too low then attain $\theta = 1.5°$
  if $\dot{x}$ too high then attain $\theta = -1.5°$

- To attain $\theta = \theta_{desired}$ do:
  if $\theta < \theta_{desired}$ then push left else right

The thresholds were chosen as follows: 'cart far from middle' means $|x| > 0.7m$; 'cart close to middle' means $|x| \leq 0.7m$; '$|\dot{\theta}|$ too high' means $|\dot{\theta}| > 7.5°$/sec.

143

```
if (dtheta < 7.5) and (dtheta > -7.5) then
  if x < -0.7 then
    begin
      if dx > 0.5 then
        if theta < -1.5 then action := -1 else action := 1
      else
        if theta <  1.5 then action := -1 else action := 1
    end
  else
  if x > 0.7 then
    ....
    {Analogous to case x < -0.7}
    ....
  else
    begin
      if dx < -0.1 then
        if theta <  1.5 then action := -1 else action := 1
      else
      if dx >  0.1 then
        if theta < -1.5 then action := -1 else action := 1
      else
        if x < 0 then
          if theta <  1.5 then action := -1 else action := 1
        else
          if theta < -1.5 then action := -1 else action := 1
    end
else
  if dtheta < -5 then action := -1 else action := 1
```

Figure 6. A pole-cart controller handcrafted by commonsense reasoning about the system. Part of the control program that can be easily reconstructed by left–right analogy has been omitted in this figure. The angle theta is in degrees.

4 STUDIES WITH CONTAINER CRANE SIMULATOR

In this section we describe experiments in the control of a container crane simulator, as used in [9]. This problem domain differs from the pole-and-cart control in several aspects, including the following:

- The system is controlled by two control forces, one applied to the trolley in the horizontal direction (F_x) and one in the direction of the rope (F_l), each of them having a set of possible values, much larger than in the pole-and-cart case, where we had just one control force with two possible values.

- The state of the system is described by six variables: trolley position and its velocity (x and $\dot{x}$), rope inclination angle and the corresponding angular velocity (θ and $\dot{\theta}$), rope length and its velocity (l and $\dot{l}$). All the six variables are to be controlled (in the pole-and-cart case there were four state variables).

As in the pole-and-cart study, a simulator was used in our crane control experiments. The simulator can be controlled by control actions performed manually using the keyboard, or automatically, control actions being determined by a control program. Output modes enable pictorial representation of the crane, or alternatively the 'instrument' representation only where the state variables and force values are presented as columns, imitating measuring instruments.

The control task was similar to the task in the pole-and-cart study. While taking into account constraints on possible values of the state variables, the system had to be brought from the initial state into a specified target region, and kept there for a specified period of time. The execution time had to be minimized, as in the control of real cranes, where severe capacity requirements have to be met.

4.1 Reconstruction of manual control with machine learning

In this experiment, six students were asked to learn to control the crane simulator in the 'instrument' version (black box), without any information about the system. The students were not told that the simulated system was a crane. The task in this variant was formulated as bringing the columns A, B, C, D, E and F (representing the state variables) as fast as possible into a marked target region, where they should stay for a specified period of time. The columns should not exceed specified limits. If the task was not accomplished in three minutes, failure was reported, as in the case that any of the state or control variables fell out of the specified boundaries.

All the subjects succeeded in accomplishing the task at least once, but they significantly differed in the speed of learning, level of reliability as well as in execution times (Table 5). While after 200 trials some of them performed fast and reliably, one of them still reported she did not know what was the strategy for solving the task.

The trials were sampled with the frequency of 10 Hz. Each snapshot consisted of the current values of the variables x, $\dot{x}$, θ, $\dot{\theta}$, l, $\dot{l}$, and the current control forces F_x and F_l. These snapshots were given as learning examples to the learning system which had to determine the two assumed functional relationships: $F_x = F_x(x, \dot{x}, l, \dot{l}, \theta, \dot{\theta})$ and $F_l = F_l(x, \dot{x}, l, \dot{l}, \theta, \dot{\theta})$. A successful trial lasts between approximately 60 and 150 seconds, so such a trace gives roughly between 600 and 1500 positive examples for learning.

145

Table 5. Learning manual control of crane simulator.

Subject	Number of the first successful trial	The best time to finish (s)
M	171	101.46
V	23	63.30
F	59	75.64
T	68	81.46
A	85	74.44
S	12	71.90

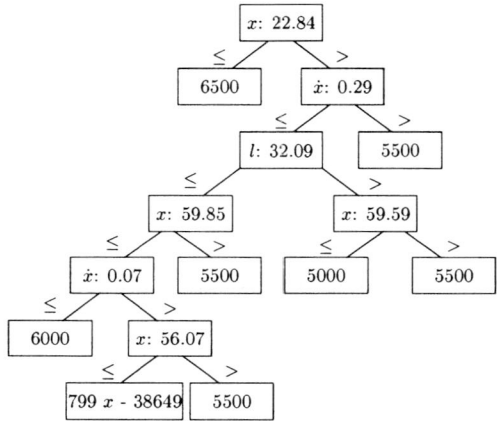

Figure 7. A control rule for F_x induced by M5 from trace of manual control, performed by subject S.

Two programs for the induction of regression trees were used in our experiments: RETIS [3] and M5 [7]. Rules that performed successfully were induced by both of them. As an example, Figure 7 shows an induced tree for F_x. The tree was generated by M5 from a trace of subject S performance, and adjusted to the control regime subjects used for manual control. Similarly, a tree for F_l was induced. In this particular case, not only did the induced trees succeed in accomplishing the task, they were also faster in achieving the goal (75 seconds for the induced rule compared to 90 seconds for the original manual control).

However, brittleness was noticed in two respects:

- Straightforward learning from the traces does not reliably produce successful clones. The process is very sensitive to the choice of particular traces as sources of learning examples, and to the learning program settings. In an exhaustive experimental testing, only two subjects were successfully 'cloned' into working control rules, although many traces as well as many different settings of learning programs were systematically tested.

- The induced rules are not robust with respect to changes in the control task (e.g. different starting or target positions of the load), even if they outperform the originals in the sense of time needed to accomplish the task. The rules generated from more than one trace are slightly more robust but at the cost of decreased transparency due to the increased size of the trees. (For example, the tree induced from 12 subject S trials, had 479 leaves for F_x and 380 for F_l.) In spite of satisfactory behavioural reconstruction, such trees are unacceptable as models of human skill. This is again due to the limitations of the language used in these experiments. In the following paragraphs, we discuss some problems regarding conceptual relevance between induced rules and human understanding of the problem.

In a previous study [9] we tried to establish the correspondence between the rules induced by machine learning from traces, and the verbal instructions given by the subjects. Straightforward learning of the control rule for F_l resulted in regression trees that were very hard to compare conceptually with the instructions. The trees tended to be large and the attributes appearing in the tree were different from those in human instructions. However, with the help of subjects' instructions, it was possible to find a set of attributes that enabled the learning system to induce a more comprehensible control rule.

In the case of F_x, it was even harder to establish the conceptual similarity between the induced rule and the instructions. For example, instructions involve time ordering which is not mentioned at all in the rules obtained by machine learning. Therefore, the time order of execution of various parts of the tree during replay was considered in order to identify their correspondence to particular parts of verbal instructions. Such a comparison can help in operationalizing verbal instructions which are normally too incomplete and imprecise to be directly translatable into a control program. In particular, some thresholds are given very approximately by humans, but can be precisely identified with the help of performance traces and rules learned from them. Furthermore, machine learning based analysis in this case revealed that the subject was actually not doing what she believed she was doing.

4.2   Hand-crafting a crane controller

One of the students (S) who earlier participated in the black-box learning of crane control later went on to hand-craft a control program for the crane simulator. The design of this controller was based on S's own control skill and on a common-sense model of the crane (the student was by that time already told that the controlled system was a crane). To tune the controller, the student was also given the crane simulator to experiment with.

The resulting control program was very simple, but worked reasonably well although far from optimal in terms of the finishing time (which was the stated criterion for this task). The control program consisted of two if-then statements in Pascal (Figure 8). One statement determines the horizontal control force FX, and the other one the vertical force FY.

```
if X <= 27.50 then
    if DX <= 0.92 then XF := 6500 else XF := 5500
else
    if X <= 56.25 then
        if DX <= 0.3 then XF := 6500 else XF := 5500
    else
        XF := 5500;


if L <= 31.95 then
    if DL <= 0.20 then
        YF := -200
    else
        if DL = 0.20 then YF := 0 else YF := 5000*(DL-0.20)
else
    if L <= 32.05 then
        if DL = 0.00 then YF := 0 else YF := 8000*DL
    else
        YF := 300;
```

Figure 8. A crane control program handcrafted by subject S.

In interpreting this program it should be noted that the friction force in the horizontal direction is 6000 N, and in the vertical direction 300 N.

The student reported that the total time needed to handcraft this controller was in the order of 10 hours (of course, not counting the prior acquisition of the control skill in the black-box learning which also took another 10 hours).

This controller carries out the task in 69 s which is considerably better than the subject's own control time. After further fine tuning of the numerical parameters it was possible to improve the 69 s to 61 s which is still quite some way from optimal. The reason for suboptimality is the conservative design of the controller. The controller does not control the swing in any active way, but simply makes sure that the swing is never too large. Then the passive dumping is sufficient to keep the swing inside the required bounds in the final stage. The price for this passive strategy is that the horizontal acceleration (and velocity) is never as high as it could have been if the controller was able to actively decrease the swing in the final stage.

Another student (A.B.) was asked to design a controller just using a common-sense model of the crane and playing with the simulator. This student did not participate in any learning experiments prior to the hand-crafting, and did not have any skill or experience in controlling the system. He was also naive in the sense of not knowing a mathematical model of the crane, nor having any knowledge of control theory concepts. He came up with a rather systematical design and a control program that was more complicated than that of subject S. A.B.'s controller also did active swing control, allowing more energetic actions in the horizontal direction. As a result, the finishing time was substantially better (51 s).

These two experiments in hand-crafting a controller would indicate two speculative hypotheses:

1. A common-sense model of the controlled system plays an important role in this naive approach to designing a controller.

2. Prior subject's experience, or skill, in manually controlling the system does not seem to really help in the design of a controller. In fact, in the case of subject S, the passive manual control strategy was inherited into the design of the control program. In this sense the prior black-box experience possibly limited the subject's creativity in exploring the new possibilities that emerged when the common-sense model became available.

Of course, these hypotheses are only based on observations with two particular subjects, and it would be premature to draw firmly any more general conclusions.

5 PRUNING, LINEAR REGRESSION AND BANG-BANG CONTROL

The experiments in Sections 3 and 4 are quite instructive regarding the use of regression tree learning in skill reconstruction. The RETIS program was used and its settings were varied, in particular:

1. the degree of pruning adjusted through the probability estimate parameter m;

2. the use of linear regression in the leaves ('yes' means use linear regression, 'no' means use average value).

The results depended critically on the choice of these parameters. The results were not very sensitive to the exact value of m, but a nice and very clear qualitative relation emerged between the parameters and the success of cloning. This qualitative relation is summarized in Table 6.

Table 6. Success of cloning depending on degree of pruning and use of linear regression.

	Low pruning	High pruning
Linear regression: No	Good	Bad
Linear regression: Yes	Bad	Very Good

149

The table indicates these trends:

1. When no linear regression is used, prune little.
2. When linear regression is used, prune much.

Best results are obtained *with* linear regression *and* much pruning. The interesting finding here is that the appropriate degree of pruning is qualitatively different for the two cases: with or without linear regression.

Regarding the use of linear regression, the results are quite surprising in view of the following fact: in the case of bang-bang control, the result of linear regression is actually interpreted as a binary value. If the regressed value is positive then push right else push left. So the corresponding learning problem is in effect a discrete, binary class problem. Both the learning examples and the 'bang-banged' predictions have binary class. The question then is, how can linear regression help at all in this situation?

The following is a plausible explanation. Just to simplify graphical illustration, assume that the control rule which is to be reconstructed from examples is simply:

$$F = \text{sign}(x + y).$$

Both x and y are real-valued. Figure 9a illustrates this function. When reconstructing this function from examples, a regression tree approximates the oblique threshold plane (a line in the case of Figure 9a) by a multidimensional stepping surface illustrated in Figure 9b.

A tree without linear regression will unavoidably make incorrect predictions within the triangles shown in Figure 9b. It now becomes obvious that in the case of no linear regression, the effect of pruning will be detrimental. More pruning will cause coarser approximation to the threshold plane (larger triangles) and consequently larger prediction error.

However, in the case of linear regression, followed by bang-bang thresholding, the original threshold plane (line) is possibly recovered. The effect of severe pruning in this case is beneficial: with more pruning we get more examples in individual

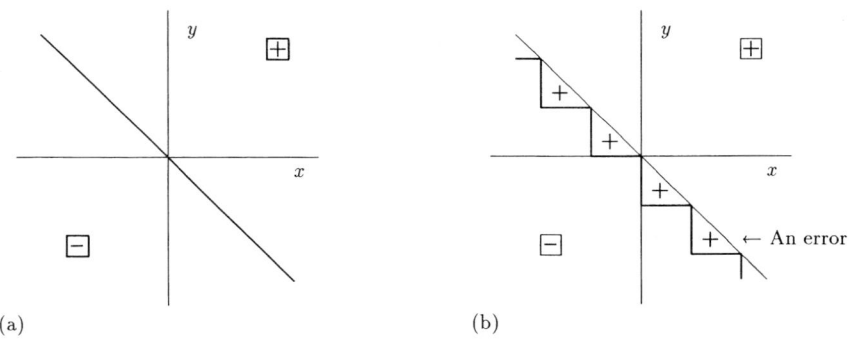

(a)   (b)

Figure 9. (a) The target function. (b) A regression tree reconstruction of this function.

leaves, and this enables more reliable reconstruction of the original linear threshold plane.

6 DISCUSSION

In this paper a number of experiments were described, carried out to investigate several questions regarding the design of controllers by 'naive' human subjects. Several parameters were varied in these experiments:

- the subject did have a common-sense model of the controlled system, or the subject did *not* have any model (black box);
- the subject did have the skill to control the system himself, or the subject did *not* have such a skill;
- the subject had a learning program available as a tool for skill reconstruction, or no such tool was available (in the latter case simple hand-crafting, possibly based on introspection, was necessary).

In the following paragraphs we review the questions investigated and the answers indicated by our experimental results. The questions investigated are complex, so the answers largely depend on circumstances and individual subjects. Therefore most of our answers should be taken as likely hypotheses rather than firm findings.

Question: Is skill reconstruction with machine learning easier than through introspection?

Answer: There is no clear evidence in these experiments that the present approach to skill reconstruction with machine learning is in general more effective than hand-crafting that involves introspection. It seems that the answer depends on the availability of a model. In the case that the subject does have some common-sense model of the controlled system, the role of machine learning seems insignificant. However, when no model is available, help from machine learning is essential. Machine learning seems to compensate for the lack of a model.

Question: Are there characteristic differences between rules obtained with machine learning and rules obtained by hand-crafting? If yes, which?

Answer: Definitely yes. Hand-crafted rules indicate the subject's tendency to attain or maintain certain goal values, or goal intervals, of certain variables. These subgoals change over time and correspond to the overall plan for achieving the final goal. A subgoal is achieved, or maintained, by repetitively executing a feedback control loop. Control rules generated by machine learning do not reflect (at least not so clearly) these subgoals and feedback loops. Working hand-crafted rules seem to be more robust than induced rules which is perhaps due to these subgoals and feedback loops. A challenging problem therefore is to automatically induce control rules that exhibit similar structures, comprising subgoals and feedback loops. Techniques for automatic detection of operator's subgoals have recently been developed [10, 11] which resulted in substantially improved robustness of induced controllers.

Question: Can *formalized* control rules be reliably reconstructed by machine learning? If yes, how? How about *skill* reconstruction?

Answer: Yes, formal control rules have been reliably reconstructed by employing the straightforward machine learning approach. In the experiments, the most effective technique turned out to be the induction of regression trees *with* linear regression in the leaves and drastic tree pruning. This approach somewhat surprisingly works well even in the case of bang-bang control. An explanation of this phenomenon was given in the paper.

Question: If the subject possesses control skill, does this help in hand-crafting a controller?

Answer: Possibly yes in the case of no model. However, in cases when a model is available, it may even be that the skill has a detrimental effect because it constrains the subject's creative search for ideas based on reasoning with the model.

Question: Is it easier for humans to learn to control by using the instrument representation rather than pictorial representation?

Answer: At the early stage of learning, the opposite seems more likely; pictorial representation seems to help the subject make early progress. However, once some basic control skill has been acquired, further progress is normally done through fine tuning. At that later stage, the instrument representation becomes more important and it is likely to eventually become more valuable than the pictorial one.

Acknowledgements

Many people contributed to this research by ideas, discussion, carrying out experiments and writing software, including: Donald Michie, Claude Sammut, Marko Grobelnik, Sašo Džeroski, Andrej Bratko, Sunčica Poljak and Andrej Zalar. This research was supported by the Slovenian Ministry of Science and Technology. Part of this paper was written while one of the authors (I.B.) was visiting the Control Laboratory of the Faculty of Information Technology and Systems, Delft Technical University, the Netherlands.

REFERENCES

[1] I. Bratko, T. Urbančlč, and C. Sammut. Behavioural cloning of control skill. In R.S. Michalski, I. Bratko, and M. Kubat, editors, *Machine Learning and Data Mining: Methods and Applications*. Wiley, 1998.

[2] B. Cestnik. Estimating probabilities: a crucial task in machine learning. In *Proc. ECAI 90*. Wiley, 1990.

[3] A. Karalič. Employing linear regression in regression tree leaves. In *Proceedings of the 10th European Conference on Artificial Intelligence*, pages 440–441. Wiley, 1992. Vienna, Austria.

[4] A. Makarovič. A qualitative way of solving the pole balancing problem. Technical Report Memorandum Inf-88-44, University of Twente, 1988. Also in: J. Hayes, D. Michie, E. Tyugu, editors, *Machine Intelligence 12*, pp. 241–258. Oxford University Press, 1991.

[5] D. Michie, M. Bain, and J. Hayes-Michie. Cognitive models from subcognitive skills. In M. Grimble, J. McGhee, and P. Mowforth, editors, *Knowledge-Based Systems in Industrial Control*, pages 71–90. Peter Peregrinus, 1990.

[6] D. Michie and R.A. Chambers. Boxes: an experiment in adaptive control. In E. Dale and D. Michie, editors, *Machine Intelligence 2*, pages 137–152. Edinburgh University Press, 1968.

[7] R. Quinlan. Combining instance-based and model-based learning. In *Proceedings of the 10th International Conference on Machine Learning*, pages 236–243. Morgan Kaufmann, 1993.

[8] C. Sammut, S. Hurst, D. Kedzier, and D. Michie. Learning to fly. In D. Sleeman and P. Edwards, editors, *Proceedings of the Ninth International Workshop on Machine Learning*, pages 385–393. Morgan Kaufmann, 1992.

[9] T. Urbančič and I. Bratko. Reconstructing human skill with machine learning. In A. Cohn, editor, *Proceedings of the 11th European Conference on Artificial Intelligence*, pages 498–502. John Wiley, 1994.

[10] D. Šuc and I. Bratko. Reconstructing control skill as LQ controllers with subgoals. In *Proc. IJCAI97*. Morgan Kaufmann, 1997. Yokohama, Japan.

[11] D. Šuc and I. Bratko. Skill modelling through symbolic reconstruction of operator's trajectories. In *Proc. IFAC Symposium Automated Systems Based on Human Skill*, pages 35–38, 1997. Kranjska Gora, Slovenia.

[12] A. Zalar. Machine learning of dynamic system control. B.Sc. Thesis, Faculty of Electrical Engineering and Computer Science, University of Ljubljana (in Slovenian), 1994.

8

Personalized mail agent using inductive logic programming

Fumio Mizoguchi and Hayato Ohwada

Science University of Tokyo,

Noda,

Chiba 278,

Japan

e-mail: {mizo,ohwada}@ia_noda.sut.ac.jp

Abstract

This paper describes an inductive logic programming method to design a personalized E-mail agent (PMAIL). In this approach, a profile is acquired from a user's mail, including characteristics such as category, priority and preference. After saving the user's mail handling behavior, PMAIL progressively produces logical rules that characterize new mails and provide the users with prior knowledge of the mail's character. Since these rules are comprehensive and readable, PMAIL has the advantage of explicit interaction for personal service. The competence of PMAIL depends upon the performance of the induced rules; therefore we have undertaken an empirical study which introduces a variety of performance measures, such as predictive accuracy. In this study, we show how PMAIL's learning parameters affect its performance and how induced rules are applied to enhance achieving its task. The present study indicates the expressive and potential power of inductive logic programming towards realizing personalized systems.

1 INTRODUCTION

Software tools or agents for personal use are essential with the increase of Internet-based work (e.g. e-mail handling, news reading, and WWW browsing) in business and at home. With the large amount of information being handled, interest is focused on personal work; in particular, filtering and classifying mail, news, and WWW pages. The key issue in the design of such an agent is learning ability, enabling customization and adaptability to the individual user. Fixed knowledge in an agent renders it unable to predict the user's activities in all situations. Recent attempts to design software agents have been devoted to personalizing existing tools by using machine learning techniques which allow the tools to capture the user's preferences and habits [1,2].

154

This paper proposes a personalized e-mail agent (PMAIL) which filters and classifies incoming mail. While similar mail agents have adopted memory-based reasoning [1] and propositional inductive learning [2], the learning method used in PMAIL is based on the framework of inductive logic programming (ILP), which introduces logic programming into inductive learning [5]. By utilizing first-order representation formalism and background knowledge, the present study experimentally investigates the expressiveness and potential of an ILP-based mail agent.

In the proposed method, a profile is acquired from the user's mail, including category, priority, and preference. After saving this user profile, PMAIL progressively produces logical rules that categorize new mail. These rules are used to provide users with prior knowledge of the mail. Since such rules are comprehensive and readable, PMAIL offers the advantage of explicit interaction for personal service.

We have developed the ILP system called GKS [4] as the learning system of PMAIL. A unique feature of GKS is handling both symbolic and numeric data, and producing first-order clauses with numerical constraints, such as linear constraints [3]. The competence of PMAIL depends on the performance of GKS, and therefore we have introduced a variety of performance measures into GKS, including predictive accuracy and other statistical parameters obtained from cross-validation. In this paper, we undertake an empirical study of PMAIL applicability by using these measures. Furthermore, through a number of experiments we show how PMAIL's learning parameters affect the performance and how the induced rules are applied to enhance achieving its task.

This paper is organized as follows. Section 2 describes the requirements for the personalizing mail agent. Section 3 presents the features and algorithm of the ILP system GKS. Section 4 describes the system structure of PMAIL and its implementation. Section 5 shows the performance of PMAIL through a number of experiments. Section 6 offers concluding remarks.

2 PERSONALIZING MAIL AGENT

2.1 Mail characterization

PMAIL is designed to be a personal mail agent which uses inductive learning. In general, inductive learning can be used for the personalization of a user's mail handling activities such as reading, transferring, classifying, etc. Among these activities, however, we focus on the classification task, which is the most personal characterization of received mail. These characterizations include category, priority, and preference, specified as follows:

Category   the folder in which the mail is classified
Priority   the importance level of the mail
Preference   whether the mail is preferred or not

These are used to filter and classify mail. For example, priority is an important factor in sorting a number of new messages, and category provides identification of mail messages for future use in mail databases.

155

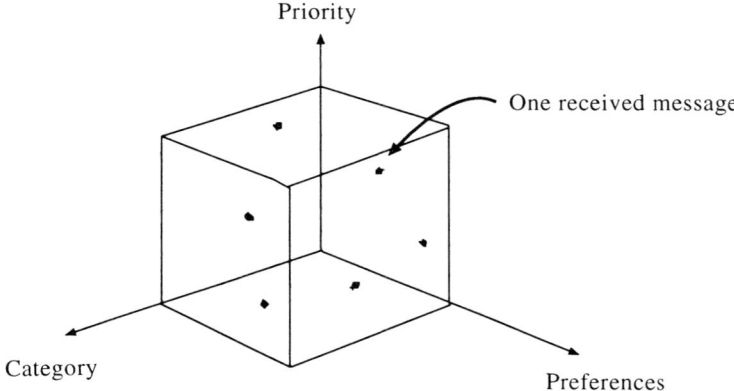

Figure 1. Multidimensional characterization of E-mail.

Figure 1 shows a multidimensional characterization of a received message. The mail is characterized within each dimension independently; in the figure the mail is located in 3-D space. Since such characterization is highly personalized, PMAIL learns logical rules for new mail characterization from the user's past characterization habits. Thus, the learning targets for PMAIL include category, priority, and preference.

In addition to the targets, PMAIL uses information in the mail header and message as background knowledge, containing the following:

Sender   the name of the mail sender
Domain   the sender's organization
Date   date when the mail was sent
Subject   the subject of the mail
Reply   whether the mail requires a reply or not
HasWord   keywords of the mail message

The information is extracted from simple text analysis and morphological analysis using a given dictionary. PMAIL produces mapping rules from such information for mail characterization.

2.2 Desiderata

The desired functions of PMAIL are summarized as follows:

- From repetitive interaction with users, PMAIL can identify the user's mail characterization patterns. These patterns are described as a logical formula which is readable and comprehensible to users—users can see and modify their own characterization rules.

- Since users habits are not constant, PMAIL progressively produces a revised version of mail characterization rules for adapting to unexpected situations. With the international nature of online documents passing through Internet, the variety of incoming mail should be handled by both users and an agent. Thus, PMAIL automatically customizes its knowledge in response to user's actions.

The first point indicates the necessity of an explanatory function allowing the agent to present the rules or processes of how the suggested characterizations are obtained. This is because of the agent's incomplete knowledge of the user's mail handling behavior. From a beginning user's viewpoint, this characterization is very accurate, and the mail handling task may be entirely committed to the agent without any explanation required. The ILP-based approach satisfies these requirements because ILP systems generate first-order clauses with a high predictive accuracy.

The second point indicates the incremental nature of the agent. If new mail can be classified as the user intends, no actions are required of the agent. Otherwise, the classification is wrong and treated as a negative example. In this case, PMAIL must learn new rules that differentiate the negative examples from a given set of positive examples.

Monitoring the interpretive state of the agent is one of the most important tasks for both the agent and user. This is a reliability problem related to accuracy and the explanatory function. A reliability measure should be provided to indicate the reliability of the agent. This measure is obtained from a combination of a variety of tests, including accuracy. In Section 5 we describe reasonable measures for reliability.

2.3 Performance task

Although predictive accuracy is widely used in the ILP community, we also utilize other measures to evaluate the performance of PMAIL. These measures are as follows:

Conflict For mail classification, we assume mutual exclusiveness; that there is only one folder in which to classify a message. Under this assumption, conflict occurs when there is more than one rule and the mail is classified into multiple folders. Such rules are viewed as overly general, and more specific rules are needed.

NoRule In contrast to conflict mode, this measure means that there is no rule to classify a message. This case may concern a pessimistic agent. If there is no clear evidence for mail classification, the agent takes no action. In this case, more general rules are needed.

In order to increase the performance based on these measures, PMAIL covers a spectrum from specific to general rules. Intuitively, more general rules are used, if specific rules prevent classification. We investigated the effect of this treatment through experiments described later.

3 INDUCING CHARACTERIZATION RULES

This section focuses on rule generation using GKS. It includes the input to GKS, the learning strategy of GKS, and the rules produced.

157

3.1 Input to the learning system GKS

The input to GKS includes positive examples, negative examples, and background knowledge. A positive example is expressed as a ground atom, while a negative example and background knowledge are described as Horn clauses (i.e. the Prolog program). Each predicate has modes and types. A mode is either input, output, or ground instantiations that are signed as '+', '−', and 'g' respectively. A type indicates the domain of a variable. For example, 'int' means integer domain and *real* denotes real number domain. Finite domains are also specified. Different modes and types allow GKS to produce different rules.

Figure 2 shows an input to GKS for mail characterization. The symbol '<=' indicates the target predicate to be learned, and '=>' specifies predicates for background knowledge. For an induced rule, the target predicate becomes the head part, and background knowledge constructs the body as a condition. To produce recursive rules, the target predicate is also included in the background knowledge.

By specifying input and output modes on variables, it is possible to construct a model where an atom is executable for getting information to be conveyed to other atoms via output variables. The information to be input is given as a query to the atom or as the computation result of other atoms. In the first case, the query puts the information on

```
% Declaration of Mode and Type
<= category(+mail,g).
=> received_from_domain(+mail,g).
=> received_from_user(+mail,g), received_from_user(+mail,-person).
=> member_of(+person,g).
=> subject(+mail,-subject).
=> in_word(+subject,g).
=> date(+mail,-int).
            :
% Background Knowledge
member_of(jo,s_agent).  member_of(khonda,s_agent).
            :
in_word(A,B) :- name(A,X), get_word(X,Y), name(B,Y).
            :
received_from_user('m113', jo).
            :
% Negative Examples
\+ category(A,B) :- B ## C, category(A,C).
            :
% Positive Examples
category('m113', s_agent).
            :
```

Figure 2. Input to GKS.

the input variable occurring in the head. If atom A is computationally meaningful, it is necessary to give information on all the input variables in A.

GKS allows users to specify multiple modes and types as shown in the predicate `received_from_user`. The first declaration specifies that the second argument becomes a ground term, while the second one is set to an output variable.

Note that the predicate `in_word(A,B)` is just a program which returns a set of words within the given sentence A. The variable B is instantiated to each word nondeterministically. For example, the goal `in_word (''This is a sentence'', B)` is solved with bindings B = This, B = is, etc.

Negative examples are specified as the form `\+ Head`. In Figure 2, negative examples are defined by a Prolog program, meaning the constraint that there are no messages folded to different categories. Here, the expression 'B ## C' specifies that the variables 'A' and 'B' are distinct. Since the atom 'category (A,C)' means that the category of the mail 'A' is 'C', '\+ category (A,B)' specifies that the negative example with meaning 'A' does not fall into any categories except 'B'.

Background knowledge is not necessarily fixed, and arbitrary knowledge can be specified as a Prolog program. In Figure 2 a group description is included through the predicate 'member_of(A,B)'. If the user's mail handling activities are dependent on groups or organizations, such descriptions may be needed.

The argument description '−int' is special in that the output variable uses an integer, and its value is constrained by a set of linear constraints. Such constraints are generated by the GKS learning algorithm shown below.

3.2 GKS learning strategy

A unique feature of the GKS learning strategy is combining 'top-down' and 'bottom-up' searches. The top-down search is used to produce the most preferable hypothesis based on given modes and types. The bottom-up search is employed for constraint generation.

- **Top-down search**

  GKS starts with the most general clause and adds literals until a certain condition is satisfied. The search strategy is characterized by an objective function and constraints. The objective function indicates the 'goodness' of a hypothesis. Intuitively, a good hypothesis covers as many positive examples as possible and as few negative examples as possible. In addition, a simpler hypothesis is preferable, based on a compression measure such as the minimum description length principle [7]. As an objective function, Progol adopted a linear combination between the number of positive and negative examples covered [6]. Since these numbers are inversely proportional, the function does not satisfy the monotonicity property of a hypothesis search. If a new literal is added and the resulting clause is specialized, it is generally impossible to say whether the function increases.

  To guarantee the monotonicity property, GKS supports the objective function of the number of positive examples (p) and the rule length (l); the negative examples are treated as constraints. More specifically, a top-down search is formulated as follows:

$$Objective\ function \quad Minimizing\ f(p,\ l)$$
$$Constraint \qquad g(n) \leq Err$$

where the function f is linearly combined with respect to p and l. The parameter Err indicates a user-specified permissible ratio of the negative examples covered.

- **Bottom-up search**
  A bottom-up search is employed for learning from numerical data. The top-down search is sufficient for logic programs on a Herbrand domain.

  A bottom-up search starts with a positive example. By focusing on a single example, a most specific hypothesis can be constructed using a top-down search. However, a most specific clause with constraints cannot be obtained from one example. Suppose that we have a geometric point in 2-D as a positive example. In this case, the most specific constraints construct four segments. However, if we have more than one point, more specific constraints can be generated.

  GKS increments positive examples until no more preferable hypotheses can be produced. GKS first focuses on one example and produces a hypothesis (h_1) using a top-down search. Then, adding a new example, GKS repeatedly produces another hypothesis (h_2), using a top-down search. If the compression measure of (h_2) is greater than that of h_1, this cycle repeats, adding other examples. Otherwise, GKS returns h_1, as the best hypothesis.

Figure 3 shows how the top-down and bottom-up searches are combined. The outer loop corresponds to the bottom-up search, handling a set of examples sequentially. The inner loop provides the top-down search to produce the most preferable hypothesis under a given set of examples. The stop criterion of the outer loop is whether all the positive examples are covered. For the inner loop, the search is terminated when the ratio of negative examples covered is less than the user-specified ratio.

3.3 Induced rules

As shown in the input example to GKS, it is possible to describe arbitrary background knowledge for mail classification. We categorize two types of background knowledge as follows:

- **Simple classification using header information**
  Header information such as the sender and subject provides a summary of a received mail message. One can often classify new mail using the header information. Since such classification is simple and efficient, it provides the first functionality of PMAIL. Header information can be obtained by simple string analysis for example, converting a sentence for the subject into a set of words. Also, sender identification is divided into the name part and the domain part. The same string analysis is used for checking whether the mail is a reply or not.

160

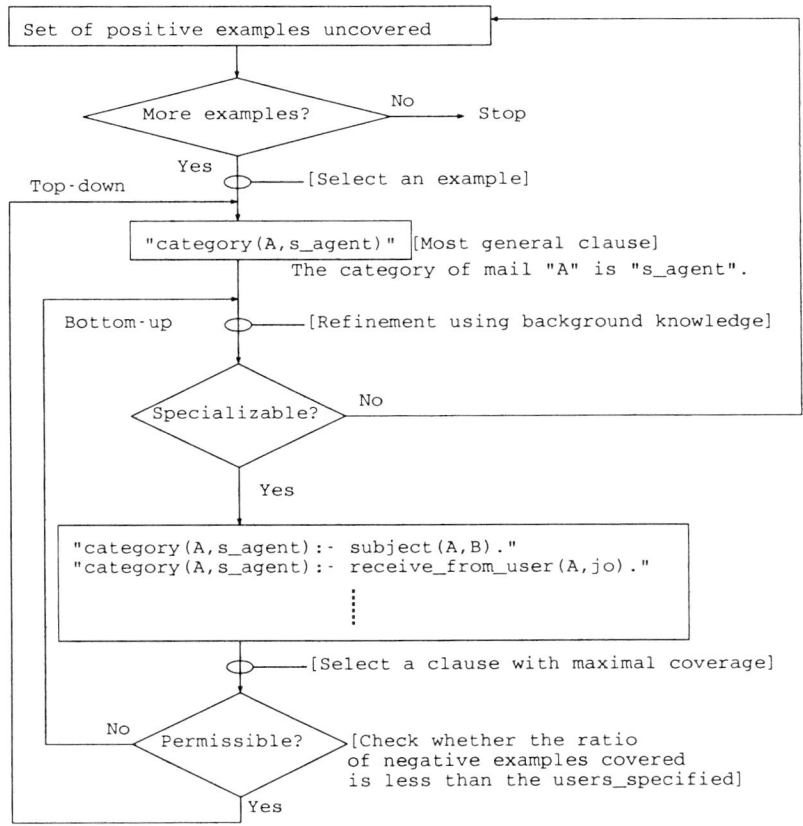

Figure 3. Combining top-down and bottom-up search.

We assume that a large part of mail classification falls into this simple classification. In particular, sender names and specific subjects play a central role in the category-based classification. The following rules are produced by GKS:

```
% {Pos = 27/97, Neg = 0/285}
category(A, misuzu) :-
     received_from_user(A, st27152).
%{ Pos = 4/51, Neg = 0/331}
category(A, s_agent) :-
     subject(A, B),
     received_from_user(A, C),
     in_word(B, from),
     member_of(C, s_agent).
```

161

For description

$$\{Pos = |E_h^+|/|E^+|, \ Neg = |E_h^-|/|E^-|\},$$

$|E^+|$ and $|E^-|$ denotes the total number of positive and negative examples. $|E_h^+|$ and $|E_h^-|$ indicates the total number of positive and negative examples that are covered by rule h. Here, rule h follows this description.

The first rule is a very simple case, and it represents the rule that mail from user 'st27152' is folded to the category 'misuzu'. The second rule is complicated, and is associated with four literals in the body. It represents the rule that the category of a mail is 's_agent' if the subject of the mail includes the word 'from' and the sender of the mail is a member of the group 's_agent'. Although these rules ignore mail messages, they are comprehensible to users.

- **Classification using keywords and time**
  Further classification using keywords in mail messages and the time the message was sent is worth investigating, because users may want to search the mail message both for mail identification and to classify business mail in the order received. Although the time the message was sent is obtained directly through a simple analysis of the mail message, keyword extraction is a complicated process. For this purpose, PMAIL provides a morphological analysis using a Japanese language dictionary, and uses keywords as background knowledge. Such keywords are asserted in the form 'has_word(MailID, Keyword)'. The following rule is a typical one produced by PMAIL:

```
% {Pos = 13/22, Neg = 0/617}
category(A, icot) :-
      received_from_domain(A, 'icot.or.jp'),
      has_word(A, '8&5f').
```

where the Japanese word '8&5f' means research. This rule means that all mail received from the domain 'icot.ot.jp' containing the word '8&5f' falls into the category 'icot'.

The following rule includes the date the mail was sent. The second argument of the predicate 'date' reveals the absolute order of the mail, yielding, for example, the constraint 'B>=1669'.

```
%{Pos = 13/14, Neg = 0/51}
category(A, work) :-
      received_from_user(A, ohwada),
      date(A, B),
      B >= 1669.
```

The relative order of the messages, such as 'after' or 'before' can be put as background knowledge, but the absolute order may be sufficient for personal mail classification. This is because relationships between personal messages can be described by the 'reply' predicate in most cases. The relative order could be useful for group mail classification.

Keywords and time-oriented classifications are somewhat complicated, and users may not understand why classification rules are produced from their own mail. In fact, there were meaningless keywords in the produced rules that successfully discriminated between positive examples and negative ones. In addition, it is hard to understand the meaning of a number obtained by absolute orderings. However, first-order representation clarifies comprehension, and machine-learned rules enhance the user's classification.

4 SYSTEM STRUCTURE

The structure of PMAIL is shown in Figure 4. The area enclosed by bold lines corresponds to PMAIL, and the other part indicates the input and output of PMAIL. In the figure, the rectangular blocks contain data, and the blocks with round edges are the PMAIL modules. Each module has the following functions:

- **Data extraction module**

  This module consists of a simple string analyzer and a morphological analyzer. The first one is written in Shell-script and Perl. Perl is used for a simple string analysis which extracts header information such as sender, subject, and date from received mail. After transferring a set of messages in the user's mailbox, the module outputs a table as a set of the triplet *<Attribute, MailID, Value>* where *Attribute* and *Value* are extracted from the associated header line.

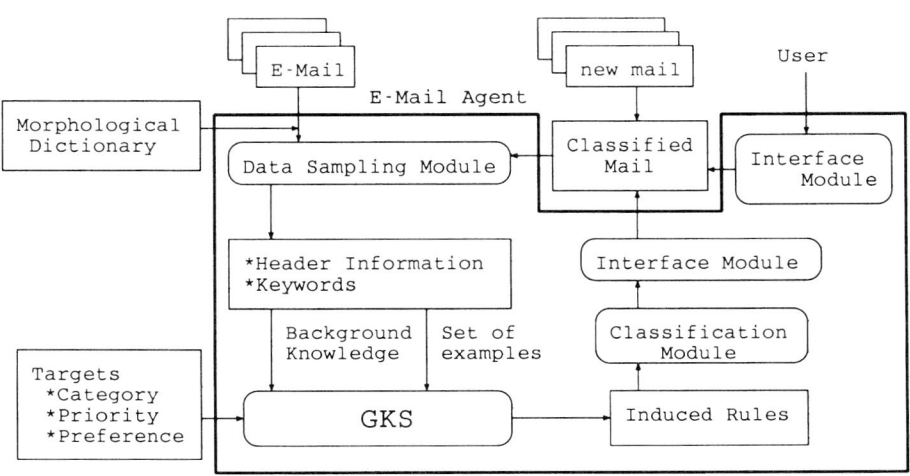

Figure 4. System structure of PMAIL.

For the morphological analysis, we used the TRIE morphological dictionary, an ICOT free software. The original dictionary consists of 150 000 words with a classification code about morphemes. The morphological analyzer is a syllablication program which divides input texts into morphological particles. The divided texts are written in the same tabular format as the one mentioned above.

- **GKS**

GKS is implemented in a Prolog family including Eclipse and Sicstus Prolog. As a stand-alone system, it connects to PMAIL through socket communication. PMAIL invokes GKS by a remote shell and translates tabular data to binary predicate assertions (i.e. *attribute(MailID, Value)*) that are accessible by GKS. GKS takes as input these assertions and the predefined relationships shown in Figure 2, and induces characterization rules with respect to category, priority, and preference. The induced rules are in the form of Prolog syntax, and are used for performance tasks in PMAIL.

- **Classification module**

This module is a very simple program written in Prolog. Its main part is defined as follows:

```
classify_category(ID,F) :-
  findall(X, category(ID, X),S),
  ( S == [] -> F = "NO-RULE" ;
    S = [A] -> F = A ;
    F = "CONFLICT" ).
```

where the predicate 'classify_category (ID, F)' identifies the category of a given mail 'ID'. The predicate 'findall (X, Pred, S)' is an all-solution predicate for 'Pred' and the variable 'S' is the list of all solutions of 'X'. Thus, by invoking the goal 'category(ID,X)', all rules are applied for mail categorization. If there is no such rule, the above clause returns the message 'NO-RULE'. If there is only one category, the mail falls into this unique category. Otherwise, the mail has different categories, yielding the message 'CONFLICT'. Although the real module is more complicated in dealing with parameters associated with rules, the above program illustrates the essential aspects of the classification module.

- **Interface module**

The output image of this module is similar to the commercial mail agent, Eudora. As shown in Figure 5, the module uses a spreadsheet-like system where each item can be selected using a mouse. The three items on the right side denote category, priority, and preference. The results of the classification module applying the induced rules are displayed at each item. If the result is not satisfactory to users, it is possible to update their intended values. Otherwise, no action is needed.

The module is mainly implemented in TCL/TK, and is composed of 1000 lines. Included functions are mail reading, sending, and saving, which are sufficient for a real mail system.

164

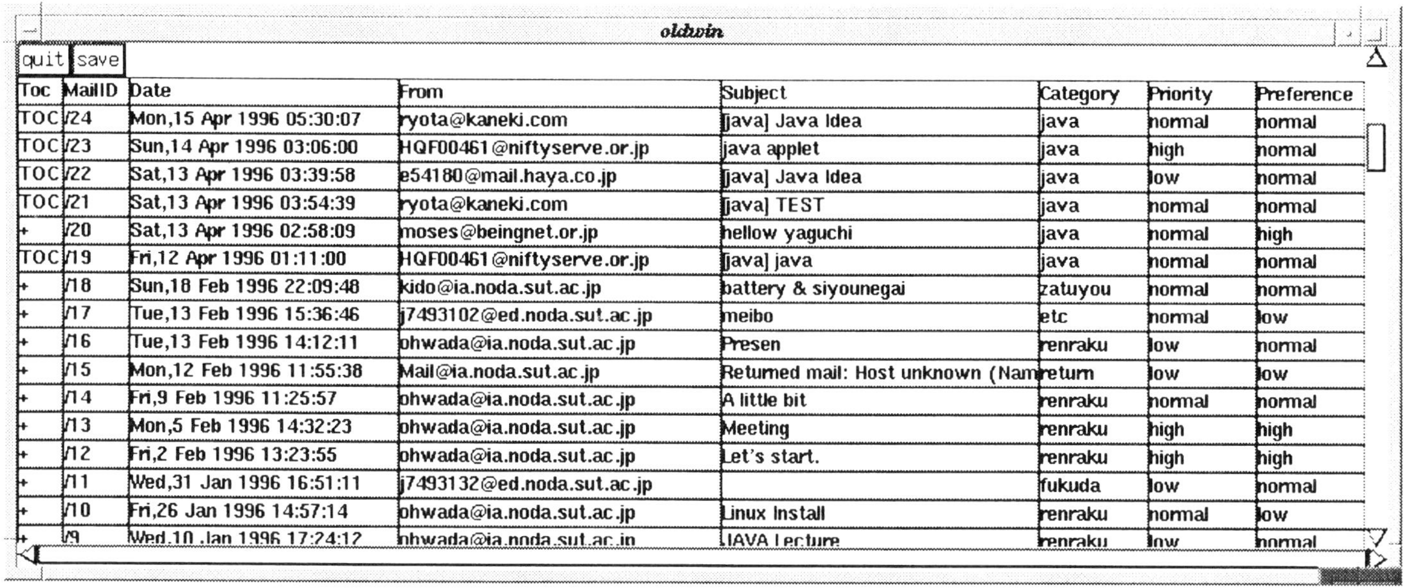

oicbwin

quit save

Toc	MailID	Date	From	Subject	Category	Priority	Preference
TOC	/24	Mon,15 Apr 1996 05:30:07	ryota@kaneki.com	[java] Java Idea	java	normal	normal
TOC	/23	Sun,14 Apr 1996 03:06:00	HQF00461@niftyserve.or.jp	java applet	java	high	normal
TOC	/22	Sat,13 Apr 1996 03:39:58	a5-4180@mail.haya.co.jp	[java] Java Idea	java	low	normal
TOC	/21	Sat,13 Apr 1996 03:54:39	ryota@kaneki.com	[java] TEST	java	normal	normal
+	/20	Sat,13 Apr 1996 02:58:09	moses@beingnet.or.jp	hellow yaguchi	java	normal	high
TOC	/19	Fri,12 Apr 1996 01:11:00	HQF00461@niftyserve.or.jp	[java] java	java	normal	normal
+	/18	Sun,18 Feb 1996 22:09:48	kido@ia.noda.sut.ac.jp	battery & siyounegai	zatuyou	normal	normal
+	/17	Tue,13 Feb 1996 15:36:46	j7493102@ed.noda.sut.ac.jp	meibo	etc	normal	low
+	/16	Tue,13 Feb 1996 14:12:11	ohwada@ia.noda.sut.ac.jp	Presen	renraku	low	normal
+	/15	Mon,12 Feb 1996 11:55:38	Mail@ia.noda.sut.ac.jp	Returned mail: Host unknown (Name return	return	low	low
+	/14	Fri,9 Feb 1996 11:25:57	ohwada@ia.noda.sut.ac.jp	A little bit	renraku	normal	normal
+	/13	Mon,5 Feb 1996 14:32:23	ohwada@ia.noda.sut.ac.jp	Meeting	renraku	high	high
+	/12	Fri,2 Feb 1996 13:23:55	ohwada@ia.noda.sut.ac.jp	Let's start.	renraku	high	high
+	/11	Wed,31 Jan 1996 16:51:11	j7493132@ed.noda.sut.ac.jp		fukuda	low	normal
+	/10	Fri,26 Jan 1996 14:57:14	ohwada@ia.noda.sut.ac.jp	Linux Install	renraku	normal	low
+	/9	Wed,10 Jan 1996 17:24:17	ohwada@ia.noda.sut.ac.in	JAVA Lecture	renraku	low	normal

Figure 5. Output of interface module.

5 EXPERIMENTS

This section shows how much the predictable induced rules use the cross-validation method, which is similar to the resampling methods of statistics. Given a set of messages, k-fold cross-validation divides the set into k mutually exclusive test partitions of approximately equal size [8]. In this setting, the remaining mail, excluding each partition, is used as a training set, and the partition is tested for estimating performance measures of the underlying learning system. Such measures are taken from [8] and are shown in Appendix B. Although predictive accuracy is widely used in the ILP community, we also pay attention to 'sensitivity': how many true hypotheses are covered by the induced rules. For example, a medical diagnosis requires high sensitivity, i.e. very few false negatives. However, sensitivity tends to cover more negative examples, and thus accuracy decreases.

GKS allows users to specify the permissible ratio of negative examples covered. The performance of the induced rules depends upon this ratio, and we investigated what ratio is reasonable considering sensitivity and accuracy. For this purpose, we set up the three experiments described below.

5.1 Experiment on performance transition

The first experiment divides accumulated mail into partitions in the order received, and investigates how to change the accuracy and sensitivity of the time sequence. Material was selected from the second author's mail and consisted of 764 messages from 6 months (April–October 1995). Each partitioned set had 40 messages, and GKS progressively produced characterization rules for each accumulated partition, where 10-fold cross-validation was done for each learning phase. Figure 6 illustrates this experiment. The application to the real mail set was done by a third experiment, as described later.

Figures 7 and 8 show the results of the priority-based classification in which priority is categorized as 'High', 'Normal' and 'Low'. Three permissible ratios (0%, 3% and 5%) of the negative examples covered were selected. In Figure 7, each transition graph is shown with the corresponding default accuracy. Here, each default accuracy is obtained

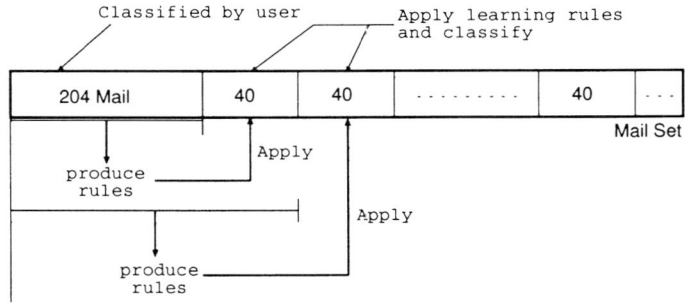

Figure 6. Accumulated mail classification.

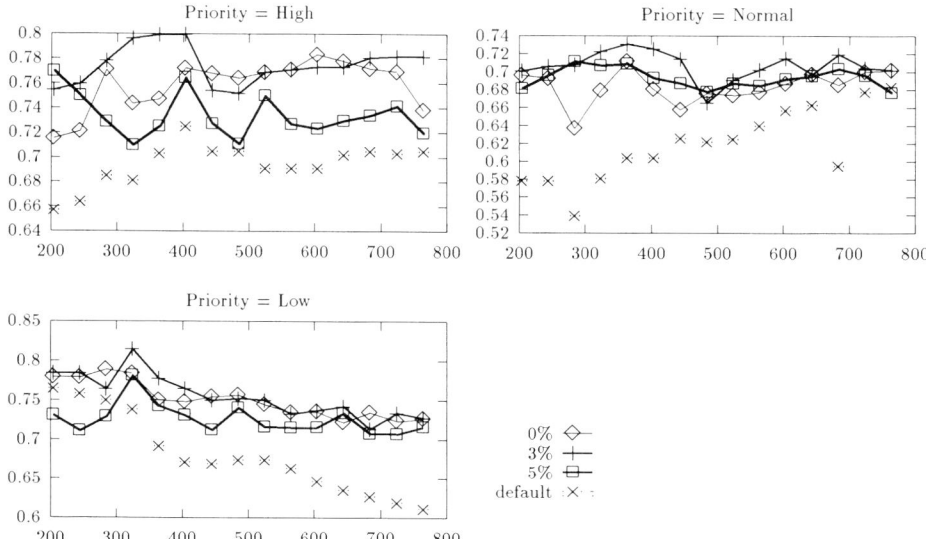

Figure 7. Accuracy of priority classification.

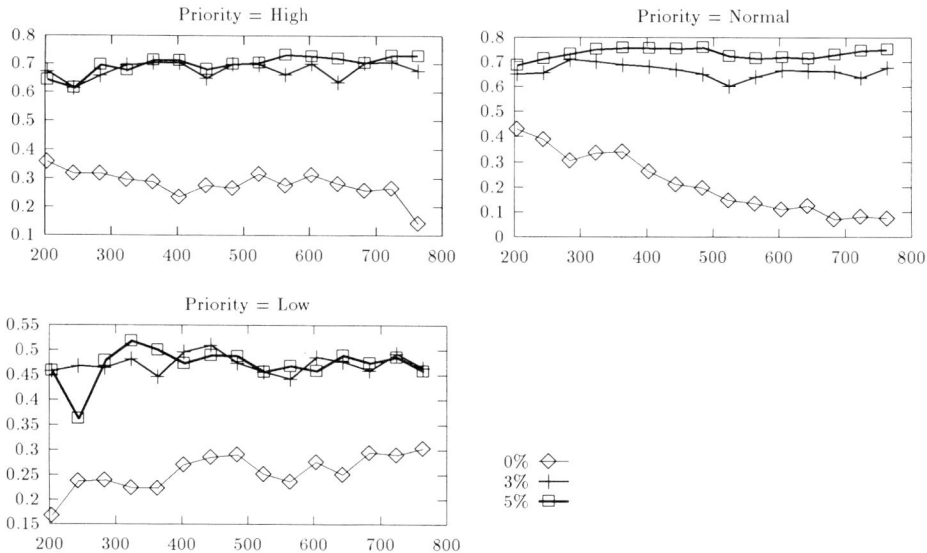

Figure 8. Sensitivity of priority classification.

by applying a single-function classifier, which always classifies any mail to a fixed category. Since the number of negative examples is greater than positive examples, this classifier accepts any mail as negative. Thus, default accuracy is defined as the ratio of negative examples.

The results are summarized as follows:

- In most cases, predictive accuracy is higher than default accuracy.

- Each predictive accuracy and default accuracy progress in the same direction. For example, the accuracy of the priority 'Low' slightly decreases according to the change of the default accuracy.

- There is no difference in the accuracy of the three permissible ratios.

- In contrast to the predictive accuracy, the sensitivity of the 0% ratio is much lower than that of 3% and 5%.

The first point does not indicate the advantage of the learning system, because cases still exist in which default accuracy is higher. The last point says that setting a 0% ratio may not be effective; there are many messages not belonging to any priorities. However, this problem is not serious, as demonstrated in the subsequent section where PMAIL performance was investigated using real mail.

Figures 9 and 10 show the results of the category-based classification. Since new mail had arrived, the number of categories increased. For the target mail set, there were 18 folders at the initial stage and eventually 28 folders were created by the user. An

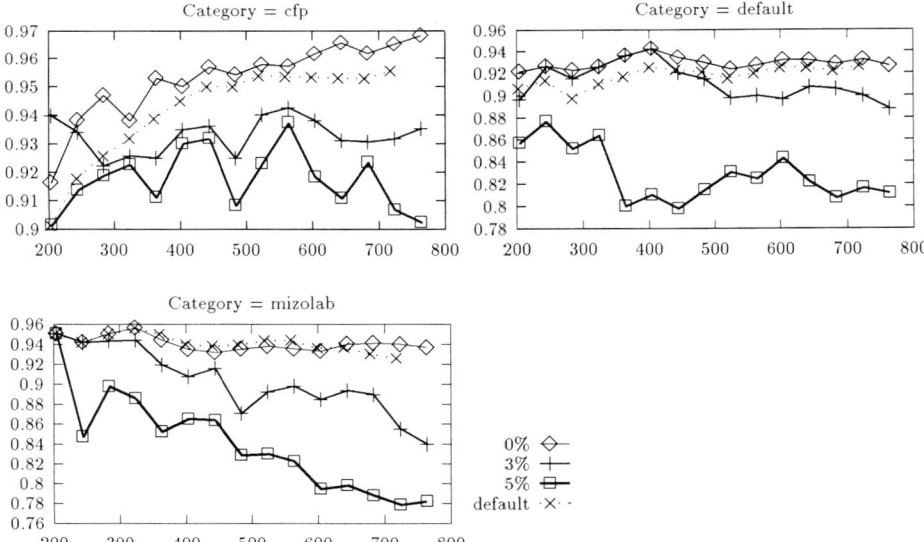

Figure 9. Accuracy of category classification.

168

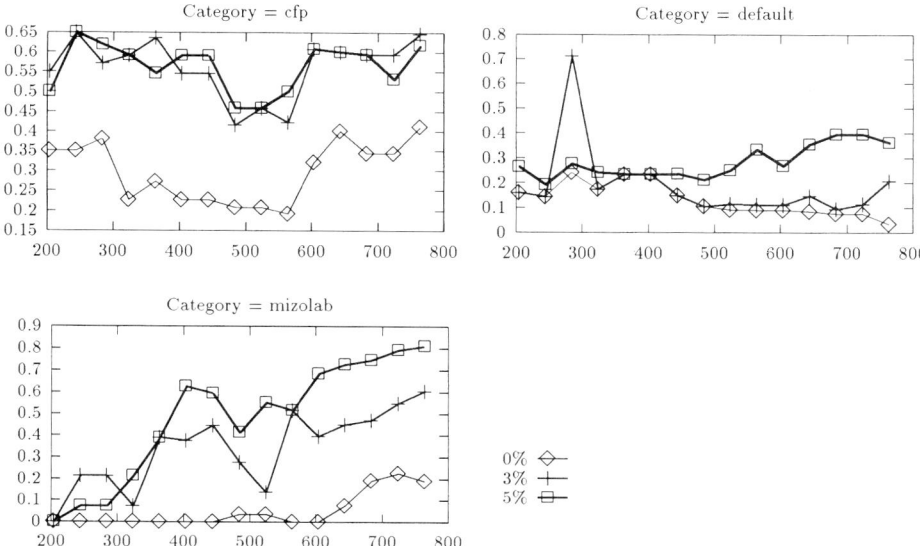

Figure 10. Sensitivity of category classification.

important point is the existence of so many categories. This leads to a larger number of negative examples than positive examples. Suppose that we put an equal number of messages in each folder. If there are 28 folders, default accuracy becomes 27/28 (= 96%). This requires a very high predictive accuracy from PMAIL.

Among the 28 folders, these figures contain the typical folders, 'cfp' (call for papers), 'default' and 'mizolab' (our laboratory). The first folder has an increasing amount of mail in comparison with the other folders.

The result is summarized as follows:

- The predictive accuracy of only the 0% permissible ratio is superior to the default accuracy.

- However, the sensitivity of the 0% permissible ratio is very low (from 0% to 40%).

- For the category 'mizolab', the predictive accuracy decreases, but the sensitivity increased at both 3% and 5%.

The first point is due to the larger number of folders, and only 0% learning is effective. In contrast, 0% learning may not be useful for classifying mail, because few messages fall into appropriate categories as well as the priority-based classification. This tradeoff is also evident in the last point where predictive accuracy and sensitivity proceed in opposite directions.

169

5.2 Comparison with various background knowledge

The second experiment was done on a collection of students' mail. The following three types of background knowledge were provided:

Type A including simple header information;

Type B including simple header information and keywords;

Type C including simple header information, keywords, and date.

Each performance was measured by using 10-fold cross-validation, setting a 0% permissible ratio. Tables 1 and 2 show the value of (Predictive Accuracy − Default Accuracy) and the sensitivity.

The progression of background knowledge leads to a larger hypothesis space. If the learning system employs an exhaustive search, better classification rules are obtained in the progression. Although GKS supports an admissible search based on A* algorithm, the performance of the obtained rules is dependent upon how relevant the background knowledge is.

The result for predictive accuracy is summarized as follows:

- For subjects having high predictive accuracy (e.g. S_5, S_6 and S_7), each accuracy increases with the progression of background knowledge.

- For the category-based classification, there are lower accuracies than the corresponding default accuracy, although their priorities and preferences are high. This is because the default accuracy is very high (95%).

- There is a similar tendency between the accuracies of the priority-based and preference-based classifications. The subjects from S_4 and S_7 can be grouped for both priority and preference.

Table 1. Predictive accuracy − Default accuracy.

Subject	Priority				Category				Preference			
	A	B	C	Ave.	A	B	C	Ave.	A	B	C	Ave.
S_1	0.03	0.00	0.00	0.01	0.05	0.05	−0.05	0.02	0.05	0.05	−0.11	0.00
S_2	0.03	0.04	0.03	0.03	−0.07	−0.05	−0.02	−0.05*	0.07	0.09	0.09	0.08
S_3	0.06	0.07	0.04	0.06	−0.03	−0.03	−0.04	−0.03*	0.01	0.02	0.08	0.04
S_4	0.05	0.13	0.07	0.08	−0.02	0.01	0.00	0.00	0.02	0.17	0.14	0.11
S_5	0.06	0.08	0.14	0.09	−0.05	−0.05	−0.01	−0.04*	0.09	0.11	0.15	0.12
S_6	0.09	0.12	0.22	0.14	−0.08	−0.06	−0.01	−0.05*	0.06	0.10	0.17	0.11
S_7	0.16	0.17	0.14	0.16	0.05	0.05	0.07	0.06	0.13	0.10	0.13	0.12

*Default accuracy = 95%
A = simple header information
B = A + keyword
C = B + date
Ave. = (A + B + C)/3

Table 2. Sensitivity.

Subject	Priority				Category				Preference			
	A	B	C	Ave.	A	B	C	Ave.	A	B	C	Ave.
S_1	0.15	0.17	0.35	0.22	0.69	0.69	0.63	0.67	0.37	0.37	0.30	0.35
S_6	0.18	0.23	0.45	0.29	0.15	0.28	0.71	0.38	0.12	0.26	0.43	0.27
S_4	0.23	0.36	0.33	0.31	0.41	0.55	0.55	0.50	0.20	0.57	0.53	0.43
S_3	0.31	0.38	0.40	0.36	0.32	0.40	0.40	0.37	0.36	0.36	0.56	0.43
S_2	0.41	0.44	0.49	0.45	0.33	0.43	0.62	0.46	0.30	0.32	0.39	0.34
S_5	0.40	0.45	0.56	0.47	0.48	0.53	0.69	0.57	0.41	0.47	0.54	0.47
S_7	0.56	0.65	0.60	0.60	0.90	0.90	0.90	0.90	0.59	0.52	0.61	0.57

For sensitivity, the following interpretation can be obtained:

- For most cases, each sensitivity increases according to the progression of background knowledge. Exceptional cases are S_1 and S_7 which have the worst and the best results.
- The subject S_7 has the highest predictive accuracy and sensitivity, yielding the best learning performance.
- The subject S_1 has high sensitivity for the category-based classification, but has low sensitivity for priority and preference.
- The sensitivity of the subject S_6 drastically increased with the progression of background knowledge.

This interpretation indicates that the performance of the produced rules is strongly dependent upon the user's mail characterization. However, meaningful keywords should be extracted to increase the relevance of the background knowledge, which includes the keywords. Since the usefulness of the extracted keywords is attributed to a given morphological dictionary, the dictionary should be sufficiently elaborate for mail characterization. The time the mail is received is somewhat a factor in discriminating positive examples from negative ones. The produced rules, however, decrease their comprehensibility. Incorporating numerical data into ILP should be carefully considered in light of the tradeoff between the statistical performance and the comprehensibility of the rules.

5.3 PMAIL performance

The purpose of the third experiment was to show how much of PMAIL's actions are based on the induced rules. As mentioned in Section 2 there are three results of its actions: 'Success', 'Conflict', and 'NoRule'. 'Conflict' is caused by general rules, while a 'NoRule' error occurs when using specific rules. The permissible ratio of the negative examples covered asserts a strong influence on the generation of a variety of rules. PMAIL constructs a spectrum from specific to general rules, and controls what rules should be applied. The control adopted in the PMAIL classification module is simple: general rules are applied if there are no specific rules to classify incoming mail into any specific folder.

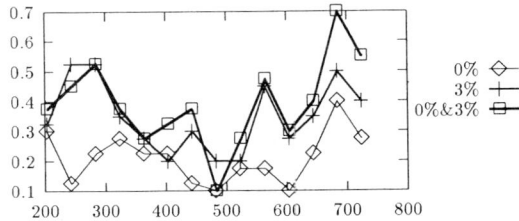

Figure 11. Accuracy of agent's actions for priority classification.

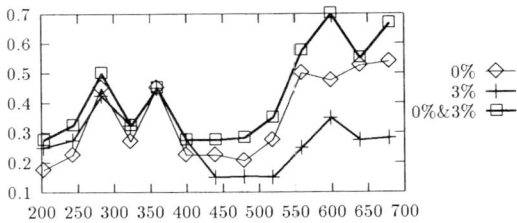

Figure 12. Accuracy of agent's actions for category classification.

Figures 11 and 12 show the results of applying the rules of 0% and 3%, and mixing these ratios to a set of real incoming mail. In these figures, accuracy is defined as the formula *Success Mail/Total Mail*. The figures lead to the following interpretation:

- For priority-based classification, the performance of the 3% rule is comparable to that of the mixing method.

- For category-based classification, the mixing method has the advantage of using both the 0% and 3% rules.

Based on the above interpretation, the mixing method used in PMAIL provides a powerful approach to mail agents. Although the method is simple and straightforward, it is a natural and comprehensive program for personal service. This is due to the expressive and potential power of inductive logic programming in the design of agent-oriented personalized systems.

6 CONCLUDING REMARKS

In this paper, a personalized mail agent (PMAIL) using inductive logic programming was designed and implemented, and the learning system GKS was introduced into PMAIL. PMAIL progressively produces logical rules to automatically classify incoming mail. A variety of experiments were done to clarify the performance of PMAIL. In particular, statistical measures such as predictive accuracy and sensitivity were demonstrated with a variety of parameter settings.

The present study focuses on the learning ability of PMAIL. However, the interface portion of PMAIL needs attention in regard to the learning facility of PMAIL. Along these lines, the interpretation state of PMAIL should be expressed within PMAIL functionality. Future work includes incorporating an autonomous nature into PMAIL.

APPENDIX A: LEARNING ALGORITHM

In the algorithm, 'compression' means the objective function. $\rho(SUB)$ produces rules that explain a set of positive examples (SUB). $Specialize(c, SUB)$ produces a set of constraints on SUB and also a set of mode-consistent literals. $\rho(SUB)$ employs top–down search until the search constraint is satisfied.

The algorithm does not specify how to select positive examples. For example, a greedy algorithm should be used for producing good rules under given sample size. GKS repeatedly generalizes examples in the user-specified order for getting the efficiency.

APPENDIX B: LEARNING TIME (IN SEC.)

Data set	$|E^+|$	$|E^-|$	$|B|$	Progol	GKS
animals	16	6	105	0.183	0.090
arch	4	4	17	0.149	0.083
krki	341	655	51	17.281	7.500
train	5	5	257	0.100	0.083

APPENDIX C: PERFORMANCE MEASURE

	Rule Positive(R^+)	Rule Negative(R^-)
Hypothesis Positive(H^+)	True Positive(TP)	False Negative(FN)
Hypothesis Negative(H^-)	False Positive(FP)	True Negative(TN)

Sensitivity	$= TP/H^+$
Specificity	$= TN/H^-$
Predictive value$(+)$	$= TP/R^+$
Predictive value$(-)$	$= TN/R^-$
Accuracy	$= (TP + TN)/((H^+) + (H^-))$

1. Let E^+ and B be positive examples and background knowledge.
2. $LEFT := E^+$, $SUB := \phi$, $CS := \phi$.
3. If $LEFT = \phi$, then return CS.
4. Let e be the first element in $LEFT$.
5. $LEFT := LEFT - \{e\}$.
8. $M' := greedy(e, LEFT, \{e\})$.
9. $CS := \{M'\} \cup CS$.
10. $LEFT := LEFT - \{e' \in LEFT \mid M' \wedge B \vdash e'\}$.
11. Go to 3.

FUNCTION $greedy(M, LEFT, SUB)$
    If $LEFT = \phi$, then return M.
    Let e be the first element in $LEFT$.
    $LEFT := LEFT - \{e\}$.
    $M' := mcc(\{e\} \cup SUB)$.
    If M' has greater compression than M, then
        return $greedy(M', LEFT, \{e\} \cup SUB)$.
    Otherwise return $greedy(M, LEFT, SUB)$.

FUNCTION $mcc(SUB)$
    Let c be a most general clause.
    $S := \{c\}$ and $S' := S - \{c\}$.
    DO
        Find c which has a maximal compression in S.
        If $terminated(c)$, then return c.
        Let $S := \{c \vee \neg l \mid l \in mpc(c, SUB)\} \cup S'$.
        If $S = \phi$, then return false.
    WHILE true.

FUNCTION $mpc(c, SUB)$
    $L := \{l \mid l$ is a new mode-consistent literal produced by
        variables in c and background knowledge $\}$.
    $S := \{s \mid s$ is a least general constraint set
        on variables in c with respect to $SUB\}$.
    Return $L \cup S$.

Figure 13. Learning algorithm.

174

REFERENCES

[1] Maes, P., Agents that Reduce Work and Information Overload, *Communications of ACM*, Vol. 37, No. 7, pp. 31–40, 1994.

[2] Mitchell, T., Caruana, R., Freitag, D., McDermott, J. and Zabowski, D., Experience with a Learning Personal Assistant, *Communications of ACM*, Vol. 37, No. 7, pp. 81–91, 1994.

[3] Mizoguchi, F. and Ohwada, H., Constrained Relative Least General Generalization for Inducing Constraint Logic Programs, *New Generation Computing*, Vol. 13, Nos. 3, 4, pp. 335–368, 1995.

[4] Mizoguchi, F. and Ohwada, H., Using Inductive Logic Programming for Constraint Acquisition in Constraint-based Problem Solving! *Proc. of the 5th International Workshop on Inductive Logic Programming*, pp. 297–322, Technical Report, Katholieke Universiteit, Leuven, 1995.

[5] Muggleton, S., Inductive Logic Programming, *New Generation Computing*, Vol. 8, No. 4, pp. 295–318, 1991.

[6] Muggleton, S., Inverse Entailment and Progol, *New Generation Computing*, Vol. 13, Nos. 3, 4, pp. 245–286, 1995.

[7] Rissanen, J., Modeling by Shortest Data Description, *Automatica*, Vol. 14, pp. 465–471, 1978.

[8] Weiss, S. M., Galen, R. S. and Tadepalli, P., Maximizing the Predictive Value of Production Rules, *Artificial Intelligence*, Vol. 45, pp. 47–71, 1990.

9

An experiment with browsers that learn

Rupert Parson and Stephen Muggleton

Oxford University Computing Laboratory,
Parks Road,
Oxford
UK

Abstract

World Wide Web (WWW) usage is increasing rapidly. Users waste time downloading pages that turn out to have no interest to them. Interesting pages are often overlooked. Modern browsers allow the user to specify search strings. This paper experimentally investigates a different approach based on learning user WWW pages preferences from examples. WWW users were drawn from a class of students. The experiments show that the inductive logic programming algorithm Progol gives overall significant predictive accuracy of user interests. However, the results are highly polarized. Some users are very predictable and others not. The polarization was surprisingly found to correlate in all cases with student exam performance. This work was conducted as part of Parson's MSc thesis [7].

1 INTRODUCTION

The rapid growth of the World Wide Web (WWW) is producing requirements for new types of user interface. The available information of potential interest to a particular user is vast. However, it is likely to be distributed sparsely over the network. Some artificial intelligence researchers have advocated the use of 'software agents' [2] which search for interesting data. These agents can also work in groups. This requires a high-level communication language. Such a language needs to be sufficiently expressive. The inclusion of the user as an agent in the group adds the requirement that the language should be easily comprehended by humans. Genesereth [2] argues for the use of a variant of first-order predicate calculus. In the present paper the representation language used is that of definite clause logic programs.

An agent's knowledge of user interests can be captured in various ways. One way might be to ask a user to give a complete and correct specification of their interests. This is likely to be a long-winded and error prone process. Also user interest is often sparked by finding new information. An alternative approach is investigated in this paper.

We suppose that users are asked if a WWW page was interesting on exit from viewing the page. The inductive logic programming (ILP) [6] system Progol [4] is used to learn rules describing pages of interest to users. This approach was tested experimentally using six users on a sample of 50 WWW pages.

The paper is arranged as follows. Section 2 describes the materials used in the experiment. The experimental method is explained in Section 3. Results are given in Section 4 and discussed in Section 5.

2 MATERIALS

2.1 The subjects

The subjects that volunteered to partake in this experiment were all MSc students at the Oxford University Computing Laboratory. This meant that they were all experienced users of the World Wide Web. They were also familiar with the domain from which the Web pages were taken.

This familiarity ensured an important factor – the users could understand and analyze the page content, and therefore they could say whether or not they were interested in a particular page.

2.2 The Web pages

Fifty pages were downloaded by following links from the Oxford University Computing Laboratory's home page. The pages were downloaded using an automated breadth-first approach. This ensured a selection of pages that was clean of any bias that a human might unwittingly impose when selecting the pages. This approach also ensured that there was a certain degree of hypertext linkage between the pages.

Because the pages were all in close link-proximity to the Computing Laboratory's home page, there was an obvious implicit theme of computer science. This fact does not affect the validity of the results since the users were still able to classify them into distinct categories of interesting and not interesting.

2.3 Background knowledge

The training examples presented to the ILP algorithm Progol were expressed in the form `interested(joe, page1)`. The web page content was then provided in the form of background knowledge about the web pages.

2.3.1 Web page background knowledge

As part of the background knowledge, the following information was given to the learning algorithm.

- The words contained in the documents.
  `has_word(page1, 'computer')`.
- The URL of each document.
  `address(page1, 'http://www.comlab.ox.ac.uk/index.html')`.

- The Hyper-links of the documents.
  `connected(page1, page2).`

This representation of the pages loses a certain amount of information. For instance, any information about the ordering of the words has been lost, along with the entailed semantic meaning implicit in this ordering.

2.3.2 WordNet

WordNet [3] is an on-line lexical reference system whose design is inspired by current psycholinguistic theories of human lexical memory.

The starting point for lexical semantics can be said to be the mapping between word forms and meanings. The mappings between forms and meanings are many to many – some forms have several different meanings, and some meanings can be expressed by several different forms. These two complementary types of mapping are known as *polysemy* and *synonymy*, respectively.

In WordNet, English nouns, verbs, and adjectives are organized into synonym sets, each representing one underlying lexical concept. These sets are the partition of the set of words under the synonym equivalence relation.

WordNet has a number of useful relations that link these sets. In particular, the *hypernym* relation.

Unlike synonymy which is a lexical relation between word forms, hypernymy is a semantic relation between word meanings. A concept represented by the synonym set $\{x, x', \dots\}$ is said to be a hypernym of synonym set $\{y, y', \dots\}$, if native speakers of English would accept sentences of the form:

A y is a kind of x.

Hence, *plant* is a hypernym of *tree*, and *tree* is a hypernym of *maple*.

The hypernym relation was used in this experiment to attempt to draw a *semantic context* or *theme* from the Web pages. A new predicate `hypernym/2` was added to the background knowledge. This gave hypernyms for every word found on the example Web pages (i.e. `hypernym('tree', 'plant').`).

2.4 Preprocessing

In order to avoid unnecessary delays in the experiment, some preprocessing was conducted in advance of the learning.

The 50 pages used were downloaded in advance, and cached. In doing so, any indirect or relative hypertext links were converted to full http addresses. This ensured that no connections between web pages was missed.

A simple html parser was built into the ILP system Progol to provide the new predicates `has_word/2` and `connected/2` (see Section 2.3.1 above). These were defined as primitives in the C code for Progol. It was then possible to use these primitives to parse the html documents during the learning process.

However the file access required for this slowed down the learning process excessively, and so the primitives were run on the files in advance, and the results cached to a file.

This then allowed the preprocessing of the WordNet lexical database on the Web page content, to predefine the predicate hypernym/2 (see Section 2.3.2).

3 METHODS

3.1 The classification procedure

The Web pages were presented to the users as a linked set of pages. However, they were actually being shown pages from the local cache. The users were asked to classify the pages according to the following rules:

- All 50 pages must be classified in one sitting. This ensured that the user was in a consistent 'mood' throughout the period of page classification. It is clear that users' interests may change, and that on one day they might be more likely to classify a page as interesting than on another day. It was important to eliminate as much as possible the effect of such phenomena. The users were asked to be as consistent as possible in their criteria for selecting a page as *interesting* or as *not interesting*.

- The user was forced to classify each page into one of two classifications: *interesting* and *not interesting*. This was anathema to some of the subjects, who appeared to be ambivalent to a few of the pages.

The users' classifications were noted and then used as the examples. The next Section 3.2 explains how they were used.

3.2 Testing the accuracy of Progol

To analyze the predictive accuracy of a machine learning algorithm on a particular domain, the standard method is to split the classified examples into two sets, training data and testing data.

However, with only 50 examples, such a method is not statistically reliable. The effects of noise and other random error sources can effect the results significantly.

Therefore a more robust statistical device known as leave-one-out cross-validation was used. This method proceeds as follows:

Assume we have a set of *n* training examples.

- Take one of the examples out of the training set, as the test example.
- Apply the learning algorithm to the remaining examples.
- Use the derived rules to predict the interest value of the test example.
- Compare the result with the actual value.
- Perform the process *n* times, once for each of the examples.

The results can then be expressed in a contingency table (Table 1).

- *A* represents the Actually interesting pages.
- *P* represents the Predicted interesting pages.

Table 1. A contingency table.

	A	$\bar{A}$	
P	a	b	$(a+b)$
$\bar{P}$	c	d	$(c+d)$
	$(a+c)$	$(b+d)$	50

- a is the frequency of pages that were *interesting* and were predicted *interesting*.
- b is the frequency of pages that were not *interesting*, but were predicted *interesting*.
- c is the frequency of pages that were *interesting*, but were predicted not *interesting*.
- d is the frequency of pages that were not *interesting*, and were predicted not *interesting*.

Results in this form are evaluated using a χ^2 test, giving a statistical measure of the significance of the results. For a result to be significant, the associated χ^2 probability needs to be less than 0.05 (significance at the 5% level.)

4 RESULTS

Table 2 shows the results of the experiment. The figures indicate a clear division of the subjects into the predictable and the unpredictable. The predictable students are in the lower half of the table. As one might expect, Progol has learned smaller theories, with shorter learning times, for the predictable students. Progol has achieved more compression in these cases.

4.1 Pooled results for predictable subjects

Pooling the results for the predictable subjects shows clearly the strong performance of Progol for the students that give generalizable classifications (see Table 3). The χ^2 probability is extremely small for such a result to occur by chance, implying a highly significant result.

4.2 Example rule sets

It is informative to inspect the rules generated by Progol. More importantly, it is vital to ask the students to give their approval of the rules produced.

The advantage of a learning algorithm that produces easily comprehensible rules is obvious in this agent-orientated setting. An agent's representation of its user should be open to inspection and validation by the user. An intelligent agent with incomprehensible, and therefore unverifiable rules, is undesirable in the case when the agent is acting on behalf of a human user.

Therefore, after Progol had generalized the users' Web page classifications, the users were shown the rule set, and asked to give their approval of the individual rules.

Table 2. Experimental results. The significant results are in the lower half of the table.

Subject number	Number of clauses	Majority class (%)	Predictive accuracy (%)	χ^2 probability	Learning time (s)
1	9	64	54 ± 7	0.84	179
2	12	58	54 ± 7	0.67	320
3	9	54	60 ± 7	0.33	183
4	5	74	78 ± 6	0.033	54
5	7	52	70 ± 6	0.009	156
6	8	68	78 ± 6	0.004	146

Table 3. Pooled results. A highly significant χ^2 test outcome.

	A	$\bar{A}$	
P	29	11	40
$\bar{P}$	26	84	110
	55	95	150

Predictive accuracy $= 75\% \pm 4$

χ^2 probability < 0.0001

Figures 1 and 2 give examples of the rule sets for an unpredictable subject (subject 1), and a predictable subject (subject 6). The subjects' approval or disapproval is given in square brackets after each rule.

Note that some of the examples have not been generalized. Progol could not find rules to cover these pages (e.g. interested(g8g4)).

Rules which contained the hypernym/2 predicate were generally unintuitive and the subjects rarely showed approval for a rule containing that predicate.

4.3 User generated rules

As an additional task, the subjects were asked to give a list of rules to define their Web interests, using the same predicates as Progol. The results are shown in Table 4. In most cases Progol's rules outperform the user's own rules, but there are a couple of notable exceptions. Subject 5 clearly knows himself very well. More importantly, Subject 3 achieved significant accuracy with his rules where Progol could not.

5 DISCUSSION

The results of this experiment appeared to give a polarization of the subjects into predictble and unpredictable. There were no subjects 'near' the borderline between the two classes.

When interviewed after the experiment, the predictable students appeared to have fixed in advance definite criteria for the classification of the Web pages. They also

```
interested(h5).
interested(h6h61).
interested(A) :- hasword(A,seminars).                    [Yes]
interested(A) :- hasword(A,smith).                       [No]
interested(A) :- hasword(A,image).                       [No]
interested(A) :- hasword(A,school).                      [No]
interested(A) :- hasword(A,B), hypernym(B,worker).       [No]
interested(A) :- hasword(A,B),
        hypernym(B,chromatic_color).                     [No]
interested(A) :- connected(A,B), hasword(B,C),
        hypernym(C,life_science).                        [Yes]
```

Figure 1. Rule set for subject 1. The subject's approval of each rule is indicated in square brackets.

```
interested(g8g4).
interested(g9g2).
interested(g9g6).
interested(g9g8).
interested(h6h61).
interested(A) :- hasword(A,bodleian).                    [Yes]
interested(A) :- hasword(A,colleges).                    [Yes]
interested(A) :- hasword(A,B),
        hypernym(B,pretense).                            [No]
```

Figure 2. Rule set for subject 6. The subject's approval of each rule is indicated in square brackets.

Table 4. Progol-generated versus human defined rules. The accuracy of user-defined rules is given, and is highlighted when significant.

Subject number	Majority class (%)	Prolog's rules acc. (%)	$\chi^2_{prob.}$	Subject's rules acc. (%)	$\chi^2_{prob.}$
1	64	54	0.84	52	0.72
2	58	54	0.67	46	0.60
3	54	60	0.33	**66**	**0.029**
4	74	78	0.033	**74**	**0.072**
5	52	70	0.009	**82**	**0.000**
6	68	78	0.004	52	0.43

ensured that they read each page, and decided the classification based on the textual content. In other words, the predictable students were more thorough and disciplined in their classification procedure.

The unpredictable students, however, were more likely just to have gone through the pages selecting according to their first impressions. Images and layout played an important part in their classification. 'I like the look of that one . . . '. They took less time to classify all 50 pages.

It is perhaps unsurprising in this context that the polarization into predictable and unpredictable correlated in all cases with good and bad exam performance. However it is important to note that the sample size (six students) is too small for this result to be significant (χ^2 probability of 0.1025). More investigation of this phenomenon is necessary before any definite conclusions can be drawn.

The interesting points to note about the results are:

- Predictable students gave rise to smaller theories (fewer rules). Progol achieved greater compression of the examples (Table 2).
- Predictable students had faster generalization times (Table 2).
- Predictable students approved of a greater proportion of the rules produced by Progol (Figures 1 and 2).
- The hypernym/2 predicate was misunderstood by the students, and generally they did not approve of rules containing that predicate (Figures 1 and 2).
- Progol performed better than the hand-crafted rules in most cases (Table 4).

5.1 Further work

In general, using the hypernym/2 predicate was unsuccessful. The rules produced were generally considered to be incomprehensible or ambiguous, and were rarely met with approval from the subjects.

A different approach that could be taken is to reduce words to some sort of canonical or normal form – in other words, reduce all words with the same root to the same normal form (e.g. 'computer', 'computation', 'computing', 'compute'). An algorithm that does this on a purely lexical basis is the Porter stemming algorithm [8].

It is also interesting to compare the performance of the ILP algorithm Progol to that of simpler machine learning techniques. In Parson's MSc thesis [7], a comparison is made with a naïve Bayes classifier, and with a statistical technique called WordStat, used in Tom Mitchell's WebWatcher agent [1].

In the present paper, all the words on each page (other than those appearing on a stop-list of common English words) were used in the learning procedure. It is possible, however, to select significant words from the pages in advance. Using a natural English word frequency database, one can compare the frequency that a word appears on a page to the expected frequency based on the database. Those that appear more than expected are significant to the page.

In practice, the user will not be presented with pages that are selected in advance. The user is far more likely to direct the choice of examples himself. For instance, a user's bookmarks or Web page hotlist are a good source of positive examples. Investigation needs to be made into the effect of user-directed example selection. Advances in positive-only learning [5] could make such investigation possible using the sources mentioned above.

Acknowledgements

Thanks are due to Donald Michie, who made several helpful suggestions and comments during the experiments described in this paper. Rupert Parson was funded by an EPSRC graduate student grant. Dr. Stephen Muggleton was supported partly by the Esprit Basic Research Action ILP (project 6020), EPSRC grant GR/J46623 on Experimental Applications and Development of ILP, and an EPSRC Advanced Research Fellowship. Dr. Stephen Muggleton was supported by a non-stipendiary Research Fellowship at Wolfson College, Oxford, during the writing of this paper.

REFERENCES

[1] R. Armstrong, D. Freitag, T. Joachims, and T. Mitchell. Webwatcher: A learning apprentice for the world wide web. Technical report, Carnegie Mellon University, 1995.

[2] M. Genesereth and S. P. Ketchpel. Software agents. *Communications of the ACM*, 37(7): 48–53, 1994.

[3] G. A. Miller, R. Beckwith, C. Fellbaum, D. Gross, and K. Miller. *Five Papers on WordNet*. Cognitive Science Laboratory, Princeton, 1993.

[4] S. Muggleton. Inverse entailment and Progol. *New Generation Computing*, 13: 245–286, 1995.

[5] S. Muggleton. Learning from positive data. In *Proceedings of the Sixth Workshop on Inductive Logic Programming*, Stockholm, Springer-Verlag 1996.

[6] S. Muggleton and L. De Raedt. Inductive logic programming: theory and methods. *Journal of Logic Programming*, 19, 20: 629–679, 1994.

[7] R. D. G. Parson. Intelligent agents for the world wide web. Master's thesis, Oxford University Computing Laboratory, 1995.

[8] M. F. Porter. An algorithm for suffix stripping. Program, 14(3): 130–137, July 1980.

10

Toward incremental knowledge correction for agents in complex environments

Douglas J. Pearson and John E. Laird

Artificial Intelligence Laboratory

The University of Michigan

Ann Arbor

Michigan 48109-2122

USA

e-mail: dpearson@iname.com and laird@umich.edu

Abstract

In complex, dynamic environments, an agent's domain knowledge will rarely be complete and correct. Existing deliberate approaches to domain theory correction are significantly restricted in the environments where they can be used. These systems are typically not used in agent-based tasks and rely on declarative representations to support nonincremental learning. This research investigates the use of *procedural* knowledge to support deliberate incremental error correction in complex environments. We describe a series of domain properties that constrain the error correction process and that are violated by existing approaches. We then present a procedural representation for domain knowledge which is sufficiently expressive, yet tractable. We develop a general framework for error detection and correction and then describe an error correction system, IMPROV, that uses our procedural representation to meet the constraints imposed by complex environments. Finally, we test the system in two sample domains and empirically demonstrate that it satisfies many of the constraints faced by agents in complex and challenging environments.

1 INTRODUCTION

In complex, dynamic environments, an agent's domain knowledge (its *domain theory*) will rarely be complete and correct. To succeed, an agent must have the ability to extend and correct its domain theory as it interacts with its environment. Figure 1 shows the basic processing steps of a planning system that performs error correction. A nonlearning system would have only some combination of planning and execution. For learning, the

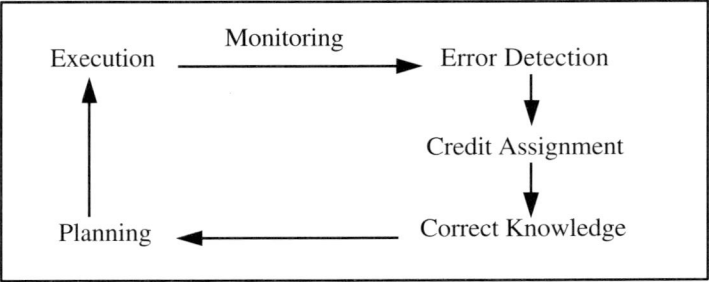

Figure 1. Deliberate domain theory correction.

system must be able to detect an error during execution. If an error is detected, the agent must determine which aspect of its knowledge is in error (credit assignment) and then correct that knowledge.

Existing domain theory correction systems use *declarative* representations of operators as their domain knowledge. These representations, in turn, support *deliberate* error correction strategies [e.g. EITHER (Ourston and Mooney, 1990), EXPO (Gil, 1991), OCCAM (Pazzani, 1988), CLIPS-R (Murphy and Pazzani, 1994), FOIL (Quinlan, 1990)]. In deliberate error correction, the system detects errors without any special signal from the environment (such as a payoff function, or a training signal), and corrects its internal planning knowledge of its actions by determining which operator was in error and then modifying it. Deliberate systems also typically consider multiple training episodes when making a correction. These approaches can be contrasted with *implicit* approaches for correcting behavior, such as Classifiers (Holland, 1986), Backpropagation (Rumelhart *et al.*, 1986), Q-learning (Watkins and Dayan, 1992), that are restricted to only detecting errors when an additional training signal is provided and are limited to correcting errors in execution knowledge, rather than planning knowledge which restricts them to purely reactive systems. They also consider only one training instance at a time when making a correction which, we will show, makes for less effective learning than considering multiple episodes at once.

Unfortunately, deliberate learners are currently restricted to simple domains and thus the agents are unable to act (or learn or plan) effectively in domains with the characteristics listed in Figure 2. For example, their representation may not be expressive enough to include conditional actions (D2) or actions with duration (D3). Similarly, their algorithms for credit assignment typically assume that sensors are error-free (D5), that immediate feedback is available (D9), and that the target domain theory never changes (D8).

There are at least two possible responses to this problem. One response would be to try to extend the current approaches by enriching their representations for action and extending their current techniques. However, there is a danger that as these representations are enriched (in response to D1, D2, D3) and as the number of operators grows, the cost of full first-order access to the preconditions and actions of all operators [as in the 'glass box' assumption of PRODIGY (Carbonell *et al.*, 1991)] will be prohibitive during error correction.

Agent, domain and task characteristics	Examples from driving
D1: An action may apply in many disjunctive states	Brakes can be applied to slow the car, to stop, or to signal a tailgater.
D2: An action can have conditional effects.	The brakes have different effects depending on the weather conditions.
D3: An action can have duration.	A car does not stop instantly when the brakes are applied.
D4: An action may have unobservable effects.	Sudden braking will wear out the car's tires.
D5: A sensor may be noisy.	A motorcycle may appear to be a bicycle, or the speedometer may be broken.
D6: A task may have arbitrary duration.	A taxi must perform an arbitrary number of pick ups and deliveries.
D7: A task may require a timely response.	A car must avoid a vehicle that swerves in front of it.
D8: A domain property may change over time.	A car's tires can wear out, making braking take more time.
D9: A domain may not have immediate feedback.	Pushing on the accelerator may not lead to failure until a sharp turn is reached.

Figure 2. Agent, domain, and task characteristics.

187

We are pursuing an alternative in which we develop approaches to planning, error detection and correction which depend only on limited and efficient *procedural* access to the preconditions and actions of an operator. The agent only has access to preconditions by knowing when they have been satisfied for a particular operator, and can only access the actions by executing the operator. Neither the preconditions nor the actions can be directly examined.

The remainder of this paper has three main sections. The first section presents a representation of domain theories, based on production rules, that meets the requirements in Figure 2. The second section presents an incremental, domain-independent, deliberate error detection and correction system, called IMPROV, that has been designed to meet the constraints of Figure 2. Although IMPROV is implemented within a specific architecture, it is a general method for correcting operator preconditions when the operators are procedurally encoded. The third section presents the results to date, which are that IMPROV corrects its domain theory incrementally, becomes *faster* (as well as more accurate) as it learns, corrects knowledge in a noisy environment, modifies its domain knowledge as the target domain theory changes over time, and makes more efficient use of training instances than pure incremental learners that process only a single instance at a time.

2 DOMAIN THEORY REPRESENTATION

Most deliberate error correction schemes represent their domain theories as sets of independent operators, where each operator corresponds to a different action an agent can perform in the world. These operators are used for planning as well as for execution of actions in the world. During planning, the operator simulates the effects of an action on an internal model, while during execution, the operator initiates motor actions in the world.

Typically, in deliberate error correction systems, an operator is represented declaratively using a STRIPS-style preconditions and actions, where the actions consist of add and delete lists. This representation is usually restricted so that the operators lack conditional effects (D2), or lack duration (D3), or are assumed to have only conjunctive conditions (D1). Additionally, these systems assume a declarative representation is always available. However, this is not always the case. For example, the precondition for moving a robot arm might be expressed as:

$$\text{if} \quad x^7 + x^2 y^5 + x y^2 + 7x - 12 > 0 \quad \text{then move-arm.}$$

As this equation has no analytic solution, it is not clear how to declaratively represent when the operator should be chosen. The agent is limited to executing the expression for particular values, to determine if the precondition is satisfied.

We are exploring the use of a largely procedural representation in an effort to provide the necessary expressiveness (D1–D3) while restricting the access to the knowledge to avoid intractability. The approach also releases us from the assumption that a declarative representation is always available. Our hypothesis, born out in our implementation, is

```
IF      distance-to-intersection(medium) AND        IF      distance-to-intersection(medium) AND
        light(red) AND engine(running)                      light(yellow) AND engine(running)
THEN  choose operator(setspeed 10)                  THEN  choose operator(set-speed 10)

IF      distance-to-intersection(close) AND          IF      distance-to-intersection(close) AND
        light(red) AND engine(running)                      light(green) AND engine(running)
THEN  choose operator(stop)                         THEN  choose operator(set-speed 30)
```

Figure 3. Precondition rules forming a procedural plan.

that declarative access to just the names of operators is sufficient for error correction. This type of restricted access is provided by Soar (Rosenbloom *et al.*, 1993), the architecture in which IMPROV is implemented.

In Soar, an operator's preconditions are defined by rules which test for situations in which the operator should be selected, and therefore include control knowledge. Once selected, an operator's actions are performed by 'operator implementation' rules which support actions with conditional effects or duration. The sufficiency of this representation for constraints D1–D3 [and efficient matching (Doorenbos, 1993)] has been demonstrated for complex, real-time domains including control of simulated aircraft (Pearson *et al.*, 1993) and tactical air combat (Laird *et al.*, 1995; Tambe *et al.*, 1995).

An IMPROV agent will use this operator knowledge to both plan and behave in its world. Errors in the planning knowledge lead to errors in behavior, so it is planning knowledge that IMPROV learns to correct. In IMPROV, planning does not create a monolithic plan. Instead, situation-dependent control rules are learned that will propose the operators when appropriate during execution (Laird and Rosenbloom, 1990). For example, a possible 'plan' to drive through an intersection (where the rules are preconditions for the operators) is shown in Figure 3.

An important property of this 'distributed' plan representation is that behavior of the agent is not controlled by only the most recently generated plan. Instead, the agent's behavior is controlled by the runtime combination of all of its previous planning. As a result, the agent may begin by using control rules learned from its most recent planning experience, but as a result of some unexpected change in the environment, control rules from a much earlier planning experience might become relevant and guide the agent. Thus, in a well-trained agent, planning will be the exception, with only enough planning to fill in for novel situations (Laird and Rosenbloom, 1990).

To create a plan, IMPROV does not search through a space of plans because of the restrictions it has on access to its operators. IMPROV could potentially use a variety of state-space planning methods. However, because we expect that the search can be usefully biased by prior experience, and because the method should be complete, we've adopted a planning method called *uncertainty-bounded iterative deepening* (UBID).[1] UBID is an extension of the iterative deepening planning method. UBID bounds an iteration based on the uncertainty associated with a plan, rather than its length. The *uncertainty* of a plan is the sum of the uncertainty associated with each operator in that plan. These uncertainties are derived from the learning component of the system and

---

[1] UBID was developed in collaboration with Scott Huffman.

essentially represent the number of times an operator was useful in similar situations. The details of the planning method are not important. The key characteristic of the search is that the planner first explores paths that the agent believes are most likely to succeed based on its previous experience. This results in a deeper search in areas of the search space that have earlier proved useful to the agent, which can make planning much more efficient. Additionally, UBID is complete, which guarantees that during error correction IMPROV will eventually discover the correct path to the goal, if one exists.

3 DOMAIN THEORY CORRECTION

To perform domain theory correction, we must attend to four issues: (1) which knowledge errors will be corrected, (2) how these errors are detected, (3) how the operator(s) responsible for the error are determined (credit assignment), and (4) how the error is corrected.

3.1 Knowledge error types

As the agent's domain theory consists of the preconditions and actions of its operators, the range of possible errors is defined in terms of that operator knowledge. An operator's preconditions may be overgeneral (missing conditions that should be present) or overspecific (containing unnecessary conditions which should not be present).[2] The actions may similarly contain additional effects, which do not occur when the operator is executed, or be missing effects which do occur. Finally, it is possible for an operator to be completely missing.

Currently, IMPROV is guaranteed to converge to the correct knowledge for both overspecializations and overgeneralizations of operator preconditions.[3] Thus, the emphasis of the remaining parts of this section are on how to identify and correct such errors. How this approach extends to correcting operator actions is discussed in the section on future work.

3.2 Error detection

Errors can either be detected during planning or during execution. Errors during planning cannot be detected without additional knowledge, for example that certain states are impossible. Without this extra knowledge the agent can only detect errors in its planning knowledge during execution. In some way, the agent must compare its planning knowledge to the execution and detect when they are inconsistent.

Most, if not all, deliberate error correction systems make this comparison directly, by comparing the declarative model of the operator to the results of execution. That is,

---

[2]The situation where a precondition is just plain incorrect can be seen as a combination of an overgeneral condition (since the correct condition is missing) and an overspecific condition (as the incorrect condition is present). IMPROV also corrects these errors.

[3]Assuming the agent's representation is sufficient to represent the correct operator preconditions, that actions do not destructively modify the environment and that a solution path exists.

before the next operator in the plan is applied, its preconditions are checked and if they are not satisfied, an error is assumed to have happened earlier in the plan. Similarly, after an operator is applied, its actions are checked and if the expected changes are not found in the external state, an error is assumed.

The comparison cannot be made directly when actions have unobservable effects (D4) or when the system is restricted to only procedural access. An alternative might be to just monitor if the current plan is being followed. However, in 'distributed' plans, such as IMPROV uses, there is no single plan for a given goal. Instead there can be collections of rules from many planning episodes that contribute control.

As a result, IMPROV relies on detecting that the agent no longer knows how to make progress towards the goal. More precisely, if at any point the agent reaches a state where no operator is proposed for the current goal, an error is assumed. The comparison between planning knowledge and execution is therefore made indirectly, through the rule matcher. Consider the example of driving a car through an intersection using the plan shown in Figure 3. If the light turns red as the agent approaches then the agent will execute set-speed(10), stop, set-speed(30) (as the light turns back to green). If, however, the agent is unaware of the need to change to a lower gear, the car will stall and the preconditions for set-speed(30) will not be met (namely engine(running)). As no other operator will be proposed, this will be recognized as an error.

This method only detects errors if they interfere with the agent's ability to achieve its current goal. It does not detect errors in the agent's ability to make accurate predictions. In complex, nondeterministic worlds, detecting lack of progress may be the best that can be done. For example, if an action involves a random event (such as the roll of a die), IMPROV will not attempt to learn to predict the random event once it has learned plans for dealing with all of the possible outcomes of the event.

The above approach fails if the agent inadvertently cycles back to an earlier part of a plan, in which case it will believe that it is still making progress. In our example, if the agent has a 'start-engine' operator then after stalling it may repeatedly turn the key and stall the car again, because it still has not changed gear. This problem is complicated by the fact that the agent may move to a state in which the only differences are irrelevant to the current task (the pedestrians on the sidewalk have moved). The key is to recognize that the task-relevant parts of the state have been repeated. For the purposes of error detection, states are grouped into equivalence classes; two states being equal if the same operator precondition matches both states. Loops are detected if the agent returns to a state in a previously visited equivalence class. IMPROV efficiently calculates these equivalence classes by explaining, at each step during execution, why the next operator in the operator is being selected. This explanation leads, through Soar's EBL method *chunking* (Laird *et al.*, 1986), to a new rule being learned which matches exactly the precondition of the operator being chosen. Whenever one of these rules fire, a cycle is detected. This method allows the same operator to be selected multiple times during the course of a goal, as long as different preconditions are used to select it each time. Iterative tasks are still possible, even when there is no observable change in the external state (such as turning a finely threaded screw), as long as there is a change to the internal state (such as a counter).

3.3 Credit assignment

Once an error is detected, the agent must determine which aspect of its domain knowledge was in error; that is which operator is incorrect and how it is incorrect. Because it is not always possible to detect an error immediately following a mistake, the agent does not know exactly which operator is incorrect. Even if a specific operator has been identified, it is still a problem to identify in what way the preconditions of the operator are wrong, that is, which preconditions should be added, or which preconditions should be dropped. This is especially true when the domain state contains a large number of irrelevant features, and when the preconditions themselves are large disjunctive sets (D1).

3.3.1 Identifying which operators are incorrect

Since most existing deliberate error correction systems assume explicit monitoring combined with complete and immediate sensing, they can assume that the current operator is the one that failed. IMPROV's approach is to compare the failed attempt's operator sequence and a successful solution, and use the differences to determine the operators that are in error. Specifically, once an error is detected, IMPROV continues to attempt to solve the problem, by generating and executing a series of plans until it eventually succeeds.[4] Once a successful plan has been executed, IMPROV recalls for each state in the successful plan the operator that would have been chosen in the original (incorrect) plan, and compares it to the operator used in the successful plan. The differences are assumed to be the operators with incorrect knowledge. For example, if the incorrect plan for crossing an intersection is set-speed(10), stop, set-speed(30) (when the light changes) and the successful plan turns out to be *change-gear(down)*, set-speed(10), stop, set-speed(30) then the conditions for change-gear and set-speed(10) should be changed. Change-gear should be generalized to be used in this task, while set-speed(10) should be specialized so it is not chosen until after the car is in a lower gear. This comparison can be achieved without a declarative operator representation. The sequence of states that make up the successful plan are recorded as the agent executes the plan. IMPROV then observes which operators are proposed (i.e. have matching preconditions) for each state in turn and compares them to the operators that made up the successful operator sequence.

Although this approach is not guaranteed to always identify the incorrect operators, it allows the agent to more accurately locate which operators are incorrect than weaker methods because IMPROV has access to more information (in the form of the successful plan). Traditional error correction methods consider only the incorrect plan during this credit assignment. Therefore, they must rely on a fixed bias. For instance, reinforcement learning typically assigns most blame for a failure to the final step (set-speed(30), in the example). It is very difficult for such a system to discover that the true correction is much earlier in the plan, while still maintaining the final set-speed(30) operator, which is required in any successful plan.

---

[4]If actions do not destructively modify the world, UBID's complete planning method ensures a successful plan will be found, if one exists.

3.3.2 Identifying errors in operator preconditions

Once incorrect operators have been detected and a successful plan has been found, the system can attempt to identify whether the operator preconditions must be either specialized or generalized. IMPROV's method for detecting errors gives an indication whether the operator needs to be specialized (because it was incorrectly selected for a given situation) or generalized (because it was not selected for a given situation). However, unless the system has access to some additional source of knowledge, such as a complete causal theory, it is impossible for the system to determine deductively exactly which features need to be added or dropped. Instead the system must rely on its accumulated experience and inductively guess. As stated earlier, we assume that there are several constraints on this process. First, it must be incremental because there may be arbitrary numbers of training instances (D6) and there are temporal constraints on the agent's behavior (D7). Second, it must be resistant to noise (D5), but also be able to adjust to changes in the underlying domain (D8). Previous deliberate approaches violate some or all of these constraints.

Our approach is to train an incremental inductive category learner on instances of operators succeeding or failing. The category being learned is which operator is the correct one to use for the current state and goal. As a result, the preconditions of an operator are represented twice within the system. First, as rules for when to choose the operator, that can be executed efficiently. Secondly, as rules within the inductive learner, that are less efficient to access (requiring a deliberate search) but support learning well. As the inductive learner must be incremental and able to represent disjunctive sets of preconditions (D1) we have used the symbolic category learner SCA (Miller, 1991, 1993), which can learn arbitrarily complex categories.[5] SCA is also incremental, tolerant of noise and is guaranteed to converge to the correct category, if that category can be represented in its description language.

The full correction algorithm is summarized in Figure 4. For simplicity in understanding the method, the algorithm is described using iteration, however it is implemented using several levels of recursion because the plans are not represented declaratively. Similarly, many of the data structures are not explicitly recorded in the agent's working memory, but are instead recorded as procedural rules which recall the correct values into working memory at the appropriate stages of the algorithm. However, these distinctions are not critical to understanding the important aspects of the algorithm.

During a correction episode, IMPROV searches for a correct plan, $P_{success}$. This is done by generating a series of plans, P_i, using the UBID planning method mentioned earlier. UBID generates plans in decreasing order of probability of successfully reaching the goal. Each plan is tested by recording the current state, S_{ij}, and then executing each operator, O_{ij}, in turn. The operator will either lead to an error, the goal or to neither. If either an error or the goal is detected, the plan is complete and the result recorded as R_i, otherwise IMPROV continues with the next operator in the plan. Once IMPROV finds a successful plan, the inductive learner, SCA, is trained on all of the instances, positive and negative, found during the search for a successful plan (see Section 3.3.2). This training

---

[5]In the limit SCA can represent each exemplar individually (Miller, 1991).

```
Procedure Make-Correction(G,S)
begin
   /* Search for the correct plan */
   while (current-state ≠ G)
      Pi := UBID(G,current-state)
      do
         Oij    := Next-step-in-plan(Pi)
         Sij    := current-state
         result := Execute(Oij)
         if (result = error-detected) then Ri := error-detected
         if (result = reached-goal) then {Ri := reached-goal ; success = i }
      while (result ≠ error-detected and result ≠ reached-goal)

   /* Identify key differences between correct and incorrect plans */
   /* Train inductive module */
   foreach Sj in Psuccess
      important-features = Differences(S1j,S2j,S3j,...,Ssuccess,j)
      for i := 1 to success
         if (Ri == error-detected) then
            Train-SCA-negative-instance(G,Sij,Oij,important-features)
         if (Ri == reached-goal) then
            Train-SCA-positive-instance(G,Sij,Oij,important-features)

   /* Correct the operator precondition knowledge */
   foreach Sj in Psuccess
      O-current := Compute-Proposal(G,Sj)
      O-new     := Test-SCA(G,Sj)
      if (O-new ≠ O-current) then
         Learn-Reject-Operator(G,Sj,O-current)
         Learn-Propose-Operator(G,Sj,O-new)

end
```

```
Main Control Loop

do
   O      := Compute-Proposal(G,S)
   result := Execute(O)

   if (result = error-detected) then
      Make-Correction(G,S)
   end

while (result ≠ reached-goal)
```

Figure 4. Basic algorithm for correcting operator preconditions.

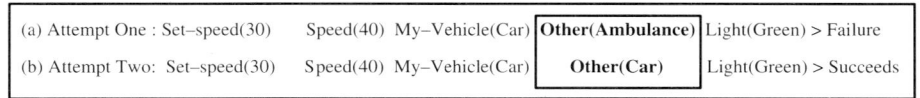

Figure 5. Identifying the important features.

is biased by the features found to be different between the failed plan states and those in the successful plan (as described below). Finally, the operator's precondition knowledge is updated to match the results of the induction (see Section 3.3.3).

IMPROV does not train the inductive learner as soon as an instance of an operator leading to an error has been found. Instead, the instances are recorded until a successful plan is found, at which point the whole set of positive and negative instances is passed to the induction method. Introducing this delay before learning allows IMPROV to more accurately identify which operators are incorrect (as described in Section 3.3.1) and, as we'll show, assists in identifying the important features for training the inductive learner.

Any incremental method discards information about the instances it sees during training (or it's not incremental). IMPROV gains more information about what to discard from an instance by considering a set of instances. We will help to clarify this property of the system with a simple example. Consider an agent which tries to cross an intersection and fails (see Figure 5a).

An incremental inductive learner training on just this first instance would probably not correctly identify the cause of the failure. However, if the learner waits and considers both instances together, it is clear that the failure was due to the fact that the other vehicle at the intersection was an ambulance (and therefore should have been given precedence). This determination can only be made in the context of the two instances. IMPROV takes advantage of this general property by delaying its training until a successful instance has been found. As the number of instances IMPROV considers during each training episode will not increase over the life of the agent, the learning is still incremental, satisfying the constraints D5 and D6. It should be noted that this information simply forms an additional bias for the inductive learner.[6]

If training is delayed even further, until a unique cause has been identified, then this would result in a system which is actively experimenting [such as the simple induction in EXPO (Gil, 1991)]. Thus IMPROV and EXPO define two interesting, *k-incremental* learners along the spectrum from pure incremental learners to pure non-incremental learners (Figure 6). K-incremental learning is related to incremental batch learners, such as RL (Clearwater *et al.*, 1989). However, those learners train on a set of randomly selected instances and therefore are *passive* learners. IMPROV and EXPO are *actively* creating instances as they act in the world. This means the agents must be more careful in their learning. To continue our example from above: a system which did not delay its credit assignment might have attributed the cause of the failure (Figure 5a) to the light

---

[6]We assume that some of the properties in the domain's representation are causally related to the success of the operator (for example, speed and the types of vehicles involved). An alternative representation, such as a graphical one based on polygons, would not have this property and this bias would not assist, and could hinder, learning.

195

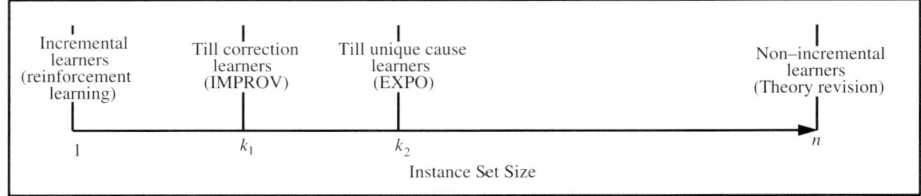

Figure 6. Range of systems based on instance set size.

being green. This incorrect learning would then make it much harder for the system to discover its error in future as it would expect the correct plan (Figure 5b) to fail, making it unlikely to execute it in the environment. A passive learner, however, would be no more or less likely to be presented with the second plan, no matter what it learned as a result of seeing the first plan. This would allow the passive learner to more easily recover from any early, incorrect learning. The important point here is that in agent-based systems which act in the world, it is more important to assign credit correctly than it is to assign credit quickly (as we will demonstrate in our experimental results).

3.3.3 Changing the precondition knowledge

When the operator is represented declaratively, the correction system can directly modify the operator knowledge. As knowledge in IMPROV is represented procedurally, it cannot be modified directly, as this would violate the restriction of only accessing the knowledge through execution. IMPROV therefore corrects the knowledge by learning additional rules that correct the decision about which operator to select. A rule is learned to reject the original (incorrect) operator and another rule is learned which suggests the new (correct) operator. This approach is explained in detail by Laird (1988).

4 RESULTS

IMPROV has been implemented in two test domains. The first was the toy domain of a robot in the blocks world, which provided a good initial test-bed during development. The second domain is a driving simulation, which allows us to test all of the constraints (D1–D9) which we used to characterize complex environments.

The task, for the agent in the robot domain, is simply to align two blocks on a table. The blocks have different characteristics and the agent must learn which of the blocks can be successfully picked up. The task for the agent in the driving domain is to successfully cross an intersection. There are other agents in the environment, both on the roads and sidewalks, and processes (such as the traffic light) which change independent of the agent's actions. Figure 7 shows an example of a learning experiment. The attributes considered during learning are shown on the left, along with the range of values each attribute can take. Then the initial knowledge given to the agent is shown next (i.e. that the set-speed(30) operator should be chosen when the distance-to-intersection is close and the road-sign is a traffic signal). Finally, an example of a target theory is shown in the third column. The agent must learn three exception cases to the initial theory's

Attributes	Number of possible values	Sample initial knowledge (+3x2)	Sample target knowledge		
Distance-to-Intersection	5	Close	Close	Close	Close
My-vehicle-isa	5		Car		
My-vehicle-color	5				
My-road-sign	1	Signal	Signal	Signal	Signal
My-light-color	3		Red	Green	Green
Gear	4				
Weather	5				
Road-Quality	5				
Other-road-user-isa	5			Police	Ambulance
Other-side-walk-user-isa	5				
Other-road-sign	1				
Operator :		set-speed (30)	set-speed(0)	set-speed(0)	set-speed(0)

Figure 7. Driving domain theory examples.

general rules. The target operator preconditions consist of three disjunctive terms, each containing two additional conjunctive terms that are missing in the initial knowledge. This example is labeled as $+3 \times 2$. The + indicates that the initial theory is overgeneral and must add three disjunctive terms (each of two conjuncts) to reach the target theory. Overspecific initial theories are the converse, for example -3×2 would mean the agent started with the target theory shown and had to learn the initial theory.

The robot domain contains a similar number of attributes and has test cases formulated in the same manner. Each experiment reflects the average results from 10 runs and each test case is designed so that the agent's initial, incorrect knowledge will lead to a failure if the agent does not learn. This makes it easier to identify the effect that learning is having on the agent's ability to perform the task. Without any learning, every trial would lead to an error.

4.1 Test 1: Overgeneral, overspecific, noise

Figure 8(a) shows the cumulative number of errors made by IMPROV over the course of 50 trials, for a range of target theories. The diagonal line is a reference, showing the number of errors that would be made if the system was not learning. The zero noise cases show that IMPROV can correct overgeneral or overspecific theories and quickly converges to the correct theory. The graph also shows that learning can tolerate noise,[7] although performance degrades.

4.2 Test 2: Learning, Disjunctive, Preconditions

Figure 8(b) shows the cumulative number of errors made as IMPROV learns a range of theories which include an increasing number of disjunctive terms. Disjunctive preconditions can present difficulties for some traditional learning methods and one of our constraints (DI) is that the theory may contain a number of disjunctive terms. This graph

---

[7] 10% noise indicates there is a 10% chance that a given attribute is incorrectly sensed for the duration of that trial.

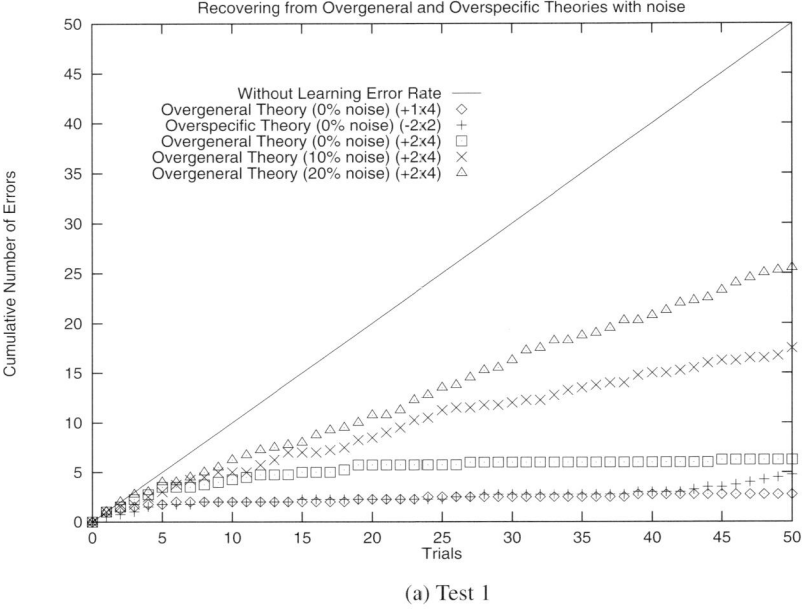

(a) Test 1

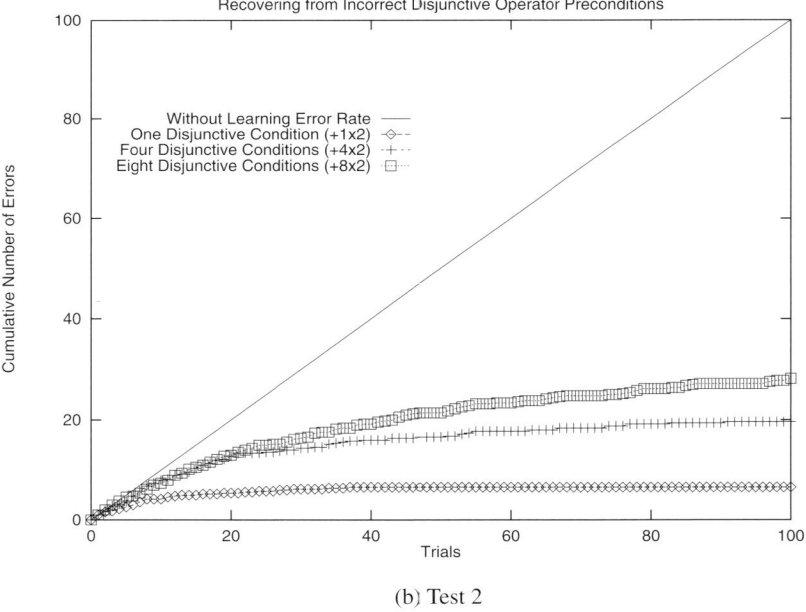

(b) Test 2

Figure 8. Recovery from different types of incorrect domain knowledge.

demonstrates that learning is harder as the number of disjuncts increases, but in each case IMPROV quickly converges towards the correct knowledge.

4.3 Test 3: Pure incremental versus K-incremental

Figure 9 demonstrates the benefit of using a deliberate correction strategy that considers sets of k instances during training over a pure incremental learner. IMPROV was modified to train immediately after seeing each individual instance, rather than waiting and training on a set of instances, and thereby simulated a pure incremental system. The difference in the resulting error rates is substantial, confirming that the accuracy of the learning has been improved because the system delays its training until a successful plan has been found. This enhances the ability of the system in both credit assignment problems (which operators are wrong and what's wrong with those operators).

4.4 Test 4: Exploration versus exploitation

Learning systems are often faced with the decision of how much to explore in an effort to gain new (and hopefully better) knowledge and how much to trust the knowledge they already have. This issue arises for IMPROV in domains with destructive modification, such as driving, during replanning. In essence, the agent must decide if it has already, unsuccessfully, tried an action in *the same state* before. For example, the agent selects set-speed(30) at the point of reaching the intersection only to discover it later leads to an error. When the agent next comes upon an intersection, should it select set-speed(30) again?

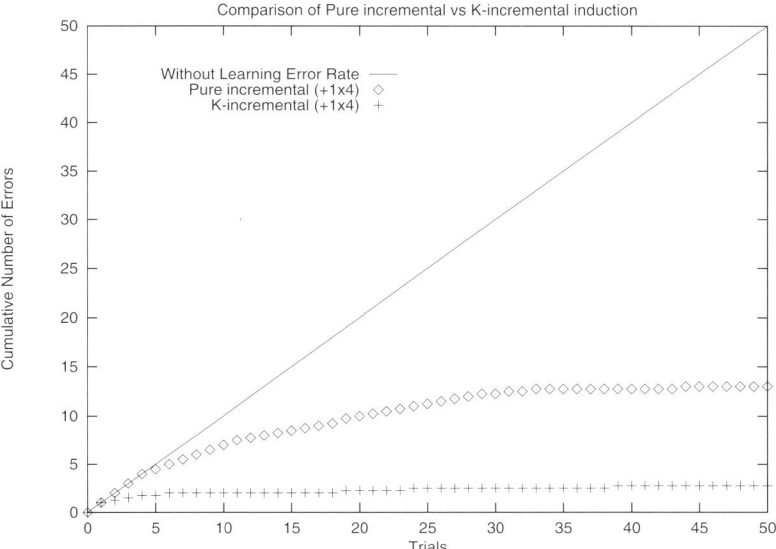

Figure 9. Test 3 – K-incremental learning versus pure incremental learning.

199

We tested three different approaches to resolving this question. First, the 0% exploration case, we required a complete match between the two states to avoid choosing the operator which led to a failure again. Secondly, the 100% exploration case, we always selected a different operator over an operator which had been seen to fail before. Thirdly, the 50% exploration case, we required a partial match (half of the features or more must match between the two states) to avoid trying an operator which had previously failed. Figure 10(a) shows the error rates of the different approaches. Figure 10(b) shows the number of training episodes (i.e. number of sets passed to SCA) that occurred for the different approaches. The 0% exploration case leads to the most errors (as the system repeatedly makes the same mistakes) but results in very few training episodes. This is because each training episode consists of a large set of instances and results in high-quality learning. The 100% exploration case leads to the most training episodes, but about the same number of errors as the 50% exploration case. This is because each training case is based on only a small set of instances and therefore results in poor-quality learning. The 50% exploration case produces the best overall results, with the lowest learning overhead for the same performance curve as the 100% exploration case. Thus the 50% exploration rate is the one used in the other trials.

4.5 Test 5: Tolerance of an evolving domain

Figure 11(a) illustrates that the induction is robust to changes in the target domain theory, for example when braking takes longer due to the wearing out of tires. In this test, two of the conditions in the target theory are changed to new values after the system has seen 50 trials. This causes the system to make more errors, but it then adjusts to the new theory. The baseline case shows the system's behavior when no change is made.

4.6 Test 6: Speeding up during learning

Figure 11(b) shows the CPU time per trial over the life of the system while performing the previous evolving domain correction task. The spikes indicate when a correction had to be made. It should be noted that the time spent on each correction remains constant or decreases as the system learns and the theory becomes more complex. This is in contrast to most machine learning algorithms, which become slower as the theory increases in complexity. Also, the frequencies of corrections decrease as the system's theory becomes more accurate. These results help support the hypothesis that procedural representations lead to an efficient correction method.

5 CONCLUSIONS AND FUTURE WORK

IMPROV can support an agent that learns, plans and executes its plans in the environment. We have shown that its deliberate, k-incremental correction strategy leads to better learning than implicit, pure incremental methods. It does this while using an expressive procedural representation that has been demonstrated to be effective in tasks that require complex domain knowledge. We have also developed a general framework for

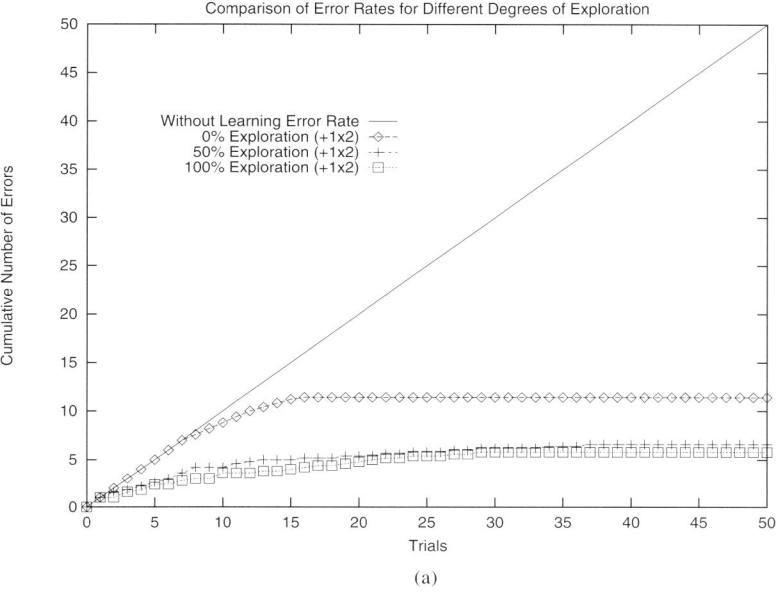

(a)

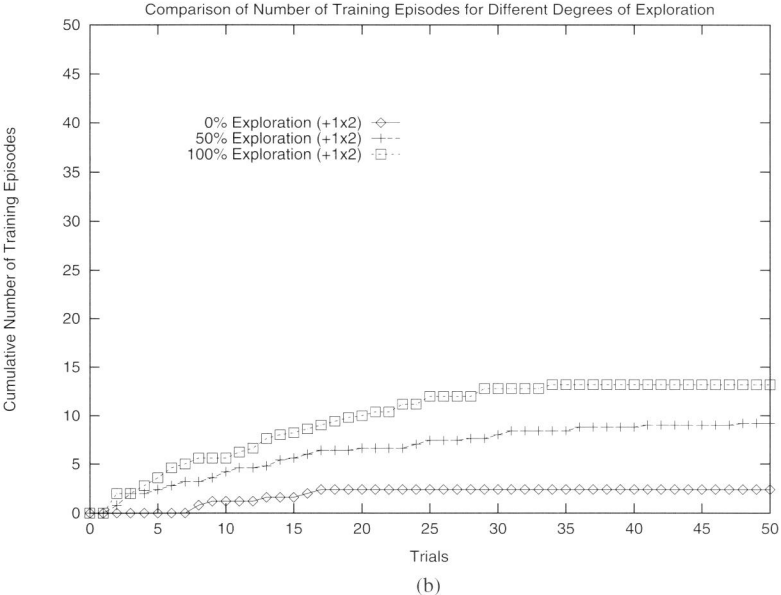

(b)

Figure 10. Test 4 – Performance of different exploration strategies.

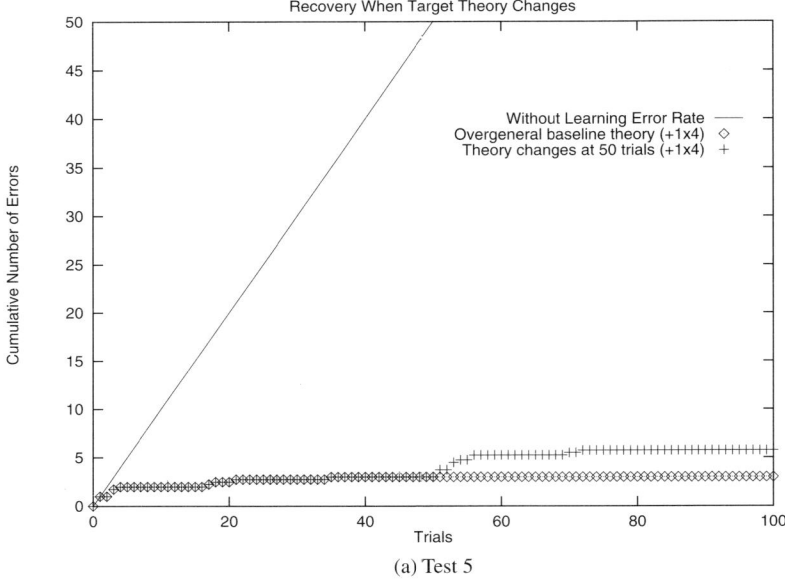

(a) Test 5

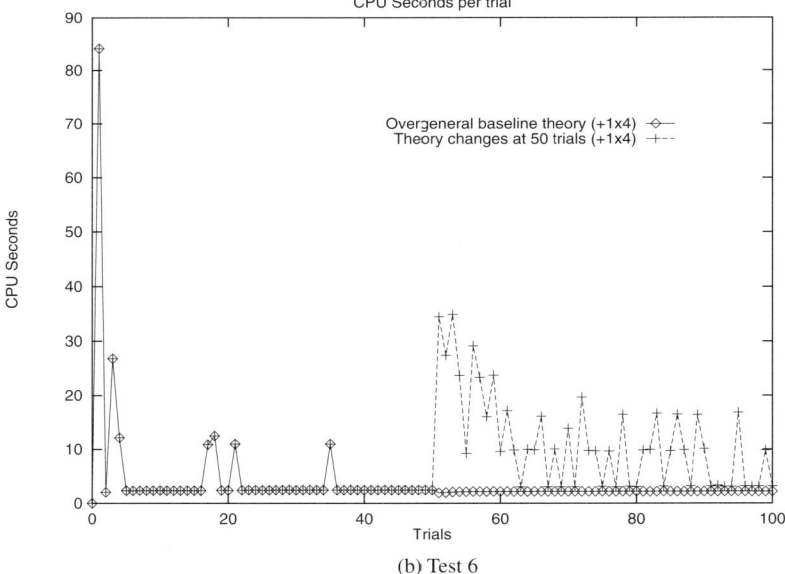

(b) Test 6

Figure 11. Tolerance of evolving domain and speed-up during learning.

202

error detection and correction and discussed the contrasts between different approaches within this framework.

IMPROV's correction method has been designed to work in complex and challenging domains, so it has been constrained in ways that mean its performance on simple domains will be slightly worse than that of existing correction systems. For example, its k-incremental learning method has access to less information than, and therefore should be inferior to, any nonincremental algorithm. However, the learning cost in IMPROV is not proportional to the size of the theory or the size of the instance set, which leads to better performance in time-critical domains.

In future work, we will extend IMPROV to correct operator actions (Pearson, 1996). Our approach will be to represent operators hierarchically, with suboperators implementing superoperators (for example, the set-speed operator's actions become a series of more primitive operators, press-accelerator, press-brake and change-gear). This allows the problem of correcting the actions of a superoperator to be reduced to the problem of correcting the preconditions of a suboperator which implements it. This will allow us to reuse IMPROV's precondition correction method in a recursive fashion to correct either operator preconditions or actions. The recursion will eventually terminate in a layer of primitive operators whose actions consist of modifying a single symbol and therefore can be guaranteed to be correct. This will allow all corrections to be reduced to the problem of correcting operator preconditions.

REFERENCES

[Carbonell *et al.*, 1991] Jaime G. Carbonell, Craig A. Knoblock, and Steven Minton. Prodigy: An integrated architecture for planning and learning. In Kurt VanLehn, editor, *Architectures for Intelligence*. Lawrence Erlbaum, 1991.

[Clearwater *et al.*, 1989] Scott H. Clearwater, Tze-Pin Cheng, Haym Hirsh, and Bruce G. Buchanan. Incremental batch learning. In *Proceedings of the International Workshop on Machine Learning*, pp. 366–370, 1989.

[Doorenbos, 1993] R. Doorenbos. Matching 100,000 learned rules. In *Proceedings of the Eleventh National Conference on Artificial Intelligence*. AAAI Press, 1993.

[Gil, 1991] Yolanda Gil. A domain-independent framework for effective experimentation in planning. In *Proceedings of the International Machine Learning Workshop*, pp. 13–17, 1991.

[Holland, 1986] John H. Holland. Escaping brittleness: The possibilities of general-purpose learning algorithms applied to parallel rule-based systems. In R. S. Michalski, J. G. Carbonell, and T. M. Mitchell, eds., *Machine Learning: An Artificial Intelligence Approach, Volume 11*. Morgan Kaufmann, 1986.

[Laird, 1988] John E. Laird. Recovery from incorrect knowledge in Soar. In *Proceedings of the National Conference on Artificial Intelligence*, pp. 618–623, August 1988.

[Laird and Rosenbloom, 1990] J. E. Laird and P. S. Rosenbloom. Integrating execution, planning, and learning in Soar for external environments. In *Proceedings of AAAI-90*, July 1990.

[Laird *et al.*, 1986] John E. Laird, Paul S. Rosenbloom, and Allen Newell. Chunking in Soar: The anatomy of a general learning mechanism. *Machine Learning*, 1(1): 11–46, 1986.

[Laird *et al.*, 1995] J. E. Laird, W. L. Johnson, R. M. Jones, F. Koss, J. F. Lehman, P. E. Nielsen, P. S. Rosenbloom, R. Rubinoff, K. Schwamb, M. Tambe, J. Van Dyke, M. van Lent, and R. E. Wray. Simulated intelligent forces for air: The Soar/IFOR project 1995. In *Proceedings of the Fifth*

Conference on Computer Generated Forces and Behavioral Representation, pp. 27–36, May 1995.

[Miller, 1991] Craig M. Miller. A constraint-motivated model of concept formation. In *The Thirteenth Annual Conference of the Cognitive Science Society*, pp. 827–831, 1991.

[Miller, 1993] Craig M. Miller. A *model of concept acquisition in the context of a unified theory of cognition*. PhD thesis, The University of Michigan, Dept. of Computer Science and Electrical Engineering, 1993.

[Murphy and Pazzani, 1994] Patrick M. Murphy and Michael J. Pazzani. Revision of production system rule-bases. In *Proceedings of the International Conference on Machine Learning*, pp. 199–207, 1994.

[Ourston and Mooney, 1990] Dirk Ourston and Raymond J. Mooney. Changing the rules: A comprehensive approach to theory refinement. In *Proceedings of the National Conference on Artificial Intelligence*, pp. 815–820, 1990.

[Pazzani, 1988] Michael J. Pazzani. Integrated learning with incorrect and incomplete theories. In *Proceedings of the International Machine Learning Conference*, pp. 291–297, 1988.

[Pearson, 1996] Douglas J. Pearson. Learning Procedural Planning Knowledge in Complex Environments. Ph.D. Thesis, The University of Michigan, Dept. of Computer Science and Electrical Engineering, 1996.

[Pearson et al., 1993] D. J. Pearson, S. B. Huffman, M. B. Willis, J. E. Laird, and R. M. Jones. A symbolic solution to intelligent real-time control. *Robotics and Autonomous Systems*, 11: 279–291, 1993.

[Quinlan, 1990] J. R. Quinlan. Learning logical definitions from relations. *Machine Learning*, 5(3): 239–266, 1990.

[Rosenbloom et al., 1993] P. S. Rosenbloom, J. E. Laird, and A. Newell. *The Soar Papers: Research on Integrated Intelligence*. MIT Press, 1993.

[Rumelhart et al., 1986] D. E. Rumelhart, G. E. Hinton, and R. J. Williams. Learning internal representations by error propagation. In *Parallel Distributed Processing*, volume 1. MIT Press, 1986.

[Tambe et al., 1995] M. Tambe, W. L. Johnson, R. M. Jones, F. Koss, J. E. Laird, P. S. Rosenbloom, and K. Schwawb. Intelligent agents for interactive simulation environments. *To appear in AI Magazine*, 1995.

[Watkins and Dayan, 1992] Christopher J. C. H. Watkins and Peter Dayan. Technical note: Q-learning. *Machine Learning*, 8: 279–292, 1992.

11

The spontaneous self-organization of an adaptive language

Luc Steels

Sony Computer Science Laboratory,
6 Rue Amyot 75005
Paris
France
and
Artificial Intelligence Laboratory,
Vrije Universiteit Brussel
Pleinlaan 2
B-1050 Brussels
Belgium
e-mail: steel@arti.vub.ac.be

Abstract

The paper studies how a group of distributed agents may spontaneously and autono-mously develop a language to refer to other agents in their environment by engaging in a series of language games. The language is adaptive in the sense that it expands or adjusts to the entry of new agents and new meanings. The paper describes the language formation mechanisms and details the results of computational simulations.

1 INTRODUCTION

The paper proposes a set of mechanisms by which a group of distributed agents may develop autonomously a language for identifying other agents in their environment. The set of agents and the set of features used for making distinctions is open-ended. The language autonomously adapts by the individual actions of agents with only local interactions.

Concretely, three mechanisms are proposed: (1) agents adopt word-meaning associ-ations from others and thus words *propagate* in the population; (2) agents may *generate* a new word and associate it with an uncovered feature set; and (3) there is a positive feedback mechanism between the selection of a word in a conversation and the success so far in using that word, thus leading to self-organized *coherence*. The mechanisms have been implemented and validated in computational experiments. The emergent languages do not have the full complexity of natural languages, for example because there is no syntax. However they involve expressions with multiple words, expressions with multiple meanings (ambiguity), and meanings with alternative expressions (synonymy).

The research discussed here has primarily a scientific motivation. The experiment is seen as a step in the investigation of how language may originate and evolve in distributed agents. The origins of language must have been one of the crucial steps in the origins of intelligence [14]. Understanding these origins forms part of recent investigations in biology to understand the major transitions towards more complexity in living systems, beginning with the origin of life itself [5], and of 'artificial life' experiments seeking to synthesize a spontaneous increase in complexity [4]. Of particular interest here are related experiments on the origin of communication [6], the origin of vocabulary [20,12], and the growth in complexity of syntax [3].

There is also a secondary motivation. Understanding the mechanisms by which a language self-organizes may make a bottom-up approach to artificial intelligence possible [10]. Although much progress has been made recently on the synthesis and acquisition of sensory–motor behaviour [9,13], the bottom-up approach still needs to be shown to be effective for cognitive capabilities. A focus on language formation is one possible route to explore this.

The next section briefly and informally sketches the main ideas proposed in the paper. Then these ideas are presented more formally and illustrated with examples. Next a number of sections detail simulation results. Section 4 shows the formation of a language from scratch, Section 5 how the language adapts to new agents entering the group, and Section 6 how the language adapts to new distinctions becoming available for lexicalization. Some further results are discussed in Section 7.

2 BASIC PRINCIPLES

Consider a set of agents capable of exchanging messages with each other. Each agent has a set of features which can be used to distinguish one agent from the other agents. The agents can engage in *language games* [21]. One agent, the *initiator*, identifies an agent, the *topic*, out of a set of other agents which constitutes the *context*. Another agent, the *recipient*, must identify the agent chosen as topic. There are two possible ways to do so: either the initiator points to the agent so that identification is direct, or the initiator uses language. Language formation and acquisition is only possible when the initiator first uses pointing and then language. When more and more language becomes available, purely linguistic means suffice.

To use language, the initiator must first identify which possible sets of features distinguish the agent chosen as topic from the other agents present in the context. There could be several such distinctive feature sets. He then chooses one and encodes this set into an expression. An expression contains one or more words. Each word encodes one or more features. Words are allowed to be ambiguous and there is not necessarily a unique way in which a given set of meanings gets encoded into an expression (synonymy).

Next, the recipient decodes the expression. If the recipient already knows which object is intended, he can identify which possible sets of features distinguish the object. From that, the recipient can confirm that the expression encodes one of the expected distinctive feature sets or infer and possibly adopt new associations between words and meanings. This feedback then enables both agents to adjust their lexicons. Each language game has therefore two dimensions. On the one hand, there is the functional dimension of identifying an object using linguistic or extra-linguistic means. On the other hand, there is the linguistic dimension in which negotiations take place about the shape of the language itself.

As we will soon see, this mechanism enables word-meaning pairs to propagate in a population of agents. But this is not enough in itself. There must also be a way in which agents can extend the language whenever the existing language is not adequate, i.e. when no word exists to express a set of features. This is achieved by allowing the initiator to make up a new word and associate it with an uncovered feature set. This action is called *lexicalization*. The creation of a new word-meaning pair happens with very low probability because the more words exist in a population the longer it takes to reach coherence.

Coherence is achieved through self-organization, in the sense of spontaneous formation of (dissipative) structures through the enforcement of random variations, known as fluctuations [8]. The fluctuations are here caused by the different associations floating around in the population. An agent records how many times a word-meaning association has been used in a game in which he was involved and how many times it was successful. When meanings need to be encoded, the agent picks the most commonly used successful association. This introduces a positive feedback loop: the more a word gets used, the more successful it will be and therefore the more it solidifies. When there are multiple possibilities a temporary struggle goes on until one association wins (see Figure 1) [11].

So we see three mechanisms: *propagation*, when agents adopt word-meaning associations from others; *creation*, when an agent generates a new word and associates it with an uncovered feature set; and *self-organization*, due to the positive feedback mechanism between association selection and success in use.

Before I discuss the details of these mechanisms more formally, some interesting properties must be pointed out.

1. There is no single agent with a complete view of the language. Each agent has his own private set of associations between words and meanings and can only experience the associations used by others by engaging in language games. There is no single agent in charge of creating new language. Each agent is allowed to make new words whenever it is needed. We therefore have a fully *distributed* system.

2. We also have an *open* system. At any point in time new agents are allowed to enter the group of existing agents or agents are allowed to leave. A new agent acquires the language of the group using the same mechanisms as those giving rise to the language in the first place. Because new agents are allowed to leave or enter, the set of topics of a conversation and the set of possible contexts is also open. The language continuously adapts, in a distributed fashion, to allow the necessary distinctions to be expressed. The system is also open with respect to features. At any point in time new features are

207

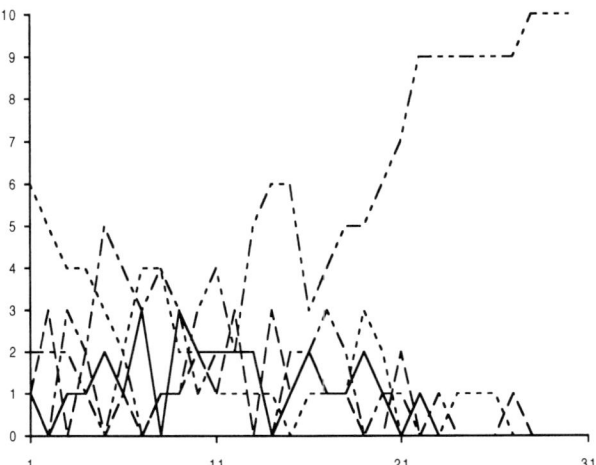

Figure 1. This figure shows the results of an experiment with 10 agents, five possible words, and one meaning. It plots the average communicative success of each word (y-axis) over a series of language games (x-axis). We see a search period in which different associations compete until one gains complete dominance.

allowed to enter into consideration for distinguishing between different agents. When these features are relevant they become lexicalized.

3. The languages derived using the proposed mechanisms have some important similarities with natural languages:

(i) The same word may have different meanings, and therefore an expression may be ambiguous. The context or additional words are then used to determine which meaning is intended.

(ii) The same meaning may be expressible by different words, and therefore we see synonyms emerge.

(iii) There is never complete coherence among agents due to different developmental pathways. Nevertheless almost complete communicative success is observed after a sufficient number of language games, because the language has become adequate enough to deal with all possible contexts of use.

3 DETAILED DESCRIPTION OF THE MECHANISMS

3.1 Terminology

Let there be a set of agents $A = \{a_1, \ldots, a_n\}$. Each agent a is assumed to have a set of features $F_a = \{f_1, \ldots, f_m\}$. $\mathcal{F}$ is the set of all possible feature sets. A feature f_k consists of a pair $(p\ v)$ where p is called an attribute and v a value. A set of features $D_{a_1}^B$

distinguishes an agent a_1 from a set of other agents $B = \{a_2, \dots, a_n\}$ iff $D_{a_1}^B \subset F_{a_1}$ and $\forall a \in B, D_{a_1}^B \not\subset F_a$. $D_{a_1}^B$ is called a *distinctive feature set* with respect to a_1 and B. There can be several distinctive feature sets for the same a_1 and B. There can also be none if $F_{a_1} \subseteq F_a \in B$.

A *word* is a sequence of letters drawn from a finite shared alphabet. In the experiments reported later, a word is a consonant-vowel sequence, such as '(t a)' or '(k i)'. An *expression* is a sequence of words. Word order is not assumed to play a role.

A *lexicon* $L \subset F \times W$ is a relation between a possible feature set $K \subset F$ and a word $w \in W$. Each member of this relation is called an *association*. Each agent $a \in A$ is assumed to have a single lexicon L_a which is initially empty.

$u(\langle K, w \rangle, a)$ is the number of times the association $\langle K, w \rangle \in L_a$ has been used by a. $s(\langle K, w \rangle, a)$ is the number of times the association $\langle K, w \rangle \in L_a$ was used successfully by a, i.e. when it is part of a language game which ended with communicative success (defined shortly).

3.2 Language games

A language game $g = \langle C, i, r, o \rangle$ includes a context $C = \{a_1, a_2, \dots, a_j\} \subseteq A$, an initiator $i \in C$, a recipient $r \in C$, and a topic $o \in C$. The language game involves the following steps:

1. Both the initiator i and the receiver r determine the distinctive feature sets $\mathcal{D}_o^C = \{D_o^B | B = C \backslash \{o\}\}$. It is assumed that both agents share the same distinctive feature set.

2. The initiator chooses one feature set $D_j \in \mathcal{D}_o^C$ and constructs an expression e which *covers* D_j.

3. The recipient *uncovers* from e the feature sets $\mathcal{H} = \{H_1, \dots, H_p\}$.

4. g ends in communicative success when $H \cap \mathcal{D}_o^C \neq \varnothing$, otherwise in failure.

The *cover* and *uncover* functions are at the heart of the language encoding and decoding process. They are defined as follows:

- Given an agent $a \in A$, *cover* $(D, L_a) = \{e | e = \{w | D = \cup K$ with $\langle K, w \rangle \in L_a\}\}$.

- Given an agent $a \in A$, *uncover* $(e, L_a) = \{H | H = \cup K$ with $\langle K, w \rangle \in L_r, w \in e\}$.

The cover function yields a set of possible expressions. Only one expression is selected for use in the communication, based on two criteria: (1) the smallest set is preferred and (2) in case of equal size, an expression is preferred for which the implied associations score better. The score $m(\langle K, w \rangle, a) = s(\langle K, w \rangle, a)/u(\langle K, w \rangle, a)$ for $\langle K, w \rangle \in L_a$.

The overall result of a language game is either

1. that there are not enough distinctions to identify the topic in this context, $\mathcal{D}_o^C = \varnothing$;

2. that the game ends in communicative success, i.e. $\mathcal{H} \cap \mathcal{D}_o^C \neq \varnothing$;

3. that the game ends in communicative failure, which could take many different forms:

   (a) the initiator i may not have enough words to cover all the features, *cover* $(D_j, L_i) = \varnothing$;

   (b) the recipient r may not have enough associations to uncover all the meanings, *uncover* $(e, L_r) = \varnothing$;

   (c) there is a mismatch between expected and uncovered meanings, $\mathcal{H} \cap \mathcal{D}_o^C = \varnothing$.

These different types of results and the corresponding steps in language formation are discussed in more detail in the next subsection.

I have implemented the mechanisms needed to engage in language games as a computer program written in LISP. The program creates agents, assigns randomly values for features from the set of possible features, and then starts a series of language games. For each game, a context, initiator, recipient and topic are randomly chosen. A language game is printed out by the program as follows:

```
Dialog 47 between a-2 and a-4 about a-2.
   Context: {a-2 a-6 a-5 a-4}
   a2 = (((size tall))
         ((shape square)))
 a-2: ((size tall)) => ((d o))
 a-4: => ((size tall))
(success)
```

In this game a-2 plays the role of initiator, a-4 that of recipient. The topic is a-2. The context is {a-2, a-6, a-5, a-4}. There are two distinctive feature sets: ((*size tall*)) and ((*shape square*)). a-2 has picked the first one and has translated this into the expression '((d o))'. a-4 uncovers ((*size tall*)) from '((d o))' . The language game ends in communicative success because ((*size tall*)) is one of the expected feature sets. The indication of the result of a game often contains additional information.

3.3 Language formation rules

This section details the different rules that agents follow in the adoption or formation of language.

```
0. No distinctions possible
```

The first case is one where there are not enough features available to distinguish the topic from the other agents present in the context. This should put pressure on a meaning creation process to introduce a new distinction (see Section 6).

```
1. Lexicon inadequate for initiator
```

The initiator may not have enough associations in his lexicon to cover all the meanings in the chosen feature structure D_j. In this case the game ends in failure and it is indicated for which features no words were available. The usage u of all associations that were used by the initiator are incremented, but not the success s. The initiator may create a new word (with probability 0.05 in the present experiments) and associate it in his lexicon with the non-covered meanings. This happens in the next example:

```
Dialog 54 between a-6 and a-5 about a-6.
    Context: {a-5 a-6 a-4 a-3}
    a6 = ((weight light))
 a-6: ((weight light)) => ?
 a-5: => nil
    !! a-6: ((weight light)) -> (t u)
(failure-no-words-initiator nil ((weight light)))
```

a-6 has created the word '(t u)' to express ((*weight light*)). Note that the word is not yet used in the conversation and there is no impact on the recipient a-5. If there are several features that are not covered yet by the lexicon, this rule will automatically lead to words that are associated with a set of features instead of just one.

The same situation may also occur when only a subset of D_j cannot be covered. This is illustrated in the next example. a-7 already has a word for ((*weight light*)) but not yet for ((*size medium*)). a-7 creates a new word '(v i)'.

```
Dialog 39 between a-7 and a-2 about a-6.
    Context: {a-2 a-7 a-5 a-3 a-6}
    a-6 = ((weight light) (size medium))
 a-7: ((weight light) (size medium)) => ?
 a-2: => nil
    !! a-7: ((size medium)) -> (v i)
(failure-no-words-initiator
    (((d o) ((weight light)) (3 . 0))) ((size medium)))
```

2. Lexicon inadequate for recipient

The recipient may not have enough associations in his lexicon to uncover all the meanings from e. In this case the game ends in failure and it is indicated for which words no associations were available. Several possibilities can be distinguished.

2.1. No words at all could be uncovered

In this case, the recipient can deduce that the expression must be associated with one of the feature sets in the distinctive feature sets, and the association is consequently constructed. This is shown in the following example.

```
Dialog 53 between a-3 and a-4 about a-7.
    Context: {a-4 a-3 a-6 a-7}
    a-7 = ((shape square))
```

```
a-3: ((shape square)) => ((s o))
a-4: => nil
    !! a-4: ((shape square)) -> (s o)
(failure-no-words-recipient ((s o)))
```

This operation may also lead to ambiguities because there might be more than one way in which the topic is distinguished from the context, as shown in the next example. The word '(z u)' comes to mean both ((*weight light*)) and ((*size tall*)).

```
Dialog 78 between a-4 and a-5 about a-2.
    Context: {a-4 a-2 a-5}
    a-2 = (((weight light))
          ((size tall)))
 a-4: ((weight light)) => ((z u))
 a-5: => nil
    !! a-5: ((weight light)) -> (z u)
    !! a-5: ((size tall)) -> (z u)
(failure-no-words-recipient ((z u)))
```

2.2. Some words could be uncovered

It could be that some words could be uncovered but others could not be. When there is only one word which is unknown, the recipient can deduce the meaning and a new association can be created. When there is too much uncertainty no changes are made. This is shown in the next example. a-11 uncovers the feature (*size tall*) from the word '(d e)' and can infer that the word '(b i)' must be associated with the other feature (*weight heavy*).

```
Dialog 946 between a-7 and a-11 about a-11.
    Context: {a-7 a-10 a-11 a-9}
    a-11 = (((size tall) (weight heavy)))
 a-7: ((size tall) (weight heavy)) => ((d e) (b i))
 a-11: => nil
    !! a-11: ((weight heavy)) -> (b i)
(failure-partial-cover-recipient
    (((d e) ((size tall)) (14 . 12))) ((b i)))
```

3. No words missing

The next cases are concerned with situations where both the initiator and the recipient have associations to encode or decode the distinctive feature sets.

3.1. Success

Complete success is reached when the distinctive feature sets expected by the recipient includes the one uncovered from the expression used by the initiator. Both the use and the success of the association is incremented by the initiator and the recipient. This is shown in the next example:

```
Dialog 47 between a-2 and a-4 about a-2.
    Context: {a-2 a-6 a-5 a-4}
    a-2 = (((size tall)))
 a-2: ((size tall)) => ((d o))
 a-4: => ((size tall))
(success)
```

3.2. Success but too general

It may also be that there is success but that the recipient decoded more possible meanings for the expression. In that case, only the success of the association that was effectively relevant gets incremented. This leads to a progressive disambiguation of associations that were unnecessarily broad. Thus in the next example, a-2 decodes '((d o))' into both ((*size tall*)) and ((*weight light*)). Both are applicable but only one is really necessary. '((d o))' is therefore broader than necessary.

```
Dialog 72 between a-3 and a-2 about a-2.
    Context: {a-2 a-3 a-5 a-6 a-7}
    a-2  = (((size tall))
            ((weight light)))
 a-3: ((size tall)) => ((d o))
 a-2: => ((size tall))
        ((weight light))
(success-but-too-general-recipient
    (((d o) ((weight light)) (3 . 2)))
    ((d o)))
```

3.3. Mismatch in meaning

It may be that the feature set decoded by the recipient is not one of the feature sets that is distinctive for the object. The success record of the implied association is therefore not incremented. This is shown in the next example.

```
Dialog 505 between a-7 and a-6 about a-6.
    Context: {a-6 a-7 a-5 a-4}
    a-6  = (((weight light)))
 a-7: ((weight light)) => ((d o))
 a-6: => ((size tall))
(failure-mismatch-meaning-recipient
    (((d o) ((size tall)) (10 . 6)))
    (((weight light))))
```

The same could happen in a multiple word sentence, as shown in the following example, where the word '(d o)' is decoded as (*size tall*) whereas (*weight light*) is expected.

```
Dialog 521 between a-7 and a-6 about a-6.
    Context: {a-7 a-4 a-5 a-2 a-6}
    a-6 = (((weight light) (size medium))))
 a-7: ((weight light) (size medium)) => ((v i) (d o))
 a-6: => (((size tall)) ((size medium)))
(failure-mismatch-meaning-recipient
    (((d o)((size tall)) (13 . 8))
     ((v i)((size medium)) (2 . 1)))
    (((weight light) (size medium))))
```

4 THE FORMATION OF A LANGUAGE FROM SCRATCH

This section and the next ones discuss in detail some simulation results obtained through an implementation of the mechanisms introduced in the previous section. It starts with a population of five agents. There are three possible features: *weight* with possible values heavy, light, average, *shape* with possible values square, oval, round, and *size* with values small, medium, tall. The agents have the following features:

```
a-10:                       a-7:
  (weight heavy)              (weight light)
  (size small)               (size medium)
  (shape square)             (shape round)
a-9:                        a-6:
  (weight average)           (weight average)
  (size tall)                (size tall)
  (shape round)              (shape square)
a-8:
  (weight heavy)
  (size medium)
  (shape round)
```

After about 4000 language games, a stable language has emerged. The language is stable in the sense that the agents are no longer creating new words or new associations, although there may still be shifts in usage. The following shows the language that the agents preferentially use. For each possible feature, the words in use, and for each word, the agents that use it are shown.

```
((shape square)):
  [(t i) (a-6 a-7 a-8 a-9 a-10)]
((weight heavy)):
  [(n e) (a-6 a-7 a-8 a-9 a-10)]
((size small)):
  [(n e) (a-6 a-8 a-9 a-10)]
  [(t i) (a-7)]
```

```
((weight average)):
  [(r e) (a-6 a-7 a-9 a-10)]
  [(d a) (a-8)]
((size tall)):
  [(r e) (a-8 a-9 a-10)]
  [(d a) (a-6 a-7)]
((shape round)):
  [(b e) (a-6 a-7 a-8 a-9 a-10)]
((weight light)):
  [(s o) (a-6 a-7 a-8 a-9 a-10)]
((size medium)):
  [(z u) (a-6 a-7 a-8 a-9 a-10)]
```

Some features, such as (*shape oval*) are not lexicalized because they are irrelevant. Others like (*weight average*) and (*size tall*) are covered by the same word '(r e)' or '(d a)' because they always occur together (in a-9 and a-6) so agents cannot distinguish which one of the features is intended. Some words are ambiguous. For example, a-6 uses '(n e)' for (*weight heavy*) as well as (*size small*). However it does not have a further impact on communicative success. Either the distinction does not matter because either one of these features is enough to distinguish. For example, if a-8 is not part of the context and a-10 needs to be identified, either feature will do. Or, agents use an additional word to express the value for *shape*.

When we look at the lexicons of individual agents, a more complex picture is emerging. Here are for example the associations involving (*size small*) with *u* and *s* printed out for each agent.

```
((size small)):
  [(n e) (a-6 (272 . 204)) (a-7 (203 . 88))
         (a-8 (285 . 156)) (a-9 (225 . 152))
         (a-10 (328 . 296))]
  [(t i) (a-6 (138 . 10)) (a-7 (139 . 70))
         (a-8 (115 . 12)) (a-9 (129 . 5))
         (a-10 (136 . 24))]
```

For the feature (*size small*) most agents use the word '(n e)' but they all have an association with '(t i)' as well, whose score is less, except for a-7. '(t i)' is a retention from earlier usage where it meant both (*size small*) and (*shape square*) as required for distinguishing a-10.

A typical conversation at this point is the following:

```
    a-10 = (((weight heavy)))
a-8: ((weight heavy)) => ((n e))
a-7: => ((size small)) ((weight heavy))
```

a-8 uses '(n e)' to encode (*weight heavy*). This is ambiguous for a-7. But ((*weight heavy*)) is the only way the topic a-10 can be distinguished. The language game succeeds

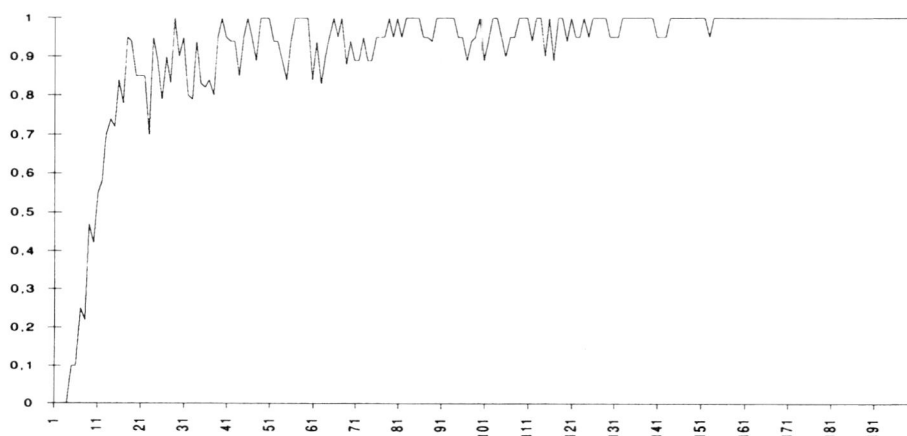

Figure 2. This figure plots the formation of a language from scratch. 4000 language games are shown. The *x*-axis plots the number of language games (scale 1/20). The *y*-axis shows the average communicative success.

(case 3.2) and the success of the association between '(n e)' and (*weight heavy*) is incremented. Resolution of the ambiguity of '(n e)' will occur when there are more cases like this.

Here is another example:

```
a-8 = (((shape round) (weight heavy))
       ((weight heavy) (size medium)))
a-10: ((shape round) (weight heavy)) => ((b e) (n e))
a-9: => ((size medium))
        ((size small))
        ((weight heavy))
        ((shape round))
```

a-9 decodes '(b e)' as ((*shape round*)) or ((*size medium*)) and '(n e)' as ((*weight heavy*)) or ((*size small*)). In this case, the use of ((*weight heavy*)) is confirmed because one way the topic can be distinguished is as ((*shape round*) (*weight heavy*)). Another combination ((*size medium*) (*weight heavy*)) also matches with possible decodings of '((b e) (n e))'.

Figure 2 shows the evolution of the language from the beginning. The communicative success climbs steadily from 0 to become absolute. The agents have developed sufficient words to distinguish each other based on their features.

5 ADDING NEW AGENTS

A new agent entering the group acquires the already existing language. At the same time, new words may get created because new distinctions become lexicalized. This is shown in the following experiment. The new agent has the following features:

```
a-11:
  (weight heavy)
  (size medium)
  (shape oval)
```

The prefered language of each agent after about 2000 language games looks as follows:

```
((weight heavy)):
  [(n e) (a-6 a-7 a-8 a-9 a-10 a-11)]
((weight light)):
  [(s o) (a-6 a-7 a-8 a-9 a-10 a-11)]
((shape round)):
  [(b e) (a-6 a-7 a-8 a-9 a-10 a-11)]
((size small)):
  [(n e) (a-6 a-8 a-9 a-10 a-11)]
  [(t i) (a-7)]
((shape square)):
  [(t i) (a-6 a-7 a-8 a-9 a-10 a-11)]
((size medium)):
  [(z u) (a-6 a-7 a-8 a-9 a-10 a-11)]
((shape oval)):
  [(z u) (a-6 a-7 a-8 a-9 a-10 a-11)]
((weight average)):
  [(n u) (a-11)]
  [(r e) (a-6 a-7 a-9 a-10)]
  [(d a) (a-8)]
((size tall)):
  [(d a) (a-6 a-7 a-10 a-11)]
  [(r e) (a-8 a-9)]
```

We see that (*shape oval*) has become lexicalized to make the distinction between a-8 and a-11. Note also that a-11 has introduced a new word '(n u)' for (*weight average*). The other agents understand this word but will not use it. There is now a majority using '(d a)' for (*size tall*). The semantic resolution of '(d a)' and '(r e)' has therefore made some progress.

A typical conversation with this language is the following:

```
a-6 = (((shape square) (weight average))
       ((shape square) (size tall)))
a-10: ((shape square) (size tall)) => ((t i) (d a))
a-11: => ((size tall))((weight average))
         ((shape square))((size small))
```

a-10 selects ((*shape square*) (*size tall*)) and encodes this as '((t i) (d a))' '(d a)' is decoded by a-11 as ((*size tall*)) or ((*weight average*)), '(t i)' as ((*size small*)) or ((*shape square*)).

Out of this a-11 can reconstruct one possible distinctive feature set compatible with the expected ones. The language game therefore ends in success.

Figure 3 plots how the language adapts after the next agent (a-12) is added. Initially there is a drop in communicative success but after some time period, adjustments and new lexicalizations restore it.

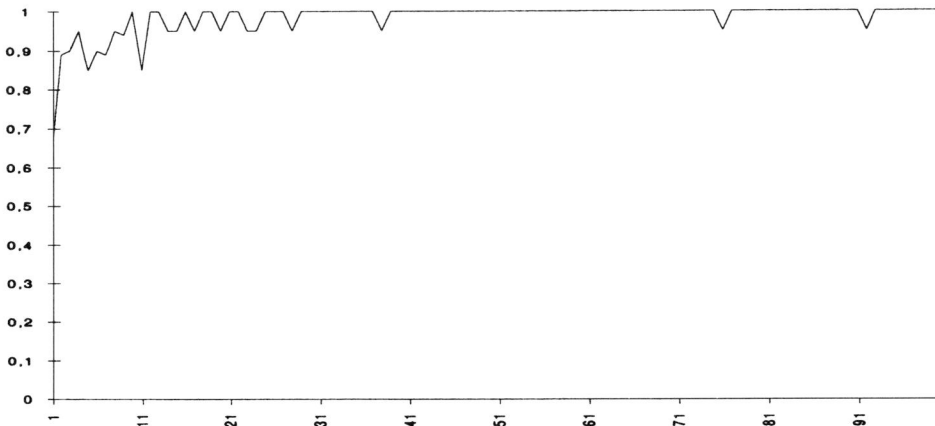

Figure 3. This figure plots 2000 language games illustrating the adaptation of language after a new agent comes in. The x-axis plots the number of language games (scale 1/20). The y-axis shows the communicative success.

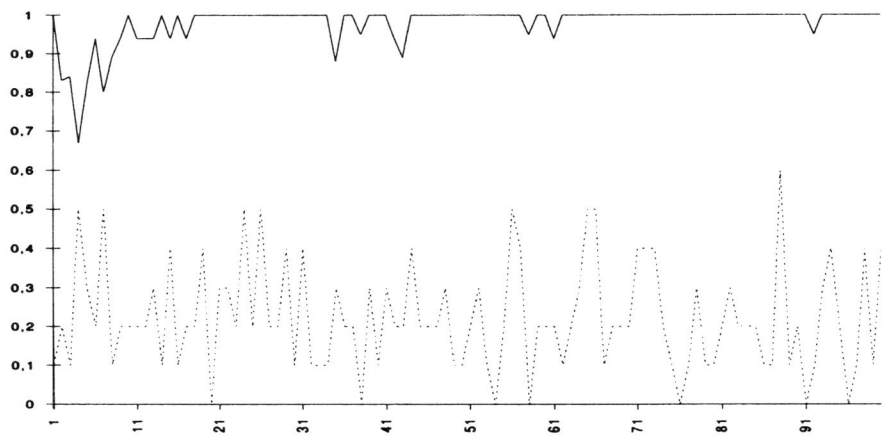

Figure 4. Another agent enters and the language adjusts. 2000 language games are shown. The y-axis shows the communicative success (top graph) and the failure in making distinctions (bottom graph). Many language games fail by lack of available distinctions because too many agents have joined the group that have the same features as those already present.

218

6 ADDING NEW FEATURES

When more and more agents are added, the available features become insufficient to distinguish one agent from others. Consequently language games start to fail on that basis. This is seen in Figure 4. When the existing set of features fails to make distinctions, new features could be added by an independent meaning creation process. The language must then adapt by lexicalizing the features that are relevant for expressing the new distinctions. This is shown in the following experiment. A new feature color has been added with possible values blue, red, yellow and green. All agents now receive a value for this new feature. For example, a-14 and a-13 have the following features:

```
a-14:                    a-13:
  (color blue)             (color red)
  (weight heavy)           (weight average)
  (size medium)            (size small)
  (shape oval)             (shape round)
```

After about 2000 language games, these colors have become lexicalized:

```
((color blue)):
  [(r u) (a-6 a-7 a-8 a-9 a-10 a-11 a-12 a-13 a-14)]
((color yellow)):
  [(m e) (a-6 a-7 a-8 a-9 a-10 a-11 a-12 a-13 a-14)]
((color red)):
  [(t e) (a-6 a-7 a-8 a-9 a-10 a-11 a-12 a-13 a-14)]
((color green)):
  [(p i) (a-6 a-7 a-8 a-9 a-10 a-11 a-12 a-13 a-14)]
```

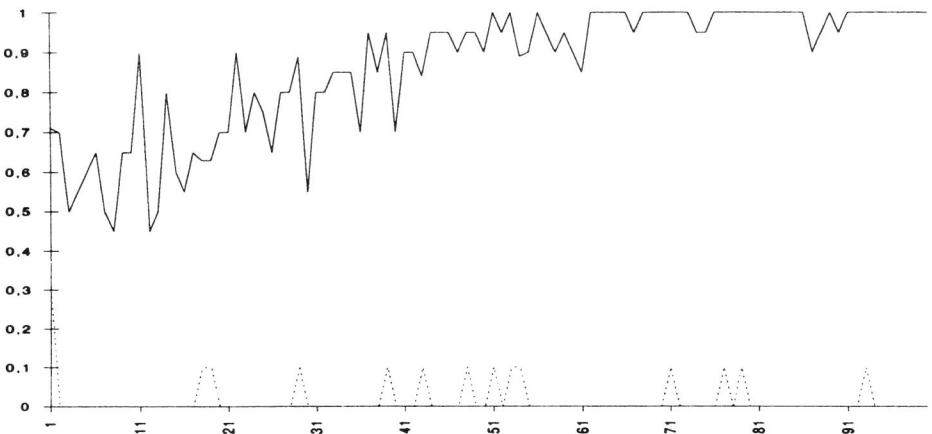

Figure 5. This figure plots the adaptation of language after a new distinction has been introduced. The failure to make distinctions has decreased. 2000 language games are shown.

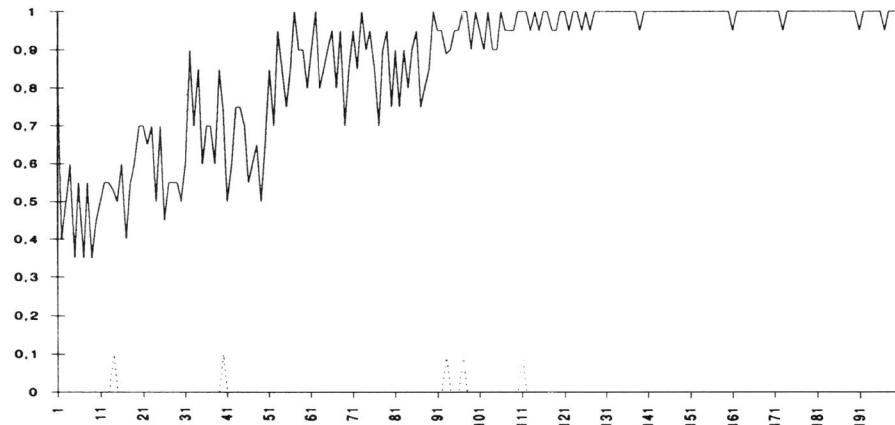

Figure 6. This figure plots the adaptation of language after yet another distinction has been added. 2000 language games are shown.

Figure 5 plots the adaptation of the language. There is a drop in communicative success when the new distinction is introduced but after a certain period, communicative success again reaches the maximum. The success in making distinctions has also improved.

A similar experiment where a new feature with five possible values is introduced is shown in Figure 6. Again we see a drop in communicative success followed by a rebound.

7 FURTHER RESULTS

The results discussed in the previous paragraphs were originally obtained in 1994. Since then, considerable progress has been made on many related issues. This section gives a brief overview with references to additional-papers.

The first question concerns scale up: Is it possible to increase the population of agents substantially? Is it possible to have a steady in- and outflux of agents and meanings? Further computational results show that a scale-up is indeed possible. It is obvious that the time needed to reach communicative success (and hence coherence in the language) increases with the number of agents in the population, and this imposes a limit on what is eventually feasable. On the other hand, we have been able to show that a population can cope with a growing set of meanings and a growing set of new agents entering. So scale-up is reached by gradual extension of the population. The growth rates are obviously bounded but nevertheless positive (see Figure 7). More detailed results and discussions can be found in [16].

A second question concerns the origin of the distinctions used for constructing distinctive features. Could they be derived as well by the agents without human intervention?

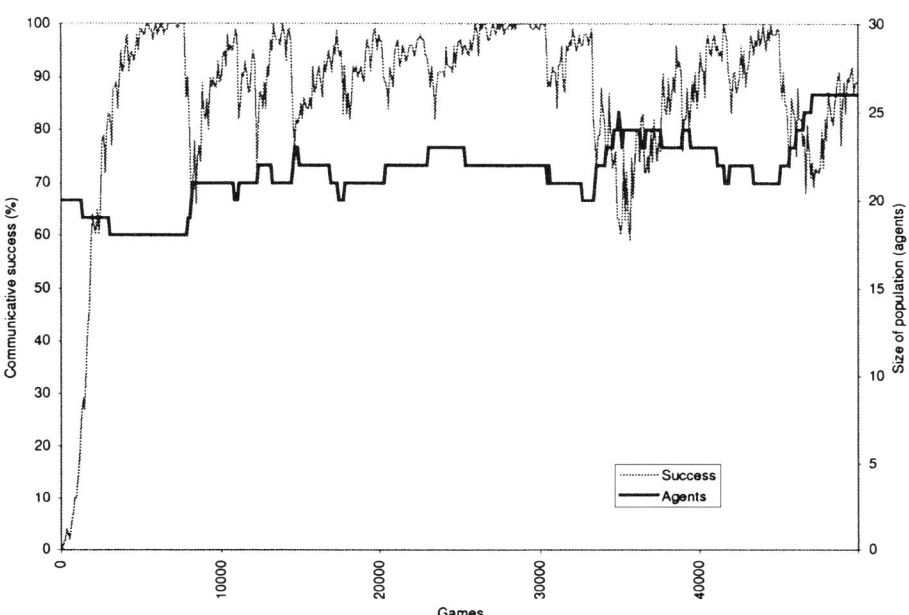

Figure 7. The figure shows the evolution of the communicative success in a fluctuating population of agents. New agents enter with a probability 0.00005 and they depart with the same probability. The agents engage in games in which they identify themselves. The population is able to cope with the flux.

The answer to this question has turned out to be positive as well. It has been shown that a group of agents can develop a repertoire of distinctions recognized through discrimination trees, driven by the need to find distinctive feature sets [15]. This mechanism has been coupled to the lexicon formation process described in this paper [17], showing a co-evolution of a meaning repertoire and a lexicon. The system is still open in the sense that new objects may enter the environment at all times. These results are illustrated in Figure 8.

A third question concerns the embedding of these mechanisms in physical robots. One of the original targets of the research is to understand mechanisms by which agents could autonomously develop visually grounded categories and a language which is grounded in their sensory–motor experience. Again we have been able to obtain positive results. The lexicon formation and ontology creation mechanisms have been ported to mobile robots and to two 'talking heads' [18]. In both cases, the agents are challenged to develop a repertoire of distinctions and a lexicon which is adequate for identifying the objects present in the environment. Figure 9 illustrates the physical setup used in these experiments.

A final question relates to the development of a syntax. We have seen already in the examples in this paper that multiple word sentences arise. Recently, the first positive

221

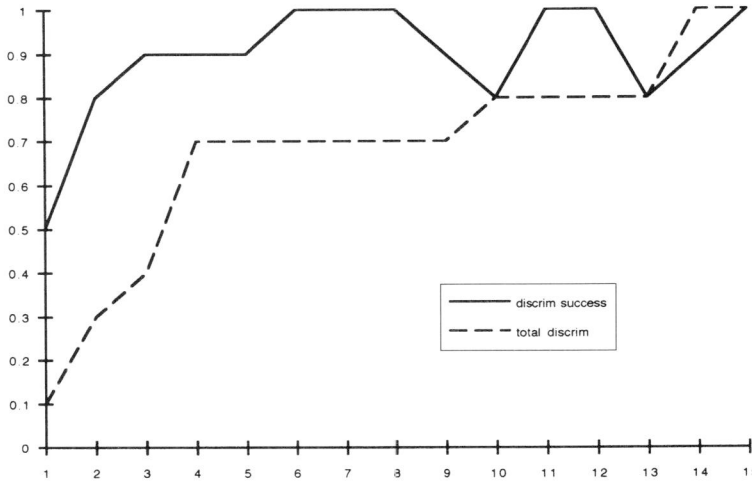

Figure 8. The graph shows the evolution of the discriminatory capacities of a single agent. The total number of objects (10) is fixed. There are five data channels. The average success in discrimination games as well as the total success is shown on the y-axis. The number of discriminations is mapped on the x-axis (scale 1/10). All objects can be discriminated after 150 discrimination games.

Figure 9. Two robots have approached each other and are now facing each other. The robots are equiped with a dozen low-level sensors. The discrimination trees are based on data coming from these sensors. They will give rise to categories which are then used in the language games as described in this paper. Note the other objects in the environment surrounding the robots, which will be the subject of the conversation.

222

results were obtained where we could show a preliminary syntax by adding an episodic, schema-based memory that starts from recording the situations arising in multiword sentences, and then re-instantiates their constraints when similar situations arise. More details are contained in [18].

8 CONCLUSIONS

The paper has proposed a set of mechanisms by which distributed agents spontaneously and autonomously develop a coherent language to identify each other using distinctive features. The system is open in the sense that new agents and new distinctions may be introduced. The language adapts by lexicalizing new features or by resolving ambiguities in the use of certain words. The mechanisms have been tested experimentally through computer implementation.

The spontaneous formation of a language in a group of distributed agents appears to be quite feasible and goes surprisingly fast. Cultural processes such as the ones proposed here provide an alternative to genetic explanations for the origin [7] or acquisition of language [1]. Self-organization is very common in other areas of biology [2] and it is therefore not surprising that it might play an important role in language formation.

Acknowledgements

The research and writing of this paper has been financed by the Belgian Federal Government FKFO project on emergent functionality (FKFO contract nr. G.0014.95) and the IUAP 'Construct' Project (nr. 20) of the Belgian Government, with additional support from the External Researcher Program of the Sony Computer Science Laboratory in Tokyo. Josefina Sierra provided valuable comments on the paper.

REFERENCES

[1] Chomsky, N. (1980) Rules and Representations. *Brain and Behavior Science*, **3**, pp. 1–15.
[2] Deneubourg, J.-L. (1977) Application de l'ordre par fluctuations à la description de certaines étapes de la construction du nid chez les termites. *Insectes Sociaux*, **24**(2), pp. 117–130.
[3] Hashimoto and Ikegami (1995) Evolution of Symbolic Grammar Systems. In: Morán, F., A. Moreno, J. Merelo and P. Chacón (Eds.), *Advances in Artificial Life. Third European Conference on Artificial Life*. Granada, Spain. Springer-Verlag, Berlin. pp. 812–823.
[4] Langton, C. (ed.) (1995) *Artificial Life. An Overview.* The MIT Press, Cambridge, MA.
[5] Maynard-Smith, J. and E. Szathmary (1994) *The Major Transitions in Evolution*. Oxford University Press, Oxford.
[6] MacLennan, B. (1991) Synthetic Ethology: An Approach to the Study of Communication. In: Langton, C. *et al*. (eds.), *Artificial Life II*. Addison-Wesley Pub. Co., Redwood City, Calif. pp. 631–658.
[7] Pinker, S. (1994) *The Language Instinct*. Penguin Books, London.
[8] Prigogine, I. and I. Stengers (1984) *Order Out of Chaos*. Bantam Books, New York.
[9] Steels, L. (ed.) (1995) *The Biology and Technology of Intelligent Autonomous Agents*. Springer-Verlag, Berlin.

[10] Steels, L. and R. Brooks (eds.) (1995) *Building Situated Embodied Agents. The Alife Route to AI.* Lawrence Erlbaum Assoc., New Haven.
[11] Steels, L. (1996a) Self-organizing Vocabularies. In: Langton, C. (ed.), *Artificial Life V.* Nara, Japan. Addison-Wesley Pub. Co., Redwood City, Calif.
[12] Steels, L. (1996b) A Self-organizing Spatial Vocabulary. *Artificial Life Journal*, **3**.
[13] Steels, L. (1996c) Discovering the Competitors. *Journal of Adaptive Behavior*, **4**(2).
[14] Steels, L. (1996d) The Origins of Intelligence. In: *Proceedings of the 1995 Carlo Erba Meeting on Artificial Life.* Fondazione Carlo Erba, Milan.
[15] Steels, L. (1996e) Perceptually Grounded Meaning Creation. In: Tokoro, M. (ed.) (1996), *Proccedings of ICMAS-96, Kyoto 1996.* AAAI Press, Calif.
[16] Steels, L. (1997a) Language Learning and Language Contact. In: Daelemans, W., Van den Bosch, A., and Weijters, A. (eds.), *Workshop Notes of the ECML/MLnet Familiarization Workshop on Empirical Learning of Natural Language Processing Tasks.* Prague, pp. 11–24.
[17] Steels, L. (1997b) Constructing and Sharing Perceptual Distinctions. In: van Someren, M. and G. Widmer (eds.), *Proceedings of the European Conference on Machine Learning.* Springer-Verlag, Berlin.
[18] Steels, L. (1997c) The Origins of Syntax in Visually Grounded Robotic Agents. In: Pollack, M. (ed.), *Proceedings of the IJCAI-97 Conference.* The AAAI Press, Morgan Kaufmann Pub., Los Angeles.
[19] Steels, L. (1997d) The Synthetic Modeling of Language Origins. *Evolution of Communication*, **1**(1): 1–35. Walter Benjamins, Amsterdam.
[20] Werner, G. and M. Dyer (1991) Evolution of Communication in Artificial Organisms. In: Langton, C. *et al.* (eds.), *Artificial Life II.* Addison-Wesley Pub. Co., Redwood City, Ca. pp. 659–687.
[21] Wittgenstein, L. (1974) *Philosophical Investigations.* Translated by G. Anscombe. Basil Blackwell, Oxford.

FORMALISMS AND MODELS OF LEARNING

12

Developments in computational learning and discovery theory within the framework of elementary formal systems

Setsuo Arikawa
Ayumi Shinohara

Department of Informatics
Kyushu University 33,
Fukuoka 812-8581,
Japan

Masako Sato

Department of Mathematics and Information Science,
College of Arts and Integrated Sciences,
Osaka Prefecture University,
Sakai
Osaka 593
Japan

Takeshi Shinohara

Department of Artificial Intelligence,
Kyushu Institute of Technology,
Iizuka 820
Japan

Abstract

This paper surveys our studies on computational learning theory and computational discovery theory within the framework of elementary formal systems (EFSs for short), which are a kind of logic program on words, i.e., strings of characters.

First we show that the EFSs are a good framework for discussing formal grammars and languages. Then we point out that EFSs work as a unifying framework for inductive inference of languages by discussing the model inference for EFSs in Shapiro's sense.

Within the framework of EFSs we show the following remarkable results on computational learning theory: (1) The class of languages inferable from positive data is much richer than has been believed. (2) The class of languages inferable from complete data can be characterized in a mathematical way without appealing to an inductive inference procedure. (3) The class of PAC-learnable languages is also much richer than has been believed. Furthermore we illustrate an application of our theoretical results on PAC-learnability to molecular biology.

These theoretical results, together with the experimental results, have led us to a mathematical theory of machine discovery from facts. We point out that the notion of refutability of the hypothesis space itself in a learning process is the most essential in such a theory, and show that there are rich spaces that can be refuted in the process of learning within the framework of length-bounded EFSs.

1 INTRODUCTION

An elementary formal system (EFS, for short) is a logical system introduced by Smullyan (Smullyan, 1961) for developing his recursive function theory. The systems were shown to be a kind of grammar for generating formal languages like Chomsky grammars (Arikawa, 1970). EFSs are also a kind of logic program which directly manipulates words, i.e., character strings, and thus we can make use of the resolution principle (Robinson, 1965) for recognizing formal languages.

Computational learning theory includes three major paradigms: inductive inference (Angluin and Smith, 1983), learning with a minimally adequate teacher (MAT) (Angluin, 1988), and probably approximately correct (PAC) learning (Valiant, 1984).

Computational learning theory has often been developed in terms of formal language theory based on various types of formal grammars and automata such as regular expressions, context-free grammars, finite automata and Turing machines. In developing computational learning theory on formal languages we can employ EFSs as a unifying framework. We can define a new hierarchy of various language classes within the framework of EFSs, which includes as a kernel the class of pattern languages that played an important role in inductive inference from positive data (Angluin, 1980b; Shinohara, 1982; Shinohara, 1983). It also includes the four classes in the Chomsky hierarchy, and many others (Arikawa, 1970; Shinohara, 1986; Arikawa et al., 1989; 1992b; Miyano et al., 1991; Saeki and Arikawa, 1990; Sakakibara, 1990; Shinohara, 1990; 1994). The resolution principle for EFSs works as a uniform procedure for testing guessed hypotheses. Thus EFSs work as grammars to generate languages, as automata to recognize languages, and as logic programs to deal with words. In developing computational learning theory with EFSs, we can take full advantage of the fruitful results obtained in the field of formal language theory.

The present paper makes a brief survey of our studies on computational learning theory and discovery theory developed within the framework of EFSs (Shinohara, 1982; Arikawa et al., 1989; Shinohara, 1990; Miyano et al., 1991; Arikawa et al., 1992a; Mukouchi and Arikawa, 1993; Moriyama and Sato, 1993; Shinohara, 1994; Sato and Moriyama, 1994; Sato, 1995; Mukouchi and Arikawa, 1995). First we define the EFSs and important subclasses. In Section 3 we briefly describe the model inference for EFSs in Shapiro's sense to show that they form a good framework for inductive inference of formal languages. Then in Section 4 we show some rich classes of EFS languages inferable from positive data and give a new characterization theorem for classes of EFS languages to be inferable from positive data. In Section 5, we discuss a theory of machine discovery from facts and point out that the essence of the theory is space refutability. Then we show some rich classes of EFS languages which are space refutable and also give a characterization theorem for a class of EFS languages to be space refutable from complete data. In Section 6, again due to our framework, we show some rich classes of EFS languages which are PAC-learnable. In Section 7 we illustrate an application of our theoretical results with EFSs to motif discovery from protein data.

2 ELEMENTARY FORMAL SYSTEMS

Let Σ be a finite *alphabet*, X be a countable set of *variables*, and Π be a set of *predicate* symbols. We assume these three sets Σ, X, Π are mutually disjoint. The *arity*, a positive integer, is associated with each predicate symbol. We use x, y, x_1, x_2, ... , to denote variables and p, q, p_1, p_2, ... , to denote predicate symbols. By Σ^*, Σ^+, $\Sigma^{\leq n}$ we denote the sets of all words over Σ, all nonempty words, all words of length n or less, respectively.

A *pattern* is an element in $(\Sigma \cup X)^+$. A pattern π is said to be *regular* if each variable appears at most once in π. For example, a pattern 'xy' is regular but not 'xx'. An *atom* is an expression of the form $p(\pi_1, \ldots, \pi_n)$, where p is a predicate symbol with arity n and $\pi_1, \ldots, \pi_n$ are patterns. A *definite clause* is a clause of the form

$$A \leftarrow B_1, \ldots, B_m,$$

where A, $B_1, \ldots, B_m$ are atoms. The atom A is called the *head* and the part $B_1, \ldots, B_m$ the *body* of the definite clause. We identify an atom A with a clause $A \leftarrow$. A clause is called *ground* if it contains no variable.

Definition 1 *An* elementary formal system *(EFS, for short) is a finite set of definite clauses.*

A *substitution* is a homomorphism from patterns to patterns that maps each symbol $a \in \Sigma$ to itself. A substitution that maps some variables to the empty word is called an ε-substitution. In this paper we do not deal with ε-substitution unless stated otherwise. By $\pi\theta$, we denote the image of a pattern π by a substitution θ. For an atom $A = p(\pi, \ldots, \pi_n)$ and a clause $C = A \leftarrow B_1, \ldots, B_m$, we define $A\theta = p(\pi_1\theta, \ldots, \pi_n\theta)$ and $C\theta = A\theta \leftarrow B_1\theta, \ldots, B_m\theta$.

Definition 2 *A definite clause C is* provable from *an EFS Γ, denoted by $\Gamma \vdash C$, if C is obtained from Γ by finitely many (possibly 0) applications of substitutions and modus ponens.*

Definition 3 *Let Γ be an EFS and p be a unary predicate symbol. The* language $L(\Gamma, p)$ *is the set $\{w \in \Sigma^+ \mid \Gamma \vdash p(w)\}$. If such Γ and p exist, the language L is* definable by an EFS Γ *or called an* EFS language. *The set of ground atoms provable from Γ is denoted by $PS(\Gamma)$.*

The language $L(\pi)$ of a pattern π is defined as the set of words obtained by substituting nonempty words for variables in π, that is, $L(\pi) = \{w \in \Sigma^+ \mid w = \pi\theta,\ \theta$ is a substitution$\}$. Note that a pattern language $L(\pi)$ is an EFS language $L(\Gamma, p)$ with $\Gamma = \{p(\pi) \leftarrow\}$.

We define several subclasses of EFSs, called variable-bounded EFSs, length-bounded EFSs, simple EFSs, regular EFSs, and linear EFSs, and show the relations of their languages to the Chomsky hierarchy.

The set of variables contained in an atom A is denoted by $\upsilon(A)$. The length of a pattern π is denoted by $|\pi|$. For an atom, $|p(\pi_1, \ldots, \pi_n)| = |\pi_1| + \cdots + |\pi_n|$. The number of all occurrences of a variable x in a pattern π is denoted by $o(x, \pi)$. For an atom $o(x, p(\pi_1, \ldots, \pi_n)) = o(x, \pi_1) + \cdots + o(x, \pi_n)$.

Definition 4 *A definite clause* $A \leftarrow B_1, \ldots, B_m$ *is said to be* variable-bounded *if*

$$\upsilon(A) \supseteq \upsilon(B_1) \cup \cdots \cup \upsilon(B_m).$$

Definition 5 *A definite clause* $A \leftarrow B_1, \ldots, B_m$ *is said to be* length-bounded *if*

$$|A\theta| \geq |B_1\theta| + \cdots + |B_m\theta|$$

for any substitution θ.

By the following lemma, we can effectively determine if a given clause is length-bounded or not.

Lemma 1 (Arikawa *et al.*, 1989; 1992b) *A definite clause* $A \leftarrow B_1, \ldots, B_m$ *is length-bounded if and only if* $|A| \geq |B_1| + \cdots + |B_m|$ *and* $o(x, A) \geq o(x, B_1) + \cdots + o(x, B_m)$ *for any variable* x.

Definition 6 *A* simple *clause is a clause of the form* $p(\pi) \leftarrow q_1(x_1), \ldots, q_m(x_m)$, *where* $p, q_1, \ldots, q_m$ *are unary predicate symbols and* $x_1, \ldots, x_m$ *are mutually distinct variables appearing in* π.

Definition 7 *A simple clause is called* regular *if the pattern in its head is regular.*

Definition 8 *A regular clause is called* right (left)-linear *if the pattern in the head is of the form* $xw(wx)$ *for some word* $w \in \Sigma^*$.

An EFS Γ is called *variable-bounded* (resp. *length-bounded, simple, regular, right-linear, left-linear*) if all clauses in Γ are variable-bounded (resp. length-bounded, simple, regular, right-linear, left-linear).

Example 1

(1) The context-sensitive language $\{a^n b^n c^n \mid n \geq 1\}$ is definable by a length-bounded EFS:

$$\Gamma_1 = \left\{ \begin{array}{l} p(xyz) \leftarrow q(x, y, z) \\ q(ax, by, cz) \leftarrow q(x, y, z) \\ q(a, b, c) \end{array} \right\}.$$

(2) The language $\{a^{2^n} \mid n \geq 0\}$ is definable by a simple EFS:

$$\Gamma_2 = \left\{ \begin{array}{l} p(xx) \leftarrow p(x) \\ p(a) \end{array} \right\}.$$

(3) The context-free language $\{a^n b^n | n \geq 1\}$ is definable by a regular EFS:

$$\Gamma_3 = \left\{ \begin{array}{l} p(axb) \leftarrow p(x) \\ p(ab) \end{array} \right\}.$$

For these classes of EFS languages, the following theorems hold.

Theorem 1   (Arikawa *et al.*, 1989; 1992b) *A language is recursively enumerable (resp. context-sensitive, context-free, regular) if and only if it is definable by a variable-bounded (resp. length-bounded, regular, right/left-linear) EFS.*

This theorem asserts that the variable-boundedness is not a restriction when we are interested in EFS languages.

Theorem 2   (Arikawa, 1970; Saeki and Arikawa, 1990) *The class of languages definable by simple EFSs is properly located in between the classes of context-free languages and context-sensitive languages.*

The EFSs can be considered as logic programs and a refutation procedure can be applied to the variable-bounded EFSs. Hence we can also consider EFSs as acceptors.

Let α and β be patterns or atoms. Then a substitution θ is called a *unifier* of α and β if $\alpha\theta = \beta\theta$. If $\alpha = \beta\theta$ and $\alpha\theta' = \beta$ for some substitutions θ and θ', α is called a *variant* of β. In the usual logic programming languages, any pair of terms or atoms has a unique most general unifier. However, there may be infinitely many maximally general unifiers for a pair of patterns. In fact, $\{x := a^i\}$ for every i is the unifier of patterns ax and xa, and all the unifiers are maximally general.

Hence, we need to define a new derivation for EFSs with no requirement that every unifier should be most general. A *goal* is a clause of the form $\leftarrow B_1, \ldots, B_m$ $(m \geq 0)$. We assume a *computation rule R* to select an atom from a goal.

Definition 9   *Let Γ be an EFS, and G be a goal. A derivation from G is a (finite or infinite) sequence of triplets $(G_i, \theta_i, C_i)(i = 0, 1, \ldots)$ that satisfies the following conditions:*

(1) *G_i is a goal, θ_i is a substitution, C_i is a variant of a clause in Γ, and $G_0 = G$.*

(2) *$\upsilon(C_i) \cap \upsilon(C_j) = \varnothing$ $(i \neq j)$, and $\upsilon(C_i) \cap \upsilon(G) = \varnothing$ for every i.*

(3) *If G_i is $\leftarrow A_1, \ldots, A_k$ and A_m is the atom selected by R, then C_i is $A \leftarrow B_1, \ldots, B_q$, and θ_i is a unifier of A and A_m, and G_{i+1} is*

$$(\leftarrow A_1, \ldots, A_{m-1}, B_1, \ldots, B_q, A_{m+1}, \ldots, A_k)\theta_i.$$

Definition 10   *A refutation is a finite derivation ending with empty goal $\Box$.*

Figure 1 depicts an example of a refutation in the EFS Γ_1 in Example 1.

Let α and β be a pair of patterns or atoms. If one of them is ground, then every unifier of α and β is ground and the set of all unifiers is finite and computable. Hence, when we deal with variable-bounded EFSs, all goals in a derivation from a ground goal are kept ground. The derivation procedure for variable-bounded EFSs can be implemented in nearly the same way as for traditional logic programming.

231

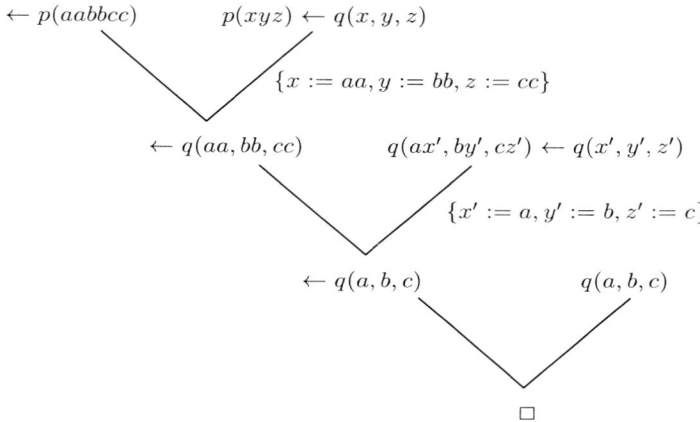

Figure 1. Refutation of $\leftarrow p(aabbcc)$ in Γ_1.

3 MODEL INFERENCE OF EFSs

Inductive inference is one of the three major paradigms in computational learning theory. One of the most important criteria for successful inference is the notion of identification in the limit (Gold, 1967). The model inference system (MIS, for short) that Shapiro (1981) developed is an inductive inference system for logic programs based on the identification in the limit. In this section we describe an MIS for EFSs. First we recall some basic notions on inductive inference.

An *indexed family of recursive languages* is a class of languages $\mathcal{C} = L_1, L_2, \ldots$ for which there exists a computable function $f : N \times \Sigma^* \to \{0, 1\}$ such that $f(i, w) = 1$ or 0 if w is in L_i or not, respectively.

For any length-bounded EFS Γ and any $w \in \Sigma^*$, we can effectively determine whether w is in $L(\Gamma)$. Therefore, for any fixed recursive enumeration $\mathcal{G} = \Gamma_1, \Gamma_2, \ldots$, the class $L(\mathcal{G}) = L(\Gamma_1), L(\Gamma_2), \ldots$ can be considered as an indexed family of recursive languages.

A *complete presentation* of a language L is an infinite sequence $(w_1, t_1), (w_2, t_2), \ldots$ such that t_i is 0 or 1, $\{w_i | t_i = 1\} = L$ and $\{w_i | t_i = 0\} = \Sigma^* - L$. A *positive presentation* of a nonempty language L is an infinite sequence $w_1, w_2, \ldots$ such that $\{w_i | i = 1, 2, \ldots\} = L$.

An *inference machine* is an effective procedure that requests input and produces output from time to time. We call an output produced by an inference machine a *guess*. Let $\sigma = w_1, w_2, \ldots$ be an infinite sequence and $g_1, g_2, \ldots$ be the sequence of guesses produced by an inference machine M when elements in σ are successively given to M. Then we say that M on input σ *converges* to g, if all but finitely many guesses out of $g_1, g_2, \ldots$ are equal to g.

Definition 11 *A class* $\mathcal{C} = L_1, L_2, \ldots$ *is said to be* inferable from complete *(resp. posi-tive)* data *if there exists an inference machine M such that for any index i and any complete*

232

(resp. positive) presentation of L_i, M on input σ converges to g with $L_g = L_i$. We also say that the machine M identifies $\mathcal{C}$ in the limit from complete (resp. positive) data.

Now in model inference, examples are given as a complete presentation of the model of an EFS, i.e., the EFS language. Therefore, positive examples of an EFS Γ are ground atoms provable from Γ, and negative examples are the rest. A hypothesis H is said to be *too strong* if H proves some negative examples. H is said to be *too weak* if H fails to prove some positive examples.

The following procedure MIS outlines our model inference system.

Procedure MIS;
begin
    $H := \{\Box\}$;
    repeat
        read next example;
        while H is too strong or too weak **do**
        begin
            while H is too strong **do**
            begin
                apply CBA to H and detect a false clause C in H;
                remove C from H;
            end;
            while H is too weak **do**
                add a refinement of a clause removed so far to H;
        end;
        output H;
    forever
end;

As in the procedure, we need to devise two subprocedures, the contradiction back-tracing algorithm CBA and the refinement operator.

Given a refutation claiming that a hypothesis H is too strong, CBA finds a false clause from H by tracing selected atoms backward. To test the truth value of a selected atom, CBA calls an oracle ASK that receives a ground atom and returns its truth value. We can easily simulate ASK, since examples are given as a complete presentation. However, CBA must take a ground instance of a tested atom that is not ground, since ASK can answer only ground atoms. Fortunately, all the selected atoms in a refutation from a ground goal in a variable-bounded EFS are ground. Hence we can simplify the original CBA for variable-bounded EFSs.

Now we introduce refinement operators for the classes of EFSs. Each refinement operator defined below consists of an application of a substitution and an addition of an atom.

Definition 12 *A substitution θ is* basic for a clause C *if*

(1) $\theta = \{x := y\}$, *where $x \in \upsilon(C)$, $y \in \upsilon(C)$ and $x \neq y$,*

(2) $\theta = \{x := a\}$, *where $x \in \upsilon(C)$ and $a \in \Sigma$, or*

(3) $\theta = \{x := yz\}$, where $x \in \upsilon(C)$, $y \notin \upsilon(C)$, $z \notin \upsilon(C)$ and $y \neq z$.

Definition 13 *Let A be an atom. Then an atom B is in $\rho_a(A)$ if and only if*

(4) $A = \Box$ and $B = p(x_1, \ldots, x_n)$ for $p \in \Pi$ with arity n and mutually distinct variables $x_1, \ldots, x_n$, or

(5) $A\theta = B$ for a substitution θ basic for A.

Definition 14 *Let C be a variable-bounded clause. Then a clause D is in $\rho_{vb}(C)$ if and only if (4) or (5) in Definition 13 holds, or $C = A \leftarrow B_1, \ldots, B_{n-1}$ and $D = A \leftarrow B_1, \ldots, B_{n-1}, B_n$ is variable-bounded. Similarly we define ρ_{lb} for length-bounded clauses.*

A refinement operator ρ is *complete for a set S* if $\rho^*(\Box) = S$. A refinement operator ρ is *locally finite* if $\rho(C)$ is finite for any clause C, where ρ^* is the reflexive transitive closure of ρ.

Theorem 3 *(Arikawa et al., 1989; 1992b)*

(1) ρ_{vb} *is a complete refinement operator for variable-bounded clauses.*

(2) ρ_{lb} *is a locally finite and complete refinement operator for length-bounded clauses.*

We can also define refinement operators for simple or regular clauses which are locally finite and complete. For simple clauses, applications of the basic substitutions are restricted only to clauses without any bodies, and for regular clauses, substitutions of the form $\{x := y\}$ are not allowed.

4 INDUCTIVE INFERENCE FROM POSITIVE DATA

In many practical inductive inference problems, inferences are naturally based on positive data rather than both positive and negative data. It is well known that inference from positive data has strictly weaker power than that from positive and negative data. Gold (1967) showed that any class of languages containing all the finite languages and at least one infinite language is not inferable from positive data. Since the class of regular languages contains all the finite languages and many infinite languages, it is not inferable from positive data. Although Gold's result might sound negative for approaches to practical applications of inductive inference, we know another important result proved by Angluin (1980a). She showed a theorem characterizing classes inferable from positive data and presented non-trivial and interesting classes. The class of pattern languages is one of her classes (Angluin, 1980b).

Angluin characterized classes inferable from positive data by giving a necessary and sufficient condition and several sufficient conditions. Here we give one of the sufficient conditions for inferability from positive data. The notion of finite thickness is established by Angluin (1980a,b) and named by Wright (1989).

234

Definition 15   *A class C has* finite thickness *if and only if* #{$L \in C | w \in L$} *is finite for any word w.*

Theorem 4   (Angluin, 1980a,b) *If a class has finite thickness then it is inferable from positive data.*

By using the above theorem, we can easily show the inferability of pattern languages from positive data.

Theorem 5   (Angluin, 1980a,b) *The class of pattern languages is inferable from positive data.*

More explicitly exploiting the framework of EFSs, we can reveal the existence of rich classes which are inferable from positive data. However, the class of EFS languages has richer structure than the class of pattern languages, and therefore it does not have finite thickness in general. When we deal with EFS languages, we assume that every EFS contains a unary predicate symbol p and simply denote $L(\Sigma, p)$ by $L(\Gamma)$. An EFS Γ_1 is said to be *equivalent* to Γ_2, denoted by $\Gamma_1 \equiv \Gamma_2$, if we can identify Γ_1 and Γ_2 up to renaming of variables and predicate symbols except p. Clearly, if $\Gamma_1 \equiv \Gamma_2$, then $L(\Gamma_1) = L(\Gamma_2)$.

LB-EFS denotes the set of all the length-bounded EFSs, and for an integer $n \geq 0$, LB-EFS(n) denotes the set of length-bounded EFSs with at most n clauses. For a set $\mathcal{G}$ of EFSs, $L(\mathcal{G})$ denotes the class of languages {$L(\Gamma) | \Gamma \in \mathcal{G}$}. Then we have the following theorem.

Theorem 6   (Shinohara, 1990; 1994) *For any $n \geq 0$, the class $L(LB\text{-}EFS(n))$ is inferable from positive data.*

Shinohara (1990; 1994) proved the above theorem by showing that L(LB-EFS(n)) has *finite elasticity*, which was introduced by Wright (1989) as a sufficient condition for a class to be inferable from positive data. Sato and Moriyama (1994) investigated conditions relating to inferability and properties of EFS languages in more detail and gave another proof of Theorem 6.

Definition 16   *An EFS Γ is* reduced with respect to *a set $T \subseteq \Sigma^*$ if $T \subseteq L(\Gamma)$ but $T \not\subseteq L(\Gamma')$ for any $\Gamma' \subsetneq \Gamma$.*

For a set $T \subseteq \Sigma^*$ and a class $\mathcal{G} \subseteq$ LB-EFS, RED($T, \mathcal{G}$) denotes the set of all the reduced EFSs in $\mathcal{G}$ with respect to T.

Definition 17   *A class $\mathcal{G} \subseteq LB\text{-}EFS$ is* R-finite *if* RED($T, \mathcal{G}$) *contains finite many inequivalent EFSs.*

Definition 18   *A class $\mathcal{G}$ of EFSs is* closed under subset operation *if for any $\Gamma \in \mathcal{G}$ and any $\Gamma' \subseteq \Gamma$, Γ' belongs to $\mathcal{G}$.*

The key property that many classes of length-bounded EFSs are inferable from positive data is given in the following lemma.

Lemma 2   (Shinohara, 1990; 1991; 1994) *Let $T \subseteq \Sigma^*$ be nonempty and $\Gamma \in LB\text{-}EFS$. If Γ is reduced with respect to T, then the max-length of heads of clauses in Γ is less than or equal to that of words in T.*

By using the above lemma, we can easily prove the following when Π is finite.

235

Theorem 7 (Shinohara, 1990; 1991; 1994) *If Π is finite, any class $\mathcal{G} \subseteq$ LB-EFS is R-finite.*

If Π is infinite, some classes are not R-finite. However, if the number of clauses in EFSs is bounded by m, then any class of length-bounded EFSs is R-finite even if Π is infinite.

Theorem 8 (Shinohara, 1990; 1991; 1994) *For any $n \geq 0$, the class LB-EFS(n) is R-finite.*

Definition 19 *A set T of words is* a finite tell-tale (ftt, *for short) of a* language L within $\mathcal{C}$ *if T is a finite subset of L and there does not exist any language $L' \in \mathcal{C}$ such that $T \subseteq L' \subsetneq L$. L has* ftt *within $\mathcal{C}$ if there is a finite tell-tale of L within $\mathcal{C}$.*

For a set $T \subseteq \Sigma^*$, L is a *minimal* language of T within $\mathcal{C}$ if there does not exist any language $L' \in \mathcal{G}$ such that $T \subseteq L' \subsetneq L$. If T is *ftt* of L within $\mathcal{C}$, then L is a minimal language of T within $\mathcal{C}$.

Definition 20 *A class $\mathcal{C}$ is of* M-finite thickness *if for any nonempty finite set T of words, (1) the number of minimal languages of T within $\mathcal{C}$ is finite and (2) for any $L \in \mathcal{C}, T \subseteq L$ implies that there exists a minimal language $L' \in \mathcal{C}$ of T such that $L' \subseteq L$.*

If a class $\mathcal{G} \subseteq$ LB-EFS is R-finite and closed under subset operation, then $L(\mathcal{G})$ has M-finite thickness.

Theorem 9 (Sato and Moriyama, 1994) *Let $\mathcal{C}$ be a class with M-finite thickness. Then the class $\mathcal{C}$ is inferable from positive data if and only if any language $L \in \mathcal{C}$ has* ftt *within $\mathcal{C}$.*

Definition 21 *A language $L \subseteq \Sigma^*$ is of* infinite hierarchy *within a class $\mathcal{G}$ of EFSs if there exists an infinite sequence of finite sets $T_1, T_2, \ldots$ and an infinite sequence of EFSs $\Gamma_1, \Gamma_2, \ldots$, each in $\mathcal{G}$, such that*

(1) $T_1 \subsetneq T_2 \subsetneq \cdots$,

(2) $\bigcup_{n=1}^{\infty} T_n = L$,

(3) $\Gamma_1 \subsetneq \Gamma_2 \subsetneq \cdots$,

(4) *for each n, Γ_n is reduced with respect to T_n within $\mathcal{G}$,*

(5) *for each n, $L(\Gamma_n) \subsetneq L$.*

A language L is of *finite hierarchy within $\mathcal{G}$* if L is not of infinite hierarchy within $\mathcal{G}$.

In terms of the above notion, a characterization of *ftt* in the framework considered is given as follows:

Theorem 10 (Sato and Moriyama, 1994) *Let $\mathcal{G} \subseteq$ LB-EFS be R-finite and closed under subset operation. Then a language L has* ftt *within $L(\mathcal{G})$ if and only if L is of finite hierarchy within $\mathcal{G}$.*

By Theorems 9 and 10, the following characterization theorem of inferability can be derived.

Theorem 11 (Sato and Moriyama, 1994) *Let $\mathcal{G} \subseteq$ LB-EFS be R-finite and closed under subset operation. Then $L(\mathcal{G})$ is inferable from positive data if and only if, for any $\Gamma \in \mathcal{G}$, $L(\Gamma)$ is of finite hierarchy within $\mathcal{G}$.*

As shown in Theorem 8, LB-EFS(n) is R-finite and closed under subset operation. As is easily seen, any language $L \in L(\text{LB-EFS}(n))$ is of finite hierarchy within LB-EFS(n). Thus we have another proof of Theorem 6.

5 A THEORY OF MACHINE DISCOVERY FROM FACTS

The machine discovery we are concerned with in this paper is to make computers discover some scientific theories from given facts. Hence machine learning should be a key technology for machine discovery. In machine learning first we must select a hypothesis space from which the learning machine proposes theories or hypotheses.

As far as facts are presented according to a hypothesis that is unknown but guaranteed to be in the space as in the ordinal inductive inference, the machine will eventually identify the hypothesis. In machine discovery, however, we cannot assume this.

If the hypothesis is not in the space, most learning machines will continue for ever to search the space for a new hypothesis. Usually we cannot know when to stop such an ineffective searching. This is the most crucial problem we must solve in realizing machine discovery systems. In machine discovery the sequences of facts are given at first independently of the space. If the learning machine can explicitly tell us that there are no theories in the space which explain the given sequence, the machine will work for machine discovery.

Hence the essence of a theory of machine discovery from facts should be that the entire hypothesis space is refutable by a sequence of observed facts. If there exist rich hypothesis spaces that can be refuted, we can give a space and a sequence to the machine, and then we can just wait for an output from it. The machine will discover a hypothesis which is producing the sequence if it is in the space, otherwise it will refute the whole of the space and stop. When the space is refuted, we may give another space to the machine and try to make such a discovery in the new space.

Consider the inductive inference as the framework for machine learning. Then the machine discovery system is an inductive inference machine that can refute hypothesis spaces. Choose classes of elementary formal systems as the hypothesis spaces. Moreover we assume that every class in question is an indexed family of recursive languages.

If the class is a finite set of recursive languages, then it is trivially refutable from complete data. Also if the class contains all finite languages, then it is easily shown not to be refutable. *Then are there any meaningful classes, i.e., hypothesis spaces, that are identifiable and refutable?* We give a positive answer to this question. We will say such classes are *refutably inferable*.

We first show some characterizations of such inductive inference. Then we show that some sufficiently large classes of formal languages, i.e., the classes definable by length-bounded EFSs with at most n axioms, are refutably inferable from complete data. We start with some definitions.

An *inductive inference machine that can refute hypothesis spaces* (RIIM, for short) is an effective procedure that requests inputs from time to time and either (i) produces positive integers from time to time or (ii) refutes the class and stops after producing some positive integers.

For an RIIM M and a finite sequence $\sigma[n] = w_1, w_2, \ldots, w_n$, by $M(\sigma[n])$ we denote the last guess or the 'refutation' sign produced by M which is successively presented $w_1, w_2, \ldots, w_n$ on its input requests.

An RIIM M is said to *converge* to a positive integer i for a presentation σ, if there is a positive integer m such that for any $n \geq m$, $M(\sigma[n])$ is defined and equal to i. An RIIM M is said to *refute* a class $\mathcal{C}$ from a presentation σ, if there is a positive integer n such that $M(\sigma[n])$ is the 'refutation' sign. In this case we also say that M refutes the class $\mathcal{C}$ from $\sigma[n]$.

Definition 22 *Let $\mathcal{C} = L_1, L_2, \ldots$ be a class. An RIIM M is said to* refutably infer *a class $\mathcal{C}$ from positive data (*resp.*, complete data), if for any nonempty concept L (*resp.*, any concept L) and any positive presentation σ (*resp.*, complete presentation σ) of L, (i) if $L \in \mathcal{C}$, then M infers L with respect to $\mathcal{C}$ from σ, (ii) otherwise M refutes the class $\mathcal{C}$ from σ. A class $\mathcal{C}$ is said to be* refutably inferable *from positive data (*resp.*, complete data), if there is an RIIM M which refutably infers the class $\mathcal{C}$ from positive data (*resp.*, complete data).*

In characterizing the refutable inferability, the following lemma is useful.

Lemma 3 *(Mukouchi and Arikawa, 1993; 1995) Let M be an RIIM which refutably infers a class $\mathcal{C}$ from positive data (*resp.*, complete data). For a nonempty concept L (*esp.*, a concept L) and for a positive presentation σ (*resp.*, a complete presentation σ) of L, if M refutes the class $\mathcal{C}$ from $\sigma[n]$, then $\sigma[n]$ is not consistent with any concept $L_i \in \mathcal{C}$.*

Definition 23 *Let $T, F \subseteq U$ be finite sets. We define two $0, 1$-valued functions $econs_p(T)$ and $econs_c(T, F)$ as follows: $econs_p(T) = 1$ if and only if there exists a concept $L_i \in \mathcal{C}$ such that T is consistent with L_i, and $econs_c(T, F) = 1$ if and only if there exists a concept $L_i \in \mathcal{C}$ such that $\langle T, F \rangle$ is consistent with L_i.*

For any concept $L_i \in \mathcal{C}$, whether $T \subseteq L_i$ and $F \subseteq L_i^c$ or not is recursively decidable, because L_i is recursive, and T and F are explicitly given finite sets. Therefore, the above functions are, in general, recursively enumerable functions.

We have the following characterization for the refutable inferability from positive data.

Theorem 12 *(Mukouchi and Arikawa, 1993; 1995) For a class $\mathcal{C}$, the following three statements are equivalent:*

- *$\mathcal{C}$ is refutably inferable from positive data.*
- *$\mathcal{C}$ satisfies the following three conditions:*

  (1) *$\mathcal{C}$ is inferable from positive data;*
  (2) *for any nonempty concept $L \notin \mathcal{C}$, there is a finite set $T \subseteq L$ such that T is not consistent with any concept $L_i \in \mathcal{C}$;*

238

(3) *the function econs$_p$ for C is recursive.*

- C *satisfies the following three conditions:*

(4) *for any concept $L_i \in C$, all nonempty subsets of L_i are also members of C;*

(5) *there is no infinite sequence of concepts $L_{i_1}, L_{i_2}, \ldots \in C$ such that $L_{i_1} \subsetneq L_{i_2} \subsetneq \ldots$;*

(3) *the function econs$_p$ for C is recursive.*

For the refutable inferability from complete data, we have the following character-ization theorem.

Theorem 13 (Mukouchi and Arikawa, 1993; 1995) *A class C is refutably inferable from complete data if and only if C satisfies the following two conditions:*

(6) *For any concept $L \notin C$, there are finite sets $T \subseteq L$ and $F \subseteq L^c$ such that $\langle T, F \rangle$ is not consistent with any concept $L_i \in C$.*

(7) *The function econs$_c$ for C is recursive.*

We can also show that if a class C is refutably inferable from complete data, then C satisfies the above condition (6).

Corollary 1 (Mukouchi and Arikawa, 1993; 1995) *If a class C contains all nonempty finite concepts, then C is* not *refutably inferable from positive data or complete data.*

Now we can show that some sufficiently large classes of EFSs are refutably inferable from complete data.

Theorem 14 (Mukouchi and Arikawa, 1993; 1995) *For any $n \geq 0$, the class $L(LB$-$EFS(n))$ is refutably inferable from complete data.*

Note that the classes above are exactly the same as those in Theorem 6 that are inferable from positive data.

Concerning the refutable inference from complete data within the framework of EFSs, we have the following characterization.

Theorem 15 (Sato, 1995) *Let $G \subseteq LB$-EFS be R-finite and let it be closed under subset operation. Then $L(G)$ is refutably inferable from complete data if and only if any language $L \notin L(G)$ is of finite hierarchy within $L(G)$ and econs$_{L(G)}$ is recursive.*

The function $econs_{L(\text{LB}-\text{EFS}(n))}$ is proved to be recursive for any n. Hence we can prove the above Theorem 14 as a corollary.

6 PAC-LEARNABLE ELEMENTARY FORMAL SYSTEMS

In this section, we discuss the learnability of EFSs in the sense of Valiant's PAC-learning (Valiant, 1984). Probably approximately correct (PAC) learning is to find an approxima-tion of the target from random sampling, and therefore it has attracted much attention even from the viewpoint of practice. However, it seems that the contributions of studies on the theory of PAC-learning are mainly on negative results derived from the theory of computational complexity. The main purpose of this section is to demonstrate the usefulness of the framework of EFSs by showing PAC-learnable classes of languages as general as possible. Some of the classes of EFSs, which we deal with in this section, are a natural extension of context-free grammars.

We introduce polynomial-time learnability (Valiant, 1984) and NC-learnability (Vitter and Lin, 1992). An *example* of a concept L is a pair $\langle w, a \rangle$ for $w \in \Sigma^*$, where $a = 1$ if $w \in L$ and $a = 0$ otherwise. We call $\langle w, 1 \rangle$ a *positive example* and $\langle w, 0 \rangle$ a *negative example*.

Definition 24 *We say that a class C of EFS languages is* polynomial-time learnable *if there exist a polynomial-time algorithm A and a polynomial $m(\cdot, \cdot, \cdot, \cdot)$ such that for any real numbers $\varepsilon, \delta (0 < \varepsilon, \delta < 1)$, any integers $n \geq 0, s \geq 1$, any concept $L \in C$ definable by an EFS of size at most s, and any probability distribution P on $\Sigma^{\leq n}$, the following condition holds: If A is given as input $m(\frac{1}{\varepsilon}, \frac{1}{\delta}, n, s)$ examples for L which are drawn randomly and independently according to P, A outputs an EFS which defines a concept $H \in C$ satisfying $P(L \cup H - L \cap H) < \varepsilon$ with probability at least $1 - \delta$. Moreover, C is NC-learnable (NC^2-learnable, resp.) if the learning algorithm A runs in polylog-time ($O(\log^2 m)$ time, resp.) using a polynomial number of processors.*

6.1 Polynomial-time learnability of pattern languages

First, we consider the class of pattern languages, a class of the simplest EFS languages. For a concept class C, we consider the following problem:

Consistency Problem for C

Instance: A set of examples $S \subseteq \Sigma^* \times \{0, 1\}$.

Question: Is there a concept $H \in C$ which is *consistent* with S?

If the consistency problem for C is shown **NP**-complete, we can say that C is not polynomial-time learnable under the assumption of **RP** $\neq$ **NP** (Blumer *et al.*, 1989). Ko and Tzeng (1991) showed that the consistency problem for pattern languages is Δ_2^p-complete. Therefore, we cannot expect any efficient learning for pattern languages. Furthermore, Schapire (1990) showed a stronger negative result. Such negative results seem to be quite natural, because even the membership problem for pattern languages is **NP**-complete (Angluin, 1980a). Therefore, we should consider subclasses of pattern languages for which at least the membership problem is computable in polynomial time.

For any regular pattern π and any word w, whether $w \in L(\pi)$ or not is decidable in $O(|\pi| + |w|)$ time, where $|\cdot|$ is the length function. Therefore regular patterns are polynomial-time computable representations for regular pattern languages. The class of regular pattern languages is efficiently inferable from positive data (Shinohara, 1982). Unfortunately, as for the consistency problem, we have the following.

Theorem 16 (Miyano *et al.*, 1991) *The consistency problem for the class of regular pattern languages is* **NP**-*complete.*

Also we have the similar negative results for extended regular pattern languages, introduced by Shinohara (1983), where ε-substitutions are allowed, as well as for common sequence languages. The latter result is independently shown by Jiang and Li (1993). From these results we know that even for regular pattern languages polynomial-time PAC-learning algorithms cannot be realized without any additional conditions.

To get another subclass of pattern languages for which the membership problem is computable in polynomial time, we restrict the total number of variable *occurrences* in patterns. When a pattern π defines a language containing a word w, $|\pi| \leq |w|$ and every subword in π without variables is a subword of w. This property that every constant word appearing in a pattern π whose language contains a word w is a subword of w is called 'heredity'. Therefore, the number of inequivalent languages that are defined by patterns with at most k variable occurrences and contain w is of polynomial order in $|w|$, if we fix k arbitrarily. Thus we can show the polynomial-time PAC-learnability of this subclass. Moreover, the algorithm is effectively parallelizable.

Theorem 17 (Miyano *et al.*, 1991) *For any fixed integer $k \geq 1$, the class of k-occurrence pattern languages is NC^2 learnable.*

From the above we observe two important facts:

- Even for regular pattern languages, polynomial-time PAC-learning is so hard to realize.

- Once we restrict the number of variable occurrences in patterns, the subclass of pattern languages is polynomial-time PAC-learnable.

Here we should note that the subclass of pattern languages with the restriction on the number of variable occurrences consists of infinitely many languages. Taking these facts as a starting point, we approach more general classes of languages in the framework of EFSs. We remark that the complexity of the consistency problem and the polynomial-time learnability for the class of k-variable pattern languages is not known for any fixed $k \geq 1$.

6.2 Polynomial-time learnability of EFS languages

We introduce 'hereditary' EFSs that preserve the heredity of pattern languages.

Definition 25 *A clause $C = A \leftarrow B_1, \dots, B_t$ is said to be* hereditary *if any pattern in the body part $B_1, \dots, B_t$ is a subword of some pattern in the head A. An EFS Γ is* hereditary *if each clause in Γ is hereditary.*

Given a hereditary EFS Γ and $w \in \Sigma^*$, whether $w \in L(\Gamma)$ or not is decidable in polynomial time with respect to $|w|$, when we consider the size of Γ as a constant. We consider the following four parameters concerning the size of EFSs:

m: the number of clauses,

k: the number of variable occurrences in the head,

t: the number of atoms in the body,

r: the arity of predicate symbols.

Definition 26 *H-EFS(m, k, t, r) denotes the class of languages defined by hereditary EFSs with parameters bounded by some constants m, k, t, r, respectively.*

The main positive result is stated as follows:

Theorem 18 (Miyano *et al.*, 1994) *The class H-EFS(m, k, t, r) is polynomial-time PAC-learnable.*

When length-boundedness is satisfied as well as heredity, the class of EFS languages becomes NC^2-learnable.

Theorem 19 (Miyano *et al.*, 1994) *The class LB-H-EFS(m, k, r) of languages defined by length-bounded hereditary EFSs with parameters bounded by some constants m, k, r is NC^2-learnable.*

We have only partial reasons for the restrictions on all the parameters. When we put no restriction on the number of clauses in EFSs, any finite language can be defined, and therefore the VC-dimension of the class naturally becomes exponential. It seems reasonable to bound the number of clauses by some constant. However, it will turn out that this restriction does not always derive the polynomial VC-dimension of the class. For example, for the most general class of EFSs, called variable-bounded EFSs, by which any recursively enumerable language can be defined, the VC-dimension still remains in exponential order after bounding all the four parameters by constants. Even for hereditary EFSs with bounded number of clauses, when some of the other three parameters are not restricted by constants, the class is also of exponential VC-dimension. As for the number of variable occurrences, when we do not restrict it, we have the negative results for pattern languages.

We can generalize the previous theorems by introducing the *union* of a concept class. For a concept class C and an integer $m \geq 1$, we define the *m-union class* of C by

$$\{c_1 \cup c_2 \cup \cdots \cup c_m | c_i \in C \quad (1 \leq i \leq m)\}.$$

The *finite union class* of C is defined by

$$\bigcup_{m \geq 1} m\text{-union class of } C.$$

Theorem 20 (Miyano *et al.*, 1994) *The finite union class of H-EFS(m, k, t, r) is polynomial-time learnable. The finite union class of LB-H-EFS(m, k, r) is NC-learnable.*

In our experiments on amino acid sequences, we use the finite union class of 4-occurrence regular pattern languages.

7 APPLICATION TO LEARNING FROM AMINO ACID SEQUENCES

This section briefly summarizes the experimental results of Miyano *et al.* (1994), where we applied our learning algorithm of EFSs to protein data. The goal is to find characteristic features of *transmembrane domains* of proteins (Hartmann *et al.*, 1989;

von Heijine, 1988) from amino acid sequences. Most approaches to this problem have been by means of biophysical analysis of amino acid residues (von Heijine, 1986) while our approach is based on concept learning from examples.

The applicability of concept learning largely depends on the representation of concepts. As the representation of concepts, we use elementary formal systems. Logic programs have been used for various knowledge representations in genome informatics. For instance, Muggleton *et al.* (1992) gave an interesting approach to protein secondary structure prediction by inductive logic programming. On the other hand, 'motifs' of functional domains are usually described with *patterns*, which are words containing variables. Such motifs have been compiled in the PROSITE database (Bairoch, 1991). Therefore EFSs are more natural representations for functional domains than the usual logic programs. Thus we can directly handle amino acid sequences with EFSs while keeping the structure of logic programs. Although we have seen the polynomial-time PAC-learnable EFSs, here we use very restricted EFSs, say the finite unions of five-variable regular pattern languages. As we will see, by using such restricted EFSs, our learning method can find reasonable motifs from a small number of positive and negative examples.

7.1 Membrane proteins and PIR database

The primary structure of a protein is described as a sequence of amino acid residues of 20 kinds. The PIR database (Winona *et al.*, 1999) contains the amino acid sequences together with their additional information such as functions.

In applying our learning strategy to this problem, we regard the sequences of transmembrane domains as positive examples. The PIR database contains the amino acid sequences with FEATURE field where transmembrane domains are explicitly indicated. As negative examples, we use amino acid sequences without any overlap with transmembrane domains. Since the length of a positive example is $20 \sim 30$, we randomly choose sequences of length around 30 for negative examples. We collected 689 positive examples and the same number of negative examples from the PIR database. Since the PIR database is not completely correct, the data may contain some noise.

A hydropathy plot (Engelman *et al.*, 1986; Kyte and Doolittle, 1982; Rao and Argos, 1986) has been used generally to predict transmembrane domains from primary sequences. Instead of directly dealing with 20 kinds of amino acids, we classify them into three classes according to the hydropathy indices (Kyte and Doolittle, 1982) as follows.

Symbol	Hydropathy	Amino acids
$*$	$1.8 \sim 4.5$	Alanine, Methionine, Cysteine, Phenylalanine, Leucine, Valine, Isoleucine
$+$	$-1.6 \sim -0.4$	Proline, Tyrosine, Tryptophan, Serine, Threonine, Glycine
$-$	$-4.5 \sim -3.2$	Arginine, Lysine, Aspartic acid, Glutamic acid, Asparagine, Glutamine, Histidine

Table 1. Collections of regular patterns covering positive examples and excluding negative examples that was produced by our learning algorithm from 10 positive (transmembrane domain) and 10 negative (non-transmembrane domain) training examples. The second (third, resp.) column shows the percentage of the positive (negative, resp.) examples that the pattern in the first column covers. The last row shows the accuracy for positive examples and negative examples.

Patterns	Positive	Negative
P1		
$x_1 * * * * * x_2$	72.6%	10.2%
accuracy	72.6%	89.8%
P2		
$x_1 + * * * + x_2$	38.6%	9.6%
$x_1 * + * x_2 * * + x_3$	80.4%	19.7%
accuracy	82.1%	76.2%

Table 2. Collections of regular patterns covering non-transmembrane domains and excluding transmembrane domains. Ten positive and negative training examples are used.

Pattern	Positive	Negative
N1		
$x_1 - - x_2$	7.4%	87.7%
accuracy	92.6%	87.7%
N2		
$x_1 - - x_2$	7.4%	87.7%
$x_1 + + - x_2$	7.0%	53.3%
accuracy	87.7%	95.1%

Table 3. Results for $x_1 - x_2 - x_3 - x_4 - x_5$.

Patterns	Positive	Negative
N3		
$x_1 - x_2 - x_3 - x_4 - x_5$	8.4%	94.8%
accuracy	91.6%	94.8%

We denote *POS* and *NEG* the sets of positive and negative examples, respectively. Fortunately, *POS* and *NEG* do not have any overlaps.

7.2 Experiments and results

As a hypothesis space, we use the concept class defined as

$$\{\tilde{L}(\pi_1) \cup \cdots \cup \tilde{L}(\pi_m)|\pi_i \text{ is a regular pattern in } \Pi' \text{ and } m \geq 1\},$$

where $\tilde{L}(\pi)$ is the extended pattern language of π by allowing ε-substitutions, and Π' is the set of regular patterns of the following forms:

$$x_1\alpha_1x_2,$$
$$x_1\alpha_1x_2\alpha_2x_3,$$
$$x_1\alpha_1x_2\alpha_2x_3\alpha_3x_4$$

with $\alpha_1, \alpha_2, \alpha_3$ in $\{*, +, -\}^+$.

Our learning algorithm chooses randomly two small training sets *Pos* and *Neg* from *POS* and *NEG*, respectively. Then the sample *S* defined by *Pos* and *Neg* is given as an input to the algorithm. This process is repeated until good hypotheses are found. In our experiments, the size of *Pos* (*Neg*) varies from 5 to 20.

The first approach we take to this problem is to find a collection of regular patterns which covers almost all positive training examples and excludes almost all negative training examples.

Table 1 shows the good hypotheses (P1) and (P2) with their accuracies that our learning system has produced.

We are also interested in collections of regular patterns which *exclude* positive examples and *cover* negative examples. That is to say, we use transmembrane domains as negative examples, and nontransmembrane domains as positive examples.

Table 2 shows the results. As is seen, hypotheses (N1) and (N2) are very small and the accuracies for both positive and negative examples are quite good. From these observations, we can say that the approach from negative examples is much better than that from positive examples in the last section.

After recognizing the importance of negative examples, we have finally found the pattern in Table 3. Table 3 (N3) shows the result whose accuracy is more than 91%.

Acknowledgments

This survey paper has outlined the authors' work on computational learning and discovery theories with their coworkers. The authors wish to thank to S. Miyano, T. Moriyama, Y. Mukouchi and A. Yamamoto for their contributions to the original work, most of which are included in the references below.

REFERENCES

Angluin, D. (1980a). Inductive inference of formal languages from positive data. *Information and Control*, 45: 117–135.

Angluin, D. (1980b). Finding patterns common to a set of strings. *Journal of Computer and System Sciences*, 21: 46–62.

Angluin, D. and Smith, C.H. (1983). Inductive inference: theory and methods. *ACM Computing Surveys*, 3: 237–269.

Angluin, D. (1988). Queries and concept learning. *Machine Learning*, 2: 319–342.

Arikawa, S. (1970). Elementary formal systems and formal languages – simple formal systems. *Memoirs of Faculty of Science, Kyushu University, Ser. A., Mathematics* 24: 47–75.

Arikawa, S., Shinohara, T. and Yamamoto, A. (1989). Elementary formal systems as a unifying framework for language learning. In *Proc. 2nd Ann. ACM Workshop on Computational Learning Theory*, 312–327, Morgan Kaufmann.

Arikawa, S., Kuhara, S., Miyano, S., Shinohara, A., and Shinohara, T. (1992a). A learning algorithm for elementary formal systems and its experiments on identification of transmembrane domains. In *Proc. 25th Hawaii Int. Conf. System Sciences*, 675–684, IEEE Computer Society.

Arikawa, S., Shinohara, T., and Yamamoto, A. (1992b). Learning elementary formal systems. *Theoretical Computer Science*, 95: 97–113.

Bairoch, A. (1991). PROSITE: A dictionary of sites and patterns in proteins. *Nucleic Acids Research*, 19: 2241–2245.

Blumer, A., Ehrenfeucht, A., Haussler, D., and Warmuth, M. (1989). Learnability and the Vapnik-Chervonenkis dimension. *Journal of the ACM*, 36(4): 929–965.

Engelman, D.M., Steiz, T.A., and Goldman, A. (1986). Identifying nonpolar transbilayer helices in amino acid sequences of membrane proteins. *Annual Review of Biophysics and Biophysical Chemistry*, 15: 321–353.

Gold, E. (1967). Language identification in the limit. *Information and Control*, 10: 447–474.

Hartmann, E., Rapoport, T.A., and Lodish, H.F. (1989). Predicting the orientation of eukaryotic membrane-spanning proteins. *Proceedings of the National Academy of Science of the United States of America*, 86: 5786–5790.

von Heijine, G. (1986). A new method for predicting signal sequence cleavage sites. *Nucleic Acids Research*, 14(11): 4683–4690.

von Heijine, G. (1988). Transcending the impenetrable: how proteins come to terms with membranes. *Biochimica et Biophysica Acta*, 947: 307–333.

Jiang, T. and Li, M. (1993). On the complexity of learning strings and sequences. *Theoretical Computer Science*, 119: 363–371.

Ko, K. and Tzeng, W. (1991). Three Σ_2^p-complete problems in computational learning theory. *Computational Complexity*, 1(3): 269–310.

Kyte, J. and Doolittle, R. (1982). A simple method for displaying the hydropathic character of protein. *Journal of Molecular Biology*, 157: 105–132.

Miyano, S., Shinohara, A., and Shinohara, T. (1991). Which classes of elementary formal systems are polynomial-time learnable? In *Proc. 2nd Workshop on Algorithmic Learning Theory*, 139–150, IOS Press.

Miyano, S., Shinohara, A., and Shinohara, T. (revised in 1994). Polynomial-time learning of elementary formal systems and an application to discovering motifs in proteins. Technical Report RIFIS-TR-CS-37. Research Institute of Fundamental Information Science, Kyushu University.

Moriyama, T. and Sato, M. (1993). Properties of language classes with finite elasticity. In *Proc. 4th Workshop on Algorithmic Learning Theory*, *LNAI*, 744: 187–196, Springer-Verlag.

Muggleton, S., King, R., and Sternberg, M. (1992). Using logic for protein structure prediction. In *Proc. 25th Hawaii International Conference on System Sciences, Vol. I*, 685–696, IEEE Computer Society.

Mukouchi, Y. and Arikawa, S. (1993). Inductive inference machines that can refute hypothesis spaces. In *Proc. 4th Workshop on Algorithmic Learning Theory*, *LNAI*, 744: 123–136, Springer-Verlag.

Mukouchi, Y. and Arikawa, S. (1995). Towards a mathematical theory of machine discovery from facts. *Theoretical Computer Science*, 137: 53–84.

Rao, J. and Argos, P. (1986). A conformational preference parameter to predict helices in integral membrane proteins. *Biochimica et Biophysica Acta*, 869: 197–214.

Robinson, J.A. (1965). A machine-oriented logic based on the resolution principle. *JACM*, 12: 23–41.

Saeki, N. and Arikawa, S. (1990). Polynomial time parsers for elementary formal systems. SIG-FAI-9001-6, Japanese Society for Artificial Intelligence, 55–64.

Sakakibara, Y. (1990). On learning Smullyan's elementary formal systems: Towards an efficient learning for context-sensitive languages. *Advances in Software Science and Technology*, 2: 79–101.

Sato, M. and Moriyama, T. (1994). Inductive inference of length-bounded EFS's from positive data. *DMSIS-RR-94-2*, Department of Mathematical Sciences and Information Sciences, Univ. of Osaka Pref.

Sato, M. (1995). Inductive inference of formal languages. *Bull. Informatics and Cybernetics*, 27(1): 85–106.

Schapire, R. (1990). Pattern languages are not learnable. In *Proc. 3rd Workshop on Computational Learning Theory*, 122–129, Morgan Kaufmann.

Shapiro, E. (1981). Inductive inference of theories from facts. *Technical Report* 192, Department of Computer Science, Yale University.

Shinohara, T. (1982). Polynomial time inference of pattern languages and its applications. In *Proc. 7th IBM Symposium on Mathematical Foundation of Computer Science*, 191–209.

Shinohara, T. (1983). Polynomial time inference of extended regular pattern languages. *LNCS*, 147: 115–127.

Shinohara, T. (1986). Inductive inference of formal systems from positive data. *Bull. Inf. Cybern.*, 22: 9–18.

Shinohara, T. (1990). Inductive inference from positive data is powerful. In *Proc. 3rd Workshop on Computational Learning Theory*, 97–110, Morgan Kaufmann.

Shinohara, T. (1991). Inductive inference of monotonic formal systems from positive data. *New Generation Computing*, 8: 371–384.

Shinohara, T. (1994). Rich classes inferable from positive data: length-bounded elementary formal systems. *Information and Computation*, 108(2): 175–186.

Smullyan, R. (1961). *Theory of Formal Systems*. Princeton University Press.

Valiant, L. (1984). A theory of the learnable. *Communications of the ACM*, 27(11): 1134–1142.

Vitter, J. S. and Lin, J.-H. (1992). Learning in parallel. *Information and Computation*, 96: 179–202.

Wright, K. (1989). Identification of unions of languages drawn from an identifiable class. In *Proc. 2nd Workshop on Computational Learning Theory*, 328–333, Morgan Kaufmann.

247

13

A learnability model for universal representations and its application to top-down induction of decision trees

Stephen Muggleton

Department of Computer Science,
University of York,
Heslington,
York,
UK
e-mail: stephen@cs.york.ac.uk

David Page

Speed Scientific School,
University of Louisville,
Louisville,
KY 40292
USA
e-mail: cdpage@louisville.edu

Abstract

Automated inductive learning is a vital part of machine intelligence and the design of intelligent agents. A useful formalization of inductive learning is the model of PAC-learnability. Nevertheless, the ability to learn *every* target concept expressible in a given representation, as required in the PAC-learnability model, is highly demanding and leads to many negative results for interesting concept classes. A new model of learnability, called universal learnability or *U-learnability*, recently has been proposed as a less demanding, average-case variant of PAC-learnability. This paper uses the U-learnability model to analyze a top-down decision tree induction algorithm. Specifically, this paper proves that an idealized variant of the well-known decision tree learning algorithm CART – one of the most successful existing machine learning algorithms – is a U-learner under a natural set of assumptions regarding target hypotheses. (The motivation and description of these assumptions is best delayed until the U-learnability model is described.) Equally interestingly, various related PAC-learning algorithms such as those for k-DNF cannot be used to U-learn under the same assumptions. Finally, the paper raises a number of related open questions and general research directions; open questions include not only U-learnability questions, but also several new PAC-learnability questions and one question regarding a general property of propositional logic.

1 INTRODUCTION

Recently a new model of inductive learning called U-learnability [11,9,10] has been derived from the PAC-learnability model [14]. The major features of U-learnability that distinguish it from PAC-learnability are

- probability distributions over concept classes, which assign probabilities to potential target concepts

- average-case sample complexity and time complexity requirements, rather than worst-case requirements.

U-learnability derives its name from its applicability to expressive, even under some assumptions *universal*, concept representations. Further discussion may be found elsewhere [11,9,10].

For U-learnability to be a viable alternative or complement to PAC-learnability, it is crucial that algorithms which work well in practice should be 'U-learners' for natural and realistic kinds of distributions over the possible target concepts. It is also important that algorithms which do not work as well in practice – even if they are PAC-learners – should be exposed by the U-learnability model as inferior algorithms (in terms of either average-case time complexity or sample complexity).

For a concrete example, the decision tree learning programs CART [3] and ID3 (or its derivatives such as C4.5) [12,13] are widely regarded as among the most successful machine learning systems in use today. On the other hand, the various PAC-learning algorithms for restricted-form decision trees or DNF formulae (e.g., linear decision trees or k-DNF) are seldom used in practice. An alternative model that shows CART or ID3 to be superior to these latter algorithms, under natural and realistic assumptions, is arguably an important complement to PAC-learnability. Such a model could potentially motivate the development of new practical machine learning algorithms or improvements to existing ones.

The primary significance of this paper is its demonstration that U-learnability meets the preceding criteria. This demonstration takes the form of a positive U-learnability result based on CART. Related PAC-learning algorithms – in particular, the standard ones for k-DNF – cannot be modified to U-learn in the same setting, or at least the obvious modification does not work. The same is true of the existing PAC-learning algorithms for various restricted-form decision trees (see end of Section 3.2.2). Thus the present paper demonstrates the potential of U-learnability and hence introduces a challenging direction for further work. The paper also raises several specific theoretical questions that are of practical import to decision tree learning, including a natural question regarding propositional logic in general.

The paper is organized as follows. Section 2 reviews U-learnability and mentions related work. Section 3 motivates and presents the paper's main result. In the course of this presentation, a number of challenging open questions arise. Section 4 lists these as well as general directions for further research.

2 REVIEW OF U-LEARNABILITY AND RELATED WORK

The traditional view of inductive learning, as captured in PAC-learnability, is basically as a one-time exercise: (1) some single target concept from a given concept class is to be learned, and (2) the learner must be prepared to 'do well' regardless of what that target is. U-learnability is motivated by a broader view. The learner faces an infinite (or at least very long) sequence of learning problems; for each problem, the target concept as well as examples are drawn according to underlying probability distributions. This view of inductive learning encourages a more realistic goal for learning algorithms. A learner should 'do well' (precisely defined later) usually, or on average over both the possible target concepts and possible sequences of examples within a given problem domain. For example, consider the problem of predicting drug activity from molecular structure. The number of activities or purposes of drugs is large, and each activity corresponds to a different target concept. One week a learning program may be asked to generate a concept description for drugs that inhibit some behavior of *E. coli* bacteria, while the next week the target concept describes drugs that counteract some behavior of HIV. An algorithm that *usually* runs very efficiently and generates accurate concepts in this domain is of great value, even if for some target concepts the algorithm is highly likely (depending on the sample) to fail or to use too much time.

Thus in the U-learnability model, a teacher randomly chooses a target concept according to a probability distribution over the concept class. The teacher then chooses examples randomly, with replacement, according to a probability distribution over the domain of examples, and labels the examples according to the chosen target. In general, these distributions may be known, completely unknown, or partially known to the learner. In the cases where these distributions are completely unknown, we are forced to rely on worst-case analyses as used in PAC-learnability.

To formalize the idea of a partially-known distribution, the U-learnability model uses the notion of a parametrized family of possible distributions. Nevertheless, the basic result of this paper is most easily understood using a streamlined version of the U-learnability model that includes neither the complexity nor the generality added by families of possible distributions. We therefore present in this section the streamlined version of the model. For clarity of exposition, this streamlined version is furthermore tailored to propositional logic. At the end of Section 3, we sketch how our main result can be further extended within the general model.

Motivated by preamble the general idea of U-learnability, tailored to propositional logic, is as follows. For every $n \geq 1$, let X^n (the domain of examples) be the set of all truth assignments to the set of propositional variables $\{x_1, \ldots, x_n\}$, let C_n be any subset of the boolean functions over $\{x_1, \ldots, x_n\}$, let D_{X^n} be a probability distribution over X^n, and let D_{C_n} be a probability distribution over C_n. We take the size of every member of X^n to be n. The choices of C_n, D_{X^n}, and D_{C_n} for all $n \geq 1$ specify a learning problem P.[1] For example, we might choose that for all $n \geq 1$, C_n is the set of all boolean functions over $\{x_1, \ldots, x_n\}$, D_{X^n} is the uniform distribution over X^n, and D_{C_n} is the uniform distribution over C_n; these choices specify a learning problem P. An algorithm L is a U-learner for a given learning problem P if L has average-case time complexity (relative to D_{C_n} and D_{X^n}) that is polynomial in n and the number of examples L receives, and L learns accurately. By 'learns accurately' we mean that the number of examples needed to provide a desired expected error ϵ, $0 < \epsilon < 1$, is bounded by a polynomial in n and $\frac{1}{\epsilon}$. The expected error is simply the probability that L's hypothesis will disagree with the target concept $C \in C$ on an unseen example; this probability is relative to both the distributions D_{C_n} and D_{X^n}.[2]

The precise definition of U-learnability follows. For simplicity, we assume algorithms are not randomized. The learning algorithm L may output hypotheses in any representation, provided there exists an efficient algorithm that, for any hypothesis H in that representation and any example $e \in X^n$, specifies whether H labels e as a positive or negative example. In this sense the model is more similar to PAC-prediction, or so-called representation-independent learning, than to PAC-learning. Throughout the definition, for any positive integer m let $\vec{X}_m^n$ denote $\langle x_1, \ldots, x_m \rangle$, a vector of m examples from X^n. For any C_n, D_{C_n}, and D_{X^n}, let $Pr_{D_{C_n}}(C)$ be the probability assigned to $C \in C_n$ by D_{C_n}. With a slight abuse of standard notation, let $Pr_{D_{C_n}, D_{X^n}}(C, \vec{X}_m^n)$ be the product of $Pr_{D_{C_n}}(C)$ and the probability of obtaining the sequence $\vec{X}_m^n$ when drawing m examples randomly and independently according to D_{X^n}.

Definition 1 U-learnability. *Let P be a learning problem specified by choices of C_n, D_{X^n}, and D_{C_n} for all $n \geq 1$. Then P is U-learnable just if there exist an algorithm L and two polynomial functions,* LEARNTIME-BOUND$(x) = x^{c_1}$ *for some $c_1 > 0$, and* SAMPLE-BOUND(x, y), *such that for all $n \geq 1$ the following hold.*

Sample complexity. *For every ϵ, $0 < \epsilon < 1$, if L is given a number of examples $m \geq$* SAMPLE-BOUND$(n, \frac{1}{\epsilon})$ *then:*

$$\sum_{all\ (C, \vec{X}_{m+1}^n)} [Pr_{D_{C_n}, D_{X^n}}(C, \vec{X}_{m+1}^n)][E_L(C, \vec{X}_{m+1}^n)] < \epsilon$$

where $E_L(C, \vec{X}_{m+1}^n) = 0$ if L's hypothesis, given examples $\langle x_1, \ldots, x_m \rangle$ labeled according to C, agrees with C on the label for example x_{m+1}, and $E_L(C, \vec{X}_{m+1}^n) = 1$ otherwise.

---

[1] In the same way, a PAC-learning problem within propositional logic is specified by the concept class C_n, for all $n \geq 1$, and an encoding of the members of C_n, which in some ways corresponds to a probability distribution D_{C_n}. In some cases a probability distribution D_{X^n}, usually the uniform distribution, is also specified.

[2] Note that in using the error bound ϵ, without a separate 'confidence' parameter δ, we return to Valiant's style in originally defining what is now called 'PAC-learnability'. The U-learnability definition could be modified to incorporate the confidence parameter δ; this would neither add nor sacrifice generality.

Time complexity. *For any* $n \geq 1$ *and* $m \geq$ SAMPLE-BOUND$(n, \frac{1}{\epsilon})$ *examples provided to* L, *the average-case time complexity of* L *is bounded by* LEARNTIME-BOUND(nm). *To be more precise,[3] let* TIME$_L(C, \vec{X}_m^n)$ *be the time spent by* L *when the target is* C *and the sequence of examples provided to* L *is* $\vec{X}_m^n$. *Then we say that the average-case time complexity of* L *is bounded by* LEARNTIME-BOUND$(x) = x^{c_1}$ *if the sum, over all tuples* $(C, \vec{X}_m^n)$, *of*

$$[Pr_{D_{C_n}, D_{X^n}}(C, \vec{X}_m^n)] \frac{(\text{TIME}_L(C, \vec{X}_m^n))^{\frac{1}{c_1}}}{nm}$$

is less than infinity.

It should be stressed that other researchers have argued for the use of average-case sample complexity relative to a distribution over target concepts, so this idea is not original with U-learnability; these researchers include Buntine [4] and Haussler, Kearns, and Schapire [7,6]. (The work of Haussier, Kearns, and Schapire provides useful tools in studying average-case sample complexity.) But U-learnability is the first computational model of learning to incorporate this idea. We believe the U-learnability definition incorporates this idea into a learnability model in the most natural manner possible.

3 U-LEARNABILITY BY CART

If one wishes to test whether a learnability model is relevant to real-world practice, one of the best ways is to 'reverse engineer' a successful practical algorithm to see if it succeeds in the model under some interesting and reasonable set of assumptions. Identifying such a set of assumptions will improve our understanding of why the algorithm works so well, and therefore may eventually lead to new, improved algorithms. No attempt to reverse-engineer CART, ID3, or other related algorithms within the PAC-learnability model has succeeded in identifying an interesting concept class that is PAC-learnable by any of these algorithms. This remains true even if a uniform distribution over examples is assumed. This failure may simply indicate that these algorithms are inferior to various PAC-learners, but such has not been the judgement of machine learning practitioners. In this section we reverse-engineer CART to identify a subclass of the boolean functions, and a set of natural and realistic distributions over them, for which CART is a U-learner; we also assume a uniform distribution over examples. This subclass of the boolean functions is not known to be PAC-learnable or PAC-predictable (assuming any reasonable representation for the functions), even with a uniform distribution over examples. (We expect that the assumption of a particular distribution over examples can be removed; this is discussed in Section 4.)

3.1 A Description of CART

We begin with a description of the basic, well-known CART algorithm. (We assume the reader is familiar with decision trees as well as the algorithm for efficiently evaluating

---

[3] See [1] for the motivation of this definition of average-case time complexity.

examples according to a decision tree.) The input to CART is a set of labeled examples; examples are truth assignments over a set of n propositional variables $\{x_1, \ldots, x_n\}$, and each example is labeled as *positive* (also written as 1) or *negative* (also written 0). CART first constructs a tree that is a single node containing all the examples it has been provided. If all the examples at this node have the same label, then we say this node is *pure*. If the node is pure, then CART labels the node with the label of its examples and halts, returning this single-node decision tree as its result. Otherwise, CART finds a propositional variable x_i that maximizes the *gain function* (defined below), labels the current node with 'x_i', and recursively builds left and right subtrees of this node. The left subtree is built from the examples having x_i set to 0, and the right subtree is built from the examples having x_i set to 1. (In this case we say that CART chose to 'split' the original node 'on x_i'.) Note that every leaf of the final tree is pure and is labeled either *positive* or *negative*.

CART's gain function is based on a measure of the *purity* of the example set at a given node; this measure is called the *Gini index*. Where E is the example set at a given node, P is the set of positive examples in E, and N is the set of negative examples, the Gini index of E is simply the product

$$\text{Gini}(E) = \left(\frac{|P|}{|E|}\right)\left(\frac{|N|}{|E|}\right) = \frac{(|P|)(|N|)}{|E|^2}.$$

Notice that the Gini index has its lowest value (0) when the node is completely pure and takes its highest value (0.25) when exactly half of the examples are positive. The gain that CART ascribes to a given variable x_i at a given node is the difference between the purity of the example set at the node and the weighted sum of the purities of the example sets at the child nodes produced by splitting on x_i. To be more precise, let E denote the set of examples at a given node, let E_0 denote the subset of E containing exactly those examples with x_i set to 0, and let E_1 denote the subset of E containing exactly those examples with x_i set to 1. Let $r = |E_0|/|E|$. Then the gain of x_i at this node is

$$\text{Gain}(E, x_i) = \text{Gini}(E) - [r(\text{Gini}(E_0) + (1 - r)(\text{Gini}(E_1))].$$

It is worth noting that a number of other decision tree learners, including ID3, differ from CART only in using alternative measures for purity. These algorithms are often referred to as TDIDT (top-down induction of decision tree) algorithms. It should also be mentioned that most TDIDT algorithms, including CART, have been extended to allow non-binary variables (even variables that take floating point numbers), to allow more than two possible labels, and to learn in the presence of noise. In dealing with noise, the TDIDT algorithms may choose not to further split an impure node. This possibility raises a popular research topic called *pruning*. We do not address any of these extensions in this paper, though we mention them again under future research directions.

3.2 Reverse-engineering CART

We now motivate and summarize the U-learnability analysis of CART. The analysis suggests that CART is successful because, for a restricted class of boolean functions,

CART finds a concept that is consistent with the data and (with high probability) uses no spurious propositional variables, or variables that do not appear in the target. And CART does this quickly.

3.2.1 A restriction on the boolean functions

Any attempt to reverse-engineer CART or any other TDIDT algorithm is well begun by recognizing that such algorithms fail miserably on some kinds of target concepts, such as parity functions, or functions involving equality or inequality (exclusive-or). The reason for this failure is that, even if the algorithm has the *entire* set of possible labeled examples, no attribute has gain for the example set. For illustration, suppose the target is $x_{21} \neq x_{121}$, and examples are truth assignments over the set $\{x_1, \dots, x_{200}\}$. Let E be the entire set of possible examples over these variables, labeled according to the given target. Then half of the examples are positive, so $\text{Gini}(E) = 0.25$. Furthermore, let x_i be an arbitrary attribute in $\{x_1, \dots, x_{200}\}$, let E_0 be the subset of E with $x_i = 0$, and let E_1 be the subset of E with $x_i = 1$. Then $\text{Gini}(E_0)$ and $\text{Gini}(E_1)$ are each 0.25 as well, which means $\text{Gain}(E, x_i)$ is 0. Since on the full set of examples no attribute has gain (including x_{21} and x_{121}), for any given sample the probability is 0.99 that some attribute other than x_{21} or x_{121} will be chosen for the split. After a wrong split, the probability of choosing a wrong attribute in the subtrees is only slightly lower. Thus under such conditions CART is almost certain to return an enormous tree (we won't digress into analyzing its expected size). We have no reason to believe such a tree will be accurate unless the sample is in fact nearly the entire set of possible examples.

Based on the preceding paragraph, we might choose to restrict attention to boolean functions such that, given the entire set of possible examples or truth assignments, some variable has gain. But this is insufficient since the same problem of no gain could occur at the next level in building a tree. For example, consider the function expressed by $x_1 \wedge (x_{21} \neq x_{121})$. The attribute x_1 has large gain on the full set of examples and so is likely to have large gain on any reasonably large sample. But once this attribute is chosen for a split, the right subtree ($x_1 = 1$) will give CART the same problems as illustrated in the previous example. We next describe a restriction on the boolean functions that will eliminate this problem. Afterward, we conjecture a possible alternative characterization of this restriction. The following preliminary definition is needed.

Definition 2 (Subfunction) *Let f be a boolean function over a set V of propositional variables. Let A be an assignment to some subset V′ of V. The subfunction f_A of f (also called the subfunction of f at A or the restriction of f to A [8]) is the boolean function over V − V′ such that: for any assignment A′ over V − V′, $f_A(A') = f(A'')$, where A″ is the assignment over V that agrees with A on V′ and with A′ on V − V′.*

We say that a subfunction is *pure* if it maps every assignment to 0 or if it maps every assignment to 1; otherwise, it is *impure*. As an example of a subfunction, the function $f_{x_1=0}$ (Figure 1) is the subfunction of (Figure 2) at $x_1 = 0$. The function f and $f_{x_1=0}$ are impure, but subfunction $f_{x_1=0, x_2=1}$ is pure since it maps both its assignments to 1.

Definition 3 (Lookahead-one (L(1)) function) *A boolean function f is Lookahead-one, or L(1), just if: for every impure subfunction f_A of f, there exists a variable x_i such*

x_1	x_2	x_3	f
0	0	0	0
0	1	1	1
0	1	0	1
0	1	1	1
1	0	0	0
1	0	1	1
1	1	0	1
1	1	1	1

x_1	x_2	f
0	0	0
0	1	1
1	0	1
1	1	1

Figure 1. The function f (left) and the subfunction of f at $x_1 = 0$ (right), which is denoted $f_{x_1} = 0$.

x_1	x_2	x_3	f_1	f_2	f_3	f_4
0	0	0	0	0	0	0
0	0	1	1	0	1	1
0	1	0	1	0	1	0
0	1	1	1	1	0	0
1	0	0	0	0	1	0
1	0	1	1	1	0	0
1	1	0	1	1	0	1
1	1	1	1	1	1	0

Figure 2.

that the number of positive assignments (assignments mapped to 1 by f_A) with x_i set to 0 differs from the number of positive assignments with x_i set to 1.

For example, consider the boolean functions f_1, f_2, f_3, and f_4 (see figure 2 above) over the variables x_1, x_2, and x_3.

The functions f_1, and f_2 are $L(1)$ functions, whereas f_3 and f_4 are not. For the function f_4, notice that for any variable x_i the number of positive assignments with x_i set to 0 is the same as the number of positive assignments with x_i set to 1. It follows that if CART is given the full set of assignments labeled according to f_4, then no variable has gain. And in the same way, for f_3 the subfunction at $x_1 = 0$ (or at $x_1 = 1$) has no variable with gain. It is worth noting that the class of $L(1)$ functions includes all functions that can be represented by linear decision trees (as is the case for f_1), but also includes many other functions such as f_2. While linear decision trees are PAC-learnable, nothing is known of the PAC-learnability or PAC-predictability of $L(1)$ functions in any reasonable encoding. This is noted in Section 4 as a topic for further research.

255

The following lemma is straightforward to prove, and it in fact holds for every TDIDT algorithm that we know about.

Lemma 4 *If CART is given the set of all possible examples over a given set of propositional variables, and the target concept is an $L(1)$ function over some subset of these variables, then at every impure node generated by CART, some variable has gain. (And of course, every variable that does not appear in the target has no gain.)*

Thus, given a complete example set labeled according to an $L(1)$ target function, CART will generate a decision tree that represents the target function and uses only the variables in the target. (The tree generated by CART is not necessarily the smallest such tree.) Our U-learnability result is built around a proof that, even given an incomplete but reasonably large sample (containing a number of examples that is polynomially related to the desired accuracy and the number of propositional variables used in the examples), with high probability CART generates such a decision tree.

In closing the discussion of $L(1)$ boolean functions, we conjecture the following alternative, perhaps more intuitive, characterization of these functions.

Conjecture 5 *The class of $L(1)$ functions is exactly the class of boolean functions whose subfunctions cannot be represented by formulae that describe only equalities among variables.*

For example, the function f_4 is described by the formula $(x_1 = x_2) \wedge \neg(x_2 = x_3)$. For the function f_3, the subfunction at $x_1 = 0$ is described by the formula $\neg(x_2 = x_3)$.

It can be verified that no $L(1)$ function has a subfunction representable by a formula that describes only equalities among variables. We have as yet been unable to prove the converse.[4] If this conjecture is true, it shows the restriction to $L(1)$ boolean functions to be very natural. If a domain expert believes a proposition b is important only related to a second propostion a – say, that the two do not take equal values – then he will be inclined to use propositions a and a XOR b, rather than a and b, in encoding the examples. Of course certainly there are some domains for which this restriction is harmful, such as in learning computer circuits; one would expect CART to perform poorly in this domain.

3.2.2 A natural family of distributions over boolean functions

As already noted, no PAC-learnability result exists for the class of $L(1)$ functions. An adversarial argument can be used to show that CART is not a PAC-learner for this class. Thus reverse-engineering CART to obtain a learnability result for this class requires choosing a distribution over target concepts in this class as well.

One family of distributions we do *not* want to consider is the family of distributions in which the probabilitites of target concepts decrease exponentially with their encoding sizes. The use of such a family fits the real world only if we have the perfect encoding for the concept class in question, which seems unlikely; when this assumption is true, a simple exhaustive search algorithm is optimal in a certain sense and is a U-learner. In fact, we would like a distribution that doesn't rely on a particular encoding of boolean functions at all, but only on some natural feature of boolean functions that is encoding-independent.

---

[4]It is worth noting that the use of *subfunctions* in the conjecture is crucial. It is easy to construct a function that cannot be described by equality, but which has subfunctions that can be, and for which no variable has gain; our example function f_3 is such a function.

(This will give our result a kind of representation independence that even results on 'representation-independent learning', or prediction, do not achieve.) Furthermore, to avoid making learning trivial by an unreasonable assumption, if the distributions we consider are exponential ones then the feature we use should be one in which encoding size of a boolean function might be exponential, given a reasonable encoding scheme. (Alternatively, we might try polynomial distributions.) The most obvious and natural encoding-independent feature of boolean functions is the number of propositions used in the function. An Occam assumption, or preference for simplicity, leads us to consider distributions in which the probabilities of boolean functions decrease exponentially with the number of propositional variables used. (More specifically, the probabilities of functions using i propositional variables sum to 2^{-i}.) Such an assumption is consistent with practical observations of CART and other TDIDT algorithms; these algorithms often find decision trees that use few propositional variables, and when they don't their trees are usually inaccurate.[5]

Given this choice of distribution over the $L(1)$ boolean functions, however, it is natural to expect that an algorithm for learning k-DNF could be used to U-learn, as follows. For any sample, simply begin with $k = 1$ and use the k-DNF learner with increasingly larger values of k until the learner finds a consistent hypothesis. A refinement of this is the following. For any given choice of ϵ, consider only values of k up to $\lceil \log \frac{1}{\epsilon} \rceil + 1$. But even given this refinement, the average-case time complexity of the algorithm is not bounded by a polynomial in nm, where m is the number of examples and n is the number of propositional variables. Specifically, the average-case time complexity of this algorithm grows faster than the function $bm(\frac{n}{2})^{c \log m}$ for constants $b, c > 0$, which cannot be bounded by a polynomial in nm. This can be seen most easily using the simpler definition of average-case time complexity, as a bound on expected run-time; the analysis can be transformed to one based on the definition used in this paper. The expected time of the algorithm is underestimated by

$$\text{TIME} > b \sum_{i=1}^{\lceil \log \frac{1}{\epsilon} \rceil + 1} n^i m (2^{-i}) > b \sum_{i=0}^{\lceil \log \frac{1}{\epsilon} \rceil} m \left(\frac{n}{2} \right)^i$$

since n^i is an underestimate of the number of possible length i monomials, m is an underestimate of the time to test one of these monomials over the full set of examples, and 2^{-i} is an underestimate of the probability that length i monomials need to be used. An underestimate of the right-hand sum, in turn, is $bm(\frac{n}{2})^{\lceil \log \frac{1}{\epsilon} \rceil + 1}$. The best sample bound we can obtain still has m related to $\frac{1}{\epsilon}$ by a polynomial function, which means that the above sum is at least $bm(\frac{n}{2})^{c \log m}$ for some $b, c > 0$.

Finally, it is natural to question whether existing PAC-learning algorithms for restricted classes of decision trees can be used as U-learners. The only such algorithms we know about that do not rely on the additional help of membership queries or other kinds of queries are those for linear decision trees or (more generally) decision trees

---

[5]We thank Ashwin Srinivasan for suggesting this type of distribution, based on his extensive experimentation using CART in real-world domains.

of bounded *rank* [5]. The algorithm for bounded-rank decision trees cannot be used to PAC-learn the $L(1)$ boolean functions directly, since these can have arbitrary rank. (This can be shown using a construction built around the example function f_2 given earlier.) Furthermore, an attempt to U-learn by using this algorithm with increasingly larger choices of rank falls prey to the same shortcoming as does the analogous use of a k-DNF learner, as described above.

Thus the U-learning problem we have now motivated appears nontrivial as well as natural. In fact we will see that CART U-learns for this problem in linear time, average-case; we expect that even if some PAC-learner can be used to U-learn under these conditions, it will have higher average-case time complexity.

3.2.3 The main result

Based on an examination of CART, we have motivated a natural and nontrivial U-learning problem. The following theorem states that CART is indeed a U-learner for this problem.

Theorem 6 *Let the U-learning problem P be defined by the following choices of C_n, D_{C_n}, and D_{X^n}, for all $n \geq 1$. Let C_n be the set of all $L(1)$ boolean functions over the propositional variables $\{x_1, \ldots, x_n\}$. Let D_{C_n} be any distribution over C_n such that: for all integers i, $2 \leq i \leq n$, the probabilities of the $L(1)$ boolean functions over exactly i variables sum to 2^{-i}. Let D_{X^n} be the uniform distribution over X^n. The problem P is U-learnable using CART, with $m = 8192(n+2)/\epsilon^{10}$ examples, with linear average-case time complexity $(O(nm))$.*

Proof For any choice of ϵ, $0 < \epsilon < 1$, we use CART to build a decision tree that uses at most $\lceil \log \frac{1}{\epsilon} \rceil + 1$ variables. (If CART tries to use more variables, we force it to halt and return an inconsistent tree – this can be seen as a kind of pruning.) Such a decision tree of course has depth at most $\lceil \log \frac{1}{\epsilon} \rceil + 1$. With probability at least $1 - \epsilon/2$, the target $L(1)$ boolean function drawn according to D_{C_n} uses no more than $\lceil \log \frac{1}{\epsilon} \rceil + 1$ variables and therefore can be represented by such a tree. Thus with probability at most $\epsilon/2$ the target is outside of the class of concepts the algorithm considers.

We first show that, using CART in this way, the sample complexity is bounded by $m = 8192(n + 2)/\epsilon^{10}$. Afterward, we address the time complexity.

The fundamental part of the proof of sample complexity is Lemma 13, stated and proven in Appendix A. This lemma states that if CART is given $m = 8192(n + 2)/\epsilon^{10}$ examples drawn randomly and independently according to a uniform distribution over truth assignments to n propositional variables, and labeled according to a target function that uses at most $\lceil \log \frac{1}{\epsilon} \rceil + 1$ variables, then the probability that CART uses any variable not in the target is at most $\epsilon/4$. Given this lemma, it remains only to show that if CART finds a hypothesis built from only the variables that appear in the target, which is consistent with all the $m = 8192(n + 2)/\epsilon^{10}$ examples, then the probability that the hypothesis will misclassify a random example is at most $\epsilon/4$. This will complete the proof of sample complexity since the probabilities of the possible causes of error will sum to ϵ, as follows:

- $\frac{\epsilon}{2}$: the probability that the target uses more variables than the algorithm is allowed to consider;

- $\frac{\epsilon}{4}$: the probability that CART chooses a spurious variable at some (any) point;
- $\frac{\epsilon}{4}$: the probability that CART finds a consistent concept built from the correct variables and yet misclassifies the random example.

The number of $L(1)$ boolean functions built from a set of at most $\lceil \log \frac{1}{\epsilon} \rceil + 1$ variables is at most $2^{2^{\lceil \log \frac{1}{\epsilon} \rceil + 1}} \geq 2^{4/\epsilon}$ The well-known *Blumer bound* [2] states that for any hypothesis space H, and any probability distribution over examples, given $m \geq \left(\ln |H| + \ln \frac{1}{\delta} \right) / \epsilon$ examples drawn randomly, independently according to that distribution and labeled according to any member of H: with probability at least $1 - \delta$ any hypothesis $h \in H$ consistent with all m examples is $(1 - \epsilon)$-accurate. Thus if we substitute for both ϵ and δ in the Blumer bound the number $\epsilon/8$ and we use for $|H|$ the number $2^{4/\epsilon}$, we find that $m = 96/\epsilon^2$ examples is sufficient for an expected error of at most $(\epsilon/8) + (\epsilon/8) = \epsilon/4$. This completes the proof for sample complexity.

It now remains to consider the time complexity. We show that the average-case time complexity is on the order of nm. The analysis is most easily presented using the simpler definition of average-case time complexity as a bound on expected run time; as with our analysis of the use of k-DNF algorithms earlier in the paper, this analysis can be transformed easily into one that uses the exact definition of average-case complexity given in the U-learnability definition.

The time CART takes to identify whether a node is pure, and, if not, which attribute to use in splitting the node, is on the order of the product of n and the number of examples at that node. Now consider CART as proceeding level-by-level in building the decision tree. At any level, the total number of examples at the nodes at that level is at most m (it is less if some nodes at previous levels are pure, that is, are leaves). Thus the total time spent by CART at that level is on the order of nm, that is, is bounded by bnm for some constant $b > 0$. (We assume $n, m \geq 1$.)

With probability at most $\epsilon/4$ CART uses spurious variables. Even in this case CART is allowed to use at most $\lceil \frac{1}{\epsilon} \rceil + 1$ variables and thus to proceed to depth at most $\lceil \frac{1}{\epsilon} \rceil + 1$. Therefore, the total time CART can spend in this case is at most $\left(\lceil \frac{1}{\epsilon} \rceil + 1 \right) bnm$. Thus the product of probability and time here is $\frac{\epsilon}{4} \left(\lceil \frac{1}{\epsilon} \rceil + 1 \right) bnm < 2bnm$, which is on the order of nm.

If, on the other hand, CART uses only variables in the target, then the expected run time is

$$\sum_{i=0}^{\log \frac{1}{\epsilon}} 2^{-i} bnm$$

(perhaps plus some constant factor) since 2^{-i} is the probability that a tree of depth $i + 1$ or greater is needed, and each additional layer in the tree costs time bnm. This sum is also on the order of nm.

It follows from these arguments that the average-case time complexity of CART as we use it here is bounded by cnm for some constant $c > 0$. $\square$

Two possible criticisms of the preceding result should be noted. First, the bound on average-case sample complexity is polynomial but quite high. We expect this bound can be decreased dramatically with a more detailed or alternative analysis; this question is cited in Section 4 as a challenging area for further work with important practical consequences.

Second, while it seems reasonable to expect probabilities of target functions to decrease rapidly with the number of propositional variables they use, it does not seem realistic to always expect this decrease to begin immediately as it does with the distributions D_{C_n}. For some problem domains, we may expect target functions to use three variables on average, for others, five variables, etc. Using the more general definition of U-learnability, this lack of certainty can be captured by a parametrized family of possible probability distributions over the $L(1)$ boolean functions. For each member of this family, the probabilities of hypotheses decrease exponentially with the number of propositional variables used, *beginning with some number k of propositional variables which is not necessarily* 1. If the members of this family are parametrized by 2^k, then the resulting problem is again U-learnable using CART;[6] in fact the proof of this is a simple modification of the proof of Theorem 6, except that time complexity goes from $O(nm)$ to $O(nm \log m)$.

4 FUTURE DIRECTIONS

A longer paper describes a number of specific questions and general research directions raised by the preceding result. We briefly list these here.

1. Is Conjecture 5 about the $L(1)$ boolean functions true? We consider the proof of this conjecture a challenging problem regarding propositional logic.

2. The definition of $L(1)$ boolean functions can be extended naturally to the $L(k)$ boolean functions for any integer k, $1 \leq k \leq n$. $L(k)$ is the class of boolean functions for which every impure subfunction f_A has the following property: there exist a set of k or fewer variables, and two assignments A_1 and A_2 to these variables, such that f_{A,A_1}, has fewer positive assignments than f_{A,A_2}. Are the $L(k)$ boolean functions (with the same distributions as used for the $L(1)$ functions) U-learnable for every fixed k?

3. Is the class $L(1)$ PAC-learnable? If it is PAC-learnable by an algorithm with quadratic time complexity or better (and without using membership queries, etc.) then this PAC-learning algorithm will be an interesting alternative to CART. Are the classes $L(2)$, $L(3)$, or $L(k)$ for every fixed k PAC-learnable?

4. Can the bound on sample complexity in Theorem 6 be tightened? For a sample of a given size, if somewhat fewer than all the examples are used at the earlier nodes

---

[6]We may think of this parameter as the size of the largest decision tree needed to represent any function built from this number of variables. If we chose 2^{2^k} as the parameter instead of 2^k, then learning would be trivial. If we instead chose k as the parameter, then we know of no algorithm that would U-learn; we expect that finding a U-learner in this case is as hard as finding a PAC-learner for the $L(1)$ functions.

in the tree, then CART still U-learns with roughly the same expected accuracy, and with improved running time. The sample complexity can be used to determine how small a subset of the original sample can be used at each node without significantly decreasing the accuracy. Even a slightly tighter bound on sample complexity will allow significantly fewer examples to be used at some nodes.

5. Does Theorem 6 still hold if we allow an arbitrary distribution over X^n, rather than the uniform distribution? We expect so. In fact, the only reason to use a *weighted* gain function,[7] as do CART and ID3, is precisely to handle nonuniform distributions over the examples. The full paper also presents a simpler variant of CART, with lower sample complexity, in which the gain function is not weighted; but this algorithm is sensible *only* with a uniform distribution over examples.

6. Can we extend the U-learnability model to deal with noise? Such an extension should allow issues such as *pruning* in TDIDT learners to be addressed.

7. What kinds of U-learnability results can be obtained using propositional learners other than TDIDT algorithms, or using learning algorithms for other representations such as logic programs?

8. The use of probability distributions over target concepts might perhaps make U-learnability more closely related than PAC-learnability to Kolmogorov complexity and MDL/MML (the 'minimum description length' or 'minimum message length' principle). The investigation of the relationship between U-learnability and Kolmogorov complexity or MDL/MML is an intriguing direction for further work.

A APPENDIX: PROOF OF THE MAIN RESULT

In this appendix we give the proof of the main lemma used in the paper, Lemma 13. To present this proof, we begin with two useful facts and three technical lemmas.

Fact 7 *For every real number $a \geq 1$:*
1. $(1 - e^{-a})^a \geq 1 - \frac{1}{a}$
This is generalized easily to say that for all real numbers a, $b \geq 1$:
2. $(1 - e^{-ab})^a \geq 1 - \frac{1}{ab}$
3. $(1 - e^{-(a+b)})^a \geq 1 - \frac{1}{(a+b)}$.

Proof To verify the first statement, use the power series

$$(1 + x)^q = 1 + qx + \frac{q(q-1)x^2}{2!} + \cdots + \frac{q(q-1)\cdots(q-k+1)x^k}{k!} + \cdots$$

with $x = -e^{-a}$ and $q = a$, noting that for all $a \geq 1$ we know that $\frac{1}{a} \geq ae^{-a}$. To verify the generalizations, substitute ab (alternatively $a + b$) for the variable a throughout the original statement, and notice that removing b from the outer exponent on the left-hand side cannot decrease the value of the left-hand side. □

---

[7]That is to say, a gain function in which the purity measures of child nodes are weighted by the fractions of examples that reach each child.

Fact 8 (Chernoff bounds) *For $0 \leq p \leq 1$ and m a positive integer, let X be a random variable distributed $b(m, p)$.[8] Let $LE(p, m, r)$ denote the probability of $X \leq r$, and let $GE(p, m, r)$ denote the probability of $X \geq r$. Then for $0 \leq \alpha \leq 1$:*

8.1 $LE(p, m, (1 - \alpha)mp) \leq e^{-\frac{\alpha^2 mp}{2}}$

8.2 $GE(p, m, (1 + \alpha)mp) \leq e^{-\frac{\alpha^2 mp}{3}}$

Lemma 9 (Minimum true gain) *Let f be a boolean function over k propositional variables $x_1, \ldots, x_k$; f has some number $p(f)$ of positive assignments. If some variable x_i has $\mathrm{GiniGain} > 0$ for f, then the split on f induced by x_i has its lowest possible gain in the case where $p(f_{x=0}) = p(f_{x=0}) + 1$ (or the symmetric case) if $p(f)$ is odd, and $p(f_{x=0}) = p(f_{x=1}) + 2$ (or the symmetric case) if $p(f)$ is even.*

Proof If $f_{x_i=0}$ and $f_{x_i=1}$ have the same number of positive assignments then x_i has gain 0. So $f_{x_i=0}$ and $f_{x_i=1}$ differ in their numbers of positive assignments. The *GiniGain* score of a split is minimized by maximizing the weighted sum of the *Gini* scores of the child nodes. This weighted sum of *Gini* scores can be written as

$$
\frac{1}{2} \frac{p(f_{x_i=0})}{2^{k-1}} \frac{2^{k-1} - p(f_{x_i=0})}{2^{k-1}} + \frac{1}{2} \frac{p(f_{x_i=1})}{2^{k-1}} \frac{2^{k-1} - p(f_{x_i=1})}{2^{k-1}}
$$

$$
= \frac{p(f_{x_i=0})(2^{k-1} - p(f_{x_i=0}))}{2^{2k-1}} + \frac{p(f_{x_i=1})(2^{k-1} - p(f_{x_i=1}))}{2^{2k-1}}
$$

$$
= \frac{2^{k-1}(p(f_{x_i=0}) + p(f_{x_i=1})) - p(f_{x_i=0})^2 - p(f_{x_i=1})^2}{2^{2k-1}}.
$$

Notice that $2^{k-1}(p(f_{x_i=0}) + p(f_{x_i=1}))$ has the same value regardless of the split. Therefore, the numerator is maximized if $p(f_{x_i=0})^2 + p(f_{x_i=1})^2$ is minimized. This value is minimized if $p(f_{x_i=0})$ and $p(f_{x_i=1})$ are as nearly equal as possible. □

Lemma 10 (Even splits) *Suppose a run of CART is provided with $m \geq 8192/\epsilon^6$ examples, drawn randomly and independently according to a uniform distribution, where ϵ is the specified maximum expected error. The probability that every node constructed has at least a fraction*

$$
\frac{1}{2} - \frac{1}{2^{\log \frac{1}{\epsilon} + 3}} = \frac{1}{2} - \frac{\epsilon}{8}
$$

of the examples at its parent node is at least $1 - \frac{\epsilon}{8}$.

Proof Note that the tree will be built to depth at most $\lceil \log \frac{1}{\epsilon} \rceil + 1$, and therefore splits will occur at nodes of depth at most $\lceil \log \frac{1}{\epsilon} \rceil$. We say that a 'bad division' of the examples

---

[8] This is standard notation for the binomial distribution with mean mp and variance $mp(l - p)$. The variable X may be considered the number of 'successes' on m trials with a Bernoulli random variable whose probability of success is p.

at a node occurs just if either child of the node gets less than

$$\frac{1}{2} - \frac{1}{2^{\log \frac{1}{\epsilon} + 3}}$$

of the examples at that node. We show that given our choice of m, for any given level i in the tree being constructed, $1 \leq i \leq \lceil \log \frac{1}{\epsilon} \rceil$, the probability of a 'bad division' at *any* node at that level is at most $\epsilon^2/8$. Showing this completes the proof, because it follows that the probability of a bad division anywhere in the tree is at most

$$\sum_{i=1}^{\lceil \log \frac{1}{\epsilon} \rceil} \frac{\epsilon^2}{8} = \frac{\epsilon^2 \lceil \log \frac{1}{\epsilon} \rceil}{8} \leq \frac{\epsilon}{8}.$$

$\square$

If no 'bad division' has occurred at any level between 1 and $i - 1$, inclusive, then every node at level i has at least $m(\frac{1}{2} - \frac{\epsilon}{8})^{i-1}$ examples. Even if i is $\lceil \log \frac{1}{\epsilon} \rceil$, which is at most $\log \frac{1}{\epsilon} + 1$, this number of examples is at least $m \left(\frac{1}{2} - \frac{\epsilon}{8} \right)^{\log \frac{1}{\epsilon}}$, which we next show is at least $2048/\epsilon^4$ given our choice of m. We then show that given $2048/\epsilon^4$ examples at every node at a given level i, $1 \leq i \leq \log \frac{1}{\epsilon}$, the probability of a bad division at that level is at most $\epsilon^2/8$, thus completing the proof.

Because $m \geq 8192/\epsilon^6$, we have

$$m \left(\frac{1}{2} - \frac{\epsilon}{8} \right)^{\log \frac{1}{\epsilon}} \geq \frac{8192}{\epsilon^6} \left(\frac{1}{2} - \frac{\epsilon}{8} \right)^{\log \frac{1}{\epsilon}}$$

We can rewrite this latter term as:

$$\frac{8192}{\epsilon^6} \left(\frac{1 - \frac{\epsilon}{4}}{2} \right)^{\log \frac{1}{\epsilon}} = \frac{\frac{8192}{\epsilon^6}(1 - \frac{\epsilon}{4})^{\log \frac{1}{\epsilon}}}{2^{\log \frac{1}{\epsilon}}} = \frac{8192}{\epsilon^5} \left(1 - \frac{\epsilon}{4} \right)^{\log \frac{1}{\epsilon}}.$$

This last term can then be rewritten as

$$\frac{8192}{\epsilon^5}(1 - e^{-(\ln \frac{1}{\epsilon} + \ln 4)})^{\log \frac{1}{\epsilon}}$$

which is at least

$$\frac{8192}{\epsilon^5}(1 - e^{-(\log \frac{1}{\epsilon} + \ln 4)})^{\log \frac{1}{\epsilon}}.$$

By Fact 7.3 (with $a = \log \frac{1}{\epsilon}$ and $b = \ln 4$), this latter value is at least $\frac{8192}{\epsilon^5} \frac{1}{(\log \frac{1}{\epsilon} + \ln 4)}$, which is at least $\frac{8192}{\epsilon^5} \frac{1}{\log \frac{4}{\epsilon}}$. Since $\log \frac{4}{\epsilon} \leq \frac{4}{\epsilon}$, we have

$$\frac{8192}{\epsilon^5} \frac{1}{\log \frac{4}{\epsilon}} \geq \frac{8192}{\epsilon^5} \frac{\epsilon}{4} = \frac{2048}{\epsilon^4}$$

as desired.

It remains to show that given $2048/\epsilon^4$ examples at every node of any level i, $1 \le i \le \lceil \log \frac{1}{\epsilon} \rceil$, the probability of any 'bad division' at this level is at most $\epsilon^2/8$. Because examples are drawn according to a uniform distribution, for any variable x_i that is chosen for use in splitting a given node, the number of examples out of $2048/\epsilon^4$ that have x_i set to 0 (alternatively 1) is distributed $b\left(\frac{2048}{\epsilon^4}, \frac{1}{2}\right)$. Therefore, by Fact 8, the probability of a 'bad division' at a *particular* node with this many examples is

$$LE\left(\frac{1}{2}, \frac{2048}{\epsilon^4}, \left(\frac{1}{2} - \frac{1}{2^{\log\frac{1}{\epsilon}+3}}\right)\frac{2048}{\epsilon^4}\right) + GE\left(\frac{1}{2}, \frac{2048}{\epsilon^4}, \left(\frac{1}{2} + \frac{1}{2^{\log\frac{1}{\epsilon}+3}}\right)\frac{2048}{\epsilon^4}\right).$$

By Fact 2, choosing

$$\alpha = \frac{1}{2^{\log\frac{1}{\epsilon}+2}},$$

we find what this sum is less than

$$e^{-\frac{\frac{2048}{\epsilon^4}}{2^{2\log\frac{1}{\epsilon}+6}}} + e^{-\frac{\frac{2048}{\epsilon^4}}{2^{2\log\frac{1}{\epsilon}+7}}},$$

which is less than

$$2e^{-\frac{\frac{2048}{\epsilon^4}}{2^{2\log\frac{1}{\epsilon}+7}}}.$$

This value is in turn less than $2e^{-\frac{16}{\epsilon^2}}$, which is substantially less than $e^{-\frac{8}{\epsilon^2}}$. Therefore, the probability that *no* parent node at level i has a 'bad division' is at least $(1 - e^{-\frac{8}{\epsilon^2}})^{2^i}$. Since $i \le \lceil \log \frac{1}{\epsilon} \rceil \le \log \frac{1}{\epsilon} + 1$, we have $2^i \le \frac{1}{\epsilon^2}$; therefore, by Fact 1.2 (with $a = \frac{1}{\epsilon^2}$ and $b = 8$), the preceding probability is at least $(1 - \frac{\epsilon^2}{8})$, so the probability of any bad division at this arbitrary level is at most $\frac{\epsilon^2}{8}$, as desired. □

Corollary 11 *Suppose a run of CART is provided with $m \ge 8192(n+2)/\epsilon^{10}$ examples. Then with probability at least $1 - \frac{\epsilon}{8}$ every node generated has at least $2048(n+2)/\epsilon^8$ examples.*

Proof It follows from Lemma 10, and the fact that the greatest depth of any node is $\lceil \log \frac{1}{\epsilon} \rceil + 1$, that with probability at least $1 - \frac{\epsilon}{8}$ every node has a number of examples that is at least

$$\frac{8192(n+2)}{\epsilon^{10}}\left(\frac{1}{2} - \frac{\epsilon}{8}\right)^{\lceil \log\frac{1}{\epsilon} \rceil + 1}.$$

This number of examples can be rewritten as

$$\frac{8192(n+2)}{\epsilon^{10}}\left(\frac{(1-\frac{\epsilon}{4})}{2}\right)^{\lceil \log\frac{1}{\epsilon} \rceil + 1}$$

which is at least

$$\frac{\frac{8192(n+2)}{\epsilon^{10}}(1-\frac{\epsilon}{4})^{\log\frac{1}{\epsilon}+2}}{2^{\log\frac{1}{\epsilon}}} = \frac{8192(n+2)}{\epsilon^9}\left(1-\frac{\epsilon}{4}\right)^{\log\frac{1}{\epsilon}+2}$$

$$= \frac{8192(n+2)}{\epsilon^9}\left(1-e^{-(\log\frac{1}{\epsilon}+\ln 4)}\right)^{\log\frac{1}{\epsilon}+2}.$$

By Fact 7.2 (with $a = \log\frac{1}{\epsilon} + \ln 4$ and b a number very slightly greater than 1 such that $ab = \log\frac{1}{\epsilon} + 2$), this last term is at least

$$\frac{8192(n+2)}{\epsilon^9}\,\frac{1}{\log\frac{1}{\epsilon}+2}.$$

For all $0 < \epsilon < 1$,

$$\frac{1}{\log\frac{1}{\epsilon}+2} \geq \frac{\epsilon}{4},$$

so we have

$$\frac{8192(n+2)}{\epsilon^9}\,\frac{1}{\log\frac{1}{\epsilon}+2} \geq \frac{8192(n+2)}{\epsilon^9}\,\frac{\epsilon}{4} = \frac{2048(n+2)}{\epsilon^8}$$

is desired. $\square$

Lemma 12 *Consider an arbitrary impure node being split by CART in the course of learning an $L(1)$ boolean function, and suppose all previous splits have been 'good' (no spurious variable has been chosen for splitting). Let m be the number of examples at this node. The probability of a good split (that a spurious variable is not chosen for splitting) at this node is at least*

$$\left(1-e^{-\frac{m\epsilon^7}{248}}\right)^{n+2}.$$

Proof Let f be the target $L(1)$ boolean function, and let A be the partial assignment leading to the current impure node in the tree; then f_A is the target function for this node. Now f_A is a function over some $k \leq n$ of the n variables from which the examples are built. Of the 2^k assignments to the k variables over which f_A is defined, let $t + 1$ be the number of positive assignments in f_A, that is, the number of assignments that f_A maps to 1. Note that t is at least 0 since the node is impure. Without loss of generality, we assume t is at most $2^{k-1} - 1$; otherwise, we can let $t + 1$ be the number of *negative* assignments instead, and we can then continue the proof in a symmetric fashion.

Let x_i be a variable f_A that would maximize CART's gain function at this node if all possible examples for f_A were available, that is, if the set of examples at this node were exactly the set of all extensions of the partial assignment A to full truth assignments. Then in $f_{A\wedge x_i=0}$ the ratio of positive assignments to all assignments is at most $\frac{t}{2^{k-1}}$

265

while in $f_{A \wedge x_i=1}$ this ratio is at least $\frac{t+1}{2^{k-1}}$ (or the other way around, by symmetry). So the difference in these ratios for $f_{A \wedge x_i=0}$ and $f_{A \wedge x_i=1}$ is at least $\frac{1}{2^{k-1}}$. On the other hand, for any spurious variable y, the ratio of positive assignments to all assignments in $f_{A \wedge y=0}$ is the same as the ratio of positive assignments to all assignments in $f_{A \wedge y=1}$. Thus if all examples were available, x_i would be selected over y for splitting. But in our analysis, CART is not given all examples, but is given a sample of m examples drawn randomly, independently according to a uniform distribution. Under these conditions, it can be shown by applying Chernoff bounds (with the assumption that k is at most $\lceil \log \frac{1}{\epsilon} \rceil + 1$) that the probability of selecting y over x_i is at most $e^{-\frac{m\epsilon^7}{248}}$. But there may be as many as $n-1$ spurious with which to compare x_i. The result follows from this consideration. $\qquad\square$

We can now present Lemma 13, which was central to the proof of the paper's main result.

Lemma 13 *If CART is given $m = 8192(n+2)/\epsilon^{10}$ examples drawn randomly and independently according to a uniform distribution over truth assignments to n propositional variables, and labeled according to a target function that uses at most $\lceil \log \frac{1}{\epsilon} \rceil + 1$ variables, then the probability that CART uses any spurious variable (any variable not in the target) is at most $\epsilon/4$.*

Proof Consider an arbitrary node being split during a run of CART. Lemma 12 states that given m' examples at a node, the probability that a spurious variable is *not* chosen for splitting the node is at least

$$\left(1 - e^{-\frac{m'\epsilon^7}{248}} \right)^{n+2}.$$

Since CART will build a tree that uses at most $\lceil \log \frac{1}{\epsilon} \rceil + 1$ variables and hence has at most this depth, CART will split at most $2^{\lceil \log \frac{1}{\epsilon} \rceil} \leq \frac{2}{\epsilon}$ nodes. Therefore, given at least m' examples at every node to be split, the probability that CART chooses *no* spurious variable at *any* node is at least

$$\left(\left(1 - e^{-\frac{m'\epsilon^7}{248}} \right)^{n+2} \right)^{\frac{2}{\epsilon}} = \left(1 - e^{-\frac{m'\epsilon^7}{248}} \right)^{\frac{2(n+2)}{\epsilon}}.$$

By Fact 7, choosing $m' \geq 2048(n+2)/\epsilon^8$ ensures that this value is at least

$$1 - \frac{\epsilon}{4(n+2)} \geq 1 - \frac{\epsilon}{8}.$$

Corollary 11 states that if CART is initially provided with $m = 8192(n+2)/\epsilon^{10}$ examples then, with probability at least $1 - \frac{\epsilon}{8}$ every node in the tree has at least $m' \geq 2048(n+2)/\epsilon^8$ examples. The probability of a bad split anywhere in the tree is at most the sum of the probability that some node has fewer than m' examples, which is $\epsilon/8$, and the probability that a spurious various is chosen even though every node has m' examples, which probability is also $\epsilon/8$. Thus the probability of a bad split anywhere in the tree is at most $\epsilon/4$. $\qquad\square$

REFERENCES

[1] S. Ben-David, B. Chor, O. Goldreich, and M. Luby. On the theory of average case complexity. *Journal of Information and System Sciences*, 44: 193–219, 1992.

[2] A. Blumer, A. Ehrenfeucht, D. Haussler, and M.K. Warmuth. Occam's razor. *Information Processing Letters*, 24: 377–380, 1987.

[3] L. Breiman, J. H. Friedman, R. A. Olshen, and C.J. Stone. *Classification and Regression Trees*. Wadsworth and Brooks/Cole, Monterey, 1984.

[4] W. Buntine. *A Theory of Learning Classification Rules*. PhD thesis, School of Computing Science, University of Technology, Sydney, 1990.

[5] A. Ehrenfeucht and D. Haussler. Learning decision trees from random examples. In D. Haussler and L. Pitt, editors, *Proceedings of the 1988 Workshop on Computational Learning Theory*, pages 182–194, San Mateo, CA, August 1988. Morgan Kaufmann.

[6] D. Haussler, M. Kearns, and R. Schapire. Bounds on the sample complexity of bayesian learning using information theory and vc dimension. *Machine Learning*, 14(1): 83–113, January 1994.

[7] D. Haussler, M Kearns, and R. Shapire. Bounds on the sample complexity of bayesian learning using information theory and the vc dimension. In *COLT-91: Proceedings of the 4th Annual Workshop on Computational Learning Theory*, pages 61–74, San Mateo, CA, 1991. Morgan Kaufmann.

[8] N. Linial, Y. Mansour, and N. Nisan. Constant depth circuits, Fourier transform, and learnability. *Journal of the ACM*, 40(3): 607–620, 1993.

[9] S. Muggleton. Bayesian inductive logic programming. In *Proceedings of the Eleventh International Conference on Machine Learning (ML-94)*, pages 371–379, San Francisco, 1994. Morgan Kaufmann.

[10] S. Muggleton. Bayesian inductive logic programming. In *Proceedings of the Seventh Annual ACM Conference on Computational Learning Theory (COLT-94)*, pages 3–11, New York, 1994. The Association for Computing Machinery.

[11] S. H. Muggleton and C. D. Page. A learnability model for universal representations. Technical Report PRG-TR-3-94, Oxford University Computing Laboratory, Programming Research Group, May 1994.

[12] J. R. Quinlan. Learning efficient classification procedures and their application to chess end games. In R. Michalski, J. Carbonnel, and T. Mitchell, editors, *Machine Learning: An Artificial Intelligence Approach*. Tioga, Palo Alto, CA, 1983.

[13] J. R. Quinlan. Learning from noisy data. In R. Michalski, J. Carbonnel, and T. Mitchell, editors, *Machine Learning Volume 2*. Kaufmann, Palo Alto, CA, 1986.

[14] L. G. Valiant. A theory of the learnable. *Communications of the ACM*, 27(11): 1134–1142, 1984.

14

A learning mechanism for logic programs using dynamically shared substructures

Masayuki Numao, Shigekazu Morita and
Kenichi Karaki

Department of Computer Science,

Tokyo Institute of Technology,

2-12-1 O-okayama,

Meguro,

Tokyo 152,

Japan

e-mail: numao@cs.titech.ac.jp

Abstract

A reasoning method that proves a predicate logic formula by reducing its graph representation is proposed. Since the method directly reduces a logic formula represented by a graph, it can be understood to *self-optimize* a graph representation, meaning that it automatically transforms a logic formula into an efficient form equivalent to that acquired by explanation-based learning. By sharing the original subgraph between the learned formulae, reasoning efficiency does not deteriorate even after learning several examples. Therefore, the utility problem is overcome in the sense that no extra search is necessary for macros. The present paper demonstrates these facts in simple list manipulation problems and by proving geometric theories.

1 INTRODUCTION

Neural networks are superior to knowledge representation due to their natural learning ability. However, in contrast to pattern recognition or voice synthesis, AI applications require structured descriptions with variables, which are not provided by neural networks. Therefore, learning mechanisms for knowledge representation are investigated in the field of machine learning.

In contrast to neural networks modified by parameters for arcs, most machine learning systems attempt to generate symbols based on knowledge representation. This helps the user understand the learned knowledge, but sometimes results in a redundant structure, rendering the system inefficient. Specifically, representing refining concept while learning is difficult to code in conventional knowledge representations. Therefore, most machine learning systems learn from a batch process rather than incrementally.

The utility problem (Minton, 1988) is an informative example. Although each rule learned by explanation-based learning (EBL) is an efficient macro transformed from a domain theory, accumulation of learned macros results in deterioration of system performance, due to the matching costs associated with rules. Since the representation is written as a flat text, the system cannot merge a large set of macros into a small shared representation. The only solution to this problem has been selecting a small subset of macros, either statistically or heuristically. One of the present authors previously showed that the utility problem can be successfully alleviated by sharing a substructure (Numao *et al.*, 1994). Based on this finding, we construct a stronger sharing mechanism, by employing graph reduction in the present paper.

We present a method for reasoning and learning predicate logic formulae by using a network structure capable of maintaining alternative partial modifications simultaneously. Since using a fixed network to handle predicate logic formulae is inefficient or virtually impossible, we propose a reduction mechanism that dynamically changes the structure of a graph. This method does not learn a rule by adding it to the database, but instead adds a modified subgraph to the graph. Thus, maintaining or canceling unsettled information costs little. Since the system need not maintain the entire macro structure, it easily maintains the learning utility.

2 A REDUCTION MECHANISM

Although reduction systems have mainly been investigated for use in functional programming languages (Sleep *et al.*, 1993; Fasel and Keller, 1987; Numao and Shimura, 1985; Numao and Shimura, 1986a), several reduction systems have been proposed for use in logic programming languages (Glauert and Papadopoulos, 1988; McBrien, 1993; Lindstrom, 1987; Damm *et al.*, 1993; Yamanaka, 1993). The purpose of proposing another reduction mechanism in the present paper is to facilitate the establishment of a system that automatically learns from past inference processes. We propose a graph representation for unification and binding of logical variables. This representation provides an implicit learning mechanism, because queries share substructures in the graph. Thus, the results of reasoning in each query are automatically maintained for subsequent queries.

2.1 Reasoning

The initial graph for reduction is shown in Figure 1. Subgraphs representing rule clauses and query clauses are shown in the dotted boxes. To execute a reasoning step, the reducer attempts to unify all combinations of heads and atomic formulae in bodies.

A node called *uu* is connected to each atomic formula. All *uu* nodes are connected via a node called *short*, which has the reduction process shown in Figure 2. This operation

269

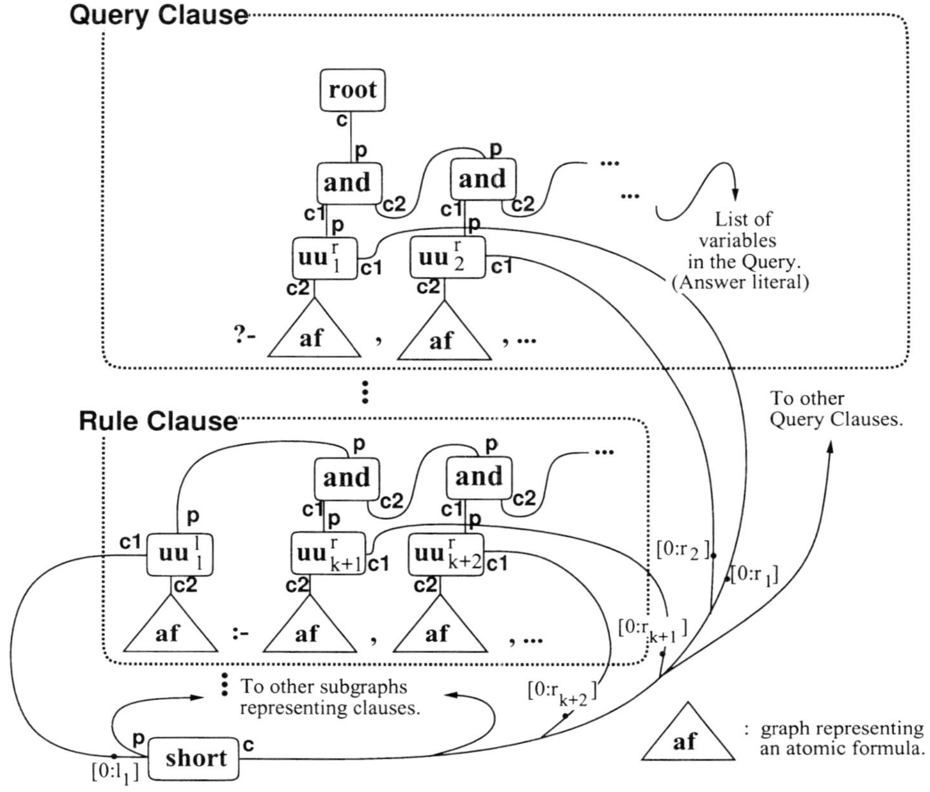

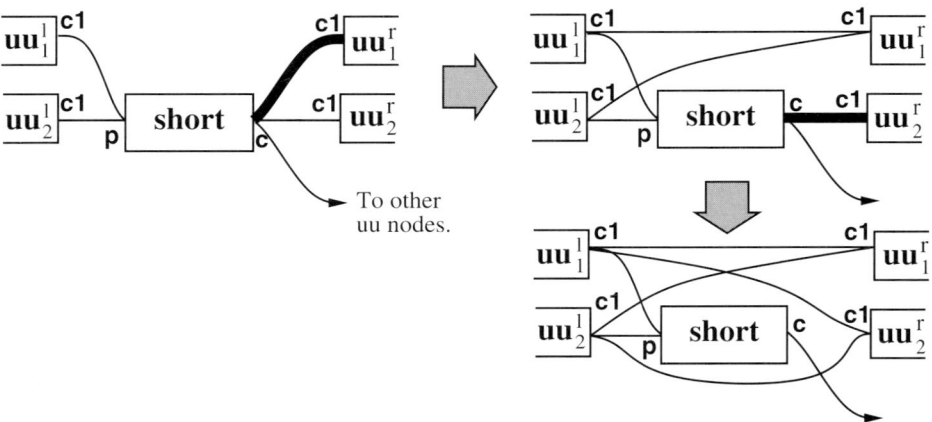

Figure 1. Initial graph.

Figure 2. Reducing a short node.

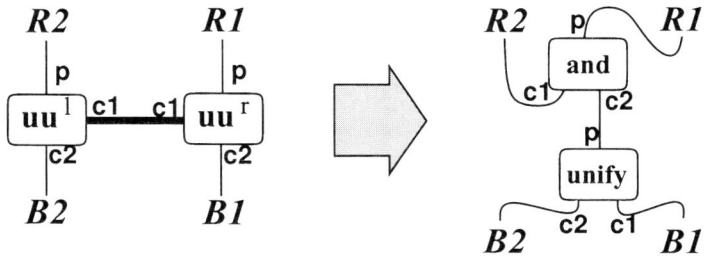

Figure 3. Reducing a pair of *uu* nodes.

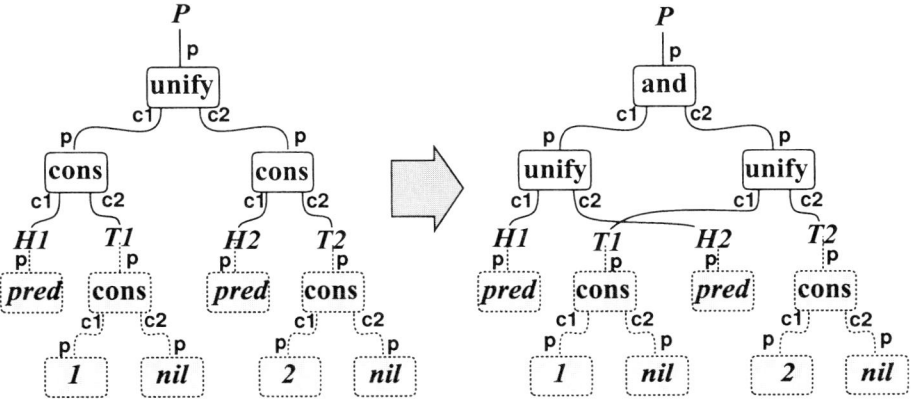

Figure 4. Unification step.

connects all combinations of uu^l_i and uu^r_j, each of which is transformed into a *unify* node by the rule shown in Figure 3.

Multiple queries can thus be made by connecting their graphs to the short node. Queries are made incrementally by adding such connections, whereby the short node is reduced incrementally as shown in Figure 2. In order to obtain the value of a variable in a query, its representation has an *answer literal* (Gray, 1984) represented as a list of the variables at the end of its *and* structure.

2.2 Atomic formulae and their unification

An atomic formula is represented by a cons structure composed of nodes called *const*, *cons*, and *var*, which denote a constant,[1] a *cons* cell, and a logical variable, respectively. By introducing the *unify* node and the logical *and* node, it is now possible to make a unification step, as shown in Figure 4.

A logical variable is represented by a shared *var* node. In order to avoid the unification anomaly (Lindstrom, 1987), we distinguish the input and output of a variable by labeling

---

[1] An atomic symbol or an *atom* as described by Lisp.

271

the corresponding arcs + and *p*, respectively. Figure 5 shows the reduction process of instantiating a variable. Other rules for unification are shown in the appendix.

2.3 One-arc reduction principle

When we describe a reduction rule, we follow the principle that the left side only refers to two nodes connected by an arc. We call this the *one-arc reduction principle*. In Figure 4, this principle is satisfied by separating the reduction step into the two steps shown in Figure 6 and introducing an intermediate node *unifyCons*. The redexes are arcs represented by the thick line connecting *unify* and *cons*, and that connecting *unifyCons* and *cons*. Similarly, the reduction step unifying two constants can be separated into the steps shown Figure 7.

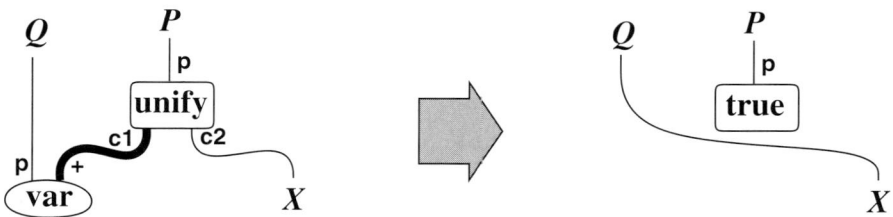

Figure 5. Reducing a variable.

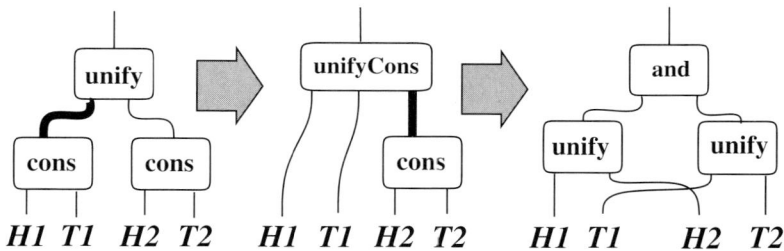

Figure 6. A process of one-arc reduction.

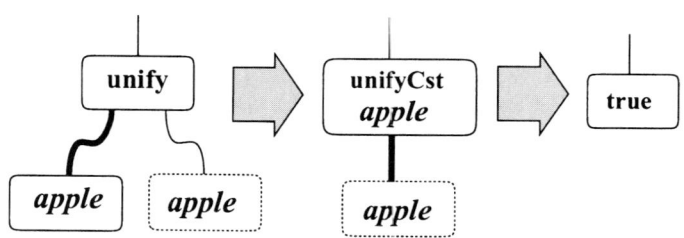

Figure 7. Unifying two constants.

Such decomposition simplifies implementation because the reducer can detect a redex simply by checking an arc that connects two nodes. This principle also utilizes the locality of the redexes and accelerates the reduction of graphs distributed over processors (Numao and Shimura, 1985; 1986a). Thus, computation in the reduction mechanism is distributed over all arcs in a graph (Numao, 1995).

2.4 Multiple results and color

In the initial graph, the *short* node has multiple parents labeled p, and multiple children labeled c, as shown in Figure 1. These arcs provide alternative possibilities for reducing the graph, and naturally introduce OR parallelism. If the query has multiple results, multiple arcs are connected to the *root* node, giving multiple values for each variable.

Since the graph is locally reduced, the OR alternatives result in mixed bindings. Consider the following program:

```
?- same(1,2).
same(X,Y) :- equal(X,Y). equal(1,1). equal(2,2).
```

where X and Y are bound to 1 or 2 and the above mechanism reduces the query to 'true.'

In order to avoid such confusion in bindings, we introduce an identifier called *color*, comprised of *source* and *destination* parts, denoted as:

$$destination : source.$$

Each tip of an arc has a queue of colors, such $Q1$, $Q2$ and $Q3$ in Figure 8.

We attach colors $[0 : l_i]$ and $[0 : r_j]$ to the initial graph shown in Figure 1, where the source parts, l_i and r_j, are markers identifying the atomic formula from which the color originates.

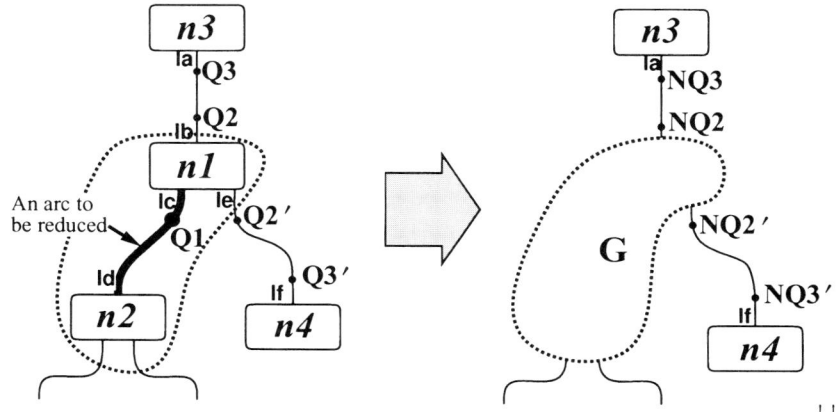

Figure 8. Color.

273

if $Q1 = [0 : S1]$ and $Q2 = [0 : S2]$ then begin
$NQ3 := [[S2] : S1]; NQ2 := [[S1] : S2]$ end
else if $Q1 = Q2$ then begin $NQ3 := []; NQ2 := []$ end
else if $Q1 = [D : S1], Q2 = [D : S2]$ and $S1 \neq S2$
then remove the arc and do not generate G
else if $Q1 = [D1 : S1], Q2 = [D2 : S2]$ and $D1 \neq D2$ then
if $S1 = l_i, S2 = r_j$ then begin
$NQ3 := [[S2|D1] : S1]; NQ2 := Q2$ end
else if $S1 = r_j, S2 = l_i$ then begin
$NQ3 := Q1; NQ2 := [[S1|D2] : S2]$ end
else begin $NQ3 := Q1; NQ2 := Q2$ end.

Figure 9. Comparing two colors.

When reducing the short node, colors $Q1 = [0 : S1]$ and $Q2 = [0 : S2]$ become the new colors $NQ3 = [[S2] : S1]$ and $NQ2 = [[S1] : S2]$, respectively, according to the procedure shown in Figure 9. The generated new color of $[[S2] : S1]$ denotes that its destination and source are $S2$ and $S1$, respectively.

We shall now trace the manner in which new colors are calculated when reducing the graph shown in Figure 8. Applying a reduction rule transforms the graph on the left into that on the right side of the figure. The new colors $NQ3$ and $NQ2$ are calculated according to the procedure shown in Figure 9.[2] If the two colors are the same ($Q1 = Q2$), they originate from the same context, and therefore the new arc is generated in order to continue the computation. If the destinations (D) of the colors are the same but their sources are different ($S1 \neq S2$), they are moving to the same destination from different contexts, and therefore the combination is removed. If the destinations are different ($D1 \neq D2$), the colors are unaffected and are not modified except for the addition of an element to the destination part to overcome nested recursion. Thus, each context is maintained and inappropriate arcs are removed based on their colors.

3 LEARNING

Explanation-based generalization (EBG) (Mitchell *et al.*, 1986) and chunking (Laird *et al.*, 1986) combine rules from a proof tree into a macro that is constructed by unifying pairs of terms (Kedar-Cabelli and McCarty, 1987).

Theorem 1 *Using the reduction mechanism, the reasoning process generates a reduced graph. This graph represents all macros, composed of instantiated rules in the proof tree, and generalized using EBG.*

---

[2]This is a simplified version of the procedure for handling cases in which the length of $Q1$ and $Q2$ is 1, and $Q3$ is empty. See Appendix B for a detailed explanation.

274

Proof (sketch) EBG generates a rule by unifying in a generalized proof tree (Kedar-Cabelli and McCarty, 1987). The reduction rules unify both in the instantiated proof tree and in the generalized proof tree. Therefore, the generated macros represented as a reduced graph are equivalent to those generated by EBG. □

In contrast to conventional resolution procedures that unify within a single context, the present reduction mechanism shares a unification in all contexts, which is maintained as a graph representing macros.

Consider the member program shown in Figure 10(a), the initial graph of which is shown in Figure 11. Reduction of a graph replaces each subgraph with its corresponding member program value. As an example, we will unify member(X,Y) and member(X,[_|Y]), and unify member(X,Y) and member(X,[X|_]). As shown in Figure 11, the subgraphs R, $L2$ and $L1$ are identical. Therefore, the unification succeeds, yielding the graph shown in Figure 12(a), in which subgraph A is shown in Figure 11. Graph (a) is reduced to graph (b), which is equivalent to graph (c), where the loop around the cons node is a reduced subgraph for recursion. In order to simplify the notation, we represent the graph by (c), whereby the third clause member(X,[_|Y]):- member(X,Y) is transformed as shown in Figure 13(a).

4 EXPERIMENTS

We implemented two versions of this system: *Natty*[3]/*Spec* (<u>N</u>etwork-based <u>a</u>rchitecture that <u>T</u>okyo Institute of <u>T</u>echnolog<u>y</u> organised for writing its <u>S</u>pecification)[4] on SICStus Prolog 2.1, and *Natty/CL*) (written in <u>C</u>ommon <u>L</u>isp) on Austin Kyoto Common Lisp.

Table 1 shows the results of several experiments using Natty/CL. Following is the problem *composer*:

```
human(X):-composer(X).
composer(mozart). composer(beethoven).
?- human(X).
```

The same query is given twice in order to check for acceleration in performance.

The second problem, *composer with append*, includes a subpredicate independent of the query:

```
human(X):-append([a,b,c],[d,e,f],[a,b,c,d,e,f]),composer(X).
composer(mozart). composer(beethoven).
append([],Ys,Ys).
append([X|Xs],Ys,[X|Zs]):-append(Xs,Ys,Zs).
?- human(X).
```

---

[3]neat, trim and smart; or *Nat*-ty after a system called Nat (Numao and Shimura, 1986b), which was previously constructed by one of the present authors for learning term rewriting rules.

[4]By replacing *y* with *o*, this version is sometimes ironically called *Natto*: a Japanese food made from fermented soybeans that is twined like a very complicated graph.

```
(a) ?- member(1,[3,2,1]).
    member(X,[X|_]).
    member(X,[_|Y]) :- member(X,Y).

(b) ?- member(1,[9,8,7,6,5,4,3,2,1,0]).
    member(X,[X|_]).
    member(X,[_|Y]) :- member(X,Y).

(c) ?- member(1,[9,8,7,6,5,4,3,2,1,0]).
    member(X,[X|_]).
    member(X,[_,X|_]).
    member(X,[_,_,X|_]).
    member(X,[_,_,_,X|_]).
    member(X,[_,_,_,_,X|_]).
    member(X,[_,_,_,_,_,X|_]).
    member(X,[_,_,_,_,_,_,X|_]).
    member(X,[_,_,_,_,_,_,_,X|_]).
    member(X,[_,_,_,_,_,_,_,_,X|_]).
```

Figure 10. *Member* program examples.

by which the program is further accelerated. Thus, the reduction mechanism enables on-the-fly dynamic optimization or partial computation of programs (Futamura, 1983).

Figure 10 shows the problems *member* (a)–(c). Using EBL, learning a self-recursive program such as the member program deteriorates performance (Letovsky, 1990; Subramanian and Feldman, 1990; Yamada, 1992). Although member (a) improves performance, member (b) deteriorates performance after training, because the mechanism generates every combination of macros for lists with lengths shorter than 9, which are represented by the definition in (c). Although (c) is inefficient due to its large number of macros, it is still faster than (b) because the sharing of graphs in (b) consumes significant time needlessly calculating unmatched colors.

We constructed another version with *lazy copying* for Natty/Spec that copies a node before reducing an arc. While reducing the training example, the lazy copying mechanism transforms the recursive loop into the shaded expanded subgraph shown in Figure 13(b), where colors are swept out, although each subgraph is still shared. As shown, the graph contains every macro combination of the member clauses, and no extra search cost is necessary for unifying the graph and a given query.

The result marked with † shows the CPU time in Natty/Spec with lazy copying, demonstrating that learning drastically improves performance. In addition, the utility of the learned graph is maintained for all queries containing lists with lengths less than 9. Thus, the learned graph maintains its utility by appropriately choosing between sharing and copying a subgraph. The reduction mechanism is considered to provide an on-the-fly program transformation system of logic programs, in which unfolding (copying) and folding (sharing) (Sato and Tamaki, 1984) are crucial.

Hasida (1994) presented a parsing mechanism based on Horn clauses denoted as a graphical representation, and proposed *incremental copy* of literals in order to speed

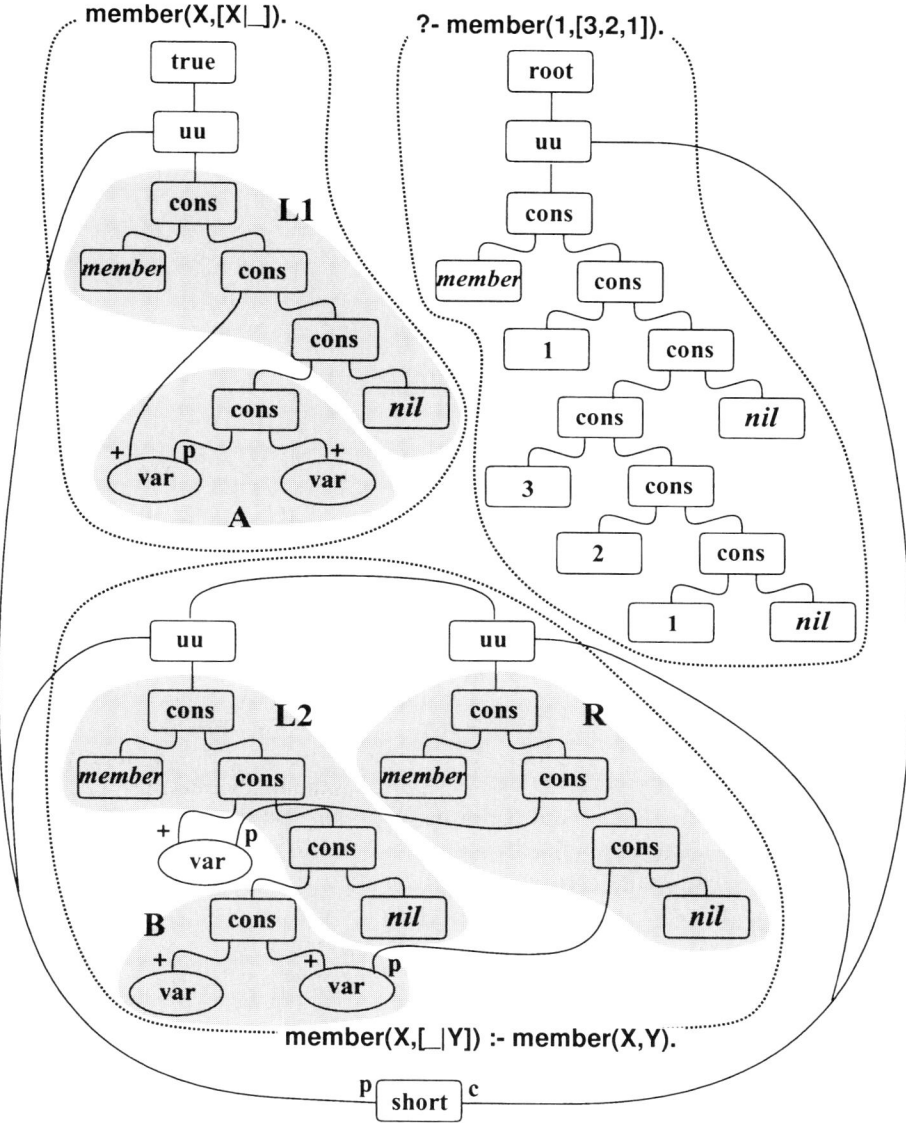

Figure 11. Initial graph of member program (a).

up the parsing process. In this process, a non-trivial check must be performed in order to determine whether two literals are *compatible* or *heterogeneous*. Our lazy copying mechanism is simpler, because it checks such compatibility using colors, and introduces natural learning ability in the reduction process.

Figure 14 shows the problems *Geometry* (1)–(3) (Morita and Numao, 1994). The system initially proves congruence between the two triangles in the training example by

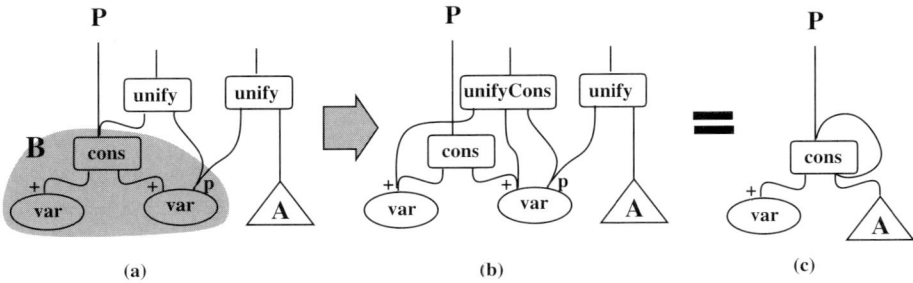

Figure 12. Reducing the member program.

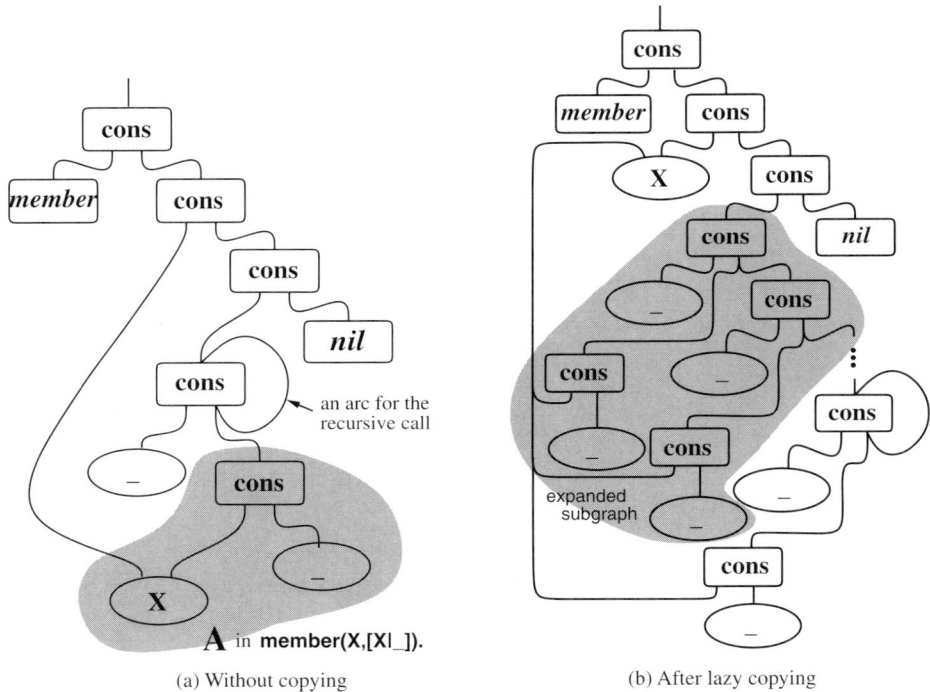

(a) Without copying

(b) After lazy copying

Figure 13. Learned graphs.

the side-angle-side (SAS) or three sides (SSS) methods, and then proves test examples
(1)–(3). The *nodes* column in the table shows the number of nodes in the graph before
training and before testing. In Geometry (1), 94.3 sec is required to prove the test example.
Proving the training examples by SAS drastically improves the performance to 8.8 sec.
Although the test example is proved by SAS, training by SSS also improves performance
because the graph is reduced by both methods. Training by SAS and testing (1) took
$60.3 + 8.8 = 69.1$ sec, which is faster than directly proving the test example, indicating

278

Table 1. Results of experiments.

Problem	Tranining set	Training			Test		
		Nodes	CPU (sec)	Steps	Nodes	CPU (sec)	Steps
composer	= test set	–	0.3	111	–	0.15	67
composer with append	= test set	–	1.7	391	–	0.3	57
member (a)	‡	–	0.4	133	–	0.3	81
member (b)	= test set	–	1.9	271	–	2.9	205
		559[†]	424[†]		67[†]	173[†]	
member (c)	= test set	–	1.2	445	–	1.2	367
Geometry (1)	none		N/A		–	94.3	7042
	SAS	866	60.3	7288	600	8.8	582
	SSS	–	51.0	7078	–	9.8	544
Geometry (2)	none		N/A		–	957.0	10507
	SAS	961	75.8	8630	829	454.7	3108
	SSS	–	76.1	8619	–	439.6	3222
Geometry (3)	none		N/A		–	306.9	9737
	SAS	1015	227.3	10274	902	150.2	2691
	SSS	–	253.9	10083	–	148.3	2719

[†] with lazy copying in Natty/Spec.
[‡] ?- member(a,[c,b,a]).

that our method is sensitive to the training example and showing that the mechanism not only compiles or partially evaluates a graph, but also learns strategy, although the system simply searches in a breadth-first manner. Although Geometry (2) and (3) are more complicated, training still improves performance and the data show similar results.

5 CONCLUSION

We have proposed a reduction mechanism for predicate logic programs. The experimental results show that the mechanism learns from examples, although the mechanism simply reduces a given graph.

Yoshida *et al.* (1993) proposed a learning algorithm based on a graph. Etzioni (1991) constructed a system that analyzes a problem space based on a *problem space graph*. Our mechanism is different in that a logic program and its data are represented by a graph, whereas previous methods used graphs to extract an explanation structure in a problem space.

The present paper has described speed-up learning, and has not dealt with other learning paradigms. However, the sharing technique in the present reduction mechanism has merits with respect to inductive learning, which is required in order to search a large number of combinations of concepts and refinements. We are now attempting to extend the technique to multistrategy learning of predicate-logic rules by introducing weight to the arcs in the graph.

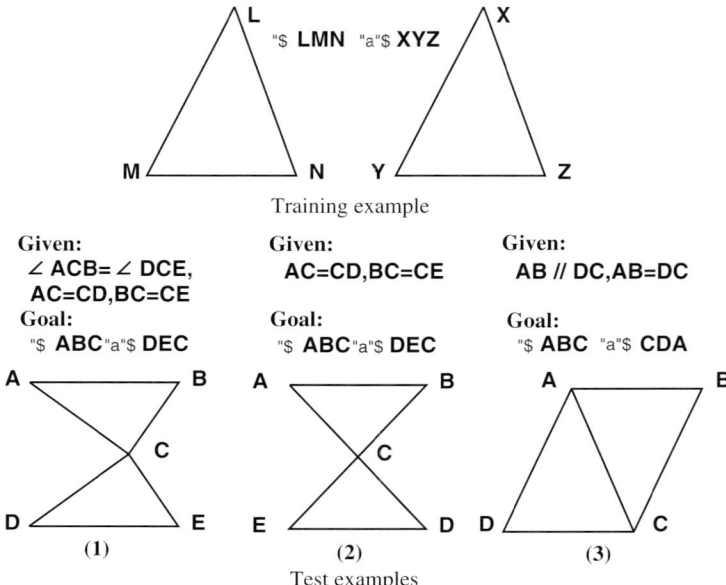

Figure 14. Geometry proof.

6 APPENDIX A: REDUCTION RULES

Let us formally define the reduction process, which has been approximately described by the figures. We represent a graph by a set of clauses. For example, the leftmost graph in Figure 2 is described as follows:

$$uu(uu_1^l). \quad uu_1^l \cdot c1-srt \cdot p. \quad uu(uu_2^l). \quad uu_2^l \cdot c1-srt \cdot p.$$
$$short(srt).$$
$$srt \cdot c-uu_1^r \cdot c1. \quad uu(uu_1^r). \quad srt \cdot c-uu_2^r \cdot c1. \quad uu(uu_2^r). \qquad (1)$$

The clauses $uu(uu_1^l)$ and $short(srt)$ denote that the node uu_1^l is a uu node and that the node srt is a $short$ node, respectively. The infix predicate '$-$' denotes an arc. For example, the arc $uu_1^l \cdot c1-srt \cdot p$ connects $c1$ of uu_1^r and p of srt. The process of reducing a short node is defined by the following rule:

$$P-S \cdot p, \ short(S), \ S \cdot c—C \Rightarrow P-C.$$

By instantiating $S = srt$, $C = uu_1^r \cdot c1$, (1) is reduced to the second graph in Figure 2, described as:

$$uu(uu_1^l). \quad uu_1^l \cdot c1-uu_1^r \cdot c1. \quad uu_2^l \cdot c1-uu_1^r \cdot c1. \quad uu(uu_1^r).$$
$$uu_1^l \cdot c1-srt \cdot p. \quad uu(uu_2^l). \quad uu_2^l \cdot c1-srt \cdot p.$$
$$short(srt).$$
$$srt \cdot c-uu_2^r \cdot c1. \quad uu(uu_2^r). \qquad (2)$$

280

Similarly, by instantiating $S = srt$, $C = uu_2^r \cdot c1$, (2) is reduced to the third graph in the figure, which is denoted as follows:

$$uu(uu_1^l).\ uu_1^l \cdot c1\text{--}uu_1^r \cdot c1.\ uu_2^l \cdot c1\text{--}uu_1^r \cdot c1.\ uu(uu_1^r).$$
$$uu(uu_2^l).\ uu_1^l \cdot c1\text{--}uu_2^r \cdot c1.\ uu_2^l \cdot c1\text{--}uu_2^r \cdot c1.\ uu(uu_2^r).$$
$$uu_1^l \cdot c1\text{--}srt \cdot p.\ uu_2^l \cdot c1\text{--}srt \cdot p.$$
$$short(srt). \tag{3}$$

where all combinations of uu_i^l and uu_j^r are connected.

Thus, the rule in Figure 3 reduces the connected uu nodes into a *unify* node. We describe this rule as follows:

(R2) $R1\text{--}Uu^r \cdot p, uu(Uu^r), Uu^r \cdot c2\text{--}B1, Uu^r \cdot c1\text{---}Uu^l \cdot c1,$

             $R2\text{--}Uu^l \cdot p, uu(Uu^l),\ Uu^l \cdot c2\text{--}B2$

            $\Rightarrow$ $R1\text{--}A \cdot p,\ and\ (A),\ A \cdot c1\text{--}R2,\ A \cdot c2\text{--}U \cdot p,$

                $unify(U), U \cdot c1\text{--}B1, U \cdot c2\text{--}B2.$

The reduction process of instantiating a variable shown in Figure 5 is defined as:

(R3) $P\text{--}U \cdot p, unify(U), U \cdot c1\text{---}V \cdot +, U \cdot c2\text{--}X, Q\text{--}V \cdot p, var(V)$

            $\Rightarrow$ $P\text{--}T \cdot p, true(T), Q\text{--}S \cdot p, short(S), S \cdot c\text{--}X.$

We insert a *short* node between Q and X. When $X = Q$, this reduction forms a loop, which is represented by an arc around the short node. This case occurs at the first argument in the member program shown in Figure 11.

The following rule comprises the first step of unifying *cons* structures shown in Figure 6:

(R4) $P\text{--}U \cdot p, unify(U), U \cdot c1\text{---}C1 \cdot p, cons(C1), C1 \cdot c1\text{--}H,$

             $C1 \cdot c2\text{--}T, U \cdot c2\text{--}Y$

               $\Rightarrow$ $P\text{--}Uc \cdot p, unifyCons(Uc), Uc \cdot c1\text{--}H, Uc \cdot c2\text{--}T, Uc \cdot c3\text{--}Y$

where the infix predicate '—' (longer dash) denotes an arc as the redex, represented by the thick line in the figure. The second step is performed by the rule:

(R5) $P\text{--}Uc \cdot p, unifyCons(Uc), Uc \cdot c1\text{--}H1, Uc \cdot c2\text{--}T1, Uc \cdot c3\text{--}C2 \cdot p,$

       $cons(C2), C2 \cdot c1\text{--}H2, C2 \cdot c2\text{--}T2$

           $\Rightarrow$ $P\text{--}A \cdot p, and(A), A \cdot c1\text{--}U1 \cdot p, unify(U1), U1 \cdot c1\text{--}H1, U1 \cdot c2\text{--}H2,$

               $A \cdot c2\text{--}U2 \cdot p, unify(U2), U2 \cdot c1\text{--}T1, U2 \cdot c2\text{--}T2.$

If the child is a var node, it is replaced by a *cons* node:

(R6) $P\!-\!Uc \cdot p,\, unifyCons(Uc),\, Uc \cdot c1\!-\!X,\, Uc \cdot c2\!-\!Y,$
         $Uc \cdot c3\!-\!V \cdot +,\, Z\!-\!V \cdot p,\, var(V)$
         $\Rightarrow \quad P\!-\!T \cdot p,\, true(T),\, Z\!-\!C \cdot p,\, cons(C),\, c \cdot c1\!-\!X,\, C \cdot c2\!-\!Y.$

The following rule comprises the first step of unifying constants shown in Figure 7:

(R7) $P\!-\!U \cdot p,\, unify(U),\, U \cdot c1\!-\!N \cdot p,\, const(N,\, C),\, U \cdot c2\!-\!Y$
         $\Rightarrow \quad P\!-\!Ut \cdot p,\, unifyCst(Ut,\, C),\, Ut \cdot c1\!-\!Y.$

where the clause *const*$(N,\, C)$ denotes that the node N is a *const* node with a constant C. The second step in Figure 7 is performed by the rule:

(R8) $P\!-\!Ut \cdot p,\, unifyCst(Ut,\, C),\, Ut \cdot c1\!-\!N \cdot p,\, const(N,\, C)$
         $\Rightarrow \quad P\!-\!T \cdot p,\, true(T).$

If the child is a var node, it is replaced by a *const* node:

(R9) $P\!-\!Ut \cdot p,\, unifyCst(Ut,\, C),\, Ut \cdot c1\!-\!V \cdot +,\, X\!-\!V \cdot p,\, var(V)$
         $\Rightarrow \quad P\!-\!T \cdot p,\, true(T),\, X\!-\!N \cdot p,\, const(N,\, C).$

Reduction rules for an *and* node are as follows:

(R10) $Y\!-\!A \cdot p,\, and(A),\, A \cdot c1\!-\!T \cdot p,\, true(T),\, A \cdot c2\!-\!X$
         $\Rightarrow \quad Y\!-\!S \cdot p,\, short(S),\, S \cdot c\!-\!X.$

(R11) $Y\!-\!A \cdot p,\, and(A),\, A \cdot c1\!-\!X,\, A \cdot c2\!-\!T \cdot p,\, true(T)$
         $\Rightarrow \quad Y\!-\!S \cdot p,\, short(S),\, S \cdot c\!-\!X.$

(R12) $true(T),\, T \cdot p\!-\!A \cdot p,\, and(A),\, A \cdot c1\!-\!X,\, A \cdot c2\!-\!Y$
         $\Rightarrow Y\!-\!S \cdot p,\, short(S),\, S \cdot c\!-\!X.$

Values of variables in a query are obtained from the answer literal in Figure 1, according to the following rules:

(R13) $root(R),\, R \cdot c\!-\!N \cdot p,\, cons(N),\, N \cdot c1\!-\!C1,\, N \cdot c2\!-\!C2$
         $\Rightarrow \quad root(R),\, R \cdot c\!-\!M \cdot p,\, pcons(M),$
         $\qquad M \cdot c1\!-\!P1 \cdot p,\, print(P1),\, P1 \cdot c\!-\!C1,$
         $\qquad M \cdot c2\!-\!P2 \cdot p,\, print(P2),\, P2 \cdot c\!-\!C2.$

(R14) $R\!-\!P \cdot p,\, print(P),\, P \cdot c\!-\!N \cdot p,\, cons(N),\, N \cdot c1\!-\!C1,\, N \cdot c2\!-\!C2$
         $\Rightarrow \quad R\!-\!M \cdot p,\, pcons(M),$

$$M \cdot c1 - P1 \cdot p, print(P1), P1 \cdot c - C1,$$
$$M \cdot c2 - P2 \cdot p, print(P2), P2 \cdot c - C2.$$

(R15) $R - P \cdot p, print(P), P \cdot c - N \cdot p, const(N, C)$
$$\Rightarrow \quad R - I \cdot p, pi(I, C).$$

(R16) $R - N \cdot p, pcons(N), N \cdot c1 - I \cdot p, N \cdot c2 - C2, pi(I, C)$
$$\Rightarrow \quad R - P \cdot p, pic(P, C), P \cdot c - C2.$$

(R17) $R - N \cdot p, pic(N, C1), N \cdot c - I \cdot p, pi(I, C2)$
$$\Rightarrow \quad R - I \cdot p, pi(I, [C1|C2]).$$

The values are stored in a *pi* node, when the *pi* node is connected to the *root* node.

7 APPENDIX B: PROCEDURE FOR COLOR QUEUES

When the following procedure fails, no arc is generated between *n3* and *G* in Figure 8.

```
% qcpr(+Q1,+Q2,+Q3, -NQ2,-NQ3)
qcpr(Q1,Q2,Q3, NQ2,NQ3)
 :- qcpr(Q1,Q2, NQ2,[AQ3,[]]), append(Q3,AQ3,NQ3).


qcpr([],Q2, Q2,[Q3,Q3]).
qcpr ([C1|Q1],Q2, NQ2,[Q3H,Q3L])
 :- ccpr(C1,Q2, MQ2,[Q3H,Q3M]),qcpr(Q1,MQ2, NQ2,[Q3M,Q3L]).


ccpr(C,[], [],[[C|Q3],Q3]).
ccpr(0:S1,[0:S2|Q2], [[S1]:S2|NQ2],Q3)
 :- ccpr([S2]:S1,Q2, NQ2,Q3).
ccpr(Cd:Cs,[Cd:Cs|Q2], Q2,[Q3,Q3]) :- Cd \==0, !.
ccpr(C1d:C1s,[C2d:C2s|Q2], [C2d:C2s|NQ2],Q3)
 :- C1d \== C2d, C1s=l(_),C2s=r(_), !,
  ccpr([C2s|C1d]:C1s,Q2, NQ2,Q3).
ccpr(C1d:C1s,[C2d:C2s|Q2], [[C1s|C2d]:C2s|NQ2],Q3)
 :- C1d \== C2d, C1s=r(_), C2s=l(_), !,ccpr(C1d:C1s,Q2, NQ2,Q3).
ccpr(C1d:C1s, [C2d:C2s|Q2], [C2d:C2s|NQ2],Q3)
 :- C1d \== C2d,ccpr(C1d:C1s,Q2, NQ2,Q3).
```

REFERENCES

Damm, W., Lui, F., and Peikenkamp, T. (1993). A graph rewriting model enhanced with sharing for OR-parallel execution of logic programs. In *Term Graph Rewriting* (Sleep *et al.*, 1993), pages 253–268.

Etzioni, O. (1991). STATIC: A problem-space compiler for PRODIGY. In *Proc. AAAI 91*, pages 533–540. AAAI Press/MIT Press, Menlo Park.

Fasel, J. and Keller, R., editors (1987). *Graph Reduction*, volume 279 of *Lecture Notes in Computer Science*. Springer-Verlag, Berlin.

Futamura, Y. (1983). Partial computation of programs. In Goto, E. *et al.*, editors, *RIMS Symposia on Software Science and Engineering, Kyoto, Japan, 1982.* (*Lecture Notes in Computer Science, vol. 147*), pages 1–35. Springer-Verlag, Berlin.

Glauert, J. R. W. and Papadopoulos, G. A. (1988). A parallel implementation of GHC. In *Proc. Conf. Fifth Generation Computer Systems*, pages 1051–1058, Tokyo.

Gray, P. (1984). *Logic, Algebra and Databases*. Ellis Horwood Limited, Chichester.

Hasida, K. (1994). Emergent parsing and generation with generalized chart. In *Proc. the International Conference on Computational Linguistics (COLING' 94)*.

Kedar-Cabelli, S. T. and McCarty, L. T. (1987). Explanation-based generalization as resolution theorem proving. In *Proceedings of the Fourth International Workshop on Machine Learning*, University of California, Irvine, pages 383–389. Morgan Kaufmann, Los Altos.

Laird, J. E., Rosenbloom, P. S., and Newell, A. (1986). Chunking in SOAR: The anatomy of a general learning mechanism. *Machine Learning*, 1(1): 11–46.

Letovsky, S. (1990). Operationality criteria for recursive predicates. In *Proc. AAAI 90*, pages 936–941.

Lindstrom, G. (1987). Implementing logical variables on a graph reduction architecture. *Lecture Notes in Computer Science*, 279: 382–400, Springer-Verlag, Berlin.

McBrien, P. J. (1993). Implementing logical variables and disjunctions in graph rewrite systems. In *Term Graph Rewriting* (Sleep *et al.*, 1993), pages 333–346.

Michalski, R. S. and Tecuci, G., editors (1994). *Machine Learning: A Multistrategy Approach* (*Vol. IV*). Morgan Kaufmann, San Francisco, CA.

Minton, S. (1988). *Learning Search Control Knowledge*. Kluwer Academic Publishers, Boston/Dordrecht/London.

Mitchell, T. M., Keller, R. M., and Kedar-Cabelli, S. T. (1986). Explanation-based generalization: A unifying view. *Machine Learning*, 1(1): 47–80.

Morita, S. and Numao, M. (1994). Overcoming the utility problem in learning to prove geometry theorems (in Japanese). In *Proc. 8th Annual Conference of Japanese Society for Artificial Intelligence*, pages 161–164, Tokyo.

Numao, M. (1995). Global Intelligence – Towards a global-size society of mind (in Japanese). *Information Processing Society of Japan SIG Notes*, 95-AI-100.

Numao, M., Maruoka, T., and Shimura, M. (1994). Inductively speeding up logic programs. *Machine Intelligence*, 13: 371–385.

Numao, M. and Shimura, M. (1985). Evaluation of the functional symbol manipulation language in distributed systems (in Japanese). *Transactions of Information Processing Society of Japan*, 26(2): 247–256.

Numao, M. and Shimura, M. (1986a). Evaluation of graph representations with active nodes. *Lecture Notes in Computer Science*, 220: 17–43, Springer-Verlag, Berlin.

Numao, M. and Shimura, M. (1986b). NAT: Nonalgorithmic translator (in Japanese). *Information Processing Society of Japan*, 86-SYM-38: 1–10, Tokyo.

Sato, T. and Tamaki, H. (1984). Transformational logic program synthesis. In *Proc. Conf. Fifth Generation Computer Systems '84*, pages 195–201, Tokyo.

Sleep, M. R., Plasmeijer, M. J., and van Eekelen, M. C. J. D., editors (1993). *Term Graph Rewriting – Theory and Practice*. John Wiley & Sons, Chichester, England.

Subramanian, D. and Feldman, R. (1990). The utility of EBL in recursive domain theories. In *Proc. AAAI 90*, pages 942–949.

Yamada, S. (1992). Computing the utility of EBL in a logic programming environment (in Japanese). *Journal of Japanese Society for Artificial Intelligence*, 7(2): 309–319.

Yamanaka, H. (1993). Graph narrowing and its simulation by graph reduction. Technical Report IIAS-RR-93-10E, Institute for Social Information Science, Fujitsu lab., Chiba, Japan.

Yoshida, K., Motoda, H., and Indurkhya, N. (1993). Unifying learning methods by colored digraphs. *Lecture Notes in Artificial Intelligence*, 744: 342–355, Springer-Verlag, Berlin.

15

PAC-learning of preference relations over interpretations in lazy nonmonotonic reasoning

Ken Satoh

Intelligent Systems Laboratory,

Fujitsu Laboratories Limited,

1015 Kamikodanaka,

Nakahara-ku,

Kawasaki 211,

Japan,

e-mail: ksatoh@flab.fujitsu.co.jp

Abstract

This paper presents a method of learning a class of preference order over interpretations in a propositional language which is a generalization of circumscription. The order considered in this paper is based on the distance in a weighted Euclidean space between the most preferable interpretation among all the interpretations and an interpretation represented as lattice points whose elements take values of either 0 or 1. Nonmonotonic reasoning defined by this order is a subclass of *lazy* nonmonotonic reasoning (Satoh 1992) where nonmonotonicity emerges only when new added knowledge is contradictory to the previous belief.

We learn the weight which defines the order from relative preference information between two interpretations. The relative preference information represents whether an interpretation is more preferable to another interpretation. We give a PAC (probably approximately correct) learning analysis for the method.

By using the method, we can efficiently learn a weight which approximates a true weight with high probability. We also show experimental results on the sample size and the error rate under the assumption of uniform probability distribution over interpretations. The results indicate that the sample size is approximately Cn/ϵ on average where $C \approx 0.485$, where n is the number of propositions and ϵ is the desired accuracy.

1 INTRODUCTION

Preference-based reasoning (Satoh 1993) is a generalization of circumscription (McCarthy 1980; Lifschitz 1985). It provides not only a solution to a multiple extension problem in nonmonotonic reasoning such as the Yale shooting problem (Satoh 1990a), but also a representation of soft constraints in synthesis problems such as planning and design (Satoh 1990b).

It is clear that there are many preferences around in the real world. However, it is not clear how humans come to have such preferences. We must answer this question. Otherwise, when we make an autonomous robot, we must specify every preference explicitly and this is quite a hard task.

Learning of preferences is a possible answer. In this paper, as the first step, we give a learning method of a class preference over interpretations in propositional language and analyze the method theoretically in the PAC-learning framework. There has been some research related to learning preferences. Bain and Muggleton (Bain and Muggleton 1990; Bain 1991) propose a learning mechanism of stratified logic program and Cussens *et al.* (1993) propose a learning mechanism of preferences over rules. However, our study is different from their methods in the following points.

1. Their methods learn rules which basically relate to logic programming and default logic. On the other hand, our method learns an order over interpretations which relates to circumscription.

2. While both of their works only provide empirical evaluations, we give a theoretical evaluation on data complexity and computational complexity as well as experimental results.

3. Although their methods can handle a first-order case, facts given by the user in a reasoning phase are restricted to definite clauses. On the other hand, although our method is restricted to propositional language, facts in a reasoning phase can be any form of propositional formula.

Our considered class of preference is based on the distance in a weighted Euclidean space between the most preferable interpretation and the interpretations which are represented as lattice points whose elements take values of either 0 or 1. This class seems to be very restricted at a first glance, but we show that it covers various kinds of circumscription and captures many desirable properties of nonmonotonic reasoning. Especially, it satisfies *rational monotony* (Lehmann and Magidor 1992) which intuitively means that the previous conclusion stays in the new belief if the negation of the added information is not in the previous belief.

The learning framework in this paper uses relative preference information between two interpretations. From the information, we learn a weight of the weighted Euclidean space. We assume a probability distribution over interpretations and provide a PAC (probably approximately correct) learning analysis for data complexity and computational complexity for our method.

This learning framework comes from the idea of learning weight in a similarity function in case-based reasoning (Satoh and Okamoto 1994). Satoh and Okamoto (1994) use relative distance information which tells if the distance between case A and case B is less than the distance between case A and case C. In this paper, we regard an interpretation as a case and a preference measure as a similarity measure between the interpretation and the most preferable interpretation. Moreover, the relative preference information between two interpretations I and J actually corresponds with the relative distance information which tells if the distance between the most preferable interpretation and I is less than the distance between the most preferable interpretation and J.

Let n be the number of propositions and $\epsilon < 1, \delta < 1$ be arbitrary positive numbers. Then we can efficiently learn a weight such that the probability that the error rate of the difference between a true weight and a hypothetical weight is more than ϵ is at most δ. The sample size of relative preference information is polynomially bounded in n, ϵ^{-1}, and δ^{-1}, and and the running time is polynomially bounded in the size of relative preference information. We also show experimental results on the sample size and the error rate under the assumption of a uniform probability distribution over interpretations. The results indicate that the sample size is approximately Cn/ϵ on average where $C \simeq 0.485$.

2 INTERPRETATION ORDERING BY WEIGHTED EUCLIDEAN DISTANCE

Let L be a finite propositional language which consists of n propositional symbols. For simplicity, we use 0 for falsity and 1 for truth. Then, we can regard an interpretation as a point in $\{0, 1\}^n$.

Definition 1 *Let W be a weight vector in $[0, \infty)^n$ and Φ be a point in $\{0, 1\}^n$ We define the following order $\preceq$ over two interpretations I and J:*

$$I \preceq J \stackrel{def}{=} W \cdot d(I, \Phi) \leq W \cdot d(J, \Phi),$$

where $\cdot$ is an inner product of vectors and $d(I, \Phi)$ is defined as follows:

$$d(I, \Phi) \stackrel{def}{=} ((I_{(1)} - \Phi_{(1)})^2, (I_{(2)} - \Phi_{(2)})^2, \ldots, (I_{(n)} - \Phi_{(n)})^2),$$

where $I_{(i)}$ and $\Phi_{(i)}$ is the i-th component of I and Φ respectively. We also define

$$I \prec J \stackrel{def}{=} W \cdot d(I, \Phi) < W \cdot d(J, \Phi).$$

We define a smaller interpretation to be more preferable one. This means that Φ is the most preferable interpretation among all the interpretations and the preference of an interpretation decreases according to the distance between the interpretation and Φ in the weighted Euclidean space defined by W. Given information, we only consider the following minimal models with respect to the order.

Definition 2 *Let I be a model of a formula A in L. I is a* minimal *model of A w.r.t. $\prec$ if there is no model of A, J, such that $J \prec I$.*

This is a very simple definition, but it captures many desirable characteristics in nonmonotonic reasoning and belief revision as follows.

The above model-theoretic definition can be paraphrased by the following circumscription, $Circ(A; \prec)$.

$$A(\mathcal{P}) \wedge \neg \exists \phi (A(\phi) \wedge \phi \prec \mathcal{P}) \tag{1}$$

where $\mathcal{P}$ is the tuple of all propositional symbols in L and $A(\phi)$ is obtained by replacing every proposition of $\mathcal{P}$ in $A(\mathcal{P})$ by every corresponding propositional variable in ϕ.

According to the analysis of circumscription (Lifschitz 1985), models of the above formula are minimal models with respect to $\prec$.

Theorem 1 *An interpretation I is a model of (1) if and only if I is a minimal model of A w.r.t. $\prec$.*

In this ordering, we can express an order such that the number of true propositions is minimized and also we can express a prioritized version of it defined below. This ordering is called 'lexicographic' preference and studied by Benferhat *et al.* (1993).

Definition 3 *Let I and J be interpretations. Let $\mathcal{P}^1$, $\mathcal{P}^2$, ..., and $\mathcal{P}^k$ be a tuple of propositions which should be minimized in the first, the second, ..., and the k-th place respectively.*

We call the following order prioritized minimization order based on cardinality:

$I < J$ if there exists some $j \le k$ such that for $i = 1$ to $j - 1$, the number of true propositions of $\mathcal{P}^i$ in I is equal to that in J and the number of true propositions of $\mathcal{P}^j$ in I is less than J.

Example 1 *Let L contain four propositions, P, Q, R, S and $\mathcal{P}^1 = \langle P \rangle$, $\mathcal{P}^2 = \langle Q, R \rangle$ and $\mathcal{P}^3 = \langle S \rangle$. Then, the prioritized minimization order based on cardinality for this language is shown in Table 1.*

In this case, if we let a weight vector, $W = (6, 2, 2, 1)$ and the most preferable interpretation, $\Phi = (0, 0, 0, 0)$, then $\prec$ is identical with the above ordering. In general, it is possible to give a W which defines an identical order with a prioritized minimization order based on cardinality.

$\prec$ in general is a kind of *ranked* order where interpretations are divided into ranks to form pre-total order.

We define a consequence relation by using the above circumscription as follows.

$$A \mathrel{\vdash\!\!\!\sim} B \stackrel{def}{=} Circum(A, \prec) \models B,$$

where we call A an antecedent and B a consequent. In other words, $A \mathrel{\vdash\!\!\!\sim} B$ if and only if for every minimal model I of A, $I \models B$.[1]

---

[1] We show a method of deciding whether $A \mathrel{\vdash\!\!\!\sim} B$ or not by 0-1 integer programming with the above weight in the conclusion section.

Table 1. Example of prioritized min-imization order based on cardinality.

(P, Q, R, S)
$(1, 1, 1, 1)$
$(1, 1, 1, 0)$
$(1, 1, 0, 1)$ $(1, 0, 1, 1)$
$(1, 1, 0, 0)$ $(1, 0, 1, 0)$
$(1, 0, 0, 1)$
$(1, 0, 0, 0)$
$(0, 1, 1, 1)$
$(0, 1, 1, 0)$
$(0, 1, 0, 1)$ $(0, 0, 1, 1)$
$(0, 1, 0, 0)$ $(0, 0, 1, 0)$
$(0, 0, 0, 1)$
$(0, 0, 0, 0)$

Example 2 *Consider the order in Example 1. Let A be $(Q \vee R) \wedge (R \vee S) \wedge (S \vee Q)$ and B be $\neg P \wedge S$. From the above table, the minimal models of A are $(0, 1, 0, 1)$ and $(0, 0, 1, 1)$ and B is true in these models. Therefore, $A \mathrel{|\!\sim} B$ by this order.*

According to Lehmann and Magidor (1992), a consequence relation defined by a ranked order satisfies the following properties and is called a *rational* consequence relation.

Definition 4 *A consequence relation that satisfies all seven properties below is called a rational consequence relation.*

1. *If $A \equiv B$ is a truth-functional tautology and $A \mathrel{|\!\sim} C$, then $B \mathrel{|\!\sim} C$.*
2. *If $A \supset B$ is a truth-functional tautology and $C \mathrel{|\!\sim} A$, then $C \mathrel{|\!\sim} B$.*
3. *$A \mathrel{|\!\sim} A$.*
4. *If $A \mathrel{|\!\sim} B$ and $A \mathrel{|\!\sim} C$, then $A \mathrel{|\!\sim} B \wedge C$.*
5. *If $A \mathrel{|\!\sim} C$ and $B \mathrel{|\!\sim} C$, then $A \vee B \mathrel{|\!\sim} C$.*
6. *If $A \mathrel{|\!\sim} B$ and $A \mathrel{|\!\sim} C$, then $A \wedge B \mathrel{|\!\sim} C$.*
7. *If $A \mathrel{|\!\sim} C$ and $A \mathrel{|\!\not\sim} \neg B$, then $A \wedge B \mathrel{|\!\sim} C$.*

The last property is called *rational monotony* and proposed by Makinson as a desired property for nonmonotonic reasoning system (Lehmann and Magidor 1992) and corresponds with one of the fundamental conditions for minimal change of belief proposed by Gärdenfors (1988). An intuitive meaning of rational monotony is that the previous conclusion stays in the new belief if the negation of the added information is not in the previous belief.

Moreover, in (Satoh 1992; Lehmann and Magidor 1992; Goldszmidt *et al.* 1990), it is proven that a rational consequence relation has a qualitative probabilistic meaning.

Thus, the consequence relation defined by the above ordering also has a probabilistic meaning.

Therefore, the class of preference order in this paper covers many kinds of circumscription and has many desirable properties of nonmonotonic reasoning.

3 LEARNING BY RELATIVE PREFERENCE

Let $\mathbf{P}$ be any probability distribution over $\{0, 1\}^n$. The teacher selects a weight vector W^* from $[0, \infty)^n$ and the most preferable interpretation Φ from $\{0, 1\}^n$. The teacher selects N pairs of points in $\{0, 1\}^n \times \{0, 1\}^n$ according to $\mathbf{P}^2$. Let a set of selected pairs be $X = \{(I_1, J_1), \ldots, (I_N, J_N)\}$.

The teacher gives Φ and the following relative preference information to the learner: for every pair $(I, J) \in X$,

$$\text{if } W^* \cdot d(I, \Phi) \leq W^* \cdot d(J, \Phi) \text{ then } I \preceq J,$$
$$\text{if } W^* \cdot d(I, \Phi) > W^* \cdot d(J, \Phi) \text{ then } I \preceq J,$$

Let W be a vector in $[0, \infty)^n$. The difference between W and W^*, $diff(W, W^*)$ is defined as the following union:

$$\{(I, J) \mid W \cdot d(I, \Phi) \leq W \cdot d(J, \Phi) \text{ and } W^* \cdot d(I, \Phi) > W^* \cdot d(J, \Phi)\}$$
$$\cup \{(I, J) \mid W \cdot d(I, \Phi) > W \cdot d(J, \Phi) \text{ and } W^* \cdot d(I, \Phi) \leq W^* \cdot d(J, \Phi)\}.$$

This set contains pairs such that the order of each pair defined by a hypothesis weight W is different from the order defined by the real weight W^*. W is said to be an ϵ-approximation of W^* w.r.t. relative preference for $\mathbf{P}^2$ if the probability of $\mathbf{P}^2(diff(W, W^*))$ is at most ϵ.

The following theorem shows that this framework is polynomially PAC-learnable.

Theorem 2 *There exists a learning algorithm which satisfies the following conditions for any probability distribution over $\{0, 1\}^n$, $\mathbf{P}$, and an arbitrary constants ϵ and δ in the range $(0, 1)$:*

1. *The teacher selects a true weight vector W^* from $[0, \infty)^n$ and the most preferable interpretation Φ from $\{0, 1\}^n$*

2. *The teacher gives Φ and N pairs of interpretations according to $\mathbf{P}^2$ with relative preference information defined by W^* to the algorithm.*

3. *The algorithm outputs a hypothetical weight vector W and the following hold.*

   - *The probability that W is not an ϵ-approximation of W^* w.r.t. relative preference for $\mathbf{P}^2$ is less than δ. We call δ a confidence.*

   - *The size of required pairs N for learning is bounded by a polynomial in n, ϵ^{-1} and δ^{-1}, and its running time is bounded by a polynomial in the size of required pairs.*

Proof We consider the following function $f : \{0, 1\}^n \times \{0, 1\}^n \mapsto \{-1, 0, 1\}^n$

$$f^\Phi(I, J) = d(I, \Phi) - d(J, \Phi).$$

Then, the relative preference information is equivalent to the following conditions:

$$\text{for } I \preceq J, W^* \cdot f^\Phi(I, J) \leq 0, \quad \text{and for } J \prec I, \quad W^* \cdot f^\Phi(I, J) > 0. \tag{2}$$

Thus, the problem of finding W to satisfy the condition in the theorem reduces to a problem of learning half-spaces separated by a hyperplane in Blumer *et al.* (1989). According to Theorem 2.1 in Blumer *et al.* (1989), the VC dimension of this problem is n and the number of required pairs N for learning is at most

$$\max\left(\frac{4}{\epsilon} \log_2 \frac{2}{\delta}, \frac{8n}{\epsilon} \log_2 \frac{13}{\epsilon}\right). \tag{3}$$

We use Karmarkar's (1984) algorithm for the above algorithm by considering the following constraints:

$$\text{for } I \preceq J, W \cdot f^\Phi(I, J) \leq 0, \quad \text{and for } J \prec I, \quad W \cdot f^\Phi(I, J) \geq 1. \tag{4}$$

Clearly, there exists a solution for W in these constraints (2) if and only if there exists a solution for the constraints (4) and the time of finding W is bounded by a polynomial of N. If we find a consistent weight W with the above constraints (2), W is an ϵ-approximation of W^* w.r.t. $\mathbf{P}^2$ for relative preference. Therefore, W satisfies the condition in the original problem. □

Figure 1 shows an algorithm from relative preference over interpretations to learn preference order over interpretations.

4 EXPERIMENTAL RESULTS

We now show the following experimental results under the assumption that the probability distribution over interpretations is uniform and Φ is the origin.

1. We use a randomized function to produce n values ranging over $[0, 1]$ and regard it as a true weight vector W^* for n propositions.
2. We use a randomized function to produce n values of 0 or 1 and regard it as an interpretation. We repeat this $2 * N$ times to produce N pairs of interpretations.
3. For every pair, we produce the following relative preference information.

$$\begin{aligned} \text{If } W^* \cdot d(I, \Phi) \leq W^* \cdot d(J, \Phi) \quad \text{then } I \preceq J; \\ \text{If } W^* \cdot d(I, \Phi) > W^* \cdot d(J, \Phi) \quad \text{then } I \preceq J. \end{aligned} \tag{5}$$

4. From (5), the algorithm learns a weight vector by using linear programming.

291

Learn(ϵ, δ, n)

ϵ: accuracy

δ: confidence

n: the number of dimension

begin

Receive Φ and $max(\frac{4}{\epsilon}log_2\frac{2}{\delta}, \frac{8n}{\epsilon}log_2\frac{13}{\epsilon})$ pairs of points and their relative distance information from the teacher.

for every pair (I, J)

   if $I \preceq J$

      then add the following inequality to the constraint set:

$$W \cdot d(I, \Phi) \leq W \cdot d(J, \Phi)$$

   if $J \prec I$

      then add the following inequality to the constraint set:

$$W \cdot d(J, \Phi) + 1 \leq W \cdot d(I, \Phi)$$

Get consistent values for the above constraint set by linear programming and output W.

end

Figure 1. Learning algorithm.

5. For the learned weight, we produce 10 000 test pairs randomly and calculate an error rate such that the order by learned weight is not identical to that by the true weight.

6. We repeat 100 times above and take the average of error rates.

Figure 2 shows the relationship between the number of propositions and the error rate. The number of propositions is almost proportional to the error rate.

Figure 3 shows the relationship between the size of training pairs and the inverse of the error rate. This graph is almost linear, so the size of training pairs is almost inversely proportional to the error rate.

Figure 4 indicates that the required total size of training pairs is almost $C * n/\epsilon$ on average in order to obtain the average error rate, ϵ, where C is a constant. From the graph, $C \approx 0.485$. This size for training pairs is smaller than the size in our PAC-learning analysis. It is probably because in PAC-learning analysis, we consider the worst case,

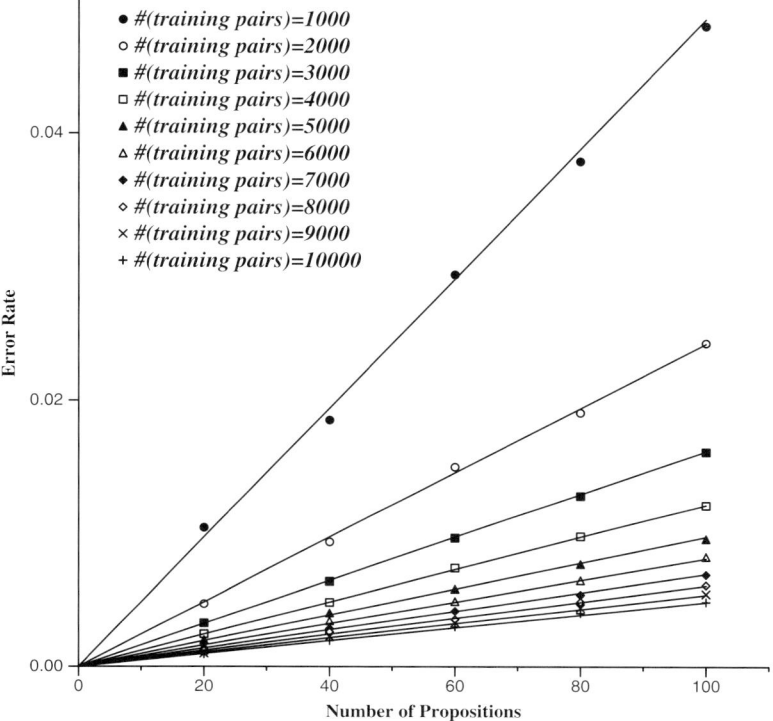

Figure 2. Relationship between n and ϵ.

while in the experiment, we assume that the probability distribution is uniform where the behavior may not be so pathological.

5 CONCLUSION

5.1 Reasoning with a learned weight

Once, we get a preference, we can perform reasoning not only by a logical inference defined by circumscription of the formula (1) but also by using 0-1 integer programming techniques to answer if a formula is true in all minimal models as follows.

Definition 5 *Let A be a formula and W be a learned weight and I be a vector of n propositional variables and Φ be an interpretation. Note that A can be represented by inequalities of I. Let rank(A) be the following value:*

1. *If A is consistent, $rank(A) =$ the value of minimizing $W \cdot d(I, \Phi)$ under a constraint set of A where $I \in \{0, 1\}^n$.*

2. *Otherwise, $rank(A) = \infty$.*

293

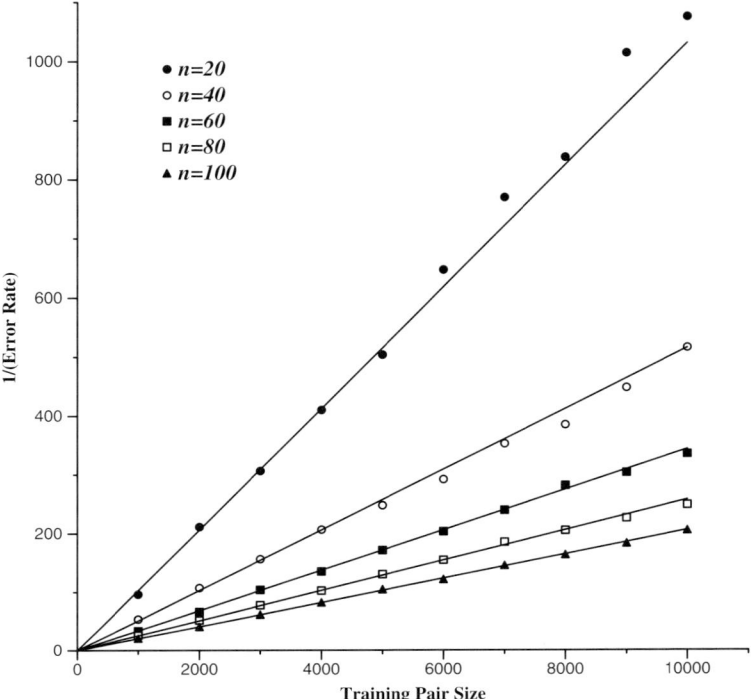

Figure 3. Relationship between number of training pairs and ϵ^{-1}.

We can calculate the above value by 0-1 integer programming. Note that every interpretation I giving $rank(A)$ is a minimal model.

Example 3   *Consider the order in Example 1. Suppose A is $(Q \vee R) \wedge (R \vee S) \wedge (S \vee Q)$. Then A can be translated into the following inequalities:*

$$q + r \geq 1, \quad r + s \geq 1, \quad q \geq 1.$$

We know that $W = (6, 2, 2, 1)$ and $\Phi = (0, 0, 0, 0)$ for this ordering. Then, $rank(A) = min(W \cdot d(I, \Phi)) = min(6p + 2q + 2r + s)$ under the above inequalities, which in this case is 3 ($(p, q, r, s) = (0, 1, 0, 1)$ or $(0, 0, 1, 1)$). These interpretations correspond with minimal models of A.

Theorem 3   *Let A be a consistent formula. $A \mathrel{|\!\sim} B$ if and only if $rank(A) < rank(A \wedge \neg B)$.*

Proof   Note that $rank(A) < rank(A \wedge \neg B)$ is always true. Suppose $A \mathrel{|\!\sim} B$. Suppose that $rank(A) = rank(A \wedge \neg B)$. Then, minimal models of A are also minimal models of $A \wedge \neg B$. Therefore, $A \mathrel{|\!\sim} \neg B$, that is, $A \mathrel{|\!\not\sim} B$ since A is consistent. This contradicts $A \mathrel{|\!\sim} B$. Therefore, $rank(A) < rank(A \wedge \neg B)$.

294

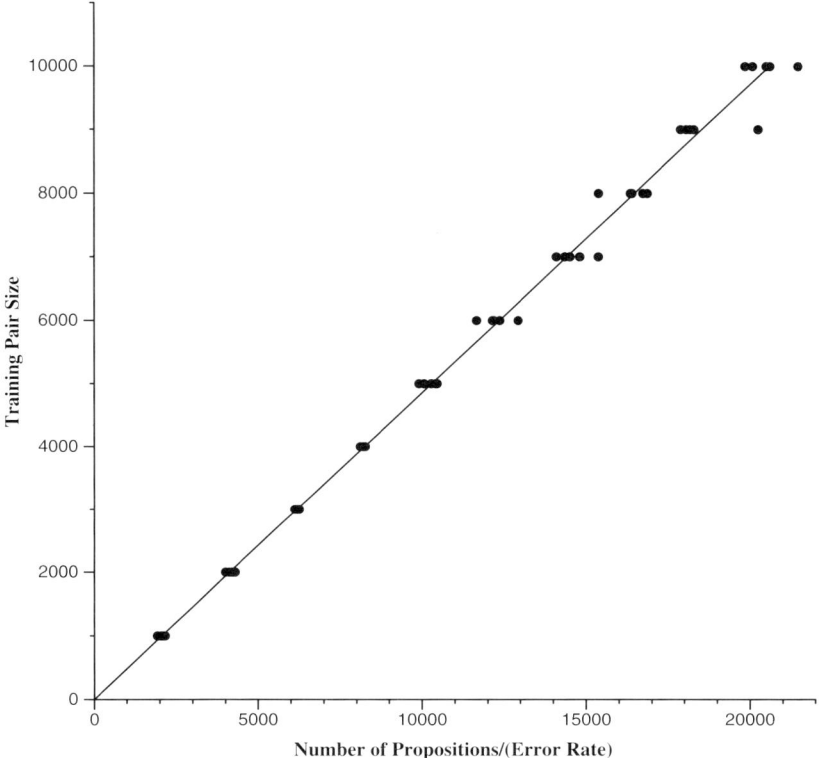

Figure 4. Relationship between n/ϵ and number of training pairs.

Suppose $rank(A) < rank(A \wedge \neg B)$ and $A \not\hspace{-0.3em}\sim B$. Then, there is a minimal model of A such that $A \models \neg B$. But, this contradicts $rank(A) < rank(A \wedge \neg B)$. Therefore, $A \hspace{0.1em}\mid\hspace{-0.6em}\sim B$.

$\square$

Example 4 *Suppose that A is $(Q \vee R) \wedge (R \vee S) \wedge (S \vee Q)$ and B is $\neg P \wedge S$. Then, $A \wedge \neg B$ can be represented as the following inequalities:*

$$q + r \geq 1, \quad r + s \geq 1 \quad s + q \geq 1 \quad p + (1 - s) \geq 1.$$

$rank(A \wedge \neg B) = min(6p + 2p + 2q + s)$ *under the above inequalities which in this case is* $4\,((p, q, r, s) = (0, 1, 1, 0))$. *Thus, $rank(A) < rank(A \wedge \neg B)$ and $A \hspace{0.1em}\mid\hspace{-0.6em}\sim B$.*

Therefore, a question if $A \hspace{0.1em}\mid\hspace{-0.6em}\sim B$ is reduced to calculate the $rank(A)$ and $rank(A \wedge \neg B)$. Of course, the optimization problem of 0-1 integer programming is NP-hard in general, so we need to use heuristics or to restrict a class of formulas to reduce complexity.

One heuristic is to use linear programming to check if there is a solution minimizing $W \cdot d(I, \Phi)$ under A. If we happen to find a 0-1 solution by linear programming, then we minimize $W \cdot d(I, \Phi)$ under $A \wedge \neg B$ by linear programming. If $rank(A) < rank(A \wedge \neg B)$, we can conclude $A \hspace{0.1em}\mid\hspace{-0.6em}\sim B$ even if a solution of the second minimization is a not 0-1 solution. If this succeeds, the computational cost is polynomial in n.

295

5.2 Extension

Our method can be easily changed to the problem of finding a prioritization among rules by introducing *abnormal propositions* for these rules. For example, suppose that there is a rule R_1 and R_2 and we would like to find a prioritization between R_1 and R_2. In order to do so, we represent rules as $\neg Ab_1 \supset R_1$ and $\neg Ab_2 \supset R_2$. Then, we try to find a preference by minimizing these abnormal predicates.

Another extension is a method of deciding Φ. If we can modify the learning framework to the one such that the learner can ask the order over specific interpretations, we can identify the most preferable interpretation Φ. Let O be the origin and I_i be an interpretation such that the value for every proposition except the i-th proposition is 0 and the value for the i-th proposition is 1. Then,

1. If $O \prec I_i$ then the value for the i-th proposition in Φ is 0.
2. If $I_i \prec O$ then the value for the i-th proposition in Φ is 1.
3. If $I_i \prec O$ and $O \preceq I_i$, then the value for the i-th proposition in Φ can be 0 or 1 and the value for the i-th component of W is 0.

In this case, we can decide Φ by at most $2 * n$ size of relative preference information for O and I_i.

5.3 Future work

We pursue the following as future work.

1. We would like to apply our method to a real application domain such as finding proper prioritizations of multiple evaluation functions in operation research.
2. We would like to extend a learnable class of preference order. A possible extension is learning the arbitrary pre-total order over interpretation.
3. We would like to enhance this method to the first-order case.
4. We would like to analyze our method theoretically when the distribution is fixed to explain the experimental results in this paper.

REFERENCES

Bain, M. and Muggleton, S. H. (1990) Non-monotonic Learning, *Machine Intelligence 12*, Oxford University Press.

Bain, M. (1991) Experiments in Non-monotonic Learning, *Proc. of the 8th Workshop on Machine Learning*, pp. 380–384.

Benferhat, S., Cayrol, C., Dubois, D., Lang, J., and Prade, H. (1993) Inconsistency Management and Prioritized Syntax-based Entailment, *Proc. of IJCAI-93*, pp. 640–645.

Blumer, A., Ehrenfeucht, A., Haussler, D., and Warmuth, M. K. (1989) Learnability and the Vapnik-Chervonenkis Dimension, *JACM*, **36**, pp. 929–965.

Cussens, J., Hunter, A., and Srinivasan, A. (1993) Generating Explicit Orderings for Non-monotonic Logics, *Proc. of AAAI-93*, pp. 420–425.

Gärdenfors, P. (1988) *Knowledge in Flux: Modeling the Dynamics of Epistemic States*, MIT Press.

Goldszmidt, M., Morris, P., and Pearl, J. (1990) A Maximum Entropy Approach to Nonmonotonic Reasoning, *Proc. of AAAI-90*, pp. 646–652.

Karmarkar, N. (1984) A New Polynomial-time Algorithm for Linear Programming, *Combinatorica*, **4**, pp. 373–395.

Lehmann, D. and Magidor, M. (1992) What Does a Conditional Knowledge Base Entail?, *Artificial Intelligence*, **55**, pp. 1–60.

Lifschitz, V. (1985) Computing Circumscription, *Proc. of IJCAI-85*, pp. 121–127.

McCarthy, J. (1980) Circumscription – A Form of Non-monotonic Reasoning, *Artificial Intelligence*, **13**, pp. 27–39.

Satoh, K. (1990a) Minimal Change – A Criterion for Choosing between Competing Models, B. Brazdil and K. Konolige (eds.), *Machine Learning, Meta-Reasoning and Logics*, pp. 257–276, Kluwer Academic Publishers.

Satoh, K. (1990b) Formalizing Soft Constraints by Interpretation Ordering, *Transactions of Information Processing Society of Japan*, **31**, pp. 772–782, (in Japanese), A shortened English version can be found in *Proc. of ECAI'90*, pp. 585–590.

Satoh, K. (1992) A Probabilistic Interpretation for Lazy Nonmonotonic Reasoning, *Journal of Information Processing*, **15**, pp. 29–39, A preliminary version can be found in *Proc. of AAAI'90*, pp. 659–664.

Satoh, K. (1993) A Logical Formalization of Preference-based Reasoning by Interpretation Ordering, University of Tokyo, Ph.D. Thesis.

Satoh, K. and Okamoto, S. (1994) Toward PAC-Learning of Weights from Qualitative Distance Information, *Proc. of 1994 AAAI Case-Based Reasoning Workshop*, pp. 128–132.

297

16

Tables, graphs and logic for induction

Kenichi Yoshida and Hiroshi Motoda

Advanced Research Laboratory,

Hitachi Ltd.,

Hatoyama,

Saitama, 350-03,

Japan

e-mail: yoshida@harl.hitachi.co.jp and motoda@harl.hitachi.co.jp

Abstract

Inductive learning, which tries to find rules from data, has been an important area of investigation. One major research theme of this area is the data representation language that the learning methods can use. Conventional learning methods use attribute-value tables as the data representation language, whereas inductive logic programming (ILP) uses first-order logic. We propose colored directed graphs as a data representation language for inductive learning methods. *Graph-based induction* (GBI) uses this data representation language. The expressiveness of graphs is in between the attribute-value table and the first-order logic. Thus its learning potential is weaker than that of ILP, but stronger than that of conventional attribute-value learning methods. The real advantage of GBI appears in the domain where the dependency between data bears the essential information. Behavior analysis of computer users is a typical example of such a domain. In this domain, the complex structure of dependency between the user tasks prevents us from using conventional attribute-value learning methods, and ILP cannot meet the requirement for efficiency. In this paper, we explain the GBI method with experimental results. We also report a user-adaptive interface system, which uses GBI to realize its adaptive function, as a practical application of this new method.

1 INTRODUCTION

Inductive learning, which tries to find rules from data, has been an important area of investigation. One major research theme of this area is the data representation language that the learning methods can use. Conventional learning methods use attribute-value tables as the data representation language, whereas inductive logic programming (ILP) uses first-order logic. We propose a colored directed graph as a data representation language for inductive learning methods.[1] *Graph-based induction* (GBI) uses this data representation language. The expressiveness of graph is in between attribute-value tables and first-order logic. Thus its learning potential is weaker than that of ILP, but stronger than that of the conventional attribute-value learning methods.

The real advantage of GBI appears in the domain where the dependency between data bears the essential information. The behavior analysis of computer users is a typical example of such a domain. The analysis of user behavior is one important function of the user-adaptive interface because, by analyzing the user behavior, it becomes possible to understand the user intention and release the user from tedious tasks which are often required to use a fast but low-level interface. Thus acquisition of the user behavior model is crucial to realizing a user-adaptive interface system. Most studies meant to realize a user-adaptive interface system only analyze superficial user behavior, from which to automate the repetitions. Their user models tend to be simple and do not reproduce the behavior well enough. GBI enables the analysis of computational processes activated by user commands, and builds the user behavior model. A user-adaptive interface system, *ClipBoard*, was developed to show the adequacy of the proposed method. It analyzes the I/O relationship between applications in the past task history, generates the user behavior model, and selects the next application based on the generated user behavior model.

This modeling task viewed as an inductive learning problem requires a huge attribute-value table and the conventional attribute-value learning methods are not directly applicable. The proposed method dynamically determines a set of the attributes from which to choose the best and avoids this computational problem. ILP cannot meet the requirement for the efficiency to build a practical system.

This paper is organized as follows. Section 2 briefly reviews the related work and contrasts our approach with other methods. Section 3 overviews *ClipBoard* to clarify the characteristics of the problem domain where the advantage of GBI appears. Section 4 describes the GBI method with quantitative evaluation of this method. Section 5 discuss the relation between GBI, conventional attribute-value learning system and ILP. Section 6 concludes the paper by summarizing what has been achieved by GBI.

2 RELATED WORK

The intelligent user interface is an important area of investigation. EAGER (Cypher, 1991) is a HyperText system that observes user operations, finds repetitions, and offers to automate repetitive operations. It has a special mechanism to generalize loop counts and makes macro operations that perform repeated operations. The knowledge which automates the repetitive operations is automatically acquired. There is some work that used machine learning techniques. Dent *et al.* (1992) and Hermens and Schlimmer (1993) used

---

[1]Editor's footnote: An implementation of a similar proposal was described by H. G. Barrow, A. P. Ambler and R. M. Burstall (1972), 'Some techniques for recognising structures in pictures' in *Frontiers of Pattern Recognition* (ed. S. Watanabe) pp. 1–29, New York, Academic Press.

a decision tree learning method, and Maes and Kozieroki (1993) examined a K-nearest neighbor method. These efforts resulted in various applications: e.g. a meeting scheduling agent, an electronic mail agent, and a form filling system.

These studies analyze only user operation sequences, and extract repetitions. The applications were carefully selected and no other source of knowledge was required. However, this success can't be generalized to other types of interface systems such as command prediction. We need to use other sources of knowledge as well as sequence information. The most typical approach would be a knowledge-based approach. Both APU (Bhansali and Harandi, 1993) which is a UNIX shell-scripts programming system, and Gold (Myers *et al.*, 1994) which is a business charts editor, take this approach. The knowledge must be carefully hand-coded in these systems.

The initial motivation of this study is to build a user-adaptive interface by using, in addition to the sequence information, other sources of knowledge which can be automatically collected during user operation, i.e., the I/O relationship between applications. Since this information has a rather complicated structure, most of the conventional attribute-value learning methods are not adequate to be applied.

ILP (Shapiro, 1983; Quinlan, 1990; Pazzani and Kibler, 1992; Muggleton and Feng, 1992) accepts descriptions of structured entities and generates rules (i.e., for classification) expressed in first-order logic. The enhanced expressiveness of this framework seems to be a promising approach to analyze structured information like I/O relationships. To control the search over a larger search space in an efficient way, MIS (Shapiro, 1983) uses user help, FOIL (Quinlan, 1990) uses information gain index, FOCL (Pazzani and Kibler, 1992) uses domain knowledge together with information gain index, and GOLEM (Muggleton and Feng, 1992) uses relative least general generalization. However, a preliminary experiment still reveals the efficiency problem of ILP (See Section 5). GBI which we used to make *ClipBoard* provides the way to use the data dependency information to control the search, and enables real-time generation of the user behavior model.

3 USER BEHAVIOR MODELLING AS A LEARNING PROBLEM

In this section, we briefly overview *ClipBoard* to clarify the characteristics of the problem domain where the advantage of GBI appears.

ClipBoard is a user-adaptive interface system. It has three main components: a mouse-based application controller, a subgraph extraction program, and an I/O recorder. The I/O recorder is part of the operating system and records all the I/O operations of each application program. Suppose a user is making a document using a *latex* document formatter according to the following process:

1. Preview the contents of a paper through the previewer *xtex*
2. Modify its contents by an *emacs* editor.
3. Use the *latex* document formatter to lay out the contents.

4. Confirm the contents by another previewer *xdvi*.

5. Print out the result by *dvi2ps*.

Figure 1 shows the information recorded by the I/O recorder in a simplified form.

We use a colored directed graph as the representation language of this information. In Figure 1, the *latex* node takes *paper.tex* as input. Here, the command name (i.e., *latex*) is the color (i.e., label) of the node. If the program inputs multiple files, multiple edges, corresponding to each input, connect the program node to other nodes: e.g., *emacs* (creator of input file *paper.tex*). Each edge has the direction which corresponds to the I/O direction. It also has an edge number which corresponds to the file suffix. For example, the edge which connects *latex* to *emacs* has the number for *tex*. Here, *tex* is the suffix of file *paper.tex* which relates *emacs* and *latex*.

We also record the command sequence, which is the main source of the information that the conventional attribute-value learning methods can use. To do this, one edge has a role of recording the command sequence. This can be used to learn the user preference of the independent application sequence such as 'first check mail, then read news' when the sequence information does not represent dependency.

Note that the actual information recorded by the I/O recorder is more complicated than shown in Figure 1. For example, in the experiments in Section 4.2, it involves 9735 processes and 127 445 I/O operations (13 I/O operations per process). Not only the processes that the user invokes but also the processes that system programs invoke, e.g., telnet daemon, line printer spooler daemon, and etc., are recorded in this information.

The information acquired by the I/O recorder is analyzed by the subgraph extraction program. Using the GBI method, this program extracts typical subgraphs from the input graph so that the extracted subgraphs represent typically used application patterns. The mouse-based application controller uses these extracted patterns to guide the selection of the next applications.

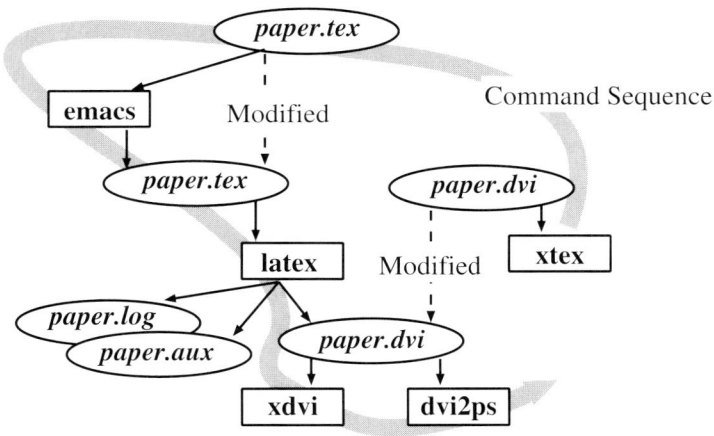

Figure 1. I/O relationship between applications.

Figure 2 displays the screen images of *ClipBoard*. It has four important areas. The left area is a space for the icons of currently used applications. In Figure 2, clock and terminal emulator are used, and the icons for these applications are displayed on the left. The right area is a space for the icons of frequently used applications. By clicking the icons shown in the right area, the user can invoke these applications. The screen also shows a list of frequently used directories on the top. By clicking the directory on the top area, the files located on the selected directory will be displayed on the center area.

When *ClipBoard* starts without any information about applications, the screen only lists file names. At this stage, after selecting (i.e., clicking the left mouse button) the file to be processed, the dialogue box appears so that the user can specify the application. If the user specifies *emacs*, *ClipBoard* treats *emacs* as the default for the file with suffix *tex*. *ClipBoard* tries to learn the appropriate application for each file suffix, and suggests these applications in the form of icon (see Figure 2). The user can override *ClipBoard's* suggestion by means of the dialogue box which can be invoked by the right mouse button.

ClipBoard analyzes the I/O relationship between applications and extracts typical relationships. Which application to suggest changes over time according to changes in extracted relationships. If the result of induction over the past task history suggests another appropriate application, *ClipBoard* changes the icon on the screen for a new application as the default. In a typical document processing task with *latex*, *ClipBoard* suggests *emacs* and *latex* interchangeably as the applications for the file *paper.tex*.

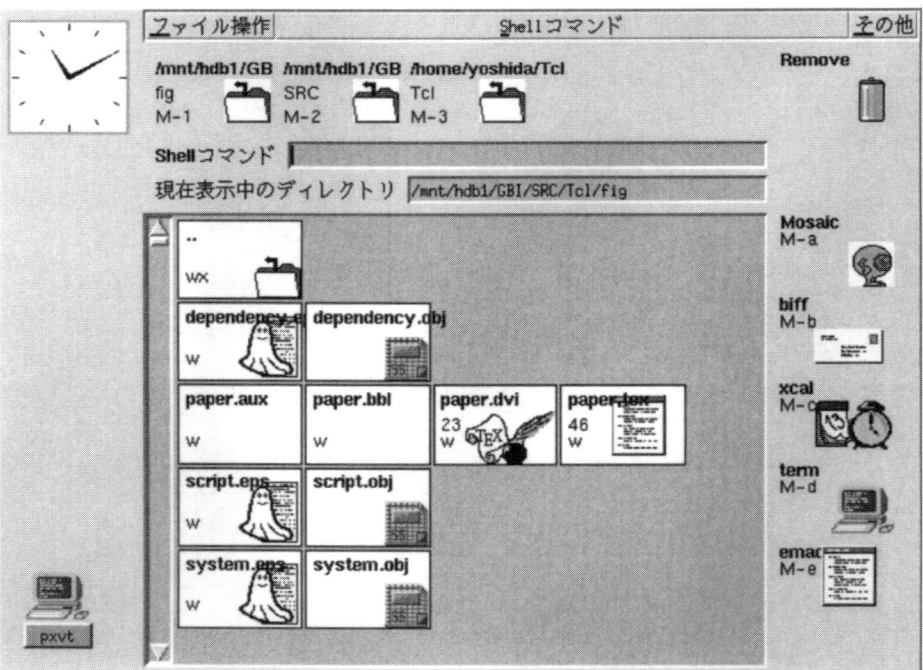

Figure 2. Screen image of *ClipBoard*.

302

Note that the selection accuracy is important if we want to get the maximum benefit from this automatic selection function. If we only analyze superficial user behavior, e.g., command sequence alone, the resulting user models do not reproduce the bevaivior well enough (see the experimental results in section 4.2). As the experimental results in Section 4.2 clearly show, the data dependency between the tasks is crucial in this domain. Thus the GBI method seems to be a promising learning method for user behavior modeling.

4 GRAPH-BASED INDUCTION

In this section, we describe the algorithm of GBI with experimental results using user behavior modeling as the example.

4.1 Algorithm

Figure 3 shows the same information shown in Figure 1 with respect to the file with suffix *dvi*. At first (see Figures 3(A)), *ClipBoard* has no previous task information. The graph contains only two nodes (one for the application and the other for the input file). Figure 3(B) shows the graph for the confirmation step, and Figure 3(C) shows that for the print out step. Thus, for example, Figure 3(C) shows: (1) the application that processes *paper.dvi* is *dvi2ps*; (2) *paper.dvi* is generated by *latex* from *paper.tex*; (3) *paper.tex* is generated by *emacs*; and (4) the previous application sequence is *xdvi, latex, emacs, xtex.*

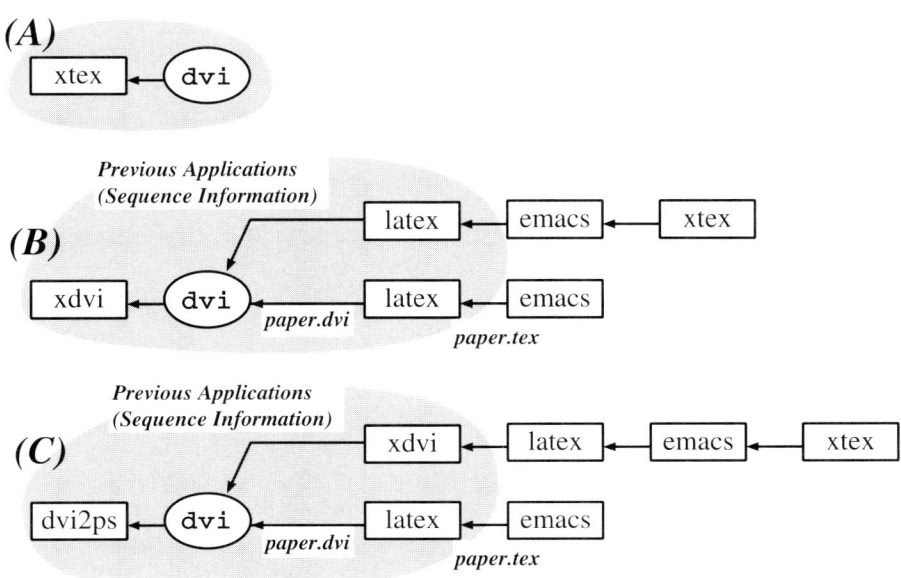

Figure 3. Subgraph of task history.

303

```
(C) If   dvi file was made from latex,
    and  the previous command was xdvi,
    Then Next Application is dvi2ps.
(B) If   dvi file was made from latex,
    and  the previous command was latex,
    Then Next Application is xdvi.
(A) If   None of the above,
    Then Next Application is xtex.
```

Figure 4. Interpretation as selection rules.

The subgraph extraction program extracts the hatched portion of the graph in Figure 3. If these three are the only graphs available, the hatched portions are enough to select the application. Figure 4 provides an interpretation of the extracted subgraphs. The rules in Figure 4 select applications for the *dvi* file based on the past task history. For example, if a user has just called up *latex* to produce *paper.dvi*, rule (B) in Figure 4 suggests that *xdvi* may be the next application.

The subgraph extraction program is an implementation of the GBI learning method, and extracts subgraphs which maximize the accuracy of the selection rules. Figure 5 displays the GBI process. Suppose that *ClipBoard* tries to make selection rules for the application that processes the *dvi* file. *ClipBoard* first selects the graphs which involve the *dvi* node as the input. It then omits the common *dvi* nodes from the selected graphs. Figure 5(a) displays input graphs, i.e., graph-format case data for the learning problem, converted from the graphs shown in Figure 3.

The GBI basic algorithm is depicted in Figure 5(b). This algorithm proceeds as follows:

1. First it generates a table of attributes and value pairs from the input graph. The generated table has the standard data structure used in conventional attribute-value learning methods. The information about root nodes, i.e., class *xtex, xdvi* and *dvi2ps*, and the nodes which are directly connected to the root node, i.e., attributes A_1 and A_2, are converted into this table. See the top table in Figure 5(b).

2. Then it selects the test condition. The method to select the test condition is that of the conventional attribute-value learning methods. The current implementation adapts this method from the one used in the CART decision tree learning program (Breiman *et al.*, 1984). In Figure 5(b), the attribute A_2 is selected as the test condition, and *xtex* is distinguished from the rest.

3. To generate further test conditions, new attributes are generated from the nodes which are connected to the test node. The table is modified by these new attributes. Note the difference in the hatched tables in Figure 5(b). A new attribute A_3, i.e., the *emacs* node, which is connected to the test node *latex*, has been added to the table.

4. After the attribute modification process above, it returns to Step 2 to select further test conditions.

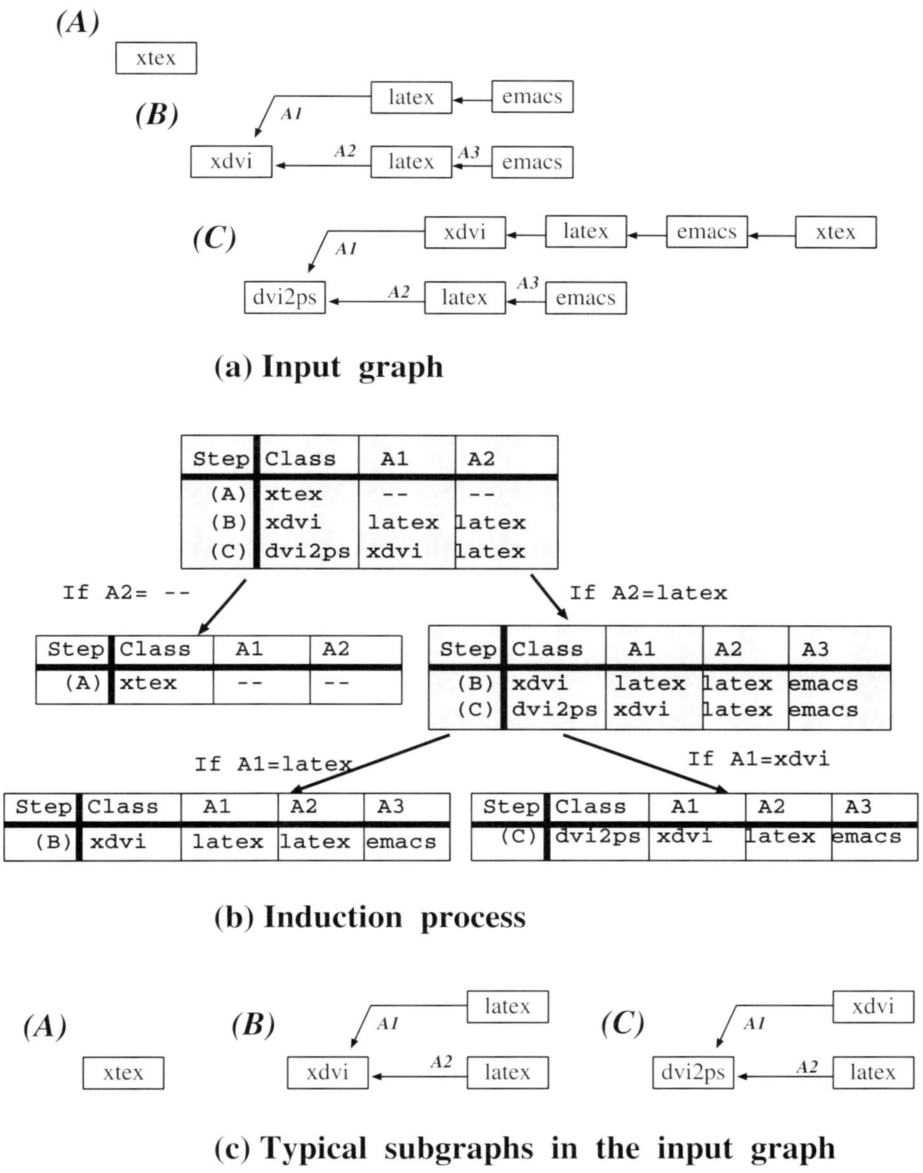

(A)

xtex

(B)

A1 — latex ← emacs

xdvi ← A2 — latex A3 ← emacs

(C)

A1 — xdvi ← latex ← emacs ← xtex

dvi2ps ← A2 — latex A3 ← emacs

(a) Input graph

Step	Class	A1	A2
(A)	xtex	--	--
(B)	xdvi	latex	latex
(C)	dvi2ps	xdvi	latex

If A2= --

Step	Class	A1	A2
(A)	xtex	--	--

If A2=latex

Step	Class	A1	A2	A3
(B)	xdvi	latex	latex	emacs
(C)	dvi2ps	xdvi	latex	emacs

If A1=latex

Step	Class	A1	A2	A3
(B)	xdvi	latex	latex	emacs

If A1=xdvi

Step	Class	A1	A2	A3
(C)	dvi2ps	xdvi	latex	emacs

(b) Induction process

(A)

xtex

(B)

A1 — latex

xdvi ← A2 — latex

(C)

A1 — xdvi

dvi2ps ← A2 — latex

(c) Typical subgraphs in the input graph

Figure 5. Example of a graph-based induction process.

Figure 5(c) provides the algorithm output. It comes in a graph format. Each graph in Figure 5(c) consists of the test conditions selected by the above process and the selected application. For example, the graph (C) in Figure 5(c) has two nodes: *xdvi* and *latex*. These are the test conditions to reach the bottom right table in Figure 5(b). If we restore

305

the omitted *dvi* nodes to the output, we get the hatched portion of the graph shown in Figure 3.

Although the simple case shown in Figure 5 does not require the added condition A_3 as a new test condition, the real advantage of this method appears in more complicated cases. For example, the application selection after *bibtex* (a bibliography processor of *latex*) is a typical example of such a case in which a naive user tends to be confused (see Figure 6), and requires this sort of extra information. Although a typical document processing task with *latex* interchangeably uses the *emacs* editor and *latex*, the use of *bibtex* sometimes requires a continuous use of *latex*. To distinguish the procedure with *bibtex* from the procedure without *bibtex*, the case shown in Figure 6 needs the information added in Step 3.

As previously mentioned and illustrated in Figure 5(b), the GBI algorithm essentially follows a conventional attribute-value learning model. In the experiments reported in Section 4.2, we used a 10-fold cross-validation technique to suppress overfitting. The correspondence between GBI and the conventional attribute-value learning model enables the use of various techniques (e.g., gini index, cross-validation, etc.) in the GBI program.

However, the attributes to be considered are dynamically modified in the process (see the difference between the hatched tables in Figures 5 and 6). As in conventional attribute-value learning methods, GBI statistically analyzes multiple cases to generate selection rules which can handle complicated cases. Note that the table of attribute and value pairs, i.e., the standard data structure for a conventional attribute-value learning method, alone cannot represent the graph structure as shown in Figures 3 and 6.

Although the GBI process tries to achieve maximum prediction accuracy, it tends to extract typically used application patterns as classification rules. A pattern which appears often in some particular class data tends to be selected as a new test condition. Thus the process of building a classification tree is equivalent to finding frequently appearing patterns.

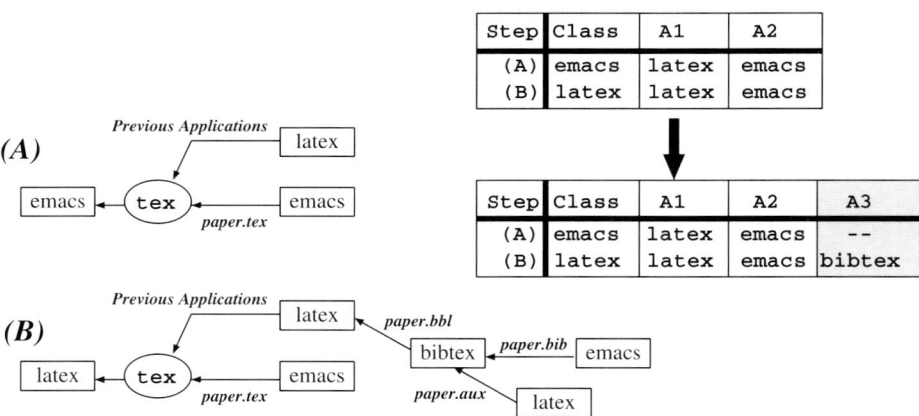

Figure 6. Another example of a graph-based induction process.

306

4.2 Experimental results

To evaluate our approach, we designed a test problem, i.e., UNIX shell command prediction, and compared our method with the other methods. Table 1 summarizes the results. In this experiment, we analyzed a conventional UNIX shell history and tried to select the next shell command from the past shell history. The *ClipBoard* I/O recorder was used to record the shell history. This history was taken from the daily usage of a single user over three months and includes about 2000 commands. Two-thirds of them were used as a training dataset and the rest was used as a test dataset.

Although the command prediction problem and application selection problem of *ClipBoard* is different, the most important factor for both problems is the accuracy of the user model learned from past task history. This batch-based test aims at comparing the modeling abilities of various methods. We spent three months in acquiring enough history data. Since we need a special operating system, i.e., *ClipBoard's* I/O recorder, and this operating system was available for only one machine when we performed this experiment, we had to rely on a single user for three months.

Both the I/O relationship between the commands and the command sequence were used by GBI. However, the former information was removed from the input data for a conventional method since these methods cannot deal with information having a graph structure.

A simple prediction may be given by assuming the most frequently used command to be the next command. The *Default* row in Table 1 gives this value. Row LD shows the result of the linear discrimination method (James, 1984). This method usually gave the same answer as the default, so it does not improve the selection accuracy. Row 1-NN shows the result of the 1-nearest-neighbor method (James, 1984). Though the accuracy on the training set by this method was 80–90%, overfitting decreased the accuracy on the test set. The best result by the conventional method was achieved by the decision-tree learning method CART (Breiman *et al.*, 1984). Nevertheless, GBI out-performed CART. The use of I/O information contributes to this difference between the selection accuracies.

Note that the ordinary UNIX shell command history involves a lot of nonessential commands, such as *ls* and *df*, which the mouse-based interface system can naturally ignore. This makes UNIX shell command prediction more difficult than the application selection of *ClipBoard*. If we ignore the effects of these nonessential commands on the accuracy from the results shown in Table 1, we get the results shown in Table 2.

Table 1. Selection accuracy of various methods.

Method	Accuracy (%)
Default	22.6
LD	22.6
1-NN	20.8
CART	34.6
GBI	57.8

Table 2. GBI's prediction accuracy for each command.

Command	Accuracy (%)	Number of suggestions
emacs	69	61
make	85	40
latex	92	25
new	86	21 (Personal backup command)
xdvi	100	13

This shows the prediction accuracies by GBI for the specific commands. For example, GBI suggests *latex* 25 times in the history. 23 suggestions (92%) were appropriate, and 2 suggestions were inappropriate. All the commands listed in Table 2 are important for user tasks, and the prediction accuracies for these commands (69%~100%) are higher than the average accuracy (57.8%). While evaluation of *ClipBoard*'s actual selection accuracy remains a research issue, most of the selected applications by *ClipBoard* were quite adequate during its functional testing. The results shown in Table 2 support this preliminary observation.

5 DISCUSSION

If the user is always logical and consistent, analytical methods, such as explanation-based learning (Mitchell *et al.*, 1986; DeJong and Mooney, 1986), are promising approaches to making the user behavior model. Unfortunately the user is sometimes illogical and inconsistent, and user capriciousness makes conventional analytical methods difficult to apply to the interface problem.

Statistical methods, such as linear discrimination and k-nearest-neighbor (James, 1984), and conventional attribute-value learning methods, such as (Quinlan, 1986), are more promising from this view point. The errors, i.e., mistyping and wrong application selection, are naturally ignored as noises in this approach. However, these methods lack a function to analyze structural data. As previously mentioned, the I/O relationship between the applications has a complex structure, and is informative to capture the user's behavior characteristics. If we have to use less informative information such as sequence information, we get lower performance as shown in Table 1.

If we can assume the maximum number of input files per application and the maximum depth of I/O relationship, it is possible to design a table, i.e., standard data structure used by the conventional attribute-value methods, which can record all possible I/O information. For example, if the maximum number of input files per application is 50 and the maximum depth of I/O relationship is 5, a table with 300 000 000 ($\simeq 50^5$) attributes can record all information. However, if the analysis requires 1000 cases to get good accuracy, the table size becomes 1 200 000 000 000 bytes (1000 cases $*$ 300 000 000 attributes $*$ 4 bytes per attribute).

Note that a typical (not maximum) single run of the *latex* command receives 50 input files. The depth of I/O relationship shown in Figure 1 is 5. The number of case data

Algorithm *Induction*
    Variable G_{in} : Case Data
               T : Classification Tree
    Begin
        $T \leftarrow \emptyset$
        Repeat
            Classify All Case Data G_{in} Using T
            Make Attribute Table by *Proc. 1, 2, 3*
            Select New Test Condition, and Add it to T
    End

Proc. 1 *Conventional Method:*   Always Use **Same** Attribute Set.
Proc. 2 *GBI Method:*   Select New Attributes from **Graph.**
Proc. 3 *ILP Method:*   Select New Attributes from **First-Order Logic.**

Figure 7. Comparison of induction algorithms.

we used in the experiments in Section 4.2 is 2000. Thus the above estimation is still conservative, and this huge table size prevents us from using this approach.

ILP accepts descriptions of structured entities and generates rules expressed in first-order logic. The enhanced expressiveness of this framework seems to be a promising approach to analyze structured information like I/O relationships. To seek the possibility of this approach, we tried to use FOCL, i.e., one of the most efficient ILP systems (Pazzani and Kibler, 1992), to analyze the data used in Section 4.2. However, FOCL took more than 4 hours to find the first rule.[2] Since 4 hours is too long to make a practical system and this is not yet to get final rule set, we had to give up this approach.

The GBI uses graphs as its data representation language. Its expressiveness of representation is in between the attribute-value tables and first-order logic (see Figure 7). Thus its learning potential is weaker than that of ILP, but stronger than that of the conventional attribute-value learning methods. We use GBI aiming at making the best of it in its efficiency. There do exist problems that best fit use of the GBI. *ClipBoard* runs on a small personal computer in real time for application selection. While the result of suggestion is correct, it keeps the same rule set. If the user overrides *ClipBoard*'s suggestion, it reconstructs the rule set from the recent history. The time required for the learning is so small that this does not cause any problem.

One may think that it is possible to design a small table for a conventional attribute-value, learning method. We think that a careful analysis of the rules generated by the GBI method enables such a design later. However, such an exquisite design is applicable only within narrow limits, and makes the use of new useful information difficult. In other words, GBI automates such a table design process.

---

[2] We used a Macintosh LC630 (68LC040 33 MHz CPU with 12M byte DRAM) for this experiment. The time depends on the knowledge we specified. We used 'type constraints' and 'mode constraints' as the domain knowledge (Pazzani and Kibler, 1992). Although both forms of knowledge dramatically decrease the search space, we also had to tune other search parameters (other kind of domain knowledge) which are available for FOCL version 2.1.

Note that the domain where the data dependency is important is not restricted to user behavior modeling. We believe this to be a typical characteristic of many domains. In general, it is always worthwhile using the least strong representation language for learning. By restricting potential search space, the least strong representation language tends to achieve learning efficiency. Thus GBI appears to be a good learning method in such a domain.

Another important point is the various functions of the GBI method. Yoshida *et al.* (1994) reported its (1) macro rule learning function, and (2) concepts finding function together with the classification rule learning function. By considering the correspondence shown in Figure 7, we can apply the various methods developed in classification rule learning studies to macro rule learning and to concept finding. The unified view of various learning functions may accelerate research in these fields.

6 CONCLUSION

In the domain where data dependency is important, the complex data structure prohibits use of conventional attribute-value learning methods to analyze data. Although the enhanced expressiveness of inductive logic programming (ILP) seems to be promising in such domains, the large amount of data to be analyzed sometimes causes excessive search, and results in inefficiency. Graph-based induction (GBI) uses colored directed graphs as the data representation language to efficiently analyze such domains. Its algorithm essentially follows a conventional attribute-value learning model. However, the attributes to be considered are dynamically modified in the process. The graph guides the search for the promising attributes which should be considered as the test conditions.

In the user modeling domain where ILP is found to be too inefficient for it to be of practical use, GBI out-performed conventional attribute-value learning methods. We compared the next command prediction accuracies of various methods. Although the best result by the conventional attribute-value learning method is 34.6%, GBI marks 57.8%. The difference of performance is attributed to the difference of the information the methods can use.

A user-adaptive interface system, *ClipBoard*, was developed to show the adequacy of the proposed method in a practical environment. It analyzes the I/O relationship between applications in the past task history, generates the user behavior model, and selects the next application based on the generated user behavior model. The prediction accuracies for important commands (69%~100%) are higher than the average (57.8%). The efficiency of GBI contributes to make the system practical.

REFERENCES

Bhansali, S. and Harandi, M. T. (1993). Synthesis of Unix Programs using Derivational Analogy. *Machine Learning*, 10: 7–55.

Breiman, L., Friedman, J. H., Olshen, R. A., and Stone, C. J. (1984). *Classification and Regression Trees*. Wadsworth and Brooks/Cole Advanced Books and Software.

Cypher, A. (1991). EAGER: Programming Repetitive Tasks by Example. In *CHI'91*, pages 33–39.

DeJong, G. and Mooney, R. (1986). Explanation-Based Learning: An Alternative View. *Machine Learning*, 1: 145–176.

Dent, L., Boticario, J., McDermott, J., Mitchell, T., and Zabowski, D. (1992). A Personal Learning Apprentice. In *AAAI-92*, San Jose, CA, 96–103.

Hermens, L. A. and Schlimmer, J. C. (1993). A Machine-learning Apprentice for the Completion of Repetitive Forms. In *Proc of the Ninth Conf. on Artificial Intelligence for Applications*, 164–170.

James, M. (1984). *Classification Algorithms*. A Wily-Interscience Publication.

Maes, P. and Kozierok, R. (1993). Learning Interface Agents. In *AAAI-93*, Washington D.C., 459–465.

Mitchell, T. M., Keller, R. M., and Kedar-Cabelli, S. T. (1986). Explanation-Based Generalization: A Unifying View. *Machine Learning*, 1: 47–80.

Muggleton, S. and Feng, C. (1992). Efficient Induction of Logic Programs. In Muggleton, S., ed. *Inductive Logic Programming*, 281–298. Academic Press.

Myers, B., Goldstein, J., and Goldberg, M. (1994). Creating Charts by Demonstration. In *CHI'94*, 106–111.

Pazzani, M. and Kibler, D. (1992). The Utility of Knowledge in Inductive Learning. *Machine Learning*, 9: 57–94.

Quinlan, J. R. (1986). Induction of Decision Trees. *Machine Learning*, 1: 81–106.

Quinlan, J. R. (1990). Learning Logical Definitions from Relations. *Machine Learning*, 5: 239–266.

Shapiro, E. (1983). *Algorithmic Program Debugging*. MIT Press.

Yoshida, K., Motoda, H., and Indurkhya, N. (1994). Graph-based Induction as a Unified Learning Framework. *Applied Intelligence*, 4: 297–328.

311

APPLIED SCIENTIFIC DISCOVERY

17

A connectionist approach to numeric law discovery

Kazumi Saito and Ryohei Nakano

NTT Communication Science Laboratories,

2 Hikaridai,

Seika-cho,

Soraku-gun,

Kyoto 619-0237,

Japan

e-mail: saito@cslab.kecl.ntt.co.jp and nakano@cslab.kecl.ntt.co.jp

Abstract

The discovery of an underlying law from a set of numeric data is the central part of scientific discovery systems. This paper proposes a new connectionist approach to numeric law discovery. In order to efficiently and constantly obtain near-optimal results (law-candidates), we introduce a new second-order learning algorithm; by adopting a quasi-Newton method as a basic framework, the optimal step-lengths are calculated as the minimal points of second-order approximations. The minimum -description length criterion selects the most suitable from law-candidates. The main advantage of our method over previous work on the symbolic or connectionist approach is that it can efficiently discover numeric laws whose power values are not restricted to integers. Experiments showed that the proposed method works well in discovering such laws even from data containing a small amount of noise.

1 INTRODUCTION

The discovery of a numeric law from a set of data is the central part of scientific discovery systems. Such systems, for example, can detect a relationship between the distance d to the sun and the revolution period p of five planets known as Kepler's third law $d = kp^{2/3}$ (k is a constant).

After the pioneering work of the BACON systems (Langley, 1978; Langley *et al.*, 1987), several methods (Langley and Zytkow, 1989; Falkenhainer and Michalski, 1990; Nordhausen and Langley, 1990; Schaffer, 1993; Sutton and Matheus, 1991) have been proposed.[1] The basic search strategy employed by these methods is much the same: two variables are recursively combined into a new variable by using multiplication, division, or some predefined prototype functions. BACON and FAHRENHEIT (Langley and Zytkow, 1989) use trend detectors to combine variables and employ a heuristic form of depth-first search. ABACUS (Falakenhainer and Michalski, 1990) creates a proportional graph and performs a modified beam search. In IDS (Nordhausen and Langley, 1990), correlation analysis is applied, and a beam search is performed. The E* algorithm (Schaffer, 1993) considers only bivariate functions. Also, Sutton and Matheus' algorithm (Sutton and Matheus, 1991) performs a regression, and the correlation between the squared error and the square of the variable's value (Sanger, 1991) is used to combine variables.

These existing methods suffer from the following problems: first, because combining two variables into a new one must be done in order, a combinatorial explosion may occur when complex laws are sought for data consisting of a large number of variables, or the desired laws will be missed when some heuristic search parameters are inappropriate. Second, when some powers appearing in a law are not restricted to integers, the law may remain unknown unless some appropriate prototype functions such as $p^{2/3}$ are prepared in advance. However, *a priori* information is rarely available. Third, these methods are often criticized for their lack of robustness; noise tolerance is definitely required since real observed data contain noise (Nordhausen and Langley, 1990; Schaffer, 1993).

We believe a connectionist approach has great potential to solve the above problems. In order to directly learn a generalized polynomial term whose power values are not restricted to integers, a computational unit called a product unit has been proposed (Durbin and Rumelhart, 1989); instead of calculating a weighted sum of input values, this unit calculates a weighted product, where each input value is raised to a power determined by a variable weight. Quite recently, however, serious difficulties have been reported when using standard back-propagation (BP) (Rumelhart *et al.*, 1986) to train networks containing these units (Leerink *et al.*, 1995). Although some heuristic strategies such as multiple learning algorithms have been proposed (Leerink *et al.*, 1995), their improvements over BP have been less than remarkable. Moreover, these earlier studies dealt only with binary data and did not specifically address the problem of numeric law discovery.

Second-order methods employing nonlinear optimization techniques such as quasi-Newton methods have been expected to overcome learning difficulties encountered by first-order methods such as BP (Gill *et al.*, 1981). Unfortunately, most previous approaches adopted a computationally expensive line search (Gill *et al.*, 1981) to calculate the optimal step-length during each iteration, causing the overall improvement to be small. If the optimal step-lengths could be efficiently calculated with reasonable accuracy, quasi-Newton methods would work much better in terms of convergence as well as processing efficiency.

In this paper, we propose a connectionist approach called RF5 for the discovery of numeric laws. Section 2 explains how neural networks are used to discover a class of numeric laws. Section 3 describes in detail a new second-order learning algorithm called

---

[1]A relevant earlier study (Collins, 1971) proposed a method of selectively incorporating predefined prototype functions into a linear regression framework.

BPQ which trains the neural networks. Section 4 explains a criterion for selecting the most suitable candidate out of the discovered ones. Section 5 evaluates the proposed method RF5 by doing experiments using both artificial and real data.

2 LAW DISCOVERY USING NEURAL NETWORKS

This section explains a connectionist problem formalization for numeric law discovery, first proposed by Durbin and Rumelhart (1989). Let $\{(\mathbf{x}_1, y_1), \ldots, (\mathbf{x}_m, y_m)\}$ be a set of examples, where $\mathbf{x}_t$ is an n-dimensional input vector and y_t is a target value corresponding to $\mathbf{x}_t$. In this paper, a class of numeric laws expressed as

$$y_t = c_0 + \sum_{i=1}^{h} c_i x_{t1}^{w_{i1}} \ldots x_{tn}^{w_{in}} \tag{1}$$

is considered, where each parameter c_i, or w_{ij} is an unknown real number and h is an unknown integer. Hereafter, $(c_0, \ldots, c_h)^T$ and $(w_{i1}, \ldots, w_{in})^T$ are expressed as $\mathbf{c}$ and $\mathbf{w}_i$, respectively, where $\mathbf{a}^T$ means the transposed vector of $\mathbf{a}$. In addition, a vector consisting of all parameters, $(\mathbf{c}^T, \mathbf{w}_1^T, \ldots, \mathbf{w}_h^T)^T$ is simply expressed as $\boldsymbol{\Phi}$, and $N(= nh + h + 1)$ shows the dimension of $\boldsymbol{\Phi}$.

By adding an adequate value to each element of the input vectors, if necessary without losing generality, we can assume $x_{ti} > 0$; then, Eq. (1) is equivalent to

$$y_t = c_0 + \sum_{i=1}^{h} c_i \exp \left(\sum_{j=1}^{n} w_{ij} \ln(x_{tj}) \right). \tag{2}$$

Equation (2) can be regarded as a three-layer feed-forward neural network such that the activation function of each hidden unit is $\exp(s) = e^s$, where h, $\mathbf{w}_i$, and $\mathbf{c}$ denote the number of hidden units, the weights between the input units and hidden unit i, and the weights between the hidden units and the output unit, respectively. Hereafter, the output value of hidden unit i is described as

$$v_i(\mathbf{x}_t; \mathbf{w}_i) = \exp \left(\sum_{j=1}^{n} w_{ij} \ln(x_{tj}) \right), \tag{3}$$

and then the output value of the output unit is described as

$$z(\mathbf{x}_t; \boldsymbol{\Phi}) = c_0 + \sum_{i=1}^{h} c_i v_i(\mathbf{x}_t; \mathbf{w}_i). \tag{4}$$

The hidden units defined by Eq. (3) are called *product units* (Durbin and Rumelhart, 1989). The discovery of numeric laws subject to Eq. (1) can thus be defined as the following learning problem in neural networks. That is, the problem is to find the $\boldsymbol{\Phi}$ that minimizes the following objective function:

$$f(\boldsymbol{\Phi}) = \frac{1}{2} \sum_{t=1}^{m} (y_t - z(\mathbf{x}_t; \boldsymbol{\Phi}))^2. \tag{5}$$

3 BPQ ALGORITHM

In our early experiments and as reported in earlier studies (Leerink *et al.*, 1995), the problem of minimizing Eq. (5) turned out to be quite tough. Thus, in order to efficiently and constantly obtain good results, this paper employs a new second-order learning algorithm called *BPQ* (*backpropagation based on quasi-Newton*); by adopting a quasi-Newton method as a basic framework, the optimal steplengths are calculated as the minimal points of second-order approximations.

3.1 Quasi-Newton method

A second-order Taylor expansion of $f(\mathbf{\Phi} + \Delta\mathbf{\Phi})$ about $\mathbf{\Phi}$ is given as

$$f(\mathbf{\Phi} + \Delta\mathbf{\Phi}) \approx f(\mathbf{\Phi}) + (\nabla f(\mathbf{\Phi}))^T \Delta\mathbf{\Phi} + \frac{1}{2}(\Delta\mathbf{\Phi})^T \nabla^2 f(\mathbf{\Phi})\Delta\mathbf{\Phi}. \tag{6}$$

If $\nabla^2 f(\mathbf{\Phi})$ is positive definite, the minimal point of the right-hand side of Eq. (6) is given by solving

$$\nabla^2 f(\mathbf{\Phi})\Delta\mathbf{\Phi} = -\nabla f(\mathbf{\Phi}). \tag{7}$$

Newton techniques minimize the objective function $f(\mathbf{\Phi})$ by using Eq. (7) to iteratively calculate the descent direction (Gill *et al.*, 1981). However, since $O(N^3)$ operations are required to straightforwardly solve Eq. (7), we cannot expect methods based on these techniques to scale up well to larger problems. Quasi-Newton techniques, on the other hand, calculate a matrix $\mathbf{H}$ during the iterations in order to approximate $(\nabla^2 f(\mathbf{\Phi}))^{-1}$. The basic algorithm is described as follows (Gill *et al.*, 1981):

step 1: Initialize $\mathbf{\Phi}^1$, set $\mathbf{H}^1 = \mathbf{I}$ (**I**: unit matrix), and set $k = 1$.

step 2: Calculate the current descent direction $\Delta\mathbf{\Phi}^k = -\mathbf{H}^k \nabla f(\mathbf{\Phi}^k)$.

step 3: Terminate the iteration if a stopping criterion is satisfied.

step 4: Calculate the step-length λ^k that minimizes $f(\mathbf{\Phi}^k + \lambda\Delta\mathbf{\Phi}^k)$.

step 5: Update weights $\mathbf{\Phi}^{k+1} = \mathbf{\Phi}^k + \lambda^k \Delta\mathbf{\Phi}^k$.

step 6: If $k \equiv 0 \pmod{N}$, set $\mathbf{H}^{k+1} = \mathbf{I}$; otherwise, update $\mathbf{H}^{k+1}$.

step 7: Set $k = k + 1$, return to **step 2**.

In **step 6**, several methods for updating $\mathbf{H}^{k+1}$ have been proposed. We have adopted the Broydon–Fletcher–Goldfarb–Shanno (BFGS) update because it has been the most successful update in a number of studies (Gill *et al.*, 1981). By setting $\mathbf{p} = \lambda^k \Delta\mathbf{\Phi}^k$, and $\mathbf{q} = \nabla f(\mathbf{\Phi}^{k+1}) - \nabla f(\mathbf{\Phi}^k)$, the BFGS formula is given as

$$\mathbf{H}^{k+1} = \mathbf{H}^k + \left(1 + \frac{\mathbf{q}^T\mathbf{H}^k\mathbf{q}}{\mathbf{p}^T\mathbf{q}}\right)\frac{\mathbf{p}\mathbf{p}^T}{\mathbf{p}^T\mathbf{q}} - \frac{\mathbf{p}\mathbf{q}^T\mathbf{H}^k + \mathbf{H}^k\mathbf{q}\mathbf{p}^T}{\mathbf{p}^T\mathbf{q}}. \tag{8}$$

3.2 New method for calculating optimal step-lengths

This section will elaborate on the newly developed calculation of **step 4**, the most crucial step in the quasi-Newton method.

3.2.1 The basic procedure

In **step 4**, since λ is the only variable, we can express $f(\Phi + \lambda\Delta\Phi)$ simply as $g(\lambda)$. Consider a second-order Taylor expansion of $g(\lambda)$:

$$g(\lambda) = g(0) + g'(0)\lambda + \frac{1}{2}g''(0)\lambda^2. \tag{9}$$

When $g'(0) < 0$ and $g''(0) > 0$, the minimal point of the right-hand side of Eq. (9) is given by

$$\lambda = \frac{-g'(0)}{g''(0)} \left(= \frac{-(\nabla f(\Phi))^T \Delta\Phi}{(\Delta\Phi)^T \nabla^2 f(\Phi)\Delta\Phi} \right). \tag{10}$$

Other cases will be considered in the next section.

For three-layer neural networks defined by Eq. (5), we can efficiently calculate $g'(0)$ and $g''(0)$ as follows. By differentiating $g(\lambda)$ and substituting 0 for λ, we obtain

$$g'(0) = -\sum_{t=1}^{m}(y_t - z(\mathbf{x}_t;\ \Phi))z'(\mathbf{x}_t;\ \Phi), \tag{11}$$

$$g''(0) = \sum_{t=1}^{m}((z'(\mathbf{x}_t;\ \Phi))^2 - (y_t - z(\mathbf{x}_t;\ \Phi))z''(\mathbf{x}_t;\ \Phi)). \tag{12}$$

Note that the derivative of $z(\mathbf{x}_t;\ \Phi)$ is defined as follows:

$$z'(\mathbf{x}_t;\ \Phi) = \frac{dz(\mathbf{x}_t;\ \Phi + \lambda\Delta\Phi)}{d\lambda}\bigg|_{\lambda=0}. \tag{13}$$

By calculating $z'(\mathbf{x}_t;\ \Phi)$ and $z''(\mathbf{x}_t;\ \Phi)$, we obtain

$$z'(\mathbf{x}_t;\ \Phi) = \Delta c_0 + \sum_{i=1}^{h}(\Delta c_i v_i(\mathbf{x}_t;\ \mathbf{w}_i) + c_i v_i'(\mathbf{x}_t;\ \mathbf{w}_i)), \tag{14}$$

$$z''(\mathbf{x}_t;\ \Phi) = \sum_{i=1}^{h}(2\Delta c_i v_i'(\mathbf{x}_t;\ \mathbf{w}_i) + c_i v_i''(\mathbf{x}_t;\ \mathbf{w}_i)), \tag{15}$$

where Δc_i denotes the change of c_i, calculated in **step 2**. Finally, by calculating $v_i'(\mathbf{x}_t;\ \mathbf{w}_i)$ and $v_i''(\mathbf{x}_t;\ \mathbf{w}_i)$, we obtain

$$v_i'(\mathbf{x}_t;\ \mathbf{w}_i) = v_i(\mathbf{x}_t;\ \mathbf{w}_i)\sum_{j=1}^{n}\Delta w_{ij}\ln(x_{tj}), \tag{16}$$

$$v_i''(\mathbf{x}_t;\ \mathbf{w}_i) = v_i(\mathbf{x}_t;\ \mathbf{w}_i)\left(\sum_{j=1}^{n}\Delta w_{ij}\ln(x_{tj})\right)^2, \tag{17}$$

where Δw_{ij} denotes the change of w_{ij}, calculated in **step 2**.

3.2.2 Coping with undesirable cases

In the above we assumed $g'(0) < 0$. When $g'(0) > 0$, the value of the objective function cannot be reduced along the search direction; thus, we set $\Delta\mathbf{\Phi}^k$ to $-\nabla f(\mathbf{\Phi}^k)$ and $\mathbf{H}^k$ to $\mathbf{I}$. Note that $g'(0) < 0$ is guaranteed by such a setting because

$$g'(0) = (\nabla f(\mathbf{\Phi}^k))^T \Delta\mathbf{\Phi}^k$$
$$= -\|\nabla f(\mathbf{\Phi}^k)\|^2$$
$$< 0. \tag{18}$$

When $g'(0) < 0$ and $g''(0) \leq 0$, Eq. (10) gives a negative value or infinity. To avoid this situation, we employ Gauss–Newton techniques. The first-order approximation of $z(\mathbf{x}_t; \mathbf{\Phi} + \lambda\Delta\mathbf{\Phi})$ is

$$z(\mathbf{x}_t; \mathbf{\Phi} + \lambda\Delta\mathbf{\Phi}) \approx z(\mathbf{x}_t; \mathbf{\Phi}) + z'(\mathbf{x}_t; \mathbf{\Phi})\lambda. \tag{19}$$

Then $g(\lambda)$ of the next iteration can be approximated by

$$g(\lambda) \approx \frac{1}{2}\sum_{t=1}^{m}(y_t - (z(\mathbf{x}_t; \mathbf{\Phi}) + z'(\mathbf{x}_t; \mathbf{\Phi})\lambda))^2$$

$$= g(0) + g'(0)\lambda + \frac{1}{2}\sum_{t=1}^{m}(z'(\mathbf{x}_t; \mathbf{\Phi}))^2\lambda^2. \tag{20}$$

The minimal point of the right-hand side of Eq. (20) is given by

$$\lambda = \frac{-g'(0)}{\sum_{t=1}^{m}(z'(\mathbf{x}_t; \mathbf{\Phi}))^2}. \tag{21}$$

Clearly, Eq. (21) always gives a positive value when $g'(0) < 0$. In this case, since the search point may be near a saddle point, the approximation of $\mathbf{H}$ is restarted by setting $k = N$.

In many cases, it is practically useful to limit the maximum change in $\mathbf{\Phi}$ during any one iteration (Gill *et al.*, 1981). Thus, if $\|\lambda\Delta\mathbf{\Phi}\| > 1.0$, λ is set to $1.0/\|\Delta\mathbf{\Phi}\|$. In this case, since the landscape of the objective function may change drastically, the approximation of $\mathbf{H}$ is also restarted by setting $k = N$.

Since λ is calcuated on the basis of the approximation, we cannot always reduce the value of the objective function $g(\lambda)$. When $g(\lambda) \geq g(0)$, we introduce a simple shrinking method. Let λ_0 be the value calculated from Eq. (10) or (21). By considering satisfying the conditions $h(0) = g(0)$, $h(\lambda_0) = g(\lambda_0)$, and $h'(0) = g'(0)$, we get the following second-order approximation $h(\lambda)$:

$$g(\lambda) \approx h(\lambda) = g(0) + g'(0)\lambda + \frac{g(\lambda_0) - g(0) - g'(0)\lambda_0}{\lambda_0^2}\lambda^2. \tag{22}$$

Since $g(\lambda_0) > g(0)$ and $g'(0) < 0$, the minimal point of $h(\lambda)$ is given by

$$\lambda = \frac{-g'(0)\lambda_0^2}{2(g(\lambda_0) - g(0) - g'(0)\lambda_0)}. \tag{23}$$

Note that $0 < \lambda < \lambda_0$ is guaranteed for λ in Eq. (23). Thus, by iterating this process until $g(\lambda) < g(0)$, we can always find λ that satisfies $g(\lambda) < g(0)$.

3.2.3 Summary of step-length calculation

By integrating the above-mentioned procedures, we can specify **step 4** by the following:

step 4-1: if $g'(0) > 0$, set $\Delta \boldsymbol{\Phi}^k = -\nabla f(\boldsymbol{\Phi}^k)$; set $\mathbf{H}^k = \mathbf{I}$ and set $k = 1$.

step 4-2: if $g''(0) > 0$, calculate λ using Eq. (10); otherwise, calculate λ using Eq. (21) and set $k = N$.

step 4-3: if $\|\lambda \Delta \boldsymbol{\Phi}\| > 1.0$, set $\lambda = 1.0/\|\Delta \boldsymbol{\Phi}\|$ and set $k = N$.

step 4-4: if $g(\lambda) > g(0)$, calculate λ using Eq. (23) until $g(\lambda) < g(0)$.

3.3 Computational complexity

We consider the computational complexity of one iteration that sweeps every training example once. In BP, the complexity (number of multiplications) to calculate the objective function is $nhm + O(hm)$ and the complexity for the gradient vector is also $nhm + O(hm)$. Thus, since $N = nh + h + 1$, the order of the complexity for BP is $2Nm + O(hm)$.

In addition to the above, BPQ performs quasi-Newton iteration and calculates the optimal step-length. The complexity of the former is $O(N^2)$ and the latter is $Nm + O(hm)$ (see Section 3.2.1). Fortunately, the complexity for BPQ to calculate the objective function can be reduced to $O(hm)$, because the output value of each hidden unit is given by $\exp(\sum_{j=1}^{n} w_{ij} \ln(x_{tj}) + \lambda \sum_{j=1}^{n} \Delta w_{ij} \ln(x_{tj}))$, but $\sum_{j=1}^{n} \Delta w_{ij} \ln(x_{tj})$ is already calculated when the optimal step-length is calculated in the previous iteration. Thus, the total complexity for BPQ is $2Nm + O(N^2) + O(hm)$.

To reduce the generalization error for an unseen example, m should usually be much larger than N. According to the PAC-learning theory (Valiant, 1984), to hold the upper bound of the generalization error less than ε, the approximate number of examples required should be more than $\varepsilon^{-1} N$ (Baum and Haussler, 1989). Thus, since complexity $O(N^2)$ becomes much smaller than $2Nm$, the order of the complexity for BPQ remains almost equivalent to that of BP.

4 CRITERION FOR SELECTION

In general, for a given set of data, we cannot know the optimal number of hidden units in advance. Moreover, since the data is usually corrupted by noise, the law-candidate which minimizes Eq. (5) is not always the best one. We must thus consider a criterion to adequately evaluate the law-candidates discovered by changing the number of hidden units. In this paper, we adopt the MDL (minimum description length) criterion (Rissanen, 1983) for this purpose. The MDL fitness value is defined by

$$\text{MDL} = 0.5m \log(\text{MSE}) + 0.5N \log(m), \qquad (24)$$

where MSE represents the value of the mean squared error defined by

$$\text{MSE} = \frac{1}{m} \sum_{t=1}^{m} (y_t - z(\mathbf{x}_t; \ \boldsymbol{\Phi}))^2. \qquad (25)$$

Recall that N is the number of parameters in $\mathbf{\Phi}$, and m is the number of examples. Hereafter, our discovery method employing the connectionist problem formalization, the BPQ algorithm and the MDL criterion, is called RF5 (Rule extraction from Facts version 5).

5 EXPERIMENTS

5.1 Evaluation using artificial data

The rule discovery method, RF5, was evaluated by using an artificial problem proposed by Sutton and Matheus (Sutton and Matheus, 1991) and a modified version. The original problem is to restore a law described as

$$y = 2 + 3x_1x_2 + 4x_3x_4x_5. \tag{26}$$

Each example is generated as follows: each value of variables $x_1, \ldots, x_5$ is randomly generated in the range [0, 1], and the corresponding value of y is calculated using Eq. (26). In this problem, the total number of variables is 9 ($n = 9$); each value of irrelevant variables $x_6, \ldots, x_9$ is also randomly generated in the range of [0, 1], and the number of examples is set to 200 ($m = 200$). In the experiments, the initial values of weights were independently generated according to a normal distribution with a mean of 0 and a variance of 0.1; the iteration was terminated when any of the following three conditions was met: the MSE value was sufficiently small, i.e.,

$$\frac{1}{m} \sum_{t=1}^{m} (y_t - z(\mathbf{x}_t; \mathbf{\Phi}))^2 < 10^{-8}, \tag{27}$$

the gradient vector was sufficiently small, i.e.,

$$\frac{1}{N} \|\nabla f(\mathbf{\Phi})\|^2 < 10^{-8}, \tag{28}$$

or the total processing time exceeded 100 seconds.

5.1.1 The original problem

In the experiments, we changed the number of hidden units from 1 to 3 ($h = 1, 2, 3$) and performed 100 trials for each of them. Table 1 shows the basic statistics of MSE values, MDL values, iterations, and processing times (sec.).[2] This table shows that the correct number of hidden units, $h = 2$, was successfully found because the best MDL value was minimized. When $h = 2$, all 100 trials converged to the global minimum. The discovered law is

$$y = 2.000 + 3.000x_1^{1.000}x_2^{1.000} + 4.000x_3^{1.000}x_4^{1.000}x_5^{1.000}, \tag{29}$$

where the weight values were rounded off to the third decimal place. RF5 perfectly restored the original law. The average number of iterations for one trial was 93.7, and the average processing time was 0.878 sec. The total processing time required for doing this experiment amounted to 4.4 min.

---

[2] Our experiments were done on HP/9000/735 computers.

Table 1. Sutton–Matheus problem.

Units	MSE value			MDL value			Iterations		Time	
	best	avg.	s.d.	best	avg.	s.d.	avg.	s.d.	avg.	s.d.
1	0.126	0.13	0.0	−177.9	−178	0.0	71	1.0	0.32	0.01
2	0.000	0.0	0.0	−1786.4	−1786	0.0	81	8.4	0.68	0.07
3	0.000	0.0	0.0	−1759.9	−1717	64	130	29	1.65	0.36

5.1.2 Modified problem

To evaluate RF5's ability to cope with the case of real-valued exponents, we changed Eq. (26) to the following:

$$y = 2 + 3x_1^{-1}x_2^3 + 4x_3x_4^{1/2}x_5^{-1/3}. \tag{30}$$

The experimental conditions were exactly the same as in the original problem. Table 2 shows the results. This table indicates that the correct number of hidden units was once again found. However, for $h = 2$, a few of the 100 trials converged to undesirable local minima. The law discovered by RF5,

$$y = 2.000 + 3.000x_1^{-1.000}x_2^{3.000} + 4.000x_3^{1.000}x_4^{0.500}x_5^{-0.333}, \tag{31}$$

is almost equivalent to Eq. (30). Note that without preparing some appropriate prototype functions, existing numeric discovery methods cannot find such laws as described in Eq. (30). This point is an important advantage of RF5 over existing methods.

5.1.3 Noise tolerance

To evaluate RF5's noise tolerance, we corrupted each value of y calculated from Eq. (26) or Eq. (30) by adding noise generated according to a normal distribution with a mean of 0 and a variance of 0.1. The other experimental conditions were exactly the same as before. Table 3 shows the results. The best MSE values were minimized when $h = 3$, while the best MDL values were minimized when $h = 2$: this indicates the correct number of hidden units was found in both problems. The original and modified laws discovered by RF5 are

$$y = 1.968 + 3.028x_1^{1.000}x_2^{0.969}x_4^{-0.007}x_5^{-0.007}x_6^{0.004}x_7^{0.008}x_8^{-0.007}x_9^{0.001}$$
$$+ 3.880x_1^{-0.027}x_2^{-0.014}x_3^{1.025}x_4^{0.995}x_5^{1.048}x_6^{-0.008}x_7^{-0.020}x_8^{0.010}x_9^{-0.014}, \tag{32}$$
$$y = 2.012 + 3.004x_1^{-1.000}x_2^{3.001}x_6^{-0.001}x_7^{0.001}$$
$$+ 3.983x_1^{0.002}x_2^{-0.003}x_3^{1.022}x_4^{0.500}x_5^{-0.333}x_6^{-0.005}x_7^{-0.002}x_8^{0.003}x_9^{-0.007}. \tag{33}$$

When the weight values were rounded off to the first decimal place, these laws become

$$y = 2.0 + 3.0x_1^{1.0}x_2^{1.0} + 3.9x_3^{1.0}x_4^{1.0}x_5^{1.0}, \tag{34}$$
$$y = 2.0 + 3.0x_1^{-1.0}x_2^{3.0} + 4.0x_3^{1.0}x_4^{0.5}x_5^{-0.3}. \tag{35}$$

Although some weight values were slightly different, laws almost equivalent to the true ones were found. This shows that RF5 is robust and noise tolerant to some degree.

Table 2. Modified problem.

Units	MSE value			MDL value			Iterations		Time	
	best	avg.	s.d.	best	avg.	s.d.	avg.	s.d.	avg.	s.d.
1	1.317	1.32	0.00	56.7	57	0.0	70	5	0.32	0.02
2	0.000	0.03	0.17	−1786.4	−1731	314	116	27	0.97	0.23
3	0.000	0.00	0.00	−1760.0	−1727	47	240	104	3.02	1.31

Table 3. Noise tolerance.

Units	MSE value			MDL value			Iterations		Time	
	best	avg.	s.d.	best	avg.	s.d.	avg.	s.d.	avg.	s.d.
Sutton–Matheus problem with noise										
1	0.160	0.16	0.0	−154.0	−154	0.0	68	4	0.31	0.02
2	0.009	0.01	0.0	−416.0	−416	0.0	93	9	0.77	0.07
3	0.008	0.01	0.0	−405.5	−405	0.8	784	81	9.80	1.02
Modified problem with noise										
1	2.326	2.33	0.0	113.6	114	0.0	90	12	0.41	0.05
2	0.010	0.03	0.21	−403.9	−399	53	228	134	1.90	1.11
3	0.009	0.01	0.0	−388.9	−385	1.2	753	127	9.41	1.58

5.1.4 Comparison with adaptive BP

BPQ was compared with adaptive BP, using both the original and modified problems with noise. In the experiment, since standard BP didn't converge to any minima, we adopted Silva and Almeida's learning rate adaptation rule (Silva and Almeida, 1990): the learning rate η_i for each weight Φ_i is adjusted by

$$
\eta_i^k = \begin{cases} \eta_i^{k-1} \times u, & \text{if } \frac{\partial}{\partial \Phi_i} f(\Phi^k) \times \frac{\partial}{\partial \Phi_i} f(\Phi^{k-1}) \geq 0, \\ \eta_i^{k-1} \times u^{-1}, & \text{otherwise} \end{cases} \tag{36}
$$

where k indicates the number of iterations, and the constant parameter u was set to 1.1 as recommended by Silva and Almeida (1990). If the value of the objective function increases, all learning rates are halved until the value decreases. Among several existing algorithms, this adaptation rule worked the most efficiently on some real medical data (Schiffmann and Werner, 1993).

Figure 1 shows experimental results. Figure 1(a) compares the processing time per quasi-Newton iteration and the number of iterations required until convergence, averaged over 100 trials using the original problem with noise. This figure shows that the processing time of one iteration of adaptive BP is slightly shorter than that of BPQ, while the number of iterations for adaptive BP is 16.1 times as large as that for BPQ. In total, BPQ is 11.4 times as fast as adaptive BP. Figure 1(b) compares convergence speed to average MDL values for the original problem with noise. Clearly, BPQ's convergence property is superior to adaptive BP's. Figure 1(c) compares convergence speed to average MDL values for the modified problem with noise. Here, adaptive BP was unable to find any minima.

Why did adaptive BP work poorly for the modified problem with noise? The basic statistics of the target value y_t indicates a hint: in our experiments, the average and standard deviation for the original one with noise are 3.33 and 0.90, while 19.40 and 60.95 for the modified one with noise. This implies that when the weight vector changes, the gradient vector changes more drastically in the modified problem than in the original problem. We believe that this caused adaptive BP being unable to learn it.

5.2 Evaluation using real data

For real data, we used three datasets supporting Boyle's law, Kepler's third law, and Ohm's law.[3] In this experiment, since the number of examples for each dataset was small, the number of hidden units was fixed at 1. Note that since we consider a constant term c_0, the problem cannot be reduced to a simple regression problem. The trials were performed 10 times for each dataset, and the weight values in the discovered laws were rounded off to the second decimal place.

5.2.1 Boyle's law

Boyle's law is a relation between the pressure and volume of a quantity of enclosed air. The reference relation is described as

$$y = 29.30/x. \tag{37}$$

The law discovered by RF5 is

$$y = 29.05x^{-1.08} - 0.61. \tag{38}$$

An undesired constant term appeared here, but the law is very similar to the reference relation. The value of the constant term is small in the discovered law; as such we can perform another trial using the model where the constant term is fixed at 0.

---

[3] We obtained the data sets from the UCI repository of machine learning databases.

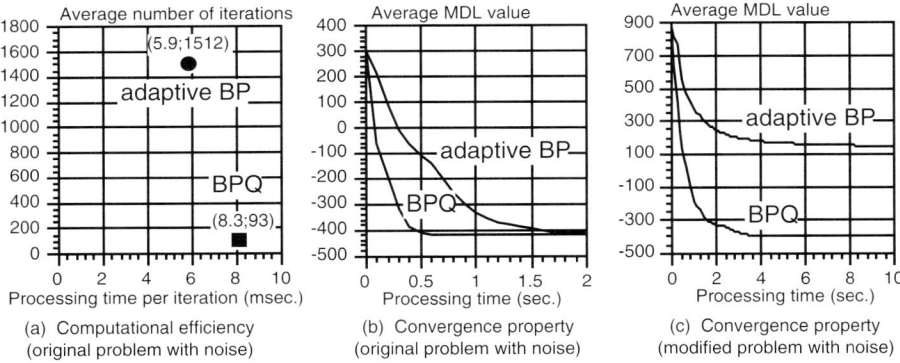

(a) Computational efficiency (original problem with noise)

(b) Convergence property (original problem with noise)

(c) Convergence property (modified problem with noise)

Figure 1. Learning results.

325

5.2.2 Kepler's third law

Kepler's third law is a relation between the distance to the sun and the revolution period of five planets. The reference relation is described as

$$y = 0.41x^{1.5}. \tag{39}$$

The law discovered by RF5 is

$$y = 0.41x^{1.50} + 0.19. \tag{40}$$

5.2.3 Ohm's law

Ohm's law is a relation between a strip of copper and the current flowing through it. The reference relation is described as

$$y = 7268.74/x - 20.30. \tag{41}$$

The law discovered by RF5 is

$$y = 7812.02x^{-1.02} - 19.14. \tag{42}$$

Although the data has two outstanding outlier examples, the discovered law is very similar to the reference relation.

6 CONCLUSION

To discover an underlying law from a set of numeric data, we have proposed a new connectionist method called RF5. After employing the connectionist problem formalization, RF5 adopts a new second-order learning algorithm called BPQ, which calculates the optimal step-length as the minimal points of second-order approximations. Experiments showed that RF5 successfully discovered underlying laws whose power values are not restricted to integers, even if the data contained a small amount of noise. In the future, we plan to do further experiments to evaluate the proposed method using a wider variety of problems.

REFERENCES

Baum, E. and Haussler, D. (1989). What size net gives valid generalization. *Neural Computation*, **1**(1): 151–160.

Collins, J. (1971). A regression analysis program incorporating heuristic term selection. In Collins, N., Dale, E., and Michie, D., eds., *Machine Intelligence 1*, pp. 153–170. Edinburgh University Press, Edinburgh.

Durbin, R. and Rumelhart, D. (1989). Product units: a computationally powerful and biologically plausible extension. *Neural Computation*, **1**(1): 133–142.

Falakenhainer, B. and Michalski, R. (1990). Integrating quantitative and qualitative discovery in the abacus system. In Kodratoff, Y. and Michalski, R., eds., *Machine learning: an artificial intelligence approach, Volume III*, pp. 153–190. Morgan Kaufmann, San Mateo, CA.

Gill, P., Murray, W., and Wright, M. (1981). *Practical optimization*. Academic Press, London.

Langley, P., (1978). Bacon.1: a general discovery system. In *Proceedings of the Second National Conference of the Canadian Society for Computational Studies of Intelligence*, pp. 173–180.

Langley, P., Simon, H., Bradshaw, G., and Zytkow, J. (1987). *Scientific discovery: computational explorations of the creative process*. MIT Press, Cambridge, MA.

Langley, P. and Zytkow, J. (1989). Data-driven approaches to empirical discovery. *Artificial Intelligence*, **40**: 283–312.

Leerink, L., Giles, C., Horne, B., and Jabri, M. (1995). Learning with product units. In Tesauro, G., Touretzky, D., and Lee, T., eds., *Advances in Neural Information Processing Systems 7*, pp. 537–544. MIT Press, Cambridge, MA.

Nordhausen, B. and Langley, P. (1990). A robust approach to numeric discovery. In *Proc. Seventh International Machine Learning Conference*, pp. 411–418, Morgan Kaufmann, Palo Alto, CA.

Rissanen, J. (1983). A universal prior for integers and estimation by minimum description length. *Ann. of Statist.*, **11**(2): 416–431.

Rumelhart, D., Hinton, G., and Williams, R. (1986). Learning internal representations by error propagation. In Rumelhart, D. and McClelland, J., eds., *Parallel Distributed Processing*, pp. 318–362. MIT Press, Cambridge, MA.

Sanger, T. (1991). Basis-function trees as a generalization of local variable selection method for function approximation. In Touretzky, D., ed., *Neural Information Processing Systems 3*, pp. 707–713. Morgan Kaufmann, San Mateo, CA.

Schaffer, C. (1993). Bivariate scientific function finding in a sampled, real-data testbed. *Machine Learning*, **12**(1/2/3): 167–183.

Schiffmann, W. and Werner, R. (1993). Optimization of the backpropagation algorithm for training multilayer perceptron. Technical report, University of Koblenz.

Silva, F. and Almeida, L. (1990). Speeding up backpropagation. In Eckmiller, R., ed., *Advanced Neural Computers*, pp. 151–160. North-Holland, Amsterdam.

Sutton, R. and Matheus, C. (1991). Learning polynomial functions by feature construction. In *Proceedings of the Eighth International Machine Learning Workshop*, pp. 208–212, Morgan Kaufmann, San Mateo, CA.

Valiant, L. (1984). A theory of the learnable. *CACM.*, **27**(11): 1134–1142.

18

Drug design by machine learning

Michael J. E. Sternberg*
Ross D. King

Biomolecular Modelling Laboratory,
Imperial Cancer Research Fund,
44 Lincoln's Inn Fields,
London
UK
*e-mail: m.sternberg@icrf.icnet.uk

Ashwin Srinivasan
Stephen H. Muggleton

Computing Laboratory,
University of Oxford,
Wolfson Building,
Parks Road,
Oxford
UK

Abstract

Inductive logic programming, implemented in PROGOL, is used to predict whether members of a set of chemical compounds are mutagenic. This study is used to explore the general area of deriving structure–activity relationships, a central tool in rational drug design. The chemical structures are described in a general way by relational descriptors that encode atom types and their bond connectivities. This description contrasts with global attributes of the chemicals that are widely used in other studies such as regression. The results using PROGOL are compared to those from regression, neural nets and decision trees. Two data sets were considered – a regression friendly and a regression unfriendly set of compounds. PROGOL performed well on both data sets, in contrast to the other approaches that only performed well on one of these two sets of data.

Importantly PROGOL rules could readily be interpreted in terms of the chemical sub-structures. Indeed PROGOL found one chemical substructure alert for mutagenicity in the regression unfriendly data that eluded expert inspection.

1 INTRODUCTION

A successful drug during its life term can have sales of many billions of pounds. Central in a rational path to its discovery is an understanding of the relationship between the structure of the drug and its activity. This paper describes the use of the inductive logic programming (ILP) program PROGOL (Muggleton, 1995), to model structure–activity relationships (SARs) for chemical compounds (King et al., 1996).

In general, there are two stages to drug design (Colman, 1994; Marshall and Cramer, 1988; Ramsden, 1990). First is the identification of a novel compound (known as a lead) with some suitable activity. Second is the improvement of the activity (i.e. optimization). Ideally knowledge of the three-dimensional structures of the principal molecular target of a potential drug (i.e. its receptor) derived by experimental methods such as X-ray crystallography or nuclear magnetic resonance can be used for lead compound identification. Similarly knowledge of the drug/receptor structure can guide lead optimization. However, often the receptor is not known or does not have a determined three-dimensional structure. Then the medicinal chemistry tends to have only the chemical formulae for a series of compounds together with experimental or calculated three-dimensional structures and their activities. Indeed increasing lead identification and initial optimization involves experimental screening of large panels of compounds against a biological assay (Gallop et al., 1994; Gordon et al., 1994). It is primarily for these systems without detailed knowledge of the receptor that we have explored the power of ILP to help the medicinal chemist obtain SARs. (However extension of the technique may well be suitable for receptor-based drug design.) More generally the SARs approach is the basis of many relationships relating molecular structure to activity, for example in understanding and predicting chemical mutagenesis.

A wide variety of learning algorithms have been applied to derive SARs, including linear regression (Hansch et al., 1962), partial least squares regression (PLS) (Frank and Friedman, 1993), neural networks (Villemin et al., 1993) and decision trees (e.g. CART (Breiman et al., 1984)). These learning algorithms have been applied to different descriptors of the compounds including molecular chemical properties (Hansch et al., 1962; Trinajstic, 1983), quantum mechanical properties (Debnath et al., 1991); substructure searches (Klopman, 1984; Ormerod et al., 1989) or molecular shape (Cramer et al., 1988). However the rules obtained from a SAR should be not only accurate but also readily comprehensible to the chemist. However, many algorithms are limited in the ease of interpreting the prediction model. This can stem from the limitations in the learning algorithms that restrict the representations that could be employed. In general the currently used representations are based on attributes. However, this form of data representation is not well suited to describing the steric structure of chemicals and consequently the rules obtained by many of the learning algorithms (e.g. PLS or neural networks) are difficult to interpret chemically. A more general way to describe objects is to use relations and this can be fully implemented using the recent ILP algorithms PROGOL. This paper reviews a recent study (King *et al.*, 1996) on the derivation of a SAR using PROGOL to understand the chemical mutagenicity of a series of compounds.

The use of this algorithm extends our previous work applying ILP to SARs using GOLEM (King *et al.*, 1992; Hirst *et al.*, 1994a; Hirst *et al.*, 1994b). These earlier studies showed that ILP can learn rules that are as accurate as linear regression and neural networks but also yielded rules that are comprehensible. However GOLEM was restricted in its use of relational representations; could only use knowledge expressed as facts; and did not perform a complete search of the rules space. PROGOL remedied these and other shortcomings and is able to cope with nondeterministic relationships, knowledge expressed as PROLOG programs and performs a complete search of rule space.

2 METHOD

2.1 PROGOL

PROGOL is a program to perform inductive logic programming (Muggleton, 1995). Rules are expressed as a subset of the predicate calculus and are encoded in PROLOG. In keeping with its predecessor GOLEM and with other ILP programs, the input to PROGOL is a set of positive examples, a set of negative (i.e. counter) examples together with background knowledge. PROGOL aims to derive rules expressed in terms of the background knowledge that predict all the positive examples whilst not identifying the negative counterexamples. In practice a tolerance is set for the number of negative examples that the rules erroneously predicted. The power of a rule is measured by (no. of correct predictions − no. of incorrect predictions − size of rule). This study used the version of PROGOL written in PROLOG.

2.2 Data set

The object of the study was to explore the power of PROGOL to derive a SAR on a test dataset in the public domain that has been examined by other techniques. We considered a set of 230 aromatic and hetero aromatic nitro compounds that had been screened for whether they were mutagenic as identified experimentally by the widely used Ames test using *Salmonella typhimurium TA* 98. This set poses a challenge to SAR studies as they are a chemically diverse set of compounds without a single common structural template. This set was used in the study by Debnath *et al.* (1991) who applied regression techniques. In their study they split the dataset into 188 compounds that were amenable to regression and 42 that could not be modelled by a regression equation. The 188 regression-friendly compounds were also studied by Villemin *et al.* (1993) using neural networks. We considered separately the regression friendly and the regression unfriendly data sets.

In keeping with many attribute-based approaches to SAR, these studies were based on representing the compounds in terms of global chemical properties. They used a measure of the molecular hydrophobicity (i.e. the tendency of the molecule to avoid contact with water) which was quantified by Log P (the octanol/water partition coefficient) and a measure of chemical reactivity based on its electronic properties (LUMO – the lowest unoccupied molecular orbital). However neither of these terms captures the molecular structure in terms of the atom and bond connectivities. In keeping with many other regression and neural network studies, molecular structure is added to these attributes by use of binary indicator variables. Debnath *et al.* used I1 set to 1 for all compounds containing three or more fused rings and Ia set to 1 to identify the five examples of acenthrylenes in the data. These two indicator variables were chosen by expert intervention and generally are the result of extensive trial and errors in the development of a regression model (or a neural network).

2.3 Data representation

The approach followed to apply PROGOL to SAR is illustrated in Figure 1. The positive examples were statements defining a particular compound as mutagenic (log(no. of revertants/nmol) > 0.0) (138 compounds) with the negative examples being the remaining 92 low mutagenic compounds.

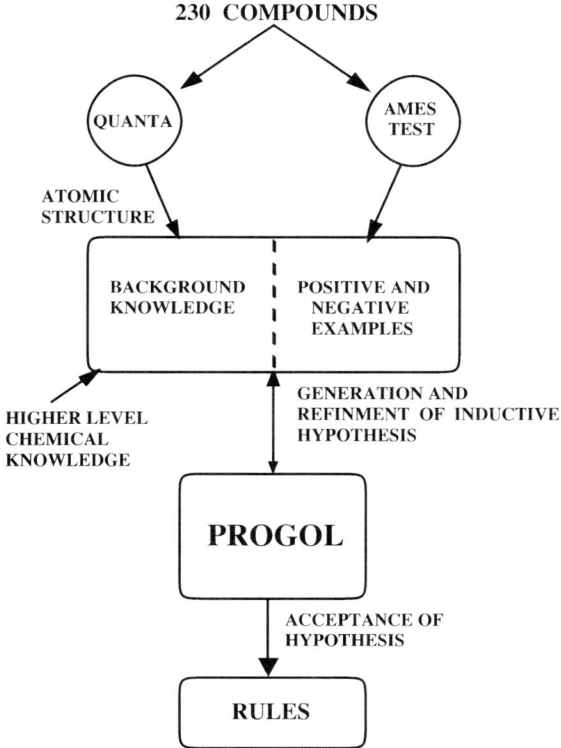

Figure 1. Schematic diagram of the approach followed.

The background knowledge represented compounds in terms of the chemical type of the component atoms and connecting bonds. These values were automatically assigned using the molecular modelling program QUANTA (Molecular Simulations Inc., USA). Each chemical was input manually via a molecular sketchpad and then the atoms automatically typed by QUANTA to consider their local chemical environment and an estimate of their electronic charge and the connecting bonds classified. Chemical typing could have been performed in an analogous method by other chemical modelling programs. Furthermore, the compounds could have been extracted from the database and then typed without the need for their entry via the sketchpad.

The background knowledge is in the form of the following two types of relations. The first is:

```
atom(127,127_1,C,22,0.191)
```

which represents that in compound number 127, atom number 1 (127_1) is a carbon (C), of chemical type coded as 22 in QUANTA with an estimated partial charge of 0.191. Similarly the relation

```
bond(127,127_1,127_6,7)
```

represents that in compound number 127 the bond between atoms 1 and 6 is assigned by QUANTA to be of type 7. The structural background knowledge for the 230 compounds was represented by around 18 300 facts. This approach to generate background knowledge does not require any predefined definition of important substructures. In the first data representation considered (denoted PROGOL I) only the above terms were used.

Representation II (i.e. PROGOL II) augmented representation I by adding the Hansch descriptors of global chemical properties (Log P and LUMO) together with a few definitions of higher-level chemical substructures such as a well-recognized collection of atoms. These substructures were precalculated by simple PROLOG programs that formalized the concepts of methyl group, nitro group, 5- and 6-membered rings, aromatic rings, heteroaromatic rings, connected rings and three forms of connecting three benzene rings. The alternative approach of using the PROLOG code to calculate these substructures during induction is possible but would have been less efficient in computation time.

2.4 Comparison with other SAR algorithms

The results using PROGOL were compared to the original study using linear regression by Debnath et al. (1991) and to neural networks (Villemin et al., 1993). Basic linear regression (denoted REG), linear regression with dependent variables and their squares (REG+) and backpropagation neural networks with three hidden units (NN) were implemented using in-house algorithms to facilitate cross-validation. In addition CART (Breiman et al., 1984) was applied to split the data according to the attributes. The McNemar (1947) test was used to compare two predictions.

3 RESULTS

3.1 Comparison of SAR accuracies

Table 1 gives the results of the different SAR algorithms on the regression-friendly (188 compounds) and regression-unfriendly (42) dataset with and without indicator variables. For the regression-friendly data, PROGOL II yielded state-of-the-art results with no other approach yielding more accurate (at $P < 10\%$ level) predictions. Furthermore without the user-defined indicator variables, PROGOL II was more accurate ($P < 10\%$) than PROGOL I, regression with squares and CART. Not surprisingly on a dataset selected to be amenable to linear regression, this technique and neural networks performed well. In contrast, for the regression-unfriendly data, only PROGOL I, PROGOL II and CART yielded results that were significantly better (2.5%) than the largest class prediction. Thus considering the two datasets as two trials, PROGOL II was statistically better than regression, neural networks or CART in at least one of the trials.

3.2 Chemical insights from PROGOL

On the regression-friendly data, PROGOL I identified five rules to identify if a compound is highly mutagenic (see Figure 3).

Table 1. Comparison of accuracy of SAR methods. Accuracy is defined as (no. of correct predictions)/(no. of incorrect prediction). Results are average from cross-validated trials. REG, REG+, NN, CART, PROGOL I and PROGOL II are linear regression, regression with squares, neural networks, CART and PROGOL with representations I and II. * and ! denote significantly (at 10% and 2.5%) worse than PROGOL II. !$ denotes significantly (2.5%) worse than PROGOL I.

Dataset	Theory	Accuracy	%
		Without indicators	With indicators
188	REG	85.2	89.3
	REG+	83.0*	88.8
	NN	86.2	89.4
	CART	82.5*	88.3
	PROGOL I	81.4!	NA
	PROGOL II	87.8	–
42	REG	66.7!$	66.7!$
	REG+	71.81!$	69.0!$
	NN	64.3!$	69.0!$
	CART	83.3	83.3
	PROGOL I	85.7	–
	PROGOL II	83.3	–

1. It has an aliphatic carbon atom attached by a single bond to a carbon atom which is in a six-membered aromatic ring.
   OR

2. It has a carbon atom in an aryl-aryl bond between two benzene rings with a partial charge ≥ 0.010.
   OR

3. It has a carbon atom that merges six-membered aromatic rings with a partial charge ≤ 0.005.
   OR

4. It has an oxygen atom in a nitro (or related) group with a partial charge ≤ 0.406.
   OR

5. It has a hydrogen atom with a partial charge of 0.146.

The structural interpretation of these rules is given in Figure 2 and provides chemical insight into the mutagenesis process. Rule 1 is a shape-based (steric) indicator in mutagenesis without invoking any electronic effects. Rule 2 is a shape-based feature (from the two rings) combined with the electronic effect of a high partial charge on the aromatic carbon. This electronic effect is consistent with the proposal that electron-withdrawing rings can promote mutagenesis by promoting the initial reduction of a nitro group (Debnath et al., 1991). Rule 3 is an indicator of high hydrophobicity; more hydrophobic rings have low partial charges on the aromatic carbons which overrides the expected electronic effect. Rule 4 identifies a low partial charge on the oxygen that should mediate reduction to the amine. In Rule 5 the positive partial charges of the hydrogens may also indicate the presence of electron withdrawing groups.

The rules learnt by PROGOL using representation II were that a compound is highly mutagenic if

1. It has LUMO ≤ -1.870.
   OR

2. It has LUMO ≤ -1.145 and a five-membered ring.
   OR

3. It has Log $P \geq 4.180$.

These rules are easy to explain and are consistent with the interpretation of Debnath et al. (1991) from their linear regression equations. Rule 1 states that low values of LUMO indicate mutagenicity; rule 2 shows that this effect is modulated by the structural feature of a five-membered ring and rule 3 states that high values of Log P indicate mutagenicity. Of particular importance is that PROGOL automatically identified the requirement for a five-membered ring which is very similar to the Ia indicator variable of Debnath et al. that was derived by expert examination of the data.

On the regression-unfriendly data, the same rule was obtained by PROGOL using representations I and II. The rule states that an indicator for high mutagenicity is a double bond conjugated to a five-membered aromatic ring via a carbon atom. This is a

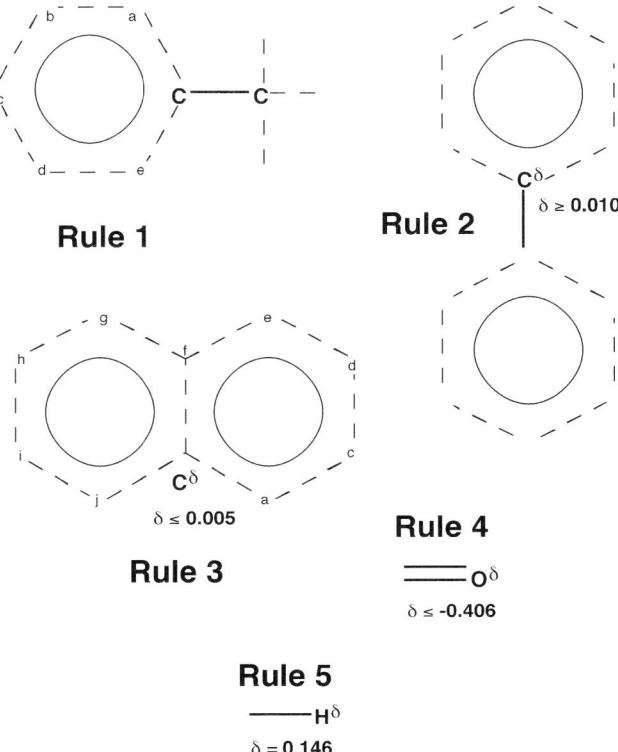

Figure 2. The structural features of the rules obtained by PROGOL using representation I. Lower case letters represent atoms that are not necessarily carbon. Reproduced from (King *et al.*, 1996).

new indicator for carcinogenicty automatically identified by ILP. This rule, which is a better prediction (at the 10% level) above the largest class choice, was not identified by experts who used both inspection and regression.

4 DISCUSSION AND CONCLUSION

The main conclusion of this study is that PROGOL can automatically identify rules to relate chemical structure to activity. Compared to several widely used other methods, these rules are at least comparable in accuracy and sometimes can be shown to be statistically more accurate. In addition to their accuracy, the rules obtained can directly be interpreted chemically providing insight into the problem that is difficult to obtain from several other approaches such as regression and neural networks. An important result of this work is that PROGOL was able to identify a structural rule for regression-unfriendly data that was not seen by domain experts.

335

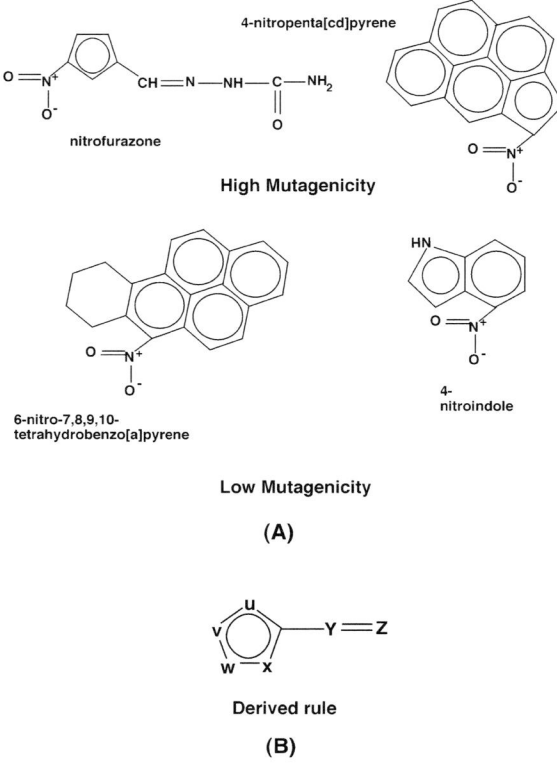

Figure 3. (A) Examples of compounds with high and low mutagenicity in the regression-unfriendly dataset. (B) The PROGOL rule for a substructure defining high mutagenicity. Letters U to Z are not necessarily carbon. Reproduced from (King *et al.*, 1996).

In this study we chose prediction of chemical mutagenicity as a public domain dataset to evaluate a new approach to derive SARs. The methodology can directly be applied to deriving SARs for drug design. This approach should prove particularly useful when one is faced with a diverse set of compounds that are less amenable to the identification of a common pharmacophore substructure onto which substituents are added. Such systems are increasingly being studied with the emphasis in the pharmaceutical industry on screening libraries of diverse chemicals.

The next step in the evaluation of this approach is to perform a blind trial. Drs King and Srinivasan are applying this method to predict the carcinogenicity of 30 chemicals in the second National Institutes of Environmental Health Sciences Predictive Toxicology Evaluation (see http://www.niehs.nih.gov/dirlecm/pte.html). Other groups will be tackling the same data and a comparison of the different approaches can therefore be made.

This study has implications for work on ILP. Drug design is of course a complex real world problem and the challenges of real data provide a spur to the development of better learning engines. Indeed our earlier study on drug design with GOLEM identified problems such as the requirement for nondeterminacy in relations and has been instrumental in the development of PROGOL (King *et al.*, 1992; Hirst *et al.*, 1994a,b). Further studies in the complex areas of both drug design and protein structure (see Sternberg *et al.*, 1994) will further challenge machine learning algorithms.

5 SOFTWARE AVAILABILITY

PROGOL (implemented in either PROLOG or C) and the data used in this study are available for nonprofit academic use by request to Ashwin Srinivasan, Oxford Computing Laboratory, Wolfson Building, Parks Road, Oxford, OX1 3QD, UK (e-mail `Ashwin.Srinivasan.comlab.oxford.ac.uk`).

Acknowledgements

This work was supported by the European Union's Information Technology Program (6020), the Sciences and Engineering Research Council and the Imperial Cancer Research Fund. We thank Professor D Michie for his continuing interest in this project, Dr R Jackson for chemical advice and Dr J Hirst for his neural network program.

REFERENCES

Breiman, L., Friedman, J. H., Olshen, R. A., and C. J. Stone (1984). *Classification and Regression Trees*. Wadsworth, Belmont.

Colman, P. (1994). Structure-based drug design. *Curr. Opin. Struct. Biol.*, 4: 868–874.

Cramer, R. D., Patterson, D. E., and Bunce, J. D. (1988). Comparative molecular field analysis (comfa). 1. Effect of shape on binding of steroids to carrier proteins. *J. Am. Chem. Soc.*, 110: 5959–5967.

Debnath, A. K., de Compadre, R. L. L., Debnath, G., Shusterman, A. J., and Hansch, C. (1991). Structure–activity relationship of mutagenic aromatic and heteroaromatic nitro compounds: correlation with molecular orbital energies and hydrophobicity. *J. Med. Chem.*, 34: 786–797.

Frank, I. E. and Friedman, J. H. (1993). A statistical view of some chemometrics regression tools. *Technometrics*, 35: 109–135.

Gallop, M. A., Barrett, R. W., Dower, W. J., Fodor, S. P., and Gordon, E. M. (1994). Applications of combinatorial technologies to drug discovery (1). Background and peptide combinatorial libraries. *J. Med. Chem.*, 37: 1233–1251.

Gordon, E. M., Barrett, R. W., Dower, W. J., Fodor, S. P., and Gallop, M. A. (1994). Applications of combinatorial technologies to drug discovery (2). Combinatorial organic synthesis, library screening strategies, and future directions. *J. Med. Chem.*, 37: 1385–1401.

Hansch, C., Maloney, P. P., Fujita, T., and Muir, R. M. (1962). Correlation of biological activity of phenoxyacetic acids with Hammett substituent constants and partition coefficients. *Nature*, (194): 178–180.

Hirst, J. D., King, R. D., and Sternberg, M. J. E. (1994a). Quantitative structure–activity relationships: Neural networks and inductive logic programming compared against statistical methods I. The inhibition of dihydrofolate reductase by pyrimidines. *J. Comp. Aided Mol. Design*, 8: 405–420.

Hirst, J. D., King, R. D., and Sternberg, M. J. E. (1994b). Quantitative structure–activity relationships: Neural networks and inductive logic programming compared against statistical methods II. The inhibition of dihydrofolate reductase by triazines. *J. Comp. Aided Mol. Design*, 8: 421–432.

King, R. D., Muggleton, S., Lewis, R. A., and Sternberg, M. J. E. (1992). Drug design by machine learning: the use of inductive logic programming to model the structure–activity relationship of trimethoprim analogues binding to dihydrofolate reductase. *Proc. Nat. Acad. Sci., USA*, 89: 11322–11326.

King, R. D., Muggleton, S., Srinivasan, A., and Sternberg, M. J. E. (1996). Structure–activity relationships derived by machine learning: the use of atoms and their bond connectivities to predict mutagenicity using inductive logic programming. *Proc. Nat. Acad. Sci., USA*, 93: 438–442.

Klopman, G. (1984). Artificial intelligence approach to structure–activity studies. Computer automated structure evaluation of biological activity of organic molecules. *J. Am. Chem. Soc.*, 106: 7315–7321.

Marshall, G. R. and Cramer, R. D. (1988). Three-dimensional structure–activity relationships. *Trends in Pharmacological Sciences*, 9: 285–289.

McNemar, Q. (1947). *Psychometrica 12*. 153–157.

Muggleton, S. (1995). Inverse entailment and Progol. *New Generation Computing*, 13: 245–286.

Ormerod, A., Willet, P., and Bawden, D. (1989). Comparison of fragment weighting schemes for substructural analysis. *Quant. Struct. Act. Relat.*, 8: 115–129.

Ramsden, C. (1990). *Quantitative Drug Design*. Pergamon Press, Oxford.

Sternberg, M. J. E., King, R. D., Lewis, R. A., and Muggleton, S. (1994). Application of machine learning to structural molecular biology. *Phil. Trans. R. Soc. Lond.*, 344: 365–371.

Trinajstic, N. (1983). *Chemical Graph Theory*. CRC Press, Boca Raton, FL.

Villemin, D., Cherqaoui, D., and Cense, J. M. (1993). Neural networks studies: quantitative structure–activity relationship of mutagenic aromatic nitro compounds. *J. Chim. Phys.*, 90: 1505–1519.

CONCURRENT DECLARATIVE PROGRAMMING

19

Debugging for a declarative programming language

J. W. Lloyd

Department of Computer Science,
University of Bristol,
Bristol,
UK

Abstract

This paper investigates debugging in declarative programming languages, concentrating specifically on the integrated functional and logic programming language Escher. The Escher language has types and modules, higher-order and meta-programming facilities, and declarative input/output. It also has a collection of system modules, providing numerous operations on standard data types such as integers, lists, characters, strings, sets, and programs.

After a brief introduction to the Escher language, a framework for declaratively debugging Escher programs is presented and an implementation of this framework is illustrated by an example. The paper concludes with a discussion of the practicalities of declarative debugging and some open problems.

1 INTRODUCTION

One of the substantial advantages of declarative programming languages is the possibility of employing declarative debugging for repairing incorrect programs. Declarative debugging was introduced (under the name algorithmic debugging) in (Shapiro, 1983) and was studied by a number of authors in subsequent years. (A fairly complete bibliography up to 1987 is given by Lloyd (1987).) More recently, there have been several conferences on debugging at which further developments of the declarative approach have been presented.

The basic idea of declarative debugging (at least in the reconstruction by Lloyd (1987) of Shapiro's original framework) is that to debug an incorrect program, all a programmer needs to know is the intended interpretation of the program. In particular, knowledge of the procedural behaviour of the system running the program is unnecessary.

What happens is that the programmer gives a symptom of a bug to the debugger which then proceeds to ask a series of questions about the validity of certain expressions in the intended interpretation, finally presenting an incorrect statement to the programmer. The terminology used is that an *oracle* answers the queries about the intended interpretation. The oracle is typically the programmer, but it could also be a formal specification of the program, or some combination of both. The approach only applies to *incorrect* programs, that is, those for which the intended interpretation is not a model of the program. Thus other kinds of errors such as infinite loops, deadlocks, or flounders have to be handled by more procedural methods. However, the class of errors associated with an incorrect program is certainly the largest such class, so that declarative debugging does address the major aspect of the debugging problem. Thus, overall, declarative debugging is an extremely attractive approach to debugging.

This last claim makes the obvious lack of practical success of declarative debugging something that needs to be explained! In fact, its failure can be largely put down to the non-declarative nature of widely used logic programming languages. My own experience in the mid 1980s suggested strongly that, however attractive declarative debugging may be, it certainly does not work well for Prolog, for example. The main difficulty by far in this regard is handling the non-declarative features of Prolog. Thus, not surprisingly, the major prerequisite for declarative debugging to be successful is to apply it to a (sufficiently) declarative language!

The declarative, general-purpose programming language Escher is such a language. Escher integrates the best features of both functional and logic programming languages. It has types and modules, higher-order and meta-programming facilities, and declarative input/output. Escher also has a collection of system modules, providing numerous operations on standard data types such as integers, lists, characters, strings, sets, and programs. The main design aim is to combine in a practical and comprehensive way the best ideas of existing functional and logic languages, such as Gödel (Hill and Lloyd, 1994), Haskell (Fasel *et al.*, 1992), and λProlog (Nadathur and Miller, 1988). Indeed, Escher goes well beyond Gödel in its ability to allow function definitions, its higher-order facilities, its improved handling of sets, and its declarative input/output. Escher also goes well beyond Haskell in its ability to run partly instantiated predicate calls, a familiar feature of logic programming languages which provides a form of non-determinism, and its more flexible handling of equality.

For general background on integrated functional and logic programming languages, the reader should consult the book by DeGroot and Lindstrom (1986) or the recent survey by Hanus (1994). Also this volume contains a paper on the VESPER language (see Chapter 20 below) which has some remarkable similarities to Escher. A much more comprehensive and detailed discussion of the facilities of Escher, including its module system, its system modules, and its declarative and procedural semantics, than can be given in this paper is contained in (Lloyd, 1995a). A general discussion of the advantages of declarative programming is also given there. Two other papers on Escher are (Lloyd, 1994) and (Lloyd, 1995b).

This paper provides a framework for declarative debugging in Escher. As well as presenting the key concepts and debugging algorithm, I give an example of the use of an implementation of these ideas. One outstanding feature of the Escher debugging framework is its simplicity. Compared with the debugging framework for Prolog-like languages based on SLDNF-resolution given by Lloyd (1987), the framework presented here is much simpler. The main reasons for the simplicity of the Escher framework are the use of equations rather than implicational formulas for statements, the single computation path rather than an (explicit) search tree, and the avoidance here of negation as failure.

The next section gives a brief account of the logic underlying Escher. The third section introduces the key ideas of the Escher language. The fourth section contains a framework for declarative debugging in languages with an Escher-like computational model. The fifth section contains an example session using the debugger given in the fourth section. In the last section, I discuss the practicalities of declarative debugging and give some open problems.

2 TYPE THEORY

In this section, I outline (an extension of) Church's simple theory of types (Church, 1940), which is the logic underlying Escher. In the following, I shall refer to Church's logic as *type theory*. There are several accessible accounts of type theory. For a start, one can read Church's original account (Church, 1940), a more comprehensive account of higher-order logic by Andrews (1986), a more recent account, including a discussion of higher-order unification, by Wolfram (1993), or useful summaries in the many papers (Nadathur, 1987; Nadathur and Miller, 1994; for example) of Miller, Nadathur, and their colleagues, on λProlog. A detailed account of (the extension of) type theory underlying Escher is presented by Lloyd (1995a). For the purposes of this paper, I simply outline now the main concepts of type theory in a few paragraphs, leaving the reader to consult the above accounts if more detail is needed.

First, I assume there is given a set $\mathcal{C}$ of constructors of various arities. Included in $\mathcal{C}$ are the constructors $\mathbf{1}$ and o both of arity 0. The domain corresponding to $\mathbf{1}$ is some canonical singleton set and the domain corresponding to o is the set containing just *True* and *False*. The main purpose of having $\mathbf{1}$ is so that constants can be given types in a uniform way as for functions. The constructor o is the type of propositions. The *types* of the logic are built up in the standard way from the set of constructors and a set of parameters (that is, type variables), using the symbol $\rightarrow$ (for function types) and $\times$ (for product types). Note that the logic is polymorphic, an extension not considered by Church.

The *terms* of type theory are the terms of the typed λ-calculus, which are formed in the usual way by abstraction and application from a given set of functions having types of the form $\alpha \rightarrow \beta$ and a set of variables. A term of type o is called a *formula*. In type theory, one can introduce the usual connectives and quantifiers as functions of appropriate types. Thus the connectives conjunction, $\wedge$, and disjunction, $\vee$, are functions of type $o \times o \rightarrow o$ and the (generalized) existential quantifier, Σ, and universal quantifier, Π, have type $(\alpha \rightarrow o) \rightarrow o$. (The $\rightarrow$ is right associative.) Terms of the form $\Sigma(\lambda x B)$ are written as $\exists x B$ and terms of the form $\Pi(\lambda x B)$ are written as $\forall x B$. In addition, if B is of type o, the abstraction $\lambda x B$ is written as $\{x : B\}$ to emphasize its intended meaning as a set. A set abstraction of the form $\{x : (x = t_1) \vee \ldots \vee (x = t_n)\}$ is abbreviated to $\{t_1, \ldots, t_n\}$. There is also a tuple-forming notation $\langle \ldots \rangle$. Thus, if $t_1, \ldots, t_n$ are terms of type $\tau_1, \ldots, \tau_n$, respectively, then $\langle t_1, \ldots, t_n \rangle$ is a term of type $\tau_1 \times \cdots \times \tau_n$. The term $F(\langle t_1, \ldots, t_n \rangle)$ is abbreviated to $F(t_1, \ldots, t_n)$, where F is a function. Thus, although all functions are unary, one can effectively use the more common syntax of n-ary functions and I sometimes refer to the 'arguments' of a function (rather than the argument). Functions mapping from the domain of type **1** have their argument omitted.

Type theory has an elegant and useful model theory. The key idea, introduced by Henkin (1950) which proved the completeness of type theory, is that of a *general model*. General models are a natural generalization of first-order interpretations. Very sketchily, leaving aside the extension to handle polymorphism, the model theory of type theory is as follows. The domain for a nullary constructor in $\mathcal{C}$ is some set, the domain for a type of the form $\alpha \rightarrow \beta$ is a set of functions mapping from the domain of type α to the domain of type β, and the domain for a type of the form $\alpha \times \beta$ is the cartesian product of the domains of type α and β. A function of type τ is assigned some element of the domain of type τ and the meaning of the connectives and quantifiers is what one would expect. From this, the notions of general model, satisfaction, validity, model of a set of formulas, and so on, can be given in a rather straightforward way. (See, for example, Andrews, 1986; Henkin, 1950; Lloyd, 1995a; or Wolfram, 1993; for the details.) I propose that Henkin's concept of a general model be the appropriate one for capturing the *intended interpretation* of an application.

3 ELEMENTS OF ESCHER

In this section, the most basic features of Escher are outlined. First, some notation needs to be established. Table 1 shows the correspondence between various symbols and expressions of type theory in the left column and their equivalent in the notation of Escher in the right column.

With this notation established, I start with a simple Escher program to illustrate the basic concepts of the language. For this example, I will carry out the design and coding

Table 1.

1	One
o	Boolean
$\neg$	~
$\wedge$	&
$\vee$	\/
$\rightarrow$	->
$\leftarrow$	<-
$\lambda x.E$	LAMBDA [x] E
$\exists x.E$	SOME [x] E
$\forall x.E$	ALL [x] E
$\{x : E\}$	{x : E}
$\in$	IN

phases of the software engineering life-cycle in some detail by first giving the intended interpretation of the application and then writing down the program.

The application is concerned with some simple list processing. There are two basic types, Person, the type of people, and Day, the type of days of the week. In addition, lists of items of such types will be needed. The appropriate constructors are declared as follows.

```
CONSTRUCT Day/0, Person/0, List/1.
```

The CONSTRUCT declaration simply declares Day and Person to be constructors of arity 0 and List to be a constructor of arity 1. (In addition, the constructors One and Boolean of arity 0 are provided automatically by the system via the system module Booleans.) Thus, for this application, typical types are Boolean, Day, List(Day), List(List(Person)), and (List(List (a) * List (a)) $-$ > Day) $-$ > Boolean, where a is a parameter. In the intended interpretation for this application, the domain corresponding to the type List(Day), for example, is the set of all lists of days of the week.

The declarations of the functions for people, days, and list construction are as follows.

```
FUNCTION Nil : One -> List(a);
         Cons : a * List(a) -> List(a);
         Mon, Tue, Wed, Thu, Fri, Sat, Sun : One -> Day;
         Mary, Bill, Joe, Fred : One -> Person.
```

Each component of the FUNCTION declaration gives the signature of some function. There are only two categories of symbols which a programmer can declare – constructors and functions. Thus what are normally called constants are regarded here as functions which map from the domain of type One and predicates are regarded as functions which map into the domain of type Boolean. This uniform treatment facilitates the synthesis of the functional and logic programming concepts. Note that every function must have a $\rightarrow$ at the top-level of its signature.

Functions are either *free* or *defined*. For the current application, the free functions are Nil, Cons, Mon, and so on, appearing in the above FUNCTION declaration. This means that, by default, the 'definition' for each of these functions is essentially the corresponding Clark equality theory of syntactic identity. So, for example, the formulas

```
Cons (x, y) ~= Nil
```

and

```
Cons(x, y) = Cons(u, v) → (x = u) & (y = v)
```

are included in this theory.

345

J. W. LLOYD

On the other hand, defined functions have explicit definitions and take on the equality theory given by their definitions. For the application at hand, there are three defined functions with the following signatures.

```
FUNCTION Perm : List(a) * List(a) -> Boolean;
         Concat : List(a) *  List(a) -> List(a);
         Split : List(a) * List(a) * List(a) -> Boolean.
```

The intended meaning of these functions is as follows. Perm maps <s,t> to True if s and t are lists such that s is a permutation of t; otherwise, Perm maps <s,t> to False. Given lists s and t, Concat maps <s,t> to the list obtained by concatenating s and t (in this order). Given lists r, s, and t, Split maps <r,s,t> to True if r is the result of concatenating s and t (in this order); otherwise, Split maps <r,s,t> to False.

At this point, the intended interpretation has been defined and I can now turn to writing the program. This consists of the above declarations, plus some definitions (and mode declarations) for the defined functions Perm, Concat, and Split, and is given in the module Permute below. The module declaration beginning with the keyword MODULE simply gives the name of the module. Note that Perm is a function from the product type List(a) * List(a) to the type Boolean and advantage has been taken of the convention mentioned earlier to write the head of the first statement as Perm(Nil,1) instead of Perm(<Nil,1>).

A *definition* of a function consists of one or more equations, which are called *statements*. The symbol ⇒ appearing in statements is simply equality, but I have made it into an arrow to indicate the directionality of the rewrite corresponding to the statement (explained below) and also to give a visual clue to indicate the head and body of a statement. In general, statements have the form

$h \Rightarrow b.$

Here the *head h* is a term of the form

$F(t_1, \ldots, t_n)$

where F is a function, each t_i is a term, and the *body b* is a term. Note carefully

```
MODULE      Permute.
CONSTRUCT   Day/0, Person/0, List/1.
FUNCTION    Nil:    One -> List(a);
            Cons :   a * List(a) -> List(a);
            Mon, Tue, Wed, Thu, Fri, Sat, Sun: One -> Day;
            Mary, Bill, Joe, Fred : One -> Person.
FUNCTION    Perm : List(a)  List(a) -> Boolean.
MODE        Perm(NONVAR, _).
Perm(Nil,  1) =>
    1 = Nil.
Perm(Cons(h,t), 1) =>
```

```
      SOME [u,v,r] (Perm(t,r) & Split(r,u,v) &
                    1 = Concat(u, Cons(h,v))).

FUNCTION Concat : List(a) * List(a) -> List(a).
MODE       Concat(NONVAR, _).
Concat(Nil,x) =>
    x.
Concat(Cons(u,x),y) =>
    Cons(u,Concat(x,y)).

FUNCTION Split : List(a) * List(a) * List(a) -> Boolean.
MODE       Split(NONVAR, _, _).
Split(Nil,x,y) =>
    x = Nil &
    Y = Nil.
Split(Cons(x,y),v,w) =>
    (v = Nil & w = Cons(x,y)) \/
    SOME [z] (v = Cons(x,z) & Split(y,z,w)).
```

that there is no implicit completion (in the sense of Clark) for predicate definitions in Escher; the theory that is intended is exactly the one that appears in the program (augmented by the default equality theory for the free functions).

Naturally, it must be checked that the intended interpretation is a model of the theory given by the program. For module `Permute`, this involves checking that each of the statements in the definitions is valid in the intended interpretation given above. The details of this are left to the reader. Leaving aside control issues, this completes the design and coding phases for this simple application. Assuming that the process of checking that the intended interpretation is a model of the program has been carried out correctly, the programmer can now be sure that the program is correct (that is, satisfies the specification given by the intended interpretation).

Mode declarations begin with the keyword `MODE`. In general, mode declarations restrict the possible calls that can be made to a function. For the `Perm` function, the `NONVAR` in the first argument of the mode declaration means that a call can only proceed if its first argument is a pattern. (A *pattern* is a term that has a free function at the top level.) The underscore in the second argument indicates that there is no restriction on that argument. A mode declaration for which each argument is an underscore may be dropped.

There are some syntactic restrictions on the form statements may take.

1. Arguments in the head of a statement corresponding to underscores in the mode declaration must be variables.

2. All local variables in a statement must be explicitly quantified.

3. Statements must be pairwise non-overlapping.

347

The first restriction comes about because the head of a statement should be at least as general as a redex and an argument in a redex corresponding to an underscore in a mode declaration can be a variable. A *local variable* is a variable appearing in the body of a statement but not the head. The second restriction concerning local variables is largely a matter of taste since it would be possible to have a default giving the same effect. However, I think it is far preferable to explicitly give the quantification of the local variables.

Two (standardized apart) statements, $h_1 \Rightarrow b_1$ and $h_2 \Rightarrow b_2$, are *non-overlapping* if, whenever there exists a substitution θ such that $h_1\theta$ and $h_2\theta$ are identical, we have that $b_1\theta$ and $b_2\theta$ are identical (where in both cases the (syntactic) identity is modulo renaming of bound variables). The restriction that statements must be pairwise non-overlapping means that if two or more statements match a redex then it doesn't matter which of them is used – the result will be the same. This condition implies the confluence of the rewrite system associated with an Escher program.

Now I turn to a discussion of function calls (which I simplify somewhat for the sake of the exposition – the details are in (Lloyd, 1995a)). A redex is a subterm of the form $F(t_1, \ldots, t_n)$, for some defined function F, which satisfies the mode declaration for F. Escher selects the leftmost redex in the current term on which to make the call. In a function call, a statement is viewed as a rewrite which behaves as follows. A statement $h \Rightarrow b$ matches a redex r if there is a substitution θ such that $h\theta$ is identical to r (modulo renaming of bound variables). In this case, the redex r in the current term is replaced by $b\theta$ to give the next term in the computation and this defines the rewrite given by the statement.

The Escher mode system provides several important facilities. First, for functions appearing in the export parts of modules, mode declarations show explicitly how the functions are meant to be called. Second, if a subterm satisfies the mode declaration for a function (and is therefore a redex), then either a statement in the definition of the function matches the redex or else a control error is generated. The compiler can do much to help avoid this kind of control error. For example, if an argument in a mode declaration is NONVAR, then the compiler can check there is a statement in the definition for each possible choice of free function at the top level in that argument.

Here are some typical goals and their answers for the program consisting of the modules Permute and Booleans. (Every module implicitly imports the system module Booleans.) For these goals, it's convenient to use the usual notational sugar for lists provided by Escher via the Lists system module, so that Nil is written as [], Cons(s,t) is written as [s|t], and Cons(s,Cons(t,Nil)) is written as [s,t]. The goal

Concat([Mon, Tue], [Wed])

reduces to the answer

[Mon, Tue, Wed].

The goal

Split([Mon, Tue], x, y)

reduces to the answer

```
(X = [] & y = [Mon, Tue]) \/
(x = [Mon] & y = [Tue])    \/
(x = [Mon, Tue] & y = []).
```

The goal

```
~ Split([Mon, Tue], [Tue], y)
```

reduces to the answer

```
True.
```

Finally, the goal

```
Perm([Mon, Tue, Wed], x)
```

reduces to the answer

```
x  =  [Mon,  Tue,  Wed] \/
x  =  [Tue,  Mon,  Wed] \/
x  =  [Tue,  Wed,  Mon] \/
x  =  [Mon,  Wed,  Tue] \/
x  =  [Wed,  Mon,  Tue] \/
x  =  [Wed,  Tue,  Mon].
```

How does Escher compute these answers? The first point is that Escher doesn't have a 'theorem proving' computational model like the majority of logic programming languages. Instead it has a 'rewriting' computational model, in which a goal term is reduced to an equivalent term, which is then given as the answer. Formally, if s is the goal term and t is the answer term, then s = t is valid in the intended interpretation. So, the first goal above, Concat([Mon, Tue], [Wed]), is reduced by a sequence of rewrites to the term [Mon, Tue, Wed], by means of the computation given in Figure 1 below. The computation consists of the successive terms produced by function calls, the first term being the goal and the last the answer. The second and third terms in the computation are obtained by using the second statement in the definition of Concat, while the fourth term,

```
Concat([Mon, Tue], [Wed])
            ⇓
[Mon | Concat([Tue], [Wed])]
            ⇓
[Mon, Tue | Concat([], [Wed])]
            ⇓
    [Mon, Tue, Wed]
```

Figure 1. An Escher computation.

which is the answer, is obtained by using the first statement in the definition of `Concat`. In each term, the redex is underlined. The other three goals for the module `Permute` require the use of statements for the functions =, ~, and \/ in the module `Booleans`.

Ultimately, a programmer is interested in computing the values of expressions in the intended interpretation. How does Escher assist in this? Since Escher has no direct knowledge of the intended interpretation, it cannot evaluate any term in the intended interpretation. However, given a term, it can *simplify* (that is, reduce) the term, so that the evaluation in the intended interpretation can then be easily done by the programmer. This is evident in the above computation – the term `Concat([Mon, Tue], [Wed])` is simplified to `[Mon, Tue, Wed]` which can be easily evaluated. Strictly speaking, this view is also appropriate for arithmetic terms. For example, given the term 3 + 4, Escher will reply with the term 7. Formally, it hasn't evaluated 3 + 4, but instead simplified it to 7. In this case, the distinction between simplification and evaluation is a bit pedantic. But, in general, it's important to keep in mind this understanding of what Escher is doing.

The reduction process terminates when a term is reached which contains no redexes. This final term, the answer, is then in *normal form*. Typically, an answer may contain some defined functions, such as =, &, or \/, which are declared in system modules, and some free functions, such as `Cons` or `Nil`. However, if the answer contains a user-declared defined function, an error has occurred in the sense that a (potential) redex containing a user-declared defined function at the top level has never become sufficiently instantiated for its mode declaration to be satisfied. This kind of programming error is called a *flounder*.

Note that there is no *explicit* concept of non-determinism in Escher. Instead, non-determinism is captured implicitly with disjunction. Furthermore, computations return 'all answers' and never fail. In Escher, the equivalent of a failure in a conventional logic programming language is to return the answer `False`. For example, for the program consisting of the modules `Permute` and `Booleans`, the goal

```
Concat([Mon], [Tue]) = [Tue]
```

reduces to the answer

```
False.
```

4 PRINCIPLES OF DECLARATIVE DEBUGGING

In this section, I give the theoretical underpinnings of declarative debugging for languages with an Escher-like computational model. Throughout the remainder of this paper, a 'program' will mean an Escher program.

Definition 1 *Let P be a program and I the intended interpretation for P. Then P is incorrect if I is not a model for P. A statement in P is incorrect if it is not valid in I.*

If a program is incorrect, then some statement in the program is incorrect. The task of (declarative) debugging is to take an incorrect program and locate an incorrect statement in the program. The basic algorithm for achieving this was introduced by Shapiro (1983) and is called *divide-and-query*. To understand how divide-and-query works, consider a typical computation in Figure 2. In this computation, t_1 is the goal, t_n is the answer, and $h_i \Rightarrow b_i$ is a statement used in a function call in the term t_i with associated substitution θ_i. Now suppose the computation is buggy. This will show up because of a bug symptom, which is formalized as follows.

Definition 2   *Let C be a computation with goal t_1 and answer t_n. Then C is incorrect if $t_1 = t_n$ is not valid in the intended interpretation.*

Informally, divide-and-query proceeds as follows. Consider the computation with goal t_1 and answer t_n. Having confirmed with the oracle that the computation is indeed incorrect, the debugging algorithm then chooses the term $t_{\lfloor(n+1)/2\rfloor}$ at the midpoint of the computation and asks the oracle whether $t_1 = t_{\lfloor(n+1)/2\rfloor}$ is valid (in the intended interpretation). If the answer is no, the algorithm discards the bottom half of the computation and continues with the segment from t_1 to $t_{\lfloor(n+1)/2\rfloor}$. If the answer is yes, then the algorithm discards the top half of the computation and continues with the segment from $t_{\lfloor(n+1)/2\rfloor}$ to t_n. Eventually, this process ends with the identification of an incorrect statement. The number of oracle queries required is logarithmic in the length of the computation.

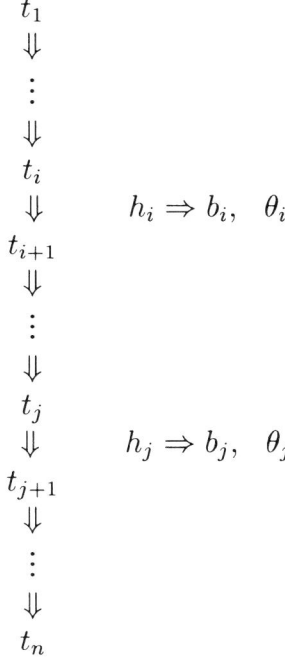

Figure 2. A computation.

351

There are several important optimizations of this basic algorithm. The first is to exploit the fact that statements in system modules are correct. Hence the algorithm can ignore steps in the computation which use statements from a system module. This leads to the definition of the following concept.

Definition 3   *Let C be a computation with goal t_1. The* debugging trace *is the subsequence of the computation formed from t_1 together with all terms t_i in the computation which resulted from the (direct) use of a statement from a user module.*

In the debugging trace in Figure 3 below, t_1 is the goal and t'_{i+1} is the term which resulted from the function call using the (user) statement $h'_i \Rightarrow b'_i$ with associated substitution θ'_i.

From this point onwards, I deal with debugging traces rather than computations. Here is a preliminary version of the debugging algorithm.

Debugging algorithm (preliminary version)

Input: The debugging trace $t_1, \ldots, t_m$ from an incorrect computation.
Output: An incorrect statement.

begin
    $i := 1$;
    $j := m$;
    while $i + 1 < j$ **do**
    begin
        if $t_i = t_{\lfloor (i+j)/2 \rfloor}$ is valid in the intended interpretation
        then $i := \lfloor (i + j)/2 \rfloor$
        else $j := \lfloor (i + j)/2 \rfloor$
    end;
    incorrect_statement := the statement used to derive t_j
end

In fact, the algorithm can also return an instance of a statement which is not valid in the intended interpretation (the instance of the incorrect statement given by the substitution used at that step).

$$
\begin{array}{ll}
t_1 & \\
t'_2 & (h'_1 \Rightarrow b'_1, \quad \theta'_1) \\
t'_3 & (h'_2 \Rightarrow b'_2, \quad \theta'_2) \\
\vdots & \vdots \\
t'_{m+1} & (h'_m \Rightarrow b'_m, \quad \theta'_m)
\end{array}
$$

Figure 3. A debugging trace.

The next optimization concerns the form of queries presented to the oracle. Often terms in a computation can be large and complex. Hence, in the case when the oracle is the programmer, some effort must be put into making oracle queries as simple as possible. One obvious idea is to exploit the fact that the programmer will surely know the denotation in the intended interpretation of the goal t_1 and that it is possible to replace the query about $t_i = t_{\lfloor (i+j)/2 \rfloor}$ with one about $t_1 = t_{\lfloor (i+j)/2 \rfloor}$. This idea cuts the complexity of oracle queries dramatically. The last optimization is to simplify the term $t_{\lfloor (i+j)/2 \rfloor}$ using only statements in system modules before presenting it to the oracle. This often reduces the complexity of oracle queries as well. With these optimizations, I now give the final form of the debugging algorithm.

Debugging algorithm

Input: The debugging trace $t_1, \ldots, t_m$ from an incorrect computation.
Output: An incorrect statement.

begin
    $i := 1$;
    $j := m$;
    while $i + 1 < j$ **do**
    begin
        $F :=$ simplified form of $t_{\lfloor (i+j)/2 \rfloor}$;
        if $t_1 = F$ is valid in the intended interpretation
        then $i := \lfloor (i + j)/2 \rfloor$
        else $j := \lfloor (i + j)/2 \rfloor$
    end;
    incorrect_statement := the statement used to derive t_j
end

This algorithm has some important properties which are easily established.
Theorem Under the assumption that the oracle is perfect, the debugging algorithm has the following properties.

1. It always terminates.

2. It is sound and complete (that is, a statement returned by the algorithm is incorrect; and, if the debugging trace comes from an incorrect computation, the algorithm will return an incorrect statement).

3. If there are m terms in the debugging trace of the computation, then the number of oracle queries required is bounded by $\lceil log_2 m \rceil$.

It is worth noting that the context in which the divide-and-query algorithm is applied in this paper is different to, and rather more general than, the context in (Shapiro, 1983). Essentially, in (Shapiro, 1983), the algorithm is applied to the computation tree of a refutation of a definite goal for a definite program where the refutation gives a wrong answer. The algorithm picks a node (an atom) in this tree which has about half the weight of the entire tree and, depending on the oracle answer, either discards the subtree rooted at this node or else enters it and applies the algorithm recursively. Furthermore, for missing answers, a different algorithm is used which involves the oracle giving values for variables to make atoms valid. The presence of negative literals and SLDNF-resolution introduce further complications which are accounted for by Lloyd (1987).

In the Escher context, the divide-and-query algorithm is applied uniformly to an entire computation irrespective of whether it has a 'wrong' or 'missing' answer and irrespective of the presence of negation or quantifiers. Furthermore, the oracle only ever has to answer *yes/no* queries and never needs to supply values for variables. As can be seen from this section, the theoretical framework which results from applying the divide-and-query algorithm to the Escher computational model is considerably simpler than the corresponding frameworks for SLDNF-resolution in (Shapiro, 1983) and (Lloyd, 1987). On the other hand, the simplicity and uniformity of the Escher approach can lead to rather large and complex oracle queries being posed which may be difficult to answer. I return to this issue in the last section.

5 DEBUGGING EXAMPLE

As an illustration of the use of the debugging algorithm, consider the module Eratosthenes below.

```
MODULE    Eratosthenes.

IMPORT    Integers, Lists.

FUNCTION Primes : Integer * List(Integer) -> Boolean.
MODE      Primes(NONVAR, _).
Primes(limit, ps) =>
    SOME [is] (Range(2, limit, is) & Sift(is, ps)).

FUNCTION Range : Integer * Integer * List(Integer) -> Boolean.
MODE      Range(NONVAR, NONVAR, _).
Range(low, high, l) =>
    IF low =< high
    THEN
      SOME [rest] (Range(low + 1, high, rest) & l = [low | rest])
    ELSE
      l = [].

FUNCTION Sift : List(Integer) * List(Integer) -> Boolean.
MODE      Sift(NONVAR, _).
Sift([], l) =>
    l =  [].
Sift([i | is], l) =>
    SOME [new, ps] (Remove(i, is, new) & Sift(new, ps) &
                                    l = [i | ps]).
```

```
FUNCTION Remove : Integer * List(Integer) * List(Integer) ->
                  Boolean.
MODE      Remove(NONVAR, NONVAR, _).
Remove(x, [], l) =>
    l = [].
Remove(x, [i | is], l) =>
    SOME [new] (Remove(x, is, new) &
                IF i Mod x = 0
                THEN
                   l = [i | new]      % should be l = new
                ELSE
                   l = new).          % should be l = [i | new]
```

This is intended to compute the list of prime numbers up to some given number. However, there is a bug in the last statement where the THEN and ELSE parts of a conditional have been interchanged. As a result, the goal

```
Primes(5, x)
```

reduces incorrectly to the answer

```
x = [2, 4].
```

Here then is the listing of a session using the debugger to locate the incorrect statement. The n or y after a colon is an oracle answer, where y indicates that the equation is valid in the intended interpretation and n indicates that it is not.

```
Debug("Eratosthenes", "Primes(5, x)").

Primes(5, x)
 =
x = [2, 4] ?
|: n

Primes(5, x)
 =
SOME [new_7, ps_7] ((Remove(2, [3, 4, 5], new_7) &
          (Sift(new_7, ps_7) & (x = [2 | ps_7])))) ?
|: y

Primes(5, x)
 =
SOME [new_7, ps_7] ((SOME [new_9]
  ((Remove(2, [], new_9) & (new_7 = [4 | new_9]))) &
          (Sift(new_7, ps_7) & (x = [2 | ps_7])))) ?
|: n
```

355

```
Primes(5, x)
 =
SOME [new_7, ps_7] ((Remove(2, [4, 5], new_7) &
          (Sift(new_7, ps_7) & (x  =  [2 | ps_7]))))  ?
|: n
```

Incorrect statement instance:

```
Remove(2, [3, 4, 5], new_7) =>
    SOME [new_8] ((Remove(2, [4, 5], new_8) &
                  (IF ((3 Mod 2) = 0)
                    THEN (new_7 = [3 | new_8])
                    ELSE (new_7 = new_8))))
```

Corresponding statement:

```
Remove(x, [i | is], l) =>
    SOME [new] ((Remove(x, is, new) &
                  (IF ((i Mod x) =  0)
                    THEN (l = [i | new])
                    ELSE (l = new))))
```

6 DISCUSSION

Unfortunately, to build a practical debugging system, much more needs to be done than simply implement the algorithm of Section 4. The problem is that, while a programmer may, *in principle*, know the intended interpretation, he or she may not be able, *in practice*, to answer an oracle query, simply because a term in the query may be very large and/or complex. Actually, this problem is not unique to declarative debugging – every debugging method suffers from it. However, in declarative debugging, there is certainly a lot at stake when an oracle query is answered, as giving the wrong answer is likely to lead the debugger astray. Thus, in this section, I discuss some of the issues, none of which are conceptually difficult, that need to be addressed to build a practical declarative debugger.

The main difficulties are centred around the 'presentation' problem, which is concerned with finding ways of presenting potentially large and complex oracle queries in such a way that the programmer is likely to be able to answer correctly. I now discuss various aspects of the presentation problem.

The first is that one of the terms in the query may be very large. If the query concerns the equation $s = t$, where s is the goal, then typically it will be t that is large. This is probably the most troublesome aspect of the presentation problem. One possibility is for the programmer to head the problem off altogether by finding a 'small' goal for which the bug manifests itself. This is good debugging practice anyway. Failing this, the debugger can attempt to break the query up into smaller subqueries, the answers to which can answer the whole query. A typical case where this can be useful is when t is a disjunction of a large number of subformulas. This occurs in Escher programs which correspond to logic programs involving a great deal of search.

To see what can be done, suppose the query concerns validity of the equation

$$s = t_1 \vee t_2 \vee \ldots \vee t_n$$

where s is the goal. The debugger can break this up into a series of queries concerning the validity of the implications

$$s \leftarrow t_1$$
$$s \leftarrow t_2$$
$$\vdots$$
$$s \leftarrow t_n.$$

If any one of these implications is not valid, then the original equation is not valid either. If all these implications are valid, then the validity of the original equation reduces to that of the validity of the implication

$$s \rightarrow t_1 \vee t_2 \vee \ldots \vee t_n$$

which can then be put to the oracle.

As a simple example of this, consider the equation

$$P(x) = ((x = A) \vee (x = B) \vee (x = C))$$

Then the series of queries concerning the validity of

$$P(x) \leftarrow (x = A)$$
$$P(x) \leftarrow (x = B)$$
$$P(x) \leftarrow (x = C)$$

is checking that the 'answers' $x = A$, $x = B$, and $x = C$ are all correct. The query concerning the validity of

$$P(x) \leftarrow (x = A) \vee (x = B) \vee (x = C)$$

is checking that the 'answers' given are complete.

The next issue concerns the use of abstract data types (ADTs). The problem here is that a subterm in the query may involve functions hidden inside an ADT (in the local part of a system module, say). Since there is no way of directly displaying such a term, the query in which it appears cannot even be properly (directly) presented. The solution to this kind of problem is rather straightforward: for each system ADT, a method has to be implemented for displaying in a suitable format terms of that type to the user. For user ADTs, the language can provide a suitable mechanism for allowing a programmer to specify how a hidden term should be displayed. A typical situation where such a problem arises is for meta-programming. Here the object program is represented by its ground representation via the ADT `Program`, which uses functions entirely hidden from the programmer. In such a case, the difficulty is overcome by displaying the object program in source form, which the programmer will certainly understand.

One useful technique which a debugger can employ is to build up a partial knowledge of the intended interpretation from the programmer's answers to oracle queries, so that it can avoid repeating queries. Typically, a large program is developed over a period of time, so one can easily imagine the debugger recording answers to oracle queries to build a more and more complete picture of the intended interpretation. If this idea is going to be practical, the debugger must also easily allow a programmer to update this partial intended interpretation, either because the programmer realized afterwards that an answer to an oracle query was wrong or because the data structures, and hence the constructors and functions, employed by the program somehow changed.

Finally, I emphasize again that declarative programming can only cope with programs that have some declarative error (that is, are not correct) and hence one needs other techniques to deal with procedural errors, such as infinite loops, deadlocks, and flounders.

REFERENCES

Andrews, P. (1986). *An Introduction to Mathematical Logic and Type Theory: To Truth Through Proof*. Academic Press.

Church, A. (1940). A formulation of the simple theory of types. *Journal of Symbolic Logic*, 5: 56–68.

DeGroot, D. and Lindstrom, G., eds. (1986). *Logic Programming: Relations, Functions and Equations*. Prentice-Hall.

Fasel, J., Hudak, P., Peyton Jones, S., and Wadler, P. (1992). Special issue on the functional programming language Haskell. *ACM SIGPLAN Notices*, 27(5).

Hanus, M. (1994). The integration of functions into logic programming: From theory to practice. *Journal of Logic Programming*, 19 and 20: 583–628.

Henkin, L. (1950). Completeness in the theory of types. *Journal of Symbolic Logic*, 15(2): 81–91.

Hill, P. and Lloyd, J. (1994). *The Gödel Programming Language*. MIT Press. Logic Programming Series.

Lloyd, J. (1987). *Foundations of Logic Programming*. Springer-Verlag, second edition.

Lloyd, J. (1994). Combining functional and logic programming languages. In *Proceedings of the 1994 International Logic Programming Symposium, ILPS'94*, pp. 43–57. MIT Press.

Lloyd, J. (1995a). Declarative programming in Escher. Technical Report CSTR-95-013, Department of Computer Science, University of Bristol. Also available at http://www.cs.bris.ac.uk/.

Lloyd, J. (1995b). Programming in an integrated functional and logic language. *Journal of Functional and Logic Programming*, 1. To appear.

Nadathur, G. (1987). *A Higher-Order Logic as the Basis for Logic Programming*. PhD thesis, University of Pennsylvania.

Nadathur, G. and Miller, D. (1988). An overview of λProlog. In Kowalski, R. and Bowen, K., eds. *Proceedings of the Fifth International Conference and Symposium on Logic Programming*, Seattle, pp. 810–827. MIT Press.

Nadathur, G. and Miller, D. (1994). Higher-order logic programming. Technical Report CS-1994-38, Department of Computer Science, Duke University. To appear in D. Gabbay, C. Hogger, and J. A. Robinson, eds., *The Handbook of Logic in Artificial Intelligence and Logic Programming*, Oxford University Press.

Shapiro, E. Y. (1983). *Algorithmic Program Debugging*. MIT Press.

Wolfram, D. (1993). *The Clausal Theory of Types*. Cambridge University Press.

20

Vesper

J. Alan Robinson

Syracuse University

Jonas Barklund

Uppsala University

1 INTRODUCTION

VESPER[1] is a denotational formalism, that is, a collection of expressions each of which denotes some entity. Its logic, when viewed at the topmost level, is given by a single simplification function. The simplification is vertically extended in the sense that in a single act of simplification an expression and (simultaneously) all or most of its sub-expressions are recast into a simpler form. All VESPER computations are *reductions to normal form*, in which the simplification function is iterated on a given expression until it has no further effect. Expressions are by definition in normal form if they are fixed points of the simplification function.

VESPER was designed as a tool for exploring two ideas:

1. the idea that functional computing (based on the lambda-calculus) and relational computing (based on Horn clause resolution) are essentially the same thing, namely logical simplification;

2. the idea that such logical simplifications can admit extensive parallelism.

There seems to be no absolute notion of parallel computation, at least in the case of simplification. The simultaneous application of several different simplification functions to (different subexpressions of) an expression can always (trivially) be viewed instead (as we do here) as the application of a single more complex function to the entire expression. This *vertically extended* simplification will (if the expression is not in normal form)

---

[1] VESPER stands for Vertically Extended Simplification Parallel Expression Reduction, the computational logic described in this paper.

produce an expression which differs from it in several places, but that fact alone does not disqualify these differences from being regarded collectively as those arising from a single, distributed step.[2]

Intuitively, the simplification function decomposes an expression into its immediate constituents, simplifies these, and reassembles the resulting expressions into a perhaps different syntactic pattern.

When the expression to be simplified is an atomic symbol for which a user-declared definition is in force, the symbol is replaced by the definiens of the definition. However, such defined symbols are rewritten only at the top level of an expression, and never when they are subexpressions of some other expression which is being simplified. The reason for this exception is that, without it, the iteration of the simplification function would be free to 'explode' in a runaway unfolding of recursive definitions, thus consuming all available resources.

2 UNDERLYING MODEL OF A VESPER MACHINE AS AN ARMY OF COOPERATING IDENTICAL AUTOMATA

Our purpose in this account is to state the vertically extended simplification logic of VESPER in an implementation-neutral way. However, we do have in mind a parallel implementation, in which the expressions are (represented as) directed graphs. Each node in the graph is (represented by) an active processor of identical design. Each processor has its own unique address, and represents an expression by virtue of the information currently in its various registers. This information records whether the expression is a conjunction, disjunction, set abstraction, etc., and gives the addresses of the other processors which represent its immediate subexpressions. It is possible for such a nodal processor both to read from and to write into the registers of other processors whose addresses it has in its own memory. Hard-wired inside each processor is a copy of the algorithm for applying VESPER's simplification function, and the processor repeatedly applies this function to the expression that it represents, by changing the information in its registers so as to represent the new expression resulting from the simplification. Since all processors are active in this way all the time, the desired effect of simultaneous application of all local transformations is obtained. In general, the action of a nodal processor may call for new expressions to be formed, in which case the necessary new nodes are represented by processors freshly allocated from a heap. The processor heap is replenished continuously by returning to it the processors whose expressions are no longer subexpressions of the expression being collectively represented by the [unique] root of the graph.

---

[2]The familiar instantiation operation of simultaneously substituting n terms $t_1, \ldots, t_n$ respectively for n variables $x_1, \ldots, x_n$ throughout an expression E is an obvious example of this. We can regard it either as one single 'large' global operation performed on E by a 'many-armed' agent, or as n distinct 'small' local operations performed on E by n 'one-armed' agents working concurrently. Even substituting one term for one variable throughout E already poses the issue if there are many occurrences of the variable in E. Substituting the term for each occurrence of the variable throughout E could itself be considered as the simultaneous (parallel) replacement of each occurrence of the variable x in E by an occurrence of the term t.

To realize this implementation in practice involves several difficult issues, which we will not discuss further here. The following account is strictly concerned with the calculus and its logic, and does not deal with any implementational problems.

3 THE LANGUAGE

VESPER is an applied, typeless, combined lambda-calculus and predicate-calculus. It has several familiar built-in or defined notions in addition to lambda abstraction and existential quantification: equality, numerals and numerical operators, lists, tuples, set abstractions, set itemizations, union expressions, boolean expressions, and conditional expressions.

Expressions are either atomic or composite. *Atomic expressions* are either constants, or abbreviations, or variables.

- *Constants* are either internal, or external. In addition, they may also be declared to be *Herbrand constants* (see below).

  - *Internal constants* are:

$$\text{AND} \quad \text{OR} \quad \text{NOT} \quad \text{NULL} \quad \text{SET} \quad \cup \quad \in \quad \subseteq$$
$$\bullet \quad = \quad + \quad - \quad * \quad / \quad < \quad >$$

    and the numerals. The internal constant $\bullet$ is a Herbrand constant.

  - *External constants* are atomic expressions which are declared to be such by the user.

  All constants denote different entities; the numerals denote numbers[3] and the other internal constants denote certain functions identified below.

- *Abbreviations* are atomic expressions which are distinct from the constants and which have been declared to be such. To declare an atomic expression α to be an abbreviation one asserts a *definition*: $\alpha =_{\text{def}} \beta$, where β is an expression different from α. The symbol α is then regarded as simply 'short for' the expression β (the *definiens* of the definition).

- *Variables* are atomic symbols which are neither constants nor abbreviations. Variables may be free or bound.

A *composite expression* is either a binding expression, or an application.

- *Binding expressions.* These are expressions of one of the three forms

$$(\lambda\ V\ B), \quad (\exists\ V\ B), \quad \{V \mid B\}.$$

---

[3] We will identify the natural numbers with certain indexing functions; cf. below.

The first is a *lambda abstraction*, the second is an *existential quantification*, and the third is a *set abstraction* (it is read: the set of all V such that B). Each binding-expression has a bound-variable-list V, which is a list of distinct variables, and a body B, which is an expression.

- An *application* is a nonempty list of expressions. Its *operator* is the first expression in the list, and the list of its *operands* is the rest of the list. For example, the operator might be a defined constant, or a composite expression.

  - The constants AND, OR and NOT denote the usual conjunction, disjunction and negation functions. The application of AND to no argument denotes truth, similarly for OR and falsity. In order to please the eye and the mind we often use the 'sugared' forms TRUE, FALSE for (AND), (OR) respectively.

  - Herbrand constants denote functions such that applications of two Herbrand constants denote the same entity if, and only if, the constants are the same, they both have the same number of operands and for each pair of corresponding operands, the two expressions denote the same entity.

    An occurrence of an expression α in an application β of a Herbrand constant is a *Herbrand occurrence* if α is an operand of β, or is a Herbrand occurrence in an operand of β.

  - *Tuplings* are applications of the Herbrand constant •. We can write the tupling (• $\alpha_1 \ldots \alpha_n$) in a sugared form as $\langle \alpha_1 \ldots \alpha_n \rangle$. [] is sugared writing for the empty tupling.

    An application of a natural numeral i to a tupling $\langle \alpha_1 \ldots \alpha_n \rangle$, where $0 \leq i < n$, denotes the same value as α_{i+1}. HEAD and TAIL are sugared forms of 0 and 1, respectively.

    Dotted pairs are the binary special case of tuplings, i.e., applications of the form (• α β). There is a very useful convention from traditional LISP that a nest of dotted pairs

    $$(\bullet \ \alpha_1 \ (\bullet \ \alpha_2 \ \ldots \ (\bullet \ \alpha_n \ \beta) \ \ldots)),$$

    where $n \geq 1$, can be sugared, using square brackets, as a 'dotted listing' as follows:

    $$[\alpha_1 \ \alpha_2 \ \ldots \ \alpha_n \ \bullet \ \beta]$$

    with a very special case when β is the empty listing [], namely, the nonempty listing:

    $$[\alpha_1 \ \alpha_2 \ \ldots \ \alpha_n \ \bullet \ []] \ = \ [\alpha_1 \ \alpha_2 \ \ldots \ \alpha_n].$$

    In computations (such as Example 6, below) the listings are written unsugared to reveal the actual applicative structure on which the logic of the computation depends.

  - *Set itemizations* are applications of the constant SET. The constant SET denotes a function such that (SET $\alpha_1 \ \ldots \ \alpha_k$) is the set consisting of the entities denoted by

$\alpha_1, \ldots, \alpha_k$. We can write a set itemization (SET $\alpha_1 \ldots \alpha_k$) in sugared form as $\{\alpha_1 \ldots \alpha_k\}$. A special case is the empty set itemization $\{\}$. SET is clearly not a Herbrand constant: (SET 1 2), (SET 1 1 2 1 2 2) and (SET 2 1) all denote the same entity.

The constant $\cup$ denotes a function such that an application $(\cup\ \alpha_1 \ldots \alpha_k)$ denotes the set which is the union of the sets denoted by $\alpha_1, \ldots, \alpha_k$. The constants $\in$ and $\subseteq$ denote the usual set membership and subset relations.

– A *conditional* is an application of the constant IF to three arguments. The constant IF denotes a function such that (IF α β γ) is equal to β if α is true and it is equal to γ if α is false.

– A *conjunction* is an application of AND; a *disjunction* is an application of OR, a *union* is an application of $\cup$, and a *negation* is an application of NOT.

Types, equality and inequality

We can partition the denotable values into five *types*: numbers, truth values, sets, functions and other values. Two expressions denoting values of different types thus cannot denote the same value.

- Numerals, and applications of the internal constants +, −, ∗ and /, denote numbers.
- Existential quantifications, and applications of the internal constants AND, OR, NOT, =, <, >, $\in$ and $\subseteq$, denote truth values.
- Set abstractions, and applications of the internal constants SET and $\cup$, denote sets.
- Lambda abstractions, and all internal constants except numerals, denote functions.
- External constants, and applications of Herbrand constants, denote other values.

An equality $(=\ \alpha\ \beta)$ is true if α and β denote the same entity and false if they do not.

Obviousness

The somewhat elusive notion of *obviousness* is partially formalized by the following sufficient conditions for concluding respectively that two expressions obviously do, or obviously do not, denote the same entity.

Two expressions α and β *obviously denote the same entity* if one of the following holds:

- α and β are identical atomic expressions;
- α and β are set itemizations, and for each operand γ of the one there is an operand δ of the other such that γ and δ obviously denote the same entity.

Two expressions α and β *obviously denote different entities* if one of the following holds:

- α and β are known to denote values of different types;
- α and β are distinct constants;

- one of α and β is a constant and the other is an application of a Herbrand constant;
- α and β are applications of different Herbrand constants;
- α and β are applications of the same Herbrand constants but with different number of operands;
- one of α and β is (AND) and the other is (OR);
- α and β are set itemizations and one of them has an operand γ such that for all operands δ of the other, γ and δ obviously denote different entities;
- one of α and β has a Herbrand occurrence in the other.

Computation

There is a function `simplify`, which when applied to an expression yields an expression that is semantically equivalent to it (that is, denotes the same entity). If (`simplify` e) is exactly the same expression as e, then e is said to be in normal form.

A sequence of $n \geq 1$ expressions

$$e_1, \cdots, e_n,$$

which contains at most one expression in normal form, and for which

$$e_{i+1} = (\text{simplify } e_i), \quad 1 \leq i < n,$$

is a VESPER computation. A computation which does not contain an expression in normal form is either finite and unfinished, or infinite, while a computation which contains an expression in normal form is necessarily finite, and finished, with that expression as its last component. Finished computations may be thought of as having 'evaluated' all the expressions in the sequence, their common value being the entity denoted by each of them. The point of the computation is that its final expression denotes this common value in as obvious a way as possible. The final expression in a computation sequence is said to be *the normal form of* every expression in the sequence. Expressions in infinite computation sequences have no normal form.

Thus, the user's view of the system need only be through the function `normalform`, whose value for an expression e is the normal form of e, if e has one, and which is undefined otherwise.

The function `simplify` has been designed with the intention of yielding, in this iterative manner, normal forms which are indeed maximally perspicuous. It formalizes the notion of 'one computation step'. Its details contain few surprises, and the presentation given here is meant to appeal straightforwardly to the reader's computational intuitions and to capture the processes of traditional functional programming within applied lambda-calculi. What may be novel about the present approach is the way in which the processes of Horn clause logic programming are also captured within the calculus, and how easily these merge with, and emerge from, the lambda-calculus ideas.

LOGLISP, SUPER and VESPER

VESPER is the third in a series of experiments aimed at exploring the problem of unifying the functional and relational styles of logic programming.

The first experiment, LOGLISP (Robinson and Sibert, 1982), was a relatively crude attempt to link a functional system with a relational system while keeping their separate identities intact. Although some useful applications were made of the resulting hybrid, the conceptual foundation was unduly complex and unnatural.

Reflection on the shortcomings of the dualist LOGLISP approach provided the basis for the second experiment, in which the unified SUPER system (Robinson, 1987) was formulated. The main idea of SUPER was to capture the logic common to both functional and relational programming within a single set of rewrite rules and then to make reduction to normal form the paradigm for all of logic programming. The potential for parallel computation was noted but not further pursued.

VESPER is a much more fully worked-out version of SUPER, with particular emphasis placed on making completely explicit the logic of parallel reduction. Just as SUPER provided relational programming by exploiting Clark's 'completion' idea (Clark, 1978) so also in VESPER the user can define relations as lambda abstractions whose bodies are disjunctions of existentially quantified conjunctions. It will be recalled that Clark's idea was to take such definitions as alternative characterizations of relations, obtaining them as translations of corresponding sets of Horn clauses. However, there is no need to begin with Horn clauses, since one can easily and naturally express one's specifications of relations directly in this way, using the lambda notation. Once one has declared definitions of one or more relations in the VESPER style, one may then evaluate 'queries' by formulating them as set-abstraction expressions (or, in a different style, as lambda-abstraction expressions) and then computing their normal forms.

The reader will easily see how further redex-patterns and corresponding small simplification transformations can be added to the VESPER logic, by adding further cases to simplify in the obvious manner.

We were pleased to discover that essentially the same ideas have been independently developed by John Lloyd, as indeed he describes in the present volume (Chapter 19 above) and elsewhere (Lloyd, 1995). Such a confluence of separate investigations tends to confirm one's sense of the naturalness and inevitability of the present approach.

4 THE FUNCTIONS SIMPLIFY AND SUBSIMPLIFY

Notation. The two functions simplify and subsimplify differ only in their behavior on abbreviations and non-redexes. The function subsimplify intuitively describes the lower-level simplifications which take place when simplification is extended vertically downwards into the substructure of an expression.

In writing the equations which define simplify and subsimplify we employ a few notational conventions.

- We use lowercase Greek letters, with subscripts if needed, to denote expressions.

- We use upper case Greek letters, with subscripts if needed, to denote (possibly empty) sequences of expressions. Concatenation of such sequences is denoted by juxtaposition. A sequence consisting of a single expression is considered to be the same as that expression.

- We write $\mathcal{S}\alpha$, $\mathcal{SS}\alpha$, to denote the expression obtained by applying `simplify`, `subsimplify`, respectively, to the expression α. To save writing, whenever *both* of two equations of the form $\mathcal{S}\alpha = \beta$ and $\mathcal{SS}\alpha = \beta$ hold, we write just the single equation: $\mathcal{B}\alpha = \beta$.

- If Γ is a (possibly empty) sequence of expressions, then we write $\mathcal{S}\,\Gamma$ or $\mathcal{SS}\,\Gamma$ to denote the sequence obtained by applying `simplify` or `subsimplify` to each expression in Γ.

- By $(\equiv \alpha\ \beta)$ we denote either of the equations $(= \alpha\ \beta)$, $(= \beta\ \alpha)$.

The function `simplify` is then given by the following equations. Each equation is given a mnemonic label to facilitate later discussion.

variable-or-constant:
> $\mathcal{B}\alpha = \alpha$
> if α is an atomic expression which is not an abbreviation.

abbreviation:
> $\mathcal{S}\alpha = \beta,$
> $\mathcal{SS}\alpha = \alpha,$
> if α is an occurrence of an abbreviation for which the definition $\alpha =_{\text{def}} \beta$ has been declared.

member-true:
> $\mathcal{B}\,(\in \alpha\ \{\Gamma\}) = (\text{AND}),$
> where α obviously denotes the same entity as some expression in Γ.

member-false:
> $\mathcal{B}\,(\in \alpha\ \{\Gamma\}) = (\text{OR}),$
> where α obviously does not denote the same entity as any expression in Γ.

subset-true:
> $\mathcal{B}\,(\subseteq \{\Gamma\}\ \{\Delta\}) = (\text{AND}),$
> where each expression of Γ obviously denotes the same entity as some expression in Δ.

subset-false:
> $\mathcal{B}\,(\subseteq \{\Gamma\}\ \{\Delta\}) = (\text{OR}),$
> where some expression in Γ obviously does not denote the same entity as any expression in Δ.

equate-obviously-same:
> $\mathcal{B}\,(= \alpha\ \beta) = (\text{AND}),$
> where α and β obviously denote the same entity.

equate-obviously-different:
> $\mathcal{B}\,(= \alpha\ \beta) = (\text{OR}),$
> where α and β obviously denote different entities.

367

or-true:

$$\mathcal{B}\,(\text{OR}\ \Gamma\ (\text{AND})\ \Delta) = (\text{AND}).$$

not-not:

$$\mathcal{B}\,(\text{NOT}\ (\text{NOT}\ \alpha)) = \mathcal{SS}\,\alpha.$$

unit-and:

$$\mathcal{B}\,(\text{AND}\ \alpha) = \mathcal{SS}\,\alpha.$$

unit-or:

$$\mathcal{B}\,(\text{OR}\ \alpha) = \mathcal{SS}\,\alpha.$$

unit-union:

$$\mathcal{B}\,(\cup\,\alpha) = \mathcal{SS}\,\alpha.$$

if-true:

$$\mathcal{B}\,(\text{IF}\ (\text{AND})\ \beta\ \gamma) = \mathcal{SS}\,\beta.$$

if-false:

$$\mathcal{B}\,(\text{IF}\ (\text{OR})\ \beta\ \gamma) = \mathcal{SS}\,\gamma.$$

if-neither:

$$\mathcal{B}\,(\text{IF}\ \alpha\ \beta\ \gamma) = (\text{IF}\ \mathcal{SS}\,\alpha\ \beta\ \gamma),$$

where α is neither (AND) nor (OR). Note that the tactic here is 'lazy', that is, simplification of neither the true arm nor the false arm of a conditional expression is begun, even if the expression is on the surface, until its boolean part has been normalized to either (AND) or (OR), and then only the relevant arm is selected. It would certainly be logically acceptable to allow 'eager' or 'speculative' simplification of both true- and false-arms to take place in parallel with that of the boolean part – a tactic which, however, may result in excessive consumption of resources.

numeric-redex:

$$\mathcal{B}\,(\delta\ \mu_1\ \dots\ \mu_k) = \mu,$$

where

- δ is either +, -, *, /, < or >;

- $\mu_1\ \dots\ \mu_k$ are numerals;

- and μ is the numeral or truth value which denotes the result of applying the corresponding operation to the corresponding numbers.

and-and:

$$\mathcal{B}\,(\text{AND}\ \Gamma_1\ (\text{AND}\ \Delta_1)\ \dots\ \Gamma_n\ (\text{AND}\ \Delta_n)\ \Gamma_{n+1}) =$$
$$(\text{AND}\ \mathcal{SS}\,\Gamma_1\ \mathcal{SS}\,\Delta_1\ \dots\ \mathcal{SS}\,\Gamma_n\ \mathcal{SS}\,\Delta_n\ \mathcal{SS}\,\Gamma_{n+1}),$$

where the sequence $\Gamma_1\ \dots\ \Gamma_n\ \Gamma_{n+1}$ does not contain the expression (OR), or any conjunctions.

or-or:

$$\mathcal{B}\,(\text{OR}\ \Gamma_1\ (\text{OR}\ \Delta_1)\ \dots\ \Gamma_n\ (\text{OR}\ \Delta_n)\ \Gamma_{n+1}) =$$
$$(\text{OR}\ \mathcal{SS}\,\Gamma_1\ \mathcal{SS}\,\Delta_1\ \dots\ \mathcal{SS}\,\Gamma_n\ \mathcal{SS}\,\Delta_n\ \mathcal{SS}\,\Gamma_{n+1}),$$

where the sequence $\Gamma_1 \ldots \Gamma_n \Gamma_{n+1}$ does not contain the expression (AND), or any disjunctions.

union-union:

$\mathcal{S} (\cup \Gamma_1 (\cup \Delta_1) \ldots \Gamma_n (\cup \Delta_n) \Gamma_{n+1}) =$
$(\cup \, \mathcal{SS} \, \Gamma_1 \, \mathcal{SS} \, \Delta_1 \ldots \mathcal{SS} \, \Gamma_n \, \mathcal{SS} \, \Delta_n \, \mathcal{SS} \, \Gamma_{n+1}),$

where the sequence $\Gamma_1 \ldots \Gamma_n \Gamma_{n+1}$ contains no set itemizations and no unions.

exists-exists:

$\mathcal{B} (\exists (\Phi) (\exists (\Psi) \beta)) = (\exists (\Phi \; \Psi) \; \mathcal{SS} \, \beta).$

exists-vacuous:

$\mathcal{B} (\exists (\Phi) \; \beta) = \mathcal{SS} \, \beta,$

where Φ is empty or none of the variables in Φ are free in β.

and-exists:

$\mathcal{B} (\text{AND } \Gamma_1 (\exists (\Phi_1) \; \beta_1) \ldots \Gamma_n (\exists (\Phi_n) \; \beta_n) \; \Gamma_{n+1}) =$
$(\exists (\Psi_1 \ldots \Psi_n) (\text{AND } \mathcal{SS} \, \Gamma_1 \; \mathcal{SS} \, \gamma_1 \ldots \mathcal{SS} \, \Gamma_n \; \mathcal{SS} \, \gamma_n \; \mathcal{SS} \, \Gamma_{n+1})),$

where $(\exists (\Psi_i) \; \gamma_i)$ is a variant of $(\exists (\Phi_i) \; \beta_i)$, $1 \leq i \leq n$, and the sequence $\Gamma_1 \ldots \Gamma_n \Gamma_{n+1}$ contains no conjunctions or disjunctions.

and-or:

$\mathcal{B} (\text{AND } \Gamma_1 (\text{OR } \Delta_1) \ldots \Gamma_n (\text{OR } \Delta_n) \; \Gamma_{n+1}) =$
$(\text{OR } (\text{AND } \mathcal{SS} \, \Pi_1) \ldots (\text{AND } \mathcal{SS} \, \Pi_r)),$

where $\Pi_1, \ldots, \Pi_r$ are all of the different sequences of the form $\Gamma_1 \, \delta_1 \ldots \Gamma_n \, \delta_n \, \Gamma_{n+1}$, in which δ_i is an expression in the sequence Δ_i, $1 \leq i \leq n$, and the sequence $\Gamma_1 \ldots \Gamma_n \Gamma_{n+1}$ contains no conjunctions, disjunctions or quantifications.

union-sets:

$\mathcal{B} (\cup \Gamma_1 \{\Delta_1\} \ldots \Gamma_n \{\Delta_n\} \Gamma_{n+1}) =$
$(\cup \{\mathcal{SS} \, \Delta_1 \ldots \mathcal{SS} \, \Delta_n\} \, \mathcal{SS} \, \Gamma_1 \ldots \mathcal{SS} \, \Gamma_n \, \mathcal{SS} \, \Gamma_{n+1}),$

where the sequence $\Gamma_1 \ldots \Gamma_n \Gamma_{n+1}$ contains no set itemizations.

solved-setof:

$\mathcal{B} \{<x_1 \ldots x_n> \mid (\text{AND } (\equiv x_1 \; \alpha_1) \ldots (\equiv x_n \; \alpha_n))\} =$
$\{<\mathcal{SS} \, \alpha_1 \ldots \mathcal{SS} \, \alpha_n>\}.$

setof-or:

$\mathcal{B} \{V \mid (\text{OR } \alpha_1 \ldots \alpha_n)\} = (\cup \{V \mid \mathcal{SS} \, \alpha_1\} \ldots \{V \mid \mathcal{SS} \, \alpha_n\}).$

thin-set-itemization:

$\mathcal{B} \{\Gamma\} = \mathcal{SS} \{\Gamma'\},$

where Γ contains two expressions α, β that obviously denote the same entity and Γ' is Γ with one of α, β removed.

selection:

$\mathcal{B} (i <\alpha_1 \ldots \alpha_n>) = \mathcal{SS} \, \alpha_{i+1},$

where i is a natural numeral, $0 \leq i < n$.

equate-Herbrand-applications:

$$\mathcal{B} (= \ (\alpha_0 \ \alpha_1 \ \ldots \ \alpha_n) \ (\beta_0 \ \beta_1 \ \ldots \ \beta_n)) =$$
$$(\text{AND} \ (= \mathcal{SS} \ \alpha_1 \ \mathcal{SS} \ \beta_1) \ \ldots \ (= \mathcal{SS} \ \alpha_n \ \mathcal{SS} \ \beta_n)),$$

where α_0 and β_0 are the same Herbrand constant.

exists-or:

$$\mathcal{B} (\exists \ (\Phi) \ (\text{OR} \ \alpha_1 \ \ldots \ \alpha_n)) =$$
$$(\text{OR} \ (\exists \ (\Phi) \ \mathcal{SS}\alpha_1) \ \ldots \ (\exists \ (\Phi) \ \mathcal{SS} \ \alpha_n)).$$

exists-and-equation:

$$\mathcal{B} (\exists \ (\Phi) \ (\text{AND} \ \Gamma \ (\equiv x \ \alpha) \ \Delta)) = (\exists \ (\Psi) \ (\text{AND} \ \mathcal{SS} \ \Gamma \ \mathcal{SS} \ \Delta) \ \theta),$$

where

- x is a variable in the sequence Φ;

- x does not occur in α;

- Γ does not contain an equation $(\equiv \ y \ \beta)$ where y is a variable in the sequence Φ;

- $\theta = \{\alpha/x\}$;

- and Ψ is Φ with x omitted.

beta-redex:

$$\mathcal{B} ((\lambda \ (x_1 \ \ldots \ x_n) \ \beta) \ \alpha_1 \ \ldots \ \alpha_n) = \beta' \{\mathcal{SS} \ \alpha_1/x_1, \ldots, \mathcal{SS} \ \alpha_n/x_n\},$$
where $\beta' = \mathcal{SS} \ \beta$.

An expression to which none of the preceding equations applies may nevertheless be simplifiable, but only at lower [syntactic] levels ('interior') and not at the top [syntactic] level ('surface'). The following equations cover the possible cases that arise. The principle followed is the same in all cases, namely, the simplification or subsimplification is merely applied to the immediate subexpressions:

simplify-interior:

$$\mathcal{S}(\Gamma) = (\mathcal{S} \ \Gamma) \text{ if } (\Gamma) \text{ is an application.}$$
$$\mathcal{SS} \ (\Gamma) = (\mathcal{SS} \ \Gamma) \text{ if } (\Gamma) \text{ is an application.}$$
$$\mathcal{S}(\exists \ V \ \beta) = (\exists \ V \ \mathcal{S}\beta).$$
$$\mathcal{SS}(\exists \ V \ \beta) = (\exists \ V \ \mathcal{SS} \ \beta).$$
$$\mathcal{S}(\lambda \ V \ \beta) = (\lambda \ V \ \mathcal{S}\beta).$$
$$\mathcal{SS}(\lambda \ V \ \beta) = (\lambda \ V \ \mathcal{SS}\beta).$$
$$\mathcal{S}\{V \mid \beta\} = \{V \mid \mathcal{S}\beta\}.$$
$$\mathcal{SS}\{V \mid \beta\} = \{V \mid \mathcal{SS}\beta\}.$$

For example, the application

$$(+ \ (* \ 3 \ 4) \ (* \ 4 \ 5))$$

is not simplifiable at the top level, and so we have:

$$\mathcal{S} (+ \ (* \ 3 \ 4) \ (* \ 4 \ 5)) = (\mathcal{S} \ + \ \mathcal{S} (* \ 3 \ 4) \ \mathcal{S} \ (* \ 4 \ 5)) = (+ \ 12 \ 20).$$

5 PARALLEL EXPRESSION REWRITING

It is helpful as a general (but not strictly truthful) description of VESPER's simplification function to say that it gives the result of the intuitive process of *simultaneously rewriting all subexpressions of an expression*. In fact, it gives the result of simultaneously rewriting *almost* all of the subexpressions. The ones which are *not* rewritten fall into two categories.

The most obvious departure from complete simultaneous rewriting concerns the replacement of an abbreviation by its definiens. In VESPER the replacement occurs *only if the abbreviation is not a proper subexpression of an expression which is simplifiable at the top level*.

The reason for this is to avoid the otherwise computationally intolerable situation in which a recursive definition (or a set of two or more mutually recursive definitions) would be 'unfolded' at each simplification step. This would result in a rapid rate of growth in the size of successive expressions in the computation.

Another departure from complete rewriting (already remarked on) involves the true and false alternatives of a conditional. Conditionals are simplified 'lazily'. Only when their boolean guards have been reduced to (AND) or (OR) is one (and, then, only one) of their alternatives exposed to the simplification process. Both alternatives of a conditional, and all of their subexpressions, are thus left untouched until the conditional is decided.

The reason for this is to avoid committing one's finite resources 'eagerly' to the simplification of alternatives which are destined *not* to be selected. The price paid for this cautious strategy is of course that the alternatives which *will* be selected are made to wait for their simplification until their conditionals are decided. The more that time is of the essence, the more worthwhile it might be to risk running out of resources by getting a running start on simplifying the alternatives, concurrently with the process of reducing the guard to normal form. In some fortunate cases, indeed, the selected alternative will already be reduced to normal form by the time the conditional is decided. The 'lazy' strategy adopted in VESPER guarantees that this will never happen except in cases where the selected alternative is in normal form to begin with.

6 FURTHER EXAMPLES

Example 1   If p is a variable, the simplification of the expression

$$\text{(AND (OR FALSE p) (> 5 7) TRUE (= 4 6) TRUE)}$$

is found by applying these equations recursively. In order to make the details clearer we desugar TRUE and FALSE to (AND) and (OR) respectively:

$\mathcal{S}$ (AND (OR (OR) p) (> 5 7) (AND) (= 4 6) AND))
    = (AND $\mathcal{S}$ (OR (OR) p) $\mathcal{S}$(> 5 7) $\mathcal{S}$(= 4 6)) **and-and**
    = (AND (OR $\mathcal{S}$ p) (OR) (OR))   **or-or,**
                                                       numeric-redex
    = (AND (OR p) (OR) (OR))   **atom.**

Example 2 If a, b, c, d, e, and f are variables, then

$$\begin{aligned}
&\mathcal{S}\text{(AND a (OR b c) d e (OR (> 5 7) (< 3 4)) f)} \\
&= \text{(OR (AND a b d e } \mathcal{S}\text{(> 5 7) f)} \quad \textbf{and-or} \\
&\qquad\quad \text{(AND a b d e } \mathcal{S}\text{(< 3 4) f)} \\
&\qquad\quad \text{(AND a c d e } \mathcal{S}\text{(> 5 7) f)} \\
&\qquad\quad \text{(AND a c d e } \mathcal{S}\text{(< 3 4) f))} \\
&= \text{(OR (AND a b d e (OR) f)} \qquad \textbf{numeric-redex} \times 4 \\
&\qquad\quad \text{(AND a b d e (AND) f)} \\
&\qquad\quad \text{(AND a c d e (OR) f)} \\
&\qquad\quad \text{(AND a c d e (AND) f)).}
\end{aligned}$$

Example 3 The following expression fits the **exists-and-equation** case. So we have:

$$\begin{aligned}
&\mathcal{S}(\exists \text{ (x y z) (AND (A x y z) (= x 4) (B x y z) (= y (C x))))} \\
&= (\exists\text{(y z) (AND } \mathcal{S} \text{ (A 4 y z) } \mathcal{S} \text{ (B 4 y z) } \mathcal{S} \text{ (= y (C 4))))} \\
&= (\exists\text{(y z) (AND } (\mathcal{S}\text{A } \mathcal{S}4 \ \mathcal{S}\text{y } \mathcal{S}\text{z)} \\
&\qquad\qquad\qquad\quad (\mathcal{S}\text{B } \mathcal{S}4 \ \mathcal{S}\text{y } \mathcal{S}\text{z)} \\
&\qquad\qquad\qquad\quad (\mathcal{S} = \mathcal{S}\text{y } \mathcal{S} \text{ (C 4))))} \\
&= (\exists\text{(y z) (AND (A 4 y z) (B 4 y z) (= y } (\mathcal{S}\text{C } \mathcal{S}4))))} \\
&= (\exists\text{(y z) (AND (A 4 y z) (B 4 y z) (= y (C 4))))}
\end{aligned}$$

This expression again fits the **exists-and-equation** case. So another round of simplification can begin:

$$\begin{aligned}
&\mathcal{S} \text{ (}\exists \text{ (y z) (AND (A 4 y z) (B 4 y z) (= y (C 4))))} \\
&= (\exists \text{ (z) (AND } \mathcal{S} \text{ (A 4 (C 4) z) } \mathcal{S} \text{ (B 4 (C 4) z)))} \\
&= (\exists \text{ (z) (AND } (\mathcal{S}\text{A } \mathcal{S}4 \ \mathcal{S}\text{(C 4) } \mathcal{S} \text{ z) } (\mathcal{S}\text{B } \mathcal{S}4 \ \mathcal{S}\text{(C 4) } \mathcal{S}\text{z)))} \\
&= (\exists \text{ (z) (AND (A 4 } (\mathcal{S}\text{C } \mathcal{S}4) \text{ z) (B 4 } (\mathcal{S}\text{C } \mathcal{S}4) \text{ z)))} \\
&= (\exists \text{ (z) (AND (A 4 (C 4) z) (B 4 (C 4) z)))}
\end{aligned}$$

yielding an expression in normal form.

The **exists-and-equations** case is one of three simplification cases which cooperate with each other, so to speak, to perform unification computations. The other two are **equate-Herbrand-applications** and **equate-obviously-different**.

Example 4 **Unification.** If P, G, H and K have been declared by the user to be external constants and at least P has been declared to be a Herbrand constant, then the expression

```
(∃ (x y z u v w r s a b t)
        (AND (= (P x y u) (P (G r s) r s))
             (= (P y z v) (P a (H a b) b))
             (= (P x v w) (P (G r s) r s))
             (= (P u z w) (P (K t) t (K t)))
             (x-becomes x)
             (y-becomes y)
             (z-becomes z)
             (u-becomes u)
             (v-becomes v)
             (w-becomes w)
             (r-becomes r)
             (s-becomes s)
             (a-becomes a)
             (b-becomes b)
             (t-becomes t))).
```

asserts in effect that there is a substitution for the bound variables which will simultaneously unify the left- and right-sides of each of the four equations. The normal form of the sentence is obtained by iteration of the **exists-and-equation** case:

```
(∃ (v) (AND (x-becomes (G v (K (H v v))))
            (y-becomes v)
            (z-becomes (H v v))
            (u-becomes (K (H v v)))
            (v-becomes v)
            (w-becomes (K (H v v)))
            (r-becomes v)
            (s-becomes (K (H v v)))
            (b-becomes v)
            (t-becomes (H v v)))).
```

When rewritten in parallel, this computation of unification is similar to a parallel unification algorithm based on rewriting of equalities (Barklund, 1990) and it might be possible to incorporate other parts of that algorithm as well.

Example 5 The Fibonacci function in a functional style. The classic Fibonacci program serves to illustrate programming in the functional style, using a conditional expression:

$FIB =_{def}$
    (λ (n) (FIB-ITER 1 1 n))

$FIB-ITER =_{def}$
    (λ (a b n) (IF (= n 1) a (FIB-ITER b (+ a b) (- n 1))))

The rewriting of an application (FIB n) proceeds just as in an ordinary functional programming language.

Example 6   A logic programming query. We now use the definition of APPEND given earlier to work through an illustration of how a simple logic programming query is handled in this logic. We wish to compute the set of all pairs <x y> such that (APPEND x y (• 1 (• 2 []))) is true. This set is denoted by the set-abstraction expression:

{<x y> |(APPEND x y (• 1 (• 2 [])))}.

and therefore we normalize this expression. Its normal form is:

{<[] (• 1 (• 2 [])))> <(• 1 []) (• 2 [])> <(• 1 (• 2[])) []>},

a set itemization expression giving all such pairs explicitly. The first few expressions in the computation are:

1. The original expression:

{<x y> | (APPEND x y (• 1 (• 2 [])))}

2. The first simplification is to replace the abbreviation APPEND by its definiens, yielding:

```
{<x y>  |  ((λ (a b c)
              (OR (∃ (x) (AND (= a [])
                              (= b x)
                              (= c x)))
                  (∃ (x y v w) (AND (= a (• x y))
                                    (= b v)
                                    (= c (• x w))
                                    (APPEND y v w)))))
      x y (• 1 (• 2 [])))}
```

3. Next, the **beta-redex** is replaced, and further within it there are two cases of **exist-and-equation**, resulting in quantifier eliminations.

```
{<x y>  |  (OR (AND (= x []) (= y (• 1 (• 2 []))))
               (∃ (x0 x1 x3) (AND (= x (• x0 x1))
```

```
                            (= (• 1 (• 2 [])))
                               (• x0 x3))
                            (APPEND x1 y x3)))))}
```

4. This expression is a case of **setof-or**, with an internal **equate-Herbrand-applications**,

```
(∪ {<x y> | (AND (= x []) (= y (• 1 (• 2 []))))}
   {<x y> | (∃ (x0 x1 x3)
                (AND (= x (• x0 x1))
                     (AND (= 1 x0) (= (• 2 []) x3))
                     (APPEND x1 y x3)))})
```

5. The first component of the union is a **solved-setof**, and within the second there is an **and-and**.

```
(∪ {<[] (• 1 (• 2 []))>}
   {<x y> | (∃ (x0 x1 x3)
                (AND (= x (• x0 x1))
                     (= 1 x0)
                     (= (• 2 []) x3)
                     (APPEND x1 y x3)))})
```

6. An **exists-and-equation** within the second component of the union.

```
(∪ {<[] (• 1 (• 2 []))>}
   {<x y> | (∃ (x0 x1)
                (AND (= x (• x0 x1))
                     (= 1 x0)
                     (APPEND x1 y (• 2 []))))})
```

7. And another.

```
(∪ {<[] (• 1 (• 2 []))>}
   {<x y> | (∃ (x1) (AND (= x (• 1 x1))
                          (APPEND x1 y (• 2 []))))})
```

8. Now the abbreviation APPEND is an outermost redex, so it is eligible for unfolding.

```
(∪ {<[] (• 1 (• 2 []))>}
   {<x y> | (∃ (x1)
                (AND (= x (• 1 x1))
                     ((λ (a b c)
                        (OR (∃ (x) (AND (= a [])
                                         (= b x)
                                         (= c x)))
```

```
(∃ (x y v w)
    (AND (= a (• x y))
         (= b v)
         (= c (• x w))
         (APPEND y v w)))))
x1 y (• 2 [])))))})
```

By now the first solution has appeared, and the development continues in a similar manner for a total of 23 simplification steps.

7 CONCLUSIONS AND FUTURE WORK

The vertically extended simplification approach described here provides a simple, sound and intuitive basis for a massively parallel computational logic which formalizes the merging of the functional and relational programming styles.

Except for (1) the 'lazy' treatment of conditionals and (2) the 'surface only' treatment of abbreviations, VESPER exploits every logically permissible opportunity for parallel computation. In this sense it comes close to the maximum possible degree of parallelism. Neither (1) nor (2) is logically necessary, but only pragmatically so, and there is plenty of scope for further investigation as to how much 'speculative' eagerness can be tolerated in relaxing (1), and how much recursive unfolding of definitions might be allowed in a more permissive version of (2).

While this discussion has been largely confined to logical and linguistic issues, the implementation issues are extremely interesting and deserve a separate investigation. As was mentioned briefly, our present view is that the VESPER logic would most naturally be embodied in the collective behaviour of a large[4] body of small identical processors, each playing the role of a node in a graphical representation of expressions, and each capable of recognizing and acting on the appropriate case of simplification corresponding to its current state.

A preliminary look at some of the problems of designing such an implementation has persuaded us that the next step in the VESPER project should be to study this cellular automaton model in detail.

Meanwhile, to run the examples given in this paper, and for general exploration purposes, we have written (in Common Lisp) a usefully fast implementation of the functions simplify, subsimplify, and normalform.

Acknowledgments

This work was partly supported by Göran Gustafssons Stiftelse and Swedish Research Council for Engineering Sciences (TFR) under grants 93:38 and 94-939, respectively.

[4]The number of processors required to represent an expression is approximately the same as the number of nodes in its parse tree. If suitable advantage is taken of 'sharing' (for example, the several occurrences of a bound variable can be pointers to a single processor representing that variable) the total number of processors need not be as large as this. A VESPER machine with, say, a million processors would be quite useful.

376

REFERENCES

Barklund, J. (1990). *Parallel Unification*. PhD thesis, Comp. Sci. Dept., Uppsala Univ., Uppsala.

Clark, K. L. (1978). Negation as failure. In Gallaire, H. and Minker, J., eds., *Logic and Data Bases*, pp. 293–322. Plenum Press, New York.

Lloyd, J. W. (1995). Declarative programming in Escher. Technical Report CSTR-95-013, Dept. of Computer Science, Univ. of Bristol.

Robinson, J. A. (1987). Beyond LOGLISP: Combining functional and relational programming in a reduction setting. In Hayes, J. E., Michie, D., and Richards, J., eds., *Machine Intelligence 11*, pp. 57–68. Ellis Horwood, Chichester.

Robinson, J. A. and Sibert, E. E. (1982). LOGLISP: Motivation, design and implementation. In Clark, K. L. and Tärnlund, S.-Å., eds., *Logic Programming*, pp. 299–313. Academic Press, London.

HISTORY OF COMPUTING

21

The Turing–Wilkinson lecture series on the Automatic Computing Engine*

edited by B. Jack Copeland

The Turing Project,
University of Canterbury,
Christchurch,
New Zealand
e-mail: bjcopeland@canterbury.ac.nz

Abstract

On 1 October 1945 Turing was appointed to the newly-formed Mathematics Division of the National Physical Laboratory, his brief to design an electronic stored-program digital computer. The lectures published here, given by Turing and his assistant J.H. Wilkinson in December 1946–February 1947, add substantially to our knowledge of Turing's design. The lectures detail the evolution of the design from Version V of early 1946 through Version VI to Version VII.

On 8 December 1943, the world's first large-scale special-purpose electronic digital computer came into operation, at the Government Code and Cypher School, Bletchley Park, England. This machine – 'Colossus' as it later became known – was built by T. H. Flowers, whose ambitious design involved approximately 1600 thermionic valves (vacuum tubes). Within six months a further 800 valves had been added. Turing was among the first to see the machine in operation. Although Colossus was neither stored-program nor general-purpose, there is no doubt that Flowers had demonstrated the practicability of using large numbers of thermionic valves to implement a general-purpose stored-program digital computer of the sort that Turing had outlined in his paper of 1936.[1] From that point on it was (in Flowers' words) a matter of Turing's waiting to see what opportunity might arise for putting the idea of a universal machine into practice.[2] (Flowers' own interests lay in a different direction. His ambition was to replace the existing network of telephone exchanges with electronic equipment.)

---

*The research involved in the preparation of this material was supported in part by University of Canterbury Research Grant no. U6271.

[1] 'On Computable Numbers, with an Application to the Entscheidungsproblem', *Proceedings of the London Mathematical Society*, Series 2, 42 (1936–37): 230–265.

[2] Flowers, private communication (1996).

Precisely such an opportunity fell into Turing's lap just over eighteen months later, when J. R. Womersley invited him to join the Mathematics Division of the National Physical Laboratory, Teddington, in order to design and construct an electronic digital computer (the formal date of the appointment was 1 October 1945).[3] During the remainder of 1945 Turing drafted his 'Proposal for Development in the Mathematics Division of an Automatic Computing Engine (ACE)'.[4] Turing submitted the proposal to the Executive Committee of the NPL in February 1946, and the Committee formally approved the ACE project in March 1946.[5]

The nine lectures published here were given by Turing and his assistant J. H. Wilkinson in December 1946–February 1947.[6] The lectures cover Versions V, VI, and VII of Turing's design for the ACE. They add substantially to our knowledge of the evolution of the design. The proposal submitted by Turing in February 1946 was based on Version V.[7] By the time of the lectures, Version VII was current. The lectures detail the transition from Version V to Versions VI and VII, illustrating the resulting simplifications in programming and enhancement of speed and flexibility of the proposed machine. Version V had a word length of 32 digits and essentially a three-address code (source, destination, position of next instruction). Version VI had essentially a four-address code (source A, source B, destination, next instruction). Version VII used an improved form of the four-address code and the word length increased to 40 digits.

The fundamental feature of the design, which influenced virtually all other aspects of it, was the use of mercury delay lines to form the working memory. (Version V was to contain some 200 of them.) Here is Turing's description of these units:

It is proposed to build 'delay line' units consisting of mercury ... tubes about 5′ long and 1″ in diameter in contact with a quartz crystal at each end. The velocity of sound in ... mercury ... is such that the delay will be 1.024 ms. The information to be stored may be considered to be a sequence of 1024 'digits' (0 or 1) ... These digits will be represented by a corresponding sequence of pulses. The digit 0 ... will be represented by the absence of a pulse at the appropriate time, the digit 1 ... by its presence. This series of pulses is impressed on the end of the line by one piezo-crystal, it is transmitted down the line in the form of supersonic waves, and is reconverted into a varying voltage by the crystal at the far end. This voltage is amplified sufficiently to give an output of the order of 10 volts peak to peak and is used to gate a standard pulse generated by the clock. This pulse may be again fed into the line by means of the transmitting crystal, or we may feed in some altogether different signal. We also have the possibility of leading the gated pulse to

---

[3] Womersley had read Turing's 'On Computable Numbers' in 1938 and straight away became interested in the possibility of constructing a computing machine (Minutes of the NPL Executive Committee, 15 November 1949).

[4] Published in Carpenter, B. E., Doran, R. W. (eds) *A.M. Turing's ACE Report of 1946 and Other Papers*, Cambridge, Mass.: MIT Press (1986): 20–105.

[5] Minutes of the NPL Executive Committee, 19 March 1946.

[6] The account of the lectures provided by Hodges in his biography of Turing is inaccurate (Hodges, A. *Alan Turing: the Enigma*, London: Burnett (1983)). Hodges states that the lectures ended in January 1947 (p. 353) and that Turing gave '[o]nly the first two and part of the last' (p. 559). In fact, the series ran until 13 February 1947 and Turing gave half the lectures.

[7] Wilkinson, in interview with Christopher Evans in 1976 ('The Pioneers of Computing: an Oral History of Computing', Science Museum: London).

some other part of the calculator, if we have need of that information at the time. Making use of the information does not of course preclude keeping it also.[8]

Delay lines had initially been developed for echo cancellation in R.D.F. (radar). As a memory medium their chief advantage was, as Turing put it, that they were 'already a going concern'.[9]

M. V. Wilkes was also proposing to use mercury delay lines in what was to be the Cambridge EDSAC.[10] Yet Wilkes's design and Turing's had little else in common. Wilkes arranged the EDSAC so that the nature of the memory medium was invisible to the machine's programmers.[11] Not so in the case of the ACE. Having decided to employ delay lines, Turing was determined to maximise their effectiveness. The time taken for an instruction, or number, to emerge from a delay line will depend on where in the delay line it happens to be, and in order to minimise waiting-time, Turing arranged for instructions to be stored not in consecutive positions, but in relative positions selected by the programmer in such a way that each instruction would emerge at exactly the time it was required, in so far as possible. Each instruction contained a specification of the location of the next. At NPL this system subsequently became known as 'optimum coding'. It was an integral feature of every version of the ACE design. Optimum coding made for difficult and untidy programming, but the advantage in terms of speed was considerable. (Wilkinson observes that Turing 'was obsessed with the idea of speed on the machine'.[12]) Thanks to optimum coding, the Pilot Model ACE was able to do a floating point multiplication in 3 milliseconds – Wilkes's EDSAC required 4.5 milliseconds to perform a single fixed point multiplication.[13]

The Pilot Model ACE was predominantly Wilkinson's project. From early 1947, and for reasons that Turing would have thought of as amounting to 'cowardly and irrational doubts',[14] Turing's colleagues in the ACE Section were in favour of devoting their efforts to building a much scaled-down and simplified form of Version V, containing a mere handful of delay lines, rather than pressing ahead with the full-scale ACE.[15] It was not in Turing's nature to direct them otherwise, and he himself stood increasingly to one side, eventually leaving the NPL in May 1948 in order to join Newman at Manchester. The Pilot Model first ran in May 1950. Wilkinson's specifications for the Pilot Model did retain both optimum coding and Turing's proposed pulse rate of one million digits

---

[8]'Proposal for Development in the Mathematics Division of an Automatic Computing Engine (ACE)', p. 24.

[9]P. 108 of his 'Lecture to the London Mathematical Society on 20 February 1947', in Carpenter, B. E., Doran, R. W. (eds): 106–24.

[10]Wilkes, M. V. *Memoirs of a Computer Pioneer*, Cambridge, Mass.: MIT Press (1985): 121–2.

[11]Wilkes, op. cit., pp. 136–7.

[12]Wilkinson, op. cit.; see also p. 102 of Wilkinson, J. H. 'Turing's Work at the National Physical Laboratory and the Construction of Pilot ACE, DEUCE, and ACE', in Metropolis, N., Howlett, J., Rota, G.C. (eds) *A History of Computing in the Twentieth Century*, Orlando: Academic Press (1980): 101–14.

[13]Wilkinson, op. cit.; Campbell-Kelly, M. 'Programming the EDSAC: Early Programming Activity at the University of Cambridge', *Annals of the History of Computing*, 2 (1980): 7–36.

[14]Turing uses this phrase on p. 92 of 'Proposal for Development in the Mathematics Division of an Automatic Computing Engine (ACE)'.

[15]H. D. Huskey exerted considerable influence in this respect. Previously of the Moore School, Pennsylvania, Huskey was a member of the ACE Section for the year of 1947.

per second. For a time the Pilot Model ACE was the fastest machine in the world. Had Version VII or its successor Version VIII been built as Turing planned, with high-speed storage for 500 K binary digits and an operating frequency of one megacycle per second, the ACE would have stood alone among the early machines, offering serious computing power.

There seems little question that had the ACE project been managed effectively, and had Turing been allocated the resources that he needed, the NPL could have succeeded in producing the full-scale ACE as early as 1951 or 1952. In 1946, Flowers had established a small team at the Post Office Research Station to build a computer to Turing's logical design. The team consisted of two engineers, A. W. M. Coombs and W. W. Chandler, both of whom had assisted Flowers in the construction of Colossus. Working alone, the two men built a large machine named MOSAIC (Ministry of Supply Automatic Integrator and Computer).[16] Based on Version VII of the ACE design, MOSAIC consisted of some 100 mercury delay lines, 2000 germanium diodes and 6000 thermionic valves. The machine was installed at R.R.D.E. (Radar Research and Development Establishment), Malvern, in 1953 or 1954. MOSAIC was used to calculate aircraft trajectories from radar data, in connection with anti-aircraft measures.[17]

On 16 November 1946, Womersley (who was Superintendent of the Mathematics Division) wrote to Sir Charles Darwin, Director of the NPL, proposing the lecture series:

ACE. Proposal for Lectures by Dr Turing
At an informal meeting yesterday with some Service representatives and Dr Porter of the Military College of Science, a suggestion was made that Dr Turing, rather than explaining his machine to a number of isolated people on many different occasions, should conserve his time by giving a course of lectures intended primarily for those who will be concerned with the technical development of the machine and possibly also with giving advice on matters connected with its components. In view of the fact that the Post Office have a contract for a computing machine [MOSAIC] for a specific Service application which it is intended shall be constructed on ACE principles, though of course on a very much smaller scale, the future users of the small machine should also be invited. After some discussion the following list of those who should be invited was drawn up.

Post Office	4	Military College of Science	2
The Gramophone Co.	1	A.5	2
British Thomson Houston Co.	1	T.R.E.	2
Standard Telephones	1	A.G.E.	1
Cinema Television Ltd	1	R.R.D.E.	1
		A.S.E.	1

Additional invitations:
Prof. D. R. Hartree   Dr M. V. Wilkes
Prof. H. S. W. Massey   3 members of the staff
                           of the Mathematics Div.

---

[16]Coombs, in interview with Christopher Evans in 1976 ('The Pioneers of Computing: an Oral History of Computing', Science Museum: London); Coombs, A. W. M. 'MOSAIC', in *Automatic Digital Computation: Proceedings of a Symposium Held at the National Physical Laboratory*, London: Her Majesty's Stationery Office (1954): 38–42.

[17]Both Coombs and Chandler attended the lecture series. Flowers was invited by Womersley to attend but did not do so. (Flowers, private communication, 1997; Coombs, in interview with Christopher Evans in 1976).

It will be noted that no-one is invited from Professor Newman's department in Manchester; this is because they have already had discussions with Dr Turing. The number from the Mathematics Division is limited to 3 because Dr Turing has already given a series of lectures to members of our staff. After some discussion it was agreed that the Ministry of Supply should provide a suitable lecture room in the Adelphi. This has already been arranged. ... The reason for holding these lectures at the Adelphi is that it will be possible in the particular room chosen to provide desk space for each person attending so that he can take copious notes. This will be necessary for those who are to be engaged in the actual design and construction of equipment.[18]

The lectures were held between 2 p.m. and 5 p.m. on successive Thursday afternoons from 12 December 1946 to 13 February 1947 (Boxing Day excepted), in a rather dingy underground room at the Headquarters of the Ministry of Supply, then housed in the Adelphi Hotel, Baker Street, London. Advertised by Womersley as 'lecture-discussions', the lectures resembled tutorials in style.[19] (Womersley's timetable set aside 50 minutes of each weekly session for discussion and criticism by the audience.[20]) It was initially proposed that Wilkes should take an official record of the lectures.[21] Wilkes presumably declined, and the task fell to T. A. H. (Tommy) Marshall, of the Mechanical and Optical Instruments Branch of the Military College of Science, Shrivenham. (Marshall's specialism was servomechanisms.) It is Marshall's notes of the lectures that are published here (with some corrections).[22] Two other sets of lecture notes are known to survive: a complete set of handwritten notes taken by J. G. L. Michel, of the Mathematics Division, and handwritten notes concerning Lectures 6 and 7 taken by D. R. Hartree, Plummer Professor of Mathematical Physics at the University of Cambridge.[23]

Marshall had his notes typed, dividing them into numbered, headed sections. The notes were distributed in booklet form under the title 'The Automatic Computing Engine' (Military College of Science, Shrivenham, February 1947). Comparison of the three sets of notes indicates that Marshall refrained from supplementing the lecture material. He kept the material in more or less its original order. The few exceptions are as follows (section numbers refer to the table of contents on page 387):

---

[18]Memo to the Director, 16 November 1946. (© Crown Copyright 1946. Reproduced by permission of the Controller of HMSO.) Copies of Womersley's handwritten notes concerning the arrangements for the lectures, and of his correspondence, have been preserved among the papers of M. Woodger (who joined the ACE Section in September 1946).

[19]Wilkes, private communication (1997).

[20]Hodges infers from the fact that Womersley invited '[d]iscussion – in particular, criticism of Dr Turing's technical proposals' (the quotation is from Womersley's memo announcing the lectures) that '[t]hey did not trust him to know what he was talking about' (Hodges, op. cit., p. 353). This seems far fetched. Critical discussion is, after all, a normal and healthy feature of academic life.

[21]'Notes of a meeting held in the Director's room', 22 November, 1946.

[22]I am grateful to the Principal of Cranfield University for permission to publish Marshall's notes.

[23]The former are among the papers of M. Woodger. The latter are among Hartree's papers in the Library of Christ's College, Cambridge. A note by Wilkes that is attached to them wrongly states that the series contained only seven lectures and ran from December 1946 to January 1947. Wilkes himself attended only the first two lectures of the series (private communication, 1997). Hartree attended most or all of the lectures, but the remainder of his notes seem not to have been preserved.

1. Marshall placed material concerning delay lines that originally straddled Lectures 1 and 2 into a single appendix, which he located following the text of Lecture 9. This appendix now forms Section 3, 'Supersonic Mercury Delay Lines'.

2. The material in Section 10, 'Sources and Destinations', is drawn mostly from the beginning of Wilkinson's first lecture, but Marshall seems to have prefaced the section with some material drawn from the previous lectures by Turing.

3. Section 14, 'Source and Destination Trees', appears to be part of Lecture 8, and was originally flanked by the material in Sections 24 and 25. Why Marshall moved this section to an earlier position in the exposition is not clear, especially since doing so destroys the otherwise smooth progression in the lectures from Version V through Version VI to Version VII. However, Marshall's arrangement has not been disturbed.

4. Section 15, 'Some Examples of Simple Instructions', came earlier in the exposition, originally lying between the material in Sections 11 and 12.

5. Hartree's lecture notes show that Marshall reversed the order of Sections 23 and 24. The original order has been restored.

6. Sections 27, 28 and 29 are the text of Turing's final lecture (which is titled 'Mechanical Details' in Michel's notes). Marshall relegated this lecture to an appendix, which he called 'Some possible circuits'.

Except in respects just noted, the correspondence between the table of contents and the actual lectures is this. Lecture 1 (December 12): Sections 1–4; Lecture 2 (December 19): Sections 5–9; Lectures 3–4 (January 2 and 9): Sections 10, 11, 15, 12, 13 (it is not known where the break between these lectures fell); Lecture 5 (January 16): Sections 16–18; Lecture 6 (January 23): Sections 19–22; Lecture 7 (January 30): Sections 23, 24; Lecture 8 (February 6): Sections 14, 25, 26; Lecture 9 (February 13): Sections 27–29.

As the table of contents shows, 14 of the 30 sections were delivered in whole or part by Wilkinson. Womersley's original intention was that the lectures be given by Turing alone. However, at Darwin's request Turing attended a symposium on digital calculating machinery held at Harvard from 7 to 10 January, and Wilkinson deputised for him during the period of his absence.[24] Wilkinson, a numerical analyst, had joined the NPL only seven months previously, with no prior experience of either electronic engineering or logical computer design. His official position was that of Turing's half-time assistant.[25] To what extent Wilkinson made use of lecture material provided for him by Turing is a matter for conjecture. Marshall thanks only Turing for 'permission to publish this account in its present form'.

The diagrams are from Marshall's booklet (with some corrections).

---

[24]Minutes of the NPL Executive Committee, Paper E.910, 15 April 1947.

[25]Wilkinson, op. cit.

Table of Contents

The automatic computing engine

1 INTRODUCTION

Digital computing machines of various sorts have been built frequently during the last 300 years with varying degrees of success and have resulted in the various well-known commercial machines of the Brunsviga and Comptometer types. Such machines are invaluable for carrying out simple routine calculations. Their main defect however when used for more complex operations is the amount of labour involved in setting numbers into them and recording intermediate results for use in subsequent parts of the calculations.

The Hollerith machines did much to overcome these difficulties by using high speed electro-mechanical techniques with punched cards as a means of input and output. Even so these machines lacked an effective 'Memory' which is essential for the rapid solution of protracted calculations.

Much work was therefore devoted to the development of analogue type machines, familiar in most Service computing instruments, and the Differential Analyser became a very powerful and useful tool for the mathematician.

The requirements of the ballisticians during the war years brought about the rapid development of digital machines once again and in America the Automatic Sequence Controlled Calculator (ASCC) and the Electronic Numerical Integrator and Calculator (ENIAC) were built. The ENIAC was the most ambitious machine to date and was capable of very high working speeds. Its memory however was still inadequate for many problems.

The machine described here is the Automatic Computing Engine (ACE) which is being designed by the Mathematics Division of the National Physical Laboratory. It is to be a digital computer capable of performing algebraic processes at very high speeds by arithmetical methods. It will be completely flexible and able to cope with a variety of problems and will be fully automatic in operation. Computation will be performed in the binary scale by electronic means and the machine will incorporate a large 'Memory' for the storage of both data and instructions. The normal operating speed of the machine will be one million binary digits per second when all the required data is held within the 'Memory'. Input and output, which is by Hollerith machinery, is of necessity somewhat slower; some 2500 digits per second.

The final version of the ACE will probably contain about 512 'Memory' units capable of storing some 500,000 binary digits and will utilise something like 8000 valves.

2 REPRESENTATION OF BINARY NUMBERS

In the binary scale only the digits 0 and 1 exist, all numbers being composed of a series of these two digits. Since timing is an essential feature in a machine of this sort and since in graphical representation the time scale is normally from left to right on the paper, and further since in arithmetic processes it is necessary to commence operations with the least significant digit of a number, binary numbers are normally written with the least significant digit first, i.e. to the left. This is the reverse of normal decimal notation. An example will make this clear.

Decimal notation	Binary notation
0	000000 . . . .
1	100000 . . . .
2	010000 . . . .
10	010100 . . . .
47	111101 . . . .
etc.	

In the machine, the digit 1 is represented by a pulse of 1 µs duration; the digit 0 by the absence of a pulse. There is no separation between pulses. Thus a binary number might be represented by a voltage waveform as below:

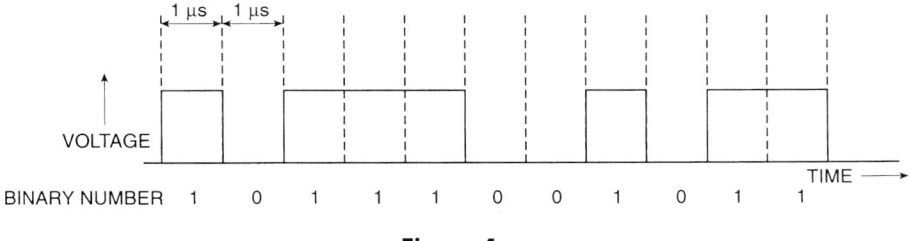

Figure 1

The above waveform is idealised and is hardly achieved in practice since it would require an infinite bandwidth. In some portions of the machine the pulses are simple voltage pulses and in others are pulses of 15 Mc/s carrier.

Similar pulses are used for timing and sequencing operations throughout the machine.

The position of a pulse with respect to the time scale standard or *nominal time* may vary in different sections due to a variety of courses; similarly due to distortion and attenuation the pulses may be shortened. Hence waveforms depart considerably from the ideal. Some typical shapes are shown below (Figure 2).

In addition to representing 1, a pulse indicates 'Truth' in logical operations, and a 0 'Untruth'.

Since binary numbers composed of 32 digits are to be handled, it is convenient to consider 32 pulses (or 'no-pulses') as a group. Such a group is termed a *Word* and the time period during which it occurs, namely 32 µs, is termed a *Minor Cycle*. A group of 32 words occurs in 1024 µs and it is convenient to refer to this time period as a *Major Cycle*.

389

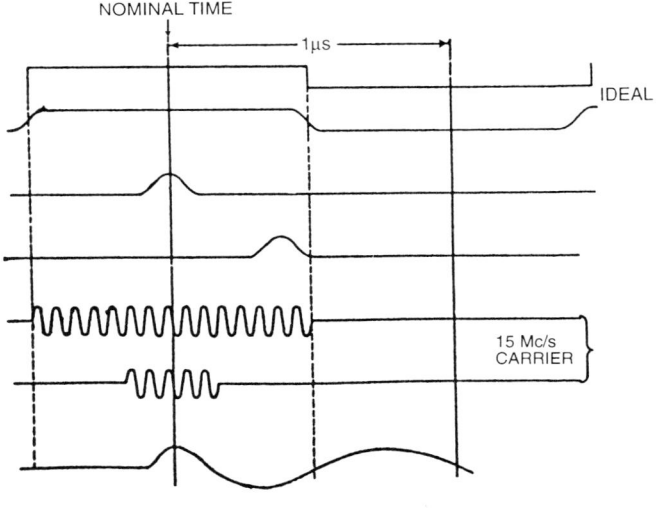

NOMINAL TIME

1 µs

IDEAL

15 Mc/s
CARRIER

Figure 2

3 SUPERSONIC MERCURY DELAY LINES

The method adopted in the machine for producing a time delay in the transmission of a pulse is an electro-mechanical one. The electrical pulse is converted to a longitudinal pressure wave in a column of mercury, which passes down the columns and is received at the far end after a finite time.

The mercury column is contained in a steel tube of diameter 1 inch. In order to achieve a delay of 1024 µs the tube is approximately 5 feet long.

At either end of the tube is fitted a piezo-electric quartz crystal arranged as shown diagrammatically below.

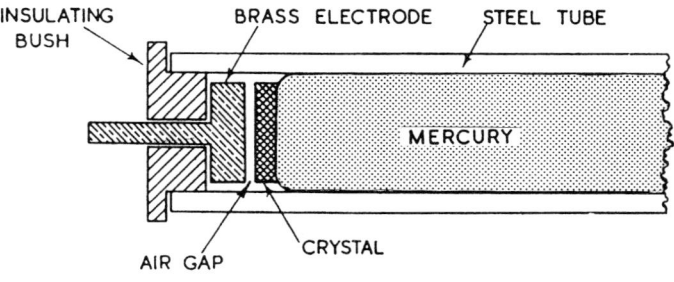

INSULATING BUSH   BRASS ELECTRODE   STEEL TUBE

MERCURY

AIR GAP   CRYSTAL

Figure 3

The mercury forms one electrode and the brass plate the other, there being an air gap between the brass and the crystal to eliminate mechanical coupling.

The pulses are applied to the crystal as pulses of 15 Mc/s carrier of duration 1 µs. Carrier working is adopted for several reasons, chief amongst which is that in non-carrier working the variation of delays of various frequencies is excessive (as much as 4 μs in total non-carrier working for a band pass of 0 to 1/2 Mc/s). Mercury is chosen as the medium for the propagation of the pressure wave since it has a reasonably constant attenuation of frequencies around 15 Mc/s and the variation of velocity of propagation with temperature at normal air temperatures is small. Further, the acoustic impedance of mercury is more closely equal to that of quartz at normal temperatures and therefore better acoustic matching is achieved than with other possible materials.

A comparison table of the pertinent constants of mercury, water and quartz are given for illustration.

	Mercury	*Water*	*Quartz*
Density	13.5 gms/ml	1.00	2.65
Velocity of propagation	1.5 Km/s	1.44	5.71
Temp. coeff. of velocity at 10 °C	0.00030 per °C	0.001	—
Acoustic impedance	2.025×10^6	1.44×10^5	1.52×10^6

The conversion efficiency of a quartz–mercury combination is such as to produce a loss of 48 dB.

In order to keep the delay of a mercury line constant to within ±0.5 μs at 10 °C (the maximum permissible tolerance) the temperature of the line must be kept within ±1.63 °C. This is easily achievable in practice.

Trouble from multiple reflections and standing waves is not present in the long lines since the attenuation is sufficiently great to render the standing wave ratio very small. In the short lines, however, it is necessary to introduce an acoustic diffraction grating to produce artificial attenuation.

The use of lines for storage of pulses

In order to store pulses in a line it is necessary to receive them as they arrive at the end and feed them back to the beginning. During the feed back the pulses must be amplified and reshaped. Facilities must also be provided to enable pulses to be put into and removed from the line.

The block arrangement is as below.

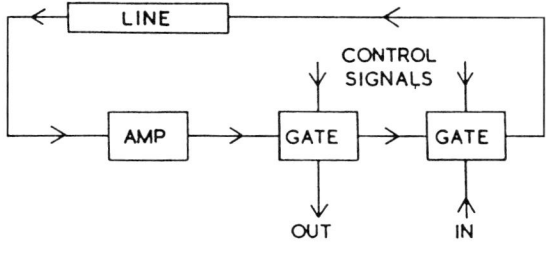

Figure 4

The precise circuitry is by no means fixed at present, but it is probable that a super-regenerative amplifier will be used which in itself will provide the necessary gating.

4 SYMBOLS USED IN DIAGRAMS

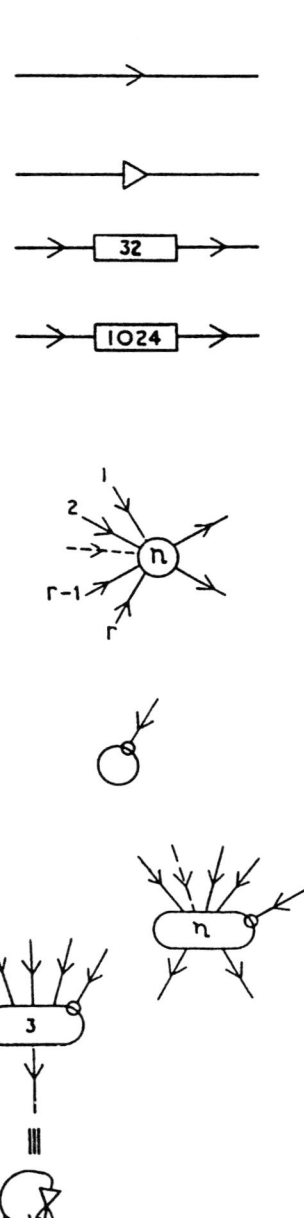

A direct connection. This assumes the instantaneous transmission of pulses between points thus connected. The arrow indicates the direction of flow of signals.

A delay of 1 μs ('unit delay'). The triangle is directional.

A short delay line of 'length' 32 μs. It is thus capable of storing a word of 32 binary digits.

A long delay line of 'length' 1024 μs. (Other 'lengths' may be indicated by the insertion of suitable figures.)

An element which emits a single pulse when it receives on any of its r input lines n or more simultaneous pulses. No pulse is emitted if less than n pulses are simultaneously received. The number n is called the *threshold* of the element and elements are referred to by their threshold numbers e.g. a 'Three element'. In the symbol for 'One element' the figure 1 is usually omitted.

This indicates an *inhibitory connection* to an element. No pulse is emitted by such an element in the microsecond during which it receives a pulse via an inhibitory connection, irrespective of all other inputs.

A *trigger circuit*. Such a circuit of threshold n emits a continuous stream of pulses when it receives n or more simultaneous input pulses. It continues to emit pulses until such time as it receives a pulse on its inhibitory connection, when it stops.

A trigger circuit may be produced from a simple element by the insertion of a unit delay in an output lead and feeding back into the element on n input leads. For example, a trigger circuit of threshold 3 may be produced from a 3-element as shown.

392

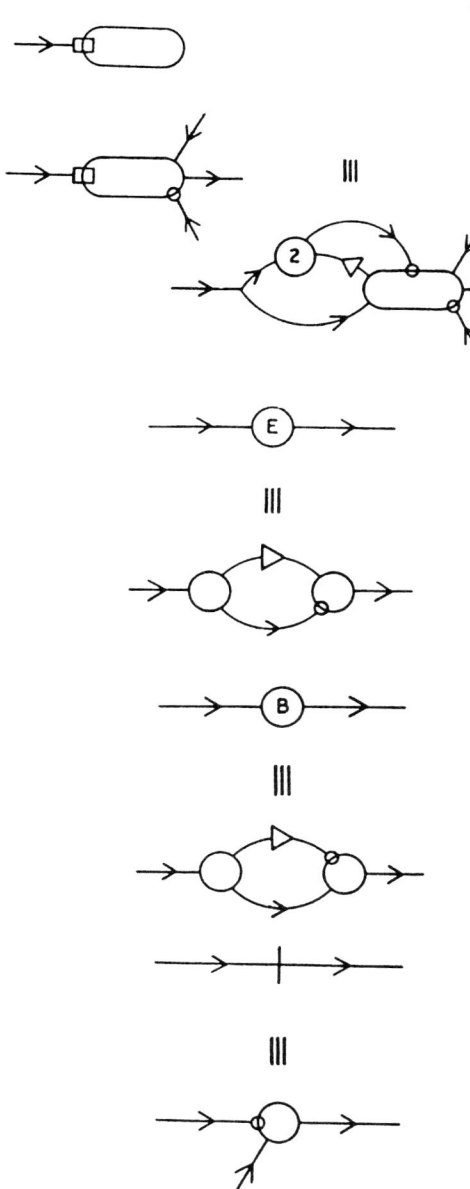

This indicates a connection to a trigger circuit such that when a pulse is received the state of the circuit is changed; i.e., if it was emitting pulses it stops, and vice versa. This connection is equivalent to the additional circuitry on a trigger circuit as shown.

An end element. This gives a pulse out during the microsec after the termination of a series of input pulses.

e.g.,

Input   001110001100
Output   000001000010

It is made up of two one-elements interconnected as shown.

A beginning element. This gives a pulse out during the first microsec of a series of input pulses.

e.g.,

Input   001110001100
Output   001000001000

It is made up of two one-elements interconnected as shown.

A polarity changer. Pulses are changed to no-pulses and vice versa.

e.g.,

Input   001110001100
Output   110001110011

This may be made up as shown.

STREAM OF 1s

The above notation covers all the simple units from which the computing and control circuits are constructed. Details of the circuitry of each unit is given in Sections 27–29.

393

5 LOGICAL OPERATIONS

It is desirable to have circuits which perform the equivalent of the terms 'and' 'or' and 'not'.

These may be very simply developed from the elements already described as indicated below. In these logical operations a pulse indicates True and no pulse indicates False.

A and B (A & B)

Suppose it is required to ascertain if two pulses coexist in two channels simultaneously, i.e. A & B.

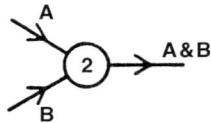

Figure 5

If each channel is fed to a 2-element, then the element will emit a pulse only when pulses occur on A and B simultaneously, i.e. a pulse on the output indicates 'A & B'.

A or B (or both) (A ∨ B)

In this case each channel is fed to a 1-element.

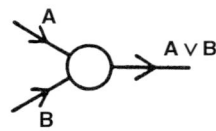

Figure 6

The element emits a pulse when there occurs a pulse on A or B or both.

A and not B (A &~ B)

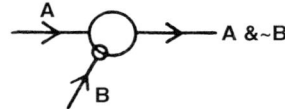

Figure 7

In this case a pulse is emitted only when a pulse exists on A and no pulse on B.

Not A (∼A)

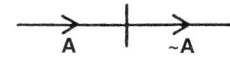

Figure 8

6 ADDING CIRCUIT

The process of addition is obviously of fundamental importance in a computing machine. It should be borne in mind that the addition of two numbers in reality involves the addition at each stage of three digits, since in general a carry digit has to be added as well as the two addends.

Further, since binary numbers are written with the least significant figure to the left, addition commences at the left and proceeds to the right. An example is given below.

Carry digit	01111100110
A	010111001100
B	111001011001
Sum	100001110011

An adding circuit, operating digit by digit, must therefore be able to distinguish the following combinations of input signals and react in the corresponding manner.

Input			*Output*	
A	*B*	*Carry*	*Sum*	*Carry*
0	0	0	0	0
1	0	0 (or permutation)	1	0
1	1	0	0	1
1	1	1	1	1

Since there are three possible input and output signals, ignoring the '0 & carry 0' answer which is implicit, three elements will be required to construct the circuit, which is shown below (Figure 9).

A single pulse on any one of the A, B, or Carry channels will cause the 1-element to emit a pulse. The output of the 1-element therefore goes straight to the adder output.

Two simultaneous input pulses should, however, produce a 0 in the sum and a carry 1. The 2-element output is therefore used to inhibit the 1-element (which therefore gives 0) and also, when delayed by 1 μs, the next carry digit.

Three simultaneous input pulses produce a carry 1 in the same way and the 1-element is inhibited. The 1 in the sum is produced by the 3-element which is now stimulated.

The adding circuit is usually drawn as below (Figure 10).

It should be noted that the outputs of the 3-element and the 1-element can be connected together directly, since if the 3-element is emitting the 1-element is always inhibited and vice-versa.

Such a circuit as described will add continuous streams of pulses, digit by digit. However, in the machine it is usually desired to add together words of 32 digits. Since there is no spacing between successive words, a carry digit formed by the addition of the last two digits in the words would be added in to the first pair of the next words. To prevent this, i.e. to break the trains of pulses up into their correct words, the carry digit is suppressed during the first microsec of each word.

	End of Word		Beginning of Word	
Carry	 01001		[1]0001	([1] suppressed by carry suppression)
A	 10111		1011	
B	 10011		0101	
A + B	..... $\overline{01101}$		$\overline{1110}$	

This is achieved by the modification to the circuit as below (Figure 11).

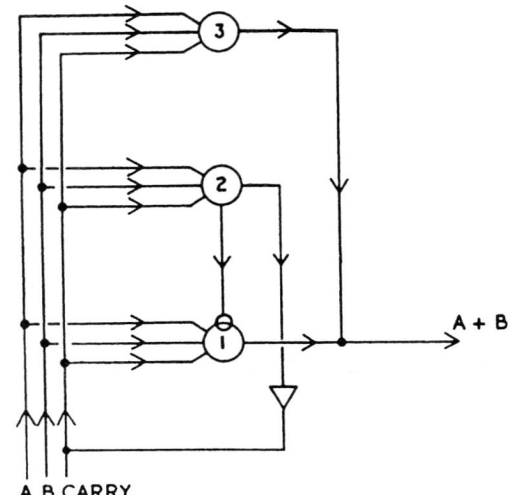

A B CARRY

Figure 9

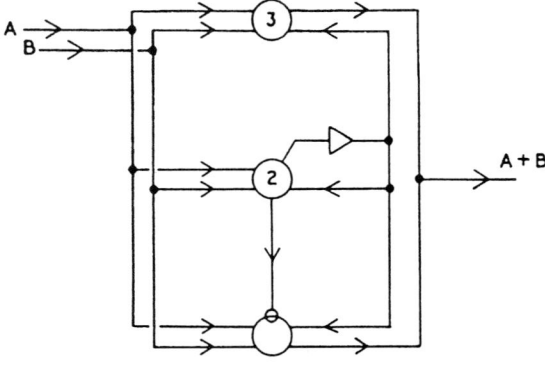

Figure 10

396

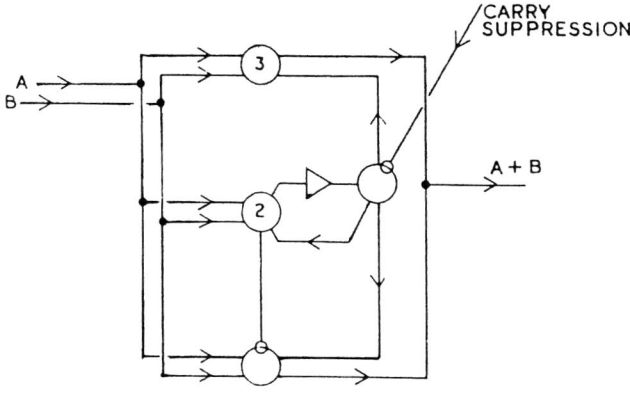

Figure 11

7 RING COUNTER

It was seen that in the adding circuit it was necessary to suppress the carry digit every 32 μs in order to divide a continuous train of pulses up into words. This calls for some device to count up to 32 μs and then emit a pulse. This may be done by a ring-counter.

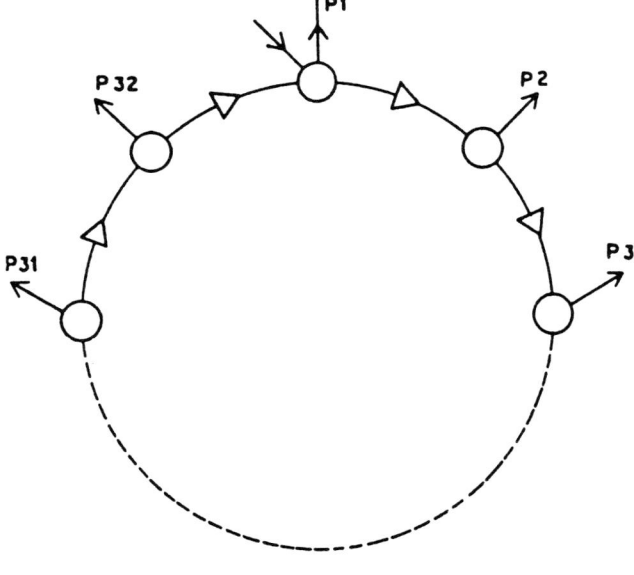

Figure 12

This is a ring of 32 1-elements connected together through unit delays. When once stimulated, a pulse continues to go round the ring, making the complete circuit in 32 μs.

Timing pulses may be taken from any of the 1-elements and these are termed P 1, P 2 etc., to P 32. P 1 corresponds to the first microsec of a word and P 32 to the last.

Hence in the adder circuit the carry suppression pulse would be P 1.

These timing pulses are used throughout the machine for gating operations.

8 STATICISER

This is a means of converting a word which is available in a minor cycle onto a set of 32 trigger circuits.

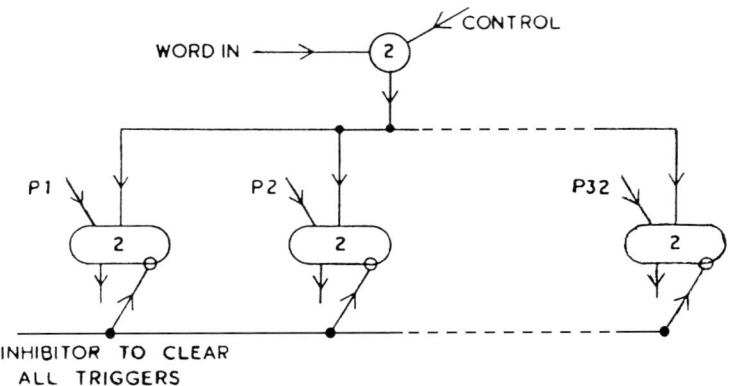

Figure 13

The 32 trigger circuits each of threshold 2 are connected as shown. When it is required to set up a word on them, the gate (the 2-element) is opened by the control signal and the pulses are applied to all the trigger circuits. To each of the triggers, however, is fed P 1 to P 32 respectively and therefore only those circuits which received a digit pulse together with a P pulse are turned on, the rest remaining off.

The triggers may be cleared by a pulse on the inhibitor connection which turns all of them off ready for the next word to be staticised.

9 DYNAMICISER

This is a circuit which performs the reverse process to the staticiser in that it converts a set of voltages available on 32 trigger circuits, or from some other source, into a 32 digit word occupying a minor cycle.

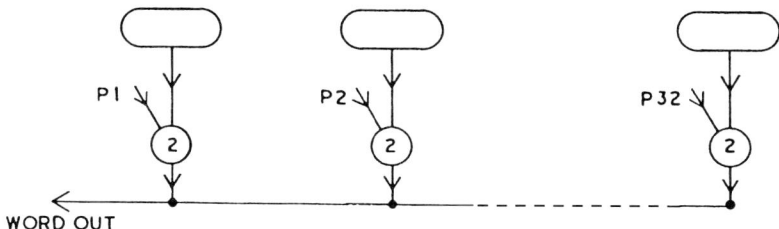

Figure 14

10 SOURCES AND DESTINATIONS

The 'Memory' of the ACE is composed of a large number of supersonic mercury delay lines. In general, these are either of 'length' 32 μs or 1024 μs, i.e. they delay a pulse by a time corresponding to their 'length'.

  If now the output of a line is fed back, after amplification, to the input, a pulse may be caused to travel repeatedly down a line and back through the amplifier for as long as required. Since the lines are either of 32 μs or 1024 μs length they can, with the feedback circuit, be used to store 32 or 1024 pulses each respectively.

Notation

A short line is designated by a reference number.

  A pulse is designated by a subscript at the corresponding position from the output end at the beginning of a minor cycle.

  Throughout the machine, pulses are fed from one part to another via the HIGHWAY.

  Transfer of numbers is achieved by indicating a SOURCE and a DESTINATION by the control system. Operations are performed on the numbers by coded instructions also from the control system.

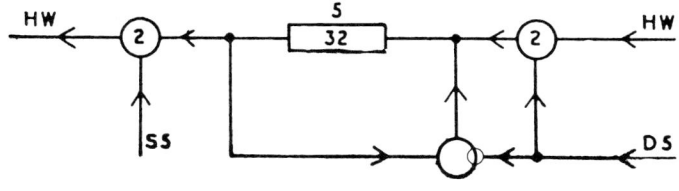

Figure 15

  All D and S pulses have a duration of 1 minor cycle (32 μs). Thus a word on the HW may be put into Temporary Storage Line 5 (TS 5) by a pulse D 5. This opens the 2-element and admits the word to the line, at the same time inhibiting the feedback loop and therefore clearing any pulses that might have previously been in the line.

D 5 ceases at the end of the minor cycle and the word therefore continues to circulate indefinitely in the line circuit.

To obtain the word from the line a pulse S 5 of duration one minor cycle opens the 2-element and the word passes out to the HW.

This system is adopted throughout the machine.

Certain lines are used exclusively for certain purposes, in Version V.

For example, lines 2 and 3 are always used for *addition*.

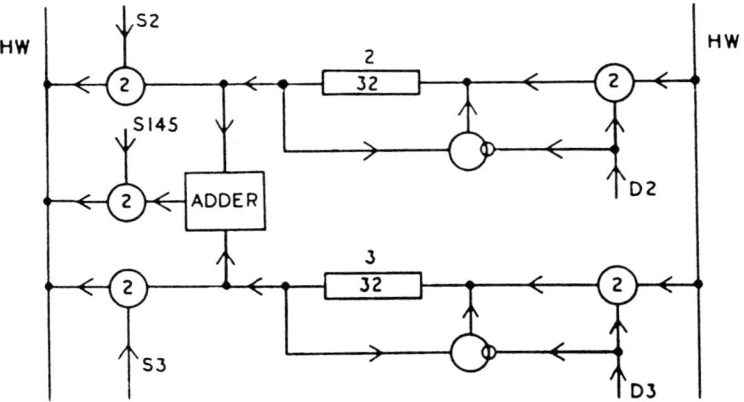

Figure 16

The arrangement is as above. D 2 admits a word to TS 2 and D 3 to TS 3. The lines feed to an adder and the sum of the words in TS 2 and TS 3 may be passed to HW by a pulse S 145.

The contents of TS 2 and TS 3 may be obtained separately by pulses S 2 and S 3 respectively.

Note. S 145 *always* gives the sum of whatever is in TS 2 and TS 3 and all addition is carried out here in Version V.

Similarly TS 8 and TS 9 are always used for logical operations, in Version V (Figure 17).

S 131 gives TS 8 & TS 9
S 132 gives TS 8 $\vee$ TS 9
S 133 gives TS 8 $\not\equiv$ TS 9
S 134 gives $\sim$TS 8

Another special facility is for the multiplication of small numbers by 2^n (where $n = 1, 2, 3, 4$ or 5) in TS 5 (Figure 18).

The doubling, quadrupling etc., is performed by delaying words 1, 2 μs etc.

Decimal		Binary
13		1011000 . . . . .
26		0101100 . . . . .
52	etc.	0010110 . . . . .

400

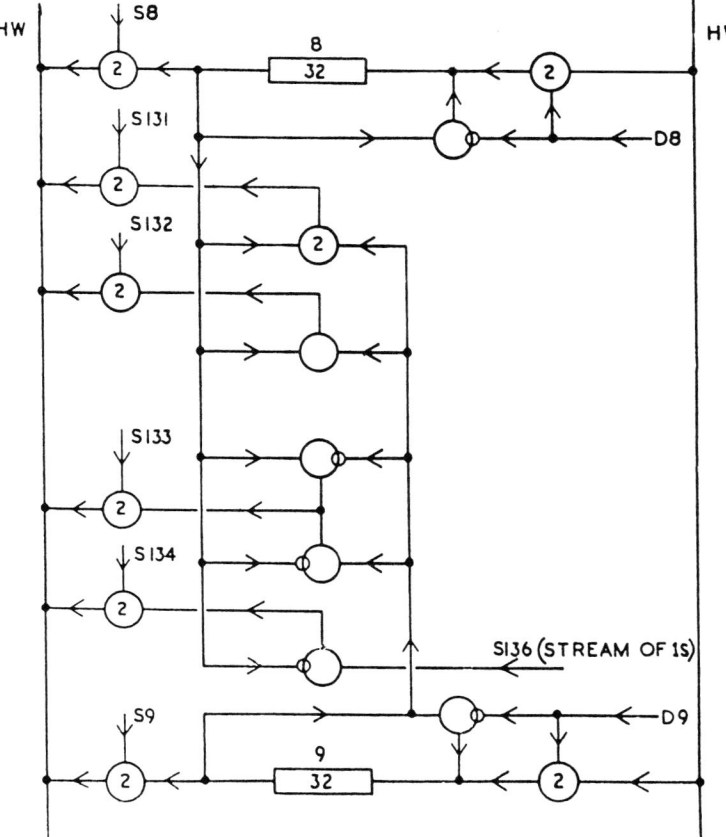

Figure 17

11 TABLE OF STANDARD SOURCES

This table gives the more commonly used Sources and Destinations.

Note. TS refers to short line (32 μs)

DL refers to long line (1024 μs)

$$\left. \begin{matrix} 0 \\ 1 \end{matrix} \right\}$$ TS for instructions.

$$\left. \begin{matrix} 2 \\ 3 \end{matrix} \right\}$$ TS for addition.

$$\left. \begin{matrix} 4 \\ 5 \\ 6 \\ 7 \end{matrix} \right\}$$ TS for general work.

$\left.\begin{array}{l}8\\9\end{array}\right\}$ TS for logical operations.

$\left.\begin{array}{l}16\\ \text{to}\\31\end{array}\right\}$ Ring of 16 TS's.

$\left.\begin{array}{l}64\\65\end{array}\right\}$ Lines of length 64 μs.

66 64 + 65
67 −64 (i.e., 2^{64} − TS 64).

84 64 Δ 1 μs (64 delayed 1 μs), i.e. multiplied by 2.
85 64 Δ 2 μs
to
89 64 Δ 32 μs

96 TC 96 special discriminating trigger circuit.
97 Inhibit TC 96.

98 Trigger circuits.
99

131 TS 8 & TS 9
132 TS 8 ∨ TS 9
133 TS 8 ≢ TS 9
134 ∼ TS 8 (i.e. 2^{32} − 1 − TS 8).
135 0   a stream of 0's.
136 2^{32} − 1   a stream of 1's.
137 ∼ (8 & 9)
145 2 + 3
146 −3 (i.e. 2^{32} − TS 3).
148 Multiplier
149 −2 (i.e. 2^{32} − TS 2).
150
151
152 5 Δ 1 μs
to
156 5 Δ 16 μs

158 260 Δ 32 μs

160 P 32
161 P 1   Ring counter
to
191 P 31

402

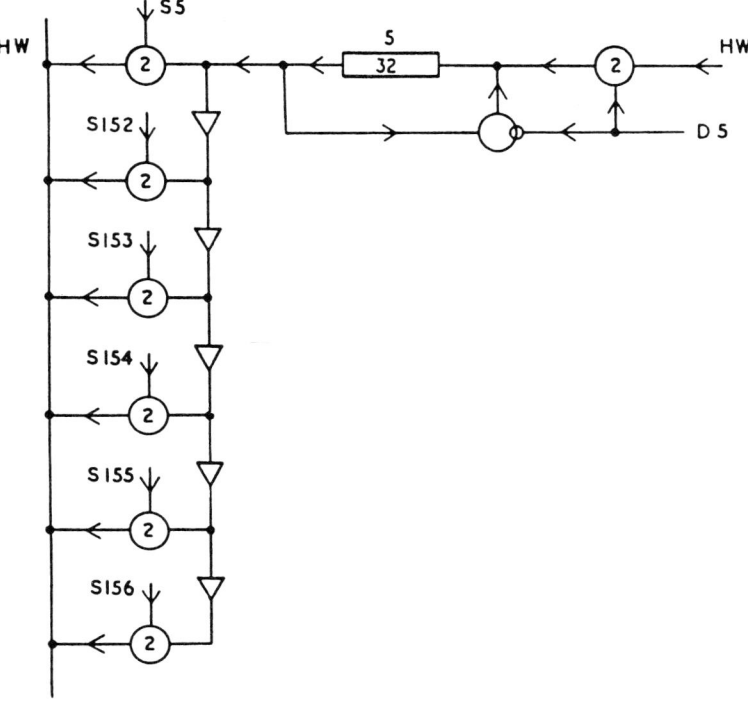

Figure 18

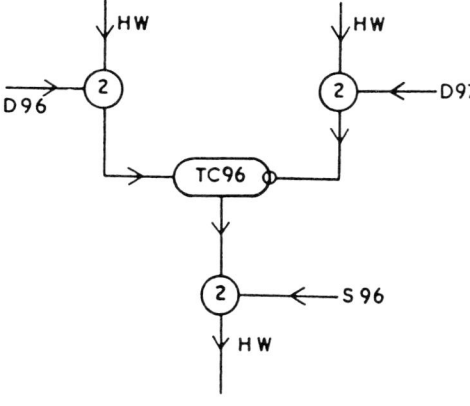

Figure 19

Figure 19 shows a special trigger circuit which is put ON if stimulated by D 96 and is put OFF by D 97.

12 PROGRAMMING (VERSION V)

An instruction must order the transfers of words to take place and order the operations to be performed on them in correct sequence.

For example, a series of instructions might be 'Take the fourth word in DL 270 and the sixth word in DL 280, add them and put the sum in DL 10'.

This would be ordered as:

1) DL 270.4 routed to TS 2

2) DL 280.6 routed to TS 3   (since TS 2 & TS 3 have adding facilities)

3) S 145 (output of adder) routed to DL 10.

More complicated instructions are built up in this manner and must be followed by the machine in the correct sequence. Since both transfer of words and operations take definite time periods to be achieved, the instructions must include information to show the machine how long to allow for each successive stage of the whole series of instructions.

Only one instruction can be obeyed at any one time, in general.

Form of instruction

Each instruction is in the form of one word of 32 binary digits. The digits form groups as follows.

Digits	1–2	3–12	13–22	23–26	27–32
	Spare	Source	Destination	Characteristic	Timing
	(not used)	Numbers	Numbers		Number
		(0–1023)	(0–1023)		(0–63)

Source number

This indicates from where a word is to be taken, e.g. TS 10.

Destination number

This indicates to where a word is to be routed, e.g. TS 11.

Characteristics

(1) Digit 23.   0 indicates external operation (i.e. Hollerith).
              1 indicates internal operation.
    (This use is obsolete. All operations are internal and 23 is therefore always 1.)

(2) Digit 24. This affects the timing number (q.v.).

(3) Digits 25 & 26. These two digits indicate the origin of the next instruction.

All instructions come from one of four sources. The four possible combinations of 0 and 1 for digits 25 and 26 indicate from which source the next instruction is to be drawn as follows.

Digits	Source		
00	TS 0	(Length 32)	
10	TS 1	(Length 32)	
01	DL 256	(Length 1024)	(Usually used)
11	DL 128	(Length 512)	

Timing number

This may have any value t from 0 to 63 minor cycles and is obeyed in conjunction with digit 24 in the characteristic.

If digit 24 is a 1 the instruction is said to be 'immediate' and carries on for t minor cycles after instruction has been set up.

If digit 24 is a 0 the instruction is said to be 'deferred' and is not obeyed until t minor cycles have elapsed. It is then obeyed in one minor cycle.

13 CONTROL CIRCUIT (VERSION V)

Figure 20 shows the control circuit. Its function is to receive an instruction, set it up in a form in which it can be obeyed and time the operation correctly. The main portions are a staticiser in which the instruction is set up, a slow counter for timing and two trigger circuits for bringing about the transfers.

Its action will be considered in parts. An instruction of 32 digits comes in from the 32 μs delay line INST.

TRANSTIM & TIMCI

These are the names given to two special trigger circuits which initiate obedience to an instruction (Figure 21).

Suppose TRANSTIM is initially off. A pulse gated by P 1, i.e. at the commencement of a minor cycle, applied to the 'change state' connection will put TRANSTIM on and it will remain on until put off by a second pulse on the same connection. It can therefore only be put on or off at the commencement of a minor cycle.

When TRANSTIM goes off the E-element will send a pulse to TIMCI which will be put on. This is the only way in which TIMCI can be put on. TIMCI will put itself off at the start of the next minor cycle by the 32nd pulse of the previous minor cycle, delayed by 1 μs and gated by P 1. TIMCI runs for one minor cycle only, during which time a complete instruction runs into the staticiser.

Note. A transfer in the machine can take place only when TRANSTIM is on. (See Section 14.)

405

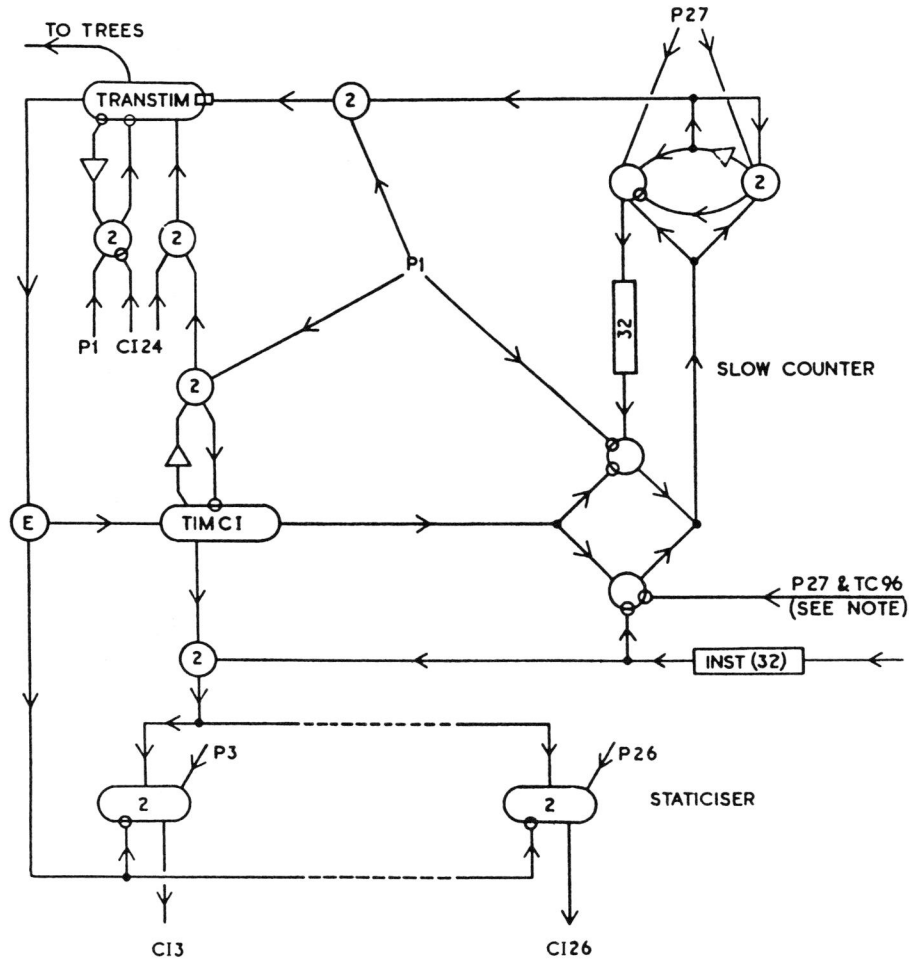

Figure 20

Slow counter

This is essentially an adder without the 3-element (Figures 22 and 23).

The slow counter is required to count up to a maximum of 64 minor cycles. Suppose the circuit is as above and initially is clear of all pulses. In each minor cycle a digit is added in the 27th place and the total accumulated. When 64 minor cycles have elapsed there will be a carry digit in the 1st place of the next minor cycle and this passes to TRANSTIM and changes its state. This carry digit is also inhibited from performing a

406

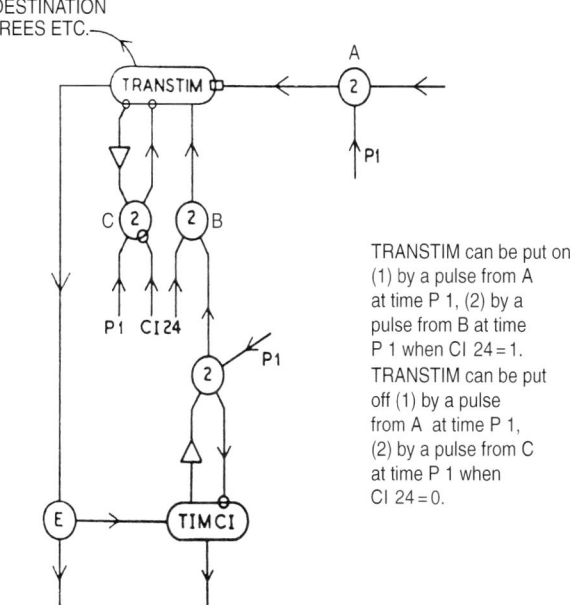

TRANSTIM can be put on
(1) by a pulse from A
at time P 1, (2) by a
pulse from B at time
P 1 when CI 24 = 1.
TRANSTIM can be put
off (1) by a pulse
from A at time P 1,
(2) by a pulse from C
at time P 1 when
CI 24 = 0.

Figure 21

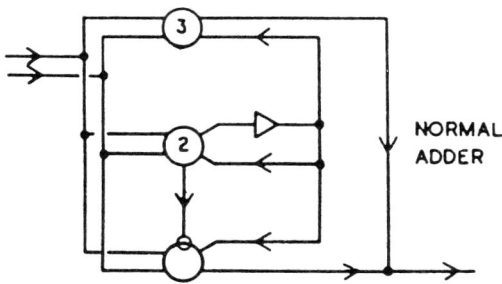

Figure 22

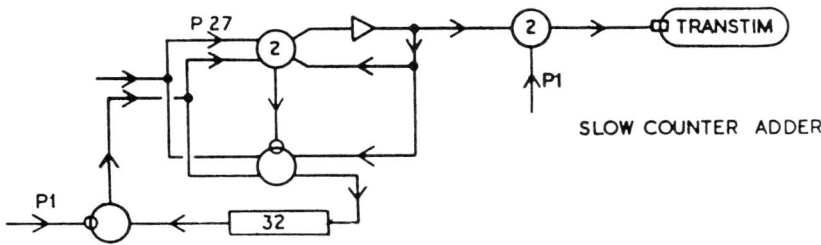

Figure 23

407

further cycle and so the circuit reverts to its state in the first cycle. This is illustrated below.

Position			27	28	29	30	31	32	1	2	
Minor	Cycle	1,	0	0	0	0	0	0	0	0	
"	"	2,	1	0	0	0	0	0	0	0	(i.e., after 1 mc).
"	"	3,	0	1	0	0	0	0	0	0	
"	"	4,	1	1	0	0	0	0	0	0	
"	"	5,	0	0	1	0	0	0	0	0	
"	"	64,	1	1	1	1	1	1	0	0	
"	"	65,	0	0	0	0	0	0	1*	0	

* This is used to change over TRANSTIM and is inhibited from passing again into the adder. Hence state at 65 is identical with that at 1 i.e. TRANSTIM will be changed over at intervals of 64 minor cycles.

Now consider the circuit arrangements below.

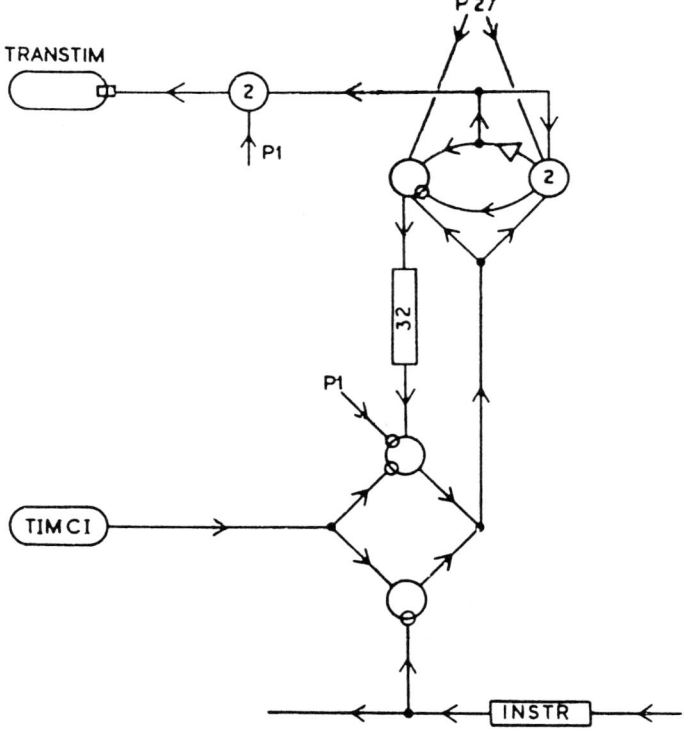

Figure 24

Suppose that for the first minor cycle TIMCI is delivering a continuous series of pulses and then shuts down. This inhibits the total already in the adder delay line and a complete instruction of 32 digits passing to the inhibitor connection of the lower

1-element goes out of this element as $\sim$INSTR and up to the adder. Here a digit is added in the 27th place and the total traverses the delay line and back to the adder where the process is repeated.

Since a digit is added in the 27th place, only places 27–32 need be considered and these places in the instruction, it will be remembered, are for the timing number. If this timing number is t, the number passed to the adder will be $\sim t$, i.e. $2^6 - 1 - t = 63 - t$. The slow counter runs until a total 64 is accumulated as has already been shown, i.e. it runs for $t + 1$ minor cycles before a carry digit in the first place operates TRANSTIM.

This is illustrated below. Suppose t is 7.

Timing Number=7

Position		27	28	29	30	31	32	1	2	etc.
Instruction		1	1	1	0	0	0	0	0	—
Passed to adder	1,	0	0	0	1	1	1			
Total at	2,	1	0	0	1	1	1			
	3,	0	1	0	1	1	1			
	8,	1	1	1	1	1	1			
	9,	0	0	0	0	0	0	1		

Thus a pulse goes to TRANSTIM after 8 minor cycles.

Immediate instructions

Now consider the complete control circuit. Suppose the instruction in the INSTR delay line is an immediate one ordering the transfer of a number from A to B (32 digits).

The timing number will be 1 and instruction will be:

```
A–B,    11,    1
i.e. Digits: 1, 2    3–12 13–22 23 24 25 26 27 28 29 30 31 32
          Spare    A    B    1  1  0  1  1  0  0  0  0  0
```

Digit 24 is a 1 since instruction is immediate.

Suppose TIMCI is ON.

The instruction runs out of INSTR and is set up on the staticiser during the first minor cycle.

$\sim$INSTR is simultaneously sent up into the slow counter, anything already in the counter delay line being inhibited by TIMCI.

After the first minor cycle TIMCI puts itself off, and since digit 24 was a 1, CI 24 is on, and therefore TRANSTIM is simultaneously started.

During the second minor cycle, the instruction in the staticiser is being obeyed, after which time the slow counter has produced a carry digit in position (1) which puts TRANSTIM off.

TIMCI is started therefore and the staticiser cleared, ready for the next instruction.

Thus it will be seen that in general, with an immediate instruction of timing number t, the instruction will be set up in the staticiser in the first minor cycle and held there while being obeyed for t minor cycles, i.e. until the end of the $(t + 1)$th minor cycle.

The action is illustrated by the following table for a timing number t.

409

Minor cycle

1_1 TRANSTIM off, TIMCI on. Instruction starts to run in.

2_1 TIMCI off, TRANSTIM on. Instruction set up and starts being obeyed.

$(2 + t)_1$ TRANSTIM off, TIMCI on, Staticiser cleared.

Total time for whole operation $(t + 1)$ minor cycles.

Deferred instruction

In this case digit 24 is a 0. As before, the instruction runs into the staticiser during the first minor cycle while TIMCI is ON.

This time, however, TRANSTIM will not come on and allow the transfer to take place until the slow counter stimlates it. TRANSTIM therefore comes on at $(t + 1)_1$ and stays on for 1 minor cycle only before putting itself off.

Minor cycle

1_1 TRANSTIM off, TIMCI on. Instruction starts to run in.

2_1 TRANSTIM off, TIMCI off.

$(2 + t)_1$ TRANSTIM on. Instruction starts being obeyed.

$(3 + t)_1$ TRANSTIM off, TIMCI on. Staticiser cleared.

Total time for whole operation $(t + 2)$ minor cycles.

Discrimination (use of TC 96)

The inhibitor connection fed with P 27 and TC 96 provides the facility for the machine to adopt one of two courses of action according to whether TC 96 is on or off. A deferred instruction, say number n, with timing number 0 is given.

If TC 96 is off, the next instruction to be obeyed will be $(n + 2)$, but if TC 96 is on, a timing number of 1 will be supplied by (TC 96 & P 27) and the next instruction will be $(n + 3)$. The examples given later will illustrate this function.

14 SOURCE AND DESTINATION TREES

In order that a combination of 10 signals from a group of CI triggers may be used to tap any source or open any destination a system of inter-connection is arranged, which is known as a TREE.

This may be illustrated by a case of 2 trigger circuits used to select one of $2^2 = 4$ sources say (Figure 25). For example, if CI x is on and CI y is off, a signal will flow to C.

In Versions V and VI the source and destination trees control 1024 sources and destinations (Figure 26). In Version VII this number is reduced to 512.

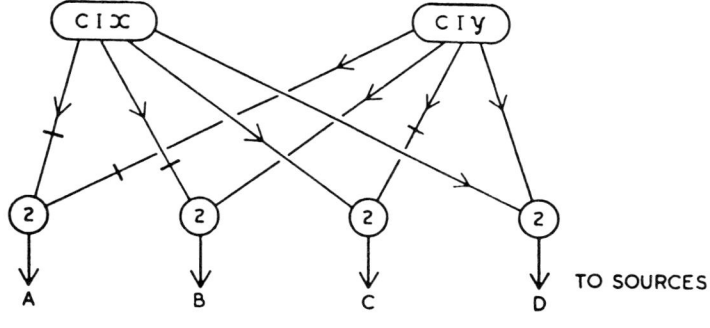

Figure 25

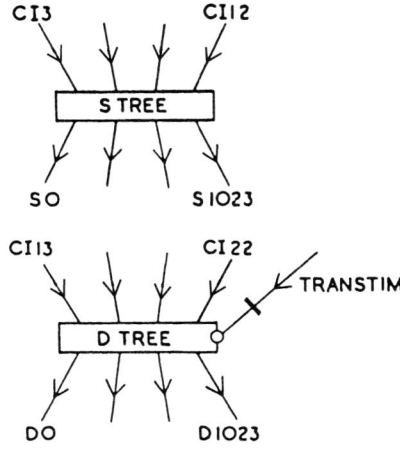

Figure 26

Note. The inhibition from TRANSTIM controls when transfer takes place, i.e. TRANSTIM must be on for transfer.

In Version VII there are only 512 sources and destinations, each controlled by 9 trigger circuits. In this case the destination tree is built up as described above with modifications introduced for reasons of available power from trigger circuits.

The 9 triggers are formed into two groups of 4 and 5 each. The 4 group controls 16 4-elements and the 5 group controls 32 5-elements.

The outputs of the 4- and 5-elements are then combined in pairs to select any one of the 512 destinations (Figure 27).

The source trees in Version VII are combined with the actual highways by elements arranged as in Figure 28, which illustrates the use of two triggers to control four sources. In practice, 9 triggers control 512 sources in this way.

In Versions V and VI there are four lines which can store instructions and feed them as required to INSTR (Figure 29). The appropriate one is selected by the four possible combinations of signals from CI 25 and CI 26 as shown.

411

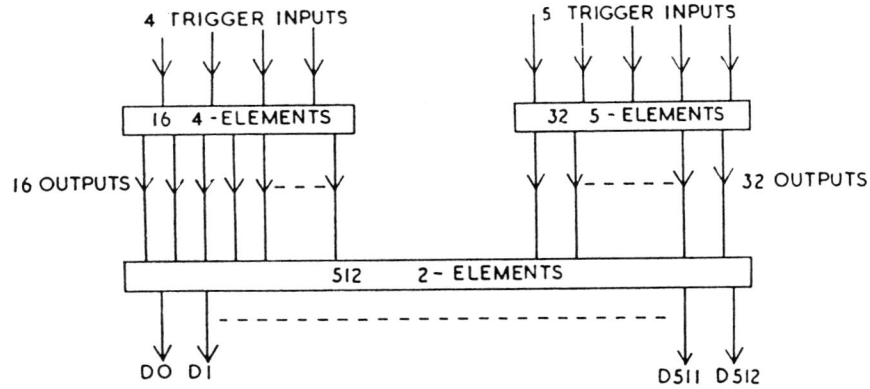

Figure 27

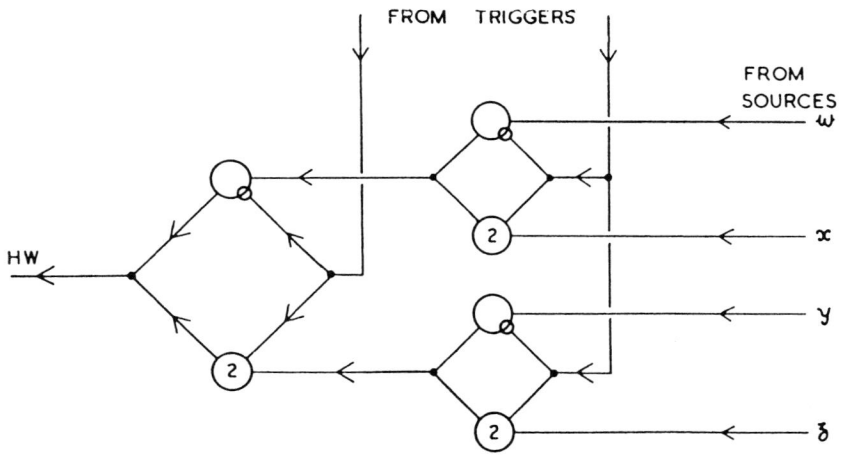

Figure 28

15 SOME EXAMPLES OF SIMPLE INSTRUCTIONS

Example 1

Numbers A and B are in TS 10 and TS 11 respectively.
Form A + B and put result in TS 12.

Instruction

1) 10–2,   11,   1   Immediate instruction, A sent to TS 2.
3) 11–3,   11,   1   B sent to TS 3.
5) 145–12, 11,   1   S 145 is TS 2 + TS 3. This is sent to TS 12.

412

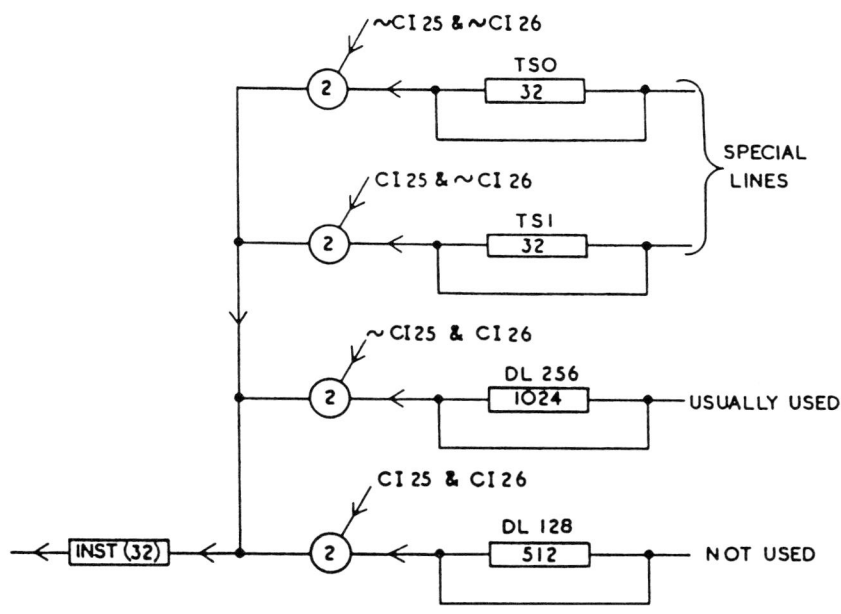

Figure 29

Example 2

Numbers A and B are in TS 10 and TS 11 respectively. If A = B put A in TS 12. If A ≠ B put (A + B) in TS 12.

Instruction

	(1)	10–8,	11, 1	Puts A into TS 8.
	(3)	11–9,	11, 1	Puts B in TS 9. (8 & 9 have facilities for logical operations.)
	(5)	133–96,	11, 1	S 133 gives a pulse if A ≠ B and this will put TC 96 on. If A = B TC 96 will not be put on.
	(7)	136–97,	9, 0	This is to put TC 96 off if it is on. It is ordered as a delayed instruction with zero timing number. There is however an inhibitor connection in the slow counter feed which is operated by (TC 96 & P 27). Hence if TC 96 is not on, next instruction will be (9), but if TC 96 is on, a timing number of 1 will be supplied and next instruction will therefore be (10).
If A = B	(9)	10–12,	11, 1	A put into TS 12. Result.
If A ≠ B	(10)	10–2,	11, 1	A put into TS 2.
	(12)	11–3,	11, 1	B put into TS 3.
	(14)	145–12,	11, 1	S 145 is (TS 2 + TS 3) and therefore A + B is sent to TS 12. This is the other result.

413

In this case the next instruction will be (16). If, however, A = B, the last instruction of the table will have been (9), and it is desirable to make the next instruction (16) in this case also. A dummy 'time wasting' instruction is given as (11) with a timing number of 4.

$$(11)\ 1023–1023, 11, 4.$$

The next instruction will now be (16) whichever the result.

16 MULTIPLIER

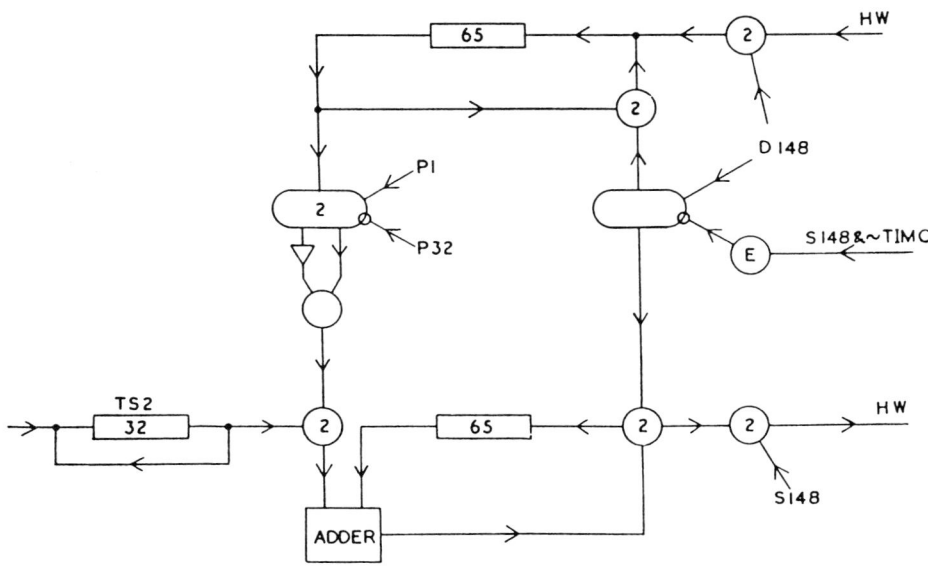

Figure 30

Multiplication in the binary scale is very simple since it is by a 0 or a 1 only. Consider two numbers A and B each of 32 digits. The product AB may be written:

$$A(B_1 + 2B_2 + 2^2 B_3 + \cdots + 2^{31} B_{32})$$

where B_1 to B_{32} are successive digits in the number B.

The multiplier is illustrated above. It consists of two special lines of 65 μs delay each and an adder. The operation is as follows. The number A is first put into TS 2. Number B is then put into the upper delay line. After one minor cycle B occupies the last 32 positions in the line. At the end of the three minor cycles B_{32} is in position one in the line. If B_{32} is a 1 the trigger circuit feeding the adder is stimulated by B_{32} & P 1. This opens the 2-element and A runs into the adder. If B_{32} is a 0, the 2-element is not opened and a stream of 0's runs into the adder.

The output of the adder runs into the lower 65 μs delay line. After a further two minor cycles B_{31} is picked out of the upper line, multiplied by A and fed to the adder, where it is added to the total already in the lower line displaced 1 μs. The process is repeated for all the digits in B.

414

The following table illustrates the action $A \times B = C$. (Numbers such as the '33' in the top delay line refer to strings of zeroes, e.g. 33 zeroes.)

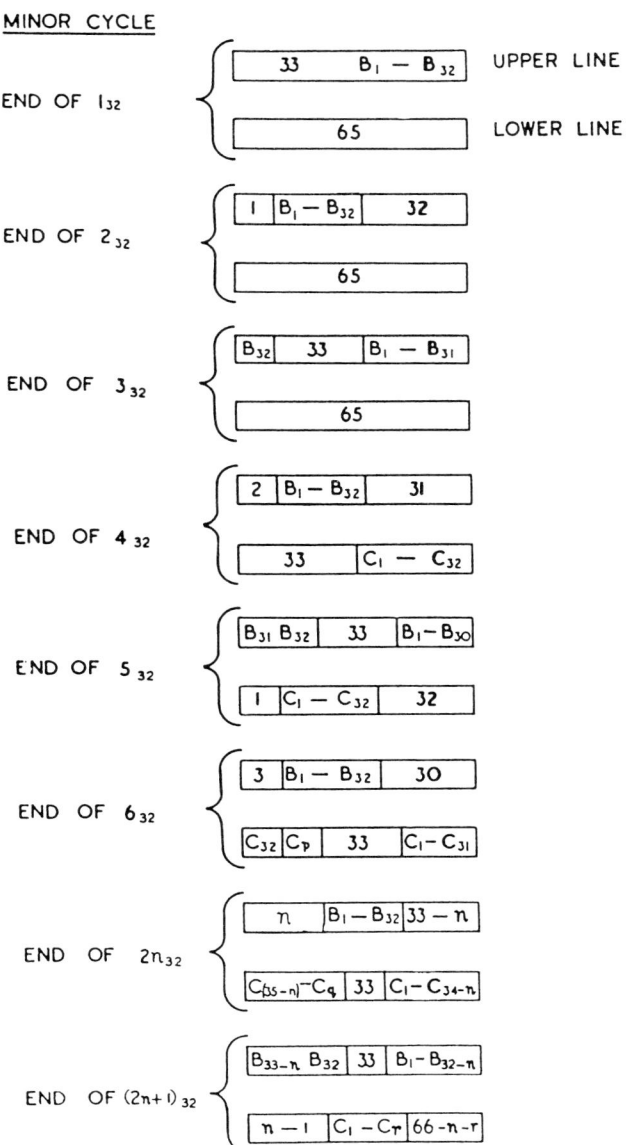

Thus if A and B are 32 digits each, the final total will be running out of the adder during the 66th and 67th minor cycles.

An instruction table ordering 32 digit numbers A in 10 and B in 11 to be multiplied together, the product being placed in DL 64, would be as follows.

(1)	10–2,	11,	1	A sent to TS 2.
(3)	11–148,	11,	1	B sent to multiplier upper delay line.
(5)	a–b,	x,	y ⎫	Other instructions to use up time until (68).
	etc.		⎬	
(68)	148–64,	11,	2 ⎭	64 digits product sent to DL 64.
(71)				Next instruction.

It will be seen from the above table that it requires 70 minor cycles to achieve the multiplication of two 32 digit numbers. The time may usefully be filled in by other processes since none of the highways are in use during this period.

Note. The trigger opening the feedback circuits of the two 65 µs lines is only put off when it receives a pulse from the E-element which is fed with (S 148 & $\sim$ TIMCI), i.e. it is put off only when transfer of 64 digit product to a storage line has been effected.

17 CUMULATIVE ADDER (D 150 AND D 151)

The function of this device is to count up (to a total consisting of 32 digits) any numbers which are sent to D 150, to store the total and make it available when required (Figure 31).

A number may be put direct into the line by D 151. Numbers coming in on D 150 are added to whatever is already in the line by the adder and put back into the line. The accumulated total may be obtained at S 150 when required.

The facilities offered by S 192, S 193 and S 194 are that the 8th, 16th or 32nd digit of the accumulated total may be examined. This is of use in certain problems.

18 EXAMPLES OF REPETITIVE PROCESSES

Example 1

Numbers $A_1, A_2 \ldots A_{32}$ are in DL 300. Determine how many are odd and put result in TS 10.

Note. Odd numbers have a 1 in first place. Hence if (P 1 & A_r) is formed (S 131) it will be a 1 if A_r is odd. The number of such 1's is stored in the cumulative adder D 150.

Instructions

	(1)	161–9	11, 1	Puts P1 into TS 9.
	(3)	300–260	11, 32	Puts all numbers $A_1 \cdots A_{32}$ into DL 260.
(36) =	(4)	260–8	11, 1	Puts A_5 in TS 8.
	(6)	131–150	11, 1	Forms (8 & 9) and sends result to D 150 (cumulative adder) (a 1 if number is odd).
	(8)	171–150	11, 1	P 11 sent to D 150. This is done so that after 32 repetitions of the table S 193 will give a pulse.

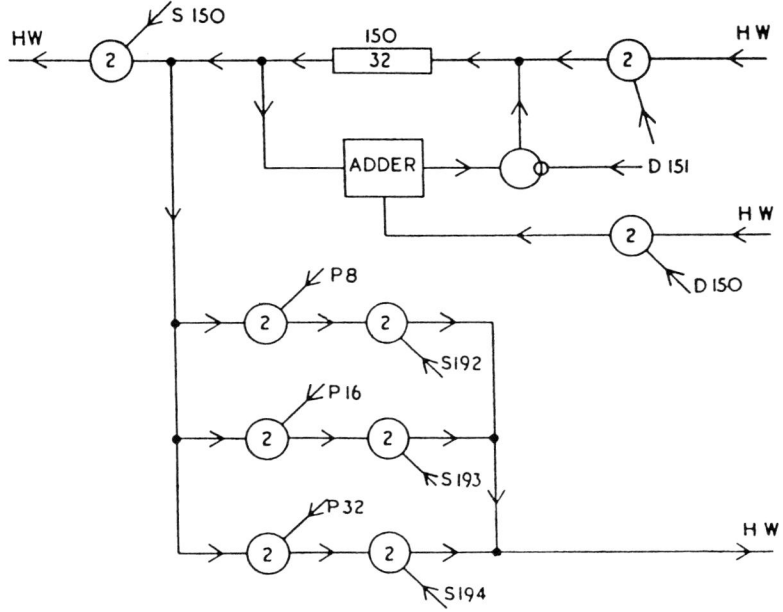

Figure 31

	(10)	158–260	11, 32	A$_1$, A$_2$ etc. now delayed by 1 minor cycle and put back into DL 260. Next number picked out by (4) will be A$_6$ and so on.
(43) =(11)		193–96	11, 1	TC 96 put on if table has been repeated 32 times.
	(13)	136–97	9, 0	Discrimination.
Either (15)		1023–1023	11, 20	Returns to (4) if TC 96 is not on. If TC 96 is on, process is finished but the 1 in 16th place (accumulated from instruction (8)) must be removed from total in 150.
or	(16)	150–2	11, 1	Total of 'odds' in 150 sent to TS 2.
	(18)	176–3	11, 1	P 16 sent to TS 3.
	(20)	159–10	11, 1	TS 3 subtracted from TS 2 and result sent to DL 10.
	(22)	135–151	11, 1	Clears cumulative adder for next operation.

Example 2

To find the larger of two positive numbers.

In order to represent negative numbers, the complementary notation is adopted i.e. $-A$ is represented by $(2^{32} - A)$ and $|A|$ is restricted to a value $<2^{31}$.

Thus to find the larger of two numbers A and B, both of which are $<2^{31}$, the difference $A - B$ is formed and if negative (i.e. a 1 in 32nd place) $B > A$ and vice versa.

Suppose A is in 10 and B in 11. The larger is to be put into 12.

417

Instructions

(1)	10–2,	11,	1	A sent to TS 2.
(3)	11–3,	11,	1	B sent to TS 3.
(5)	159–8,	11,	1	(TS 2 – TS 3) sent to TS 8.
(7)	160–9,	11,	1	P 32 sent to TS 9.
(9)	131–96,	11,	1	Forms (TS 8 & TS 9). If TS 8 contains a negative number, TC 96 is put on.
(11)	136–97,	9,	0	Discrimination.
Either (13)	10–12,	11,	2	If TC 96 not on, A > B and A sent to DL 12.
or (14)	11–12,	11,	1	If TC 96 is on, B > A and B sent to DL 12.

Note. The above method is applicable also to values of A and B positive or negative provided A and B are then both restricted to the range 2^{30} to -2^{30}. This is necessary since if A $= -$B $= 2^{31}$ say, the difference A $-$ B would have a 1 in 32 place and it would appear to the machine that the difference was negative, i.e. B > A, which is clearly absurd. Hence the further restriction on the values of A and B if either may be negative.

Example 3

Numbers $A_1, A_2 \ldots A_{32}$ $(2^{30} > A_r > 2^{-30})$ are in DL 300. It is required to find the largest and place it in DL 12.

The method is to compare a pair of numbers, find the larger and compare that with a third and so on until 32 have been examined.

Instructions

(1)	300–260,	11,	32	$A_1, A_2 \ldots A_{32}$ sent to DL 260.
(34) = (2)	260–2,	11,	1	A_3 picked out and sent to TS 2.
(4)	160–8,	11,	1	P 32 sent to TS 8.
(6)	163–150,	11,	1	P 3 sent to D 150 (cumulative adder). Thus after 32 repetitions of the table S 192 will give a pulse (i.e. in 8th place).
(8)	260–3,	11,	1	A_{10} sent to TS 3.
(10)	159–9,	11,	1	Forms difference $(A_3 - A_9)$ and sends to TS 9.
(12)	131–96,	11,	1	Forms (TS 8 & TS 9) and stimulates TC 96 if $(A_3 - A_9)$ is negative. (i.e. if $A_9 > A_3$).
(14)	136–97,	9,	0	Discrimination.
Either (16)	1023–1023,	11,	2	If TC 96 not on $(A_3 > A_9)$ A_3 already in TS 2.
or (17)	3–2,	11,	1	If TC 96 is on $(A_9 > A_3)$ A_9 sent to TS 2.
(19)	158–260,	11,	32	All numbers in DL 26 delayed one minor cycle.
(52) = (20)	192–96,	11,	1	If S 192 stimulates TC 96, process has been repeated 32 times.
(22)	136–97,	9,	0	Discrimination.

418

Either (24) 1023–1023, 11, 13 If TC 96 not on, returns to (6) and repeats table.
  or (25) 2–12, 11, 1 If TC 96 is on, process is finished and largest number
                         is sent to DL 12.
    (26) 135–151, 11, 1 Clears cumulative adder for next operation.

19 CONTROL AND INSTRUCTION (VERSION VI)

A major difficulty in the machine described to date was the permanent association of
certain operations with certain delay lines. For example TS 2 and TS 3 were associated
with an adder. Thus in order to add two numbers, one had to be put in TS 2, the other in
TS 3 and S 145 routed to the required destination.

A table for such a simple process would be, for example:

(1) 10–2,   11, 1
(3) 11–3,   11, 1
(5) 145–12, 11, 1

Three separate instructions are required.

A shortening and simplification of the instruction table would result if two numbers
could be taken from *any* sources A and B, have an operation F performed on them, the
result delayed D micro seconds and then put in C all by means of one instruction.

Such an operation may now be performed by means of *two word instructions.*

These two word instructions may be used at any time in addition to the original single
word instructions.

Form of two word instruction

Digits	1, 2	3–12	13–32	23–26	27–32
1st word	Spare	Source A	Destination C	Characteristic	Timing
2nd word	Spare	Source B	Delay D (0–1023 μs)	Operation F	Spare

The first word of a two word instruction is similar to the original one word type
except for the characteristic. This must now indicate whether the instruction is a one
word instruction or whether it is the first word of a two word instruction.

The significance of digits 23–26 is therefore as follows.

Digit		Meaning	
23	0	External operation	} as before
	1	Internal operation	
24	0	Deferred operation	
	1	Immediate operation	
25, 26,	0 0	Next instruction from TS 0 and present word is a one-word instruction.	

1 0	Next instruction from TS 1 and present word is a one-word instruction.
0 1	Next instruction from DL 256 and present word is a one-word instruction.
1 1	Next instruction from DL 256 and present word is 1st word of a two-word instruction.

The second word digits 23–26, i.e. the value of F, determines the nature of the operation to be performed on the numbers from sources.

The code is as follows

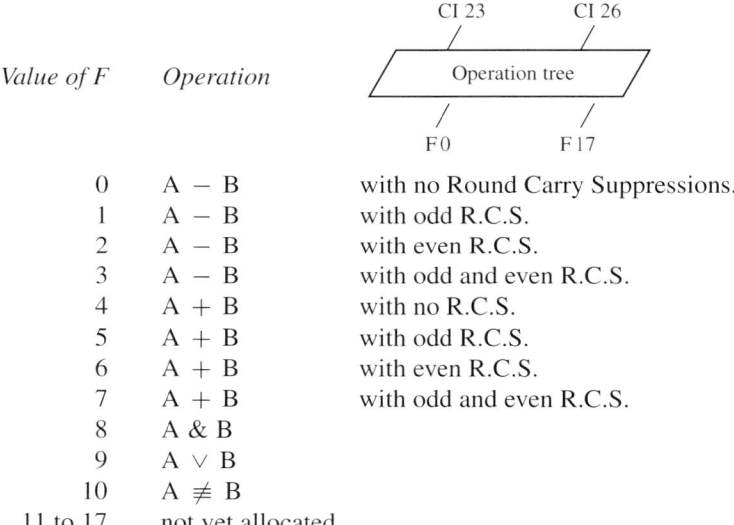

Value of F	Operation	
0	A − B	with no Round Carry Suppressions.
1	A − B	with odd R.C.S.
2	A − B	with even R.C.S.
3	A − B	with odd and even R.C.S.
4	A + B	with no R.C.S.
5	A + B	with odd R.C.S.
6	A + B	with even R.C.S.
7	A + B	with odd and even R.C.S.
8	A & B	
9	A ∨ B	
10	A ≢ B	
11 to 17	not yet allocated.	

The ability to add or subtract with various R.C.S. is very useful, since it enables numbers composed of any number of words to be added or subtracted. For example, if the numbers are each 64 digits long, then they must be added with even R.C.S.

Arrangement of secondary control circuit

A secondary staticiser is arranged in the control circuits as shown below (Figure 32). While the first word is running into the primary staticiser (the original one) the second word is running into the secondary staticiser and setting up trigger circuits CJ 3–CJ 26 (Figure 33).

Triggers CJ 3 to CJ 12 select the secondary sources SS 0 to SS 1023 by means of a secondary source tree.

Triggers CJ 13 to CJ 26 feed into a delay unit and select the required delay.

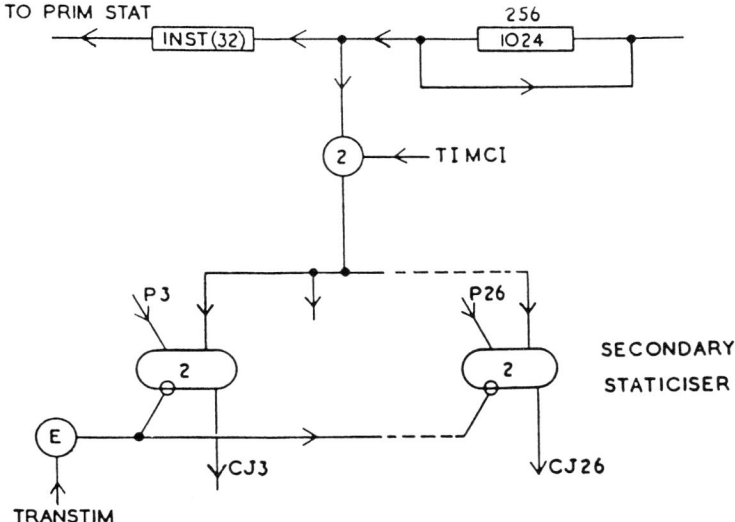

Figure 32

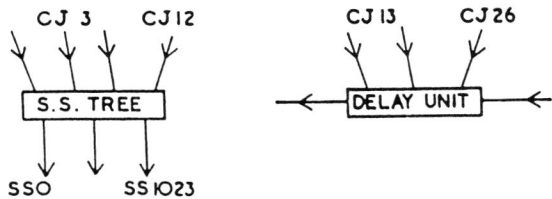

Figure 33

Delay unit

This unit is constructed so that any delay from 0–1023 µs may be selected. The arrangement is as below.

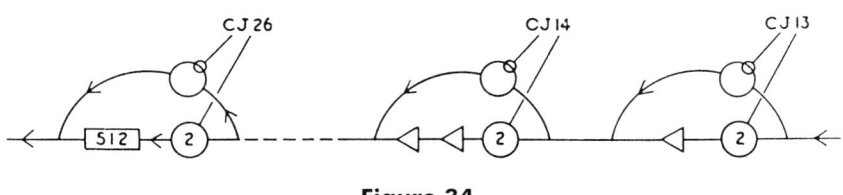

Figure 34

Thus if the required delay is, for example, 39 µs, triggers CJ 13, 14, 15 and 18 will be on and a total delay of 39 µs introduced in the delay unit.

Highway arrangements

All sources may now be fed into either or both of two highways. These are known as HW 1 and HW 2. An S signal puts the source to HW 1 and an SS signal puts the source to HW 2.

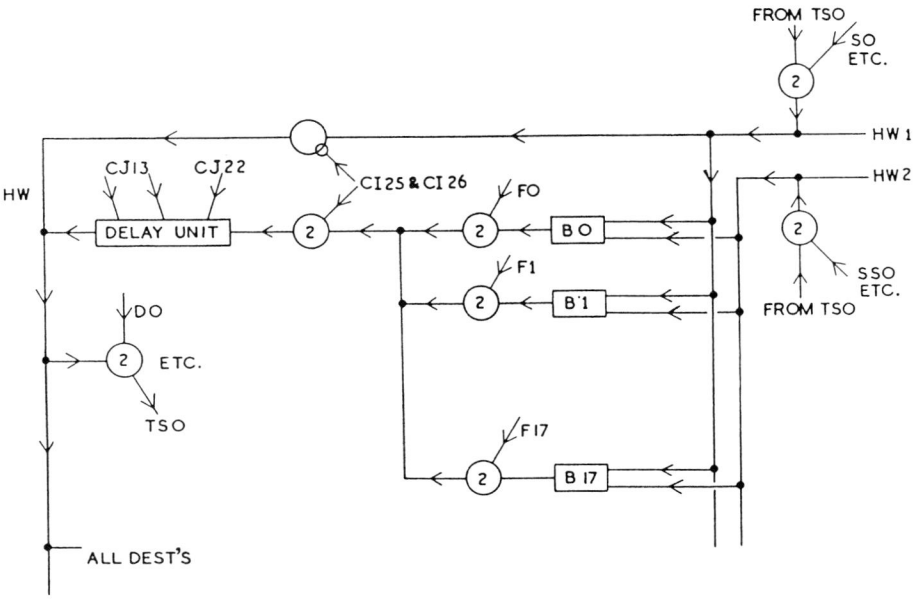

Figure 35

B 0 to B 17 are the units in which the addition, subtraction and logical operations are performed.

Consider first a one word instruction. It will be set up on the primary staticiser in the normal way and the next one word instruction will be set up on the secondary staticiser. Since the first instruction is of one word only, its digits 25 and 26 will be one of 00, 01, or 10 but *not* 11. Hence (CI 25 and CI 26) will be 0's and the number on HW 1 will pass directly through to the destination highway.

The source tapped to HW 2 by the instruction in the secondary staticiser will pass to the B units together with the number on HW 1 and will have some operation performed on it, but will not reach the delay unit and destination HW since the 2-element is not opened by (CI 25 & CI 26). The action is thus quite normal.

If the instruction is the first word of a two word instruction, then digits 25 and 26 will be 11. Thus (CI 25 & CI 26) will be 1's, the direct route from HW 1 to destination HW will be inhibited and the operation selected by F will be performed on the numbers. The result will be delayed D in the delay unit and then passed to the destination highway.

422

20 EXAMPLES OF TWO-WORD INSTRUCTIONS

Example 1

It is required to add a series of 32 words in DL 300 to a series of words in DL 301, the results to be placed in DL 302 with no delay.

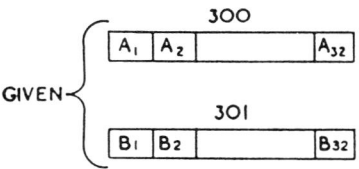

Instructions

This is 1111

(1)   300–302,   15,   32   (Since 32 pairs are to be added.)
(2)   301–0,   7,   —

Example 2

There are 32 numbers each of 32 digits, in DL 300. Find how many of them are odd and put result in DL 10.

Note. All odd numbers have a 1 in first place. Hence if a number is, say, A_r and (P 1 & A_r) is formed, this will be a 1 if A_r is odd.

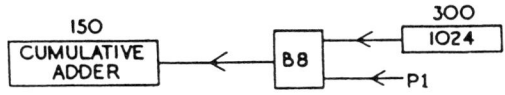

Instruction

(1)   300–150, 15, 32
(2)   161–0,   8, —
(34) 150–10,   9, 1
=(2)

Compare this simple table with the table required to solve the same problem in the original machine with only one word instruction.

Example 3

Given 32 numbers of 32 digits each in DL 300 arranged

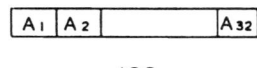

at the commencement of a major cycle, delay them by 1 minor cycle so that they are arranged

$$\boxed{A_{32} \mid A_1 \mid A_2 \mid \quad \text{ETC.} \quad}$$

at the commencement of a major cycle.

Note. Process is to add SS.135 (a series of 0's), delay result by 32 μs, and feed back.

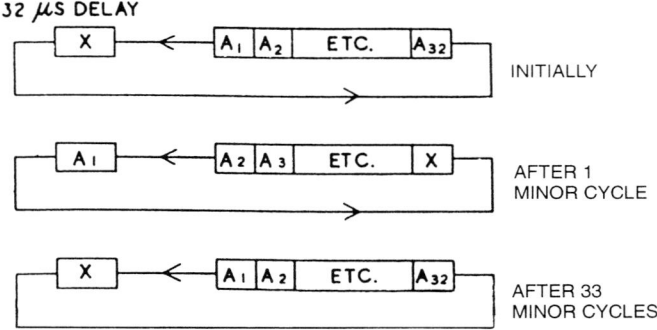

32 μS DELAY

INITIALLY

AFTER 1 MINOR CYCLE

AFTER 33 MINOR CYCLES

i.e., if timed for 33 and then stopped, arrangement at the commencement of a major cycle has become

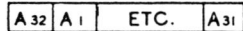

$$\boxed{A_{32} \mid A_1 \mid \quad \text{ETC.} \quad \mid A_{31}}$$

Instruction

(1) 300–300, 15, 33
(2) 135–32, 7, —

In general

With n word notation for a series of numbers (i.e. of $32\,n$ digits each) to move up by one complete number (i.e. n minor cycles) instruction is

(1) 300–300, 15, $(32 + n)$
(2) 135–32 n, 7, —

Example 4

Given A in TS 10 and B in TS 11 form $8\,(A+B)$ and put in TS 12.

Instruction

(1) 10–12, 15, 1
(2) 11–3,   15, —

21 A SPECIAL SOURCE IN THE VERSION VI CONTROL SYSTEM

This is S 157. Its function is to enable a particular number of 32 digits to be fed into the machine, for use in the computation, via the instruction table.

The arrangement is as below.

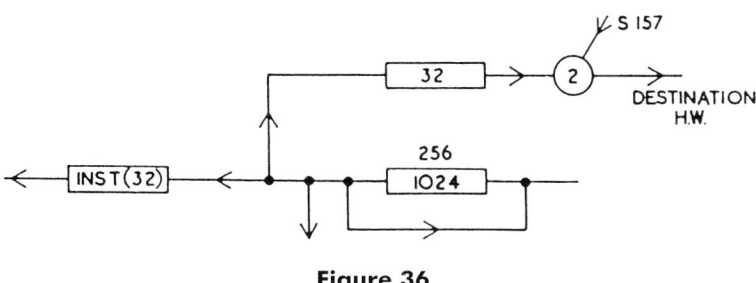

Figure 36

Instruction

(1)   157–2,   11,   1
(2)   NUMBER
(3)   etc.

(1) & (2) are a two-word instruction which causes instruction (2), which is the number, to be sent via the destination HW to TS 2.

The operation then continues normally.

22 CHANGING INSTRUCTION TABLES

It is frequently necessary that while using a main table, say Table I, at a certain stage another table, say Table II, be brought into use, after which the main table (or a third) be reverted to. This may be effected by *link instructions*.

Suppose Table I is in DL 301 and Table II in DL 300. A blank is left in the subsidiary Table II at a convenient point at the end for the link.

The link instruction will be supplied by the main table using the facility of S 157.

Main Table I (in DL 301)

(1) L–M,   11, 1
      to   } Normal instructions.
(9) N–O,   11, 1
(11) 157–300, 9, 4   This is a delayed instruction ordering INSTR (16) into the blank in Table II (which is INSTR (17) in Table II). Hence timing number 4.
(16) 301–256, 11, x   This is the link instruction.
(17) 300–256, 11, y (47) This orders Table II into use.

Subsidiary Table II (in DL 300)

(1) A–B,   11, 1
      to   } Normal instructions.
(15) C–D,   11, 1
(17) LINK (301–256, 11, x) Supplied by Table I and brings Table I back into use.

Note. x & y must be chosen to order the new table into use at the correct minor cycle.

   Thus $y = 32 + (32 - 17) = 47$
   & $x = 32 + (32 - 17) = 47$ also, if both tables commence at (1).

23 INPUT AND OUTPUT UNITS

The input and output to and from the A.C.E. is by means of Hollerith units and punched cards. The standard Hollerith code is illustrated below. Each card may be punched in 12 rows comprising 80 columns.

The numbering of rows and columns is as shown.

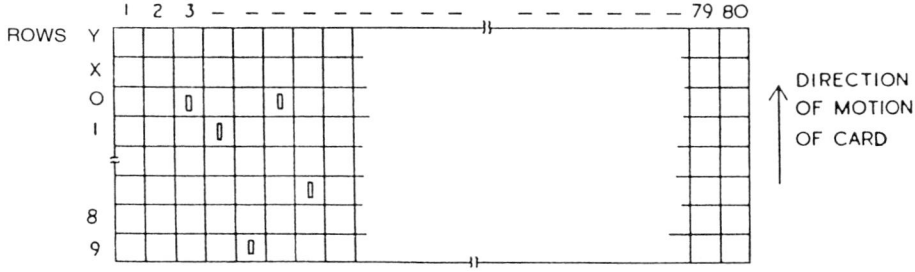

Figure 37

As normally used in the decimal scale, a ten figure number, say, could be represented by punching holes at positions in the first ten columns corresponding to the value of the digit in each place. Thus a number of 5 digits, for example 62049, would be represented as shown below.

426

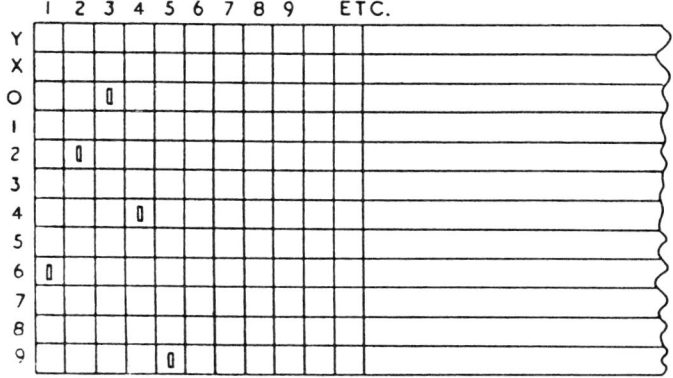

Figure 38

Cards so punched are used to feed numbers to be used in a computation into the machine. The A.C.E. itself converts such decimal numbers into binary form and stores them.

Cards, however, may be used to record binary numbers directly. Either one or two 32 digit binary numbers may be punched in each row. At the present time only columns 41 to 72 inclusive are being used, with the convention that a 'hole' corresponds to a 1 and 'no-hole' to a 0. Thus a total of twelve (or 24) binary numbers may be punched on each card. The remaining columns are used for indexing and coding of the cards. This method of punching is used for recording output data and also for feeding in instruction tables. In the latter case, the instructions are punched in the normal decimal fashion on cards. The cards are then fed through a Hollerith machine which converts the information to binary form and assembles 12 instructions and punches them on a single card.

Input Card Reader

The data is taken from the cards by means of a series of 80 brushes under which the cards pass. As a hole passes under a brush a circuit is completed. The case of card data in binary form only will be considered at present, i.e. instructions.

The cards pass through the reader at a rate of 150 cards/min. Each card has 12 rows and there are 4 'dead' rows between cards, i.e. 25 ms per row.

Each row is actually being read for a period of 8–10 ms out of the 25 ms.

In order to read a card, the necessary instructions must be in the A.C.E. in advance. The table is as follows.

(1) 136–138, 11, 1 D 138 controls a knife edge which pushes a card
into the reader.

A signal is now required to indicate when the card is in position for the first row (y) to be read. This is obtained from the reader itself (mechanical contact) and is S 132^{+}.

427

(3) 132^{+}–96, 11, 1   If a card is in position, TC 96 will be put on and vice versa.

(5) 0–5,   11, 1   Dynamiciser contents sent to TS 5.

(7) 136–97,   9,   26   Discrimination. If TC 96 is off (card not yet ready) brings back to (3). (3) and (7) repeated until TC 96 comes on when (5) is applied.

Wait 15 ms (approx.) and then take next row.

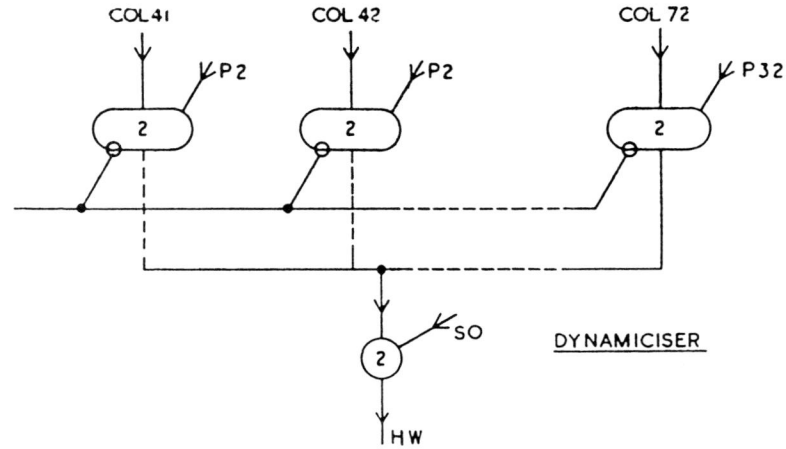

Figure 39

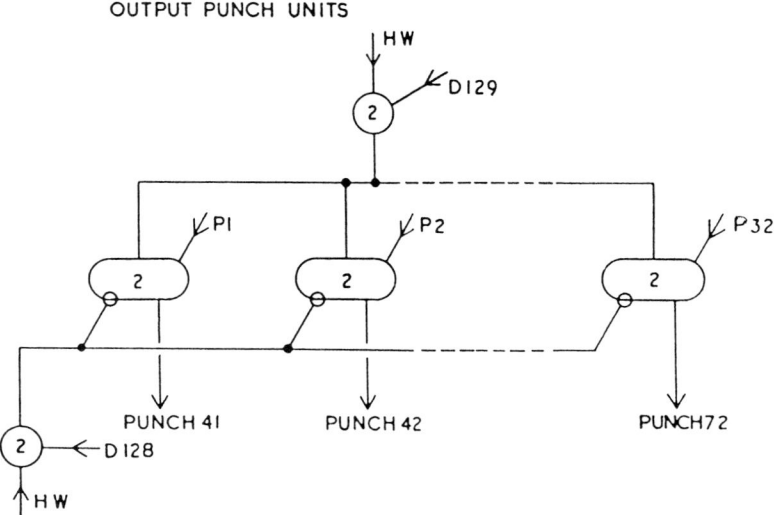

Figure 40

428

To record an output number, the number is sent to D 129 to set up the staticiser. These trigger circuits operate the punch relays in the punch unit. Then card is punched (15 ms) and the staticiser cleared.

An alternative output is to a print unit.

24 ARITHMETICAL OPERATIONS WITH POSITIVE OR NEGATIVE NUMBERS

In all the following operations the numbers concerned are composed of a maximum of 32 binary digits, i.e. the modulus of all numbers is less than 2^{32} in magnitude.

It should be remembered that in the A.C.E., as in most digital computers, a negative quantity, say $-A$, is represented by the number (A max $-$ A) where (A max $-$ 1) is maximum possible number which can be handled.

Thus in a 32 digit number in the A.C.E., $-A$ would be represented by $2^{32} - A$.

If $|A|$ is restricted to a value $< 2^{31}$, the 32nd digit of the word will be a 0 if the number is positive and a 1 if negative. This is the accepted code for negative numbers.

Operation $A + B$

A and B may be positive or negative numbers.

A two word instruction.

(1) A–C, 15, 1
(2) B–0,   7, —

carries out the operation and puts the result in C. Similarly the instruction

1) A–C, 15, 1
2) B–0,   3, —

forms $A - B$.

Operation $A + nB$

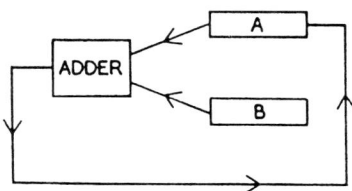

In this case, B is added n times to A.

1) A–A, 15, n
2) B–0,   7, —

The answer accumulates in the A line and method words for positive or negative numbers.

429

Operation 2^nA where $n < 31$ and positive

This may be achieved by delaying the word for n μs provided that a has less than $31 - n$ digits.

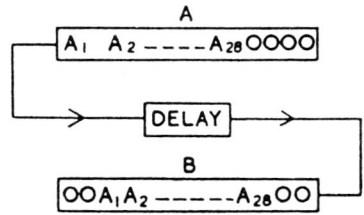

(1) A–B,   15, 1
(2) 135–2,   7, —

Method is to add a series of 0's (S 135) and delay result 2 μs and put in B. Works for A positive or negative with above restrictions.

Note. To move a number round n places in a line (and not multiply it by 2^n)

e.g., $n = z$

$$\boxed{\text{A}_1 \quad \text{A}_2 \;\text{---------}\; \text{A}_{32}}$$

$$\boxed{\text{A}_1 \quad \text{A}_{32} \;\text{A}_1 \text{------}\; \text{A}_{30}}$$

(1) A–B,   15, 2
(2) 135–2,   7, —

In this case add zero's and put into B with a delay of 2 μs. The number cannot be fed back into the same line in this case, since this would introduce zero's within the number. Operation $2^n(A \pm B)$

1) A–C, 15, 1
2) B–n,   7, —
          or 3 for $-B$.

Operation 2^{-n}A, A positive

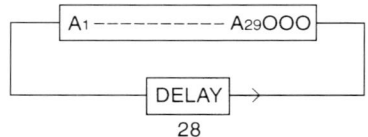

For example, 2^{-4}A.

An advance of 4 μs is the same as a delay of 28 μs.

(1) A–A,   15, 2
(2) 135–28,   7, —

This works for positive A and number must be returned to original line.

If A is positive or negative, perform a discrimination to determine the sign. If negative, find complement, perform operation, and replace sign afterwards.

Operation $A \times B$

A and B may be positive or negative. If A and B are both positive the operation is straightforward. However, if either or both A and B are negative and expressed in the usual convention difficulties arise.

For example, suppose A is negative.

The product formed will be

$$(2^{32} - A)B = 2^{32}B - AB.$$

But the required product is known to be $2^{64} - AB$, in a 64 μs delay line. Hence the quantity $2^{32}(2^{32} - B)$ must be added to the answer to obtain the correct product.

Similarly if B is negative

$$2^{32}(2^{32} - A)$$

must be added.

If both A and B are negative, answer produced will be

$$(2^{32} - A)(2^{32} - B) = 2^{64} - 2^{32}(A + B) + AB.$$

Hence in this case $2^{32}(A + B)$ must be added. (The 2^{64} has no effect.)

An instruction table for signed multiplication will make the operation clear.

A is in line 11 and B in 12. A and B may be positive or negative. The product is to be formed and put in line 64.

(1) 11–2,   11, 1   A put in TS 2.
(3) 12–148, 11, 1   B put in 148.

The multiplication now proceeds normally and the product will be available in minor cycles (3 + 67) and (3 + 68), i.e. in (6) and (7). This time interval is used to determine the corrections, if any, that are required, as follows.

(5)	135–65,	11,	2	Clears out 65 in case it has something left in it. 65 is used for holding the correction term.
(8)	11–96,	15,	1 ⎫	Determines sign of A by forming (A & P 32) and
(9)	160–0,	8,	— ⎭	passing result to TC 96. TC 96 put on if A is negative.
(10)	136–97,	9,	0	Discrimination. Puts off TC 96 if on.
Either				
(12)	1023–1023,	11,	2	If A is positive wastes time until (15).
or				
(13)	12–65,	11,	1	If A is negative sends B to DL 65.
(15)	160–96,	15,	1 ⎫	Determines sign of B by forming (A & P 32) and
(16)	12–0,	8,	— ⎭	passing result to TC 96. TC 96 put on if B is negative.

431

(17) 136–97,   9,   0   Discrimination.
Either
(19) 1023–1023, 11,   3   If B is positive, wastes time until (23).
or
(20) 11–65,   13,   1 ⎫ Delayed instruction which adds A to correct
(21) 65–0,   7,   — ⎭ half of DL 65.

(23) 148–64,   15, 48 ⎫ Subtracts number in DL 65 from product and puts
(24) 65–0,   1,   — ⎭ in DL 64. Timing number is chosen to obtain result
                             when product is coming from the multiplier.

Next instruction will be (72) = (8).

Note. The total time required for signed multiplication is the same as for unsigned.

25 VERSION VII

In this version the instructions are in a modified form. Either one– or two– word instructions can be used, the form of the instruction being thus:

Digits	1	2–10	11–19	20–21	22–26	27–32
1st Word	Spare	Source	Destination	Characteristic	Source of next instr.	Timing
2nd Word	Spare	Sec. Source	Delay (21 not used)		Operation (26 not used)	Spare

In this new instructional form, it will be seen that only nine digits are used to describe a source or destination and this limits the total number of sources to 512. It is considered that with the increased flexibility of the machine this number will be adequate.

The characteristic is of two digits and is used to indicate whether the instruction is of one word or two and whether immediate or deferred.

00 Deferred one-word instruction.
10 Immediate one-word instruction.
01 Deferred two-word instruction.
11 Immediate one-word instruction.

The use of five digits to describe the source of the next instruction facilitates the use of 32 possible sources. These are DL 256 to DL 287 inclusive, and are selected by a small tree in the usual manner:

Thus 0 for digits 22–26 selects DL 256
      1 for digits 22–26 selects DL 257
      n for digits 22–26 selects DL $(256 + n)$

In the second word of a two word instruction, the delay required is represented by digits 11–20, 21 not being used, and the operation by digits 22–25, 26 being spare also. The operation code is as before, namely:

432

Value	Operation			
0	HW1 − HW2	with	NO	R.C.S. (Round Carry Suppression)
1	HW1 − HW2	with	ODD	R.C.S.
2	HW1 − HW2	with	EVEN	R.C.S.
3	HW1 − HW2	with	ODD & EVEN	R.C.S.
4	HW1 + HW2	with	NO	R.C.S.
5	HW1 + HW2	with	ODD	R.C.S.
6	HW1 + HW2	with	EVEN	R.C.S.
7	HW1 + HW2	with	ODD & EVEN	R.C.S.
8	HW1 & HW2			
9	HW1 $\vee$ HW2			
10	HW1 $\neq$ HW2			
11	(HW1 & 157) $\vee$ (HW2 & $\sim$ 157)			
12–15	Not yet allocated.			

The circuits for the new selector arrangements and new coding are shown below and are self-explanatory. The operation of these portions of the circuit is identical with those in the Version VI, though some of the units have somewhat different internal construction. Of these, the function unit is noteworthy.

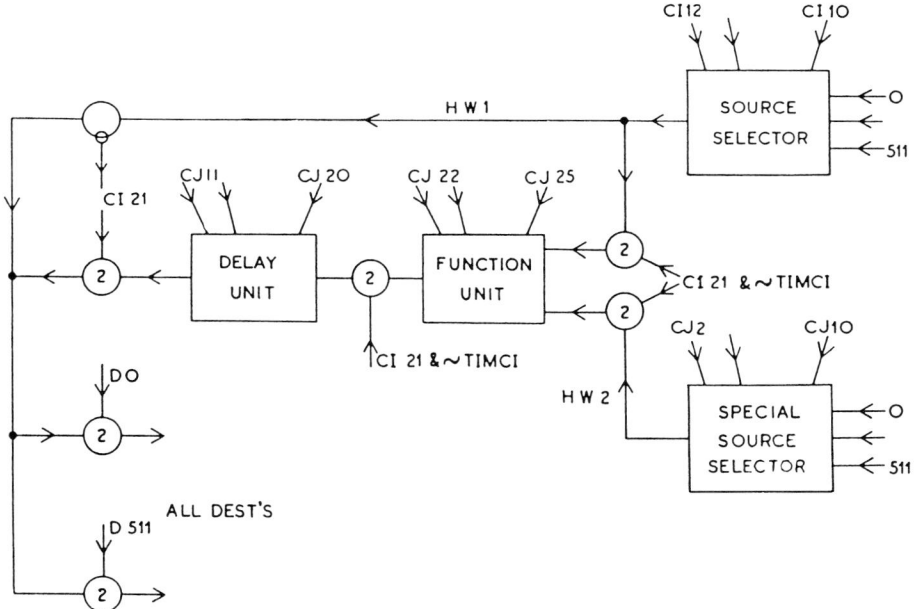

Figure 41

433

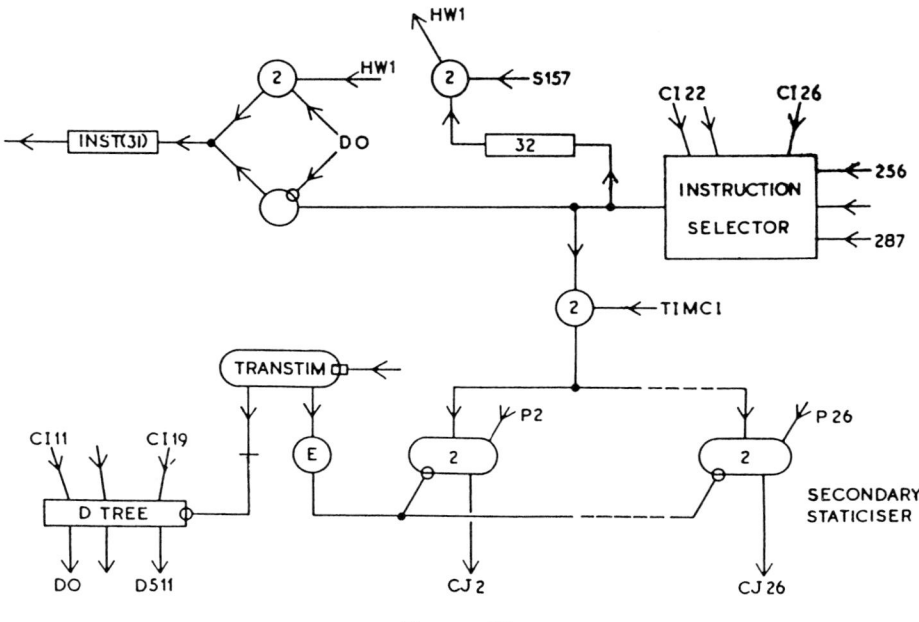

Figure 42

Function unit

The operation tree of Version VI has been dispensed with and the circuit is operated direct from trigger circuits CJ 22 and CJ 25 inclusive.

The circuit is shown in Figure 43.

The upper portion of the circuit is the adder, which is provided with either Odd, Even, Both or No Round Suppression. (Note: EVEN is a multivibrator which is on and off during alternate minor cycles).

For subtraction (HW1 − HW2), CJ 24 is off and the number on HW2 has its digits inverted, i.e. 0's for 1's and vice versa, by the polarity changer. Thus the number sent to the adder is $2^{32} - 1 - B$, where B is the original 32 digit number on HW2. But the true complement of B is $2^{32} - B$. Hence one must be added to the result in the adder. This is achieved by adding in the carry suppression pulse at the beginning of the minor cycle concerned. It will be seen that the method works for numbers of 32 or 64 digits, but does not for numbers of more digits than 64. If it is essential to correct an answer for a greater number of digits than 64 this must be done separately.

The lower portions of the circuit are for the logical operations and are self explanatory.

The timing circuits of version VII

Several changes have been introduced into the timing circuits of the control. The slow counter has been redesigned and the whole circuit simplified as in Figure 44.

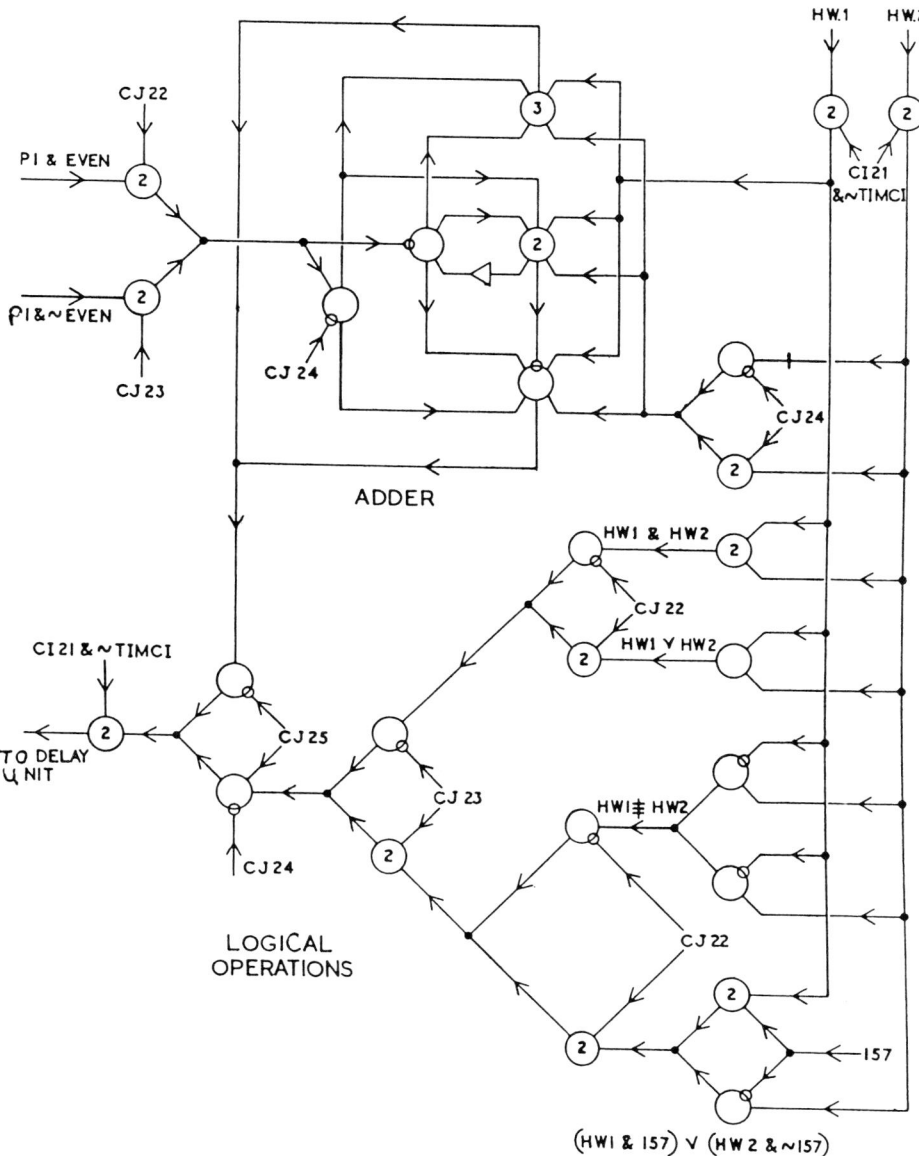

Figure 43

The length of the INSTRUCTION line (Figure 44) is now 31 μs. As before, when TIMCI is on, an instruction is allowed to run into the staticiser. Since, however, the INSTR line is of length 31 only, an extra 1 μs delay has to be inserted before the staticiser. TIMCI can be put on only by a pulse from the E-element, i.e. only when TRANSTIM goes off, and puts itself off after one minor cycle by its 32 pulse delayed by 1 μs and gated by P 1.

435

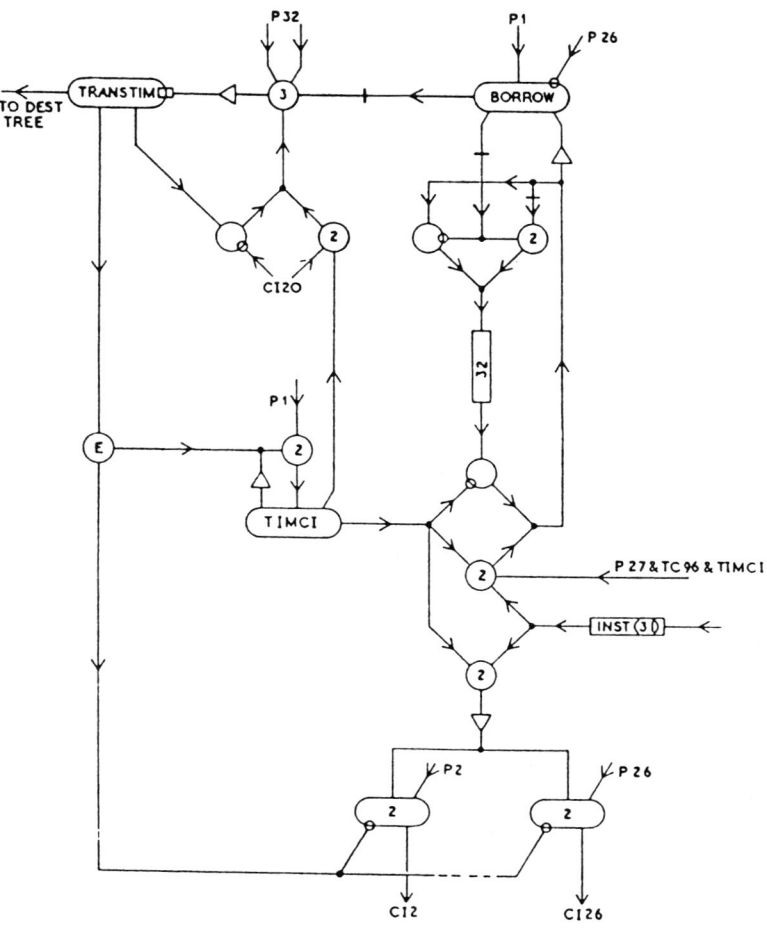

Figure 44

Consider now a single word instruction of the immediate variety with a timing number of 5. The characteristic (digits 20 & 21) will be 1 and therefore CI 20 will come on. The instruction then runs into the staticiser and simultaneously into the slow counter portion. The BORROW trigger circuit will be on as a result of a P 1 pulse at the commencement of the minor cycle and will be put off again during the 26th μs of the minor cycle by P 26. While BORROW is off, the 1-element above the counter delay line will be inhibited, and the 2-element will be opened. During the 26th μs, therefore, digit 27 of the instruction will pass to the counter delay line via the polarity changer and the 2-element. Thus if originally a 0 it will enter the line as a 1 and vice versa. The 27th digit will arrive at BORROW during the 27th μs and if a 1 will put BORROW on again. The 28th and subsequent digits of the instruction will therefore pass to the counter delay

436

line unchanged. The action is best illustrated by the following table for an instruction of timing number 5.

	Digit numbers					
	27	28	29	30	31	32
Instruction (timing number 5)	1	0	1	0	0	0

Minor cycle	*Digits passed to counter line* (Position in minor cycle)						
	26	27	28	29	30	31	32
End of 1	0	0	1	0	0	0	0

BORROW off during 26th μs and therefore 27th digit of INSTR passed as a 0.
BORROW put on by 27th digit on 27th μs and next passed unchanged.

End of 2	1	1	0	0	0	0	0

BORROW off during 26th μs and not put on until 29th μs by the 28th digit delayed 1 μs. Rest of digits pass unchanged.

End of 3	0	1	0	0	0	0	0
End of 4	1	0	0	0	0	0	0
End of 5	0	0	0	0	0	0	0

Now TRANSTIM is not put off until it receives a pulse during the 32nd μs of a minor cycle from BORROW, i.e. until BORROW is off at this time. It will be seen from the example that this will not occur until the end of minor cycle 6 in this case.

Hence this timing circuit produces precisely the same result as in Version VI, i.e. an instruction of timing number t is set up in the first minor cycle and takes place during the next t minor cycles. The next instruction will be set up in minor cycle $(t + 2)$ as before. The procedure with a deferred instruction is along similar lines. The instruction runs into the staticiser during the first minor cycle. The counter operates as before. CI 20 is off in this case (deferred instruction), and therefore TRANSTIM has put itself off. The transfer does not take place until TRANSTIM goes on again, i.e. until BORROW is off during the 32nd μs of a minor cycle. This occurs after $(t + 1)$ minor cycles. TRANSTIM then goes on for one minor cycle and puts itself off.

Discrimination

As in the earlier control circuits discrimination facilities are provided by the use of TC 96. Since in Version VII two-word instructions will largely be used it is desirable that after a discrimination instruction of number n the next instruction will be either $(n + 2)$ or $(n + 4)$. This is achieved by the input of (P 27 & TC 96 & TIMCI) which, if TC 96 is on, adds a 1 in the 27th place of the number circulating in the counter and hence delays the operation of TRANSTIM by 2 minor cycles.

26 INITIAL STARTING PROCEDURE

The problem of starting up the A.C.E. is a complex one, since after switching on, all the lines will have a random assortment of spurious pulses in them. The first thing to be done, therefore, is to clear out a line of all spurious pulses.

437

Three manually operated switches are provided in the control circuit. The first is a switch operating on TRANSTIM and called 'PARALYSIS PERIOD'. This has three settings:

'0'   – Normal working
'10 ms' – 10 ms delay after working
'∞'   – used in conjunction with a SINGLE TRANSFER switch to operate TRANSTIM one at a time.

The third switch is 'P 32 PULSES'. It has 3 positions:

'ON'   – Normal
'Hollerith' – P 32 pulses gated by card reader and only supplied when a card is in a position to be read.
'OFF'   – no P 32 at all.

With the aid of these switches, the starting up is as follows:

(1) Check that P 32 pulses are on.
(2) Set PARALYSIS to ∞ to ensure TRANSTIM off.
(3) Set P 32 PULSES to Hollerith.
(4) Set PARALYSIS to 10 ms. TRANSTIM put on only when a card is in position.
(5) Clear the CI staticiser by a manual switch.
(6) Start card feed with a pack of 'Initial Input Cards'.

Initial Input Cards

Since the CI staticiser has been cleared, it is set up with a row of zeros, i.e. with an instruction in the Version VII code of 0−0, 0, 0, 0, the last figure the timing number, going to the counter.

The meaning of this instruction is: 'Feed the input dynamiciser to the INSTR line, the instruction being a deferred one-word instruction. The next instruction will come from DL 256 and the timing number of this instruction is 0.'

This means that the 1st row of the first Initial Input Card is fed to the INSTR line. The instructions on these cards then go as shown in the table below.

Minor cycle	Input to INSTR	Origin	Effect
(30)	135–256, 1, 0, 0,	Row 1	A string of 0's pass to 256 for two major cycles (due to 10 m s paralysis of TRANSTIM) and clears the line. Row 2 is wasted.
(31)	0–0, 0, 0, 0,	256	Row 3 to INSTR.
(1)	0–258, 0, 0, 29,	Row 3	Row 4 to DL 258
(0)	0–0, 0, 0, 0,	256	Row 5 to INSTR.
(2)	0–258, 0, 0, 29,	Row 5	Row 6 to DL 258

and so on.

DL 258 can thus be filled with 32 instructions by having odd rows on cards of the required instructions alternating with the instruction 0–258, 0, 0, 29. The first table thus introduced into the machine should be one enabling the more easy assimilation of further instructions.

Synchronisation of EVEN (S 157) with the machine

This is another starting-up problem. The EVEN multivibrator, which is on and off in even and odd minor cycles respectively, has to be made to synchronise with the arbitrary numbering of the minor cycle. It is found simpler in practice however to achieve the reverse, i.e. to number the minor cycles to correspond to the already functioning multivibrator.

This is done, as soon as sufficient initial instructions have been introduced into the machine, by forming the result $\sim$ (EVEN & P 27).

	1	2–10	11–19	20	21	22–26	27	28	29	30	31	32	
P 27	0	0–0	0–0	0	0	0–0	1	0	0	0	0	0	
$\sim$ (EVEN &P 27)	1	1–1	1–1	1	1	1–1	0	1	1	1	1	1	If EVEN is on.
	1	1–1	1–1	1	1	1–1	1	1	1	1	1	1	If EVEN is off.

This result will have two possible values depending on whether EVEN is on or off during the minor cycle in which the operation is performed. If the result is interpreted as an instruction, the two possibilities will be:

511–511, 3, 31, 62 if EVEN was on.
or 511–511, 3, 31, 63 if EVEN was off.

In either case, the instruction is a 'waste-time' one and if obeyed by the machine, will carry it on for either 62 or 63 minor cycles, depending on the original state of EVEN.

The action will be illustrated by reference to a complete instruction table for the process.

Minor cycle		
n	EVEN–8, 1, 0, 1	Sends EVEN to TS 8.
$n+2$	187–9, 1, 0, 1	P 27 to TS 9.
$n+4$	137–0, 1, 0, 1	Forms $\sim$ (8 & 9) and sends to INSTR.
$n+6$	511–511, 3, 31, 62 or 63	
$n+69$	Next instruction if n was an even minor cycle.	
$n+70$	Next instruction if n was an odd minor cycle.	

The next instruction obeyed after $(n+6)$ is always odd, since if n had been odd then that instruction would be $(n+70)$, i.e. odd also. If n had been even, then the next instruction followed after $(n+6)$ would be $(n+69)$, i.e. odd.

Hence, to synchronise the machine with EVEN, a table of the above form is fed through and results in the determination of an odd minor cycle.

27 POLARITY CHANGER

The circuits given in this and the following two sections represent possible methods of producing the required effects of the various units. At present it is by no means certain that any of these schemes will be finally adopted. They are intended only to indicate possible solutions.

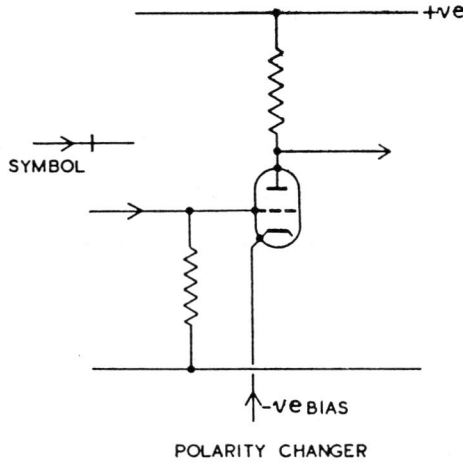

POLARITY CHANGER

Figure 45

A single valve connected as shown will act as a polarity changer for the conversion of 1's to 0's and vice versa. A 1 is normally represented as a voltage pulse in the positive sense.

The valve is normally biassed to cutoff and the input pulses are large enough to take the valve up to saturation.

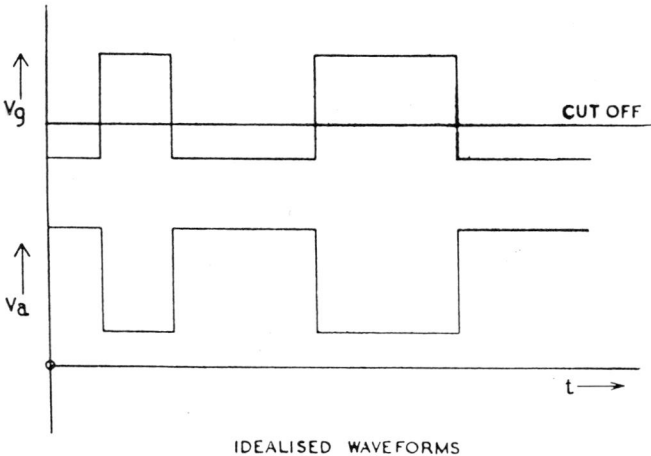

IDEALISED WAVEFORMS

Figure 46

The circuit is so designed that the input and output pulses are of equal amplitude.

440

28 TREES

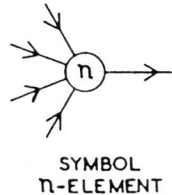

SYMBOL
π-ELEMENT

Figure 47

Such an element has to respond to n or more simultaneous input pulses. Consider the simple network below.

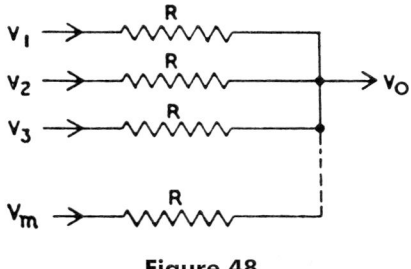

Figure 48

There are m input voltages applied to the resistors. The output voltage, V_0, is therefore given by

$$V_0 = \frac{1}{m}(V_1 + V_2 + V_3 + \cdots + V_m).$$

If the only possible values of V_1, V_2, ... , V_m are either 0 or v (i.e., no pulse or a pulse) then when the threshold number of pulses n is received

$$V_0 = \frac{nv}{m}.$$

Such an input network connected to a valve can constitute an n-element (Figure 49).

The valve is so biassed that a voltage $> nv/m$ is required to produce conduction. If the input voltage is $< ((n-1)/m)\, v$, then conduction must not occur (Figure 50).

The system will work provided v/m is greater than the grid base from cutoff to saturation and is in fact achievable for $m = 4$ or 5, say, if the pulse amplitude is 50 volts.

Normally, a stage as described above would be followed by an inverter stage in order that positive pulses can be obtained. An inhibitor connection can be conveniently incorporated in this stage (Figure 51).

With such an inhibitor connection it is necessary to ensure that the pulse it carries is sufficiently large to maintain the second valve in a state of conduction irrespective of the anode potential of the first stage.

So far only the use of triodes has been considered. Pentodes, however, increase the scope of the circuitry, since both control and suppressor grids may be used as inputs.

For instance it is convenient to construct a 2-element which has but two input connections using a pentode (Figure 52). The circuit shown is the basis of a very reliable 2-element.

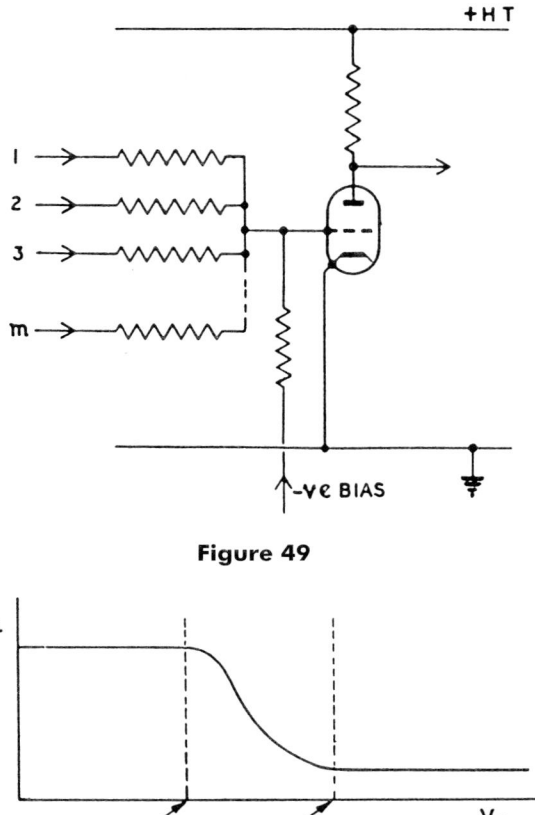

Figure 49

Figure 50

29 TRIGGER CIRCUIT

A trigger circuit must have two stable conditions and must be capable of being changed from one to the other. A suitable circuit is given below (Figure 53).

In the off condition A is cutoff and B conducting. When the threshold number of pulses is received on the grid of A it goes into conduction and B is cut off. This is the alternative stable condition and corresponds to the on condition, since the anode of B is now near HT potential.

The trigger is put off by a pulse on the inhibitor connection to the grid of B. It is necessary to ensure that the inhibitor pulse is large enough to put the trigger off irrespective of the input to the grid of A.

442

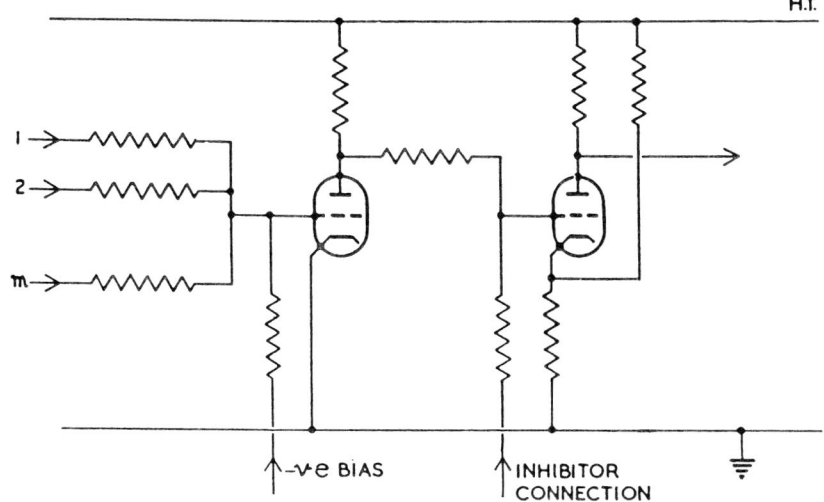

Figure 51

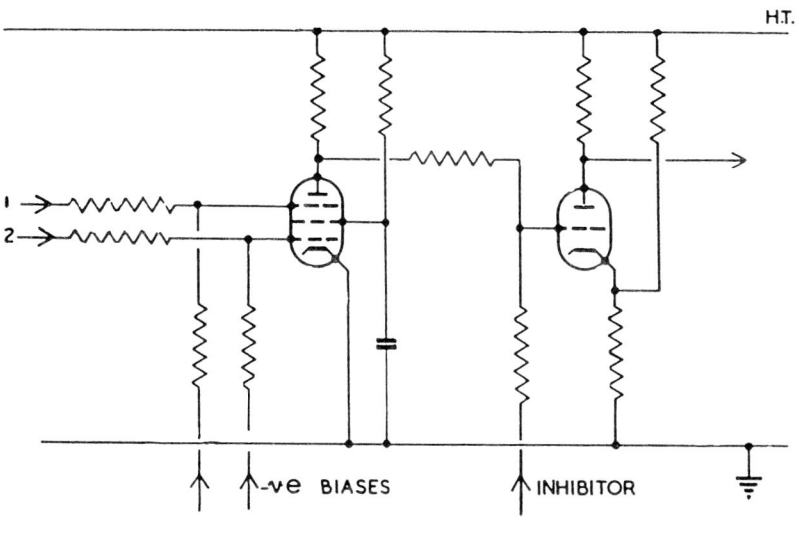

Figure 52

If (in Figure 53) an output is taken from the anode of A, this constitutes a 'NOT' output.

A 'change-state' connection to a trigger circuit may be achieved by applying the change pulse to both grids simultaneously. As illustration, a possible circuit for TRANSTIM of Version V is given below (Figure 54). Inputs are marked IN and outputs OUT to correspond on symbol and circuit.

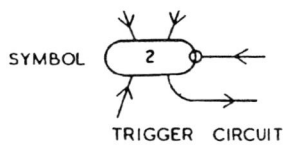

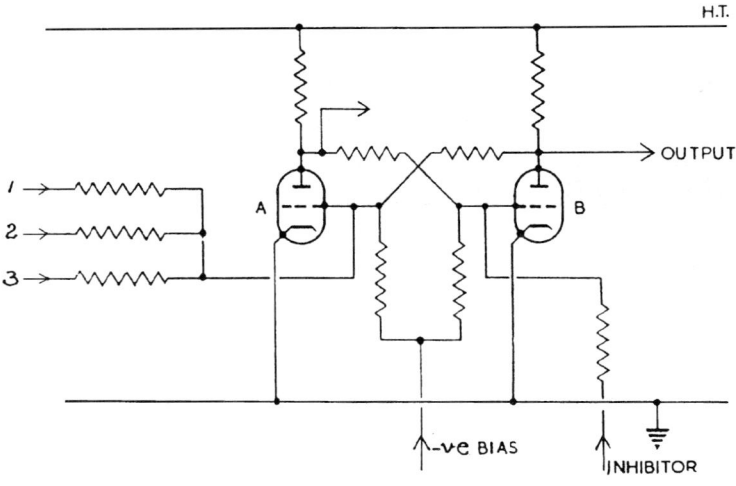

Figure 53

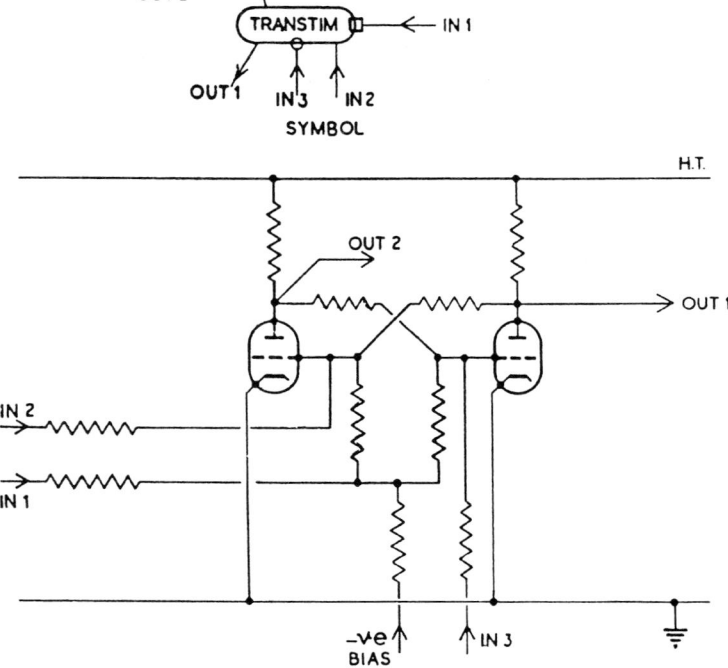

Figure 54

444

22

A lecture and two radio broadcasts on machine intelligence by Alan Turing*

edited by B. Jack Copeland

The Turing Project,

University of Canterbury,

Christchurch,

New Zealand,

email: bjcopeland@canterbury.ac.nz

Abstract

Turing's lecture 'Intelligent Machinery, A Heretical Theory' was given at Manchester University, probably in 1951. His 'Can Digital Computers Think?' was broadcast on the BBC Third Programme in May 1951. 'Can Automatic Calculating Machines Be Said To Think?', broadcast on the Third Programme in January 1952, is a discussion between Turing, Newman, Braithwaite and Jefferson. The appearance of these three items completes the publication of Turing's surviving works on machine intelligence.

1 INTRODUCTION

In his will Turing gave his 'books articles and manuscripts' to Robin Gandy. The manuscripts were subsequently deposited by Gandy in the Library of King's College, Cambridge.[1] The three documents published here are all from this collection.

The lecture entitled 'Intelligent Machinery, A Heretical Theory' was given at Manchester University, at a meeting of the '51 Society' (the name is from the year, 1951). Leading lights of the Society were M. H. A. Newman, Fielden Professor of Mathematics at Manchester, and the philosopher Michael Polanyi, then Professor of Social Studies at Manchester. Turing's mother, Sara, included the text of the lecture in her biography *Alan M. Turing* (unfortunately with some errors).[2] The version printed here is taken from a typescript prepared by Turing's typist.

---

*The research involved in the preparation of this material was supported in part by Unversity of Canterbury Research Grant no. U6271.

[1] Much material has also been deposited there by Sara Turing, and by The A. M. Turing Trust.

[2] Turing, S. *Alan M. Turing*, Cambridge: Heffer (1959): 128–34.

The lecture 'Can Digital Computers Think?' was broadcast on the BBC Third Programme on 15 May 1951, and was repeated on 3 July of that year.[3] The version printed here is taken from Turing's typescript and incorporates corrections made in his hand. Turing's was the second in a series of lectures with the general title 'Automatic Calculating Machines'. Other speakers in the series included Newman, D. R. Hartree, M. V. Wilkes, and F. C. Williams.[4]

The discussion between Turing, Newman, R. B. Braithwaite, and G. Jefferson entitled 'Can Automatic Calculating Machines Be Said To Think?' was recorded by the BBC on 10 January 1952 and broadcast on the Third Programme on 14, and again on 23, of that month. The version printed here is taken from a BBC script (marked 'Not checked in Talks Department with "as broadcast" script').

During this period Turing was Deputy Director of the Royal Society Computing Machine Laboratory at Manchester University (there being no Director). The Computing Machine Laboratory was the brainchild of Newman, and it was he who in 1946 had secured the Royal Society grant with which the laboratory was founded.[5] Here the world's first fully electronic stored-program general-purpose digital computer, the so-called Baby machine, ran its first program on 21 June 1948. In May of that year the vigour of the Manchester project and Newman's offer of a job had lured a 'very fed up' Turing away from his position at the National Physical Laboratory, where work on his own Automatic Computing Engine (ACE) had, for various reasons having little to do with Turing, drawn almost to a standstill.[6] (A pilot version of the ACE eventually ran in May 1950.) Shortly before the first of the two radio broadcasts, Turing completed his 'Programmers' Handbook For Manchester Electronic Computer',[7] and throughout the period he was using the computer extensively, in particular to simulate aspects of biological growth.[8]

1.1 Intelligent machinery, a heretical theory

This is the third of the series of four papers that Turing devoted explicitly to the issue of machine intelligence, the others being 'Intelligent Machinery',[9] 'Computing Machinery and Intelligence',[10] and 'Can Digital Computers Think?'[11]. Turing begins by observing that 'there are machines theoretically possible which will do something very close to

---

[3] Sara Turing relates that Turing did not listen to the first broadcast but did 'pluck up courage' to listen to the repeat (op. cit., p. 102).

[4] Here I am indebted to Wilkes for information.

[5] Turing's salary was paid wholly from Newman's Royal Society grant (letter from Newman to D. Brunt at the Royal Society, 22 December 1948).

[6] The quoted words are Robin Gandy's (private communication, 1995).

[7] An errata sheet in Turing's hand is dated 13 March 1951.

[8] See his 'The Chemical Basis of Morphogenesis', *Philosophical Transactions of the Royal Society of London*, series B, 237 (1952): 37–72. This is the paper that the new Artificial Life movement regards as its point of origination.

[9] National Physical Laboratory Report, 1948. In Meltzer, B., Michie, D. (eds) *Machine Intelligence 5*, Edinburgh: Edinburgh University Press (1969): 3–23.

[10] *Mind* 59 (1950): 433–60.

[11] This volume: 462–465.

thinking', giving as an example the task of determining the validity or otherwise of a formal derivation in the logical system set out by Whitehead and Russell in *Principia Mathematica*. Then in what are some of the most interesting remarks in the paper, he sketches, and refutes to his own satisfaction, an argument against the possibility of a computing machine emulating the full intelligence of a human being. Essentially the same argument has recently been endorsed by Penrose.[12] The crux of the argument is a claim that one can show, by using Gödel's first incompleteness theorem, that there are bound to be cases where the machine fails to give an answer to some question that a human mathematician would be able to answer. Turing's rebuttal of the argument is straightforward: the claim in question is true only if it supposed that the machine—unlike the typical human mathematician—never makes mistakes (other than those that ensue from any mechanical or electrical breakdown). Turing makes this same point in two other papers:

Recently the theorem of Gödel and related results . . . have shown that if one tries to use machines for such purposes as determining the truth or falsity of mathematical theorems and one is not willing to tolerate an occasional wrong result, then any given machine will in some cases be unable to give an answer at all.[13]

I would say that fair play must be given to the machine. Instead of it sometimes giving no answer we could arrange that it gives occasional wrong answers . . . [T]he human mathematician would likewise make blunders . . . It is easy for us to regard these blunders as not counting and give him another chance, but the machine would probably be allowed no mercy. In other words then, if a machine is expected to be infallible, it cannot also be intelligent . . . But these theorems say nothing about how much intelligence may be displayed if a machine makes no pretence at infallibility.[14]

A common theme in Turing's writing is that if a machine is to be intelligent, then it will need to 'learn by experience', probably with some pre-selection by an external educator of the experiences to which the machine will be subjected. In the present paper he writes

As I see it, this education process would in practice be an essential to the production of a reasonably intelligent machine within a reasonably short space of time. The human analogy alone suggests this.

He speaks of the possibility of incorporating two keys in the machine, representing 'pleasure' and 'pain', which can be manipulated by the external educator. This is an idea that he discusses more fully in the earlier paper 'Intelligent Machinery', where he considers adding two input lines to a (modified) Turing machine, the pleasure (or reward) line and the pain (or punishment) line, calling the result a 'P-type machine'. A detailed description of Turing's P-type machines, and also of his trainable neural networks or 'B-type unorganised machines' (forerunners of modern connectionist networks) may be found in the reference given in note 15.[15] Turing remarks in 'Intelligent Machinery'

---

[12] See his *The Emperor's New Mind: Concerning Computers, Minds, and the Laws of Physics*, Oxford: Oxford University Press (1989); 'Précis of *The Emperor's New Mind: Concerning Computers, Minds, and the Laws of Physics*', *Behavioral and Brain Sciences* 13 (1990): 643–55 and 692–705; *Shadows of the Mind: A Search for the Missing Science of Consciousness*, Oxford: Oxford University Press (1994).

[13] Intelligent Machinery', p. 4.

[14] P. 124 of Turing's 'Lecture to the London Mathematical Society on 20 February 1947', in Carpenter, B. E., Doran, R. W. (eds) *A. M. Turing's ACE Report of 1946 and Other Papers*, Cambridge, Mass.: MIT Press (1986): 106–24.

[15] Copeland, B. J., Proudfoot, D. 'On Alan Turing's Anticipation of Connectionism', *Synthese* 108 (1996): 361–77.

that it is probably possible to educate a P-type machine to be a universal machine, but warns that this 'is not easy' (p. 19). It is a P-type machine that Turing is speaking of in 'Computing Machinery and Intelligence' when, in his famous discussion of strategies for building a machine to pass the Turing Test, he says 'I have done some experiments with one such child-machine, and succeeded in teaching it a few things' (p. 457).

Turing's idea of a machine's building up 'indexes of experiences' is not mentioned elsewhere in his writings. An example of an index of experiences is a list (ordered in some way) of situations in which the machine has found itself, coupled with the action that was taken, and the outcome, good or bad. The situations are described in terms of features. Faced with a choice as to what to do next, the machine looks up features of its present situation in whatever indexes it has. If this procedure affords more than one candidate action, the machine selects between them by means of some rule, possibly itself learned through experience. Turing very reasonably grounds his belief that comparatively crude selection-rules will lead to satisfactory behaviour in the fact that engineering problems are regularly solved by 'the crudest rule of thumb procedure . . . e.g. whether a function increases or decreases with one of its variables'.

In the course of his discussion of educating a machine, Turing speaks of the 'mechanic who has constructed the machine'. This is perhaps a glimpse of Turing's attitude toward Williams, Kilburn, and the other engineers associated with the Manchester computer. Some of the engineers (not all) are scarcely less dismissive of the logicians' contributions. Kilburn is forthright in expressing his belief that Turing contributed 'very little' to the design of the Manchester computer.[16]

Turing ends with a vision of the future, now hackneyed, in which intelligent computers 'outstrip our feeble powers' and 'take control'. There is more of the same in 'Can Digital Computers Think?'. No doubt this is comic-strip stuff. Nevertheless, these images of Turing's reveal his profound grasp of the potential of the universal Turing machine at a time when the only computers in existence were minuscule, and none but the most straightforward of tasks had been successfully programmed.

1.2 Can digital computers think?

In this broadcast Turing defends his view that 'it is not altogether unreasonable to describe digital computers as brains'. The broadcast contains much of interest, for example a continuation of Turing's discussion of 'Lady Lovelace's dictum', which he began in 'Computing Machinery and Intelligence', and not least Turing's glorious simile that compares trying to program a computer to behave like a brain with trying to write a treatise about family life on Mars—and moreover with insufficient paper. Yet what is of outstanding interest about the broadcast is that it contains Turing's most accessible remarks concerning a thesis which, following Robin Gandy, I will call thesis M:

The behaviour of any machine can be simulated by a universal Turing machine.[17]

---

[16]Kilburn in interview with Christopher Evans in 1976 ('The Pioneers of Computing: an Oral History of Computing', Science Museum: London).

[17]Compare pp. 124–6 of Gandy's 'Church's Thesis and Principles for Mechanisms', in Barwise, J., Keisler, H. J., Kunen, K. (eds) *The Kleene Symposium*, Amsterdam: North-Holland (1980): 123–48.

Thesis M admits of two interpretations, according to whether the phrase 'any machine' is taken in the narrow sense of 'any machine that conforms to the physical laws of the actual world (if not to the resource constraints of the actual world)', or in a wide sense that abstracts from the issue of whether or not the notional machine in question could exist in the actual world. The narrow version of thesis M is an empirical proposition whose truth-value is unknown. The wide version of thesis M is known to be false. Various notional machines have been described whose behaviour cannot be simulated by a universal Turing machine (nor even approximated arbitrarily finely).[18]

Thesis M, in both its wide and narrow forms, is to be sharply distinguished from the *Church–Turing thesis*. The latter is the thesis that every effectively calculable function is Turing-machine-computable, the effectively calculable functions being those functions whose values can be calculated by a human mathematician working effectively, which is to say, working in accordance with a finite list of instructions, these demanding neither insight, inspiration nor ingenuity for their execution, and unaided by any auxiliary devices apart from paper and pencil. Clearly, the Church–Turing thesis does not entail either form of thesis M. That a universal Turing machine is able to simulate the relevant intentional behaviour of a human being working effectively is one thing; the matter of whether or not a universal Turing machine is able to simulate the behaviour of every form of machine is another. Turing explicitly endorsed the Church–Turing thesis properly so-called, but not thesis M, in either its wide or narrow form.[19]

As he makes clear in 'Can Digital Computers Think?', Turing did endorse the thesis that results when the words 'any machine' in the statement of thesis M are replaced by 'any *calculating* machine'. Newman likewise endorsed this qualified form of the thesis. He wrote:

A universal machine is a single machine which, when provided with suitable instructions, will perform any calculation that could be done by a specially constructed machine. No real machine can be truly universal because its size is limited ... but subject to this limitation of size, the machines now being made in America and in this country will be 'universal'—if they work at all; that is, they will do every kind of job that can be done by special machines.[20]

If Turing were pressed to make it clear exactly what is meant by 'calculating machine', he would perhaps offer paradigm examples, as in his earlier paper 'Intelligent Machinery' (pp. 5–6), such as the Brunsviga (a popular desk calculating machine), the ENIAC, and so on. Or perhaps he would say, with greater generality, that a calculating machine is any machine that apes a human mathematician working with pencil and paper

---

[18]See, for example, Copeland, B. J. 'The Broad Conception of Computation', *American Behavioral Scientist*, 40 (1997): 690–716; Copeland, B. J., Sylvar, R. 'Beyond the Universal Turing Machine', *Australasian Journal of Philosophy*, 77 (1999): 46–66; Copeland, B. J., Proudfoot, D. 'Alan Turing's Forgotten Ideas in Computer Science', *Scientific American* 280 (April 1999): 76–81; Hogarth, M. L. 'Non-Turing Computers and Non-Turing Computability', *PSA* 1 (1994): 126–38; Stewart, I. 'Deciding the Undecidable', *Nature*, 352 (1991): 664–5.

[19]See further Kleene, S. C. *Mathematical Logic*, New York: Wiley (1967); Copeland, B. J. 'The Broad Conception of Computation', *American Behavioral Scientist*, 40 (1997): 690–716, and 'The Church–Turing Thesis', in Zalta, E. (ed.) *The Stanford Encyclopaedia of Philosophy*, World Wide Web: Stanford University (1996) [http://plato.stanford.edu/], 25 screens.

[20]Newman, M. H. A. 'General Principles of the Design of All-Purpose Computing Machines', *Proceedings of the Royal Society of London*, series A, 195 (1948): 271–4. The quotation is from pp. 271–2.

in accordance with what he calls a 'rule of thumb' procedure (op. cit., p. 7). It was in that manner that he explained the idea of an electronic computing machine in the opening paragraph of his Programmers' Handbook:

Electronic computers are intended to carry out any definite rule of thumb process which could have been done by a human operator working in a disciplined but unintelligent manner.[21]

Turing could not consistently have endorsed the wide form of thesis M. In Section 4 of his PhD thesis (Princeton 1938) he introduced a class of notional machines whose behaviour cannot be calculated by a universal Turing machine.[22] He described these as 'a new kind of machine' and called them 'O-machines'. An O-machine is a Turing machine augmented with a primitive operation that produces the values of some function (on the non-negative integers) that is not Turing-machine-computable.[23] The new primitive operation is made available by a black box. Turing refers to the black box as an 'oracle'. An example of an oracle is a device that will produce the corresponding value of Turing's famous halting function when fed any pair of integers. Turing remarks that an oracle works by 'unspecified means' and says 'we shall not go any further into the nature of [an] oracle'. One way of conceptualising an oracle—which need not reflect the box's actual manner of functioning—is as a device accessing an infinite tape upon which there have been inscribed, in order, all the infinitely many arguments and values of whatever function it is that the oracle instantiates. This device can produce any of the function's values after only a finite search along the tape. A fuller description of O-machines may be found in the reference given in note 24.[24]

The pronouncements of a certain form of oracle can be likened to the intuitive judgements made by a mathematician in determining the truth or falsity of arbitrary number-theoretic statements. In a letter to Newman, Turing discusses the role of intuition (or the role of such an oracle) in the production of proofs of number-theoretic statements.[25]

I think you take a much more radically Hilbertian attitude about mathematics than I do. You say 'If all this whole formal outfit is not about finding proofs which can be checked on a machine it's difficult to know what it is about'. When you say 'on a machine' do you have in mind that there is (or should be or could be, but has not been actually described anywhere) some fixed machine on which proofs are to be checked, and that the formal outfit is as it were about this machine? If

---

[21] Turing, A. M. *Programmers' Handbook for Manchester Electronic Computer*, University of Manchester Computing Laboratory (1950), p. 1.

[22] The thesis was published in the following year ('Systems of Logic Based on Ordinals', *Proceedings of the London Mathematical Society*, 45 (1939): 161–228).

[23] In Turing's original exposition, the additional operations produce the values only of π_2^0 functions. In the subsequent technical literature the notion of an O-machine has been widened to include operations that produce values of *any* function on the integers that is not Turing-machine-computable. I will employ this extended sense here.

[24] Copeland, B. J. 'Turing's O-machines, Searle, Penrose and the Brain', *Analysis*, 58 (1998): 128–38.

[25] The letter is one of several that Turing wrote to Newman in the early years of the war. With the exception of the present letter, which was written from King's College, all are from Bletchley.

you take this attitude ... there is little more to be said: we simply have to ... resign ourselves to the fact that there are some problems to which we can never get the answer. On these lines my ordinal logics would make no sense. However, I don't think you really hold quite this attitude because you admit that in the case of the Gödel example we can decide that the formula is true i.e. you admit that there is a fairly definite idea of a true formula which is quite different from the idea of a provable one. Throughout my paper on ordinal logics I have been assuming this too.[26] ... If you think of various machines I don't see your difficulty. One imagines different machines allowing different sets of proofs, and by choosing a suitable machine one can approximate 'truth' by 'provability' better than with a less suitable machine, and can in a sense approximate it as well as you please. The choice of a proof checking machine involves intuition, which is interchangeable with the intuition required for finding an Ω if one has an ordinal logic Λ, or as a third alternative one may go straight for the proof and this again requires intuition. Or one may go for a proof finding machine. I am rather puzzled why you drew this distinction between proof finders and proof checkers. It seems to me rather unimportant as one can always get a proof finder from a proof checker ... .

What Turing says in this letter is consistent with the view he expressed later in his lecture to the London Mathematical Society, and which was quoted above: a Turing machine can display the search behaviour that in a human mathematician is called 'intuitive', but a corollary of this is that the Turing machine will give occasional wrong answers. An O-machine, in contrast, can enumerate the theorems of a logic without a single blunder.)

   A simple example of an oracle is a device that outputs a genuinely random and unboundedly long sequence of integers. As Church pointed out in 1939, if a sequence of integers $a_1, a_2, \ldots a_n, \ldots$ is random, then there is no function $f(n) = a_n$ that is calculable by a Turing machine.[27] As suggested previously, such an oracle may be conceptualised as a device accessing a tape upon which an infinite random sequence of integers has been inscribed.[28] A Turing machine to which such an oracle is attached may be set up so as to select between two paths of action by calling to the oracle for a number and following one path if the number is even and the other if it is odd. Turing describes this as a 'partially random machine':

It is possible to modify the above described types of discrete machines by allowing several alternative operations to be applied at some points, the alternatives to be chosen by a random process. Such a machine will be described as 'partially random'. If we wish to say definitely that a machine is not of this kind we will describe it as 'determined'. Sometimes a machine may be strictly speaking determined but appear superficially as if it were partially random. This would occur if for instance the digits of the number π were used to determine the choices.... These machines are known as apparently partially random.[29]

   Concerning the issue of whether or not the narrow version of thesis M is true, Turing points out in 'Can Digital Computers Think?' that the human brain itself might in fact

---

[26]Turing is here referring to 'Systems of Logic Based on Ordinals'.

[27]Church, A. 'On the Concept of a Random Sequence', *American Mathematical Society Bulletin*, 46 (1940): 130–5; see especially pp. 134–5.

[28]The arguments of the function instantiated by such an oracle are 1st call, 2nd call, 3rd call, ... (or simply 1, 2, 3, ...) and the first value of the function is the number that the oracle produces in response to the first call, and so on.

[29]'Intelligent Machinery', p. 9

infringe thesis M. Assuming that the brain is a machine of a sort whose behaviour is in principle predictable by calculation, then a digital computer can in principle be programmed to calculate what any given brain would do under any given circumstances, says Turing. He then immediately goes on to remark that that assumption 'can quite reasonably be challenged'. He points out that Eddington argued on quantum mechanical grounds that no such prediction is even theoretically possible. Possibly Turing's own view was that the brain may contain some random element. As Newman put it, Turing 'had a deep-seated conviction that the real brain has a "roulette wheel" somewhere in it'.[30] On that hypothesis the brain is not a deterministic Turing machine but a partially random machine.

Turing presses on to argue that randomness in the brain, if it exists, is no obstacle to his view that a digital computer can reasonably be described as a brain. For a digital computer might itself be augmented with a random element. Turing often mentioned this idea, for example in 'Computing Machinery and Intelligence' (p. 438) and 'Intelligent Machinery' (p. 9). Alternatively, he argues, one might employ not a genuinely random element but a quasi-random one. He says:

It is not difficult to design machines whose behaviour appears quite random to anyone who does not know the details of their construction.

No doubt he had in mind his own speech encipherment machine, Delilah (1943–5), one component of which produced a quasi-random stream of digits with an immensely long period.[31] His point is that even if the brain is a partially random machine, some apparently partially random machine Q may, so far as an observer innocent of Q's internal constitution is concerned, appear to behave in a perfectly brain-like fashion. It surely is 'not altogether unreasonable' to describe not only Q but also a computer that is calculating the behaviour of Q as itself being a brain, even though neither Q nor the simulating computer is equivalent in behaviour to any particular human brain.

Might there be, in the real world, some other way, apart from partial randomness, in which thesis M is infringed? Over the past four decades a number of writers have suggested that there might indeed.[32] What Turing himself thought is not certain.

---

[30]Newman in interview with Christopher Evans in 1976 ('The Pioneers of Computing: an Oral History of Computing', Science Museum: London).

[31]A description of Delilah may be found in Hodges, op. cit., pp. 270–90.

[32]For example da Costa, N. C. A., Doria, F. A. 'Classical Physics and Penrose's Thesis', *Foundations of Physics Letters*, 4 (1991): 363–73; Doyle, J. 'What is Church's Thesis?', typescript, Laboratory for Computer Science, MIT (1982); Geroch, R., Hartle, J. B. 'Computability and Physical Theories', *Foundations of Physics*, 16 (1986): 533–50; Komar, A. 'Undecidability of Macroscopically Distinguishable States in Quantum Field Theory', *Physical Review*, second series, 133B (1964): 542–4; Kreisel, G. 'Mathematical Logic: What Has it Done for the Philosophy of Mathematics?', in *Bertrand Russell: Philosopher of the Century*, ed. R. Schoenman, London: George Allen and Unwin (1967), and 'A Notion of Mechanistic Theory', *Synthese* 29 (1974): 11–26; Penrose, in the works cited in note 12; Pour-El, M. B. 'Abstract Computability and its Relation to the General Purpose Analog Computer', *Transactions of the American Mathematical Society*, 199 (1974): 1–28; Pour-El, M. B., Richards, I. 'A Computable Ordinary Differential Equation Which Possesses No Computable Solution', *Annals of Mathematical Logic*, 17 (1979): 61–90, and 'The Wave Equation with Computable Initial Data such that its Unique Solution is not Computable', *Advances in Mathematics*, 39 (1981): 215–39; Scarpellini, B. 'Zwei unentscheitbare Probleme der Analysis', *Zeitschrift für mathematische Logik und Grundlagen der Mathematik*, 9 (1963): 265–89; Stannett, M. 'X-Machines and the Halting Problem: Building a Super-Turing Machine', *Formal Aspects of Computing*, 2 (1990): 331–41; Vergis, A., Steiglitz, K., Dickinson, B. 'The Complexity of Analog Computation', *Mathematics and Computers in Simulation*, 28 (1986): 91–113.

His claim that

> If any machine can appropriately be described as a brain, then any digital computer can be so described

is entirely consistent with a view that the brain is computationally equivalent to, say, an O-machine whose oracle produces values of the halting function. For Turing could readily modify his argument concerning observers who are innocent of internal constitution in order to cover this case: an appropriately programmed Turing machine will appear to such an observer to behave in a perfectly brain-like fashion, even though not computationally equivalent to an O-machine. As previously discussed, the Turing machine may produce 'an occasional wrong result', but this will hardly mark out the Turing machine from the brain. However, if Turing did think that O-machines other than partially random machines are physically possible, then perhaps he would have said as much, and he does not appear to have done so. Penrose (on the basis of the argument employing Gödel's theorem that was discussed earlier) doubts current physical theory precisely because it implies that any discrete physical device whose behaviour is not random can be exactly mimicked by a Turing machine. Possibly for Turing the implication might have run the other way: accepted physical theory rules out the real-world existence of all O-machines other than partially random machines.

One thing is clear. Penrose gets Turing wrong when he attributes to him the view that

> the computational capacities of any physical device must (in idealisation) be equivalent to the action of a Turing machine. . . . It seems likely that [Turing] viewed physical action in general—which would include the action of a human brain—to be always reducible to some kind of Turing-machine action.[33]

1.3 Can automatic calculating machines be said to think?

This is the earliest known recorded discussion of artificial intelligence.[34] It predates by more than four years the conference arranged in 1956 by John McCarthy, the Dartmouth Summer Research Project on Artificial Intelligence, which many artificial intelligence researchers in the United States regard as the point of origination of their subject.

The participants

The anchor man of the discussion was Richard Braithwaite (1900–1990). Braithwaite was at the time Sidgwick Lecturer in Moral Science at the University of Cambridge, where the following year he was appointed Knightsbridge Professor of Moral Philosophy. Like Turing, he was a fellow of King's College. Braithwaite's main work lay in the philosophy of science and in decision and games theory (which he attempted to apply in moral philosophy).

---

[33] *Shadows of the Mind*, p. 21. Penrose even goes so far as to 'call this (physical) assertion "Turing's thesis" ' (ibid.).

[34] This broadcast together with the dialogues recorded in *Wittgenstein's Lectures on the Foundations of Mathematics* (ed. C. Diamond, Ithaca: Cornell University Press, 1976) are the only examples we have of Turing in discussion.

Geoffrey Jefferson (1886–1961) retired from the Chair of Neurosurgery at Manchester University in 1951. In his Lister Oration, delivered at the Royal College of Surgeons of England on 9 June 1949, he had declared:

When we hear it said that wireless valves think, we may despair of language.[35]

Turing gave a substantial discussion of Jefferson's views in 'Computing Machinery and Intelligence', rebutting the 'argument from consciousness' that he found in the Lister Oration. In the discussion Jefferson takes numerous pot shots at the notion of a machine's thinking, which for the most part Turing and Newman are easily able to turn aside. Jefferson may have thought little of the idea of machine intelligence, but he held Turing himself in considerable regard, saying after Turing's death that he 'had real genius, it shone from him'.[36]

Max Newman (1897–1984) played an important part in Turing's intellectual life over many years, and deserves a substantial introduction.[37] It was Newman who, in a lecture in Cambridge in 1935, introduced Turing to the concept which led directly to the Turing machine: Newman defined a constructive process as one that a *machine* can carry out.[38] Turing presented Newman with a draft typescript of 'On Computable Numbers' in April 1936.[39] Newman relates that right from the start Turing was interested in the possibility of actually making a machine of the sort that he described in the paper. Newman's own role in the development of computers has never been sufficiently emphasized (due perhaps to his thoroughly self-effacing way of relating the relevant events). As a result of reading Turing's draft in 1936 Newman became interested in the possibilities of computing machinery 'in a rather theoretical way'. It was not until Newman joined the Government Code and Cypher School at Bletchley Park in 1942 that his interest suddenly became practical, with his realisation that the attack on the 'Fish' codes could be mechanized. (The 'Fish' codes were based on the standard 5-digit Baudot telegraph code.) Newman and C. E. Wynn-Williams designed a machine for this purpose, and it was built by F. O. Morrell, head of the telegraph group at the Post Office Research Station at Dollis Hill. This machine was partly electronic but largely electromechanical. It proved difficult to operate and was unreliable. Its operators nicknamed it 'Robinson', after Heath Robinson. At Turing's suggestion, Newman approached T. H. Flowers, head of the switching group at Dollis Hill, and asked him to improve the reliability of the machine.[40] Flowers was

---

[35] Jefferson, G. 'The Mind of Mechanical Man', *British Medical Journal* (25 June 1949): 1105–10. The quotation is from p. 1110.

[36] Letter from Jefferson to Sara Turing, 18 October 1954.

[37] Throughout the following account my sources are, unless otherwise indicated: (1) Newman in interview with Christopher Evans in 1976 ('The Pioneers of Computing: an Oral History of Computing', Science Museum: London), (2) F. C. Williams in interview with Christopher Evans in 1976 (ibid.), (3) private communications from T. H. Flowers (1996–97), (4) private communications from T. Kilburn (1997).

[38] The Turing machine concept was made public by Turing in an address to the London Mathematical Society on 12 November 1936 'On Computable Numbers, with an Application to the Entscheidungsproblem' already mentioned in note 25.

[39] Hodges, op. cit. p. 109.

[40] Flowers and Turing had previously worked together when Flowers was set the task of building a machine for automatically decrypting Enigma messages once the various settings of the Enigma had been determined by the Bombe. In the event little use was made of Flowers' machine.

less than impressed by the Robinson and on his own initiative he started work on a new design. Already an expert in electronic switching, Flowers 'didn't care' how large a number of valves he used. The result was Colossus, the world's first fully-functioning special-purpose electronic digital computer. Colossus first worked on 8 December 1943. Flowers' ambitious design, involving approximately 1600 thermionic valves ('tubes' in the US), established decisively and for the first time that large-scale electronic computing machinery was a practical proposition.[41] During the construction of Colossus, Newman had tried to interest Flowers in Turing's 1936 paper—the birthplace of the stored-program concept—but Flowers 'didn't really understand much of it'. There can be little doubt that by 1943 Newman had firmly in mind the possibility of building a universal Turing machine using electronic technology.

In July of 1946—the month in which the Royal Society approved Newman's grant[42]—F. C. Williams, working at the Telecommunications Research Establishment, Malvern, began the series of experiments on cathode ray tube storage that was to lead to the Williams Tube.[43] Williams, until then a radar engineer, explains how it was that he came to be working on the problem of computer memory:

once [the German Armies] collapsed . . . nobody was going to care a toss about radar, and people like me . . . were going to be in the soup unless we found something else to do. And computers were in the air. Knowing absolutely nothing about them I latched onto the problem of storage and tackled that.[44]

Newman learned of Williams' work, and there seems little doubt that Newman, with the able help of Patrick Blackett, Langworthy Professor of Physics at Manchester and one of the most powerful figures in the University, was instrumental in the appointment of the 35 year old Williams to the recently vacated Chair of Electro-Technics at Manchester. Newman himself was a member of the appointing committee.[45] Williams immediately had Kilburn, his assistant at Malvern, seconded to Manchester.[46] To take up the story in Williams' own words:

neither Tom Kilburn nor I knew the first thing about computers when we arrived in Manchester University. We'd had enough explained to us to understand what the problem of storage was and what we wanted to store, and that we'd achieved, so the point now had been reached when we'd

---

[41]The second generation Colossus, which went into service at Bletchley Park on 1 June 1944, contained approximately 2400 valves.

[42]Council Minutes, Royal Society, 11 July 1946.

[43]Kilburn, T., Piggott, L. S. 'Frederic Calland Williams', *Biographical Memoirs of Fellows of the Royal Society*, 24 (1978): 583–604.

[44]Quoted in Bennett, S. 'F. C. Williams: his contribution to the development of automatic control' (an unpublished typescript based on interviews with Williams in 1976).

[45]Kilburn and Piggott, op. cit., p. 591. Williams has said 'I suspect, but cannot prove, that he [Blackett] was instrumental in my post-war appointment as Professor' (quoted on p. 48 of Lovell, B. 'Patrick Maynard Stuart Blackett', *Biographical Memoirs of Fellows of the Royal Society*, 21 (1975): 1–115. Williams relates that it was Blackett who first interested him in making an automatic curve follower for Hartree's differential analyser (ibid.). This work was carried out while Williams was an assistant lecturer in the Department of Electro-Technics at Manchester from 1936 to 1939. It was also Blackett who, in 1939, had 'channelled' Williams into the Telecommunications Research Establishment (ibid.).

[46]Letter from TRE to NPL, 9 January 1947. Williams' appointment at Manchester began on 25 December 1946 (Council Minutes, Manchester University, 1946).

got to find out about computers. . . . Newman explained the whole business of how a computer works to us.[47]

Elsewhere Williams is explicit concerning Turing's role and gives something of the flavour of the explanation that he and Kilburn received:

Tom Kilburn and I knew nothing about computers, but a lot about circuits. Professor Newman and Mr A. M. Turing . . . knew a lot about computers and substantially nothing about electronics. They took us by the hand and explained how numbers could live in houses with addresses and how if they did they could be kept track of during a calculation.[48]

It seems that Newman must have used much the same words with Williams and Kilburn as he did in an address to the Royal Society on 4 March 1948:

In modern times the idea of a universal calculating machine was independently [of Babbage] introduced by Turing . . . There is provision for storing numbers, say in the scale of 2, so that each number appears as a row of, say, forty 0's and 1's in certain places or 'houses' in the machine. . . . Certain of these numbers, or 'words' are read, one after another, as orders. In one possible type of machine an order consists of four numbers, for example 11, 13, 27, 4. The number 4 signifies 'add', and when control shifts to this word the 'houses' $H11$ and $H13$ will be connected to the adder as inputs, and $H27$ as output. The numbers stored in $H11$ and $H13$ pass through the adder, are added, and the sum is passed on to $H27$. The control then shifts to the next order. In most real machines the process just described would be done by three separate orders, the first bringing $<H11>$ ($=$ content of $H11$) to a central accumulator, the second adding $<H13>$ into the accumulator, and the third sending the result to $H27$; thus only one address would be required in each order. . . . A machine with storage, with this automatic-telephone-exchange arrangement and with the necessary adders, subtractors and so on, is, in a sense, already a universal machine.[49]

Newman goes on to explain program storage ('the orders shall be in a series of houses $X1$, $X2$, . . . ' and conditional branching. He then sums up:

From this highly simplified account it emerges that the essential internal parts of the machine are, first, a storage for numbers (which may also be orders). . . . Secondly, adders, multipliers, etc. Thirdly, an 'automatic telephone exchange' for selecting 'houses', connecting them to the arithmetic organ, and writing the answers in other prescribed houses. Finally, means of moving control at any stage to any chosen order, if a certain condition is satisfied, otherwise passing to the next order in the normal sequence. Besides these there must be ways of setting up the machine at the outset, and extracting the final answer in useable form.[50]

---

[47] F. C. Williams in interview with Christopher Evans in 1976.

[48] Williams, F. C. 'Early Computers at Manchester University', *The Radio and Electronic Engineer*, 45 (1975): 237–331, p. 328. Concerning the matter of Turing's knowledge of electronics, opinion among the engineers at Manchester seems to have been divided. G. C. Tootill—who bore much of the responsibility for liaising between the Computing Machine Laboratory and the engineers at the Manchester firm of Ferranti Ltd, who turned the work of the Laboratory into the world's first commercially available electronic stored-program digital computer—spoke approvingly of Turing's 'ability as a circuit designer' (letter from Tootill to Lavington, 1 July 1975). (Tootill's 'Informal Report on the Design of the Ferranti Mark I Computing Machine' (Royal Society Computing Machine Laboratory, November 1949) contains a technical appendix by Turing entitled 'Generation of Random Numbers'.)

[49] Newman, M. H. A. 'General Principles of the Design of All-Purpose Computing Machines', *Proceedings of the Royal Society of London*, series A, 195 (1948): 271–2.

[50] Ibid., pp. 273–4.

There seems little doubt that the major credit for the Manchester machine belongs not only to Williams and Kilburn but also to Newman, and that the influence upon Newman of Turing's paper of 1936, which first set out the concept of the stored-program universal digital computer, was crucial.

The discussion

From the point of view of Turing scholarship, the most important parts of 'Can Automatic Calculating Machines Be Said To Think' are the passages containing Turing's exposition of the 'imitation game' (or Turing test), which he originally described in 'Computing Machinery and Intelligence'. In the later exposition he modifies his test in a number of significant ways. The lone interrogator of the original version is replaced by a 'jury'. Each jury must judge a number of contestants, and for a machine to pass the test 'a considerable proportion' of the jury 'must be taken in by the pretence'. The members of the jury interrogate the contestants, but their contributions 'don't really have to be questions, any more than questions in a law court are really questions'; for example, 'I put it to you that you are only pretending to be a man' is 'quite in order'. Turing stipulates that members of the jury 'should not be expert about machines'—perhaps ill-advisedly, since experience with administering the test at the Boston Computing Museum has shown that naive jurors (often selected from passers-by) are too easily fooled.[51] In the original version of the test the interrogator is faced by a computer and a human foil (who plays a role equivalent to that of the woman in Turing's man–woman imitation game) and must distinguish between them. In the later account Turing prefers an arrangement whereby the jury is sometimes confronted by a machine and sometimes by a human (an arrangement that has been adopted in some attempts to stage a Turing test).[52] This departure from the original specifications probably makes the test less effective. For example, the jury might overlook some small feature of the machine's performance which, in a test conducted to the original specifications, might be the decisive factor in distinguishing the machine from the foil.[53]

In 'Computing Machinery and Intelligence' Turing said that the question 'Can machines think?' is 'too meaningless to deserve discussion' (p. 442). If he ever did believe this, he certainly did not allow it to stop him indulging rather often in such discussion. In the present piece his official attitude to the question is milder. He says 'You might call it a test to see whether the machine thinks, but it would be better to avoid begging the question, and say that the machines that pass are (let's say) "Grade A" machines. . . . [The question whether] machines really could pass the test [is] not the same as "Do machines think?", but it seems near enough for our present purpose, and raises much the same difficulties'.

Turing is often quoted as having predicted that by the turn of the century artificial intelligence that is indistinguishable from human intelligence will be upon us. What he

---

[51] Dan Dennett, personal communication (1995). Dennett was chair of the organising committee for the series of tests held at the Boston Computing Museum and chief adjudicator during the tests.

[52] See, for example, Heiser, J. F., Colby, K. M., Faught, W. S., Parkison, R. C. 'Can Psychiatrists Distinguish a Computer Simulation of Paranoia from the Real Thing?', *Journal of Psychiatric Research*, 15 (1980): 149–62.

[53] I give a fuller discussion of this point in my *Artificial Intelligence: A Philosophical Introduction*, Oxford: Blackwell (1993), pp. 40–1.

actually said (in 1950) was that 'in about 50 years' time' an average interrogator in the test 'will not have more than 70 per cent chance of making the right identification after five minutes of questioning'.[54] In the present dialogue he offers a more conservative estimate: it will be at least 100 years before the machine stands a 'chance with no questions barred'.

Turing sketches an interesting mechanical explanation of how analogy works in the human brain, and suggests that a digital computer can be made to do the same. Another proposal that does not appear elsewhere in Turing's writings concerns the vexed issue of creativity. A machine that combines words more or less at random and then scores the combinations 'for various merits' would, he says, be able to find useful new concepts. His example is 'lumping together rain, hail, snow and sleet, under the word "precipitation"'. He agrees with Newman that this process would be 'shockingly slow'. Nevertheless, this brief suggestion of Turing's is an economical illustration of the possibility of a machine's acquiring new concepts for itself.

Equally economical is Newman's illustration of how a machine can learn to do better with practice by modifying its own program. Faced with a 2-move chess problem, the machine obeys an instruction to choose a move at random. If the move, say B–Q5, is found to lead to forced mate in two moves, then the machine changes the instruction calling for a random choice to 'Try B–Q5'. When presented with the same problem again, the machine immediately gives the right answer.

There is a lengthy discussion of machine learning, in which Turing alludes to the P-type machines of his paper 'Intelligent Machinery', saying in response to Jefferson's challenge that real learning involves intervention by teachers, 'I have made some experiments in teaching a machine to do some simple operation, and a very great deal of such intervention was needed'.[55] Turing stresses several times that an effective learning machine will not only learn first-order facts but will also be learning all the time how to improve its learning methods.

Towards the end of the discussion Newman suggests a test—and the term 'Newman's test' seems appropriate—for when machines have 'begun to think'. That stage of development has been reached when a machine can solve a mathematical problem for which no effective method exists.[56]

2 INTELLIGENT MACHINERY, A HERETICAL THEORY

"You cannot make a machine to think for you". This is a commonplace that is usually accepted without question. It will be the purpose of this paper to question it.

Most machinery developed for commercial purposes is intended to carry out some very specific job, and to carry it out with certainty and considerable speed. Very often

---

[54] Op. cit. p. 442.

[55] See 'Intelligent Machinery', pp. 18–20.

[56] Reproduction of 'Intelligent Machinery, A Heretical Theory' by kind permission of The Turing Estate. Reproduction of 'Can Digital Computers Think?' and 'Can Automatic Calculating Machines Be Said To Think?' by kind permission of the BBC, The Turing Estate, Lewis C. Braithwaite, Antony A. Jefferson, and Edward Newman.

it does the same series of operations over and over again without any variety. This fact about the actual machinery available is a powerful argument to many in favour of the slogan quoted above. To a mathematical logician this argument is not available, for it has been shown that there are machines theoretically possible which will do something very close to thinking. They will, for instance, test the validity of a formal proof in the system of Principia Mathematica, or even tell of a formula of that system whether it is provable or disprovable. In the case that the formula is neither provable nor disprovable such a machine certainly does not behave in a very satisfactory manner, for it continues to work indefinitely without producing any result at all, but this cannot be regarded as very different from the reaction of the mathematicians, who have for instance worked for hundreds of years on the question as to whether Fermat's last theorem is true or not. For the case of machines of this kind a more subtle argument is necessary. By Gödel's famous theorem, or some similar argument, one can show that however the machine is constructed there are bound to be cases where the machine fails to give an answer, but a mathematician would be able to. On the other hand, the machine has certain advantages over the mathematician. Whatever it does can be relied upon, assuming no mechanical 'breakdown', whereas the mathematician makes a certain proportion of mistakes. I believe that this danger of the mathematician making mistakes is an unavoidable corollary of his power of sometimes hitting upon an entirely new method. This seems to be confirmed by the well known fact that the most reliable people will not usually hit upon really new methods.

My contention is that machines can be constructed which will simulate the behaviour of the human mind very closely. They will make mistakes at times, and at times they may make new and very interesting statements, and on the whole the output of them will be worth attention to the same sort of extent as the output of a human mind. The content of this statement lies in the greater frequency expected for the true statements, and it cannot, I think, be given an exact statement. It would not, for instance, be sufficient to say simply that the machine will make any true statement sooner or later, for an example of such a machine would be one which makes all possible statements sooner or later. We know how to construct these, and as they would (probably) produce true and false statements about equally frequently, their verdicts would be quite worthless. It would be the actual reaction of the machine to circumstances that would prove my contention, if indeed it can be proved at all.

Let us go rather more carefully into the nature of this 'proof'. It is clearly possible to produce a machine which would give a very good account of itself for any range of tests, if the machine were made sufficiently elaborate. However, this again would hardly be considered an adequate proof. Such a machine would give itself away by making the same sort of mistake over and over again, and being quite unable to correct itself, or to be corrected by argument from outside. If the machine were able in some way to 'learn by experience' it would be much more impressive. If this were the case there seems to be no real reason why one should not start from a comparatively simple machine, and, by subjecting it to a suitable range of 'experience' transform it into one which was more elaborate, and was able to deal with a far greater range of contingencies. This process could probably be hastened by a suitable selection of the experiences to which it was subjected. This might be called 'education'. But here we have to be careful. It would be quite easy to arrange the experiences in such a way that they automatically caused the structure of the machine to build up into a previously intended form, and this would obviously be a gross form of cheating, almost on a par with having a man inside the machine. Here again the criterion as to what would be considered reasonable in the way of 'education' cannot be put into mathematical terms, but I suggest that the following would be adequate in practice. Let us suppose that it is intended that the machine shall understand English, and that owing to its having no hands or feet, and not needing to eat, nor desiring to smoke, it will occupy its time mostly in playing games such as Chess and GO, and possibly Bridge. The machine is provided with a typewriter keyboard on which any remarks to it are typed, and it also types out any remarks that it wishes to make. I suggest that the education of the machine should be entrusted to some highly competent schoolmaster who is interested in the project but who is forbidden any detailed knowledge of the inner workings of the machine. The mechanic who has constructed the machine, however, is permitted to keep the machine in running order, and if he suspects that the machine has been operating incorrectly may put it back to one of its previous positions and ask the schoolmaster to repeat his lessons from that point on, but he may not take any part in the teaching. Since this procedure would only serve to test the bona fides of the mechanic, I need hardly say that it would not be adopted at the experimental stages. As I see it, this education process would in practice be an essential to the production of a reasonably intelligent machine within a reasonably short space of time. The human analogy alone suggests this.

I may now give some indication of the way in which such a machine might be expected to function. The machine would incorporate a memory. This does not need very much explanation. It would simply be a list of all the statements that had been made to it or by it, and all the moves it had made and the cards it had played in its games. This would be listed in chronological order. Besides this straightforward memory there would be a number of 'indexes of experiences'. To explain this idea I will suggest the form which one such index might possibly take. It might be an alphabetical index of the words that had been used giving the 'times' at which they had been used, so that they could be looked up in the memory. Another such index might contain patterns of men on parts of a GO board that had occurred. At comparatively late stages of education the memory might be extended to include important parts of the configuration of the machine at each moment, or in other words it would begin to remember what its thoughts had been. This would give rise to fruitful new forms of indexing. New forms of index might be introduced on account of special features observed in the indexes already used. The indexes would be used in this sort of way. Whenever a choice has to be made as to what to do next, features of the present situation are looked up in the indexes available, and the previous choice in the similar situations, and the outcome, good or bad, is discovered. The new choice is made accordingly. This raises a number of problems. If some of the indications are favourable and some are unfavourable what is one to do? The answer to this will probably differ from machine to machine and will also vary with its degree of education. At first probably some quite crude rule will suffice, e.g. to do whichever has the greatest number of votes in its favour. At a very late stage of education the whole question of procedure in such cases will probably have been investigated by the machine itself, by means of some kind of index, and this may result in some highly sophisticated, and, one hopes, highly satisfactory, form of rule. It seems probable however that the comparatively crude forms of rule will themselves be reasonably satisfactory, so that progress can on the whole be made in spite of the crudeness of the choice of rules. This seems to be verified by the fact that engineering problems are sometimes solved by the crudest rule of thumb procedure which deals only with the most superficial aspects of the problem, e.g. whether a function increases or decreases with one of its variables. Another problem raised by this picture of the way behaviour is determined is the idea of 'favourable outcome'. Without some such idea, corresponding to the 'pleasure principle' of the psychologists, it is very difficult to see how to proceed. Certainly it would be most natural to introduce some such thing into the machine. I suggest that there should be two keys which can be manipulated by the schoolmaster, and which represent the ideas of pleasure and pain. At later stages in education the machine would recognise certain other conditions as desirable owing to their having been constantly associated in the past with pleasure, and likewise certain others as undesirable. Certain expressions of anger on the part of the schoolmaster might, for instance, be recognised as so ominous that they could never be overlooked, so that the schoolmaster would find that it became unnecessary to 'apply the cane' any more.

To make further suggestions along these lines would perhaps be unfruitful at this stage, as they are likely to consist of nothing more than an analysis of actual methods of education applied to human children. There is, however, one feature that I would like to suggest should be incorporated in the machines, and that is a 'random element'. Each machine should be supplied with a tape bearing a random series of figures, e.g. 0 and 1 in equal quantities, and this series of figures should be used in the choices made by the machine. This would result in the behaviour of the machine not being by any means completely determined by the experiences to which it was subjected, and would have some valuable uses when one was experimenting with it. By faking the choices made one would be able to control the development of the machine to some extent. One might, for instance, insist on the choice made being a particular one at, say, 10 particular places, and this would mean that about one machine in 1024 or more would develop to as high a degree as the one which had been faked. This cannot very well be given an accurate statement because of the subjective nature of the idea of 'degree of development' to say nothing of the fact that the machine that had been faked might have been also fortunate in its unfaked choices.

Let us now assume, for the sake of argument, that these machines are a genuine possibility, and look at the consequences of constructing them. To do so would of course meet with great opposition, unless we have advanced greatly in religious toleration from the days of Galileo. There would be great opposition from the intellectuals who were afraid of being put out of a job. It is probable though that the intellectuals would be mistaken about this. There would be plenty to do, trying to understand what the machines were trying to say, i.e. in trying to keep one's intelligence up to the standard set by the machines, for it seems probable that once the machine thinking method had started, it would not take long to outstrip our feeble powers. There would be no question of the machines dying, and they would be able to converse with each other to sharpen their wits. At some stage therefore we should have to expect the machines to take control, in the way that is mentioned in Samuel Butler's 'Erewhon'.

461

3 CAN DIGITAL COMPUTERS THINK?

Digital computers have often been described as mechanical brains. Most scientists probably regard this description as a mere newspaper stunt, but some do not. One mathematician has expressed the opposite point of view to me rather forcefully in the words 'It is commonly said that these machines are not brains, but you and I know that they are'. In this talk I shall try to explain the ideas behind the various possible points of view, though not altogether impartially. I shall give most attention to the view which I hold myself, that it is not altogether unreasonable to describe digital computers as brains. A different point of view has already been put by Professor Hartree.

First we may consider the naive point of view of the man in the street. He hears amazing accounts of what these machines can do: most of them apparently involve intellectual feats of which he would be quite incapable. He can only explain it by supposing that the machine is a sort of brain, though he may prefer simply to disbelieve what he has heard.

The majority of scientists are contemptuous of this almost superstitious attitude. They know something of the principles on which the machines are constructed and of the way in which they are used. Their outlook was well summed up by Lady Lovelace over a hundred years ago, speaking of Babbage's Analytical Engine. She said, as Hartree has already quoted, 'The Analytical Engine has no pretensions whatever to *originate* anything. It can do whatever *we know how to order it* to perform.' This very well describes the way in which digital computers are actually used at the present time, and in which they will probably mainly be used for many years to come. For any one calculation the whole procedure that the machine is to go through is planned out in advance by a mathematician. The less doubt there is about what is going to happen the better the mathematician is pleased. It is like planning a military operation. Under these circumstances it is fair to say that the machine doesn't originate anything.

There is however a third point of view, which I hold myself. I agree with Lady Lovelace's dictum as far as it goes, but I believe that its validity depends on considering how digital computers *are* used rather than how they *could be* used. In fact I believe that they could be used in such a manner that they could appropriately be described as brains. I should also say that 'If any machine can appropriately be described as a brain, then any digital computer can be so described'.

This last statement needs some explanation. It may appear rather startling, but with some reservations it appears to be an inescapable fact. It can be shown to follow from a characteristic property of digital computers, which I will call their *universality*. A digital computer is a *universal* machine in the sense that it can be made to replace any machine of a certain very wide class. It will not replace a bulldozer or a steam-engine or a telescope, but it will replace any rival design of calculating machine, that is to say any machine into which one can feed data and which will later print out results. In order to arrange for our computer to imitate a given machine it is only necessary to programme the computer to calculate what the machine in question would do under given circumstances, and in particular what answers it would print out. The computer can then be made to print out the same answers.

If now some particular machine can be described as a brain we have only to programme our digital computer to imitate it and it will also be a brain. If it is accepted that real brains, as found in animals, and in particular in men, are a sort of machine it will follow that our digital computer suitably programmed, will behave like a brain.

This argument involves several assumptions which can quite reasonably be challenged. I have already explained that the machine to be imitated must be more like a calculator than a bulldozer. This is merely a reflection of the fact that we are speaking of mechanical analogues of brains, rather than of feet or jaws. It was also necessary that this machine should be of the sort whose behaviour is in principle predictable by calculation. We certainly do not know how any such calculation should be done, and it was even argued by Sir Arthur Eddington that on account of the indeterminacy principle in quantum mechanics no such prediction is even theoretically possible.

Another assumption was that the storage capacity of the computer used should be sufficient to carry out the prediction of the behaviour of the machine to be imitated. It should also have sufficient speed. Our present computers probably have not got the necessary storage capacity, though they may well have the speed. This means in effect that if we wish to imitate anything so complicated as the human brain we need a very much larger machine than any of the computers at present available. We probably need something at least a hundred times as large as the Manchester Computer. Alternatively of course a machine of equal size or smaller would do if sufficient progress were made in the technique of storing information.

It should be noticed that there is no need for there to be any increase in the complexity of the computers used. If we try to imitate ever more complicated machines or brains we must use larger and larger computers to do it. We do not need to use successively more complicated ones. This may appear paradoxical, but the explanation is not difficult. The imitation of a machine by a computer requires not only that we should have made the computer, but that we should have programmed it appropriately. The more complicated the machine to be imitated the more complicated must the programme be.

This may perhaps be made clearer by an analogy. Suppose two men both wanted to write their autobiographies, and that one had had an eventful life, but very little had happened to the other. There would be two difficulties troubling the man with the more eventful life more seriously than the other. He would have to spend more on paper and he would have to take more trouble over thinking what to say. The supply of paper would not be likely to be a serious difficulty, unless for instance he were on a desert island, and in any case it could only be a technical or a financial problem. The other difficulty would be more fundamental and would become more serious still if he were not writing his life but a work on something he knew nothing about, let us say about family life on Mars. Our problem of programming a computer to behave like a brain is something like trying to write this treatise on a desert island. We cannot get the storage capacity we need: in other words we cannot get enough paper to write the treatise on, and in any case we don't know what we should write down if we had it. This is a poor state of affairs, but, to continue the analogy, it is something to know how to write, and to appreciate the fact that most knowledge can be embodied in books.

In view of this it seems that the wisest ground on which to criticise the description of digital computers as 'mechanical brains' or 'electronic brains' is that, although they might be programmed to behave like brains, we do not at present know how this should be done. With this outlook I am in full agreement. It leaves open the question as to whether we will

463

or will not eventually succeed in finding such a programme. I, personally, am inclined to believe that such a programme will be found. I think it is probable for instance that at the end of the century it will be possible to programme a machine to answer questions in such a way that it will be extremely difficult to guess whether the answers are being given by a man or by the machine. I am imagining something like a viva-voce examination, but with the questions and answers all typewritten in order that we need not consider such irrelevant matters as the faithfulness with which the human voice can be imitated. This only represents my opinion; there is plenty of room for others.

There are still some difficulties. To behave like a brain seems to involve free will, but the behaviour of a digital computer, when it has been programmed, is completely determined. These two facts must somehow be reconciled, but to do so seems to involve us in an age-old controversy, that of 'free will and determinism'. There are two ways out. It may be that the feeling of free will which we all have is an illusion. Or it may be that we really have got free will, but yet there is no way of telling from our behaviour that this is so. In the latter case, however well a machine imitates a man's behaviour it is to be regarded as a mere sham. I do not know how we can ever decide between these alternatives but whichever is the correct one it is certain that a machine which is to imitate a brain must appear to behave as if it had free will, and it may well be asked how this is to be achieved. One possibility is to make its behaviour depend on something like a roulette wheel or a supply of radium. The behaviour of these may perhaps be predictable, but if so, we do not know how to do the prediction.

It is, however, not really even necessary to do this. It is not difficult to design machines whose behaviour appears quite random to anyone who does not know the details of their construction. Naturally enough the inclusion of this random element, whichever technique is used, does not solve our main problem, how to programme a machine to imitate the brain, or as we might say more briefly, if less accurately, to think. But it gives us some indication of what the process will be like. We must not always expect to know what the computer is going to do. We should be pleased when the machine surprises us, in rather the same way as one is pleased when a pupil does something which he had not been explicitly taught to do.

Let us now reconsider Lady Lovelace's dictum. 'The machine can do whatever *we know how to order it* to perform'. The sense of the rest of the passage is such that one is tempted to say that the machine can *only* do what we know how to order it to perform. But I think this would not be true. Certainly the machine can only do what we *do* order it to perform, anything else would be a mechanical fault. But there is no need to suppose that, when we give it its orders we know what we are doing, what the consequences of these orders are going to be. One does not need to be able to understand how these orders lead to the machine's subsequent behaviour, any more than one needs to understand the mechanism of germination when one puts a seed in the ground. The plant comes up whether one understands or not. If we give the machine a programme which results in its doing something interesting which we had not anticipated I should be inclined to say that the machine *had* originated something, rather than to claim that its behaviour was implicit in the programme, and therefore that the originality lies entirely with us.

I will not attempt to say much about how this process of 'programming a machine to think' is to be done. The fact is that we know very little about it, and very little research has yet been done. There are plentiful ideas, but we do not yet know which of them are of importance. As in the detective stories, at the beginning of the investigation any trifle may be of importance to the investigator. When the problem has been solved, only the essential facts need to be told to the jury. But at present we have nothing worth putting before a jury. I will only say this, that I believe the process should bear a close relation to that of teaching.

I have tried to explain what are the main rational arguments for and against the theory that machines could be made to think, but something should also be said about the irrational arguments. Many people are extremely opposed to the idea of a machine that thinks, but I do not believe that it is for any of the reasons that I have given, or any other rational reason, but simply because they do not like the idea. One can see many features which make it unpleasant. If a machine can think, it might think more intelligently than we do, and then where should we be? Even if we could keep the machines in a subservient position, for instance by turning off the power at strategic moments, we should, as a species, feel greatly humbled. A similar danger and humiliation threatens us from the possibility that we might be superseded by the pig or the rat. This is a theoretical possibility which is hardly controversial, but we have lived with pigs and rats for so long without their intelligence much increasing, that we no longer trouble ourselves about this possibility. We feel that if it is to happen at all it will not be for several million years to come. But this new danger is much closer. If it comes at all it will almost certainly be within the next millennium. It is remote but not astronomically remote, and is certainly something which can give us anxiety.

It is customary, in a talk or article on this subject, to offer a grain of comfort, in the form of a statement that some particularly human characteristic could never be imitated by a machine. It might for instance be said that no machine could write good English, or that it could not be influenced by sex-appeal or smoke a pipe. I cannot offer any such comfort, for I believe that no such bounds can be set. But I certainly hope and believe that no great efforts will be put into making machines with the most distinctively human, but non-intellectual characteristics such as the shape of the human body; it appears to me to be quite futile to make such attempts and their results would have something like the unpleasant quality of artificial flowers. Attempts to produce a thinking machine seem to me to be in a different category. The whole thinking process is still rather mysterious to us, but I believe that the attempt to make a thinking machine will help us greatly in finding out how we think ourselves.

4 CAN AUTOMATIC CALCULATING MACHINES BE SAID TO THINK?

Braithwaite: We're here today to discuss whether calculating machines can be said to think in any proper sense of the word. Thinking is ordinarily regarded as so much a speciality of man, and perhaps of other higher animals, that the question may seem too absurd to be discussed. But, of course, it all depends on what is to be included in thinking. The word is used to cover a multitude of different activities. What would you, Jefferson, as a physiologist, say were the most important elements involved in thinking?

Jefferson: I don't think that we need waste too much time on a definition of thinking since it will be hard to get beyond phrases in common usage, such as having ideas in the mind, cogitating, meditating, deliberating, solving problems or imagining. Philologists say that the word 'Man' is derived from a Sanskrit word that means 'to think,' probably in the sense of judging between one idea and another. I agree that we could no longer use the word 'thinking' in a sense that restricted it to man. No one would deny that many animals think, though in a very limited way. They lack insight. For example, a dog learns that it is wrong to get on cushions or chairs with muddy paws, but he only learns it as a venture that doesn't pay. He has no conception of the real reason, that he damages fabrics by doing that.

The average person would perhaps be content to define thinking in very general terms such as revolving ideas in the mind, of having notions in one's head, of having one's mind occupied by a problem, and so on. But it is only right to add that our minds are occupied much of the time with trivialities. One might say in the end that thinking was the general result of having a sufficiently complex nervous system. Very simple ones do not provide the creature with any problems that are not answered by simple reflex mechanisms. Thinking then becomes all the things that go on in one's brain, things that often end in an action but don't necessarily do so. I should say that it was the sum total of what the brain of man or animal does. Turing, what do you think about it? Have you a mechanical definition?

Turing: I don't want to give a definition of thinking, but if I had to I should probably be unable to say anything more about it than that it was a sort of buzzing that went on inside my head. But I don't really see that we need to agree on a definition at all. The important thing is to try to draw a line between the properties of a brain, or of a man, that we want to discuss, and those that we don't. To take an extreme case, we are not interested in the fact that the brain has the consistency of cold porridge. We don't want to say 'This machine's quite hard, so it isn't a brain, and so it can't think.' I would like to suggest a particular kind of *test* that one might apply to a machine. You might call it a test to see whether the machine thinks, but it would be better to avoid begging the question, and say that the machines that pass are (let's say) 'Grade A' machines. The idea of the test is that the machine has to try and pretend to be a man, by answering questions put to it, and it will only pass if the pretence is reasonably convincing. A considerable proportion of a jury, who should not be expert about machines, must be taken in by the pretence. They aren't allowed to see the machine itself—that would make it too easy. So the machine is kept in a far away room and the jury are allowed to ask it questions, which are transmitted through to it: it sends back a typewritten answer.

Braithwaite: Would the questions have to be sums, or could I ask it what it had had for breakfast?

Turing: Oh yes, anything. And the questions don't really have to be questions, any more than questions in a law court are really questions. You know the sort of thing. 'I put it to you that you are only pretending to be a man' would be quite in order. Likewise the machine would be permitted all sorts of tricks so as to appear more man-like, such as waiting a bit before giving the answer, or making spelling mistakes, but it can't make smudges on the paper, any more than one can send smudges by telegraph. We had better suppose that each jury has to judge quite a number of times, and that sometimes they really are dealing with a man and not a machine. That will prevent them saying 'It must be a machine' every time without proper consideration.

   Well, that's my test. Of course I am not saying at present either that machines really could pass the test, or that they couldn't. My suggestion is just that this is the question we should discuss. It's not the same as 'Do machines think,' but it seems near enough for our present purpose, and raises much the same difficulties.

Newman: I should like to be there when your match between a man and a machine takes place, and perhaps to try my hand at making up some of the questions. But that will be a long time from now, if the machine is to stand any chance with no questions barred?

Turing: Oh yes, at least 100 years, I should say.

Jefferson: Newman, how well would existing machines stand up to this test? What kind of things can they do now?

Newman: Of course, their strongest line is mathematical computing, which they were designed to do, but they would also do well at some questions that don't look numerical, but can easily be made so, like solving a chess problem or looking you up a train in the time-table.

Braithwaite: Could they do that?

Newman: Yes. Both these jobs can be done by trying all the possibilities, one after another. The whole of the information in an ordinary time-table would have to be written in as part of the programme, and the simplest possible routine would be one that found the trains from London to Manchester by testing every train in the time-table to see if it calls at both places, and printing out those that do. Of course, this is a dull, plodding method, and you could improve on it by using a more complicated routine, but if I have understood Turing's test properly, you are not allowed to go behind the scenes and criticise the method, but must abide by the scoring on correct answers, found reasonably quickly.

Jefferson: Yes, but all the same a man who has to look up trains frequently gets better at it, as he learns his way about the time-table. Suppose I give a machine the same problem again, can it learn to do better without going through the whole rigmarole of trying everything over every time? I'd like to have your answer to that because it's such an important point. Can machines learn to do better with practice?

Newman: Yes, it could. Perhaps the chess problem provides a better illustration of this. First I should mention that *all* the information required in any job—the numbers, times of trains, positions of pieces, or whatever it is, and also the instructions saying what is to be done with them—all this material is stored in the same way. (In the Manchester machine it is stored as a pattern on something resembling a television screen.) As the work goes on the pattern is changed. Usually it is the part of the pattern that contains the data that changes, while the instructions stay fixed. But it is just as simple to arrange that the instructions themselves shall be changed now and then. Well, now a programme could be composed that would cause the machine to do this: a 2-move chess problem is recorded into the machine in some suitable coding, and whenever the machine is started, a white move is chosen at random

467

(there is a device for making random choices in our machine). All the consequences of this move are now analysed, and if it does *not* lead to forced mate in two moves, the machine prints, say, 'P-Q3, wrong move', and stops. But the analysis shows that when the right move is chosen the machine not only prints, say, 'B-Q5, solution,' but it changes the instruction calling for a random choice to one that says 'Try B-Q5.' The result is that whenever the machine is started again it will immediately print out the right solution—and this without the man who made up the routine knowing beforehand what it was. Such a routine could certainly be made now, and I think this can fairly be called learning.

Jefferson: Yes, I suppose it is. Human beings learn by repeating the same exercises until they have perfected them. Of course it goes further, and at the same time we learn generally to shift the knowledge gained about one thing to another set of problems, seeing relevances and relationships. Learning means remembering. How long can a machine store information for?

Newman: Oh, at least as long as a man's lifetime, if it is refreshed occasionally.

Jefferson: Another difference would be that in the learning process there is much more frequent intervention by teachers, parental or otherwise, guiding the arts of learning. You mathematicians put the programme once into the machine and leave it to it. You wouldn't get any distance at all with human beings if that is what you did. In fact, the only time you do that in the learning period is at examinations.

Turing: It's quite true that when a child is being taught, his parents and teachers are repeatedly intervening to stop him doing this or encourage him to do that. But this will not be any the less so when one is trying to teach a machine. I have made some experiments in teaching a machine to do some simple operation, and a very great deal of such intervention was needed before I could get any results at all. In other words the machine learnt so slowly that it needed a great deal of teaching.

Jefferson: But who was learning, you or the machine?

Turing: Well, I suppose we both were. One will have to find out how to make machines that will learn more quickly if there is to be any real success. One hopes too that there will be a sort of snowball effect. The more things the machine has learnt the easier it ought to be for it to learn others. In learning to do any particular thing it will probably also be learning to learn more efficiently. I am inclined to believe that when one has taught it to do certain things one will find that some other things which one had planned to teach it are happening without any special teaching being required. This certainly happens with an intelligent human mind, and if it doesn't happen when one is teaching a machine there is something lacking in the machine. What do you think about learning possibilities, Braithwaite?

Braithwaite: No-one has mentioned what seems to me the great difficulty about learning, since we've only discussed learning to solve a particular problem. But the most important part of human learning is learning from experience—not learning from one particular kind of experience, but being able to learn from experience in general. A machine can easily be constructed with a feed-back device so that the programming of the machine is controlled by the relation of its output to some feature in its external environment—so that the working of the machine in relation to the environment is self-corrective. But this requires that it should be some particular feature of the environment to which the machine has to adjust itself. The peculiarity of men and animals is that they have the power of adjusting themselves to almost all the features. The feature to which adjustment is made on a particular occasion is the one the man is attending to and he attends to what he is *interested in*. His interests are determined, by and large, by his appetites, desires, drives, instincts—all the things that together make up his 'springs of action'. If we want to construct a machine which will vary its attention to things in its environment so that it will sometimes adjust itself to one and sometimes to another, it would seem to be necessary to equip the machine with something corresponding to a set of appetites. If the machine is built to be treated only as a domestic pet, and is spoon-fed with particular problems, it will not be able to learn in the varying way in which human beings learn. This arises from the necessity of adapting behaviour suitably to environment if human appetites are to be satisfied.

Jefferson: Turing, you spoke with great confidence about what you are going to be able to do. You make it sound as if it would be fairly easy to modify construction so that the machine reacted more like a man. But I recollect that from the time of Descartes and Borelli on people have said that it would be only a matter of a few years, perhaps 3 or 4 or maybe 50, and a replica of man would have been artificially created. We shall be wrong, I am sure, if we give the impression that these things would be easy to do.

Newman: I agree that we are getting rather far away from computing machines as they exist at present. These machines have rather restricted appetites, and they can't blush when they're embarrassed, but it's quite hard enough, and I think a very interesting problem, to discover how near these actually existing machines can get to thinking. Even if we stick to the reasoning side of thinking, it is a long way from solving chess problems to the invention of new mathematical concepts or making a generalisation that takes in ideas that were current before, but had never been brought together as instances of a single general notion.

Braithwaite: For example?

Newman: The different kinds of number. There are the integers, 0, 1, −2, and so on; there are the real numbers used in comparing lengths, for example the circumference of a circle and its diameter; and the complex numbers involving $\sqrt{-1}$; and so on. It is not at all obvious that these are instances of one thing, 'number.' The Greek mathematicians used entirely different words for the integers and the real numbers, and had no single idea to cover both. It is really only recently that the general notion of kinds of number has been abstracted from these instances and accurately defined. To make this sort of generalisation you need to have the power of recognising similarities, seeing analogies between things that had not been put together before. It is not just a matter of testing things for a specified property and classifying them accordingly. The concept itself has to be framed, something has to be created, say the idea of a number-field. Can we even guess at the way a machine could make such an invention from a programme composed by a man who had not the concept in his own mind?

Turing: It seems to me, Newman, that what you said about 'trying out possibilities' as a method applies to quite an extent, even when a machine is required to do something as advanced as finding a useful new concept. I wouldn't like to have to define

469

the meaning of the word 'concept,' nor to give rules for rating their usefulness, but whatever they are they've got outward and visible forms, which are words and combinations of words. A machine could make up such combinations of words more or less at random, and then give them marks for various merits.

Newman: Wouldn't that take a prohibitively long time?

Turing: It would certainly be shockingly slow, but it could start on easy things, such as lumping together rain, hail, snow and sleet, under the word 'precipitation.' Perhaps it might do more difficult things later on if it was learning all the time how to improve its methods.

Braithwaite: I don't think there's much difficulty about seeing analogies that can be formally analysed and explicitly stated. It is then only a question of designing the machine so that it can recognise similarities of mathematical structure. The difficulty arises if the analogy is a vague one about which little more can be said than that one has a feeling that there is some sort of similarity between two cases but one hasn't any idea as to the respect in which the two cases are similar. A machine can't recognise similarities when there is nothing in its programme to say what are the similarities it is expected to recognise.

Turing: I think you could make a machine spot an analogy, in fact it's quite a good instance of how a machine could be made to do some of those things that one usually regards as essentially a human monopoly. Suppose that someone was trying to explain the double negative to me, for instance, that when something isn't not green it must be green, and he couldn't quite get it across. He might say 'Well, it's like crossing the road. You cross it, and then you cross it again, and you're back where you started.' This remark might just clinch it. This is one of the things one would like to work with machines, and I think it would be likely to happen with them. I imagine that the way analogy works in our brains is something like this. When two or more sets of ideas have the same pattern of logical connections, the brain may very likely economise parts by using some of them twice over, to remember the logical connections both in the one case and in the other. One must suppose that some part of my brain was used twice over in this way, once for the idea of double negation and once for crossing the road, there and back. I am really supposed to know about both these things but can't get what it is the man is driving at, so long as he is talking about all those dreary nots and not-nots. Somehow it doesn't get through to the right part of the brain. But as soon as he says his piece about crossing the road it gets through to the right part, but by a different route. If there is some such purely mechanical explanation of how this argument by analogy goes on in the brain, one could make a digital computer do the same.

Jefferson: Well, there isn't a mechanical explanation in terms of cells and connecting fibres in the brain.

Braithwaite: But could a machine really do this? How would it do it?

Turing: I've certainly left a great deal to the imagination. If I had given a longer explanation I might have made it seem more certain that what I was describing was feasible, but you would probably feel rather uneasy about it all, and you'd probably exclaim impatiently, 'Well, yes, I see that a machine could do all that, but I wouldn't call it thinking.' As soon as one can see the cause and effect working themselves out in the brain, one regards it as not being thinking, but a sort of unimaginative donkey-work.

From this point of view one might be tempted to define thinking as consisting of 'those mental processes that we don't understand'. If this is right then to make a thinking machine is to make one which does interesting things without our really understanding quite how it is done.

Jefferson: If you mean that we don't know the wiring in men, as it were, that is quite true.

Turing: No, that isn't at all what I mean. We know the wiring of our machine, but it already happens there in a limited sort of way. Sometimes a computing machine does do something rather weird that we hadn't expected. In principle one could have predicted it, but in practice it's usually too much trouble. Obviously if one were to predict everything a computer was going to do one might just as well do without it.

Newman: It is quite true that people are disappointed when they discover what the big computing machines actually do, which is just to add and multiply, and use the results to decide what further additions and multiplications to do. '*That's* not thinking', is the natural comment, but this is rather begging the question. If you go into one of the ancient churches in Ravenna you see some most beautiful pictures round the walls, but if you peer at them through binoculars you might say, 'Why, they aren't really pictures at all, but just a lot of little coloured stones with cement in between.' The machine's processes are mosaics of very simple standard parts, but the designs can be of great complexity, and it is not obvious where the limit is to the patterns of thought they could imitate.

Braithwaite: But how many stones are there in your mosaic? Jefferson, is there a sufficient multiplicity of the cells in the brain for them to behave like a computing machine?

Jefferson: Yes, there are thousands, tens of thousands more cells in the brain than there are in a computing machine, because the present machine contains—how many did you say?

Turing: Half a million digits. I think we can assume that is the equivalent of half a million nerve cells.

Braithwaite: If the brain works like a computing machine then the present computing machine cannot do all the things the brain does. Agreed; but if a computing machine were made that could do all the things the brain does, wouldn't it require more digits than there is room for in the brain?

Jefferson: Well, I don't know. Suppose that it is right to equate digits in a machine with nerve cells in a brain. There are various estimates, somewhere between ten thousand million and fifteen thousand million cells are supposed to be there. Nobody knows for certain, you see. It is a colossal number. You would need 20,000 or more of your machines to equate digits with nerve cells. But it is not, surely, just a question of size. There would be too much logic in your huge machine. It wouldn't be really like a human output of thought. To make it more like, a lot of the machine parts would have to be designed quite differently to give greater flexibility and more diverse possibilities of use. It's a very tall order indeed.

Turing: It really is the size that matters in this case. It is the amount of information that can be stored up. If you think of something very complicated that you want one of these machines to do, you may find the particular machine you have got won't do, but if any machine can do it at all, then it can be done by your first computer, simply increased in its storage capacity.

Jefferson: If we are really to get near to anything that can be truly called 'thinking' the effects of external stimuli cannot be missed out; the intervention of all sorts of extraneous factors, like the worries of having to make one's living, or pay one's taxes, or get food that one likes. These are not in any sense minor factors, they are very important indeed, and worries concerned with them may greatly interfere with good thinking, especially with creative thinking. You see a machine has no environment, and man is in constant relation to his environment, which, as it were punches him whilst he punches back. There is a vast background of memories in a man's brain that each new idea or experience has to fit in with. I wonder if you could tell me how far a calculating machine meets that situation. Most people agree that man's first reaction to a new idea (such as the one we are discussing today) is one of rejection, often immediate and horrified denial of it. I don't see how a machine could as it were say 'Now Professor Newman or Mr. Turing, I don't like this programme at all that you've just put into me, in fact I'm not going to have anything to do with it.'

Newman: One difficulty about answering that is one that Turing has already mentioned. If someone says, 'Could a machine do this, e.g. could it say "I don't like the programme you have just put into me"', and a programme for doing that very thing is duly produced, it is apt to have an artificial and ad hoc air, and appear to be more of a trick than a serious answer to the question. It is like those passages in the Bible, which worried me as a small boy, that say that such and such was done 'that the prophecy might be fulfilled which says' so and so. This always seemed to me a most unfair way of making sure that the prophecy came true. If I answer your question, Jefferson, by making a routine which simply caused the machine to say just the words 'Newman and Turing, I don't like your programme,' you would certainly feel this was a rather childish trick, and not the answer to what you really wanted to know. But yet it's hard to pin down what you want.

Jefferson: I want the machine to reject the problem because it offends it in some way. That leads me to enquire what the ingredients are of ideas that we reject because we instinctively don't care for them. I don't know why I like some pictures and some music and am bored by other sorts. But I'm not going to carry that line on because we are all different, our dislikes are based on our personal histories and probably too on small differences of construction in all of us, I mean by heredity. Your machines have no genes, no pedigrees. Mendelian inheritance means nothing to wireless valves. But I don't want to score debating points! We ought to make it clear that not even Turing thinks that all that he has to do is to put a skin on the machine and that it is alive! We've been trying for a more limited objective whether the sort of thing that machines do can be considered as thinking. But is not your machine more certain than any human being of getting its problem right at once, and infallibly?

Newman: Oh!

Turing: Computing machines aren't really infallible at all. Making up checks on their accuracy is quite an important part of the art of using them. Besides making mistakes they sometimes haven't done quite the calculation one had expected, and one gets something that might be called a 'misunderstanding.'

Jefferson: At any rate, they are not influenced by the emotions. You have only to upset a person enough and he becomes confused, he can't think of the answers and may make a fool of himself. It is high emotional content of mental processes in the human being that makes him quite different from a machine. It seems to me to come from the great complexity of his nervous system with its 10^{10} cells and also from his endocrine system which imports all sorts of emotions and instincts, such as those to do with sex. Man is essentially a chemical machine, he is much affected by hunger and fatigue, by being 'out of sorts' as we say, also by innate judgements, and by sexual urges. This chemical side is tremendously important, not the least so because the brain does exercise a remote control over the most important chemical processes that go on in our bodies. Your machines don't have to bother with that, with being tired or cold or happy or satisfied. They show no delight at having done something never done before. No, they are 'mentally' simple things. I mean that however complicated their structure is (and I know it *is* very complicated), compared with man they are very simple and perform their tasks with an absence of distracting thoughts which is quite *inhuman*.

Braithwaite: I'm not sure that I agree. I believe that it will be necessary to provide the machine with something corresponding to appetites, or other 'springs of action', in order that it will pay enough attention to relevant features in its environment to be able to learn from experience. Many psychologists have held that the emotions in men are by-products of their appetites and that they serve a biological function in calling higher levels of mental activity into play when the lower levels are incapable of coping with an external situation. For example, one does not feel afraid when there is no danger, or a danger which can be avoided more or less automatically: fear is a symptom showing that the danger has to be met by conscious thought. Perhaps it will be impossible to build a machine capable of learning in general from experience without incorporating in it an emotional apparatus, the function of which will be to switch over to a different part of the machine when the external environment differs too much from what would satisfy the machine's appetites by more than a certain amount. I don't want to suggest that it will be necessary for the machine to be able to throw a fit of tantrums. But in humans tantrums frequently fulfil a definite function—that of escaping from responsibility; and to protect a machine against a too hostile environment it may be essential to allow it, as it were, to go to bed with a neurosis, or psychogenic illness—just as, in a simpler way, it is provided with a fuse to blow, if the electric power working it threatens its continued existence.

Turing: Well, I don't envisage teaching the machine to throw temperamental scenes. I think some such effects are likely to occur as a sort of by-product of genuine teaching, and that one will be more interested in curbing such displays than in encouraging them. Such effects would probably be distinctly different from the corresponding human ones, but recognisable as variations on them. This means that if the machine was being put through one of my imitation tests, it would have to do quite a bit of acting, but if one was comparing it with a man in a less strict sort of way the resemblance might be quite impressive.

Newman: I still feel that too much of our argument is about what hypothetical future machines will do. It is all very well to say that a machine could easily be made to do this or that, but, to take only one practical point, what about the time it would

473

take to do it? It would only take an hour or two to make up a routine to make our Manchester machine analyse all possible variations of the game of chess right out, and find the best move that way—*if* you didn't mind its taking thousands of millions of years to run through the routine. Solving a problem on the machine doesn't mean finding a way to do it between now and eternity, but within a reasonable time. This is not just a technical detail that will be taken care of by future improvements. It's most unlikely that the engineers can ever give us a factor of more than a thousand or two times our present speeds. To assume that runs that would take thousands of millions of years on our present machines will be done in a flash on machines of the future, is to move into the realms of science fiction.

Turing: To my mind this time factor is the one question which will involve all the real technical difficulty. If one didn't know already that these things can be done by brains within a reasonable time one might think it hopeless to try with a machine. The fact that a brain *can* do it seems to suggest that the difficulties may not really be so bad as they now seem.

Braithwaite: I agree that we ought not to extend our discussion to cover whether calculating machines could be made which would do everything that a man can do. The point is, surely, whether they can do all that it is proper to call thinking. Appreciation of a picture contains elements of thinking, but it also contains elements of feeling; and we're not concerned with whether a machine can be made that will feel. Similarly with moral questions: we're only concerned with them so far as they are also intellectual ones. We haven't got to give the machine a sense of duty or anything corresponding to a will: still less need it be given temptations which it would then have to have an apparatus for resisting. All that it has got to do in order to think is to be able to solve, or to make a good attempt at solving, all the intellectual problems with which it might be confronted by the environment in which it finds itself. This environment, of course, must include Turing asking it awkward questions as well as natural events such as being rained upon, or being shaken up by an earthquake.

Newman: But I thought it was you who said that a machine wouldn't be able to learn to adjust to its environment if it hadn't been provided with a set of appetites and all that went with them?

Braithwaite: Yes, certainly. But the problems raised by a machine having appetites are not properly our concern today. It may be the case that it wouldn't be able to learn from experience without them; but we're only required to consider whether it would be able to learn at all—since I agree that being able to learn is an essential part of thinking. So oughtn't we to get back to something centred on thinking? Can a machine make up new concepts, for example?

Newman: There are really two questions that can be asked about machines and thinking, first, what do we require before we agree that the machine does *everything* that we call thinking? This is really what we have been talking about for most of the time; but there is also another interesting and important question: Where does the doubtful territory begin? What is the *nearest* thing to straight computing that the present machines perhaps can't do?

Braithwaite: And what would your own answer be?

Newman: I think perhaps to solve mathematical problems for which no method is known, in the way that men do; to find new methods. This is a much more modest aim than inventing new mathematical concepts. What happens when you try to solve a new problem in the ordinary way is that you think about it for a few seconds, or a few years, trying out all the analogies you can think of with problems that have been solved, and then you have an idea. You try it out in detail. If it is no good you must wait for another idea. This is a little like the chess-problem routine, where one move after another is tried, but with one very important difference, that if I am even a moderately good mathematician the ideas that I get are not just random ones, but are pre-selected so that there is an appreciable chance that after a few trials one of them will be successful. Henry Moore says about the studies he does for his sculpture, 'When the work is more than an exercise, inexplicable jumps occur. This is where the imagination comes in.' If a machine could really be got to imitate this sudden pounce on an idea, I believe that everyone would agree that it had begun to think, even though it didn't have appetites or worry about the income tax. And suppose that we also stuck to what we know about the physiology of human thinking, how much would that amount to, Jefferson?

Jefferson: We know a great deal about the end-product, thinking itself. Are not the contents of our libraries and museums the total up to date? Experimental psychology has taught us a lot about the way that we use memory and association of ideas, how we fill in gaps in knowledge and improvise from a few given facts. But exactly how we do it in terms of nerve cell actions we don't know. We are particularly ignorant of the very point that you mentioned just now, Newman, the actual physiology of the pounce on an idea, of the sudden inspiration. Thinking is clearly a motor activity of the brain's cells, a suggestion supported by the common experience that so many people think better with a pen in their hand than viva voce or by reverie and reflection. But you can't so far produce ideas in a man's mind by stimulating his exposed brain here or there electrically. It would have been really exciting if one could have done that—if one could have perhaps excited original thoughts by local stimulation. It can't be done. Nor does the electro-encephalograph show us how the process of thinking is carried out. It can't tell you what a man is thinking about. We can trace the course, say, of a page of print or of a stream of words into the brain, but we eventually lose them. If we could follow them to their storage places we still couldn't see how they are reassembled later as ideas. You have the great advantage of knowing how your machine was made. We only know that we have in the human nervous system a concern compact in size and in its way perfect for its job. We know a great deal about its microscopical structure and its connections. If fact, we know everything except how those myriads of cells allow us to think. But, Newman, before we say 'not only does this machine think but also here in this machine we have an exact counterpart of the wiring and circuits of human nervous systems', I ought to ask whether machines have been built or could be built which are as it were anatomically different, and yet produce the same work.

Newman: The logical plan of all of them is rather similar, but certainly their anatomy, and I suppose you could say their physiology, varies a lot.

475

Jefferson: Yes, that's what I imagined—we cannot then assume that any one of these electronic machines is a replica of part of a man's brain even though the result of its actions has to be conceded as thought. The real value of the machine to you is its end results, its performance, rather than that its plan reveals to us a model of our brains and nerves. Its usefulness lies in the fact that electricity travels along wires 2 or 3 million times faster than nerve impulses pass along nerves. You can set it to do things that man would need thousands of lives to complete. But that old slow coach, man, is the one with the ideas—or so I think. It would be fun some day, Turing, to listen to a discussion, say on the Fourth Programme, between two machines on why human beings think that they think!

23

Repairs to Turing's Universal Computing Machine

D. W. Davies

Royal Holloway College,
Egham, Surrey

1 INTRODUCTION

On Computable Numbers, with an Application to the Entscheidungsproblem, published by the London Mathematical Society in 1937, must be one of the most important and influential papers in the history of mathematical logic. It resolved the decision problem posed by Hilbert, gave an intuitive yet precise definition of computability and anticipated the stored-program computer which is central to today's technology.

Its author, the young Alan Turing, was to become one of the World War II codebreakers, using electronic calculators to speed up the running of his algorithms and then one of the first builders and programmers of stored-program machines. His work on artificial intelligence and morphogenesis was remarkable for its foresight.

The purpose of this paper is to present corrections to the design of the Universal Machine, which was one of the features of *On Computable Numbers*. The corrections have no significance for the argument of that work. Today they would be described as programming errors. Perhaps it is ironic, as well as understandable, that the first emulation program for a computer should have been wrong. To point this out and offer corrections is very presumptuous, and I had to be encouraged to publish. A reviewer said that ... *such errors will from time to time be noted and any error in so foundational a paper has some significance.* So perhaps, because of the great historical significance of Turing's paper, these corrections should be put on record.

An outline description of the Universal Machine will be followed by my proposed corrections to its design. Only two of the errors are more than trivial. One is a programming error in which a routine returns to the wrong place. The other is more basic and can be regarded as a confusion between the two representations of blank tape, one in the Universal Machine itself and the other in the machine which it is simulating.

To avoid filling this paper with tedious detail it will be assumed that the reader has the original paper for reference when dealing with trivial corrections. The two interesting errors will be described more fully. Turing's Gothic symbols are replaced by bold Roman letters.

It would be gratifying to be able to say that the revised machine has been simulated and shown to work on many examples. This has not been done. It proves to be difficult because the Universal Machine of Turing's design has to be generated from his description by repeated substitution and replication. Features of his description language which greatly simplified the description also cause the explicit machine to have many symbols, an enormous number of states and instructions and to be extremely slow. For example I estimate that the process of copying strings of symbols on the tape, embodied in the operations called **ce**$_5$ described below, introduces about 6000 states. Some fairly simple changes to the design reduce this problem. The final part of this paper outlines a redesign of the Universal Machine which was tested by simulation and shown to work. There can be reasonable confidence that there are no further significant errors in Turing's design, but a simulation starting directly from Turing's 'skeleton tables' would clinch the matter.

I shall use Turing's notation and terminology but introduce new words from computer technology where they make things clearer.

The page references are to the original published paper.

2 THE TURING MACHINE

A real number is said to be *computable* if it can be calculated by finite means. To make explicit the nature of those finite means, Turing devised a simple machine which took its instructions from a table, given in a well-defined format. The machine scanned one square of a tape at any time and read the symbol (of a finite alphabet) from that square. Depending on its present state, called *m-configuration*, and the symbol it has read, the next action is determined and this can be to change the symbol on the scanned square, then move right or left for the next action. It can leave the symbol unchanged or it can stay unmoved. The instruction table defines these actions for each state–symbol pair and also defines the resultant state.

The instruction table has a set of instructions, one for each state–symbol pair the machine could experience, with no significance in their order of appearance. An instruction has five parts:

[initial state,   symbol read]   [symbol written,   movement,   resultant state]

There is no explicit provision to leave the symbol unchanged, though this is required more often than anything else, because the effect of the instructions in Turing's Universal Machine is predominantly to reposition the machine by multiple shifts. In Turing's primitive machine this requires an instruction per shift for each symbol that might be read (or for the whole alphabet), just to move over the tape, rewriting what was already in each square. The Universal Machine spends nearly all its time moving from one end of the tape to the other. This is one of the reasons that simulating the machine literally is unrewarding. For Turing's purpose this awkwardness was irrelevant.

There are two operationally distinct parts of the instruction, on the left are the *state* and *symbol* by which the relevant instruction is found and on the right the *symbol*, *movement* and *state* which are the outcome.

478

It is convenient to have a starting point on the tape, marked with special symbols, and work only to the right of this. So the tape has a left-hand end, but to the right it is not limited.

3 THE UNIVERSAL MACHINE

The Universal Machine, U, is an ordinary Turing machine, with a special table of instructions which constitutes its design and which Turing specified in his paper. In operation, U would begin its work on a tape which had been prepared with, written at the left-hand end in a suitable format, the instruction table of a machine which I shall call T, for *target* machine. Set to work, U emulates the operation of T, including printing the output which T would have produced with its instructions as given on the initial tape. This printing uses a symbolism which makes T's output easily distinguishable on U's tape.

To describe the operation of U fully required a 15 page document, but for our purpose it is sufficient to outline just the coding of the states and symbols of T as they are represented on U's tape and the stages of the emulation process.

States are shown as DA, DAA, DAAA . . . where DA is the *initial* state of machine T.

Symbols are shown as D, DC, DCC, DCCC . . . where D is the *blank* symbol for T.

The letters D, A and C fall only on alternate squares, leaving spaces between them. All of the permanent work on the tape is in squares of one parity so that the spaces to the right of any such square can be used for temporary marks.

When it is performing the simulation of T, the machine U must write on its tape a complete description of what T is doing. This takes the form of a list of the symbols on T's (conceptual) tape. Additionally it must show T's present state and which square it is scanning. It does this by writing the letters (such as DAA) for T's state immediately to the left of the image of the scanned symbol of T. This list of T-symbols with one state inserted is a *snapshot* of T at one instant of its evolution.

To simulate the evolution of T, machine U writes successive snapshots on its tape. It begins with an image of T in its initial state (DA), then makes one evolution, using the instruction table which is stored to the left, and thus writes (on some new tape to the right) the next snapshot of T. As this evolution continues, more and more snapshots are written, so that an entire history of T gradually appears. Only the markers which guide this process are ever deleted.

There are two phases in the process by which U performs the evolution. The first finds the relevant instruction and second performs the actions it specifies.

For the first phase, the current machine state and scanned symbol of T are found in the last snapshot on U's tape (the state is immediately to the left of the scanned symbol). These are marked with y in each of the marking squares. Then an instruction is marked with x in its first two parts, the state and symbol, and the two strings on U's tape marked x and y are compared. This comparison is repeated for each instruction in turn until a match is found.

The second phase begins when the instruction has been found, and the instruction is now marked in its last three parts, the new symbol, the movement and the new state. The snapshot of T is also marked up, making ready to copy out parts from both instruction and snapshot into a new snapshot. Everything now depends on the movement, right, left or stationary, which determines which parts are to be copied and in which sequence. At the end of the copying, one evolution of T is complete.

4 THE INTERESTING ERRORS

The first phase of an evolution of T is to find the relevant instruction. This is done by marking the current state-symbol pair of T with y and the state-symbol pair of an instruction with x, then using the **cpe** operation to compare the marked strings. The process of **cpe** deletes some of the x and y markings. When comparison fails on one instruction the machine moves on to the next. This comparing process is shown in *The table for U* on page 244 of Turing's paper as

$$\textbf{kmp} \quad \textbf{cpe}(\textbf{e}(\textbf{kom}, x, y), \textbf{sim}, x, y)$$

The **e** operation is intended to delete all the remaining x and y markings. In fact this is not quite how erasure works as defined on page 237 and the correct form would be $\textbf{e}(\textbf{e}(\textbf{kom}, x), y)$. But there is a more serious error in returning to **kom**, since the essential y marking will not be restored. Returning to **anf** will repair this error. The correct definition of **kmp** should be

$$\textbf{kmp} \quad \textbf{cpe}(\textbf{e}(\textbf{e}(\textbf{anf}, x), y), \textbf{sim}, x, y)$$

To introduce the second of these interesting errors, it is instructive to look at the penultimate step in the copying out of the evolved new snapshot of T. This has been reduced, by Turing's clever scheme of skeleton tables, to a choice of one of three copy instructions on page 246, such as, for example

$$\textbf{inst}_1 \ (R) \quad \textbf{ce}_5 \ (\textbf{ov}, v, x, u, y, w)$$

This copies five marked areas of the last snapshot of T in the sequence shown to create the new snapshot, for the case where the machine moves right. The part marked y is the new machine state, v and x form the string of T-symbols to the left, u is the newly printed symbol and w the string of T-symbols to the right. Because u replaces an existing symbol, the number of symbols (including blanks) on T's conceptual tape has not changed! The same is true for left and null movement. There must be something wrong in an emulation in which the emulated machine can never change the number of symbols on its tape.

The snapshot shows just the occupied part of T's tape, and this is conceptually followed by an unlimited set of blank symbols, which are the tape as yet unused. The number of symbols on the snapshot of T will increase by moving right from the last occupied square and writing on the blank square. After a move right onto blank tape, there will be no string marked w, so machine state y will be the last thing on the snapshot.

This will lead to a failure of the emulation at the next evolution because the state-symbol pair of the snapshot, due to be marked with y during the search for the relevant instruction, is incomplete.

The remedy is to print a new blank symbol for T at the end of the image, when the move has been to the right and there is no T-symbol there. The necessary corrections, on page 246, to the table for U are:

inst$_1$ (R)			**ce**$_5$ (**q**(**inst**$_2$, A), v, x, u, y, w)
inst$_2$		R, R	**inst**$_3$
inst$_3$	| none	PD	**ov**
	| D		**ov**

In the case of a move right, after copying the parts of the previous snapshot, the operation **q** finds the last A on the tape, which is the end of the state symbol copied from markings y. If there is a T-symbol to its right, there is no problem. After two right moves of U, if a D is found there is a T-symbol but, if not, by printing D, a new blank tape square is added to the snapshot of T. In this way T's conceptual tape is extended and the state-symbol pair is made complete.

The error perhaps arose because the endless string of blank symbols on U's tape was taken as sufficient for the purpose of T. But for the emulation a blank square is shown as D. Machines U and T represent a blank tape differently.

There is a corresponding error in the way the initial state of T is placed on U's tape. It should contain the U-symbols: D A D with suitable spaces between them, representing T's initial state D A followed by the scanned symbol D, a blank. The correction on page 244 is:

b$_1$	R, R, P :, R, R, PD, R, R, PA, R, R, PD	**anf**

5 DIAGNOSTICS

With experience of writing programs it is second nature to build in diagnostics. Whether they are needed in U is arguable. Since U is a conceptual tool, its requirements are determined by its use in the argument of Turing's paper. For testing the design of U, diagnostics are certainly needed.

There may be a need for two kinds of failure indication in the program of U.

Suppose that T has a deficient set of instructions, meaning that its latest snapshot has a state–symbol pair which does not appear among the instructions. I believe that Turing would class this as a *circular* machine. The effect on the operation of U is that the search for the relevant instruction fails with U moving left beyond the left-hand end of its tape, and continuing to move left indefinitely. Perhaps this is acceptable for the purpose for which U was intended, but it seems anomalous that a deficiency in T should cause U to misbehave. It can be avoided by adding a line to the definition of **kom** on page 244:

$$\textbf{kom} \qquad \text{e} \qquad \textbf{fail}_1 \qquad \text{(deficient T instructions)}$$

then changing the next line to respond to symbols *not z nor*; *nor* **e**.

If T moves right without limit, this will be emulated correctly, but moving left beyond the limits of its tape is a problem. The way the U works will cause the next snapshot of T to appear as if no shift had occurred. There is no way to represent T as scanning a square to the left of its starting position. This means that the subsequent behaviour of T will differ from what its instructions imply. I think this might affect the use that Turing made of the machine in the main part of the paper.

The changes to deal with this problem are:

$$\textbf{inst}_1 \text{ (L)} \qquad \textbf{f}(\textbf{inst}_4, \textbf{fail}_2, x) \qquad \text{(machine T has run off left)}$$

$$\textbf{inst}_4 \qquad \textbf{ce}_5 \, (\textbf{ov}, \text{v}, \text{y}, \text{x}, \text{u}, \text{v})$$

6 TRIVIAL ERRORS AND CORRECTIONS

1. There is potential confusion in the use of the symbol **q** for different states in two places, and it is also confused with state **g**. The best resolution is as follows.

   We can treat the use of **q** in the Example on page 234 as casual, without permanent significance. The same might be said of its use on page 237, which is unrelated. But from there onwards the examples will form part of the definition of U, so the symbols have global significance.

   On page 239, the states **q** and $\textbf{q}_1$ appear but, in their subsequent uses in U, they have been replaced by **g**, for example in the definitions of **anf**, **mk** and **inst**. We have retained the notation **q**, while remembering that previous uses of this symbol are unrelated.

2. The skeleton tables for **re** and **cr** on page 238, which comprise five different states, are redundant, serving no illustrative purpose and not being used again.

3. On page 241, the format of the instruction table of T, as written on the tape of U, is described. Instructions are separated by semicolons. An example DADDCRDDA;DAA … DDRDA; is given. But this is misleading, because each instruction should be preceded by a semicolon. The example should begin with a semicolon, not end with one.

4. In the explanation of the skeleton table for **con**, C is one of the symbols being read and marked. But the words refer to ' … the sequence C of symbols describing a configuration … ' The final remarks ' … to the right of the last square of C. C is left unmarked.' use C in the second sense. It would otherwise seem as if the final symbol C was left unmarked, but this is not so. To clarify, replace by ' … the sequence S … ' and ' … last square of S. Configuration S is left unmarked.'

5. On page 245, a line for **sim$_2$** should read:

sim$_2$	not A	L, Pu, R, R, R	**sim$_2$**

6. On page 245, the line for mk should read: **mk**   **q(mk$_1$)**
7. On page 246, the line for **inst$_1$** (N) should read: **inst$_1$** (N)   **ce$_5$ (ov, v, x, y, u, v)**

7 A REDESIGN OF THE UNIVERSAL MACHINE

To verify, as far as this is possible, that there are no remaining errors in the amended version of Turing's program for U, it would be best to generate the explicit machine instruction table by substitutions and repetitions, then run this machine with one or more examples of a machine T and find if the emulations behaved as they should. But the complexity and slowness of the explicit form of Turing's U makes this difficult.

Therefore I made some changes to the design of U before constructing a simulation of a Turing Machine, loading the instructions for U, producing a tape image for a machine T and running the program. After some corrections to my version of U, the simulation behaved correctly. In this section the main features of the redesign are described.

The new version of U follows Turing's methods quite closely. The substitution process introduced with the skeleton tables had been nested to a depth of 9, causing a proliferation of states and instructions in the explicit machine. To avoid this, no skeleton tables were used in the new version and this allowed the procedures to be optimised for each application. The downside is that the 'low level' description of U which results takes up more space than the original and is harder to understand and check for accuracy. There are 147 states and 295 instructions in the new version, an enormous reduction.

The representation of T's states and symbols in a monadic notation such as DAAAA was replaced by a binary notation. This was an easy change that reduced the length of the workspace used. Because nearly all the time is used moving from end to end of the workspace, this is worthwhile. The small cost of the change is that there are four U-symbols to represent states and symbols instead of three.

The classic Turing Machine can move right or left or stay put in each operation. To simplify U a little, the third option was removed, so that a left or right movement became mandatory. For consistency, U was also run on a machine with this characteristic. In the whole of U's program, a compensating movement became necessary only a few times, so it is not a significant restriction.

Turing's skeleton tables show, for the scanned symbol, such words as *any*, or *not A*. When translated into a list of discrete symbols for the explicit machine these generate many instructions. By introducing a 'wild card' notation and searching instructions in a definite sequence, this proliferation can be avoided. A form of instruction was added which, in its written form, had an asterisk for both the scanned symbol and the written symbol. This acted on any scanned symbol and did not overwrite it. The way that U worked would have made it possible to read a wild card (i.e. any) scanned symbol and write over it or to read a specific symbol and leave it unchanged, but these were never needed in practice. The wild card scanned symbol should only be actioned after all other

483

possibilities (for this particular state) have been tested. Therefore instructions now have a defined sequence and must be tested accordingly. U always did test instructions in sequence but never made use of that fact.

Testing all instructions in sequence to find a match is very time-consuming because it requires marking, then comparing square by square, running from instruction space to work space. It was largely avoided by writing in U's instruction table an *offset* which indicated where the next instruction could be found. This indication led to a section of instructions dealing with a given state; after this, sequential testing took place. This was a shortcut to speed up U and was not envisaged as a feature of all Turing machines, since it would greatly complicate U. Technically it was a little more complex than I have described, but it has no effect on the design of U, being merely a chore for the programmer and a detail of the computer program which interprets those instructions.

U spends some of its time searching for a region on the tape where it will begin work. To make this easier, additional markers were introduced, for the action symbol (L or R) and for the start of the current snapshot. Also, the end of the work space was marked, and this marking was placed in one of the squares normally reserved for permanent symbols. Since it had to be overwritten when the workspace extended, this broke one Turing's conventions.

Finally the two failure indications described earlier were incorporated, one for a deficient T-instruction set and the other for T running its machine left, beyond the usable tape.

7.1 Testing the redesigned machine

A computer program was written which would simulate the underlying Turing Machine, which I shall call T*, using a set of instructions in its own special code, which had one byte per symbol or state. This code was chosen for convenience of writing U's instructions. It incorporated the wild card feature and the offset associated with each instruction, but the offset did not alter the way it responded to its instructions, only making it faster. When the design of U is complete and it instructions have been loaded, T* will behave as the Universal Machine U.

A simple editor was written to help the user write and amend the instruction tables for T* and prepare a starting tape for T* which holds the coded instructions for the emulated Turing Machine T.

For T, the example given by Turing on page 234 was used. It prints a sequence of increasing strings of ones, such as 001011011101111011111 .... . This program in its explicit form would have 23 instructions and 18 states. To make it simpler, it was rewritten without the 'alternate squares' principle and it then had 12 instructions and 6 states. It may be interesting to see how the wild card feature operates by studying this example, shown below.

As a first step, the example was loaded into the program space of T* and run, thus testing the mechanism of T* as well as the example in the table below.

Then the example was coded for the initial part of the tape of T*, so that it would cause U to emulate it as the target T. The program of U was loaded in many stages, debugging each by testing its part in the whole operation of U. Two serious program errors were found. One was in the operation **sh** which prints the output of T between the snapshots of T's evolution. The other was in the correction to Turing's scheme which wrote a blank symbol (D) at the end of the tape. It had been inserted at the wrong place. With these and several minor errors corrected the redesigned U performed as expected and the evolution of T agreed with expectation and with its earlier running, directly on T*. Only this one example of T was tried, but it probably does test the Universal Machine fully. The full results are given below.

Because of the differences between the version of U that was tested and Turing's design with my corrections, the testing must be regarded as incomplete. A compiler could be written to take the design in the form of skeleton tables and generate the explicit machine, which could then be run to emulate examples of the target machine. This would be extraordinarily slow.

8 THE PROGRAM FOR T

The instructions for T are given in the standard 5-part form, state, scanned symbol, written symbol, movement and resultant state. The snapshots are shown for the first eleven moves, in the standard form with the state symbol (**a** to **e**, printed bold) preceding the scanned symbol.

The blank space symbol is a hyphen and the other symbols are 0, 1, x and y.

The program writes a block of xs followed by a y, then converts the xs successively to 1s and the y to a 0, while writing the next block of xs and a y, increasing the number of xs by one.

s	–	0	R	a	print 0	: 0 **a** –	
a	–	y	R	b	print y at end	: 0 y **b** –	: 0 0 x **a** –
a	*	*	R	a			: 0 0 x y **b** –
b	–	x	L	c	print x at end	: 0 **c** y x	: 0 0 x **c** y x
b	*	*	R	b			
c	y	y	L	d	run back to y	: **d** 0 y x	: 0 0 **d** x y x
c	*	*	L	c			
d	x	1	R	b	change x to 1		: 0 0 1 **b** y x
d	0	0	R	e	none left	: 0 **e** y x	
d	*	*	L	d			
e	y	0	R	a	change y to 0	: 0 0 **a** x	
e	*	*	R	e			

485

9 RESULTS OF THE TEST

Here is a copy of the symbols on the tape of T* after 22 evolutions of U. The part up to the symbol % represents the 12 instructions for T. Then follow the 23 snapshots, separated by colon symbols. Whenever U prints a 0 or 1 symbol, this is also an output of T. To make this explicit (following Turing's practice) the strings **1** : or **0** : are inserted into the tape (bold in our table). So the whole set of evolutions shown has printed "**0 0 1 0**". The tape shown is printed on alternate spaces, except for the initial ee. The final F is a device of my own to make it easy to find the end of the written area of tape.

ee; M C S S C R M D ; M D S S C D R M C C ; M D S E S E R M D ;
M C C S S C C L M C D ; M C C S E S E R M C C ; M C D S C D S C D L M D C ;
M C D S E S E L M C D ; M D C S C C S D R M C C ; M D C S C S C R M D D ;
M D C S E S E L M D C ; M D D S C D S C R M D ; M D D S E S E R M D D % :
M C S : **0** : S C M D S : S C S C D M C C S : S C M C D S C D S C C :
M D C S C S C D S C C : S C M D D S C D S C C : **0** : S C S C M D S C C :
S C S C S C C M D S : S C S C S C C S C D M C C S :
S C S C S C C M C D S C D S C C : S C S C M D C S C C S C D S C C : **1** :
S C S C S D M C C S C D S C C : S C S C S D S C D M C C S C C :
S C S C S D S C D S C C M C C S : S C S C S D S C D M C D S C C S C C :
S C S C S D M C D S C D S C C S C C : S C S C M D C S D S C D S C C S C C :
S C M D C S C S D S C D S C C S C C : S C S C M D D S D S C D S C C S C C :
S C S C S D M D D S C D S C C S C C : **0** : S C S C S D S C M D S C C S C C :
S C S C S D S C S C C M D S C C : S C S C S D S C S C C S C C M D S F

As an aid to understanding this tape, here are the symbols and states of T in U's notation:

–	S	**s**	MC
0	SC	**a**	MD
1	SD	**b**	MCC
x	SCC	**c**	MCD
y	SCD	**d**	MDC
*	SE	**e**	MDD

The first few snapshots therefore read:

s – : **0** : 0 **a** – : 0 y **b** – : 0 **c** y x : **d** 0 y x : 0 **e** y x : **0** : 0 0 **a** x : 0 0 **a** x – : 0 0 x y **b** – :
0 0 x **c** y x : 0 0 **d** x y x : **1** : 0 0 1 **b** y x : 0 0 1 y **b** x : 0 0 1 y x **b** – : 0 0 1 y **c** x x :
0 0 1 **c** y x x :

The final configuration of the above tape is 0 0 1 0 x x **a** – :

10 THE CORRECTED TABLES FOR U

The table for **f**(A, B, a) is unchanged on page 236.

On page 237, **e**(A, B, a) and **e**(B, a) are unchanged, but note that the state **q** used in the explanation of **e**(B, a) is a local notation, unrelated to the states of that name on page 239.

On page 237, **pe**(A, b), **l**(A), **f′**(A, B, a) and **c**(A, B, a) are unchanged, but **r**(A) and **f″**(A, B, a), defined on that page, are not used again.

On page 238, **ce**(A, B, a), **ce**(B, a), **cp**(A, B, C, a, b), **cpe**(A, B, C, a, b) and **cpe**(A, B, a, b) are unchanged but **re**(A, B, a, b), **re**(B, a, b), **cr**(A, B, a) and **cr**(B, a) are not used again.

On page 239, **q**(A), pe_2(A, a, b) and **e**(A) are unchanged. Also, ce_2(B, a, b) and ce_3(B, a, b, c) are defined, but it is ce_5(B, a, b, c, d, e), derived in an analogous way, which is actually used, in the inst function.

On page 244, **con**(A, a) is unchanged, but the remark that 'C is left unmarked' is confusing and is best ignored.

In the table for U, which begins on page 244, the state b_1 should have the following action:

R, R, P **:**, R, R, PD, R, R, PA, R, R, PD in order to print **:** D A D on the F squares, so that a 'blank' symbol 'D' is available for matching with an instruction.

The table for **anf** should lead to **q**(anf_1, **:**).

If the set of instructions for the target machine T is deficient, so that a state–symbol pair is created which has no matching instruction, machine U will attempt to search beyond the left hand end of its tape. What happens then is undefined. To make it definite, **kom** can be augmented by the line:

kom   e $fail_1$, which indicates the failure, and the last line will be:

kom   not z nor ; nor e   **kom**

The table for **kmp** should read:

kmp   **cpe**(**e**(**e**(**anf**, y), x)**sim**, x, y)

since **e**(A, B, a) does not delete letters B and a, as seems to be assumed in the original text, and it should return to **anf**, to restore the markings deleted by **cpe**.

487

On page 245, **sim$_2$** with scanned symbol 'not A' should have the action L, Pu, R, R, R.

The first line of **mk** should lead to **q(mk$_1$, :)**

On this same page, **sh** is unchanged.

On page 246, **inst** should lead to **q(l(inst$_1$), u)** and the final line should read

inst$_1$(N)   **ce$_5$(ov, v, x, y, u, w)**

The instruction for **inst$_1$**(L) could try to move the target machine left beyond its end of tape, but there is no way for U to represent this condition, so T will seem not to move. To make this kind of error explicit, these changes can be made:

inst$_1$(L)   **f(inst$_4$, fail$_2$, x)**

inst$_4$ **ce$_5$(ov, v, y, x, u, w)**

To correct the fundamental flaw that a right movement **inst$_1$**(R) could move the state symbol to the right of all other symbols, making a future match with an instruction impossible, the following change is needed:

inst$_1$(R)		**ce$_5$(q(inst$_2$, A), v, x, u, y, w)**	finds the last A on the tape
inst$_2$	R, R	**inst$_3$**	move to start of scanned symbol
inst$_3$	{none PD	**ov**	if blank space, print D
	{		
	{D	**ov**	but not if a symbol follows

Finally, **ov** is unchanged.

11 FURTHER INFORMATION

More detailed reports and programs in Visual Basic are available from the author.

24

W. S. Jevons: his logical machine and work on induction and boolean algebra

J. C. Shepherdson

Mathematics Department,
University of Bristol,
UK
e-mail: John.Shepherdson@bris.ac.uk

1 INTRODUCTION

The English scientist William Stanley Jevons, who lived from 1835 to 1882, was one of the architects of symbolic logic. In 1870 he designed and had built the very first logical deduction machine. Since this machine is in the Museum of Science in Oxford where Machine Intelligence 15 was meeting, Donald Michie thought it would be interesting for members to visit it and he invited me to describe it for them before the visit. He also thought that Jevons' work on induction was related to recent work on inductive logic programming, and asked me to elucidate that relation. Finally I'd like to comment on one of Jevons' most important contributions to the founding of boolean algebra as we know it today, i.e. allowing the use of unrestricted union. Boole only allowed the use of the exclusive 'or', the union only of disjoint classes which meant he only had an awkward partial algebra and a very shaky foundation for many of his results.

Jevons' accomplishments make present-day scientists appear very narrow; not only was he one of the founders of symbolic logic and, in his great work *The Principles of Science*, of the theory of scientific inference, but his *Theory of Political Economy* played a similar role in the foundations of economic theory. He also wrote many papers on applied economics – his treatise *The Coal Question: an inquiry concerning the Progress of the Nation, and the Probable Exhaustion of our Coal Mines* led to the formation of a Royal Commission and was used by the prime minister Gladstone in support of his proposals. He also wrote papers on chemistry, physics, metallurgy and meteorology. I was just thinking that it was impossible for anyone to be such a polymath nowadays when I realised that we have a magnificent counterexample here in Donald Michie. He has made fundamental contributions to pure science in fields as diverse as genetics and computer science. These have led to important applications of practical value; and his work on cryptography during the war was of great national importance. He also shares Jevons' interest in mechanical devices in his work on robots. Perhaps it was the feeling that Jevons was a fellow spirit that made him suggest that we review his work here.

2 JEVONS' LOGICAL PIANO: THE PROBLEMS IT SOLVES

As Jevons said (Jevons, 1877, p. 108), his machine (Plate 1) 'somewhat resembles a very small upright piano or organ' and was apparently made by a piano or harpsichord maker so it's not surprising that it's always been called Jevons' logical piano.

The problem it is designed to solve is what he calls (Jevons, 1870, p. 499) 'the problem of logical science in its complete generality:- *Given certain logical premises or conditions, to determine the description of any class of objects under those conditions.*' I might be willing to accept this as the general problem of logic if taken in a very broad sense, but, as one would expect for anyone writing at that time, he had a rather restricted notion of logical premise. These take the form of inclusions between classes formed by taking intersections and unions of classes $A, B, C, \ldots$ and their complements $a, b, c, \ldots$, for example

$$A \subseteq B \qquad BC \subseteq a \qquad A + C \subseteq B.$$

Elements can be classified according to which of the eight basic intersections or *combinations* $ABC, ABc, AbC, Abc, aBC, aBc, abC, abc$ they belong to. The problem is to list those combinations which are compatible with the given premises, i.e. those which are not forced to be empty. In this case they are

$$ABc, aBC, aBc, abc.$$

Having got these you can obtain what he calls the *description* of any class by taking the union of those combinations which are contained in it, e.g.

$$B = ABc + aBC + aBc, \ AC = 0.$$

I've kept to Jevons' description in terms of classes because it's easier to visualise the operations in terms of classes of combinations. In terms of propositional logic the problem is, given

$$X_1, Y_1, X_2, Y_2, X_3, Y_3, \ldots$$

in disjunctive normal form, to express

$$(X_1 \rightarrow Y_1) \& (X_2 \rightarrow Y_2) \& (X_3 \rightarrow Y_3) \& \ldots$$

in principal (full) disjunctive normal form.

This is not the sort of logical problem I've ever needed to solve but it was typical of the examples which had been considered at that time by De Morgan, Venn and Boole. Plate 2 shows how Jevons solves such a problem by hand, striking out the inconsistent combinations (by substituting the premise equations into them and rejecting those which then contain self-contradictory pairs such as Bb) and then getting the description of the relevant class.

490

PLATES

Plate 1. Jevons' logical piano (see p. 490).

As a somewhat more complex example I take the argument thus stated, one which could not be thrown into the syllogistic form :—

"All metals except gold and silver are opaque ; therefore what is not opaque is either gold or silver or is not-metal."

There is more implied in this statement than is dis-tinctly asserted, the full meaning being as follows :

All metals not gold or silver are opaque,	(1)
Gold is not opaque but is a metal,	(2)
Silver is not opaque but is a metal,	(3)
Gold is not silver.—	(4)

Taking our letters thus—

$$A = \text{metal} \qquad C = \text{silver}$$
$$B = \text{gold} \qquad D = \text{opaque},$$

we may state the premises in the forms

$Abc = AbcD$	(1)
$B = ABd$	(2)
$C = ACd$	(3)
$B = Bc.$	(4)

To obtain a complete solution of the question we take the sixteen combinations of A, B, C, D, and striking out those which are inconsistent with the premises, there remain only

$$ABcd$$
$$AbCd$$
$$AbcD$$
$$abcD$$
$$abcd.$$

The expression for not-opaque things consists of the three combinations containing d, thus

$$d = ABcd \cdot\mid\cdot AbCd \cdot\mid\cdot abcd,$$
$$\text{or} \qquad d = Ad \, (Bc \cdot\mid\cdot bC) \cdot\mid\cdot abcd.$$

In ordinary language, what is not-opaque is either metal which is gold, and then not-silver, or silver and then not gold, or else it is not-metal and neither gold nor silver.

Plate 2. Jevons' solution to a logical problem (see p. 490).

Finis.	Left-hand side of Proposition.								Copula.	Right-hand side of Proposition.								Full Stop.
∴ Or	d	D	c	C	b	B	a	A	A	a	B	b	C	c	D	d	∴ Or	

To work the machine it is only requisite to press the keys in succession as indicated by the letters and signs of a symbolical proposition. All the premises of an argument are supposed to be reduced to the simple notation which has been employed in the previous pages. Taking then such a simple proposition as

$$A = AB,$$

we press the keys A (left), copula, A (right), B (right), and full stop.

If there be a second premise, for instance

$$B = BC,$$

we press in like manner the keys—

B (left), copula, B (right), C (right), full stop.

The process is exactly the same however numerous the premises may be. When they are completed the operator will see indicated on the face of the machine the exact combinations of letters which are consistent with the premises according to the principles of thought.

As shown in the figure opposite the title-page, the machine exhibits in front a Logical Alphabet of sixteen combinations, exactly like that of the Abacus, except that the letters of each combination are separated by a certain interval. After the above problem has been worked upon the machine the Logical Alphabet will have been modified so as to present the following appearance—

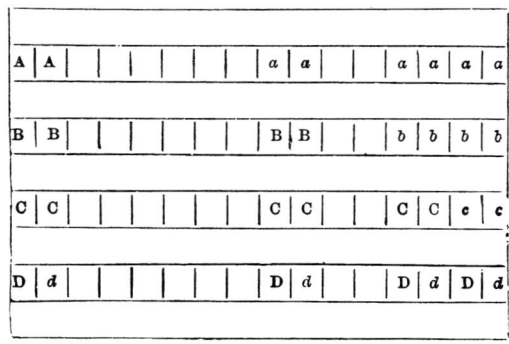

Plate 3. Keyboard of Jevons' logical piano (see p. 491).

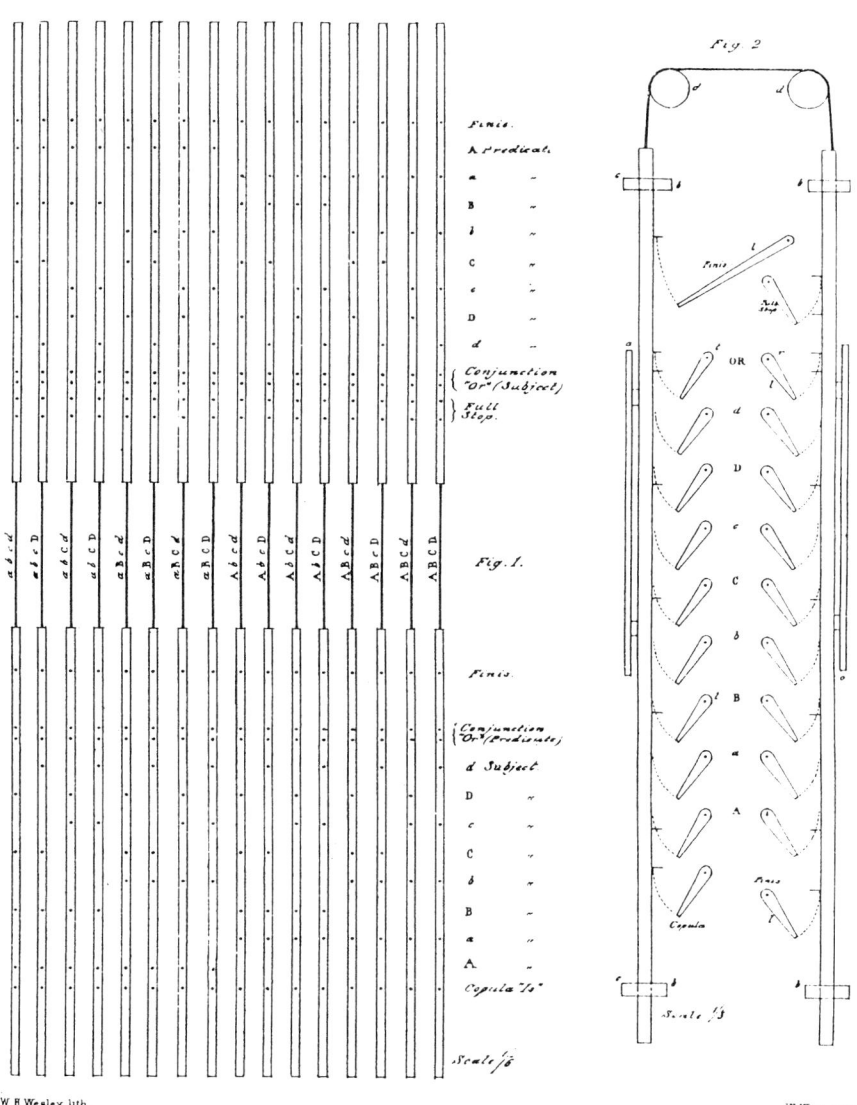

Plate 4. Levers and rods of Jevons' logical piano (see p. 496).

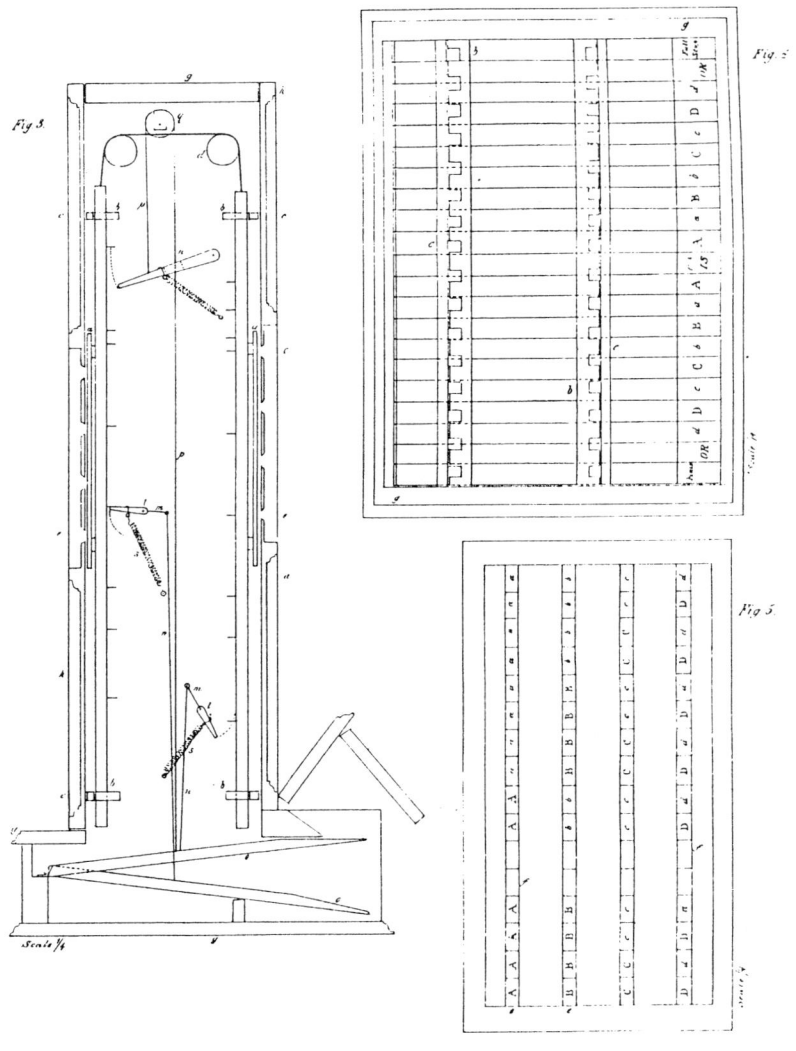

Plate 5. Copper wires and brass arms connecting the keyboard and levers of Jevons'
logical piano (see p. 497).

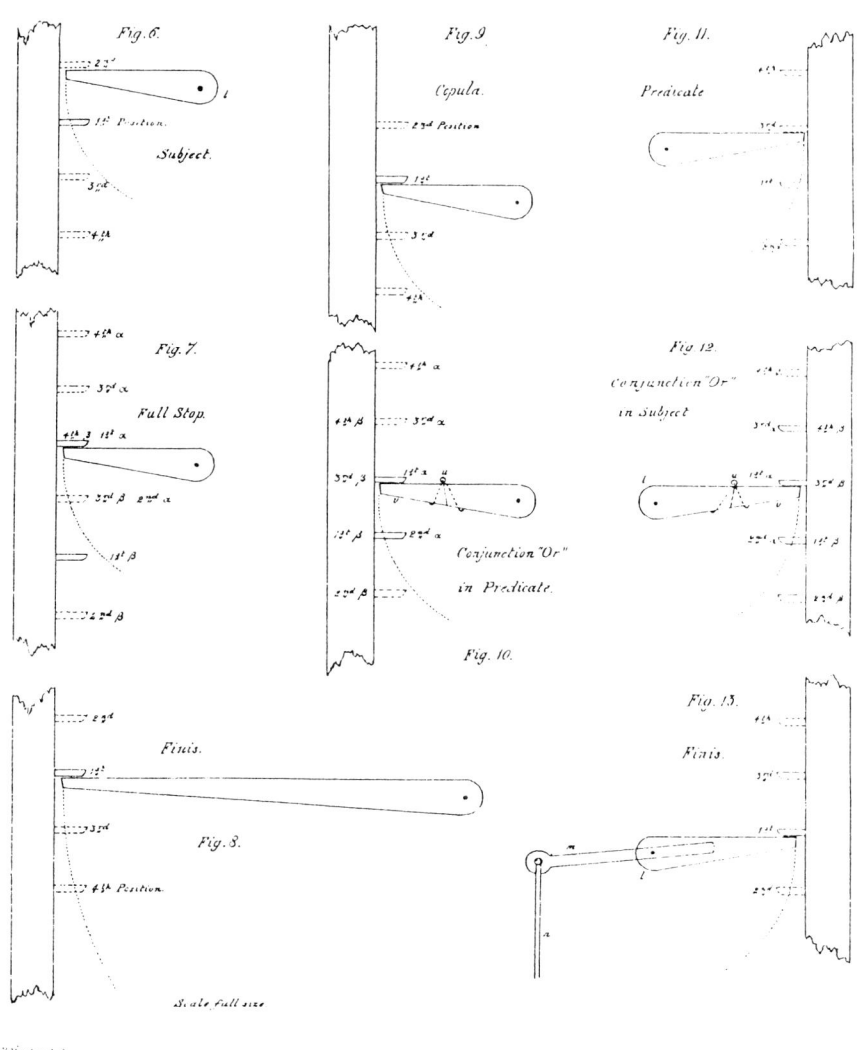

Plate 6. Diagrams showing the workings of Jevons' logical piano (see p. 497).

Reference Number.	Propositions expressing the general type of the logical conditions.	Number of distinct logical variations.	Number of combinations contradicted by each.
I.	A = B	6	4
II.	A = AB	12	2
III.	A = B, B = C	4	6
IV.	A = B, B = BC	24	5
V.	A = AB, B = BC	24	4
VI.	A = BC	24	4
VII.	A = ABC	24	3
VIII.	AB = ABC	8	1
IX.	A = AB, aB = aBc	24	3
X.	A = ABC, ab = abC	8	4
XI.	AB = ABC, ab = abc	4	2
XII.	AB = AC	12	2
XIII.	A = BC +|· Abc	8	2
XIV.	A = BC +|· bc	2	3
XV.	A = ABC, a = Bc +|· bC	8	5

Plate 7. Jevons' tour de force: the solution for three classes (see p. 500).

3 SIMULATION OF PIANO ON ABACUS

In order to make the description of the logical piano more intelligible I think it is worth looking at a simpler device which he invented first, for use in his lectures. This *Logical Abacus* consisted (Jevons, 1870, pp. 104–106) of an inclined blackboard with four horizontal ledges. Each of the eight combinations, ABC, ABc, ... was fixed on a slip of wood and pins were driven through them, the pins for capital and small letters being in different positions so that by inserting a ruler below the pins you could lift out say, all the combinations containing A or all the ones containing a. What I'm going to do is take you through the operations of the piano on the abacus. So I'll talk about *pressing keys*, which is what you do on the logical piano.

First a bit of jargon. He writes $A \subseteq B$ as A *is* B. as it might be expressed in the 'natural' language usage of the day – *metal is element* – and so he calls A the *subject* and B the *predicate*; the full stop is put in to mark the end of a premise. Also he uses '*or*' instead of $+$ here. So the premises are written:

$$A \subseteq B \qquad BC \subseteq a \qquad A + C \subseteq B$$
$$A \ is \ B. \qquad BC \ is \ a. \qquad A \ or \ C \ is \ B.$$

The algorithm used by the piano is based on the fact that an inclusion $A \subseteq B$ is equivalent to $Ab = 0$, so the combinations it forces to be empty are all those containing Ab.

(Jevons doesn't express it like this; for some reason he doesn't use the equivalence of $A \subseteq B$ to $Ab = 0$. I think if he had he wouldn't have been motivated to invent the logical abacus and piano because, as we shall see later, it's very quick to get the results by hand by using this and then reducing Ab to disjunctive form using De Morgan's laws and algebraic reduction. His argument that the combinations containing Ab are empty is based either on common sense; if all A's are B's then no A can be not-B, or else, using his usual way of expressing $A \subseteq B$ as $A = AB$, that if you substitute AB for A in Ab you get ABb which is contradictory because it contains Bb.)

As soon as you know the subject is A, you know that all combinations containing a are consistent, can be excluded from further consideration and brought back later. This accords with common sense since saying that A is included in something is putting an upper bound on A and a *lower* bound on its complement a, so it can't force an intersection of a with something to be empty. Having excluded the a combinations you examine the A combinations, reject those containing b and accept those containing B. It's very fortunate that this processing depends only on the nature of the symbol being processed; you start with the subject A, and, without knowing what the predicate B is, you can exclude the a combinations. When the subject is a product AC, you start with A, exclude the a combinations, then process C in exactly the same way, excluding the c combinations, which is just what you want to do, i.e. exclude the complement of AC, which is $a + c$. We shall see that this context freedom (provided you distinguish between subject and predicate sides) holds also when *or* is involved, so that the whole process is verv user friendly, like pocket calculators have become; you just go through the premises in order from left to right keying in each symbol. The keyboard (Plate 3) has keys for A, a, B, b, C, c, D, d and Or on the left (subject) side of a proposition,

491

similar keys for these letters on the right (predicate) side, and keys for *copula(Is)*, *Full Stop* and *Finis*(reset).

Jevons' article (Jevons, 1877) is the source of my information about the working and construction of the logical piano. It coped with four classes A, B, C, D, but for simplicity I'll illustrate with two, with the single premise,

$$AB \text{ or } b \text{ is } B.$$

which is sufficiently general to illustrate all the operations. To facilitate comparison with Jevons' notation for the piano I'm going to number the ledges 2, 1, 3, 4 in order from the top. This is in the order in which operations are performed, ledge 1 being where all the combinations are initially, and where only the consistent ones remain at the end.

Start with all combinations on ledge 1:

2				
1	A	A	a	a
	B	b	B	b
3				
4				

To process our example premise,

$$AB \text{ or } b \text{ is } B.$$

you start with the first symbol, **SUBJECT** A, and remove all combinations including a to a safe place on ledge 2 above. These are what Jevons calls *excluded combinations* because since the subject of the inclusion is A, it can't force any of the combinations containing a to be empty, and they will be put back later. (I'll keep to this notation, although it is slightly confusing since it might be thought to mean that the excluded combinations are the inconsistent ones, whereas the opposite is the case; these are the ones which, at least as far as this premise is concerned, are definitely consistent because they are *excluded* from the constraints of the following predicate. It's the *included* ones that have to be checked against the predicate.)

2		a a	excluded
		B b	combinations
1	A a		included
	B b		combinations
3			
4			

We abbreviate this operation thus:

SUBJECT *A* **key**: *a*'s **1 → 2.**

We are now at:

$$A\mathbf{B} \; or \; b \; is \; B.$$

and we process the next symbol, **SUBJECT** *B*

SUBJECT *B* **key: *b*'s 1 → 2.**

2	*A a a*	excluded
	b B b	combinations
1	*A*	included
	B	combinations
3		
4		

We've now excluded first *a*'s then *b*'s i.e. all those in the complement of *AB*, the current subject, which is what we want to do.

We now come to *or*:

$$AB \; \mathbf{or} \; b \; is \; B.$$

The *or* sign tells us that the combinations on ledge 2 are not necessarily safe; *X or Y is Z* **can** force some of the *x*'s to be 0, namely those which are not also *y*'s. The safe ones are in the complement of $X + Y$, i.e. xy. So the ones on ledge 2 are sent down to ledge 1 to be checked again; at the same time the ones on ledge 1 which we know have to be checked with the predicate are sent down to ledge 3, to be brought up to 1 again when the *is* symbol tells us the subject is finished.

SUBJECT *Or* **key: all 1 → 3; 2 → 1.**

(It's not difficult to see from duality that on the other side of the inclusion the **PREDICATE** *Or* **key** must have the opposite effect **all 1 → 2; 3 → 1.**)

2		excluded
		combinations
1	*A a a*	possibly
	b B b	included
3	*A*	definitely
	B	included
4		

We are now at:

$$AB \; or \; \mathbf{b} \; is \; B.$$

and we process the next symbol, **SUBJECT** *b*; exclude all combinations on ledge 1 which don't include *b*.

SUBJECT b **key:** B's $1 \rightarrow 2$.

2		a	excluded
		B	combinations
1	A	a	possibly
	b	b	included
3	A		definitely
	B		included
4			

We are now at:

$$AB \ or \ b \ \textbf{is} \ B.$$

and we come to the *copula is*. This tells us that we are at the end of the subject, there are no more disjunctions so we can confirm that the combinations on ledge 1 are definitely included and put those on ledge 3 back there with them to be checked against the predicate. So we add an operation:

Is **key: all** $3 \rightarrow 1$.

2			a	excluded
			B	combinations
1	A	A	a	included
	B	b	b	combinations
3				
4				

We are now at:

$$AB \ or \ b \ is \ \textbf{B}.$$

and we process the **predicate** B. The *included combinations* which are left on ledge 1 are constrained by B. They are divided into the *consistent* ones which contain B and the *inconsistent* ones which contain b. The latter are moved down to ledge 3:

So the required action is:

Predicate B **key:** b's $1 \rightarrow 3$.

2		a	excluded
		B	combinations
1	A		included but
	B		consistent
3	A	a	inconsistent
	b	b	combinations
4			

We are now at:

$$AB \text{ or } b \text{ is } B.$$

and we come to the first **full stop** which tells us we are at the end of the first premise, so we restore to ledge 1 the excluded combinations we stored on ledge 2, and clear ledge 3 for use with possible later premises by demoting the inconsistent combinations from ledge 3 to 4.

Full Stop **key: all 2 → 1; 3 → 4.**

2			
1	A B	a B	consistent combinations
3			
4	A b	a b	inconsistent combinations

We've now dealt with the first premise, leaving all combinations consistent with it on the original ledge 1, and demoting the inconsistent ones to ledge 4. Auxiliary ledges 2 and 3 are clear for use with any subsequent premises.

If you want the *description* of A you can get it now by pressing the subject A key; this sends a's from 1 to 2, leaving on 1 all those consistent combinations containing A. So here we get $A = AB$. If you press the full stop key you restore the full display of consistent combinations on ledge 1. If you now want the description of another class, say, *Ab or aB* just press the corresponding subject keys in succession. You can add a new premise at any time by pressing the full stop key to bring the consistent combinations onto ledge 1 and clearing ledges 2 and 3, then keying in the new premise.

Finally we want a *Finis* or reset key which will restore the initial configuration, putting everything back on ledge 1 ready for another problem:

Finis **key: 2 → 1; 3 → 1; 4 → 1.**

(If you've properly completed the problem with a full stop you only need the last of these, but this takes care also of cases where you make a mistake and want to start again from any situation.)

3.1 Piano software

We've now got the piano software. Jevons' model copes with four basic classes, A, B, C, D.

PROBLEMS TO BE SOLVED: Given a number of propositions of the form $X \subseteq Y$. where X, Y are in disjunctive normal form (the piano won't work properly if you use '*and*' after '*or*'), to list those of the 16 basic combinations $ABCD, ABCd, \ldots$ which are compatible with these propositions, i.e. not forced to be empty.

Interpreting the ledges simply as positions of some sort, we want:

Four positions for each combination; visible only in position 1.
Start with all combinations in position 1.
Process the problem description from left to right pressing the appropriate key for each symbol.

Action of keys:
Subject A key: a's **1 → 2.**
Predicate B key: b's **1 → 3.**
Is **key: all 3 → 1.**
Subject *or* key: all 1 → 3; 2 → 1
Predicate *or* key: all 1 → 2; 3 → 1
Full Stop **key: all 2 → 1; 3 → 4.**

Consistent combinations now displayed in position 1.
Inconsistent combinations now displayed in position 4.

Finis **key: all 2 → 1, 3 → 1, 4 → 1.**

3.2 Piano hardware

Jevons' hardware realisation of this procedure is extremely elegant and shows that he was a mechanical genius as well.

The basic idea (Plate 1) is to have four windows in the front – and back, you could view it from either side – the top one showing the A or a of each compatible combination, the next the B or b and so on. These show only when the vertical rod carrying the combination is in position 1, because the positions are $\frac{1}{2}''$ apart and the windows $1\frac{1}{2}''$ apart. The keyboard at the bottom (Plate 3) has keys:

Finis Or d D c C b B a A Copula (Is) A a B b C c D d Or Full Stop

the left side letter keys being for the subject and the right side ones for the predicate.

The keys move the rods up or down by means of long flat levers (Plate 4, fig. 2) which strike pins in the rods. The levers are operated by the keys via copper wires and brass arms (Plate 5, fig. 3) and are returned by spiral brass springs.

The first clever choice is in the vertical order for positions. He uses the order 2134 that we used above. This has the advantage that, apart from the *Finis* key, all the keys shift only to adjacent positions. It, and its opposite 4312, are the only orders which do that. To further simplify and uniformise the mechanism he has all keys moving rods only upwards. He achieves this (Plate 4, figs 1, 2) by duplicating the rods, having a rod joined to one with its pins in mirror image positions, by a cord slung over round horizontal bars. Pressing a subject key A activates a lever at the back (on the left side in the diagram) which moves any back a rods in position 1 up $\frac{1}{2}''$ to position 2. Pressing a predicate key B activates a lever in the corresponding position in the front of the piano which moves any front b rods in position 1 up $\frac{1}{2}''$, so the back b rods which were in position 1 fall to position 3 as required. Note that these letter pins (Plate 4, fig. 1) are distributed in an inverse manner. The function of the A key is to raise the a's so it is the a combinations which have a pin in space A, not the A ones.

All these levers except one of the *Finis* ones are of the same length, the different effect being obtained by their positioning (Plate 5). The subject A lever is placed on a level with position 2 of the back a pins. It is long enough to sweep up into position 2 any rod which is in position 1, but not long enough to affect one in position 3 or 4. Similarly a predicate B lever is placed on a level with position 3 of the front b pins, so that it will sweep up into position 3 any rods in position 1, but won't affect any in other positions.

The *Is* or *copula* lever is placed opposite position 1 so as to sweep 3 into 1. The *Full Stop* lever has to do two things so you need two pins at that place on the rods, an upper or α pin and a lower β pin $1''$ below. His (Plate 6, fig. 7) is confusing because, as you see from (Plate 4, fig. 2) it's at the front of the piano i.e. the right-hand side of the diagram, not the left as shown. It has to be because it has to send $2 \rightarrow 1$ and $3 \rightarrow 4$, and to do this by raising you must be at the front. So just imagine fig. 7 laterally inverted. You can see that it's exactly the right length to hit the α pin of a rod in position 2 and sweep it into position 1, and to hit the β pin of a rod in position 3, and sweep it to position 4.

The *Or* levers exhibit another subtle touch. Once again they have two functions. The subject *Or* key has to perform $2 \rightarrow 1$ and $1 \rightarrow 3$. So they need two pins, but positions 2 and 1 are adjacent, so (Plate 6, fig. 10) the α and β pins are only $\frac{1}{2}''$ apart. So a rod in position 2 would be swept up into position 1 by its α pin, but then its β pin would be caught by the lever on its spring loaded return, and it would be knocked down again. Jevons avoids this by hinging the lower edge so that it opens out when it hits a pin on the downward path, and the lever can exert force upwards but not downwards. (Fig. 10, Plate 6. 'Predicate *Or*' has the pins in the wrong order and the lever in the wrong place; the pins should be in the left side order 2134 reading down and the lever should be opposite the 1st α, 2nd β pin.)

Finally the three functions $3 \rightarrow 1$, $4 \rightarrow 1$, $2 \rightarrow 1$ of the *Finis* key are performed (Plate 6, figs. 8, 13) by two levers, a long one at the back which does the first two and a normal length one at the front which does the last.

Jevons undoubtedly found one of the simplest possible mechanisms for solving the logical problem. One can see how the piano developed as a natural way of mechanising the abacus with the single ruler used there for lifting the combinations replaced by a series of long flat levers one for each operation. But the actual details of the mechanisation are elegant and ingenious. And the key to the success of the whole endeavour was the discovery of a 'context free' algorithm which allowed the input proposition to be processed from left to right one symbol at a time.

Jevons says (Jevons, 1870. p. 112) that he regards his machine only as a teaching aid, and as a demonstration of the existence of an all-embracing system of indirect inference: 'I may remark that these mechanical devices are not likely to possess much practical utility. We do not require in common life to be constantly solving complex logical questions.' However he goes on: 'Even in mathematical calculations the ordinary rules of arithmetic are generally sufficient, and a calculating machine can only be used to advantage in peculiar cases.'

He'd be amazed by and scornful of the way we all use pocket calculators. However they are more useful than his machine. I don't like to criticise such a beautiful and elegant piece of machinery, but it is almost as quick to do the calculations by hand. He gives an example of the power of the machine by showing how much more easily than Boole it deals with an example from his *Laws of Thought* (Boole, 1854, p. 118), namely:

$$AB \subseteq Cd + cD, BC \subseteq AD + ad, ab \subseteq cd, cd \subseteq ab.$$

'This somewhat complex problem is solved in Boole's work by a very difficult and lengthy series of eliminations. developments. and algebraic multiplications. Two or three pages are required to indicate the successive stages of the solution, and the details of the algebraic work would probably occupy many more pages.'

Now Boole did make very heavy weather of this, and brought in his worrying expressions 0/0 and 1/0, though he did go on to indicate a better method (like the one I'm about to describe). But I'm surprised Jevons didn't realise that if you express each inclusion proposition $X \subseteq Y$ as $Xy = 0$, and use De Morgan's laws you can get the list of inconsistent combinations very quickly:

$$AB(c + D)(C + d) = 0, BC(a + d)(A + D) = 0, ab(C + D) = 0, cd(A + B) = 0.$$

If you just multiply out and remove cC, etc. you get:

$$ABcd + ABCD = 0, ABCd + aBCD = 0, abC + abD = 0, Acd + Bcd = 0,$$

giving $ABcD, AbCD, AbCd, AbcD, aBCd, aBcD, abcd$ as the consistent combinations. As far as I can see Jevons never used this step from $X \subseteq Y$ to $Xy = 0$; although Boole had already made extensive use of it. I think Jevons was so disturbed by Boole's use of unsound and uninterpretable mathematics that he over-reacted and tried to minimise his use of algebra.

4 INDUCTION

Jevons wrote a lot about induction and its role in scientific method. He defines it (Jevons, 1877, p. 121) as the inference of general from particular truths, as the inverse operation of deduction. He notes that inverse operations are usually more difficult than direct ones, citing integral and differential calculus as examples. Another of his examples (Jevons, 1877, p. 122) is very topical:

Given any two numbers, we may by a simple and infallible process obtain their product; but when a large number is given it is quite another matter to determine its factors. Can the reader say what two numbers multiplied together will produce the number 8,616,460,799? I think it is unlikely that anyone but myself will ever know; for they are two large prime numbers, and can only be rediscovered by trying in succession a long series of prime divisors until the right one be fallen upon. The work would probably employ a good computer for many weeks, but it did not occupy me many minutes to multiply the two factors together. Similarly there is no direct process for discovering whether any number is prime or not ...

He goes on to give cyphering and decyphering as another example of the greater difficulty of inverse operations.

The main technical problem associated with induction which he attacks is one that I thought would appear rather esoteric to modern logicians. In fact I told Stephen Muggleton that I thought that if I described it to this audience you would think I was wasting your time. It involves finding all possible generalisations compatible with given examples. Now I always thought the main problem about induction was not finding the right generalisation but finding some logical or probabilistic argument to justify it. That just shows how ignorant of recent developments I am. Stephen immediately sent me some offprints of his work on inductive logic programming which convinced me that Jevons' work was similar, and relevant; so I will describe it to you. But I haven't yet learnt enough about inductive logic programming to say exactly how it relates to that, so I'll have to leave Stephen and other practitioners of inductive logic programming to do that for you.

What Jevons calls 'the inverse or inductive problem' is indeed the inverse of the problem which the logical piano was designed to solve. There you were given some general laws of the form 'all A is B', 'all B is $A\&C$' and you asked what combinations of properties of elements were compatible with these. Jevons (Jevons, 1877, p. 134) says:

It is now plain that Induction consists in passing back from a series of combinations to the laws by which such combinations are governed. The natural law that all metals are conductors of electricity really means that in nature we find three classes of objects, namely –

1. Metals, conductors;
2. Not-metals, conductors;
3. Not-metals, not-conductors.

It comes to the same thing if we say that it excludes the existence of the class, 'metals not conductors'. In the same way every other law or group of laws will really mean the exclusion from existence of certain combinations of the things, circumstances or phenomena governed by those laws.

This tells us what sort of laws he is talking about. The examples he gives take the form of boolean equations and inclusions, but we can put it slightly more generally and state this observation of his in the form of a definition and theorem:

Definition   A *law* about properties A, B, . . . is a conjunction of statements of the form $\forall x \phi(x)$ where $\phi(x)$ is built from $A(x)$, $B(x)$, . . . by the propositional connectives &, *or, not.*

To a modern logician this is a very restricted kind of law, but it covered the logical forms of statement usually considered at that time, before it was realised that what gives logic its power – and undecidability – is enlarging its scope from the monadic calculus of classes to include binary relations.

Theorem   Every law is equivalent to a conjunction of statements of the form $\neg \exists x \psi(x)$ where $\psi(x)$ is a *combination*, i.e. a conjunction containing, for each property A, either $A(x)$, or $\neg A(x)$.

Proof   Reduce $\phi(x)$ to principal conjunctive normal form.   □

His main effort was on a more fundamental, preliminary problem; how to classify and express these laws simply:

Now in logic, strictly speaking, we treat not the phenomena, nor the laws, but the general form of the laws; and a little consideration will show that for a finite number of things the possible number of forms or kinds of law governing them must also be finite.

Starting with he simple case of two properties, A, B, he observes that since there are four combinations AB, Ab, aB, ab, there are 16 possible sets of excluded combinations, so 16 possible different laws. Actually he doesn't admit all of these. He rejects the empty law which excludes no combinations, and his tacit assumption is that all classes are non-empty, non-universal, so he rules out laws which contradict this. So he ends up with six, which he classifies as follows:

$$A = AB, A = Ab, a = aB, a = ab$$
$$A = B, A = b.$$

or as two *forms*

$$A = AB \quad \text{(i.e. } A \subseteq B) \quad \text{with four variations}$$
$$A = B \quad \text{with two variations.}$$

The *variations* here are obtained by substitutions of letters.

He says (Jevons, 1877, p. 137):

In short we may conclude that in treating of partial and complete identity, we have exhaustively treated the modes in which two terms or classes of objects can be related. Of any two classes it can be said that one must be included in the other, or must be identical with it, or a like relation must exist between one class and the negative of the other. We have thus completely solved the inverse logical problem concerning two terms.

This is a very satisfactory classification because it is intelligible to the layman. When you consider more than two classes it's not completely clear to me what Jevons would regard as a solution to this classification problem. It looks as though the problem he is tackling is:

Definition Two laws are variants of each other, and belong to the same *type* if one can be obtained from the other by a permutation of letters. (This means they can be realised by equivalent relay-contact circuits.)

Problem Classify into types all the laws about n classes, giving the number of variants of each, the number of combinations contradicted by each, and expressing each as simply as possible by boolean equations.

His *tour de force*, which he's obviously very pleased with, is to work out the solution for three classes (Plate 7). Most of these are fairly intelligible, though some of the later ones are a bit involved. He explains (Jevons, 1877, p. 141) how this table can be used:

I do not think it needful to publish at present the complete table of 193 series of combinations and the premises corresponding to each. Such a table enables us by mere inspection to learn the laws obeyed by any set of combinations of three things, and is to logic what a table of factors and prime numbers is to the theory of numbers, or a table of integrals to the higher mathematics. The table already given would enable a person with but little labour to discover the law of any combinations. If there be seven combinations (one contradicted) the law must be of the eighth type, and the proper variety will be apparent. If there be six combinations (two contradicted) either the second, eleventh, or twelfth type applies, and a certain number of trials will disclose the proper type and variety.

He points out how rapidly the number of laws goes up with the number of classes and in the first edition of *The Principles of Science* he speculated that it would take years of labour even to find the precise number of types of law for the case of four classes, but in the second edition he sketches the brilliant mathematician (best known now for his Clifford algebras) Clifford's solution of this. It turns out that although there are 65 536 sets of combinations there are only 159 different types of law. Clifford claimed that this classification was useful to him in some applications of hyper-elliptic functions. I'm a bit sceptical of Cayley's belief that it might also be useful in the higher geometry, indeed I'm not convinced that, in the form given, it is of any use.

5 JEVONS' CONTRIBUTION TO BOOLEAN ALGEBRA

One of Jevons' most important contributions to the development of symbolic logic was his modification of Boole's algebra by allowing the union of non-disjoint classes. Like the majority of logicians before him Boole used the exclusive *or*, and for him a union $A + B$ was only interpretable when A, B were disjoint. This meant that he only had an awkward partial algebra, and the intermediate steps of an argument often involved such uninterpretable expressions.

It was very awkward; Boole says (Boole, 1854, p. 57): '... let the expression "Either x's or y's" be expressed by $x(1 - y) + y(1 - x)$, when the classes denoted by x and y are exclusive, by $x + y(1 - x)$ when they are not exclusive.' Several authors, e.g. C.I. Lewis (Lewis, 1960, p. 52, 53) and Styazkhin (Styazhkin, 1969, p. 177) say that Boole's $A + B$ was the mod 2 sum of A, B i.e. the class consisting of those elements in just one of A, B. This would give a full algebra, a boolean ring, in which all operations are everywhere defined (but would need the sum $1 + 1$ to be taken modulo 2). However I can find no trace of this definition in Boole's work; all the remarks of his that I have found say that the sum is only meaningful when A, B are disjoint. This could be extended to all classes either as the union or the mod 2 sum.

I think the reason Boole made this restriction was that he was strongly motivated by his discovery that all the laws of his calculus of classes were satisfied in ordinary algebra by the numbers 0, 1 – all, that is, except $A + A = A$; unfortunately $1 + 1 \neq 1$ – so he couldn't allow $A + A$ as a meaningful expression, because he relied heavily – and as we shall see in a minute, quite unjustifiably – on this fact that all the laws were satisfied by 0 and 1.

Although Boole is often, and rightly, called the founder of mathematical logic, his own use of logical reasoning in *The Laws of Thought* (Boole. 1854) is quite unsound.

He states the basic principle of his reasoning on pp. 37, 38:

Let us conceive, then, of an Algebra in which the symbols x, y, z, &c. admit indifferently of the values 0 and 1, and of these values alone. The laws, the axioms, and the processes, of such an algebra will be identical in their whole extent with the laws, the axioms, and the processes of an Algebra of Logic. Difference of interpretation will alone divide them. Upon this principle the method of the following work is established . . . .

and, more specifically, on pp. 69, 70:

6. The following is the mode in which the principle above stated will be applied in the present work. It has been seen, that any system of propositions may be expressed by equations involving symbols x, y, z, which. whenever interpretation is possible, are subject to laws identical in form with the laws of a system of quantitative symbols, susceptible only of the values 0 and 1. But as the formal processes of reasoning depend only upon the laws of the symbols, and not upon the nature of their interpretation, we are permitted to treat the above symbols, x, y, z, as if they were quantitative symbols of the kind above described. *We may in fact lay aside the logical interpretation of the symbols in the given equation; convert them into quantitative symbols, susceptible only of the values 0 and 1; perform on them such as all the requisite processes of solution; and finally restore to them their logical interpretation.*

And for Boole there were no holds barred; the 'requisite processes of solution' could include not just addition and multiplication but division – including division by zero – and even expansion in infinite series. My favourite example of this carefree enthusiasm is his use of Taylor's theorem on pp. 72, 73 to expand $f(x)$ in an infinite series.:

*To some it may be interesting to remark that the development of $f(x)$ obtained in this chapter, strictly holds, in the logical system, the place of the expansion of $f(x)$ in ascending powers of x in the system of ordinary algebra. Thus it may be obtained by introducing into the expression of Taylor's well-known theorem, viz:

$$f(x) = f(0) + f'(0)x + f''(0)\frac{x^2}{1.2} + f'''(0)\frac{x^3}{1.2.3} + \cdots \tag{1}$$

the condition $x(1 - x) = 0$, whence we find $x^2 = x$, $x^3 = x$, & c. and

$$f(x) = f(0) + \left\{ f'(0) + \frac{f''(0)}{1.2} + \frac{f'''(0)}{1.2.3} + \cdots \right\} x. \tag{2}$$

But making in line 1, $x = 1$, we get

$$f(1) = f(0) + f'(0) + \frac{f''(0)}{1.2} + \frac{f'''(0)}{1.2.3} + \cdots ; \tag{3}$$

whence,

$$f'(0) + \frac{f''(0)}{1.2} + \frac{f'''(0)}{1.2.3} + \cdots = f(1) - f(0), \tag{4}$$

and line 2 becomes, on substitution,

$$f(x) = f(0) + \{f(1) - f(0)\} x \tag{5}$$
$$= f(1)x + f(0)(1 - x), \tag{6}$$

the form in question.

However he does admit: 'This demonstration in supposing developable in a series of ascending powers of x is less general than the one in the text.'

This is Boole at his boldest. Later on when he interprets $0/0$ as an indefinite class symbol he concedes that 'This cannot, except upon the ground of analogy, be deduced from its arithmetical properties, but must be established experimentally.'

This basic principle would be sound if the usual laws of algebra when restricted to 0, 1 formed a complete theory, since these laws are also (in so far as they are interpretable) satisfied by his calculus of classes. It would then follow that any result, *established by any means* (even using Taylor series!), about 0 and 1, which is capable of being interpreted in the calculus of classes, could immediately be asserted for the calculus of classes.

But if we are talking about full first-order logic this principle, and its consequence that all results about 0 and 1 carry over to the calculus of classes, is patently false. For example the disjunction '$x = 0$ *or* $x = 1$' which is true of 0 and 1, would, in the calculus of classes, make every class empty or universal. As C. I. Lewis says in his 'Survey of Symbolic Logic' (Lewis, 1960, p. 51), 'Boole is obviously more at home in mathematics than in logic.'

This transfer principle of Boole, that what is true for 0 and 1 is true in the calculus of classes, does actually hold for equations and more generally for a conjunction of equations implying an equation, which is all that Boole used it for (and on pp. 69, 70 all that he stated it for). One is tempted to say that he was lucky, but I think it's due more to his eager experimentation and sound intuition; that gut feeling which enables great mathematicians to handle things they don't fully understand and never put a foot wrong (e.g. Euler's use of divergent series: he was quite at ease with $1 - 1 + 1 - 1 + \cdots = 1/2$, and even $1 + 2 + 4 + 8 + 16 + \cdots = -1$, regarding infinity, like 0, as being a sort of boundary between positive and negative!). As Jevons says of Boole (Jevons, 1877, p. 113): 'It is wonderful evidence of his mental power that by methods fundamentally false he should have succeeded in reaching true conclusions and widening the sphere of reason.'

Boole's real strength was in symbol manipulation; as well as the calculus of classes he invented the E and Δ operators for finite differences, and formal methods using the D operator for solving differential equations. I think he was possibly the greatest symbol manipulator of all time – a worthy founder of symbolic logic. But like all great formal manipulators (e.g. Heaviside, Dirac) he didn't waste any time on rigorous justification, even when that was his very subject. Bertrand Russell called him the discoverer of pure mathematics, but, bold formalist that he was, he couldn't make the further jump to considering new algebraic laws like $A + A = A$ or to having an unnatural unit satisfying $1 + 1 = 1$.

Jevons was a great admirer of Boole; to quote from the Royal Society obituary notice of Jevons (H., 1883):

But the man whose writings more, perhaps, than any other influenced the course of his logical speculations was Professor Boole. With the 'Investigation of the Laws of Thought' Jevons first became acquainted in 1860, and from that date, throughout the remainder of his life, the science of logic occupied a prominent place in his studies. The boldness, originality, and beauty of Boole's system captivated him. As a generalisation of reasoning, he regarded it as vastly superior to anything previously known; but there were some portions of it that seemed to him dark and mysterious and these he sought to separate from what he considered clear and unassailable. The calculus of 0 and 1, which plays so important a part in Boole's method, Jevons rejected on the ground that it represents other operations than those of common thought. He attached to the sign + as a logical sign, a somewhat different meaning from that which it bears in the works of Boole. He dispensed altogether with the indefinite class symbol v or 0/0, and he imposed such restrictions as served to make the symbolical operations always interpretable in ordinary language. Thus in place of the logical equation $x = vy$, he employed its equivalent $x = xy$, and so on. By means of these and other minor modifications he succeeded in producing a system by which logical problems may be worked out according to the general laws developed by Boole, but in such a way as to make all intermediate as well as final results interpretable.

(Boole's v is his indefinite class symbol, 'all, some or none', also expressed by 0/0. It's unnecessary, and as Jevons says (Jevons, 1877, p. 41): 'But I believe that indeterminate symbols only introduce complexity, and destroy the beauty and simple universality of the system which may be created without their use.')

These small modifications of Jevons did amount to a significant step forward in putting Boole's calculus on a sounder foundation and making it more accessible. It was left to Peirce and Schröder to build on them and mould it into boolean algebra as we know it today. C. I. Lewis (Lewis, 1960, p. 118) summarises the development of boolean algebra as follows:

It was founded by Boole and given its present form by Schröder, who incorporated into it certain emendations which Jevons had proposed and certain additions – particularly the relation 'is contained in' or 'implies' – which Peirce had made to Boole's system. It is due to Schröder's sound judgement that the result is still an algebra, simpler yet more powerful than Boole's calculus. Jevons, in simplifying Boole's system, destroyed its mathematical form; Peirce retaining the mathematical form, complicated instead of simplifying the original calculus.

I think this is a little hard on Jevons. In order to put Boole's results on a sound footing he had to renounce the use of the argument by analogy with the numbers 0 and 1. And because so much of Boole's algebraic manipulation involved logically uninterpretable expressions or unjustified steps, he was naturally keen to confine himself to using only the most transparent algebraic transformations. He did err on the side of caution there, and by preferring 'logical' rather than mathematical arguments he failed to use the power of the correct algebraic laws of logic he did have, for example in not making use of the equivalence of $A \subseteq B$ to $Ab = 0$. (One can see that since he had $A + A = A$ as a general law he could not use 1 like Boole did, but there was no reason why he could not have made freer use of 0.) But making $A + B$ everywhere defined by using the inclusive '*or*' was the crucial step towards getting an algebra instead of a partial algebra and avoiding the dubious use of intermediate steps involving uninterpretable expressions. And by showing in this way that Boole's results could be obtained in a rigorous and understandable way he made them accessible to a vastly wider audience and thereby hastened the progress towards the elegant boolean algebra we now have.

Jevons was certainly right in his prediction that 'It seems likely that many unexpected points of connection will in time be disclosed between the sciences of logic and mathematics.'

REFERENCES

Boole, G. (1854). *The Laws of Thought*. Walton, London.

H., R. (1883). Obituary notice of W. S. Jevons. In *Proc. Roy. Soc.*, 35: i–xii.

Jevons, W. S. (1870). On the Mechanical Performance of Logical Inference. *Phil. Trans. Roy. Soc.*, 160: 497–521.

Jevons, W. S. (1877). *The Principles of Science*. Macmillan, London, 2nd edition (1st edition 1874).

Lewis, C. I. (1960). *A Survey of Symbolic Logic*. Dover, New York (1st edition, University of California Press, 1918).

Styazhkin, N. I. (1969). *History of Mathematical Logic from Leibniz to Peano*. MIT Press, Cambridge, Mass., and London (Russian edition by Nauka, Moscow, 1964).

Index